Freedom of Speech
in the United States

Congress shall make no law respecting an establishment of religion, or prohibiting the free exercise thereof; or abridging the freedom of speech, or of the press; or the right of the people peaceably to assemble, and to petition the Government for a redress of grievances.

—First Amendment, United States Constitution

Freedom of Speech in the United States

THOMAS L. TEDFORD
University of North Carolina at Greensboro

RANDOM HOUSE NEW YORK

First Edition

987654321

Copyright © 1985 by Random House, Inc.

LIBRARY OF CONGRESS CATALOGING IN PUBLICATION DATA

Tedford, Thomas L.
  Freedom of speech in the United States.

  Includes bibliographies and index.
  1. Freedom of speech—United States—History.
I. Title.
KF4772.T43   1985   323.44'3'0973   84-27681
ISBN 0-394-33256-3
ISBN 0-8093-1220-4 (Southern Illinois University Press : lib.
bdg.)

Cover illustration: An engraving from an 1871 issue of *Leslie's
Illustrated Weekly* depicting female suffragists petitioning a
congressional committee on behalf of voting rights for
women. Library of Congress.
Manufactured in the United States of America

To the memory of my father, L. C. Tedford, whose life as a minister was made possible by the liberty of speech.

Foreword

It is hard to realize that more than two decades have passed since I started teaching a course in Freedom of Speech at Northwestern University and almost as long since my first book on the subject was published. During those years there has been an explosion of interest in the First Amendment, fueled initially by the protest activities of the civil rights and anti-Vietnam war movements of the 1960s, then by Watergate and the ensuing exposures of massive government surveillance of the political activities of American citizens, and more recently by the challenges of the radical right to what many of us had thought were firmly established constitutional principles. A subject which was once the almost exclusive domain of professors and students of law, with a scattering of course offerings in departments of political science and journalism, has become the concern of a wide range of people in many fields of study and in a variety of occupations.

Public school officials, librarians, and authors find themselves caught up in censorship battles over books and other reference materials and needing to know more about their legal rights and responsibilities. Activists in the environmental movement and other social causes, and whistleblowers seeking to expose political or corporate corruption, find themselves sued for libel for innocent errors they may have communicated, and they wonder if they are protected by the First Amendment. City councils attempt to restrict the kind of programming that will be carried over the cable television channels being installed in their communities and are hauled into court by cable companies who claim that their rights of free speech and those of their subscribers are being violated. Members of Congress and state legislators ponder over what, if anything, can be done within constitutional limits to prevent the undermining of our electoral process by the spending of vast amounts of money by political action committees and others on TV advertisements which smear their opponents as often as they enlighten the voters about the qualifications of the candidates they support. Broadcasters call for deregulation of the airwaves in the name of the First Amendment, and their listeners and viewers wonder whether they will have access to a diversity of viewpoints in the media if rules like the Fairness Doctrine are abandoned. Police crack down on so-called "adult" bookstores and movie houses, while the patrons insist that adult Americans ought to be able to read and see whatever they please. High school and college newspaper editors clash with faculty advisers or school administrators over stories that the former wish to print and the latter wish to suppress. Majors in speech communication, like their print-media counterparts in departments of journalism, seek a better understanding of the legal rights and responsibilities of those who engage in the processes of public and interpersonal communication. Freedom of speech has become a vital business for everyone, not just an intellectual romping ground for lawyers and judges.

But there are reasons for the study of freedom of speech beyond learning how to know and to defend one's own First Amendment rights and those of others. To understand the history of the struggle for freedom of expression from classical to modern times is to understand the history of democracy itself—a body of knowledge without which one cannot claim to be a well-educated citizen of a free society. To explore the tensions between the freedom to communicate without restraint and competing social interests, such as those of personal privacy and national security, is to confront some of the most difficult and important ethical dilemmas of the contemporary world and thereby to increase one's sensitivity to what it means to be humane. In other words, the study of freedom of speech is not just some form of vocational training. Rather, it is to partake of a liberal arts education in the very best sense of that phrase.

It is in that spirit, and that tradition, that Thomas Tedford has written this book. He has placed the exposition of contemporary problems in freedom of speech in its proper historical context, providing the reader with a long-range perspective on what otherwise might seem to be isolated issues. His coverage of the subject is both comprehensive and concise—he wastes no words but omits nothing of significance. He has compressed a huge amount of material into digestible chunks of information, beautifully organized into a series of chapters, each of which addresses a major subdivision of the general topic and each of which culminates in a set of questions and exercises that provide students and teachers with creative devices for assimilating the concepts of that chapter. And through it all, Tedford writes with clarity, style, and a sense of humor.

About a year ago I was faced with the question of whether to revise and update my 1976 *Freedom of Speech* textbook, which had been designed, on a more modest scale, to fulfill the purposes to which Tedford's book is directed. By that time I had read the manuscript for about half of the chapters for this book, which Tedford had sent to me for my comments. I knew that a third edition of my book would be competing for the same readers as this one, but with the disadvantage of being not nearly so comprehensive. I decided that the students in my own classes, as well as those in other schools, would be better served by this book than a revision of my own, because Tedford had said it all and said it so well. The old adage that "If you want it done right, do it yourself" had proven entirely wrong in this instance. I was, in fact, relieved and happy that I could retire from this particular enterprise comfortable in the knowledge that a successor volume of such outstanding quality was to be available to serious students of the First Amendment.

Franklyn S. Haiman
Northwestern University

Preface

I began work on *Freedom of Speech in the United States* in the summer of 1980, with the purpose of making available to students who had little, if any, legal background a clearly organized, readable historical survey and up-to-date analysis of free-speech issues and cases in the United States. Although I hope that the result will be useful to attorneys and to students and professors in schools of law, the book was written with the layperson in mind. This is not to say that the text makes no use of "legal jargon," for such use is inevitable in a study of this type. However, an effort is made to explain the many specialized terms and to illustrate their use so that the student, with the help of the glossary (Appendix III) and a good dictionary, should be able to follow the legal controversies that are an inherent—and fascinating—part of the study of freedom of speech.

Specifically, the book was written to be used as a text in college and university courses with titles such as "Freedom of Speech," "Communication and the Law," "Media Law," "Intellectual Freedom and Censorship," and the like—which are being offered with increasing frequency in departments of speech communication, journalism, media studies, communication studies, library science, and political science. The book differs from the usual "media law" text in a number of ways, including its liberal arts components (e.g., Chapters 1 and 2 on the history of free speech in Western society), its emphasis upon freedom of expression in its many variations—from the traditional spoken and written word to nonverbal forms of communication—and its inclusion of chapters on several topics that are only briefly mentioned (or not mentioned at all) in the typical "media law" book, namely: political heresy; provocation to anger; time, place, and manner constraints; and institutional controls upon freedom to communicate (prison, the military, and free speech in the schools).

PLAN OF THE BOOK

In order to accomplish the goal of explaining the fundamentals of freedom of speech in the United States, the text is divided into four main sections. Part I, "Historical Development," assists the reader in placing our contemporary theory and practice of communication freedom within the flow of history. Chapter 1 surveys the ancient origins of many free-speech questions in the societies of Greece and Rome, then moves to English history in order to examine the roots of Anglo-American libertarian philosophy out of which our freedom of speech grew. Chapter 2 provides an overview of the evolution of freedom of thought and expression in America from the colonial period to World War I—the conclusion of this war being the historical point at which the U.S. Supreme Court began to become deeply and permanently involved in deciding a wide variety of First Amendment cases.

Part II, "Constraints upon the Content of Speech," studies the evolution of Supreme Court thinking from 1919–1920, the years immediately following World War I, to the present day, with a focus on the content of the speech in question. The various areas of speech content include sedition, slander and libel, invasion of privacy, religio-moral heresy (ranging from blasphemy to obscenity), provocation to anger, and commercial advertising.

Part III, "Special Issues," addresses those problems of communication freedom that are not basically content-centered but arise out of special situational factors or because of problems unique to the medium of communication. Such issues include those of time, place, and manner of expression (with attention to nonverbal communication and the First Amendment); constraints upon communication imposed by institutions (in prisons, the military, and in the schools); prior restraint; the conflict between the free press and an accused person's right to a fair trial; copyright laws and the freedom to communicate; broadcasting; and access to the media as a First Amendment right.

Finally, Part IV, "Conclusion," consists of one brief chapter that summarizes the free-speech philosophies of four leading First Amendment theorists of the twentieth century—Zechariah Chafee, Jr., Alexander Meiklejohn, Thomas I. Emerson, and Franklyn S. Haiman. Students are then urged to continue their study of communication rights by reading and by taking courses in communication ethics.

Special Features of the Book

On the basis of my experience in teaching a junior-senior-graduate course in Freedom of Speech and Censorship at the University of North Carolina at Greensboro for the past fifteen years, I established for myself at the beginning of the project several standards of organization and presentation that I thought would be helpful to those using the text. These include a clear, logical outline for each chapter and the publication of the basic points of that outline at the opening of the chapter that it organizes. Within each chapter, internal "in brief" summaries follow each major unit of subject matter, with an overall summary at the end of the chapter. In addition, a unique feature of the text is that all First Amendment landmark cases, plus a number of other cases important to the subject (note that not all abstracts are of *landmark* cases), are abstracted in a standard format that makes it easy for the student to grasp the essentials of the case at a glance. Exercises, a list of suggested term-paper topics, and a list of readings conclude each of the twelve chapters of the text.

To further assist the student, several charts and diagrams are placed at strategic spots in the text to help explain in a visual way the issues being discussed. Examples are the historical summary charts appearing at the ends of Chapters 1 and 2. Similarly, the appendices provide short explanations, complete with diagrams, of the federal court system (including the basic citation system) and of the various tests employed by the courts in deciding free-speech cases. A glossary of terms and a table of cases complete the study aids. However, readers should not overlook the more than fifty photographs and illustrations that help to make the history of freedom of speech "come alive" with drawings and photographs of numerous personalities and events.

ACKNOWLEDGMENTS

My gratitude is extended to the many individuals who encouraged me in the research and writing of *Freedom of Speech in the United States* and who were so generous with their time in reviewing the manuscript. In particular, I am grateful to my colleagues at the

University of North Carolina at Greensboro who awarded me a research leave to work full time on the book in the fall of 1981 and to the University Graduate Research Council for a financial grant that supported the project in its early stages. The support of my department colleagues was also important, particularly that of John Lee Jellicorse, Head of the Department of Communication and Theatre, and Ethel Glenn, Director of the Division of Communication Studies, in which I teach. In addition to protecting my time, Dr. Glenn also reviewed portions of the manuscript. Further on-campus support came from the staff of the Walter Clinton Jackson Library of the University of North Carolina at Greensboro, where most of the research was done, and from Tim Barkley and Sylvia Eidam of the university's Learning Resources Center, who assisted in the preparation of most of the photographs and illustrations used in the book.

For reading and making suggestions on the manuscript itself, I am especially indebted to Franklyn S. Haiman of Northwestern University, who reviewed eleven of the book's twelve chapters and whose wise counsel and advice were invaluable in improving the quality and accuracy of the text. Also, my thanks goes to Ruth McGaffey of the University of Wisconsin—Milwaukee, who reviewed approximately half of the manuscript, and to Greensboro attorneys Michael K. Curtis and William O. Moseley, Jr., for their suggestions concerning the chapter on defamation. And for her patience and many points of helpful advice, my appreciation goes to Elizabeth R. Hunt, who typed the manuscript.

Finally, I was fortunate to have the guidance of the experienced, dedicated professionals at Random House who have worked closely with me during the past two years, as the manuscript was being completed. These include Kathleen Domenig, Kirsten Olson, Kathy Bendo, Fred Burns, and Roth Wilkofsky. To close, a personal word of thanks goes to my wife, Ann, whose unfailing encouragement over the past four years of work on the book has been an essential part of the total project.

Thomas L. Tedford
Greensboro, N.C.

Contents

CHAPTER 5
Religio–Moral Heresy: From Blasphemy to Obscenity *146*

CHAPTER 6
Provocation to Anger *206*

CHAPTER 7
Commercial Speech *233*

Part I

HISTORICAL DEVELOPMENT

CHAPTER 1

Freedom of Speech: The Classical
and English Heritage

CHAPTER 2

Freedom of Speech in America
to World War I

CHAPTER 1

Freedom of Speech: The Classical and English Heritage

"That is the slave's lot, not to speak one's thought."

—Euripides, *Phoenician Women, v. 392.*

Herbert J. Muller records that the first known use of the word "freedom" occurs in a manuscript from the twenty-fourth century B.C. in which King Urukagina of the Sumerian city of Lagash issued decrees that "established the freedom" of his citizen-subjects by restoring liberties which tyrants had denied them. Improvements that this "first social reformer known to history" made in the lives of the people included ridding the city of tax collectors, ending the corruption of priests, and providing special protection for widows and orphans.[1] Nowhere does the record show, however, that this benevolent monarch established the liberty thought by many persons throughout history to be the most essential—liberty of speech. For that salient development one must journey from Urukagina's Lagash over sixteen centuries to Athens, where democracy was invented, then follow the thread of freedom of expression to Republican Rome, eventually to England, and finally to the United States. Such a journey is the purpose of this chapter and the next. Each society is examined for the constraints it has placed upon speakers, the content of expression, and—in some instances—the time, place, and manner of speaking.[2]

Later, with the invention of the printing press, constraints directed at the medium of communication become significant. The section on licensing of the press in England discusses this development.

I. FREEDOM OF SPEECH IN ANCIENT ATHENS

Freedom of speech had its birth in Athens during the archaic period (c. 800–600 B.C.), when the aristocratic rulers allowed certain classes of citizens to communicate their opinions without fear. This right was expanded under the reforms of Solon (c. 594 B.C.) and Cleisthenes (c. 507 B.C.), reaching a zenith during the golden age under Pericles (c. 443–429 B.C.). The citizens of Athens were permitted great freedom of expression, both in governmental bodies such as the council, the assembly, and the courts, and in society at large—including the areas of philosophy and the arts. Max Radin, a classical scholar whose interests include freedom of speech in Greece, illustrates the extent of artistic liberty permitted by recounting that the dramatist Aristophanes criticizes one Cleonymus, an Athenian politician, by calling him a "glutton," "perjurer," "catamite," "flatterer," "informer," "swindler," and "one who throws away his shield in battle" (i.e., a *coward*). Although calling a fellow Athenian a "shield thrower" was considered defamatory under Athenian law (see Chapter 4 for an explanation of "defamation," including both slander and libel), Aristophanes impudently uses the term *five* times in reference to Cleonymus; the response of Cleonymus to the insult is not known.[3]

So outstanding was Athens' reputation for

---

[1]Herbert J. Muller, *Freedom in the Ancient World* (New York: Harper & Row, 1961), pp. 40–41. Note: Muller is also the author of a companion volume, *Freedom in the Western World* (New York: Harper & Row, 1963).

[2]Chapters 1 and 2 focus upon how ordinary citizens and the leaders of minority religious and political movements have been constrained and their ideas suppressed. No effort is made to cover special organizational or institutional controls, such as those applied to military personnel, prisoners, and persons in hospitals or mental institutions.

[3]Max Radin, "Freedom of Speech in Ancient Athens," *American Journal of Philology* 43 (1927): 223–224.

personal freedom that artists, philosophers, teachers, and statesmen were drawn from afar to the creative ferment of this remarkable city-state. Euripides pens his admiration when he has unhappy Phaedra, in *Hippolytus* (421), express her hopes for her sons by crying, "But free with tongues unfettered, flourish they, their home yon burg of glorious Athens." Even Plato, who unabashedly provides for censorship in his *Republic,* has Socrates in the *Gorgias* (461) praise Athens as a city "where there is the greatest liberty of speech in all Greece . . . ."

Despite the high degree of freedom of speech permitted in Athens, that liberty was not absolute. Radin observes that as far as is known there never was "a community in which a man might say whatever he pleased. Even those who at various times have pleaded for great freedom of utterance, have always hastened to add qualifications."[4] The citizens of Athens were no exception, for they imposed restrictions upon speakers, content, and—in the case of defamation—the time and place of utterance.

Control of Communicators in Athens

General Controls over the Population at Large

A degree of freedom of speech existed in Athens prior to the reforms of Solon. Those who owned land were eligible for citizenship and for participation in the assembly, where freedom of speech was practiced, and those nobles who advised the king or aristocratic ruler were permitted freedom to speak in the aristocratic council.

Solon expanded liberty of speech when he rewrote the Athenian Constitution in 549 B.C., for he mandated that all classes of citizens, including those who owned no land, be

permitted to participate in the assembly. Furthermore, he abolished the aristocratic council and replaced it with an elected one. These reforms extended the right of free speech to all *citizens,* whether rich or poor. But the designation "citizen" excluded the 60 percent of the population which fell in these four groups: (1) males under eighteen years of age, (2) women, (3) resident aliens, and (4) slaves. Even in Athens, freedom of expression was for the minority!

Specific Controls over Those Who Held Citizenship

The Athenians took measures to punish their fellow citizens whose conduct made them *unworthy* to participate in self-government. In a sense, they developed a system of prior restraint—the stopping of speech before it reaches an audience—which forced irresponsible orators from public life. The first group subject to this system was composed of citizens who had failed to discharge their financial obligations to the treasury or who had been convicted of committing a crime. Such persons could be prohibited from speaking in either the courts or in the assembly; if they continued to speak, they were subject to arrest and punishment. In some cases they suffered total disenfranchisement.

The second group was composed of those whose dishonorable acts had not already been made the subject of a criminal prosecution. In these cases, the Athenians exercised a procedure called *scrutiny of orators* to determine the worthiness of those who spoke regularly in the assembly. If an orator was suspected of a dishonorable act, he could upon demand of another citizen be prosecuted *(scrutinized),* and, if found unworthy, disqualified from speaking in either the assembly or in the courts. Dishonorable acts covered by the procedure of *scrutiny* included offenses against parents, military offenses, the prostitution of

[4]Ibid., p. 215.

FIGURE 1.1. SOLON DICTATING HIS LAWS.

The wise lawgiver Solon expanded freedom of speech in Athens when he rewrote the Athenian Constitution in 549 B.C. *He extended the right of free speech to all citizens, even the poor. However, he did make it a crime to slander the dead or to defame living persons if the slanderous remarks were made in temples, during festivals, in courts of law, or in public offices.*

From John C. Ridpath, History of the World *(1901).*

one's body, and squandering of one's inheritance.[5]

Control of Content in Athens

Qualifications also existed upon what the people of Athens could say without fear of legal action. Solon provided for a small fine as punishment for those who were found guilty of *slander* ("speaking evil") of the dead, and slander of the living if spoken in temples, during festivals, in courts of law, or in public offices.[6] "Speaking evil" of the dead under all circumstances, and of the living if uttered in temples and during festivals, was also considered *impious* speech, a concept later to be expanded in Europe and in England into a variety of religio-moral "heresies," including blasphemy, profanity, and obscenity (the Greeks, however, had no obscenity laws).

The general prohibitions of Solon were made specific in later years by legislation that increased the amount of the fine and listed certain *actionable words*. These included words that accused a person of being (1) a murderer, (2) an abuser of his parents, or (3) a coward in battle. In addition, Athenians were forbidden to slander a magistrate in a court of law or to defame those who worked "in the marketplace."[7] Despite these controls, few cases of slander were actually tried. Bonner explains this in his *Aspects of Athenian Democracy* by noting two customs: first, the citizens of Athens viewed suits for slander with disfavor, regarding the accuser in such suits as

[5]Robert J. Bonner, *Aspects of Athenian Democracy* (New York: Russell & Russell, 1967; reprint of the 1933 edition), pp. 81–84. Bonner notes that the Athenians also applied *scrutiny* to magistrates.

[6]Ibid., p. 70. Also Halford Ryan, "Free Speech in Ancient Athens," in *Free Speech Yearbook: 1972,* ed. Thomas L. Tedford (New York: Speech Communication Association, 1973), pp. 20–30. Note: Slander as later defined in the English common law refers to spoken defamation, i.e., words which tend to destroy the good name and reputation of another, especially if the words are false and malicious in nature.

[7]Bonner, pp. 70–74; and Radin, p. 229.

"mean and litigious"; and second, suits for private defamation were arbitrated, with the parties involved being brought together for "an opportunity for retraction and forgiveness" before a bitter lawsuit was embarked upon. Finally, even though laws to punish slander were "on the books," Athenian orators who respected the dead and who avoided actionable words "could indulge in the widest range of personality and invective without danger of outraging public opinion."[8]

If Athens was the birthplace of freedom of speech, it was also the birthplace of the concept of "chilling effect" (i.e., intimidation of would-be orators) in relation to free expression. The citizens were protective of their democracy, and so concerned about attempts to overthrow it, that they enacted legislation to punish those speakers whose proposals were judged as "deceiving the people, giving bad advice, and promoting inexpedient or unconstitutional legislation." Bonner explains that these provisions were designed to make orators personally responsible for what they said in public, just as Athenian judges were held responsible for their decisions. For example, an orator could be impeached for giving "bad advice," such as deliberately misleading his audience after being bribed by an enemy (to the Athenians, such rhetoric was comparable to betrayal of a military post).[9]

Perhaps the best example of a policy which had a chilling effect upon freedom of speech during the period under consideration comes from the Greek colony of Thourioi, located on the coast of southern Italy. This pleasant city-state, to which the Greek historian Herodotus came to live while finishing his *History* and where tradition says he remained until his death, acted to discourage attempts to change its constitution. As explained by Greek scholar Kathleen Freeman, "The original code of laws . . . contained a provision to prevent tampering with the laws, namely that the person wishing to propose an amendment of an existing law must speak with his head in a noose; if he or she failed to convince, the noose was tightened instantly and the complainant was strangled."[10] Furthermore, the Athenians, in an act of intolerance that stains their reputation even to this day, condemned Socrates to death for teaching disrespect for the official religion and for "corrupting the youth"—charges which amounted to the crime of *sedition*.[11]

The "Doctrine of Place" in Athens

As mentioned earlier, Solon specified in his code that a small fine be assessed as punishment for speech which defamed a living person in any of four special situations: *in temples, during festivals, in courts of law,* or *in public offices.* Like the late Justice Hugo Black of the U.S. Supreme Court, Solon conceived of a doctrine of *place,* arguing that, in special circumstances or in special places, certain messages or types of protest should be prohibited.

Athens in Brief

In summary, restrictions upon freedom of speech in Athens centered upon speaker, con-

---

[8]Bonner, pp. 73–74.

[9]Ibid., pp. 80–84. Note: Elements of what were identified as two crimes in the English common law—*sedition* and *treason*—were present in the early Greek legislation discussed above. "Sedition" refers to speech that is critical of the government, whereas "treason" refers to overt acts against the government, including giving aid and comfort to the enemy. For more, see the expanded definitions in the glossary.

[10]Kathleen Freeman, *Greek City-States* (London: Macdonald, 1950), p. 35.

[11]See I. F. Stone, "I. F. Stone Breaks the Socrates Story," *New York Times Magazine,* April 8, 1979, pp. 22 ff.

FIGURE 1.2. THE DEATH OF SOCRATES, *BY JACQUES LOUIS DAVID.* The Death of Socrates, *as imagined by the French painter Jacques Louis David (1748–1825), shows Socrates about to drink the cup of hemlock, a poison sometimes used for executions in ancient times. The Greeks became so incensed at Socrates' sharp criticisms of religion and democracy that they indicted, tried, convicted, and executed him for sedition in the year 399* B.C. *At the time of his death, Socrates was seventy years of age.*
Metropolitan Museum of Art, Wolfe Fund, 1931 (all rights reserved).

tent, and place of communication. Speakers were restricted by granting freedom of expression to citizens only (about 40 percent of the total population) and by providing for the punishment of those judged "unworthy" or "dishonorable" yet who continued to speak in public. Content was restricted by laws and customs that provided for the punishment of impiety, sedition, and defamation. In addition, the speaker who deceived the people, gave bad advice, or attempted to promote unconstitutional legislation could be punished. Certain times and places were controlled, for the slander of the living was actionable if spoken in temples, during festivals, in courts of law, or in public offices. Despite these limitations, freedom of expression flourished in Athens, for, as Bonner stresses, "no laws or penalties could have fully enforced responsibility for public utterances. . . . Popular government would have languished and failed if every citizen stood in danger of the law every time he ventured to speak in public."[12]

II. FREEDOM OF SPEECH IN THE ROMAN REPUBLIC

Freedom of speech in Republican Rome differed considerably from that which developed in Athens, with its "pure democracy" embodied in an assembly open to all citizens. The representative democracy of Rome derived its authority from the people who thought of liberty *(libertas)* and civic responsibility *(civitas)* as one. To the Roman, there was no basic conflict between the individual and the state, for the free and responsible citizen possessed certain rights which the state

[12]Bonner, p. 84.

was able to protect so long as its people practiced *civitas*. Because the Romans believed so strongly in social responsibility and abhorred lawlessness, they willingly accepted more state control over their lives than did the Athenians, and certainly more than do individuals in modern liberal democracies. One result was that the Romans thought of freedom of speech as a right rather than a civil liberty.[13]

Despite the absence of legal guarantees of freedom of speech in Rome, a tradition of tolerance developed during the Republic that in practice permitted a high degree of free expression by the population. Laura Robinson, following an intense analysis of available sources, concludes that writers of satirical verse, poets (many of whom—such as Lucilius, Catullus, and Trebonius—criticized public and private citizens *by name*), pamphleteers, writers of biased history, and creators of political lampoons suffered no state censorship.[14] On the other hand, some controls were exercised over who could speak and on message content. Also, Roman censorship of the theater, a state-established institution, is well documented and is a forerunner of contemporary debates over government control of expression in state-financed institutions such as public libraries, public schools and colleges, city auditoriums, and state-subsidized broadcasting.

[13]Arnaldo Momigliano, review of Laura Robinson's *Freedom of Speech in the Roman Republic,* in the *Journal of Roman Studies,* 32 (1942), p. 124. Momigliano cites Kloesel as follows: "Liberty is nowhere explicitly associated with freedom of speech in Republican Rome, although, of course, many institutions of which the Romans were consciously proud, depended on liberty of speech." Also, see Ch. Wirszubski, *"Libertas" as a Political Idea at Rome During the Late Republic and Early Principate* (Cambridge: Cambridge University Press, 1950), pp. 1–24.

[14]Laura Robinson, *Freedom of Speech in the Roman Republic* (Published Ph.D. dissertation, Johns Hopkins University, 1940).

Control of Communicators in Rome

The procedure followed in the assembly of the people resulted in the control of public speakers, significantly restricting the common citizen's freedom of speech. The republican constitution provided that the assembly serve as the supreme legislature as well as the "supreme court" (i.e., the assembly was the final place to which an accused could appeal a conviction).[15] However, the ordinary people who participated in the assembly did *not* have the right to speak—they came to listen to debates by magistrates, senators, and barristers, after which they voted. In this way the right to speak was controlled by those in power. In fact, as Momigliano observes, "the right of free speech was well protected only for the governing class."[16]

Roman senators fared much better. When the senate convened, the presiding consul called upon the members to speak in order of rank, which meant that those of low rank were rarely allowed to speak. Senators could not demand to be heard but had to await their turn, although when called upon they could speak as long as they wished upon any subject concerning public affairs. Wirszubski concludes that, as a result, "There was freedom of speech in the Senate, but in fact not for all the senators."[17]

Control of Content in Rome

Whether or not the law of the Twelve Tables, Rome's first written law codified in 451 B.C., provided punishment for seditious libel or for the defamation of private persons remains a matter of speculation. Few fragments of the Twelve Tables are extant, and none

[15]Wirszubski, p. 18.
[16]Momigliano, p. 124.
[17]Wirszubski, p. 21.

FIGURE 1.3. FREEDOM OF SPEECH IN THE ROMAN SENATE.
Cicero's Oration Against Catiline, *a turn-of-the-century engraving based upon a painting by Theodor Grosse, shows Cicero exercising his right of free speech in the Roman senate as he accuses former government official Catiline (left foreground) of conspiracy. Under the rules of the Roman senate, freedom of speech was permitted, although on many occasions that body's seniority system functioned to deny the floor to senators of low rank. Also, as one can imagine, not all debates were as dramatic as the one pictured here.* Frontispiece of Plutarch's Lives and Writings, Colonial Company (1905).

concern libel. Frank and Robinson argue that the early law did not punish seditious libel or defamation and that therefore Romans had full freedom of speech. Momigliano, in spirited disagreement, cites a considerable body of scholarship to support his conclusion that some forms of libel were indeed serious offenses under the Twelve Tables—perhaps even capital crimes in some cases.[18] Whatever the facts might be in this dispute, the record reveals that the Romans tolerated a considerable degree of criticism of both government officials and private persons, for few libel cases ever came to trial.

The orators who spoke in the assembly and the senate were permitted to communicate their opinions with little fear of legal action. Orations often went beyond argument into defamation and even invective, much to the delight of most of the listeners. In one instance, Cicero attacked his opponent Piso with a tirade in which he called the piqued Piso a "plague," "beast," "funeral pyre of the state," "mud," "dog of Clodius," "trunk of a tree," "donkey," "hog," and "piece of rotten flesh."[19]

Similarly, extreme license of language was practiced in the Roman courts, although here suits for defamation were permitted either by tradition or by law. In practice, however, such suits were not encouraged; few came to trial—and then only in unusual circumstances such as a verbal attack upon the reputation of a powerful aristocratic woman. The Roman courts also tolerated hearsay and irrelevant evidence which was of a defamatory nature, as illustrated by one courtroom record in which the defendant was described as a "par-

[18]Tenny Frank, "Naevius and Free Speech," *American Journal of Philology* 48 (1927): 105–110. Also, see Robinson and Momigliano.

[19]Robinson, pp. 39–40.

ricide," "fratricide," "lover of his sister," and "desecrator of religious ceremonies."[20] Robinson concludes that the "lawyers of the Republic enjoyed license beyond modern conception."[21]

Control of Speech in a Roman Institution

An interesting legal restriction upon freedom of speech developed in Rome's state-supported theater. The first recorded case of repression in the theater occurred in 206 B.C., when the comic poet Gnaeus Naevius made fun of the Metelli brothers, both of whom served as consuls, and was arrested, tried, and convicted of slander. Whether Naevius was tried under a specific law against slander, or under some other law that was "stretched" in order to silence the upstart, remains uncertain. Naevius was not freed, however, until he had published *two* retractions, and his conviction had a distinct "chilling effect" upon other playwrights, including Plautus and Terence, two well-known Roman dramatists. In later years a definite law was enacted prohibiting playwrights and actors from defaming a citizen *by name*. Two suits based upon this law are on record, one a successful prosecution of a mime in 136 B.C. and the other an unsuccessful effort made thirty-six years later.[22]

The law prohibiting insulting (i.e., "slandering") a person by name from the stage demonstrates that the Romans were certainly sensitive to issues of defamation, even though they chose not to prosecute many cases. Furthermore, by placing special legal restraints upon the speech of those who worked in a state-supported enterprise, the

Romans identified an issue that generates disagreement even today.[23]

Rome in Brief

In summary, restrictions upon freedom of speech in Rome focused upon the communicator, message content, and what could be said from the stage of the state-supported theater. Public communicators were controlled by rules concerning who could speak in the assembly of the people and by a seniority system in the senate. Libelous expression was constrained to some extent, although the record is not clear about the existence or enforcement of specific laws governing sedition or defamation in the assembly and the senate; however, defamation was actionable if it occurred in the courts. Finally, in the state-run theater, the Romans decreed punishment for any person who defamed another by name from the stage.

III. FREEDOM OF SPEECH IN ENGLAND

The crumbling of the Roman Republic and the birth of the Empire under Augustus Caesar in 27 B.C. resulted in a shift of governmental control from democratic institutions to one-man rule. Augustus, who was tolerant of dissent, nevertheless agreed to the strengthening of the law of high treason. Tiberius, who permitted considerable personal criticism, allowed critics of others in government to be punished. Caligula announced a

---

[20]Ibid., p. 33.
[21]Ibid., p. 37.
[22]Ibid., pp. 1–11.

[23]For example, one argument advanced to support North Carolina's 1963 "Speaker-Ban Law," which prohibited "known communists" from speaking on the campus of any state-supported college or university, was that Communists could exercise their freedom of speech in society at large but that *tax-supported* schools need not provide them with a platform.

policy of leniency early in his administration, but he soon revoked it in anger over the dissenting opinions that resulted. His harsh repression included having one author burned alive in the amphitheater. Claudius suspended the law of treason, but Nero reinstated it and used it often, deporting his critics and burning manuscripts of which he disapproved. Following the tolerant Vespasian, Domitian applied the law of high treason with terrible results, including such acts as having the historian Hermogenes Tarsus, whose writings had displeased the emperor, put to death and *his secretaries crucified*.[24]

The pattern of "dissent by permission" established by the Roman emperors became the accepted practice throughout Europe and the British Isles for more than seventeen centuries, during which time no Western nation extended to its citizens a legal guarantee of freedom of expression. In keeping with this practice, the established Christian church, having won *its* battle against persecution by the authorities, set out to persecute others whom it deemed unorthodox or heretical.[25] The Inquisition of the thirteenth through the eighteenth centuries was the result.

Early in the thirteenth century, at about the same time that the Inquisition was beginning in earnest on the Continent, an event of great import to the development of civil liberties occurred in England. In June of 1215 King John, who had conducted himself more like a tyrant than a benevolent monarch, was forced to sign the Magna Carta ("Great Charter"), a document now recognized as the foundation of constitutional liberty for both England and the United States. Although this charter did not mention freedom of speech, it did plant significant seeds of liberty by declaring that justice was not to be sold, denied, or delayed and that no freeman could be deprived of life or property except by peer judgment and by the law of the land. The word "liberty" appears several times in the document, and the final paragraph states "that all the men in our kingdom have and hold all the aforesaid liberties, rights, and concessions . . . forever . . . ."

Subsequent reaffirmations and liberal interpretations of the Magna Carta gave support to the evolution of political liberty, including freedom of speech. In this respect, there is no *direct* line of free-speech theory traceable from Athens and Rome to England; the English, in effect, had to learn the principles and practice of freedom of expression "all over again." Once the idea of liberty of thought and speech took root, however, its growth was steady and its branches reached to the American colonies, blooming in 1791 with the ratification of the Bill of Rights. Meanwhile, following John's signing of the Magna Carta, the powers of church and state in England managed for centuries to restrain the developing liberty of speech by imposing controls upon public communicators, message content, and the medium of the printing press.

---

[24]Robinson, pp. 80–83.

[25]Leo Pfeffer, *Church, State, and Freedom*, rev. ed. (Boston: Beacon Press, 1967), pp. 10–20. Pfeffer notes that a spirit of persecution of the unorthodox "pervaded the Middle Ages," reflecting the thinking "of Augustine and Aquinas, who taught that salvation could be achieved through compulsion, and that oppression and persecution of heretics was not merely the right but the holy duty of the Church" (p. 20).

Control of Communicators in England

Freedom of speech as a *civil liberty* depends upon the right of citizens to function as public communicators with legal guarantees in operation at two levels. First, each citizen must be protected by law from arbitrary arrest and imprisonment; second, the law must support *each* citizen's right to serve as a communicator, not limiting the privilege to a powerful few. With regard to the first of these levels, the arbitrary arrest and secret imprisonment of a speaker is one way to eliminate the source of a message and hence the message itself. This procedure has been used for centuries (and is still used by some governments) to silence critics of the "establishment." The Anglo-American democratic tradition makes such jailings illegal, and the means for enforcing the tradition is called the writ of habeas corpus. The Latin term *habeas corpus* means "you have the body"; in practice, it provides that those who make an arrest can be required to bring the arrested person (i.e., "the body") to a judicial officer who has the authority to decide whether or not the individual is legally detained.[26] If the judge determines that an unlawful arrest has been made, he or she can set the citizen free.

The second requirement for free speech to be a civil liberty is that the law guarantee *all* citizens the right to speak and write. In England, the removal of constraints upon citizens who wished to express themselves evolved slowly according to three phases: first, the monarch and the high clergy were the only individuals who could speak without fear of punishment; later, freedom of debate was granted to the members of Parlia-

ment; and finally, freedom of speech was assured for all citizens of the realm.

Strict Control by the King and the Clergy

Monarchs and church officials were the only persons who could speak without fear of punishment for many centuries in England. A 1620 "Proclamation against excesse of Lavish and Licentious Speech of matters of State," issued by James I, illustrates the accepted view, for the king asserts that political issues "are no Theames, or subjects fit for vulgar persons, or common meetings."[27] Likewise, the clergy, whether Catholic or Anglican, taught that the only source of theological truth was *competent authority*, by which term they meant, of course, themselves.

Free Speech as a Parliamentary Right

The English Bill of Rights of 1689 expanded freedom of speech to include members of Parliament in their *official capacity* during a legislative session. To many—especially those in Parliament—adequate freedom of speech was achieved by this guarantee, even though the legislative privilege excluded the majority of the citizens of the kingdom.[28] Jealous of their new freedom, both houses of Parliament declared that although *they* needed freedom of speech, the average citizen did not, and that unwarranted criticism of the lawmakers would be punished. Commons was particularly harsh, asserting in its rules of 1701 "that to print, or publish any Books or

---

[26]The idea of habeas corpus predates the Magna Carta, although its general acceptance did not come until four hundred years after King John signed the charter. In 1641, when Parliament acted to abolish the Star Chamber, it approved a procedure of habeas corpus to check the legality of detentions authorized by the king or his Privy Council. A few years later, in the Habeas Corpus Act of 1679, Parliament firmly implanted the writ in English statute law. The United States Constitution, Article I, Section 9:2, guarantees the writ to all Americans in this language: "The Privilege of the Writ of Habeas Corpus shall not be suspended unless when in Cases of Rebellion or Invasion the public Safety may require it."

[27]Leonard Levy, *Freedom of Speech and Press in Early American History: Legacy of Suppression* (New York: Harper & Row, 1963), p. 5; originally published as *Legacy of Suppression* (Cambridge, Mass.: Harvard University Press, 1960).

[28]Fredrick S. Siebert, *Freedom of the Press in England: 1476–1776* (Urbana, Ill.: University of Illinois Press, 1952; paper edition, 1964), pp. 275–276 and 368–374. Also see Levy, pp. 5–6.

Libels, reflecting upon the Proceedings of the House of Commons, or any member thereof, for, or relating to, his service therein, is a high violation of the Rights and Privileges of this House of Commons."[29] A number of newspaper publishers were tried and convicted of publishing stories critical of the legislators. Levy explains that the "guilty parties were summoned, examined, and tried in a summary fashion; their criminal publications were burned by the hangman at the order of the house, the party humiliated, usually on his knees, and forced to pay costs."[30] In addition, a critical speaker or publisher could be imprisoned indefinitely by the Lords, and for the life of the session by the Commons. During most of the eighteenth century the Parliament was the principal deterrent to freedom of speech in England, although the common law courts assisted in suppressing political dissent.[31]

Freedom of Speech Becomes a Civil Liberty

During the final quarter of the eighteenth century, Parliament quietly ceased its sedition prosecutions and dropped its restrictions upon the reporting of debates by the press, and in 1792 the legislators approved Fox's Libel Act, which gave the jury more authority in sedition cases.[32] Licensing, which had ended in 1694, was buried for good by the great jurist Sir William Blackstone, who asserted in his *Commentaries* of 1765–1769 that freedom of speech existed when there was no prior restraint upon publishing, although "criminal matter" such as "blasphemous, immoral, treasonable, schismatical, seditious, or scandalous" speech could be punished after

publication.[33] Sedition trials in the common law courts did continue with regularity until the passage of the Reform Bill of 1832, after which they gradually diminished; by the 1860s most efforts at government control of speakers and writers had ended and freedom of speech was finally accepted as a civil liberty by the government of England.[34]

Control of Content in England

The English, like the Greeks, adopted legal controls over three types of speech, each of which was called a *libel:* sedition, defamation, and blasphemy.[35] Unlike the Greeks, the English expanded blasphemy to cover a number of "religio-moral heresies," including messages considered "disgusting," "immoral," "lewd," or sexually stimulating. This extension was classified as a separate type of illegal speech and for a time did not have a name. With the help of a Latin dictionary, however,

[29]Siebert, p. 371.
[30]Levy, p. 16.
[31]Siebert, p. 368.
[32]Fox's Libel Act is discussed in more detail in the next section, concerning content.

[33]William Blackstone, *Commentaries on the Laws of England,* vol. 4 (Oxford: Clarendon Press, 1769), p. 151. Note: Censorship in advance of publication is called *prior restraint,* whereas a penalty applied after publication is called *post facto* punishment.
[34]Siebert, p. 5. Note: Zechariah Chafee, Jr., in *Free Speech in the United States* (Cambridge, Mass.: Harvard University Press, 1941), p. 27, states that 1832 marks the triumph of democratic thought in England. The Reform Bill of that year, sometimes described as a modern Magna Carta, made Parliament into a truly democratic body by eliminating unfair, arbitrary systems of representation. However, it did not extend the right to vote to all citizens, Working-class males who lived in towns were not enfranchised until 1867, and working men who lived in rural districts could not vote until 1884. Women were ineligible to vote in England until 1918, and then only married women and female university graduates over thirty years of age were enfranchised. Universal suffrage for women twenty-one years of age and older was not achieved in England until 1928.
[35]The term "libel" is derived from the Latin *libellus,* meaning "little book" (a pamphlet, journal, letter, placard, etc.). "Libel" is used in English common law to describe any prohibited message, not just personal insult (see Levy, pp. 9–10). The resulting "four libels" of the common law are seditious libel, private libel, blasphemous libel, and obscene libel.

FIGURE 1.4.   SIR WILLIAM BLACKSTONE.
*Sir William Blackstone (1723–1780), famous
English jurist, published his influential four-
volume* Commentaries on the Laws of
England *at intervals during the years 1765–
1769. In volume 4, Blackstone asserted that
freedom of speech existed when there was an
absence of prior restraint; however, he provided
for the punishment of "criminal matter" (such as
blasphemy, treason, and sedition) after it was
published or otherwise communicated.*
Library of Congress.

FIGURE 1.5.   CHARLES JAMES FOX.
*Charles James Fox (1749–1806), British
statesman and orator, drafted the bill that was
approved by Parliament in 1792 and became
known as Fox's Libel Act. This act provided
that in sedition trials truth must be accepted as a
defense; also, that the jury rather than the judge
was to determine whether the speech or
publication in question was seditious or not.
Although Fox's statute did not put an end to
sedition prosecutions in England, it did make the
job of the government prosecutor more difficult,
thereby helping to reduce the number of
convictions for the "crime" of criticizing the
government.*
J. R. Green's Short History of the English People, *vol. 4
(1894).*

a name was soon agreed upon—*obscene libel*.[36] In this way the "four libels" of the Anglo-American legal tradition were established. To help keep the historical and generic relationships clear, both blasphemy and obscenity are discussed in the explanations to follow as forms of religio-moral heresy, although the structure of the four libels is retained.

Seditious Libel

The most severe restrictions upon expression were applied to sedition—the "crime" of criticizing the king and other government officials, the form of government, or the laws, symbols, or politics of the government. Sedition was first prohibited by statute in 1275, when Parliament made it illegal to communicate "any false news or tales whereby discord or occasion of discord or slander may grow between the king and his people or the great men of the realm." The statute was reenacted in 1379.[37] For the next six hundred years the publication of political opinion critical of those in power was subject to government restriction. The rationale for suppressing messages of political criticism was stated by Chief Justice Holt in a 1704 sedition trial. Speaking or writing which reflected upon the government must be punished, Holt argued, because if speakers and writers "should not be called to account for possessing the people with an ill opinion of the government, no government can subsist. For it is very necessary for all governments that the people should have a good opinion of it."[38]

The doctrine of sedition was often enforced to the extreme, for it became a capital offense to even *imagine* the death of the king.[39] During the seventeenth and eighteenth centuries, hundreds of persons were prosecuted for seditious libel, including one William Twyn who printed a book approving the right of revolution. For this Twyn was convicted of sedition, including imagining the death of the king, and was sentenced to be hanged, emasculated, disemboweled, quartered, and beheaded.[40] With such examples before them, there is little wonder that many English speakers and writers carefully practiced the art of self-censorship.

To help control seditious speech, the English monarchs established the Privy Council with its judicial arm, the Court of the Star Chamber.[41] Beginning in 1542, the council and the Star Chamber vigorously pursued those who published seditious opinions, searching out those whose speech included "lewd and naughty matters" (a term referring to political opinions, not sex), "unfitting worddes," "unsemely words," or "evil opinions."[42] Their victims were tried without a jury, and torture was used to exact confessions. These practices so alienated the public that in 1641 Parliament enacted legislation to abolish the Star Chamber.

Following the abolition of the king's prerogative court, the crown and others in government who wished to suppress dissent be-

---

[36]G. D. Nokes, *A History of the Crime of Blasphemy* (London: Sweet and Maxwell, 1928), p. 51. Note: The English discovered the name for the new heresy in the Latin term *obscenus,* meaning "offensive," "repulsive," or "disgusting." Before long, "obscenity" was stretched to reach numerous depictions of sexual activity, including "normal" sexual intercourse. By this imposition of the term *obscenus* upon normal sexual activity, the Anglo-American legal mind has contributed greatly to the view that sex is "dirty."

[37]Levy, p. 7.

[38]Ibid., p. 10.

[39]This seventeenth-century "crime" is similar to that defined by a law instituted by the government of imperial Japan during the 1930s which made it a crime to "think dangerous thoughts."

[40]Levy, p. 11.

[41]The Star Chamber was the king's prerogative court, separate from the traditional local and county courts. The name "Star Chamber" refers to the *room* in which this court sat, the walls of which were decorated with stars. Because of the many injustices propagated by this body, the term "star-chamber proceeding" has come to mean any unfair or arbitrary trial or hearing. See Siebert, pp. 28–29.

[42]Ibid., p. 29

gan to prosecute sedition cases in the common law courts, where they developed four procedures to facilitate their efforts. First, *general warrants* were authorized for the search of homes and offices. Second, *the grand jury was bypassed* by the attorney general, who was permitted to issue an "information" attesting to the libelous nature of the material. Third, *truth was rejected* as a defense, with the explanation that truthful criticism was more of a danger to the government than was false comment. Finally, the trial jury was permitted to determine *only the fact of publication* but was not allowed to determine whether the content of the message was seditious; the trial judge, who was, of course, an officer of the very government being criticized, retained the authority to determine the dangerous nature of the expression. Levy points out that under this system, one's home could be forcibly entered and searched for objectional manuscripts, the victim could be indicted without any participation by the grand jury, the truth of the message was not permitted as a defense (in fact, punishment for telling the truth was more severe than for telling a falsehood), and the judge—not the jury—determined the seditious nature of the viewpoints in question.[43]

In 1792 Charles James Fox secured parliamentary approval of a libel act providing that truth was to be accepted as a defense in cases of sedition and that the jury rather than the judge was to decide whether or not the content of the material was seditious. Fox's Libel Act did improve matters somewhat, but it did not put an end to sedition prosecutions, since many officials of the government continued to equate criticism with subversion. Hundreds of communicators were prosecuted after 1792, including Tom Paine for publishing the *Rights of Man*. Furthermore, the arbitrary nature of sedition prosecutions in England was an historic fact known to America's Founding Fathers and was a considerable influence in their decision to add the Bill of Rights to the Constitution.

Private Libel

Both Roman and German law provided for punishment of defamatory speech, and both traditions influenced early Anglo-Saxon law, which was sometimes harsh in exacting punishment, including such measures as "excision of the tongue" of the guilty party.[44] For many years the church preempted temporal (i.e., state) courts in the area of defamation, trying the cases on the principle that "defamation is a purely spiritual offence" which can only be punished in an ecclesiastical court.[45] By 1482 certain types of defamation suits were being heard in the common law courts, and by 1535 these courts were hearing private libel cases with some regularity. Eventually, defamation became a temporal offense heard almost entirely in the common law courts. The temporal courts evolved three principles for trying these cases: (1) the "defamatory" message had to be communicated to a third party to be actionable; (2) spoken defamation (slander) was less serious than printed defamation (libel) because speech is heard by so few, whereas printed material can be widely disseminated and is therefore more damaging; and (3) truth was accepted as a defense.[46]

---

[44]Less severe punishments included fines and "humiliating" confessions, such as requiring an offender to "hold his nose and call himself a liar." See Theodore F. T. Plucknett, *A Concise History of the Common Law,* 5th ed. (Boston: Little, Brown, 1956), p. 483.

[45]Plucknett, pp. 492–493. The church courts based their disapproval of private libel upon the teachings of the books of Exodus and Leviticus in the Old Testament. For example, the ninth commandment says, "Thou shalt not bear false witness against thy neighbour" (Exodus 20:16). Also see Exodus 23:1; Leviticus 5:4; Proverbs 22:1; Ecclesiastes 7:1.

[46]Ibid., pp. 490 ff.; also Levy, p. 9.

[43]Levy, pp. 12–13.

FIGURE 1.6.   JOHN MILTON.

FIGURE 1.7.   JOHN STUART MILL.

John Milton (1608–1674, above left), famous English writer and statesman, published his argument in opposition to censorship in an unlicensed and therefore illegal tract in 1644. Entitled Areopagitica, *the essay set forth in tactful prose Milton's four reasons for the abandonment of prior restraint by Parliament, as follows: (1) it is a tool developed and used by those held in low regard (such as the opponents of the Reformation); (2) it weakens character (since the study of various points of view helps to build character); (3) it does not work (the ideas being censored become known despite efforts to suppress them); and (4) it discourages learning and the search for truth. Although Milton had reservations about extending freedom of speech to everyone (for example, he argued that liberty of expression should be denied to Catholics), his argument is a landmark in the development of a philosophy of political freedom that encompasses the right to communicate. The best-known lines from* Areopagitica *are these:* "And though all the winds of doctrine were let loose to play upon the earth, so Truth be in the field, we do injuriously by licensing and prohibiting to misdoubt her strength. Let her and Falsehood grapple; who ever knew Truth put to the worse in a free and open encounter?"

John Stuart Mill (1806–1873, above right), English philosopher and economist, set forth his classic argument in support of freedom of speech in the essay On Liberty, *first published in 1859. Here, Mill reaffirmed and added strength to the ideas on liberty of thought and discussion so cautiously argued by Milton more than two hundred years earlier. Freedom of speech is justified, asserted Mill, for three basic reasons: (1) the censored opinion may be true and the accepted opinion may be in error; (2) even truth needs to be challenged and tested, else it becomes a* "dead dogma"; *and (3) there is probably some degree of truth in all opinions. Mill's oft-quoted line from* On Liberty *is:* "If all mankind minus one, were of one opinion, and only one person were of the contrary opinion, mankind would be no more justified in silencing that one person, than he, if he had the power, would be justified in silencing mankind."

Milton, *from Todd's* Poetical Works of John Milton *(1842). Mill, from* Harper's Magazine, *September 1873.*

Traditional Religio-Moral Heresy:
Blasphemous Libel

The suppression of heretical opinions was one of the early concerns of the Roman Catholic church, both on the Continent and in England. Church authorities in England used various means to eliminate "false teachings," including burning objectionable books and excommunicating their authors, publishers, and sellers. When these efforts proved inadequate, the leaders of the church approached Parliament, which in 1414 gave its approval for ecclesiastical officials to proceed in open court against those who disseminated blasphemous libel. Later, the licensing of printers was added to the weapons of the church in its battle against erroneous religious beliefs.

In 1529 Henry VIII, who had not yet broken with the church of Rome, showed his approval of the work of the church censors by issuing a proclamation against the "heretical and blasphemous books" of Martin Luther and other "heretics," decreeing that no person in England was to sell or to receive any manuscript that was against "the faith catholic, or against the holy decrees, laws, and ordinances of holy church, or in reproach, rebuke, or slander of the king, his honorable council, or his lords spiritual or temporal. . . ."[47] Two years later Henry abolished the Roman church as the official religion of the realm and established the Church of England (i.e., Anglican) *with himself as its head,* an act that instantly made the merger of church and state official. With the king the head of both temporal and spiritual affairs in the land, blasphemy became a concern of the state, whereas it had previously been primarily a concern of the clergy. Subsequently, some judges claimed that the doctrines of Christianity were part of the common law of England.

Lord Birkett, former lord justice of appeal, explains that the common-law crime of "blaspheming God" came to mean any message denying God's "existence or providence or contumeliously reproaching Jesus Christ or vilifying or bringing into disbelief or contempt or ridicule Christianity in general or any doctrine of the Christian religion or the Bible or the Book of Common Prayer."[48]

Gradually, prosecutions for blasphemous expression fell into disrepute in England. An 1842 decision by Justice Coleridge states that the common law does not prohibit "reverently doubting or denying" the doctrines of Christianity, and a subsequent decision by the same judge affirms that the fundamentals of religion may be attacked provided "the decencies of controversy are observed."[49] The issue was almost, but not entirely, put to rest in the 1917 case of *Bowman* v. *Secular Society Ltd.,* which was appealed to the House of Lords. In an opinion written by Lord Sumner, the changing attitudes of society are noted: "The words, as well as the acts, which tend to endanger society differ from time to time in proportion as society is stable or insecure . . . . In the present day reasonable men do not apprehend the dissolution or downfall of society because religion is publicly assailed . . . ."[50]

---

[47]Siebert, pp. 42–45.

[48]Lord Birkett, "The Changing Law," in *"To Deprave and Corrupt": Original Studies in the Nature and Definition of "Obscenity,"* ed. John Chandos (New York: Association Press, 1962), p. 82.

[49]Ibid., p. 83. Note: Birkett says that blasphemy technically remains an indictable misdemeanor at common law in England. (During the 1970s officials of the Church of England threatened legal action under the common-law crime of blasphemy against a European filmmaker who announced that he would film a pornographic *Life of Christ* in England. The film was never made.)

[50]Ibid., p. 83.

The Expansion of Religio-Moral Heresy:
Obscene Libel

One of the earliest manuscripts of Anglo-Saxon literature includes a collection of "obscene" riddles that were "lovingly collected by a monk and included in a work intended to be a work of piety." Riddle No. 44 reads:

> A strange thing hangs by a man's thigh under its master's clothes. It is pierced in front, is stiff and hard, has a good fixed place. When the man lifts his own garment up above the knee, he wishes to visit with the head of this hanging instrument the familiar hole which it, when of equal length, has often filled before.[51]

As this example, and numerous others which could be cited, indicate, the church in early English history and in the Middle Ages was so preoccupied with its efforts to suppress blasphemy that, as St. John-Stevas asserts, it was "certainly not worried about obscenity."[52] To cite another case, Boccaccio's *Decameron,* a fourteenth-century collection of bawdy stories, was banned by the pope *not* because of obscenity but because it satirized the clergy and was, therefore, considered blasphemous. Even the well-organized censorship program of the Catholic church during the sixteenth century, which included the publication of the first *Index* of banned books in 1564, was concerned primarily with theological "error," not sexual material.

The few obscenity prosecutions that occurred in England during the seventeenth century were conducted in the ecclesiastical courts, so that by the end of that century the tradition was established that the appropriate body for the punishment of naughty stories, bawdy poems, and public cursing was the church. In confirmation of this custom, an English judge in a state court *dismissed* an obscenity prosecution in 1708 because "there was no law to punish it," since the correct place for such matters to be handled was a "spiritual court." The effect of this decision was reversed, however, in 1727, when a different state court proceeded to convict Richard Curl for publishing a naughty volume entitled *Venus in the Cloister, or the Nun in Her Smock.* The lord chief justice ruled in this case that obscene libel was a concern of the secular authorities if it "reflects on religion, virtue, or morality," or if it "tends to disturb the civil order of society." Thus did the church-crime of "obscenity" enter the common law. As Ernst and Schwartz emphasize, "Throughout these earliest English precedents there is a strong link between the prosecution for obscenity and the fear of blasphemy or sedition, mostly blasphemy."[53]

The spread of Methodism and the evangelical revival of the late 1700s spurred an interest among conservative Christians in purifying the literature of England, and in 1802 Thomas Bowdler and others founded the Society for the Suppression of Vice.[54] Among the purposes of the society: "To prevent the profanation of the Lord's Day, prosecute blasphemy and suppress blasphemous publications, bring the trade in obscene books to a halt, close disorderly houses and suppress fortune tellers."[55] From 1802 to 1807 between thirty and forty successful prosecutions for obscenity were recorded by the society. In 1857 Parliament officially recognized

---

[51]Norman St. John-Stevas, "The Church and Censorship," in Chandos, p. 92. The answer to the riddle: "a key."

[52]Ibid., p. 92.

[53]Birkett, p. 80; and Morris L. Ernst and Alan U. Schwartz, *Censorship: The Search for the Obscene* (New York: Macmillan, 1964), p. 9. Also, Haig A. Bosmajian, comp., *Obscenity and Freedom of Expression* (New York: Burt Franklin, 1976), p. ii.

[54]The term "bowdlerize" comes from the activity of Thomas Bowdler, who sought to remove from literature those words which he thought unfit for "decent people." His most famous effort at expurgation was an edition of Shakespeare carefully pruned of "indecencies."

[55]St. John-Stevas, p. 104.

the common-law crime of obscene libel by passing the Obscene Publications Act (sometimes called "Lord Campbell's Act," after the bill's author and leading proponent, Lord Chief Justice John Campbell) which provided a procedure for the search, seizure, and destruction of obscene publications.

The 1868 case of *Regina* v. *Hicklin* is important to the legal history of obscene libel, for in this case Lord Cockburn enunciated the landmark "Hicklin Rule" for determining obscenity: "Whether the tendency of the matter charged as obscenity is to deprave and corrupt those whose minds are open to such immoral influences, and into whose hands a publication of this sort may fall."[56] This test—which made its way to the United States, where it was widely accepted until the middle of the twentieth century—allowed the prosecution of any work that contained isolated passages which some judge or jury might believe harmful to children. Numerous English prosecutions under the Hicklin formulation were successful until the 1950s when juries began to balk at enforcing the test. However, obscene libel remains illegal in England, having been reaffirmed by Parliament in 1959, with the passage of the Obscene Publications Act. The 1959 statute did liberalize the law by providing that no publisher could be convicted of obscenity if the defense shows that the material in question is "for the public good" (i.e., that it has value to science, literature, art, or learning).[57]

Technological Constraints: The Licensing of the Press and the First Copyright Law

The invention of printing by Johann Gutenberg in 1450 was a major development in the history of freedom of speech. Prior to Guten-

berg, the primary means of communication were the human voice and hand-copied manuscripts, neither of which was of pressing concern as a free-speech issue because neither was effective in reaching mass audiences. Restrictive legislation centering upon media began in response to Gutenberg's marvelous machine, and in contemporary times such legislation remains an important matter because of developments in broadcasting and other electronic means for reaching large audiences.

Controls upon communication media have been advanced for at least three reasons: technological necessity, message-control reinforcement, and monetary profit. Twentieth-century regulations concerning the broadcasting spectrum illustrate the first, the licensing policies of the church and the state in England during the sixteenth and seventeenth centuries illustrate the second, and copyright laws are illustrative of the third.

The technology of the printing press spread rapidly throughout Europe following Gutenberg's success, so that by 1500 over a thousand printers were at work on the Continent. In 1476 William Claxton set up the first printing press in England (the infamous Star Chamber was born only eleven years later), and before long several presses were operating in and around London. Not only were manuscripts being published in England but many books were also being imported. In 1520 a shipment of "heretical" books arrived from the Continent, and the alarmed clergy responded vigorously by establishing a system of *licensing* to control both the printing presses and the manuscripts which they produced. In the beginning, this system of prior restraint was focused upon trying to suppress blasphemy; it included the conduct of anti-heresy demonstrations such as one held in 1521 at St. Paul's in London, during which a number of Luther's writings were

[56]*Regina* v. *Hicklin* (1868), in Bosmajian, p. 3.
[57]Lord Birkett, p. 82.

FIGURE 1.8.   KING HENRY VIII.
King Henry VIII (1491–1547), ruler of England from 1509 until his death in 1547, abolished the Catholic church and established the Church of England with himself as the head. In the Proclamation of 1538, Henry took control of the system of licensing of the press, which had previously been the domain of church censors. For more than 150 years following this action, and including the reigns of Henry's daughters Mary and Elizabeth, prior restraint of the press was the law of the land in England.
Green's Short History of the English People (1893).

FIGURE 1.9.   QUEEN MARY I.
Queen Mary I (1516–1558), Henry's daughter by his first wife, Catherine of Aragon (before his death, Henry married six times), remained a faithful Catholic even while her father was attempting to banish that religion from the kingdom. During her short reign (1553–1558), she earned the name of "Bloody Mary" for her efforts to reestablish Catholicism as the official religion of the realm. More than 275 Protestants were executed for heresy, most of them burned at the stake, as a result of Mary's crusade. She died of cancer in 1558.
Green's Short History of the English People (1893).

FIGURE 1.10. QUEEN ELIZABETH I.
Queen Elizabeth I (1533–1603), Henry's daughter by his second wife, Anne Boleyn, strengthened the system of prior restraint of the press inherited from her father and her half-sister Mary. Elizabeth effectively employed the powers of church, state, and private enterprise (especially the Stationers' Company) to control printing. She died in 1603 at the age of seventy.
Green's Short History of the English People *(1893).*

publicly burned.[58] Meanwhile, King Henry watched the work of the clergy with growing interest, occasionally voicing support for their censorious activities. Finally he could restrain his enthusiasm no longer, and in the Proclamation of 1538 (issued seven years after he had established the Church of England with himself as its head), Henry took over the licensing system, dismissing the ecclesiastic censors and installing members of his own Privy Council. Owning a printing press and publishing a book now needed the approval of the crown.

Following Henry's death and the reign of Edward VI (1547–1553), Henry's daughter Mary ascended to the throne of England, ruling during the brief period of 1553–1558. Queen Mary I, also known as the Catholic Mary and "Bloody Mary" because of her

persecution of Protestants in her attempt to reestablish the Roman Catholic religion in England, gave her wholehearted approval to the practice of censorship. In 1557 she moved to strengthen the licensing system by granting to the private Stationers' Company, a London-based guild of printers, bookbinders, and booksellers, a charter of incorporation that included a grant of monopoly over what was published in England. This royal decree was, in effect, *England's first copyright law,* for it provided that the "ownership of copy" be vested in the Company of Stationers. In exchange for this grant, which served to greatly enhance the wealth of those who comprised the Stationers' organization, the company agreed to help control the publication and distribution of "seditious" and "blasphemous" materials in England. In short, the crown helped the Stationers to become wealthy by a grant of monopoly in publishing and bookselling, and the Stationers in turn helped the crown to suppress religious and political heresy.[59]

The charter of monopoly that Queen Mary gave to the Stationers was reconfirmed by

[58]Siebert, p. 42.

[59]See Lyman Ray Patterson, *Copyright in Historical Perspective* (Nashville, Tenn.: Vanderbilt University Press, 1968). Also, Siebert, chapter 3, "The Stationers' Company."

Queen Elizabeth in her decree of 1559. In this decree, Elizabeth provided the company with a "perpetual lease" (i.e., publications were given a form of permanent copyright, with no date of expiration) over most materials published in England, including such items as maps, portraits, and even statutes. One can easily understand the financial stake that the Company of Stationers had in this monopoly, which lasted for about 150 years, expiring in 1694 when Parliament refused to extend the licensing process.

When Parliament allowed licensing to die at the end of the seventeenth century, the royal grant of copyright died with it. Among publishers and book merchants, chaos prevailed. In response to the legal vacuum created by the absence of a copyright law, Parliament approved the first legislative copyright act in Anglo-American history— the Statute of Anne, which became effective in the year 1710. Years of debate followed concerning how to interpret various provisions of the new law; and in 1774 the Statute of Anne was given a landmark interpretation by the House of Lords, which declared that by act of Parliament copyright was no longer a publisher's right, as had been the case under the decrees of Mary and Elizabeth, but an *author's* right. The House of Lords also said that the concept of copyright as a "perpetual lease" had been rejected by Parliament in the Statute of Anne, and that henceforth copyright was for a definite but limited period of time as determined by act of law (i.e., as set by a vote of the Parliament). In this decision of 1774 the old monopoly of the Company of Stationers was forever broken. Furthermore, the Statute of Anne as interpreted by the House of Lords became the basis for American copyright law. (For a discussion of the free-speech issues raised by copyright, see Chapter 10, "Technology and Free Speech.")

The most effective enforcement of censor-ship by means of licensing during the Tudor period was practiced by Henry's daughter, Queen Elizabeth, who by the royal injunction of 1559 and the Star Chamber Decree of 1586 effectively strengthened the practice of prior restraint. Elizabeth employed a three-sided system based upon the Privy Council, which was directly under her control, the ecclesiastical authorities, and the Stationers' Company. Her approach, which combined state, church, and the business community, was more effective than previous efforts in controlling what was published and distributed in England. The regulations developed under Elizabeth's rule included these four: *first,* all printers had to register their presses with the Stationers' Company; *second,* with the exception of Oxford and Cambridge, all printing had to be done in London; *third,* the number of printing apprentices was strictly controlled, and the appointment of new master printers required official permission; *finally,* the wardens of the Stationers' Company were authorized to search for and seize unlawful presses and books.[60]

For 156 years, from Henry's royal licensing proclamation of 1538 to the refusal of Parliament in 1694 to reenact the Printing Act, government after government attempted to control the spread of religious and political opinion by supervising the presses of England. But opposition was growing, and numerous unlicensed pamphlets stating that opposition were in circulation by the middle of the seventeenth century, including John Milton's famous *Areopagitica* published in 1644 without a license (see Figure 1.6). By the end of the seventeenth century, licensing had been abolished, and with its abolition the crown yielded its prerogative powers over the press. Furthermore, the power of the Sta-

---

[60]Siebert, pp. 69–70.

tioners' Company as a trade monopoly had been eliminated by England's first parliamentary copyright law, the Statute of Anne (1710), so that England entered the second decade of the eighteenth century with the press freed from prior restraint and from the copyright monopoly enjoyed for so many years by the Stationers' Company.

England in Brief

In summary, British controls upon speakers and writers were liberalized at two levels. At the first level, the adoption of the writ of habeas corpus provided protection from arbitrary arrest and imprisonment for those persons who were the originators of unpopular opinions. At the second level, freedom of speech for *all* citizens was gradually accepted in three phases: initially, only monarchs and high clergymen could speak with impunity; then, by authority of the Bill of Rights of 1689, members of Parliament gained the right to speak in their capacity as lawmakers; finally, common citizens gradually gained freedom of speech as a civil liberty during the thirty-year period between the Reform Act of 1832 and the ending of the government's sedition prosecutions in the early 1860s.

Controls over the content of expression paralleled those of ancient Athens, with prosecutions for sedition, defamation, and blasphemy being paramount. Eventually, the British added a fourth type of forbidden message—obscene libel—which grew out of trials for blasphemy and profanity in the church courts, entering the common law in 1727 with the conviction of Richard Curl. Furthermore, the British attempted to control the printing press as a medium of communication for 156 years, from King Henry VIII's licensing decree of 1538 until 1694, when Parliament refused to renew the Printing Act, thus ending censorship by licensing.

In a related matter, the monopoly copyright privilege of the Stationers' Company, granted and sustained by royal decrees under Queen Mary and Queen Elizabeth in return for company help in the control of printing, was ended by Parliament and replaced with a more democratic copyright law, the Statute of Anne (1710).

CONCLUSION

An examination of the summary chart for this chapter (Figure 1.11) reveals some interesting parallels in how Athens, Rome, and England responded to the practice of freedom of expression. In each society, freedom to speak evolved slowly—as did democratic government itself—moving from monarch to aristocracy to common citizen. Even after reaching commoners, liberty of speech was not necessarily permitted for all persons. In Athens the right to speak was granted to those who were *citizens,* thereby excluding 60 percent of the population who did not hold citizenship (women, males under eighteen years of age, aliens, and slaves). In Rome, the ordinary citizen did more listening than speaking where matters of government were concerned. And in England, freedom to express one's opinion expanded gradually from monarch to member of Parliament to common person in an evolutionary process that was not completed until almost 1900.

Furthermore, all three societies placed constraints upon speech content, especially that considered seditious or defamatory. Athens provided for the punishment of impiety (blasphemy), as did England with its ecclesiastical cum civil statutes severely condemning antichurch expression, including the sinful ideas of "obscenity." When technological advance produced the printing press, the English responded with a licensing system in an

FIGURE 1.11. **Summary of Communication Restrictions for Athens, Rome, and England.**

Government	Communicator Constraints	Content Constraints	Medium and Channel Constraints	Time, Place, and Manner Constraints
Athens	(a) Evolved from king to aristocratic council to all citizens. (b) "Citizen" excluded women, males under 18, aliens, and slaves (those excluded composed 60% of the population).	Had laws to punish (a) sedition, (b) private libel, (c) blasphemy.	None noted.	Under Solon's law, a small fine was levied for slander if spoken (a) in temples, (b) during festivals, (c) in courts of law, (d) in public offices.
Rome	(a) Evolved from king to aristocrats (patricians) to all citizens. (b) Restrictions upon who could speak in the assembly. (c) Seniority system in the senate restricted orators.	Had laws to punish (a) sedition, (b) private libel.	None noted.	In the state-supported theater, defaming a person *by name* from the stage was prohibited.
England	Evolved from king to Parliament to citizen. Freedom of speech was established as a civil liberty by 1860.	Had laws to punish (a) seditious libel, (b) private libel, (c) blasphemous libel, (d) obscene libel. (These are called the "four libels" of the English common law.)	(a) Licensing of the press from 1538 to 1694 (156 years). (b) Copyright ordained by royal decree, 1557. (c) Copyright revised by Parliament (the Statute of Anne, 1710).	See Note[1] below.

[1] The historical literature on freedom of speech rarely mentions constraints of time, place, and manner of communication. For legal developments in the United States, see the summary chart at the end of Chapter 2, as well as Chapter 8, which takes up subjects of time, place, and manner.

attempt to control both the presses themselves and the materials that came from those presses. The effort of the English to require government supervision of the technology of the printing medium was a forerunner of contemporary systems of control by government of a variety of communications media, including radio, television, and film. In addition, English censorship produced the first copyright laws in Anglo-American history— the very first being the royal decree of Queen Mary in 1557 granting a charter of monopoly to the Stationers' Company, later preempted by Parliament with the Statute of Anne, which went into effect in 1710. The Statute of Anne, as interpreted by the House of Lords in a landmark decision of 1774, is the basis of American copyright law.

Finally, minor constraints upon the time, place, and manner of expression are documented for Greece and Rome. Solon decreed that the Athenians should not speak ill of one another at certain times (during festivals) or in certain places (temples, courts of law, and public offices). And the Romans crafted a law to punish playwrights and actors who defamed a citizen by name from the stage. An examination of the developing theories and practice of freedom of speech in the American colonies, and, after the Revolutionary War, in the United States, is the subject of the chapter to follow.

EXERCISES

A. Classroom projects and activities.

1. Points of view for discussion by the class.

a. Sir William Blackstone in his *Commentaries* of 1765–1769 argued that a society had freedom of speech when there was *no prior restraint* upon what could be said or published; however, "criminal matter" such as blasphemy, sedition, or defamation could be punished *after* being communicated (under laws approved by the people's representatives and, presumably, known to the offending speaker or publisher). Is the absence of prior restraint an adequate standard for protecting freedom of speech? Discuss.

b. Who is closer to the truth in his point of view, John Milton or John Stuart Mill, in these statements?

Milton argues in *Areopagitica:* "And though all the winds of doctrine were let loose to play upon the earth, so Truth be in the field, we do injuriously by licensing and prohibiting to misdoubt her strength. Let her and Falsehood grapple; whoever knew Truth put to the worse in a free and open encounter?"

Mill, on the other hand, argues in *On Liberty:* "It is a piece of sentimentality that truth, merely as truth, has any inherent power denied to error of prevailing against the dungeon and the stake. Men are not more zealous for truth than they often are for error . . . . The real advantage which truth has consists in that, when an opinion is true, it may be extinguished once, twice, or many times, but in the course of ages there will generally be found persons to rediscover it . . . until it has made such a head as to withstand all subsequent attempts to suppress it."

2. Invite a professor of classical history (or three professors, one each from history, classical literature, and classical rhetoric) to explain the working of democracy in Athens and Rome, including the place of freedom of speech in both governments.

3. Invite a faculty member who specializes in classical rhetoric (or a panel of several such specialists) to explain to the class the major contributions to rhetorical theory of Plato, Aristotle, Cicero, and Quintilian. Why is Quintilian important, even though he lived and taught following the collapse of the Roman Republic? Who among the four classical figures mentioned above took strong stands on ethics in public communication?

4. Invite a professor of theater to address the class concerning theater censorship in England under the Tudors (during the time that licensing was in effect). Can any parallels be drawn to contemporary efforts to constrain theater, film, and television in the United States?

5. Divide the class into two groups. Have those in the first group each prepare an abstract of John Milton's *Areopagitica* (1644) and those in the second group each prepare an abstract of Mill's "On Liberty of Thought and Discussion" (Chapter 2 of *On Liberty*, 1859). Limit the abstracts to 500 to 600 words and submit to the instructor for grading. Discuss the major views of Milton and Mill in class.

B. Topics for research papers or oral reports.

1. Sedition in Ancient Athens: The Trial and Execution of Socrates.

2. Censorship in Plato's *Republic*.

3. Plato on the Ethics of Persuasion. (Begin with a careful reading of these two Platonic dialogues: *Gorgias* and *Phaedrus*.)

4. Aristotle (or Cicero or Quintilian) on Ethics in Public Communication.

5. The Struggle of Galileo Galilei (1564–1642) for Academic Freedom.

6. A Short History of the Inquisition in Europe.

7. Freedom of Expression and the Church of England.

8. Benedict de Spinoza on Freedom of Thought and Expression. (Begin with a study of his *Theologico-Political Treatise*, published in 1670.)

9. A History and Analysis of the Writ of Habeas Corpus. (Include an evaluation of the writ's relationship to freedom of speech; see the article by Wells in the reading list.)

10. Censorship of the Bible in Europe and England prior to 1800.

11. Censorship of the Elizabethan Stage.

12. The Influence of the English Common Law upon Freedom of Speech in the United States.

13. England's Thomas Bowdler and the Society for the Suppression of Vice.

14. John Milton's Fight Against Licensing of the Press. (Include a careful study of Milton's classic essay *Areopagitica*.)

15. John Stuart Mill: Advocate of Liberty of the Press.

16. The Levellers Movement and Civil Liberties in Seventeenth-Century England.

17. The Stationers' Company and Freedom of the Press in England (1557–1694).

18. The Persecution of Catholics by King Henry VIII.

19. The Persecution of Protestants by Queen Mary I.

20. Sedition Prosecutions in Nineteenth-Century England: What Forces Brought Them to an End?

SELECTED READINGS

Bonner, Robert J. *Aspects of Athenian Democracy*. New York: Russell & Russell, 1967 (reprint of 1933 edition).

Chandler, Daniel R. "A Comparison of John Milton's *Areopagitica* with Thomas Erskine's Addresses on Free Speech." In *Free Speech Yearbook: 1978*, pp. 98–112. Edited by Gregg Phifer. Falls Church, Va.: Speech Communication Association, 1979.

Cherwitz, Richard A., and Hikins, James W. "John Stuart Mill's *On Liberty*: Implications for the Epistemology of the New Rhetoric." *Quarterly Journal of Speech* 65 (February 1979): 12–24.

Enos, Richard L. "When Rhetoric Was Outlawed in Rome: A Translation and Commentary of Suetonius's Treatise on Early Roman Rhetoricians." *Speech Monographs* 39 (March 1972): 37–45.

Flory, Joyce V. "Philosophical Assumptions Underlying Plato's Theory of Freedom of Speech: A Comparison with the Theory of Democratic Individualism." In *Free Speech Yearbook: 1974,* pp. 45–53. Edited by Alton Barbour. New York: Speech Communication Association, 1975.

Fowell, Frank, and Palmer, Frank. *Censorship in England.* New York: B. Blom, 1969. (A recommended source on censorship of the theater.)

Frank, Joseph. *The Levellers.* Cambridge, Mass.: Harvard University Press, 1955.

Freeman, Kathleen. *Greek City-States.* London: Macdonald, 1950.

Gillett, Charles. *Burned Books: Neglected Chapters in British History and Literature.* 2 vols. New York: Columbia University Press, 1932.

Hair, Paul. *Before the Bawdy Court.* London: Paul Elek, 1972.

Holorenshaw, Henry. *The Levellers and the English Revolution.* New York: Fertig, 1971.

Levy, Leonard W. *Treason Against God: A History of the Offense of Blasphemy.* New York: Schocken, 1981.

Nokes, G. D. *A History of the Crime of Blasphemy.* London: Sweet and Maxwell, 1928.

Patterson, Lyman R. *Copyright in Historical Perspective.* Nashville, Tenn.: Vanderbilt University Press, 1968.

Plucknett, Theodore F. T. *A Concise History of the Common Law.* 5th ed. Boston: Little, Brown, 1956.

Robinson, Laura. *Freedom of Speech in the Roman Republic.* Published Ph.D. dissertation, Johns Hopkins University, 1940.

Ryan, Halford. "Free Speech in Ancient Athens." *Free Speech Yearbook: 1972,* pp. 20–30. Edited by Thomas L. Tedford. New York: Speech Communication Association, 1973.

Siebert, Fredrick S. *Freedom of the Press in England: 1476–1776.* Urbana, Ill.: University of Illinois Press, 1952. (Paper edition, 1964).

Stone, I. F. "I. F. Stone Breaks the Socrates Story." *New York Times Magazine,* April 8, 1979, pp. 22 ff.

Taylor, F. S. *Galileo and Freedom of Thought.* London: Watts, 1938.

Thomas, Donald. *A Long Time Burning: The History of Literary Censorship in England.* New York: Praeger, 1969.

Thorson, Thomas L., ed. *Plato: Totalitarian or Democrat?* Englewood Cliffs, N.J.: Prentice-Hall, 1963.

Wells, M. "Habeas Corpus and Freedom of Speech." *Duke Law Journal* 1978 (January 1978): 1307–1351.

Wirszubski, Ch. *"Libertas" as a Political Idea at Rome During the Late Republic and Early Principate.* Cambridge: Cambridge University Press, 1950.

CHAPTER 2

Freedom of Speech in America to World War I

" . . . I will now tell you what I do not
like. First the omission of a bill of rights,
providing clearly, and without the aid of
sophism, for freedom of religion, freedom of
the press, protection against standing armies,
restriction of monopolies, the eternal and
unremitting force of the habeas corpus laws,
and trials by jury in all matters of fact triable
by the laws of the land. . . . Let me add,
that a bill of rights is what the people are
entitled to against every government on
earth . . . and what no just government
should refuse, or rest on inference."

—Thomas Jefferson to James Madison, December 20, 1787.[1]

Leonard W. Levy begins his study of freedom of speech in prerevolutionary America
by stating that the "persistent image of colonial America as a society in which freedom
of expression was cherished is an hallucina-
tion of sentiment that ignores history. . . . The American people simply did
not understand that freedom of thought and
expression means equal freedom for the other
fellow, especially the one with hated ideas."[2]
The intolerance to which Levy refers was
brought from the Old World to the New by
the early settlers, and—as in England—centered upon the issues of *who* was to be allowed to speak, what religious and political
ideas were to be permitted, and to what degree *prior restraint of the press* was to be practiced. The struggle over these and related issues of freedom to communicate continued
into the nineteenth century and were particularly controversial in the period of the Civil
War. Even during the first two decades of the
twentieth century, guarantees of freedom of
expression for all citizens—including labor
organizers and antiwar dissidents—remained
more a neglected promise than an established
practice. In order to survey these developments and thereby help place contemporary
free-speech debates within the flow of history, this chapter summarizes key issues of
(1) the colonial period; (2) the period in
which the Bill of Rights was adopted; and (3)
the years from 1798 to 1917, covering the
Alien and Sedition Acts, the Civil War, and
ending with World War I, which set the stage
for the landmark *Schenck* case of 1919, discussed early in Chapter 3.

I. FREEDOM OF SPEECH IN COLONIAL AMERICA

Control of Communicators in the Colonies

The development of freedom of speech as a
civil liberty followed a pattern in the colonies
similar to that which occurred in the mother
country. To begin with, certain powerful individuals, such as clergymen and royal governors, were the only persons who could
speak without fear of punishment. Later, the
elected colonial assemblies gained freedom of
speech for themselves, but they were hesitant
to extend it to the people. Finally, the War of
Independence was won and the Constitution
and the Bill of Rights ratified, granting freedom of speech to all persons.

Controls upon the sources of religious
expression were severe in the Puritan colo-

---

[1]Thomas Jefferson, *The Writings of Thomas Jefferson,*
ed. Andrew A. Lipscomb and Albert E. Bergh, vol. 6
(Washington, D.C.: The Thomas Jefferson Memorial
Association, 1903–1904), pp. 387–389. Note: This quotation is from one of several letters to Madison from Jefferson that helped persuade Madison to support the addition of a bill of rights to the U.S. Constitution.

[2]Leonard Levy, *Freedom of Speech and Press in Early
American History: Legacy of Suppression* (New York: Harper & Row, 1963), p. 18; originally published as *Legacy
of Suppression* (Cambridge, Mass.: Harvard University
Press, 1960).

nies of Massachusetts, New Hampshire, and Connecticut as well as in the Anglican colonies of Virginia and the Carolinas. In Massachusetts one had to be certified as "orthodox in the fundamentals of religion" before being allowed to participate in political affairs and to vote. Furthermore, legislation was enacted against Quakers and other "heretics," leading in at least one instance to the execution of several Quakers for heresy. The persecutions in New Hampshire and Connecticut were likewise vigorous.[3]

Church-state union was practiced in Virginia and the Carolinas, where the royal governor, like the king of England, acted as head of both the Anglican establishment and the temporal government. In 1612, Governor Thomas Dale of Virginia demonstrated his authority over both church and state by publishing eight "Lawes Divine, Moral and Martial," two of which placed restrictions upon communicators. In the first of these laws, Dale warned all clergymen that they must preach only what is orthodox or lose their ministerial posts. And in the second, the pious governor ordered every person in the colony to visit an Anglican minister to be examined for religious orthodoxy and, if found "unsound" in doctrine, to submit to church instruction. "If any refused to go to the minister," Dale warned, "he should be whipt."[4] The authorities in Virginia and the Carolinas also restricted the sources of religious dissent by banishing many Puritan and Quaker clergymen and by expelling *all* Catholic priests who ventured into Anglican territory. As an added measure, Catholic citizens were barred from public office. The late Supreme Court

Justice Hugo Black, writing about this period in American history, states:

> Catholics found themselves hounded and proscribed because of their faith; Quakers who followed their conscience went to jail; Baptists were peculiarly obnoxious to certain dominant Protestant sects; men and women of varied faiths who happened to be in a minority in a particular locality were persecuted because they steadfastly persisted in worshipping God only as their own consciences dictated. And all of these dissenters were compelled to pay tithes and taxes to support government-sponsored churches whose ministers preached inflammatory sermons designed to strengthen and consolidate the established faith by generating a burning hatred against dissenters.[5]

The chief oppressors of political dissent in prerevolutionary America were the elected assemblies, although the royal governors and their councils were also active from time to time in the search for sedition. Contrary to the folklore about colonial America, the colonial courts were the least active in efforts to stamp out minority political opinion.[6] In other words, the members of the colonial assemblies followed the lead of their brothers in the English Parliament, insisting upon freedom of speech as a special "legislative privilege" for themselves but opposing the extension of the privilege to ordinary citizens.

---

[3]Leo Pfeffer, *Church, State, and Freedom,* rev. ed. (Boston: Beacon Press, 1967), pp. 73–77.

[4]Ibid., pp. 77–78. Note: Dale's laws were so severe that complaints were made in England and the laws eventually abolished.

[5]*Everson* v. *Board of Education,* 330 U.S. 1 (1947), at p. 10.

[6]Levy, pp. 20–21. Note: Whereas the common law courts attempted the prosecution of "not more than half a dozen" persons for political dissent prior to the Revolution, the provincial assemblies prosecuted "scores of persons, probably hundreds," for speeches and writings critical of the proceedings or of individual members (pp. 19–21). This abuse of power by the elected assemblies was a factor in the decision of the Founding Fathers to adopt a form of government in which the legislature was constrained by a written Constitution.

FIGURE 2.1 *BANISHED FROM MASSACHUSETTS, 1660.*
"Move on, or stay and hang," the sheriff (right, with raised, clenched fists) cried in John Greenleaf Whittier's poem, commissioned to be published in Harper's Weekly *with this engraving of a picture by E. A. Abbey.* Banished *depicts a family of "Friends," the name by which Quakers addressed each other, being driven from their Massachusetts home. Whittier's poem in its entirety follows.*

Over the threshold of his pleasant home
  Set in green clearings passed the exiled
    Friend,
  In simple trust, misdoubting not the end.
"Dear heart of mine!" he said, "the time has
  come
To trust the Lord for shelter." One long gaze
  The goodwife turned on each familiar
    thing—
  The lowing kine, the orchard blossoming,
The open door that showed the hearth-fire's
  blaze—
And calmly answered, "Yea, He will provide."
  Silent and slow they crossed the homestead's
    bound,
  Lingering the longest by their child's grave-
    mound.
"Move on, or stay and hang!" the sheriff cried.
They left behind them more than home or land,
And set sad faces to an alien strand.

Safer with winds and waves than human wrath,
  With ravening wolves than those whose zeal
    for God
  Was cruelty to man, the exiles trod
Drear leagues of forest without guide or path,
Or, launching frail boats on the uncharted sea,
  Round storm-vexed capes, whose teeth of
    granite ground

The waves to foam, their perilous way they
  wound,
Enduring all things so their souls were free.
Oh, true confessors, shaming them who did
  Anew the wrong their Pilgrim fathers bore!
  For you the Mayflower spread her sail once
    more,
Freighted with souls, to all that duty bid
Faithful as they who sought an unknown land,
O'er wintry seas, from Holland's Hook of
  Sand!
Aquidneck's isle, Nantucket's lonely shores,
  And Indian-haunted Narragansett saw
  The wayworn travellers round their camp
    fires draw,
Or heard the plashing of their weary oars.
And every place whereon they rested grew
  Happier for pure and gracious womanhood,
  And men whose names for stainless honor
    stood,
Founders of States and rulers wise and true.
The Muse of history yet shall make amends
  To those who freedom, peace, and justice
    taught,
  Beyond their dark age led the van of thought,
And left unforfeited the name of Friends.
O mother State, how foiled was thy design!
The gain was theirs, the loss alone was thine.

From Harper's Weekly, March 15, 1884.

The Virginia House of Burgesses initiated the practice of legislative supremacy in matters of freedom of speech when the members decided, in 1620, that a Captain Henry Spellman was guilty of speaking "treasonable words" and voted to strip him of his rank. The Massachusetts legislature, sitting as a court in 1635, banished the Baptist Roger Williams for the crime of disseminating "dangerous opinions" against the government (among other "dangerous" beliefs, Williams advocated the separation of church and state). Between 1706 and 1720 the General Assembly of New York punished four citizens for seditious reflections on the assembly. The Pennsylvania Assembly of 1758 ordered the arrest of the Reverend William Smith, a prominent Anglican minister, and William Moore, a county judge, for collusion in libeling the *previous* assembly, and before a trial could be held, voted that they were guilty![7] As these and other cases illustrate, freedom of speech in both religious and political matters was not a civil liberty but a right reserved to a powerful few in much of colonial America.[8]

Control of Content in the Colonies

Neither private libel nor obscenity were significant free-speech concerns in colonial America,[9] although both were eventually written into the statutes of the states following independence. Obscenity, for example, is mentioned hardly at all during the colonial period. Massachusetts did enact a statute in 1712 making it a crime to publish any "filthy, obscene, or profane song, pamphlet, libel, or mock sermon," but this prohibition was directed more at blasphemy and profanity than at erotic sexual materials.[10] The first American prosecution for obscenity did not occur until 1815, in Philadelphia. The two types of speech that were vigorously suppressed during colonial times were blasphemy and sedition, both of which merit special attention at this point.

Blasphemous Libel

The Puritan colonies of New England—Massachusetts, New Hampshire, and Connecticut—were governed according to theocratic principles (i.e., by clergymen claiming divine sanction). The laws of Massachusetts illustrate how the Puritan clergy sought to suppress religious opinions of which they disapproved. In 1641, the General Court of Massachusetts adopted the principle that the "civil authority" of the state had the duty to see that "the people be fed with wholesome and sound doctrine." In 1646, the same body, declaring that "damnable heresies . . . ought to be duly restrained," adopted the Act Against Heresy, which punished persons who denied the immortality of the soul, the resurrection, or the need for re-

---

[7]Ibid., p. 57.

[8]For a more detailed study of cases, see Levy, chapter 2, "The American Colonial Experience," and Nat Hentoff, *The First Freedom: The Tumultuous History of Free Speech in America* (New York: Delacorte Press, 1980), chapters 5, 6, and 17.

[9]A number of reasons can be given for the absence of much heat over defamation and obscenity in the colonies, including (1) the widely scattered, primarily rural nature of the population; (2) the limited number of print-

ing presses; and (3) the overriding concern of clergy and government officials for suppressing other types of expression, viz., blasphemy and sedition.

[10]Cited by Supreme Court Justice William Brennan in America's landmark censorship decision, *Roth* v. *U.S.*, 354 U.S. 476 (1957). Brennan recognizes the religious basis of this statute, commenting "Thus, profanity and obscenity were related offenses."

pentance. Those who attempted to convert others to these or other heresies were banished from the colony.[11]

In the southern colonies, where the Church of England was official, similar restrictions upon religious expression were imposed. Virginia's Governor Thomas Dale (mentioned previously) in his 1612 "Lawes Divine, Moral and Martial," asserted that *death* was the penalty for speaking "impiously of the Trinity . . . or against the known articles of Christian faith," or for "blaspheming God's holy Name." Other punishments devised by the governor included having a bodkin "thrust through the tongue" for cursing and being subjected to a public whipping for speaking derisively of "God's holy word" or for speaking disrespectfully of a minister.[12]

Even the more liberal colonies of Maryland, Rhode Island, and Pennsylvania defined "tolerance" to mean only that *other Christians* could worship as they chose; they did not provide protection for the opinions of non-Christians or those who might oppose the beliefs and practices of established Christian groups. Maryland's ironically named Act of Toleration of 1649 decreed the *death penalty* and the forfeiture of property for any person who "shall hence forth blaspheme God . . . or deny our Savior Jesus Christ to be the Son of God, or shall deny the Holy Trinity . . . or shall use or utter any reproachful speeches, words or language concerning the Holy Trinity. . . ."[13] And in William Penn's state, the Great Law of 1682 provided that profanity be punished and that church attendance be required in order to prevent the growth of "looseness, irreligion and Atheism."[14]

Seditious Libel

At the same time that church and state were joined in trying to suppress blasphemy in the New World, the various governors and the elected assemblies were busy attempting to stamp out criticism of more temporal matters. In 1660 the House of Burgesses of Virginia had a citizen imprisoned for speaking "scandalous, mutinous, and seditious" words (he had been critical of a tax bill), and in 1699 the Governor's Council had four citizens arrested and punished for communicating an "evil opinion" of the government.[15] In nearby Maryland, a group of dissidents under the leadership of one John Coode issued a statement in 1689 condemning the existence of harsh laws against "mutinous and seditious" speeches, thus indicating a free-speech problem in that state.[16] Further north, the first governor of New York instituted prosecutions for sedition early in the seventeenth century, a policy that remained in effect for almost one hundred years. Similar attempts to control speech critical of the government were in effect in seventeenth-century Pennsylvania and Massachusetts, leading Levy to observe that "liberty of expression in principle or practice barely existed, if at all, in the American colonies during the seventeenth century."[17]

Matters gradually improved in the eighteenth century, although prosecutions for sedition did not occur despite the growing sympathy for freedom of expression. In 1754 the Massachusetts legislature ordered that a pamphlet that represented a "false, scandalous Libel reflecting upon the Proceedings of

---

[11]Pfeffer, p. 75.
[12]Ibid., pp. 77–78.
[13]Ibid., p. 83.
[14]Ibid., p. 89.

[15]Levy, p. 22.
[16]Ibid., p. 23.
[17]Ibid., p. 34.

the House in general, and on many worthy Members in particular," be burned by the hangman, and that warrants for the arrest of the alleged author be issued. In Virginia, the House of Burgesses punished ten men for signing a "seditious paper," and in North Carolina the assembly, having voted that an article which appeared in the *Gazette* was a "false, seditious, and Malicious Libel," imprisoned the author of the piece.[18]

The trial of newspaper publisher John Peter Zenger in New York in 1735 did not change things greatly, although the jury's verdict of "not guilty" did demonstrate that the citizens of the colony were sometimes sympathetic to those who verbally attacked the king's representatives, especially if the criticism was true. Zenger had written critical comments about Governor William Cosby, accusing him of incompetence, favoritism, tampering with trial by jury, and rigging elections. The governor ordered Zenger prosecuted for sedition. Early in the trial the judge explained to the jury that, under the common law, the jury was to decide only the fact of publication, whereas he, the judge, would determine whether or not Zenger's expression was seditious. The citizen jury ignored the judge's instructions and accepted the argument of Andrew Hamilton, Zenger's persuasive attorney, that *truth* was a defense and, to the consternation of the judge and the governor, acquitted Zenger. Although this decision did not alter the common law (it came fifty-seven years before Fox's Libel Act), it did add weight to the argument that citizens should have the freedom to speak more freely concerning the conduct of government officials.[19]

Control of Printing in the Colonies

The licensing of the press was never as well organized in the colonies as in England, although there were local exceptions. Prior restraint upon printing is recorded in Massachusetts, New York, and Pennsylvania as late as the 1720s and in Virginia until the latter part of the seventeenth century. No doubt there were other locations where licensing was practiced upon occasion. The colonies ended their licensing procedures at about the same time that Parliament refused to renew prior restraint laws in England, so that by 1725 licensing was no longer an issue in America.[20]

The Colonies in Brief

In summary, during the early years of colonial America only high government officials and leading clergymen could function freely as public communicators. Later, the members of the popular assemblies gained freedom of debate. However, freedom of speech for all citizens did not become an official government policy until the ratification of the Bill of Rights in 1791, and even then—as later chapters will demonstrate—many decades were to pass before the promise of the First Amendment became a reality. Second, colonial authorities vigorously suppressed opinions they believed to be blasphemous or seditious, although they paid little attention to private libel or obscenity. Finally, the authorities of Massachusetts, New York, Pennsylvania, and Virginia practiced control over the press as a medium of communication by enforcing policies of licensing until early in the eighteenth century. Those colonies that did practice licensing abandoned their efforts at about the same time that Parliament ended the procedure in England.

[18]Ibid., pp. 75–76.
[19]For more on the Zenger case, see Hentoff, pp. 63–68; also, Levy, pp. 126–134.

[20]See Levy, pp. 18–87, for a more detailed discussion.

II. THE ADOPTION OF THE CONSTITUTION AND THE BILL OF RIGHTS

On Monday, September 17, 1787, following an intense and sometimes bitter debate, the delegates to the Constitutional Convention unanimously resolved that the result of their work should be submitted to "the United States in Congress assembled, and that it is the opinion of this convention, that it should afterwards be submitted to a convention of delegates, chosen in each state by the people thereof . . . for their assent and ratification." Nine of the thirteen states were required to ratify the proposed document before it became the supreme law of the new nation.

The first state to ratify was Delaware (December 7, 1787), followed by Pennsylvania, New Jersey, Georgia, Connecticut, Massachusetts, Maryland, and South Carolina. New Hampshire was the ninth state to act, voting approval on June 21, 1788, thereby putting the Constitution into effect. Virginia, New York, and North Carolina were reluctant to support the document because it lacked guarantees of certain civil liberties that the representatives of these states believed were vital. When promises were made that a bill of rights would be developed by the Congress and submitted to the states as amendments to the original Constitution, both Virginia and New York ratified. North Carolina waited until the Congress actually approved the bill of rights before voting affirmatively. (The thirteenth state, Rhode Island, did not ratify until May of 1790.)

Although the original Constitution did not mention certain individual liberties desired by the people—such as freedom of religion, and freedom of speech—it did specify others. For example, the Constitution of 1788 provides the following guarantees:

1. The writ of habeas corpus cannot be suspended except in times of critical emergency, such as rebellion or invasion (I, 9:2).

2. No bills of attainder are permitted (I, 9:3. Note: A bill of attainder is a procedure in English law by which the king or the Parliament tried a person for crimes such as treason *without recourse to the courts;* such persons were often condemned to severe punishment, including death).

3. No ex post facto laws are allowed (I, 9:3).

4. Titles of nobility are illegal (I, 9:8).

5. All crimes against the United States, except impeachment, must be tried by a jury in the state where the crime was committed (III, 2:3).

6. Strict limitations are placed upon the definition, trial, and punishment of treason (III, 3:1–2).

7. A republican form of government is guaranteed to the citizens of every state (IV, 4).

8. No religious test is allowed as a qualification for holding office (VI, 3).

The original Constitution also granted Congress the authority to enact copyright legislation, although the document does not require that such a law be approved. Article I, Section 8:8 of the Constitution, without specifically employing the term "copyright," provides that "Congress shall have Power . . . To promote the Progress of Science and useful Arts, by securing for limited Times to Authors and Inventors the exclusive Right to their respective Writings and Discoveries." This provision, the wording of which reflects the influence of the English Statute of Anne as interpreted by the House of Lords in 1774, was given life by the Congress with the enactment of the Copyright Act of 1790. Among other things, this law provided to the author-creator a legal right of copy for a period of fourteen years, renewable under specified conditions for one additional period of fourteen years. The statute, as amended in 1831, was the basis for the landmark decision of the U.S. Supreme Court on copyright in *Wheaton* v. *Peters* (1834), a development discussed later in the chapter under "Constraints upon Media and Channels."

As promised, the First Congress began work on a bill of rights during the summer of 1789. James Madison took the lead in the House of Representatives, and on June 8, 1789, proposed twelve amendments to the Constitution which were based upon suggestions received earlier from several state representatives. Madison's original amendment to protect religious and communication freedoms was composed of three sections, as follows:

> The civil rights of none shall be abridged on account of religious belief or worship, nor shall any national religion be established, nor shall the full and equal rights of conscience be in any manner, or on any pretext, infringed.
>
> The people shall not be deprived or abridged of their right to speak, to write, or to publish their sentiments, and the freedom of the press, as one of the great bulwarks of liberty, shall be inviolable.
>
> The people shall not be restrained from peaceably assembling and consulting for their common good; nor from applying to the legislature by petitions, or remonstrances, for redress of their grievances.[21]

A select committee of the House, with Madison as one of its members, was assigned the task of studying proposals for a bill of rights. Madison's ideas for the protection of freedom of religion and freedom of speech against encroachment by the *federal* government were agreed to in principle; however, his three phrases were reduced to one, thus shortening the statement by more than half.

On a second but related matter, Madison argued that the states, too, should be required to guarantee certain rights, including "equal rights of conscience," "freedom of the press," and "trial by jury in criminal cases" to all citizens. The committee agreed, and after adding the phrase "freedom of speech" to Madison's list, reported back to the House that "No State shall infringe the equal rights of conscience, nor the freedom of speech or of the press, nor of the right of trial by jury in criminal cases."[22] The twelve amendments, including the restrictions upon the states, were approved by the House and forwarded to the Senate for final action.

In the Senate, those who believed that the Constitution already contained too many restrictions upon states rights managed to have Madison's constraints upon the states deleted; the other sections of the proposed bill of rights were approved by the Senate and sent to the states for ratification. As a result, the Bill of Rights of 1789 placed controls upon the federal government but *not upon state governments* in vital civil liberties areas (the states were to provide safeguards in their own constitutions). In the area of freedom of speech, the First Amendment limited federal authorities *only* until 1925, when the U.S. Supreme Court, in the case of *Gitlow* v. *New York,* employed the due process clause of the Fourteenth Amendment (adopted in 1868) to apply the First Amendment to the states. In *Gitlow,* Madison's argument of 1789 finally prevailed.[23]

---

[21]*Annals of Congress* (House), June 8, 1789, I:434.

[22]Levy, p. 222.
[23]*Gitlow* v. *New York*, 268 U.S. 652 (1925).

FIGURE 2.2. THOMAS JEFFERSON.

FIGURE 2.3. JAMES MADISON.
At the urging of Thomas Jefferson, James Madison came to believe that a bill of basic rights—to include liberty of speech—should be added to the federal Constitution of 1788. In the summer of 1789, in his capacity as a member of the House in the First Congress, Madison led the Congress in the development of the rights amendments that were proposed to the states, thus earning the title Father of the Bill of Rights. In 1791 the first ten amendments to the Constitution were ratified by the states, and the long-debated Bill of Rights became a reality. Jefferson was later elected as the nation's third president (1801–1809), to be followed in that office by Madison, who served as president from 1809 until 1817.
Both pictures from The Writings of Thomas Jefferson, The Thomas Jefferson Memorial Foundation (1903).

By December of 1791 three-fourths of the states—the required number for ratification—had approved ten of the twelve proposed amendments in the Bill of Rights. The two that were never ratified included an amendment to limit the number of members of the House of Representatives and another to prevent Congress from raising its salaries without an election intervening. The First Amendment which emerged from the ratification process reads:

> Congress shall make no law respecting an establishment of religion, or prohibiting the free exercise thereof; or abridging the freedom of speech, or of the press; or the right of the people peaceably to assemble, and to petition the Government for a redress of grievances.

III. FREEDOM OF SPEECH IN THE NEW NATION: FROM THE ALIEN AND SEDITION ACTS TO WORLD WAR I

The adoption of the Constitution and the Bill of Rights marked a high point in the centuries of struggle for democracy and civil liberties; never before had a people managed to adopt principles that so eloquently proscribed the powers of those who govern, thereby assuring (or so it would seem) the personal freedoms of the governed. Years later the British statesman William Gladstone would describe the American Constitution as "the most wonderful work ever struck off at a given time by the brain and purpose of man."[24] Yet the ink was hardly dry upon the first ten amendments to that Constitution before conflicts over civil liberties emerged. In the area of freedom of speech, the intense disputes that developed were the result of at least five interacting factors:

1. International affairs, particularly (a) disagreements with France from 1793 to 1800, and the resulting Alien and Sedition Acts passed by the Congress in 1798, and (b) World War I, which America entered in 1917, and the resulting Espionage Acts of 1917 and 1918.
2. The Civil War, including prewar abolitionist controversies, wartime constraints in both North and South, and post-Civil War repression of blacks and their sympathizers, particularly in the South.
3. The feminist movement and related controversies concerning the rights of women.

4. The growth of the publishing industry, resulting in an increase in suits for private libel, and, at the same time, the codification of the common law of defamation by state legislatures.
5. Post-Civil War moral crusades leading to the adoption of strict federal and state laws aimed at the suppression of "immoral" expression.

During the 118 years between the adoption of the Alien and Sedition Acts and the explosion of state and federal antisedition activity upon the entry of America into World War I, the U.S. Supreme Court rarely heard cases concerning the First Amendment. In those few cases that it did hear, the Court issued few landmark decisions. However, those in power who wished to suppress the spread of opinions with which they disagreed were enthusiastically at work, using means both legal and extralegal to constrain both speaker and speech.

Control of Communicators

Other than the suspension of the writ of habeas corpus on several occasions by both the North and the South during the Civil War, the most significant method of source control during the nineteenth century was to prevent certain *groups* of persons from functioning as advocates. As if to imitate the Greeks—who did not extend the right of free speech to aliens, women, and slaves—the white male "establishment" of the United States constrained the same three groups. This was accomplished through formal legislation, social pressures, and extralegal intimidation and violence. Formal legislation was at the forefront of early efforts to control the public communication of aliens, for in the summer of 1798—only seven years following the ratification of the First Amendment—the Fed-

---

[24]Constitution Sesquicentennial Commission, *History of the Formation of the Union Under the Constitution* (Washington, D.C.: U.S. Government Printing Office, 1941), p. 127.

eralist-controlled Congress approved the Alien and Sedition Acts as a means of striking back at France, with which America was having a major foreign policy dispute (many articulate opponents of President Adams and the Federalists were French citizens living in the United States); furthermore, numerous immigrants from other European nations, and from England and Ireland, were attracted to the policies of the Democratic Republicans, led by Thomas Jefferson, and were seen by the Federalists as a threat to their control of the government. The measures against aliens, therefore, served the dual purposes of revenge upon France and protection for the incumbent party.

The Alien and Sedition Acts of 1798 consisted of four parts, the first three of which threatened aliens as public communicators; the fourth part concerned seditious content and is detailed in the next section of this chapter. For the sake of a clear overview, however, all four should be seen as the parts of a unified effort:

1. *The Naturalization Act* of June 18, 1798, changed from five to fourteen years the period of residence required for citizenship. (This act was repealed in 1802, when the naturalization law of 1795 was reenacted.)[25]

2. *The Alien Act* of June 25, 1798, which permitted the president to expel from the country any alien whom he believed "dangerous to the peace and safety of the United States" or whom he suspected of "treasonable or secret machinations against the government." (This act was allowed to expire in June of 1800, as set forth in the original law.)[26]

3. *The Alien Enemies Act* of July 6, 1798, which empowered the president in time of war to have any alien who was subject to an enemy power "apprehended, restrained, secured and removed." (This was a permanent statute and *remains in force* as a part of the president's wartime emergency power.)[27]

4. *The Sedition Act* of July 14, 1798, which included punishment for "any false, scandalous and malicious" writing against the government. (This act was allowed to expire on March 3, 1801, as set forth in the original law.)[28]

Thirteen years following the expiration of the Alien Act, former President John Adams noted in a letter to Jefferson that he had not applied the law in a single instance.[29] Nevertheless, the law did have a chilling effect upon hundreds of aliens, including numerous critics of Adams and the Federalists, who felt threatened and therefore either fled the country or went into hiding until the act expired.[30]

In addition to aliens, America's women composed a second group of persons who were discriminated against as potential sources of discourse. Abigail Adams stated the issue succinctly in March of 1776 when, in a letter to her husband, John Adams, she anticipated American independence and the writing of a Constitution and new statutes: " . . . [in future lawmaking, do] not put such unlimited power into the hands of the husbands. Remember, all men would be tyrants if they could. If particular care and attention is not paid to the ladies, we are determined to foment a rebellion, and will not

---

[25]1 *Statutes at Large* 566–569.
[26]1 *Statutes at Large* 570–572.

[27]1 *Statutes at Large* 577–578.
[28]1 *Statutes at Large* 596–597. Note: The full text of the Sedition Act is given elsewhere in this chapter.
[29]James Morton Smith, *Freedom's Fetters: The Alien and Sedition Laws and American Civil Liberties* (Ithaca, N.Y.: Cornell University Press, 1956), p. 159.
[30]For more on the exodus, see ibid., chapter 9, "The Hunters and the Hunted," especially pp. 159–162.

FIGURE 2.4. *WOMEN SPEAKERS BEFORE A COMMITTEE OF CONGRESS.* This nineteenth-century engraving pictures a group of female suffragists testifying in favor of voting rights for women before the Judiciary Committee of the House of Representatives, January 11, 1871. The expressions of skepticism on the faces of the men effectively depict the mood of the times concerning public advocacy by women. The engraving was published in Leslie's Illustrated Weekly, February 4, 1871. *Library of Congress.*

hold ourselves bound by any laws in which we have no voice or representation."[31]

Although the ratification of the Bill of Rights in 1791 guaranteed all citizens, women included, the legal right to speak, write, and publish, the extralegal pressures of the male-dominated society effectively prevented most females from functioning as effective speakers. As Ellen Carol DuBois points out in her study of the early feminist movement, the women of the United States suffered from "lack of public skills; lives marked by excessive domesticity; husbands and fathers hostile to their efforts; the material pressures of housekeeping and child-rearing; and the deep psychological insecurity bred by all these factors."[32]

Women were denied not only the vote but also, for the most part, education, along with career opportunities in the professions, in the established churches, and in government. To secure a formal education, which included learning how to write and speak effectively, was difficult if not impossible for a woman. No American college would admit women until 1833, when Oberlin broke with tradition and enrolled female students; however, for a number of years females at Oberlin were *not allowed to speak in class.*[33] Even a number of abolitionist societies refused to open their membership to females, and when a group of American women attended the World Anti-Slavery Convention in London in 1840, the indignant male organizers of the event assigned them to the galleries and *denied them permission to speak.*[34]

Despite intimidating extralegal pressures, women such as Susan B. Anthony, An-

[31]From *Familiar Letters of John Adams and His Wife, Abigail Adams, During the Revolution,* ed. Charles Francis Adams (1876); cited in Eve Cary and Kathleen W. Peratis, *Woman and the Law* (Skokie, Ill.: National Textbook, 1977), pp. 1–2.

[32]Ellen Carol DuBois, *Feminism and Suffrage: The Emergence of an Independent Women's Movement in America, 1848–1869* (Ithaca, N.Y.: Cornell University Press, 1978), p. 24.

[33]Cary and Peratis, p. 5.

[34]J. R. Pole, *The Pursuit of Equality in American History* (Berkeley, Calif.: University of California Press, 1978), p. 301.

toinette Brown, Mary Grew, and Elizabeth Cady Stanton persisted in their efforts to be heard in the public forum. In a letter of September 10, 1855, to Susan B. Anthony, Mrs. Stanton eloquently addressed the issue when she affirmed her determination to speak freely, even though her father had temporarily disinherited her because of her attempts to lecture in public:

> To think that all in me of which my father would have felt a proper pride had I been a man, is deeply mortifying to him because I am a woman . . . has stung me to a fierce decision—to speak as soon as I can do myself credit. But the pressure on me just now is too great. [My husband] Henry sides with my friends who oppose me in all that is dearest to my heart. They are not willing that I should write even on the woman question. *But I will both write and speak.*[35]

And write and speak she did, together with other brave and dedicated women, until "the ladies" were no longer considered oddities when they advocated their beliefs. As women acquired good educations and improved their skills of communication, they became more effective in the public forum—so effective, in fact, that they persuaded the nation to adopt the Woman Suffrage Amendment to the Constitution in 1920.

Blacks in America, both as slaves and as free persons, composed a third group of potential speakers to be suppressed. Of the three groups discussed here—aliens, women, and blacks—the latter suffered most severely, particularly in the South.[36] White society controlled blacks in two important ways:

first, by denying or severely limiting educational opportunities, thereby reducing the prospect that a black could communicate effectively in public; and second, by using persuasion, repressive laws, and extralegal intimidation and force to constrain those blacks who did manage to become literate.

Although many citizens in the North were sympathetic to the educational and civil liberties ambitions of blacks, not all shared this humane view. In some cases private schools for Negroes were threatened or forcibly closed, college admission for Negroes was often denied, and Negro speakers were sometimes threatened by mobs. Some theological schools in the North would not admit Negro ministerial students. However, it was in the southern states that blacks endured the greater repression.

The general method for the control of blacks was the slave code, which by 1835 was in use throughout the slaveholding sections of the nation. The code included the following provisions: (1) rebelling or plotting an insurrection was punishable by death; (2) slaves could not leave their plantations without written passes; (3) slaves could not assemble for social events, such as dancing, without the presence of a white man; (4) firearms, horses, horns, and drums could not be owned by slaves; (5) black preachers could not speak to their fellow blacks without the presence of a white man (and in some states could not preach to fellow blacks at all); (6) except in Maryland, Tennessee, and Kentucky, Negroes could not be taught how to read and write; (7) all slave owners were required to keep white persons on their plantations; and (8) free blacks were to be kept away from slaves. These rules, and others similar to them, were enforced by armed patrols of white citizens which were activated at the slightest hint of trouble.[37]

[35] *Stanton Letters,* cited in DuBois, p. 26. [Emphasis supplied.]

[36] Note: Constraints upon the communication rights of racial minorities have not been limited to blacks, of course. The American Indian, who was not granted full citizenship until 1924, faced similar barriers, as did Orientals, Mexicans, Irish, Puerto Ricans, and others.

[37] Clement Eaton, *The Freedom-of-Thought Struggle in the Old South* (New York: Harper & Row, 1964), p. 114.

A few examples serve to illustrate the difficulty faced by blacks who wished to serve as communicators in the antebellum South. Prior to 1862, Georgia prohibited the licensing of Negroes to the ministry.[38] In South Carolina, Negroes were punished by death upon the third conviction for possession of abolitionist literature.[39] In 1829, the North Carolina General Assembly voted to require free Negroes serving as stewards or mariners to stay aboard their ships while docked in North Carolina ports, thus preventing them from speaking to any North Carolina black.[40] Last, the southern attitude toward the education of blacks was particularly narrow, since the literate black was a potential source of an effective abolitionist message. As one speaker in the Virginia House of Delegates put it in 1832, "We have, as far as possible, closed every avenue by which light can enter . . . [the Negro mind]. If we could extinguish the capacity to see the light, our work would be completed; they would then be on a level with the beasts of the field, and we should be safe."[41]

After the Civil War, when southern whites discovered that enfranchised Negroes were not going to vote as directed by their former masters, the repression of black sources of dissent became even more determined. By ridicule, economic pressure, and vigilante action, whites fought to "keep Negroes in their place." Racist preachers, writers, political orators, and newspaper editors opposed civil liberties for blacks, using their rhetorical skills to sustain their opinions. The ridicule of white supremacist Ryland Randolph, editor of the *Independent Monitor* of Tuscaloosa, Alabama, is typical. Writing in 1868, Randolph jibes: "If [a Negro] . . . attends barbecues let his province be to wait on the tables and brush off flies. He befits the speaker's stand about as well as a skunk would suit a sofa. Let him squall aloud for . . . [the candidates he supports] to his heart's content, for it is like a donkey braying for his food. . . ."[42] Others resorted to violence rather than to ridicule and economic pressure, so that for decades most blacks in the former slaveholding states remained nonvoting, poorly educated, intimidated souls untutored in the art of effective persuasion. A century was to pass before the chant of "freedom now" and the dramatic civil rights advocacy of the 1960s—together with sympathetic rulings from the Supreme Court and the passage of strong civil rights legislation by the Congress—managed to break the bonds of racist constraint forged during Reconstruction and the years immediately thereafter. Even then, the "decade of dissent" of 1960–1970 was not without its costs, for many sources of that dissent were threatened and assaulted; some were murdered, including black communicators Medgar Evers and Martin Luther King, Jr.

Control of Content

The First Amendment's command that "Congress shall make no law . . . abridging the freedom of speech" seems clear; unfortunately it is not, as witnessed by

---

[38]Stephen A. Smith, "Freedom of Expression in the Confederate States of America," in *Free Speech Yearbook: 1978,* ed. Gregg Phifer (Falls Church, Va.: Speech Communication Association, 1978), p. 27.

[39]Russel B. Nye, *Fettered Freedom: Civil Liberties and the Slavery Controversy, 1830–1860* (East Lansing, Mich.: Michigan State College Press, 1949), p. 124.

[40]Eaton, p. 115.

[41]Cited in Nye, p. 71.

[42]Allen W. Trelease, *White Terror: The Ku Klux Klan Conspiracy and Southern Reconstruction* (New York: Harper & Row, 1971), pp. xl–xli. Note: Trelease documents numerous instances of vigilante attacks upon black communicators and their Caucasian sympathizers during the period of Reconstruction.

FIGURE 2.5. *"OF COURSE HE WANTS TO VOTE THE DEMOCRATIC TICKET!"* A potential black voter in the South being threatened by so-called Democratic *"reformers"* who are saying, *"You're as free as air, ain't you? Say you are, or I'll blow yer black head off!"* This 1876 engraving illustrates well the plight of southern blacks within a decade of the conclusion of the Civil War. Published as an editorial cartoon by Harper's Weekly, *the engraving ridiculed the two-faced attitude of certain politicians of the South who agreed in public that blacks should be "free" but who added that the federal government need not enforce that freedom, since the states would take care of things.*

Harper's Weekly, *October 21, 1876.*

the hundreds of essays, books, editorials, debates, and legal opinions on the subject. Furthermore, numerous laws have been passed at both the state and federal levels to proscribe the communication freedoms of American citizens. The disparity between principle and practice is grounded in history, for even the Founding Fathers were in disagreement about how to interpret the specifics of the Bill of Rights—the First Amendment in particular. Near the conclusion of his carefully documented study on *Freedom of Speech and Press in Early American History,* Leonard Levy remarks that the nation's founders were "sharply divided and possessed no clear understanding" of what they meant by freedom of speech.[43] Levy's finding is confirmed when both common law and statutory constraints upon content are examined for the period of 1791 to the Espionage Acts of World War I. As if to show complete agreement with the English view that freedom of

speech existed when there was an absence of prior restraint (but that punishment could be inflicted *after* publication), Americans celebrated their newfound liberty by proceeding to prosecute at common law, or by newly passed statute law, speech thought to be seditious, defamatory, or blasphemous.

Seditious Libel

In the summer of 1798, just a few days before the Congress passed the first of the alien and sedition bills, Thomas Jefferson described the increasing efforts of the Federalists to punish their political opponents as a "reign of witches."[44] Jefferson's characterization fits four major First Amendment crises in American history, the first, of course, being the period of the Alien and Sedition Acts. The second "reign of witches" occurred in the years before, during, and immediately after the Civil War, and the third was the period of 1917 into the 1920s, during

[43]Levy, p. 248.

[44]Letter from Jefferson to John Taylor of Philadelphia, June 1, 1798. Jefferson, vol. 10, p. 46.

THE SEDITION ACT OF JULY 14, 1798

The Alien and Sedition Acts were enacted by the Federalists in order to strike back at the French (the United States was engaged in a foreign policy dispute with France, and there were many French aliens in the country) and to silence domestic critics of President John Adams, himself a Federalist. The sedition bill was enforced with more vigor than were the three alien laws. At least twenty-four newspaper editors and one congressman—all supporters of the Democratic Republicans, led by Thomas Jefferson—were arrested and tried under the Sedition Act. A number were convicted and were fined or jailed. This repressive law, which was unpopular with the general public, was allowed to expire as set forth in the original measure on March 3, 1801—ironically, just one day before the inauguration of Thomas Jefferson as third president of the United States.

Section 1. *Be it enacted by the Senate and House of Representatives of the United States of America, in Congress assembled,* That if any persons shall unlawfully combine or conspire together, with intent to oppose any measure or measures of the government of the United States, which are or shall be directed by proper authority, or to impede the operation of any law of the United States, or to intimidate or prevent any person holding a place or office in or under the government of the United States, from undertaking, performing or executing his trust or duty; and if any person or persons, with intent as aforesaid, shall counsel, advise or attempt to procure any insurrection, riot, unlawful assembly, or combination, whether such conspiracy, threatening, counsel, advice, or attempt shall have the proposed effect or not, he or they shall be deemed guilty of a high misdemeanor, and on conviction, before any court of the United States having jurisdiction thereof, shall be punished by a fine not exceeding five thousand dollars, and by imprisonment during a term not less than six months nor exceeding five years; and further, at the discretion of the court may be holden to find sureties for this good behaviour in such sum, and for such time, as the court may direct.

Sec. 2. *And be it further enacted,* That if any person shall write, print, utter or publish, or shall cause or procure to be written, printed, uttered or published, or shall knowingly and willingly assist or aid in writing, printing, uttering or publishing any false, scandalous and malicious writing or writings against the government of the United States, or either house of the Congress of the United States, or the President of the United States, with intent to defame the said government, or either house of the said Congress, or the said President, or to bring them, or either of them, into contempt or disrepute; or to excite against them, or either or any of them, the hatred of the good people of the United States, or to stir up sedition within the United States, or to excite any unlawful combinations therein, for opposing or resisting any law of the United States, or any act of the President of the United States, done in pursuance of any such law, or of the powers in him vested by the constitution of the United States, or to resist, oppose, or defeat any such law or act, or to aid, encourage or abet any hostile designs of any foreign nation against the United States, their people or government, then such person, being thereof convicted before any court of the United States having jurisdiction thereof, shall be punished by a fine not exceeding two thousand dollars, and by imprisonment not exceeding two years.

Sec. 3. *And be it further enacted and declared,* That if any person shall be prosecuted under this act, for the writing or publishing any libel aforesaid, it shall be lawful for the defendant, upon the trial of the cause, to give evidence in his defence, the truth of the matter contained in the publication charged as a libel. And the jury who shall try the cause, shall have a right to determine the law and the fact, under the direction of the court, as in other cases.

Sec. 4. *And be it further enacted,* That this act shall continue and be in force until the third day of March, one thousand eight hundred and one, and no longer: Provided, that the expiration of the act shall not prevent or defeat a prosecution and punishment of any offence against the law, during the time it shall be in force.

1 Statutes at Large 596–597.

and in the aftermath of World War I. The final "reign of witches" centers around World War II and includes the prewar Alien Registration Act of 1940 and the postwar Internal Security Act of 1950 as well as the search for "subversion" by Senator Joseph McCarthy in the late 1940s and the early 1950s. During each of the four periods, *seditious messages* were the objects of the "witches" hunt.

Although the Alien Acts were not vigorously enforced, the opposite was true of the Sedition Act of 1798 (see box). This law, which provided penalties for "writing, printing, uttering or publishing any false, scandalous and malicious writing . . . against the government of the United States," was enthusiastically prosecuted, particularly in the New England and mid–Atlantic states, where Federalists were in control. At least twenty-four Republican editors, one congressman, and a number of private citizens were prosecuted under the Sedition Act, including Benjamin Bache, grandson of Benjamin Franklin and editor of the leading Republican paper, the Philadelphia *Aurora;* editors of the Boston *Independent Chronicle,* the New York *Argus,* the Richmond *Examiner,* and the Baltimore *American;* and Republican Congressman Matthew Lyon, who had publicly criticized President Adams. In addition, the *Time Piece* and the *Mount Pleasant Register,* both anti-Federalist newspapers in New York, ceased publication as a result of the prosecutions, while in New London, Connecticut, the *Bee* suspended publication for five months in 1800 while its editor served time in prison for sedition.[45]

In a comic episode that was counterproductive to the Federalist cause, an intoxicated Luther Baldwin of Newark, New Jersey, articulated his opinion of the controversy—within hearing distance of Federalist sympathizers—by saying that he didn't care if someone fired a cannon through President Adams' ass! For this remark Baldwin was arrested, tried, and convicted for speaking seditious words "tending to defame the President and Government of the United States." Upon conviction he was fined, assessed court costs, and placed in a federal jail until the fine and court fees were paid.[46] With wicked glee the Republican press told the nation of the conviction of this "dangerous" drunkard, and within days the now sober fellow became a hero to the Jeffersonians. Continuing the attack, the New York *Argus* dryly assured its readers that Baldwin was no real danger to the president, for no person would think of "firing at such a disgusting a target" as the ass of John Adams.[47]

The constitutional issues inherent in the Alien and Sedition Acts never reached the Supreme Court during the years the laws were in force, although a number of Federalist judges in lower courts (including three Supreme Court justices who were hearing cases in circuit courts) did rule that the acts did not violate the Constitution.[48] Popular

---

[45]James Morton Smith, *Freedom's Fetters,* pp. 176–187.

[46]Ibid., pp. 270–271.

[47]Ibid., p. 273.

[48]During the twentieth century several justices of the U.S. Supreme Court have commented on the Alien and Sedition Acts. In his dissent in *Abrams* v. *United States,* 250 U.S. 616 (1919), at 630, Justice Holmes states: "I wholly disagree with the argument of the Government that the First Amendment left the common law as to seditious libel in force. History seems to me against the notion. I had conceived that the United States through many years had shown its repentance for the Sedition Act of 1798 by repaying fines that it imposed." In 1964, writing for the majority in *New York Times* v. *Sullivan,* 376 U.S. 254 (1964), at 276, Justice Brennan states: "Although the Sedition Act was never tested in this court, the attack upon its validity has carried the day in the court of history. . . . [There exists] a broad consensus that the Act, because of the restraint it imposed upon criticism of government and public officials, was inconsistent with the First Amendment."

opposition to the legislation was a factor in the defeat of the Federalists in the election of 1800. The newly elected President Jefferson soon pardoned all those convicted under the Alien and Sedition Acts. However, this first free-speech crisis in the new republic clearly demonstrates the tenuous health of the First Amendment at the beginning of the nineteenth century, soon reconfirmed by events that led to the war between the states.

The suppression of "sedition" before, during, and after the Civil War focused upon two types of messages: those that urged freedom and justice for blacks and those wartime messages that were critical of the government, whether of the Union or of the Confederacy. During the 1820s, debates over slavery became more and more heated; by the early 1830s, abolitionists began to organize societies so that they could speak effectively against the evils of involuntary servitude. Predictably, the legislatures of the southern states responded with laws designed to punish the communication of abolitionist arguments.

The Virginia Act of 1836 is typical of the restraints placed upon freedom of speech by the southern states. The statute begins by acknowledging the source of the subversive opinion as "certain abolition and anti-slavery societies and evil disposed persons, being and residing in some of the non-slaveholding states." Article 1 then provides that any member or agent of an abolitionist society who comes to Virginia to advocate "by speaking or writing, that the owners of slaves have no property in the same," or to "advise the abolition of slavery," is guilty of a high misdemeanor. Such persons, upon convic-

tion, could be punished by a fine of $200 and imprisoned for up to three years.[49]

Meanwhile, many conservatives in the North, partly from prejudice and partly from a belief that northerners should "mind their own business," did what they could to discourage the work of the antislavery organizations. This attitude was reversed to a great degree during the late 1830s and early 1840s in response to harsh antiabolitionist legislation in the South and mob violence against opponents of slavery in both North and South. An event that occurred near St. Louis, Missouri, on the night of November 7, 1837, was especially influential in changing conservative attitudes in the North.

Elijah P. Lovejoy, a native of Maine and a graduate of Princeton Theological Seminary, moved to St. Louis, Missouri, in the early 1830s to edit the *Observer,* a religious newspaper. The paper was not affiliated with any abolitionist society and generally published religious news and opinion. Occasionally, however, editor Lovejoy stated his antislavery views, including an occasion in 1836 when he bitterly condemned a racist mob for burning a Negro alive. Soon thereafter he was driven out of St. Louis by threats, moving his press to nearby Alton, Illinois, where it was forthwith burned by a mob. Lovejoy's replacement press was burned also, as was his third. In November of 1837 his fourth press arrived and was placed in a warehouse for safekeeping. On the night of November 7 a mob of about thirty men marched on the warehouse and set it ablaze. While fighting the blaze, Elijah Lovejoy was shot and killed. The mob finished burning the warehouse and later destroyed what was left of the press, throwing the pieces in the river. As Nye points out in *Fettered Freedom,* "The Alton tragedy rocked the North to its foundations," for Lovejoy had been murdered in a *free* state. From that point forward, "aboli-

---

[49]Harold L. Nelson, ed., *Freedom of the Press from Hamilton to the Warren Court* (Indianapolis: Bobbs-Merrill, 1967), p. 175.

tionism and freedom of the press merged into a single cause."[50]

After the Civil War began, officials in both the Union and the Confederacy permitted a surprising degree of freedom of expression, although there were notable exceptions in both camps. Northerners who opposed the Lincoln administration during the war years were referred to as "Copperheads," and the "Copperhead press" was often vehement in its criticisms of the president, the members of his cabinet, and the military execution of the war. On a number of occasions military men and others sympathetic to the Union cause assaulted the editors or destroyed the equipment—or both—of antigovernment newspapers. In one such case, Ambrose S. Kimball, editor of the *Essex County Democrat* of Haverhill, Massachusetts, was seized in his home by members of a mob, tarred and feathered, and ridden through town on a rail for publishing anti-Union sentiment. He was released after taking an oath that he would "never again write or publish articles against the North and in favor of secession."[51]

In 1863, Union General A. E. Burnside closed the *Chicago Times* for its extreme "Copperheadism," but after three days the paper was allowed to resume publication when Lincoln, on behalf of "liberty of the press," revoked the general's order.[52] Lincoln's libertarianism was temporarily interrupted on May 18, 1864, when two antiadministration newspapers in New York, the *World* and the *Journal of Commerce,* published

a bogus presidential proclamation claiming that a new draft of 400,000 men was imminent. An outraged president, after a conference with his cabinet, ordered the two newspapers closed and their owners arrested and imprisoned. The Independent Telegraph System, which had transmitted the story, was seized by the military and its transmissions stopped.[53] Fortunately for most other Copperhead papers, the measures taken in the bogus proclamation case were the exception rather than the rule, thanks in large part to the patience and democratic beliefs of Abraham Lincoln.

The Constitution of the Confederate States of America, ratified on March 29, 1861, included a freedom-of-speech clause identical in language to that of the First Amendment to the U.S. Constitution. However, this did not prohibit the government, the military, and some private citizens exercising extralegal constraints from attempting to control seditious speech during the war. The Congress, for example, passed several restrictive laws, including one to punish anyone who tried to entice desertion from the military and another to imprison or execute anyone caught communicating with the Union "with intent to injure the Confederate States of America."[54] Southern military authorities occasionally attempted to silence dissent by arresting reporters, threatening newspapers, or issuing decrees of censorship under the cloak of martial law. In North Carolina, troops ac-

---

[50]Nye, p. 119. For a more complete account, see Nye, chapter 4, "Abolitionism and Freedom of the Press." Note: The nineteenth-century orator Wendell Phillips delivered his famous "Murder of Lovejoy" speech in response to the Illinois incident; see the exercises at the end of this chapter. Also, in January of 1838 nineteen of the members of the murderous mob were tried for riot and found not guilty.

[51]Nelson, p. 223. For other examples see pp. 222–227.

[52]Ibid., pp. 230–232.

[53]Note: The false proclamation was the result of a hoax perpetrated by a stock market manipulator named Joseph Howard, who hoped to profit from the news of the draft. The editors and owners of the two newspapers and the telegraph company were not parties to the hoax (although they were negligent about confirming the announcement before publication), a fact that led many citizens to conclude that the government's actions were unjust. See Nelson, pp. 232–247.

[54]Smith, "Freedom of Expression in the Confederate States," p. 20.

tually destroyed the offices of the antiadministration *Raleigh Standard*. Instances of repression were numerous yet unpredictable in Richmond, the capitol of the Confederacy; likewise, a number of censorship efforts were made in eastern Tennessee, a stronghold of Union sentiment. Among the many persons punished for sedition in Richmond was a Unitarian minister who was jailed for praying that "this unholy rebellion should be crushed out."[55] And in eastern Tennessee, despite vigorous prosecutorial activity against the publication of "sedition," few people were convicted. As a rule, sympathetic judges released the prisoners or friendly juries refused to find guilt. In all of this, no official, organized pattern of restraint was evidenced. As Stephen A. Smith, whose scholarship includes a thorough study of freedom of speech in the Confederate states, concludes, "freedom of expression, when measured by prevailing practices in the United States during the same period, was no more repressed in the Confederacy than in the United States."[56]

During the years between the conclusion of the Civil War and the turn of the century, the most sustained restraint upon sedition occurred in the South, where a combination of economic pressure and organized terror effectively eliminated almost all civil rights advocacy on behalf of blacks. This intimidation lasted well into the twentieth century, as witnessed by the violent reactions of many southerners to black demands for equal justice during the 1960s.

Meanwhile, the growth of the labor movement and the attraction which that phenomenon had for a variety of radical anarchists, socialists, and other antiestablishment groups resulted in the passage of laws similar to those enacted during the sedition controversy

of one hundred years earlier. This time, however, the repressive legislation was approved, not by the United States Congress but by the legislatures of a number of *states*. Starting with the strike against the McCormick Harvester Company in 1886 and the bomb explosion and riot in Chicago's Haymarket Square during a rally in support of that strike, many state officials expressed alarm at the "seditious activities" of union organizers and their radical supporters. The issue became one of national concern when President William McKinley was assassinated by anarchist Leon Czolgosz in September of 1901.

In 1905 the Industrial Workers of the World (or IWW; nicknamed the "Wobblies") organized for the express purpose of abolishing capitalism and forming the working people of America into a Marxist-type industrial society. To get their message to the workers, the Wobblies spoke in the streets and in other open places where groups of lumbermen, migrant workers, or factory employees could be found. Attempts by employers and local police to censor the Wobblies caused numerous free-speech confrontations in communities from coast to coast. Consequently, the IWW was driven to make the First Amendment a key issue in its organizational campaigns. Local officials all too often ignored their oath to uphold the Constitution of the United States and assaulted, imprisoned, starved, and even tortured advocates of the Wobbly philosophy. Finally, the IWW movement was destroyed by a series of raids conducted by the federal government soon after America entered World War I.[57]

Because of labor and social unrest in some

---

[55]Ibid., p. 25.
[56]Ibid., p. 29.

[57]Terry W. Cole, "The Right to Speak: The Free Speech Fights of the Industrial Workers of the World," in *Free Speech Yearbook: 1978*, pp. 113–117. For additional information on the Wobblies, see the readings at the end of this chapter.

FIGURE 2.6. THE ASSASSINATION OF PRESIDENT MCKINLEY.
President William McKinley was shot by anarchist Leon Czolgosz on September 6, 1901, while attending a reception at the Pan-American Exposition, Buffalo, New York. Czolgosz, depicted with a handkerchief draped over his right hand to conceal the small pistol he used, had stalked McKinley for several days before the shooting occurred. Eight days later, McKinley died from the wounds. Czolgosz was promptly tried, convicted, and executed for murder. He went to his death unrepentant, claiming that all governmental leaders of the world should be eliminated in order that the ultimate freedom of anarchy should prevail.

Many states passed criminal anarchy laws in response to the murder of President McKinley. The thinking of the time was reflected in an editorial published by Harper's Weekly *on October 5, 1901, a month following McKinley's death: "Words that incite to crime are . . . criminal acts. The regular anarchist is . . . a potential murderer, at least a potential inspirer of murder. . . . We have treated him leniently because we have a theory that it is well to permit people like the anarchist to blow off steam; and this liberty, or license, of speech is a safety-valve. But we have made a mistake. . . . [The advocacy of anarchy] is a crime, and every speech made in behalf of destruction of government should be followed by imprisonment."*

Etching from Murat Halstead's The Illustrious Life of William McKinley, *privately printed, 1901 (as originally published in* Leslie's Illustrated Weekly*).*

parts of the country during the four decades preceding World War I, a number of states including New York, New Jersey, Wisconsin, and California passed antisedition statutes of their own. These state sedition acts are called *criminal anarchy* or *criminal syndicalism* laws. In general, their purpose is to pun-ish at the state level what the Alien and Sedition Acts of 1798, and, later, the federal Espionage Acts of 1917 and 1918 sought to punish at the national level. During the years following the conclusion of World War I, the Supreme Court handed down several important opinions concerning the First Amendment in cases that originated with attempts to enforce these state sedition statutes.[58]

Private Libel

Following the American Revolution, the law of private libel became a more important public communication issue than it had been during the colonial period. This was so because of the growing population, the increase in the number of newspapers and other publications, and the formal organization of state governments, which required the ratification of constitutions and the development of state legal codes (in the United States all defamation statutes are at the *state level*—there are no federal laws of slander and libel). The First Amendment to the Constitution did not restrain the states from codifying the common-law crime of defamation, as witnessed by the enactment of statutes punishing slander and libel by New Jersey (1799), New York (1820), and Massachusetts (1827). Also, the states of Pennsylvania, Delaware, Tennessee, Kentucky, Ohio, Indiana, and Illinois were among the first to provide for defamation suits in their constitutions.[59]

During the nineteenth century most, if not all, of the states added the offense of defamation to their legal codes. By the beginning of the twentieth century, according to a leading text on the subject, case law on defamation had become so complex that aspiring attorneys needed to know about (1) libels by means of writing, printing, pictures, and effigies; (2) oral defamation (slander); and (3) numerous subject types, including imputation of crime; imputation of a want of chastity or the commission of adultery or fornication; imputation of disease; and insults and criticisms affecting persons in offices, professions, and trades.[60] To the present time, the defamation of private persons is excluded from the protection of the First Amendment.[61]

Religio-Moral Heresy

In an English blasphemy case of 1676, presiding judge Lord Hale announced that "Christianity being parcel of the laws of England, therefore to reproach the Christian religion is to speak in subversion of the law."[62] This view, widely accepted by English and American colonial judges, was confirmed by Lord Mansfield in a 1767 decision in which he wrote: "The eternal principles of natural religion are part of the common law; the essential principles of revealed religion are part of the common law; so that any person reviling, subverting, or ridiculing them may be prosecuted at common law."[63] Following the American Revolution, this tradition concerning blasphemy was accepted in many state courts, as were the common-law traditions governing seditious libel and private libel. Although a number of states did codify antiblasphemy laws, others simply used the common law to punish those whose speech "maliciously reviled God or religion."[64] For years, the First Amendment's assurances of freedom of speech, and of the separation of church and state, had little deterrent effect upon pious prosecutors, judges, and jurors.

In 1811 a citizen whose name was Ruggles

---

[58]See Chapter 3, and these two cases in particular: *Gitlow* v. *New York* (1925) and *Whitney* v. *California* (1927).
[59]James Kent, *Commentaries on American Law*, vol. II (New York: O. Halsted, 1827), pp. 16–19. Reprinted by Da Capo Press, 1971.

[60]Martin L. Newell, *The Law of Slander and Libel in Civil and Criminal Cases*, 4th ed. (Chicago: Callaghan and Company, 1924), pp. vii–xii. Note: Newell's authoritative study was first published in 1890; the 1924 edition runs more than 1,000 pages.
[61]In the case of *New York Times* v. *Sullivan*, 376 U.S. 254 (1964), the U.S. Supreme Court made it much more difficult for *public officials* to successfully prosecute defamation cases (see Chapter 4).
[62]*Rex* v. *Taylor*, cited in Nelson, p. 51.
[63]*Chamberlain* v. *Evans*, cited in Nelson, p. 52.
[64]Pfeffer, p. 663.

was tried in New York for the common-law offense of blasphemy. According to the record, Ruggles had publicly stated that "Jesus Christ was a bastard and his mother was a whore." In confirming the conviction, the judge announced:

> The reviling is still an offense because it tends to corrupt the morals of the people, and to destroy good order. . . . The people of this State, in common with the people of this country, profess the general doctrines of Christianity . . . and to scandalize the author of these doctrines is not only . . . extremely impious, but . . . in gross violation of decency and good order.[65]

A similar trial occurred in Boston in 1834, when the court found Abner Kneeland guilty of blasphemy for circulating a newspaper that contained opinions contrary to the Christian religion. In his speech to the jury, the state prosecutor asserted that the courts must prevent "moral poison" by serving as "moral Boards of Health." Furthermore, argued the Commonwealth's attorney:

> The law does say, that no man shall in a scurrilous, indecent, scandalous, obscene manner blaspheme God or the Christian Religion as contained in the Holy Scriptures. . . . [T]hat when the Constitution and Laws establish the existence and providence of God and the Christian Religion and recognize them as part of the Law of the land, no man shall impiously and contumeliously reproach them—no man shall in a vulgar, sneering and scoffing manner promulgate doctrines destructive of the peace of society . . . .[66]

Harold Nelson states in his introduction to *Freedom of the Press from Hamilton to the Warren Court* that about two dozen blasphemy cases are reported for the nineteenth century, including the *Ruggles* and *Kneeland* cases mentioned above. Although this was by no means a "reign of terror" against religious dissent, the trial records do serve as a reminder of how the First Amendment was ignored by many government officials. In contemporary times the religio-moral offense of blasphemy is rarely prosecuted (see Chapter 5), although fifteen states continue to carry antiblasphemy laws on their books.[67] When prosecutions are attempted, they occur at the state level; as with defamation, there are no federal blasphemy statutes.

While attempts to suppress blasphemy remained few in number and in the twentieth century have all but ceased, the opposite is true for speech thought to be sexually immoral or "impure"—expression labeled under the common law as "obscene." In the years before the Civil War, as happened during the colonial period, there were few arrests for "obscenity"; those which did occur were at the state level. The first trial resulting from such an arrest took place in 1815 in Philadelphia, Pennsylvania, when Jesse Sharpless was charged and convicted under the common law (there were as yet no state or federal obscenity statutes) for exhibiting "for money, to persons . . . a certain lewd, wicked, scandalous, infamous, and obscene painting, representing a man in an obscene, impudent, and indecent posture with a woman."[68] Six years later the Supreme

---

[65] *The People* v. *Ruggles,* cited in Pfeffer, p. 665.

[66] "Report of the Arguments of the Attorney of the Commonwealth, at Trials of Abner Kneeland, for Blasphemy, in the Municipal and Supreme Courts, in Boston, January and May, 1834," cited in John McCormick and Mairi MacInnes, *Versions of Censorship* (Garden City, N.Y.: Doubleday, 1962), pp. 167–168.

[67] These are Delaware, Maryland, Maine, Massachusetts, Michigan, Nebraska, New Hampshire, New Jersey, North Dakota, Ohio, Oklahoma, Pennsylvania, Rhode Island, South Dakota, and Vermont; reported in "Blasphemy," *Columbia Law Review* 70 (1970): 694–733.

[68] Haig A. Bosmajian, comp., *Obscenity and Freedom of Expression* (New York: Burt Franklin, 1976), p. iii.

Court of Massachusetts upheld the common-law conviction of Peter Holmes for publishing John Cleland's *Memoirs of a Woman of Pleasure* (also known as *Fanny Hill*) because the book was "lewd, wicked, scandalous, infamous and obscene."[69] At about this time, the states began to write the common law of obscene libel into the statute books. Franklyn S. Haiman notes in *Freedom of Speech* that Vermont was the first state to codify the law of obscenity, doing so in 1821. Connecticut adopted an antiobscenity statute in 1834, and Massachusetts followed with a similar act in 1835.[70] Eventually, all of the states approved laws against obscenity, although definitions and details varied from state to state. However, unlike what happened with private libel and the religio-moral offense of blasphemy—both of which were omitted from the federal criminal code—the United States government soon entered the arena of sexual censorship.

In 1842 Congress passed the first federal obscenity statute in the form of Section 28 of the Tariff Act. This section barred the "importation of all indecent and obscene prints, paintings, lithographs, engravings and transparencies" into the United States. It has been amended several times to add items such as photographs, films, and phonograph records to the list; it currently appears as part of the *U.S. Code*.[71] The second federal censorship law was the Postal Act of March 3, 1865, Section 16 of which declares that "no obscene book, pamphlet, picture, print, or other publication of a vulgar and indecent character,

shall be admitted into the mails of the United States." It, too, has been amended a number of times, primarily by the "Comstock Act" of 1873, and is now a part of the *U.S. Code*.[72] Neither of these early laws defined "obscenity," nor did they provide enforcement machinery. Consequently, there was for a time little organized federal censorship, a fact which in the early 1870s became an obsessive concern of a young, puritanical retail clerk in New York City—Anthony Comstock.

A veteran of the Civil War and in his early twenties, Anthony Comstock arrived in New York City in 1867. There, he secured a job as a clerk in a dry-goods store. So disturbed was Comstock by the reading materials passed around by his fellow employees that he tracked down one supplier of "indecent literature" and had him arrested. Encouraged by this success, he determined to rid the city of all such "filth," and with a zeal unequaled in American history became the nation's premier crusader against "vice." In 1873, at the age of twenty-eight, he successfully enlisted the support of several prominent New Yorkers, including financier J. P. Morgan and soap magnate Samuel Colgate, in founding the New York YMCA's Committee for the Suppression of Vice (later to be renamed the New York Society for the Suppression of Vice). As news of this development spread, procensorship Watch and Ward Societies were formed in numerous communities throughout the United States.

Also in 1873, Comstock almost single-handedly lobbied through Congress a detailed statute to prohibit the mailing of "obscene" communications or any materials concerning birth control or abortion (see Figure 2.7). Later, as an unpaid postal inspector, he worked evangelistically to help enforce the

---

[69]Ibid. Note: In 1966 the U.S. Supreme Court ruled that Cleland's book was not obscene; see *Memoirs* v. *Massachusetts*, 383 U.S. 413 (1966).

[70]Franklyn S. Haiman, *Freedom of Speech* (Skokie, Ill.: National Textbook Company, 1976), p. 112.

[71]For the 1842 law, see 5 *Statutes at Large* 566–567. The current law as approved in the Tariff Act of 1930 appears at 19 *U.S. Code* Sec. 1305(a).

[72]The 1865 law is found at 13 *Statutes at Large* 507. The current law is found at 18 *U.S. Code* Sec. 1461.

new law. Numerous prosecutions followed.[73] "Obscene" works banned over the years by either the Customs Office or the U.S. Post Office include Daniel Defoe's *Moll Flanders,* Voltaire's *Candide,* Jean-Jacques Rousseau's *Confessions,* Honoré de Balzac's *Droll Stories,* Walt Whitman's *Leaves of Grass,* Gustave Flaubert's *November,* Havelock Ellis' *Studies in the Psychology of Sex,* Marie Stopes' *Contraception* and *Married Love,* James Joyce's *Ulysses,* D. H. Lawrence's *Lady Chatterley's Lover* and *Women in Love,* Sinclair Lewis' *Elmer Gantry,* Henry Miller's *Tropic of Cancer,* Lillian Smith's *Strange Fruit,* Ernest Hemingway's *For Whom the Bell Tolls,* Erich Maria Remarque's *All Quiet on the Western Front,* and Erskine Caldwell's *Tobacco Road* and *God's Little Acre.*[74] With minor legislative changes, the Comstock Act remains a part of the federal law. The obscenity provisions, as interpreted by the Supreme Court, have been upheld.[75]

Two cases decided by the U.S. Supreme Court in 1896 complete the system of restraint placed upon sexual expression prior to World War I. In the first case, the conviction of New York publisher Lew Rosen for mailing "indecent" pictures of females in violation of the Comstock Act was upheld by the Supreme Court. In its decision, the Supreme Court accepted the trial judge's use of Lord Cockburn's ruling in the 1868 English case of *Regina* v. *Hicklin,* which defines "obscenity" as that which has a *tendency* "to deprave and corrupt those whose minds are open to such immoral influences, and into whose hands a publication of this sort may fall."[76] Consequently, this "most susceptible person" standard became the accepted one in both federal and state courts throughout the nation during the first thirty years of the twentieth century.

In the second case, the Supreme Court *overturned* the conviction of Dan K. Swearingen, who had been found guilty in a federal district court of Kansas of mailing a newspaper that contained an "obscene, lewd, and lascivious" article. The offending piece charged an unnamed—but, evidently, a readily identifiable—person with being a "red headed mental and physical bastard," and a "black hearted coward" who would "sell a mother's honor with less hesitancy and for much less silver than Judas betrayed the Saviour, and who would pimp and fatten on a sister's shame with as much unction as a buzzard gluts in carrion."[77] While agreeing that the language was extreme, the Supreme Court ruled that no obscenity was involved. "Obscenity," said the Court, does not apply to words that are simply "coarse and vulgar," but it does concern language addressing "that form of immorality which has relation to sexual impurity."[78]

Although the Supreme Court's *Rosen* and *Swearingen* decisions are not "landmark cases" in the legal sense, they are milestones in the evolutionary development of controls

[73]See James C. N. Paul and Murray L. Schwartz, *Federal Censorship: Obscenity in the Mail* (New York: The Free Press of Glencoe, 1961); and Paul S. Boyer, *Purity in Print: The Vice-Society Movement and Book Censorship in America* (New York: Scribner's, 1968).

[74]Anne Lyon Haight and Chandler B. Grannis, *Banned Books: 387 B.C. to 1978 A.D.,* 4th ed. (New York: Bowker, 1978), pp. 25–83. Note: None of the writings in this list is currently classified as obscene by customs or the post office.

[75]In *Roth* v. *U.S.,* 354 U.S. 476 (1957); for more details, see Chapter 5, on religio-moral heresy. Note: In the early part of this century, British playwright George Bernard Shaw coined the term "Comstockery" in response to attempts to censor novels and plays in the United States; this so angered the aging Comstock that he singled out Shaw's productions for police action whenever possible.

[76]*Rosen* v. *U.S.,* 161 U.S. 29 (1896). Note: Rosen did not challenge the constitutionality of the Comstock Act, basing his appeal on technical and procedural grounds.

[77]*Swearingen* v. *U.S.,* 161 U.S. 446 (1896); see footnote at 446.

[78]Ibid., at 450.

FIGURE 2.7. ANTHONY COMSTOCK.
In 1873, Anthony Comstock, antivice crusader from New York, lobbied through Congress the Obscene Literature and Articles Act, which became known as the Comstock Act. With minor legislative changes made over the years, this law remains in effect, as recorded at 18 U.S. Code Sec. 1461. Although parts of the statute have been declared unconstitutional (such as the prohibitions upon the distribution of birth control information), the obscenity provisions have been upheld as interpreted by the U.S. Supreme Court, primarily in Roth v. U.S. *(1957) and* Miller v. California *(1973). The original act can be found at 17 Statutes at Large 598–600.*

The Comstock Act made it illegal to advertise for sale or to disseminate in the District of Columbia or in U.S. territories or to import or send through the mails "any obscene book, pamphlet, paper, writing, advertisement, circular, print, picture, drawing or other representation, figure, or image on or of paper or other material, or any cast, instrument, or other article of an immoral nature, or any drug or medicine, or any article whatever, for the prevention of conception, or for causing unlawful abortion . . . ."
Although this law did not define the terms "obscenity" or "immorality," it did provide for a prison term of up to five years and a fine of up to $2,000. (The current federal obscenity statute increases the punishment to a prison term of up to ten years and a fine of up to $10,000.)
Library of Congress.

upon sexual speech. In *Rosen,* the Court interpreted the Comstock Act so as to make it illegal in the United States to mail anything that a jury might find sexually provocative to a *child.* And in *Swearingen,* the Court—without realizing it—climaxed three centuries of evolution of the Anglo-American concept of the "obscene." That which began as a seventeenth-century church punishment for the *sin* of communicating an immoral or blasphe-

mous thought had now become the state *crime* of communicating an erotic one.

Constraints upon Media and Channels

Three significant developments of the nineteenth century continue to influence legal controls over the means of communication in the United States: (1) the Supreme Court's landmark decision of 1834 concerning copyright law, (2) the enactment of federal statutes to prohibit the importation or mailing of "obscene" and "immoral" messages, and (3) the development of electronic means of communication, especially radio. The *first* of these was the Supreme Court's landmark copyright decision in the 1834 case of *Wheaton* v. *Peters*, which upheld the authority of Congress, as set forth in the Constitution, to *create* copyright regulations by statute (i.e., to originate such laws fresh and new), thereby rejecting the argument that the Copyright Act simply confirmed the common law in the area of copyright.[79] The practical effect of the Court's opinion was to clarify that *copyright law in the United States is whatever the Congress says it is*—not what tradition had confirmed.

Although the issue of whether or not copyright infringed upon the freedom of the press as guaranteed by the First Amendment was not raised by the decision of 1834, the outcome of the case was to confirm a theory of copyright which held a number of inherent problems—in the form of unasked and therefore unanswered questions—for the future. Among these is the central question of how to resolve the incompatibility between the First Amendment and copyright law. This question, generally ignored by legal scholars, lawmakers, and the courts until recent years, has begun to attract serious attention in the legal profession. An overview of contemporary issues and cases is discussed in Chapter 10 under "Copyright Law and the First Amendment."

The *second* development was the approval by Congress of strict laws governing what may be imported into the country and what may be sent through the mails. These statutes—the Tariff Acts and the Comstock Act and its revisions—were designed to support the censorship of "immoral" expression, serving the same social purpose as did the licensing of printing presses in sixteenth- and seventeenth-century England. With minor changes, federal controls upon the channel of imports and the channel of the mails remain in effect in the United States.

The *third* development grew out of technological innovation, primarily in the area of the electronic media. Visual and aural means of communicating over great distances had been used for centuries (e.g., smoke signals, the semaphore, and drums) before Samuel F. B. Morse invented the telegraph in 1837. Morse's "electronic semaphore" was put to wide military and civilian use before 1860 and was placed under strict military control by both North and South during the Civil War. Reporters in Washington, D.C., for example, had to secure the clearance of military censors before sending any news item by telegraph (as a rule, no permission was required for use of the slower postal system).

The invention of the telephone by Alexander Graham Bell in 1875, and the wireless telegraph (radio) by Guglielmo Marconi in 1895, raised new issues of media control. The first federal legislation concerning Marconi's invention was the Wireless Ship Act of 1910, which required most American ships to be equipped with a radio transmitter as a safety measure. The Radio Act of 1912 was the first federal statute that required radio operators in the United States to secure a license; unfortunately, this act did not provide for the su-

---

[79]*Wheaton* v. *Peters*, 33 U.S. 591 (1834). Note: Wheaton, a former Supreme Court reporter, sued Peters, who succeeded Wheaton as reporter of the Court, for issuing a new six-volume set of formerly published Court opinions, including those that had been collected and edited by Wheaton. Wheaton claimed that he had a common-law right of ownership over those opinions, which he had previously edited. The Supreme Court disagreed, ruling that tradition did not rule in the area of copyright in the United States and, furthermore, that Supreme Court opinions belonged to the public and could not be copyrighted.

pervision of frequencies used, an oversight that soon produced chaos in the growing field of broadcasting. Landmark legislation of a comprehensive nature was eventually required. Since this legislation came after the end of World War I, it is considered in Chapter 11, on broadcasting.

Constraints of Time, Place, and Manner

In 1897 the U.S. Supreme Court decided a case of time, place, and manner which served as legal precedent on the use of public places for speechmaking until it was overruled by a more liberal Court in 1939.[80] The case was *Davis* v. *Massachusetts*—often called the Boston Common case—that began when minister William F. Davis preached a sermon on the Common of the City of Boston without a permit as was required by law. For this, Davis was fined and required to pay court costs. The Massachusetts Supreme Court upheld the conviction.

Upon appeal to the U.S. Supreme Court, Davis argued that his First Amendment rights had been violated and that the law under which he had been convicted was unconstitutional. The Supreme Court rejected the minister's claim and upheld the constitutionality of the Boston ordinance. In so ruling, the Court said that government was entrusted with the supervision of public places and had complete control over their use, including their use for speechmaking. "For the legislature absolutely or conditionally to forbid public speaking in a highway or public park," said the Court, "is no more an infringement of the rights of a member of the public than for the owner of a private house

to forbid it in his house." Forty-two years would pass before the High Court would liberalize this restrictive decision.

The United States in Brief: 1798–1917

In summary, despite the ratification of the First Amendment, government at either the national or state level attempted to control the public communication of aliens, women, and blacks during the first 130 years of the republic. The English common law concerning forbidden expression was accepted to a large degree in the United States, so that in one form or another laws were enforced to punish sedition, defamation, and the religio-moral "crimes" of blasphemy and obscenity. Although licensing of the press was a dead issue, other forms of media and channel constraints were practiced, including copyright, import and mail restrictions, and the licensing of radio transmitters, beginning with the Radio Act of 1912. Governmental units were given support in the control of speechmaking in public places by the Supreme Court's decision of 1897 upholding a Boston ordinance requiring that a permit be secured before a public place was used for speaking. Throughout this time of national ferment, which included the Civil War, the U.S. Supreme Court treated the First Amendment with benign neglect, announcing no "ringing defenses" of the revolutionary command which initiates the nation's Bill of Rights: "Congress shall make no law . . . abridging the freedom of speech, or of the press."

CONCLUSION

A review of the summary chart (Figure 2.8) on communication restrictions in Western culture—covering the societies discussed in both Chapters 1 and 2—tempts one to observe that for constraints over communica-

---

[80]*Davis* v. *Massachusetts*, 167 U.S. 43 (1897). This decision was rejected by the Supreme Court and public places opened for speech purposes in *Hague* v. *CIO*, 307 U.S. 496 (1939). For more on this development, see Chapter 8, on time, place, and manner.

tors and speech content, "the more things changed, the more they remained the same." The evolution of controls upon speakers and writers followed a similar pattern in each society, evolving from authoritarian selection to democratic freedom for all persons; also, the types of expression forbidden in each society were, with some exceptions, remarkably the same. Media controls became significant with the development of communication technology, beginning with Gutenberg's printing press in 1450 and extending to the development of the telegraph and radio in the nineteenth century (thus setting the stage for the growth of "media law" in the twentieth century).

In the years following World War I, the courts accepted the right of all persons—including women, blacks, and even resident aliens—to believe as they wish without fear of police repression and to function as communicators in the give and take of democratic debate.[81] This has not meant, however, that the *opinions* expressed have always been given the full protection of the Constitution. In fact, most twentieth-century constraints upon freedom of speech have arisen in the area of speech content. A close look at these content restrictions is the subject of the next five chapters.

EXERCISES

A. Classroom projects and activities.

1. Discuss the summary chart at the end of Chapter 2, which covers Athens, Rome,

[81]Extralegal pressures continue to emerge from time to time. Only recently, for example, have homosexuals dared to openly advocate a change in public attitudes toward homosexuality and in laws punishing homosexual conduct. In a midcentury decision, the U.S. Supreme Court did make it clear—in *American Communications Association* v. *Douds,* 339 U.S. 382 (1950)—that in America "one may not be imprisoned or executed because he holds particular beliefs."

England, and America to 1917. How valid is the statement that in matters of free speech, "the more things change the more they remain the same"? Do you believe that your freedom of expression is greater (or less) today than it was for those who lived before you, particularly in the United States?

2. Invite several local clergymen, whose views range from "liberal" to "conservative," to come to the class for a panel discussion of blasphemy. Announce this topic to each clergyman invited: "Blasphemy: How I Define It and What I Think Should Be Done About It." After the participants have stated their positions, discuss the matter in class. Have attitudes changed much since the sixteenth and seventeenth centuries? (This project is also suitable for Chapter 5.)

3. The plays of George Bernard Shaw were targeted for suppression by Anthony Comstock after Shaw coined the term "Comstockery" to describe literary censorship in America. Study, then abstract in about six hundred words, Shaw's argument against censorship as set forth in the preface to his short play *The Shewing-Up of Blanco Posnet.* Discuss Shaw's ideas in class.

4. Have each student in the class read Wendell Phillips's famous oration, "The Murder of Lovejoy," delivered in Faneuil Hall, Boston, on December 8, 1837. Discuss both the content of the speech and its rhetorical techniques. (Be sure to read a short article in a good encyclopedia on Wendell Phillips and Elijah Lovejoy.) "The Murder of Lovejoy" is reprinted in a number of speech anthologies, including A. Craig Baird, *American Public Addresses: 1740–1952* (New York: McGraw-Hill, 1956), pp. 138–144.

5. In the debate over adoption of the Bill of Rights, several persons, including Alexander Hamilton, argued that no offi-

FIGURE 2.8. **Summary of Communication Restrictions for Athens, Rome, England, and America to 1917.**

Government	Communicator Constraints	Content Constraints	Medium and Channel Constraints	Time, Place and Manner Constraints
Athens	(a) Evolved from king to aristocratic council to all citizens. (b) "Citizen" excluded women, males under 18, aliens, and slaves (those excluded composed 60% of the population).	Had laws to punish (a) sedition, (b) private libel, (c) blasphemy.	None noted.	Under Solon's law a small fine was levied for slander if spoken (a) in temples, (b) during festivals, (c) in courts of law, (d) in public offices.
Rome	(a) Evolved from king to aristocrats (patricians) to all citizens. (b) Restrictions upon who could speak in the assembly. (c) Seniority system in the senate restricted orators.	Had laws to punish (a) sedition, (b) private libel.	None noted.	In the state-supported theater defaming a person *by name* from the stage was prohibited.
England	Evolved from king to Parliament to citizen. Freedom of speech was established as a civil liberty by 1860.	Had laws to punish (a) seditious libel, (b) private libel, (c) blasphemous libel, (d) obscene libel. (These are called the "four libels" of the English Common law.)	(a) Licensing of the press from 1538 to 1694 (156 years). (b) Copyright ordained by royal decree, 1557. (c) Copyright revised by Parliament (the Statute of Anne, 1710).	See Note[1] below

Government	Communicator Constraints	Content Constraints	Medium and Channel Constraints	Time, Place and Manner Constraints
Colonial America	Evolved from governors to assemblies to citizens. Freedom of speech established as a civil liberty by Bill of Rights (1791).	Had laws to punish (a) sedition, (b) blasphemy. (Paid little attention to private libel and obscenity.)	Some licensing, including colonies of Mass., N.Y., Pa., and Va.; licensing efforts ended prior to 1725 (licensing in colonies never as effective as in England).	See Note[1] below.
U.S.A. 1788 to 1917	Despite Bill of Rights, many persons were denied the right to speak, including members of these groups: (a) aliens, (b) women, (c) blacks.	Had laws to punish (a) sedition, (b) private libel, (c) blasphemy, (d) obscenity.	(a) First U.S. copyright law (1790). (b) Laws to control importing and mailing of "immoral" items and literature. (c) Radio Act of 1912.	"Boston Commons" case of *Davis* v. *Mass.* decided by U.S. Supreme Court in 1897; upheld right of absolute control of government over public places, including use for speech purposes.

[1] The historical literature on freedom of speech rarely mentions constraints of time, place, and manner of communication. For legal developments in the United States (which have occurred primarily during the twentieth century) see Chapter 8, which takes up the subject of time, place, and manner.

cial list of rights was needed, for personal freedom rested ultimately upon public opinion and depended upon the love of liberty within the hearts and minds of the nation's citizens. Would America be better off without a written First Amendment? Discuss.

6. Read a good essay on the common law in a standard encyclopedia, such as the *Britannica* or the *Americana*. Invite a law professor or local attorney to address the class on the influence of the English common law upon American law, with particular emphasis upon civil liberties.

7. Invite a panel of professional women who are active in the women's movement in your community; ask them to discuss their problems in being accepted as communicators of worthwhile ideas. What types of subtle pressures are exerted to "keep them in their place"? (The same exercise can be done with a panel made up of

blacks or some other minority.) Have things changed much since the nineteenth century? If so, in what ways have matters improved?

8. Study the First Amendment to the Constitution, then rewrite it with the intent of making it clearer and more applicable to contemporary society. Have each student make copies of his or her "improvement" and distribute them to others in the class. Discuss the results. Would you be willing to exchange the wording of the First Amendment with any of the suggestions made by your classmates? Explain your answer.

9. In class discussion, compare and contrast the "original" First Amendment proposed by James Madison with the one that was finally ratified (Madison's original proposal is given in Chapter 2 under the heading "The Adoption of the Constitution and the Bill of Rights"). Which of the two versions do you like better? Why?

10. During the course, keep a scrapbook (a loose-leaf notebook is recommended) of contemporary examples of efforts to control freedom of expression. Divide the scrapbook into these sections:

(a) Content controls
   (1) Political heresy
   (2) Defamation and privacy
   (3) Religio-moral heresy
   (4) Provocation to anger
   (5) Commercial speech
(b) Time, place, manner, and institutional constraints
(c) Issues of prior restraint and free press–fair trial
(d) Issues of technology, including copyright and broadcasting
(e) Issues of ethics in public communication

Remember to record complete bibliographical information for each item you clip for the project.

B. Topics for research papers or oral reports.

1. America's Anthony Comstock and the New York Society for the Suppression of Vice.

2. The Salem Witchcraft Trials and Freedom of Conscience in the Puritan Colonies (Massachusetts, seventeenth century).

3. The Trial of John Peter Zenger (New York, 1735) and Its Influence upon Freedom of Speech in America.

4. What Did Our Founding Fathers *Really* Mean by "Freedom of Speech"? (From the reading list, see Levy, *Freedom of Speech and Press in Early American History*.)

5. A Short History of Postal Censorship in the United States. (From the reading list, see Paul and Schwartz on *Federal Censorship*.)

6. Thomas Jefferson and Freedom of Speech: What Did He Really Believe? (From the reading list, see Levy, *Jefferson and Civil Liberties*.)

7. James Madison: Apostle of Freedom of Expression.

8. Anthony Comstock vs. Robert G. Ingersoll: Conflict over the "Suppression of Vice."

9. Theodore Schroeder: Father of the Free Speech League (1911).

10. The Battle of the Feminists for Recognition as Public Communicators in Nineteenth-Century America.

11. Terrorist Organizations in the South During the Nineteenth Century: The Suppression of Black Communicators. (Be sure to include the Ku Klux Klan; from the reading list, see Trelease, *White Terror*.)

12. Jefferson and Madison Against the Alien and Sedition Acts: The Kentucky and Virginia Resolutions of 1798–1799.

13. Elijah P. Lovejoy: Martyr for Abolition and Freedom of the Press. (From the reading list, see Dillon, *Elijah P. Lovejoy*.)

14. Abraham Lincoln and Freedom of the Press. (From the reading list, see the studies by Sprague and Harper.)
15. The Free-Speech Rhetoric of the Industrial Workers of the World (the "Wobblies"). (From the reading list, see the article by Terry Cole and the books by Conlin, Kornbluh, and Renshaw.)

SELECTED READINGS

Berns, Walter. "Freedom of the Press and the Alien and Sedition Laws: A Reappraisal." In *The Supreme Court Review: 1970,* pp. 109–159. Edited by Philip B. Kurland. Chicago: University of Chicago Press, 1970.

Boyer, Paul S. *Purity in Print: The Vice-Society Movement and Book Censorship in America.* New York: Scribner's, 1968.

Brant, Irving. *The Bill of Rights: Its Origin and Meaning.* Indianapolis: Bobbs-Merrill, 1965.

Broun, Heywood, and Leech, Margaret. *Anthony Comstock: Roundsman of the Lord.* New York: Boni, 1927.

Chafee, Zechariah, Jr. *Free Speech in the United States.* Cambridge, Mass.: Harvard University Press, 1941.

Cole, Terry W. "The Right to Speak: The Free Speech Fights of the Industrial Workers of the World." In *Free Speech Yearbook: 1978,* pp. 113–118. Edited by Gregg Phifer. Falls Church, Va.: Speech Communication Association, 1978.

Conlin, Joseph. *Bread and Roses Too: Studies of the Wobblies.* Westport, Conn.: Greenwood Press, 1969.

Dillon, Merton. *Elijah P. Lovejoy: Abolitionist Editor.* Urbana, Ill.: University of Illinois Press, 1964.

Duker, William F. *A Constitutional History of Habeas Corpus.* Westport, Conn.: Greenwood Press, 1980.

Eaton, Clement. *The Freedom-of-Thought Struggle in the Old South.* New York: Harper & Row, 1964.

Haight, Anne Lyon, and Grannis, Chandler B. *Banned Books: 387 B.C. to 1978 A.D.* 4th ed. New York: Bowker, 1978.

Harper, Robert S. *Lincoln and the Press.* New York: McGraw-Hill, 1951.

Hentoff, Nat. *The First Freedom: The Tumultuous History of Free Speech in America.* New York: Delacorte Press, 1980.

Kornbluh, Joyce L., ed. *Rebel Voices: An I.W.W. Anthology.* Ann Arbor, Mich.: The University of Michigan Press, 1964.

Levy, Leonard W., ed. *Freedom of the Press from Zenger to Jefferson.* Indianapolis: Bobbs-Merrill, 1966. (Companion volume to Nelson.)

Levy, Leonard W. *Freedom of Speech and Press in Early American History: Legacy of Suppression.* New York: Harper & Row, 1963. (Originally published as *Legacy of Suppression* by Harvard University Press, 1960.)

Levy, Leonard W. *Jefferson and Civil Liberties: The Darker Side.* New York: Quadrangle, 1973.

Nelson, Harold L., ed. *Freedom of the Press from Hamilton to the Warren Court.* Indianapolis: Bobbs-Merrill, 1967.

Nelson, Harold L. "Seditious Libel in Colonial America." *American Journal of Legal History* 3 (1959): 160 ff.

Nye, Russel B. *Fettered Freedom: Civil Liberties and the Slavery Controversy, 1830–1860.* East Lansing, Mich.: Michigan State College Press, 1949.

Paul, James C. N., and Schwartz, Murray L. *Federal Censorship: Obscenity in the Mail.* New York: The Free Press of Glencoe, 1961.

Pfeffer, Leo. *Church, State, and Freedom.* Rev. ed. Boston: Beacon Press, 1967.

Renshaw, Patrick. *The Wobblies.* Garden City, N.Y.: Doubleday, 1967.

Smith, James Morton. *Freedom's Fetters: The Alien and Sedition Laws and American Civil Liberties.* Ithaca, N.Y.: Cornell University Press, 1956.

Smith, Stephen A. "Freedom of Expression in the Confederate States of America." In *Free Speech Yearbook: 1978,* pp. 17–37. Edited by Gregg Phifer. Falls Church, Va.: Speech Communication Association, 1978.

Sprague, Dean. *Freedom Under Lincoln.* Boston: Houghton Mifflin, 1965.

Trelease, Allen W. *White Terror: The Ku Klux Klan Conspiracy and Southern Reconstruction.* New York: Harper & Row, 1971.

Part II

CONTROLS UPON THE CONTENT OF SPEECH

CHAPTER 3

Political Heresy: Sedition in the United States Since 1917

"The absence of seditious libel as a crime is the true pragmatic test of freedom of speech."
                                                    —Harry Kalven, Jr.[1]

On March 18, 1981, Robert Hill was arrested by a security officer of Miami-Dade Community College, Miami, Florida, for selling copies of the *Revolutionary Worker,* newspaper of the Revolutionary Communist party, on the campus. The arresting officer justified his action by stating that he had found "violence" in the newspaper, as well as threats to overthrow the government of the United States. Hill was jailed and charged with violating Florida's criminal anarchy law; a local judge set bond at $5,000. (The Florida statute makes it a felony to distribute printed material advocating the overthrow of the government and provides for up to fifteen years in prison upon conviction.) In response to the incident, a Miami member of the American Civil Liberties Union accused local authorities of arresting Robert Hill "for the outrageous crime of distributing a newspaper." A check by reporters revealed that similar charges were pending in Atlanta, Georgia, against vendors of the *Revolutionary Worker.*[2] Regardless of the outcome of these cases, and others similar to them, contemporary efforts to suppress political dissent should come as no surprise to those who have carefully studied the first two chapters of this book. The 1981 police action against Hill simply raises the ancient question anew: How much criticism of the government should a society permit?

Efforts to suppress antigovernment dissent, an activity characterized by Thomas Jefferson as a "reign of witches," have occurred during four periods of American history since the adoption of the Constitution. As noted in Chapter 2, the first "witches' reign" developed during the presidency of John Adams, when the Alien and Sedition Acts were in effect (1798–1800); the second occurred prior to, during, and following the Civil War, particularly in the South. The third and fourth periods of political repression belong to the twentieth century and are in large part the subjects of this chapter. The third, centering around America's entry into World War I, was in response to the *federal* Espionage Acts of 1917 and 1918, plus *state* criminal anarchy and criminal syndicalism laws passed during the first quarter of this century to control the activities of "labor extremists," "anarchists," and "radicals." Finally, the fourth "reign of witches" was born out of the anti-Communist hysteria following World War II (sometimes described as the "McCarthy era," in reference to the tactics of Communist-hunter Joseph McCarthy, U.S. senator from Wisconsin) and includes federal efforts to enforce the antisedition sections of the Smith Act, passed in 1940. The third and fourth "witches' reigns" are of utmost importance to the study of freedom to communicate in the United States, for as Franklyn S. Haiman points out, "With respect to the law of freedom of speech, most of the judicial precedents that need concern us today are the product of only the last half century, for it is primarily since 1917 that the U.S. Supreme Court has been writing opinions which give us guidance in interpreting the free speech clause of the First Amendment."[3]

[1]Harry Kalven, Jr., *The Negro and the First Amendment* (Columbus: Ohio State University Press, 1965), p. 16.
[2]*Newsletter on Intellectual Freedom,* May 1981, p. 72.

[3]Franklyn S. Haiman, *Freedom of Speech* (Skokie, Ill.: National Textbook Company, 1976), p. xiii.

I. FROM WORLD WAR I TO WORLD WAR II: THE SUPPRESSION OF SEDITION IN AMERICA, 1917–1940

Soon after America declared war against Germany in 1917, the Congress passed the Espionage Act, primarily for the purpose of preventing sabotage and the communication of military secrets to the enemy. Section 3 of the act of 1917, however, did provide for the punishment of speech which had the *intent* (1) to interfere with the operation of the military; (2) to promote the success of the nation's enemies; (3) to "attempt to cause insubordination, disloyalty, mutiny, or refusal of duty, in the military or naval forces of the United States"; or (4) to interfere with the draft. Upon conviction, a person could be fined up to $10,000, imprisoned for up to twenty years, or both.[4] Several months later, top officials of the Justice Department concluded that the 1917 law, while effective in silencing some who openly and clearly opposed the war, failed to get at informal, casual, or "impulsive" messages of disloyalty.[5] The remedy was the Amendment of May 16, 1918, which added to the original statute a variety of types of speech that could be punished (see box).

Under the Espionage Acts of 1917 and 1918, more than two thousand prosecutions took place, with almost any antiwar comment being a potential source of government suspicion. In his definitive study of the period, Zechariah Chafee, Jr., details how it became a crime to criticize the war bond effort, to describe the draft as unconstitutional, or to state that war was in opposition to the teachings of Christ. One citizen, opposed to the war, was convicted for writing in a personal letter that "I am for the people and the government is for profiteers," whereas others were punished for criticizing the Red Cross or the YMCA. A German-American who had not purchased Liberty bonds and who justified his action by explaining that he did not support either side in the war was arrested for the remark.[6]

At the state level, a number of sedition laws were already on the books before 1917; however, the patriotic fervor that swept the country during the war, plus the fear of Bolsheviks and other "radicals" following the armistice, caused an additional number of states to approve similar statutes. By 1925 about two-thirds of the states had criminal anarchy or criminal syndicalism laws on the books. Court decisions emerging from litigation concerning these federal and state laws initiated what Thomas Emerson describes as "the remarkable development of First Amendment doctrine which has continued to the present day."[7]

None of the appeals from convictions under the wartime Espionage Acts was decided by the U.S. Supreme Court until after the war was over. The armistice was signed on November 11, 1918, and two months later, on January 9 and 10, 1919, *Schenck* v. *U.S.*, the first of the Espionage Act cases, was argued before the Supreme Court. On March 3, 1919, with Justice Holmes speaking for a unanimous Court, Schenck's conviction was upheld in a landmark decision.

A more detailed examination of the opinion of Justice Holmes is revealing. Following his description of the contents of Schenck's antidraft leaflet and the facts concerning its

---

[4]40 *Statutes at Large* 219.
[5]Zechariah Chafee, Jr., *Free Speech in the United States* (Cambridge, Mass.: Harvard University Press, 1941), pp. 39–40.

[6]Ibid., pp. 51–60.
[7]Thomas I. Emerson, *The System of Freedom of Expression* (New York: Random House, 1970), pp. 63–64.

THE MAY 16, 1918, AMENDMENT TO THE ESPIONAGE ACT OF 1917

The Espionage Act of June 15, 1917, passed by Congress about two months after the United States declared war upon Germany, was directed primarily at acts of sabotage and the protection of military secrets. However, the 1917 law did make it illegal to communicate opinions aimed at interference with the armed forces (such as encouraging insubordination) or with obstructing the draft (Schenck, for example, was convicted under the 1917 act of conspiring to obstruct the draft). A year later, Congress expanded the sedition language of the Espionage Act and added a constraint upon the delivery of mail to persons suspected of violating the act. These two changes are given in full below. (The 1918 amendment was repealed in 1921.)

Title I, Section 3 of the 1917 Espionage Act was amended so as to read as follows:

Sec. 3. Whoever, when the United States is at war, shall willfully make or convey false reports or false statements with intent to interfere with the operation or success of the military or naval forces of the United States, or to promote the success of its enemies, or shall willfully make or convey false reports or false statements, or say or do anything except by way of bona fide and not disloyal advice to an investor or investors, with intent to obstruct the sale by the United States of bonds or other securities of the United States or the making of loans by or to the United States, and whoever, when the United States is at war, shall willfully cause or attempt to cause, or incite or attempt to incite, insubordination, disloyalty, mutiny, or refusal of duty, in the military or naval forces of the United States, or shall willfully obstruct or attempt to obstruct the recruiting or enlistment service of the United States, and whoever, when the United States is at war, shall willfully utter, print, write, or publish any disloyal, profane, scurrilous, or abusive language about the form of government of the United States, or the Constitution of the United States, or the military or naval forces of the United States, or the flag of the United States, or the uniform of the Army or Navy of the United States, or any language intended to bring the form of government of the United States, or the Constitution of the United States, or the military or naval forces of the United States, or the flag of the United States, or the uniform of the Army or Navy of the United States into contempt, scorn, contumely, or disrepute, or shall willfully utter, print,

circulation, he argued that "the document would not have been sent unless it had been intended to have some effect, and we do not see what effect it could be expected to have upon persons subject to the draft except to influence them to obstruct the carrying of it out." The landmark doctrine of clear and present danger was stated in the final part of the opinion.

Justice Holmes *delivered the opinion of the Court:*

. . . We admit that in many places and in ordinary times the defendants, in saying all that was said in the circular, would have been within their constitutional rights. But the character of every act depends upon the circumstances in which it is done. . . . **The most stringent protection of free speech would not protect a man in falsely shouting fire in a theater, and causing a panic. It does not even protect a man from an injunction against uttering words that may have all the effect of force. . . . The question in every case is whether the words used are used in such circumstances and are of such a nature as to create a clear and present danger that they will bring about the substantive evils that**

write, or publish any language intended to incite, provoke, or encourage resistance to the United States, or to promote the cause of its enemies, or shall willfully display the flag of any foreign enemy, or shall willfully by utterance, writing, printing, publication, or language spoken, urge, incite, or advocate any curtailment of production in this country of any thing or things, product or products, necessary or essential to the prosecution of the war in which the United States may be engaged, with intent by such curtailment to cripple or hinder the United States in the prosecution of the war, and whoever shall willfully advocate, teach, defend, or suggest the doing of any of the acts or things in this section enumerated, and whoever shall by word or act support or favor the cause of any country with which the United States is at war or by word or act oppose the cause of the United States therein, shall be punished by a fine of not more than $10,000 or imprisonment for not more than twenty years, or both: *Provided,* That any employee or official of the United States Government who commits any disloyal act or utters any unpatriotic or disloyal language, or who, in an abusive and violent manner criticizes the Army or Navy or the flag of the United States shall be at once dismissed from the service. Any such employee shall be dismissed by the head of the department in which the employee may be engaged, and any such official shall be dismissed by the authority having power to appoint a successor to the dismissed official.

Title XII was amended by adding the following section:

Sec. 4. When the United States is at war, the Postmaster General may, upon evidence satisfactory to him that any person or concern is using the mails in violation of any of the provisions of this Act, instruct the postmaster at any post office at which mail is received addressed to such person or concern to return to the postmaster at the office at which they were originally mailed all letters or other matter so addressed, with the words "Mail to this address undeliverable under Espionage Act" plainly written or stamped upon the outside thereof, and all such letters or other matters so returned to such postmasters shall be by them returned to the senders thereof under such regulations as the Postmaster General may prescribe. Approved, May 16, 1918.

40 Statutes at Large 553–554.

Congress has a right to prevent. It is a question of proximity and degree. When a nation is at war many things that might be said in time of peace are such a hindrance to its effort that their utterance will not be endured so long as men fight, and that no court could regard them as protected by any constitutional right. It seems to be admitted that if an actual obstruction of the recruiting service were proved, liability for words that produced that effect might be enforced. The Statute of 1917 . . . punishes conspiracies to obstruct as well as actual obstruction. If the act (speaking, or circulating a paper), its tendency and the intent with which it is done, are the same, we perceive no ground for saying that success alone warrants making the act a crime. . . .

Judgments affirmed.

As a careful reading of the *Schenck* decision reveals, (1) the clear-and-present-danger doctrine was *announced*, but (2) the traditional bad-tendency rule was *used* to justify the result. Justice Holmes states that if the "tendency" is to obstruct the draft, then punishment of those who communicated the message is justified.

On March 10, 1919, seven days following

FIGURE 3.1. THE SUPREME COURT OF 1919. The "Schenck Court" of 1919, with the names of the two liberal voices—Holmes and Brandeis—noted in boldface type, is as follows, with names given from left to right. Front row, seated: Justice William R. Day, Justice Joseph McKenna, Chief Justice Edward D. White, **Justice Oliver Wendell Holmes, Jr.,** *and Justice Willis Van Devanter. Back row, standing:* **Justice Louis D. Brandeis,** *Justice Mahlon Pitney, Justice James C. McReynolds, and Justice John H. Clarke.* Library of Congress.

LANDMARK CASE
Schenck v. United States, 249 U.S. 47 (1919)
Decided March 3, 1919

Vote: 9 to 0 for sustaining the conviction of Schenck.

Majority Opinion By: Justice Holmes.

Concurring Justices: Chief Justice White, Justices McKenna, Day, Van Devanter, Pitney, McReynolds, Brandeis, and Clarke.

Dissenting Justices: (none)

Justices Not Participating: (none)

Summary: Defendant Charles T. Schenck, general secretary of the Socialist party, was charged with three counts of violating the Espionage Act of June 15, 1917. The charges were: (1) conspiracy to obstruct the draft by circulating a document (leaflet) which urged resistance to the draft; (2) conspiracy to use the mails to circulate the document; and (3) actually mailing copies of the antidraft leaflet. Schenck was convicted, and both the U.S. Court of Appeals and the U.S. Supreme Court upheld his conviction. The announcement of the new clear-and-present-danger test by Justice Holmes did not save Schenck, for the Court, relying more upon "bad tendency" than upon "clear and present danger," voted unanimously that Schenck's leaflet created enough of a threat to merit punishment.

Rule Established; Significance of Case: This is classified as a landmark case because in it the clear-and-present-danger test was announced (although it was not vigorously applied) by the Court for the first time in its history. The new test was *not* firmly established by its announcement, for the conservative majority on the Court for the next two decades simply interpreted the words "clear and present danger" to mean "bad tendency" and voted accordingly. In effect, *Schenck* put the new test "on the table," where it was debated for years before being generally accepted by the majority of Supreme Court justices.

the birth of the clear-and-present-danger doctrine in *Schenck,* two more Espionage Act convictions were sustained by a unanimous Court, demonstrating clearly the shaky legs upon which the new test stood. Justice Holmes continued as spokesman for the Court, and—in *Frohwerk* v. *United States* and *Debs* v. *United States*—demonstrated that he had not yet realized the liberalizing potential of the clear-and-present-danger test.[8]

Jacob Frohwerk, publisher of the *Missouri Staats Zeitung,* a pro-German newspaper, was convicted in trial court of conspiracy to violate the Espionage Act of 1917 by printing twelve articles opposed to America's entry into the war, the combined effect of which was intended "to cause disloyalty, mutiny, and refusal of duty in the military and naval forces of the United States." For this he was fined and sentenced to ten years in federal prison. In agreement with the trial court, Justice Holmes cited *Schenck* to establish "that a person may be convicted of a conspiracy to obstruct recruiting by words of persuasion"; then he proceeded to use the put-out-the-spark argument of the bad-tendency doctrine to condemn Frohwerk.

Justice Holmes *delivered the opinion of the Court:*

> . . . But we must take the case on the record as it is, and on that record it is impossible to say that it might not have been found that the circulation of the paper was in quarters where a little breath would be enough to kindle a flame, and that the fact was known and relied upon by those who sent the paper out. . . . But a conspiracy to obstruct recruiting would be criminal even if no means were agreed upon specifically by which to accomplish the intent. It is enough if the parties agreed to set to work for the com-

mon purpose. That purpose could be accomplished or aided by persuasion . . . .

In the second decision of March 10, 1919, Socialist leader Eugene V. Debs had been convicted in trial court of violating the 1918 amendment to the Espionage Act by delivering an antiwar speech which *tended* to obstruct the conscription of men for the armed forces. For the crime of making this antiwar speech, Debs was sentenced to ten years in federal prison. Among other things, Debs had praised several activists who had been prosecuted for their opposition to the war, then he told his audience, "You have your lives to lose . . . ; you need to know that you are fit for something better than slavery and cannon fodder." Justice Holmes's opinion sustaining the conviction did not mention the clear-and-present-danger test but it noted the *tendency* of Debs' antidraft remarks and ruled the remarks criminal because their "reasonably probable effect" was to "obstruct the recruiting service."[9]

Exactly eight months following *Frohwerk* and *Debs,* and after considerable reflection by Justices Holmes and Brandeis on the meaning of "clear and present danger," the important case of *Abrams* v. *United States* was decided by the Court. Unlike the previous Espionage Act convictions, all of which were affirmed unanimously, *Abrams* produced a 7-to-2 split, with Justices Holmes and Brandeis, in the first of several famous dissents, advocating a more liberal interpretation of the clear-and-present-danger doctrine.

Justice John Clarke, author of the majority opinion, described the content of the pro-Russian leaflet distributed by Abrams and his friends, noting that the purpose of the publication "was to persuade the persons to whom

[8]*Frohwerk* v. *United States,* 249 U.S. 204 (1919), and *Debs* v. *United States,* 249 U.S. 211 (1919).

[9]*Debs* v. *U.S.,* at 216.

FIGURE 3.2. EUGENE V. DEBS.
Eugene Victor Debs, Socialist candidate for president of the United States in the campaigns of 1900, 1904, 1908, and 1912, was convicted in 1918 of making a seditious antiwar speech and sentenced to a term in the federal prison in Atlanta. On appeal, the U.S. Supreme Court upheld his conviction. In 1920 he ran for president while still in prison and issued this campaign photograph, showing him in prison garb standing before the prison doors. He received almost one million votes in the election of 1920. On Christmas Day, 1921, elderly and ill, Debs was released from prison by President Warren G. Harding.

Abrams v. United States, 250 U.S. 616 (1919)
Decided November 10, 1919

Vote: 7 to 2 for sustaining the conviction of Abrams and his four associates.

Majority Opinion By: Justice Clarke.

Concurring Justices: Chief Justice White, Justices McKenna, Day, Van Devanter, Pitney, and McReynolds.

Dissenting Justices: Holmes and Brandeis.

Justices Not Participating: (none)

Summary: Jacob Abrams and four other defendants, all Russian citizens living in the United States, were convicted under the 1918 Amendment to the Espionage Act of conspiring to unlawfully "utter, print, write, and publish" seditious messages during time of war, including the advocacy of "curtailment of production of things and products . . . necessary and essential to the prosecution of the war." The unlawful messages were contained in two antiwar leaflets distributed in and around New York City. The trial court sentenced the defendants to twenty years in prison, and the Supreme Court, using the bad-tendency doctrine, upheld the conviction.

Rule Established; Significance of Case: Although no rule was established, the case is significant because of the Holmes-Brandeis dissent, first of a series of persuasive Holmes-Brandeis arguments (continued in *Gitlow* and *Whitney*) rejecting the doctrine of bad tendency and urging use of the more liberal clear-and-present-danger standard.

it was addressed to turn a deaf ear to patriotic appeals . . . and to cease to render . . . assistance in the prosecution of the
war." He then stated the bad-tendency rationale by which the majority concluded that
the convictions were justified.

Justice Clarke *delivered the opinion of the
Court:*

It will not do to say, as is now argued, that
the only intent of these defendants was to prevent injury to the Russian cause. Men must be
held to have intended, and to be accountable
for, the effects which their acts were likely to
produce. Even if their primary purpose and intent was to aid the cause of the Russian Revolution, the plan of action which they adopted
necessarily involved, before it could be realized,
defeat of the war program of the United States,
for the obvious effect of this appeal, if it should
become effective, as they hoped it might,
would be to persuade persons of character such
as those whom they regarded themselves as addressing, not to aid government loans and not
to work in ammunition factories, where their
work would produce "bullets, bayonets, cannon" and other munitions of war, the use of
which would cause the "murder" of Germans
and Russians.

In dissent, Justice Holmes, in an opinion
joined by Justice Brandeis, argued for a reversal of the convictions. He first reviewed
the charges against Abrams and his codefendants, then summarized the contents of the
two leaflets in question. Both leaflets, for example, opposed the use of "working-class"
soldiers to fight for capitalism, and both were
sharply critical of President Wilson for sending American troops to Russia in support of
anti-Communist forces there. The second
leaflet, headed "Workers—Wake Up," urged
those who were sympathetic to the Russian
Revolution to take part in a general strike,
then concluded: "Woe unto those who will

be in the way of progress. Let solidarity live!
The Rebels."

Justice Holmes then explained his understanding of "intent" by stating that the term
"as vaguely used in ordinary legal discussion
means no more than knowledge at the time
of the act that the consequences said to be intended will ensue"; since there was no chance
that the "consequences" of Abrams' message
would, in fact, occur, there was, therefore,
no genuine danger.

Justice Holmes, *dissenting:*

I never have seen any reason to doubt that the
questions of law that alone were before this
court in the cases of *Schenck, Frohwerk,* and
Debs . . . were rightly decided. I do not doubt
for a moment that by the same reasoning that
would justify punishing persuasion to murder,
the United States constitutionally may punish
speech that produces or is intended to produce
a clear and imminent danger that it will bring
about forthwith certain substantive evils that
the United States constitutionally may seek to
prevent. The power undoubtedly is greater in
time of war than in time of peace because war
opens dangers that do not exist at other times.

But, as against dangers peculiar to war, as
against others, the principle of the right to free
speech is always the same. It is only the present
danger of immediate evil or an intent to bring
it about that warrants Congress in setting a
limit to the expression of opinion where private
rights are not concerned. Congress certainly
cannot forbid all effort to change the mind of
the country. Now nobody can suppose that the
surreptitious publishing of a silly leaflet by an
unknown man, without more, would present
any immediate danger that its opinions would
hinder the success of the government arms or
have any appreciable tendency to do so.

The most persuasive words of Justice
Holmes's argument were saved for the final
two paragraphs. In language more eloquent

than usual, he spoke in defense of freedom of speech.

Justice Holmes, *dissent continued:*

In this case sentences of twenty years' imprisonment have been imposed for the publishing of two leaflets that I believe the defendants had as much right to publish as the government has to publish the Constitution of the United States now vainly invoked by them. Even if I am technically wrong, and enough can be squeezed from these poor and puny anonymities to turn the color of legal litmus paper,—I will add, even if what I think the necessary intent were shown,—the most nominal punishment seems to me all that possibly could be inflicted, unless the defendants are to be made to suffer not for what the indictment alleges, but for the creed that they avow,—a creed that I believe to be the creed of ignorance and immaturity when honestly held, as I see no reason to doubt that it was held here, but which, although made the subject of examination at the trial, no one has a right even to consider in dealing with the charges before the court.

Persecution for the expression of opinions seems to me perfectly logical. If you have no doubt of your premises or your power and want a certain result with all your heart you naturally express your wishes in law and sweep away all opposition. To allow opposition by speech seems to indicate that you think the speech impotent, as when a man says that he has squared the circle, or that you do not care whole-heartedly for the result, or that you doubt either your power or your premises. But when men have realized that time has upset many fighting faiths, they may come to believe even more than they believe the very foundations of their own conduct that the ultimate good desired is better reached by free trade in ideas,—that the best test of truth is the power of the thought to get itself accepted in the competition of the market; and that truth is the only ground upon which their wishes safely can be carried out. That, at any rate, is the theory of our Constitution. It is an experiment, as all life

is an experiment. Every year, if not every day, we have to wager our salvation upon some prophecy based upon imperfect knowledge. While that experiment is part of our system I think that we should be eternally vigilant against attempts to check the expression of opinions that we loathe and believe to be fraught with death, unless they so imminently threaten immediate interference with the lawful and pressing purposes of the law that an immediate check is required to save the country. I wholly disagree with the argument of the government that the 1st Amendment left the common law as to seditious libel in force. History seems to me against the notion. I had conceived that the United States through many years had shown its repentance for the Sedition Act of July 14, 1798, by repaying fines that it imposed. Only the emergency that makes it immediately dangerous to leave the correction of evil counsels to time warrants making any exception to the sweeping command, "Congress shall make no law abridging the freedom of speech." Of course I am speaking only of expressions of opinion and exhortations, which were all that were uttered here; but I regret that I cannot put into more impressive words my belief that in their conviction upon this indictment the defendants were deprived of their rights under the Constitution of the United States.[10]

Over the next five years, and despite the arguments of Justice Holmes in *Abrams,* the majority of Supreme Court judges held to their view that an expression of political dissent could be punished in those instances where they perceived a tendency in that dissent to somehow threaten the government. The philosophy of the High Court's majority was extended to the level of state law in 1925 in the case of *Gitlow* v. *New York,* the first of

[10]In November 1921, after serving two years of their twenty-year sentence, the five codefendants in *Abrams* were released from federal prison on condition that they return to Russia at their own expense. Chafee, note 43, p. 140.

LANDMARK CASE
Gitlow v. New York, 268 U.S. 652 (1925)
Decided June 8, 1925

Vote: 7 to 2 for sustaining the conviction of Gitlow.
Majority Opinion By: Justice Sanford.
Concurring Justices: Chief Justice Taft, Justices Van Devanter, McReynolds, Sutherland, Butler, and Stone.
Dissenting Justices: Holmes and Brandeis.
Justices Not Participating: (none)
Summary: Benjamin Gitlow, a radical socialist, published and distributed 16,000 copies of a "Left Wing Manifesto" that urged the establishment of socialism by strikes and "class action . . . in any form." He was convicted in the courts of New York for violating the *state's* criminal anarchy statute (whereas Schenck, Frohwerk, Debs, and Abrams had been convicted of violating the *federal* law). Gitlow's attorneys argued that the First Amendment to the U.S. Constitution applied to state law by way of the due process clause of the Fourteenth Amendment. The Court, while agreeing with the innovative Fourteenth Amendment argument, upheld the conviction anyhow, asserting that Gitlow presented a degree of danger to the state which even the First Amendment could not excuse. Holmes and Brandeis, in dissent, argue that no *genuine* danger was created by the "Left Wing Manifesto."

   Rule Established; Significance of Case: This is a landmark decision, not because Gitlow's conviction was upheld (see Justice Sanford's classic statement of the doctrine of bad tendency) but because for the first time in American history the Court ruled that the First Amendment was binding upon the states (see the views of James Madison, in Chapter 2) as well as upon the federal government. Also, Justices Holmes and Brandeis enter a significant dissent which continues their argument for more freedom of speech under the clear-and-present-danger doctrine.

several appeals accepted by the Court from convictions under state criminal anarchy and criminal syndicalism statutes.

Justice E. Terry Sanford, speaking for the Court's seven-man majority, explained that Gitlow was found guilty in the courts of New York of violating that state's Criminal Anarchy Law. He used the language of the New York statute to explain what was meant by the charge: "Criminal anarchy is the doctrine that organized government should be overthrown by force or violence, or by assassination of the executive officials of government, or by any unlawful means. The advocacy of such doctrine either by word of mouth or writing is a felony." In defense of the statute, he asserted that it "does not pe-

nalize the utterance or publication of abstract 'doctrine' or academic discussion having no quality of incitement to any concrete action. . . . What it prohibits is language advocating, advising, or teaching the overthrow of organized government by unlawful means."

Justice Sanford then ruled on the issue that created a *landmark* case out of one which otherwise would have been routine—that is, the question of whether or not *state* laws are to be judged by the standards of the First Amendment to the *federal* Constitution. In answer to this question, he announced: **"For present purposes we may and do assume that freedom of speech and of the press— which are protected by the 1st Amend-**

FIGURE 3.3 WILLIAM Z.
FOSTER AND BENJAMIN
GITLOW.
In both 1924 and 1928 the
Workers Communist Party of
the United States nominated
William Z. Foster (on left) as
its presidential candidate and
Benjamin Gitlow (on right) as
its vice-presidential candidate. In
the photograph, both are shown
on the speaker's platform at
Madison Square Garden on
November 4, 1928. The fact
that Gitlow had earlier been
convicted of violating New
York's criminal anarchy statute
and that the U.S. Supreme
Court had upheld that conviction
in 1925 did not deter the
Workers Communist party from
nominating him a second time.
UPI/Bettmann Archive.

ment from abridgment by Congress—are
among the fundamental personal rights
and 'liberties' protected by the due process clause of the 14th Amendment from
impairment by the states.''[11] This landmark interpretation of the Court in *Gitlow*
means that after 1925 any citizen of any state
could invoke the protection of the First
Amendment to the U.S. Constitution against
state laws that attempt to constrain freedom
of expression. (Of course, the determination
of constitutionality is made by the courts.)

[11]The language of the Fourteenth Amendment (ratified in 1868) referred to by Justice Sanford is as follows:
"No State shall make or enforce any law which shall
abridge the privileges or immunities of citizens of the
United States; nor shall any State deprive any person of
life, *liberty,* or property, without due process of
law . . . ." [Emphasis supplied.]

Having quietly but dramatically altered the
law by applying the First Amendment to the
states, Justice Sanford returned to his reasons
for upholding the conviction of Gitlow; and
in so doing, he provided a classic summary
of the concept of bad tendency.

Justice Sanford *delivered the opinion of the
Court:*

. . . That utterances inciting to the overthrow of organized government by unlawful
means present a sufficient danger of substantive
evil to bring their punishment within the range
of legislative discretion is clear. Such utterances,
by their very nature, involve danger to the public peace and to the security of the state. They
threaten breaches of the peace and ultimate revolution. And the immediate danger is none the
less real and substantial because the effect of a
given utterance cannot be accurately foreseen.

The state cannot reasonably be required to measure the danger from every such utterance in the nice balance of a jeweler's scale. A single revolutionary spark may kindle a fire that, smoldering for a time, may burst into a sweeping and destructive conflagration. It cannot be said that the state is acting arbitrarily or unreasonably when, in the exercise of its judgment as to the measures necessary to protect the public peace and safety, it seeks to extinguish the spark without waiting until it has enkindled the flame or blazed into the conflagration. It cannot reasonably be required to defer the adoption of measures for its own peace and safety until the revolutionary utterances lead to actual disturbances of the public peace or imminent and immediate danger of its own destruction; but it may, in the exercise of its judgment, suppress the threatened danger in its incipiency. . . .

In dissent, Justice Holmes (joined by Justice Brandeis) continued the argument begun in *Abrams* for a more liberal interpretation of the First Amendment. While agreeing with the majority that the First Amendment should apply to the states, he stressed that no real threat was created by the distribution of Gitlow's "Left Wing Manifesto."

Justice Holmes, *dissenting:*

Mr. Justice Brandeis and I are of opinion that this judgment should be reversed. . . . If what I think the correct [interpretation of the clear-and-present-danger] test is applied, it is manifest that there was no present danger of an attempt to overthrow the government by force on the part of the admittedly small minority who shared the defendant's views. **It is said that this Manifesto was more than a theory, that it was an incitement. Every idea is an incitement. It offers itself for belief, and, if believed, it is acted on unless some other belief outweighs it, or some failure of energy stifles the movement at its birth. The only difference between the expression of an opinion and an incitement in the narrower sense is the speaker's enthusiasm for the result. Eloquence may set fire to reason. But whatever may be thought of the redundant discourse before us, it had no chance of starting a present conflagration.** If, in the long run, the beliefs expressed in proletarian dictatorship are destined to be accepted by the dominant forces of the community, the only meaning of free speech is that they should be given their chance and have their way.

Two years after *Gitlow,* a second state sedition controversy reached the Supreme Court, resulting in the by now predictable decision to sustain the conviction. Unlike the votes in *Abrams* and *Gitlow,* however, this one was unanimous, at least in a technical sense, for Justices Holmes and Brandeis voted with the majority, although their concurring opinion reveals that they preferred to dissent. Just as earlier decisions showed that the term "clear and present danger" could, in practice, mean "bad tendency," so did the case of *Whitney* v. *California* demonstrate that a "concurrence" could, in fact, function as a "dissent."

Justice Sanford, who authored the majority opinion in *Gitlow,* is again spokesman for the Court. He begins by defining the crime of criminal syndicalism as set forth in the California statute.

Justice Sanford *for the Court:*

Section 1. The term "criminal syndicalism" as used in this act is hereby defined as any doctrine or precept advocating, teaching or aiding and abetting the commission of crime, sabotage . . . or unlawful acts of force and violence or unlawful methods of terrorism as a means of accomplishing a change in industrial ownership or control, or effecting any political change.

Section 2. Any person who . . . organizes or assists in organizing, or is or knowingly becomes a member of, any organization, society, group or assemblage of persons organized or assembled to advocate, teach or aid and abet

Whitney v. California, 274 U.S. 357 (1927)
Decided May 16, 1927

Vote: 9 to 0 for sustaining the conviction of Whitney.

Majority Opinion By: Justice Sanford.

Concurring Justices: Chief Justice Taft, Justices Holmes, Van Devanter, McReynolds, Brandeis, Sutherland, Butler, and Stone.

Dissenting Justices: (none)

Justices Not Participating: (none)

Summary: Miss Anita Whitney, Wellesley graduate and niece of former Supreme Court Justice Stephen J. Field, was about sixty years of age when she was convicted of violating the California Criminal Syndicalism Act for her active membership in the Communist Labor Party (CLP). The CLP had approved a platform which favored the takeover of the government by "revolutionary class struggle" rather than by parliamentary means despite the public opposition of Miss Whitney, who voted against the proviolence platform (but who, nevertheless, remained in the party). The Supreme Court upheld her conviction on grounds similar to those stated in *Gitlow*. Reluctantly, Justice Brandeis concurred with the majority because of the failure of Whitney's attorneys to properly argue the clear-and-present-danger test. However, the concurring opinion of Justice Brandeis (joined in by Justice Holmes) should be read as a form of dissent.

Rule Established; Significance of Case: Although no rule is established by this decision, the case is significant because Justices Brandeis and Holmes explain in more than usual detail why they believe the clear and present danger test should be adopted by the Court. (Study the Brandeis opinion carefully.)

criminal syndicalism . . . is guilty of a felony and punishable by imprisonment.

Following a review of the facts of the case, which included the information that Miss Whitney publicly stated to her fellow Communists that she opposed violence as a means of bringing about political change, the Court sustained her conviction because she retained her membership in the Communist Labor party despite her disagreement with the organization over the issue of violence. As Justice Sanford stated, "The essence of the offense . . . is the combining with others in an association . . . . It partakes of the nature of a criminal conspiracy." Thus, in a legal irony explicitly overruled in the 1969 *Brandenburg* decision (discussed later in this chapter), the nonviolent, nondangerous Anita

Whitney was sent to prison because, somehow (as Justice Sanford reasoned), her membership held the potential for "joint action" and was therefore a "greater danger to the public peace and security" than if she acted alone to advocate the teachings of communism.[12]

In concurring, Justices Brandeis and

---

[12]A few months following the decision of the U.S. Supreme Court, Governor C. C. Young of California pardoned Miss Whitney, stating that the Communist Labor party was all but dead in California, and that no clear and present danger existed from either the party or from Miss Whitney. The governor concluded his pardon message as follows: "Miss Whitney, lifelong friend of the unfortunate, is not in any true sense a 'criminal,' and to condemn her, at sixty years of age, to a felon's cell is an action which is absolutely unthinkable." Chafee, p. 353.

Holmes pointed out that Miss Whitney and her attorneys could have made clear and present danger an important issue in the case, but they did not. As Justice Brandeis said, she did not claim that the conviction "was void because there was no clear and present danger of serious evil . . . . Under these circumstances the judgment of the state court cannot be disturbed." (In other words, the responsibility for raising the right issues rests with the defense; since the "right" issues were not raised, Justices Brandeis and Holmes felt obligated by legal precedent to concur with the majority on technical grounds.) However, voting with the majority did not mean agreement with the reasoning of the majority; to the contrary, Justices Brandeis and Holmes used the concurring opinion as a way of stating their disagreement with the arguments set out by the majority.

At the outset, Justice Brandeis (with whose concurring opinion Justice Holmes joined) stated his belief that the nation's founders supported the practice of freedom of speech for three basic reasons: individual development and happiness, to facilitate the search for political truth, and as a tool of democracy. His brief comment concerning each is as follows:

1. *Individual development and happiness.* "Those who won our independence believed that the final end of the state was to make men free to develop their faculties . . . . They valued liberty both as an end and as a means. They believed liberty to be the secret of happiness and courage to be the secret of liberty."

2. *As a means of discovering political truth.* "[The founders also] believed that freedom to think as you will and to speak as you think are means indispensable to the discovery and spread of political truth; that without free speech and assembly discussion would be futile; that with them, discussion affords ordi-

narily adequate protection against the dissemination of noxious doctrine . . . ."

3. *As a tool of democracy.* "[Furthermore, they believed] that public discussion is a political duty; and that this should be a fundamental principle of the American government. . . . Believing in the power of reason as applied through public discussion, they eschewed silence coerced by law—the argument of force in its worst form. Recognizing the occasional tyrannies of governing majorities, they amended the Constitution so that free speech and assembly should be guaranteed."

Justice Brandeis then moved to the central point of his opinion—the way in which he and Justice Holmes interpreted the clear-and-present-danger test.

Justice Brandeis, *concurring:*

Fear of serious injury cannot alone justify suppression of free speech and assembly. Men feared witches and burned women. It is the function of speech to free men from the bondage of irrational fears. To justify suppression of free speech there must be reasonable ground to fear that serious evil will result if free speech is practiced. There must be reasonable ground to believe that the danger apprehended is imminent. There must be reasonable ground to believe that the evil to be prevented is a serious one. . . . In order to support a finding of clear and present danger it must be shown either that immediate serious violence was to be expected or was advocated, or that the past conduct furnished reason to believe that such advocacy was then contemplated.

Those who won our independence by revolution were not cowards. They did not fear political change. They did not exalt order at the cost of liberty. To courageous, self-reliant men, with confidence in the power of free and fearless reasoning applied through the processes of popular government, no danger flowing from speech can be deemed clear and present, unless the incidence of the evil apprehended is so imminent that it may befall before there is opportunity for full discussion. If there be time to expose through discussion the falsehood and fallacies, to avert the evil by the processes of education, the remedy to be applied is more speech, not enforced silence. Only an emergency can justify repression. Such must be the rule if authority is to be reconciled with freedom. Such, in my opinion, is the command of the Constitution. It is, therefore, always open to Americans to challenge a law abridging free speech and assembly by showing that there was no emergency justifying it.

Moreover, even imminent danger cannot justify resort to prohibition of these functions essential to effective democracy, unless the evil apprehended is relatively serious. Prohibition of free speech and assembly is a measure so stringent that it would be inappropriate as the means for averting a relatively trivial harm to society. A police measure may be unconstitutional merely because the remedy, although effective as means of protection, is unduly harsh or oppressive. Thus, a state might, in the exercise of its police power, make any trespass upon the land of another a crime, regardless of the results or of the intent or purpose of the trespasser. It might, also, punish an attempt, a conspiracy, or an incitement to commit the trespass. But it is hardly conceivable that this court would hold constitutional a statute which punished as a felony the mere voluntary assembly with a society formed to teach that pedestrians had the moral right to cross unenclosed, unposted, waste lands and to advocate their doing so, even if there was imminent danger that advocacy would lead to a trespass. The fact that speech is likely to result in some violence or in destruction of property is not enough to justify its suppression. There must be the probability of serious injury to the state. Among freemen, the deterrents ordinarily to be applied to prevent crime are education and punishment for violations of the law, not abridgment of the rights of free speech and assembly.

By this time, one might wonder—with considerable justification—whether any per-

son convicted under the seditious speech sections of the Espionage Acts of 1917 and 1918, or under the various state sedition statutes, was set free on First Amendment grounds by the United States Supreme Court. To review the six cases analyzed so far:

1. Charles Schenck (for circulating an antidraft leaflet during the war), conviction *upheld* (1919).
2. Jacob Frohwerk (who published antiwar columns in his Missouri newspaper), conviction *upheld* (1919).
3. Socialist leader Eugene Debs (who made an antiwar speech), conviction *upheld* (1919).
4. Jacob Abrams and four colleagues (who distributed antiwar leaflets in and around New York City), convictions *upheld* (1919).
5. Benjamin Gitlow (who distributed copies of a "Left Wing Manifesto" in New York), conviction *upheld* (1925).
6. Anita Whitney (for remaining a member of the California branch of the Communist Labor party after the party adopted a proviolence position over Whitney's protests), conviction *upheld* (1927).

De Jonge v. Oregon (1937): A First Amendment Victory

The arguments of Justices Holmes and Brandeis were beginning to have some effect, however; so that ten years after *Whitney* a reversal was finally achieved.[13] Defendant Dirk De Jonge, a member of the Communist party, was convicted under the Oregon Criminal Syndicalism Act after making a speech at a public meeting in which he was critical of the conduct of the police of Port-

---

[13]*De Jonge* v. *Oregon*, 299 U.S. 353 (1937). Note: Brandeis was still on the Court, although Holmes had retired in 1932 and had died in 1935.

land, Oregon, toward striking longshoremen (among the charges: police shooting of strikers and illegal raids upon the homes and offices of strikers and their supporters). At no time during the speech did De Jonge advocate illegal conduct or criminal syndicalism, yet he was convicted in trial court, and the Oregon Supreme Court upheld his conviction. In a unanimous decision written by Chief Justice Charles Evans Hughes, the U.S. Supreme Court reversed De Jonge's conviction on January 4, 1937.

Chief Justice Hughes *delivered the opinion of the Court:*

It follows from these considerations that, consistently with the Federal Constitution, peaceable assembly for lawful discussion cannot be made a crime. The holding of meetings for peaceable political action cannot be proscribed. Those who assist in the conduct of such meetings cannot be branded as criminals on that score. The question, if the rights of free speech and peaceable assembly are to be preserved, is not as to the auspices under which the meeting is held but as to its purpose; not as to the relations of the speakers, but whether their utterances transcend the bounds of the freedom of speech which the Constitution protects. . . . We are not called upon to review the findings of the state court as to the objectives of the Communist Party. Notwithstanding those objectives, the defendant still enjoyed his personal right of free speech and to take part in a peaceable assembly having a lawful purpose, although called by that Party. The defendant was none the less entitled to discuss the public issues of the day and thus in a lawful manner, without incitement to violence of crime, to seek redress of alleged grievances. That was of the essence of his guaranteed personal liberty.

Political Heresy, 1917–1940, in Brief

As the period between World War I and World War II comes to an end, what can be said of the evolution of First Amendment doctrine by the United States Supreme Court? Four points stand out.

1. To begin with, the Court was *at last* deeply involved in interpreting the free-speech language of the U.S. Constitution.

2. Next, this beginning provided Justices Oliver Wendell Holmes and Louis D. Brandeis the opportunity to argue that the liberty of speech ought to be expanded beyond the narrow constraints of the traditional bad-tendency doctrine; the result was the "educational debate" over the clear-and-present-danger proposal, a factor which slowly influenced the Court to become more liberal in matters of political dissent.

3. Third, the willingness of the Court in *Gitlow* to use the Fourteenth Amendment as a means of applying the First Amendment to the states is of great importance to the development of free-speech doctrine in the United States.

4. Finally, the majority of justices during the period remained "conservative" and refused to interpret the First Amendment so as to protect outspoken critics of war, or of conscription, or of America's form of government. Although new doctrine was evolving, old doctrine ruled. The 1920s and the 1930s were not happy times for political mavericks in the United States.

II. FROM THE SMITH ACT OF 1940 TO THE PRESENT: THE HAZARDOUS ROAD TO EXPANDED FREEDOM FOR POLITICAL DISSENT

On December 8, 1941, the day after the surprise attack by Japan upon Pearl Harbor, President Franklin D. Roosevelt delivered his "Declaration of War Address" to a joint session of Congress. With a grimness unmatched since his "First Inaugural Address" in 1933, in which he announced the waging of economic warfare upon the Great Depression, Roosevelt began: "Yesterday, December 7th, 1941—a date which will live in infamy—the United States of America was suddenly and deliberately attacked by naval and air forces of the Empire of Japan." Noting that the attack occurred while Japanese representatives were still talking peace in Washington, Roosevelt continued: "Indeed, one hour after Japanese air squadrons had commenced bombing in the American island of Oahu, the Japanese Ambassador to the United States and his colleague delivered to our Secretary of State a formal reply to a recent American message." The reply, the president emphasized, "contained no threat or hint of war or of armed attack."[14] Upon hearing that his nation's envoys were still negotiating at the time of the attack, American-educated Admiral Isoroku Yamomoto, Japan's brilliant naval tactician who had planned the Pearl Harbor venture, noted with dismay that the apparent treachery of the attackers would instill in Americans "a terrible resolve."

Yamomoto was correct. In the days following Pearl Harbor, wrote columnist Arthur Krock of the *New York Times,* you could almost hear the unity of Americans "click into place." Even Senator Burton K. Wheeler of Montana, a strong isolationist in the years prior to the Japanese attack, reversed his position and declared that "the only thing now is to do our best to lick hell out of them."[15] The angry, determined response of the citizenry was so overwhelming that there was almost no antiwar dissent in the United States during the war years of 1941–1945 (a distinct contrast with the World War I period and its aftermath, during which more than two thousand sedition prosecutions were recorded). The issue of political heresy was not dead, however, for after the war ended America experienced its fourth "reign of witches" in the form of a revived fear—some would even describe it as "hysteria"—of Soviet communism. The legal basis for the postwar attack upon alleged Communist subversion in America was the Alien Registration Act voted by Congress on June 28, 1940, more than a year before the United States entered World War II.

Zechariah Chafee, Jr., describes the Alien Registration Act of 1940, usually called the Smith Act because the antisedition section was authored by Representative Howard W. Smith of Virginia, as providing "the most drastic restrictions on freedom of speech ever enacted in the United States during peace."[16] Its five sections had the following purposes:

Section 1, to punish speech that attempted to create disloyalty among members of the military.

Section 2, to punish speech advocating the "necessity, desirability, or propriety" of overthrowing the government by force and to make it illegal to organize any group to teach the overthrow of the government.

Section 3, to punish any person who conspires with others to violate this act.

Section 4, to allow seizure of printed matter intended for use in violation of this act (a proper search warrant must be secured).

Section 5, the penalty provision (originally a maximum fine of $10,000 and imprisonment for up to ten years, later increased to a maximum fine of $20,000 and up to twenty years in prison).[17]

[14]In *Great American Speeches, 1898–1963,* ed. John Graham (New York: Appleton-Century-Crofts, 1970), pp. 71–72.

[15]Both quotations from Ronald H. Bailey, *The Home Front: U.S.A.* (Alexandria, Va.: Time-Life Books, 1977), p. 23.

[16]Chafee, p. 441.

[17]54 *Statutes at Large* 670–671 (1940); currently in 18 *U.S. Code* Sec. 2385. For a detailed analysis, see Chafee, pp. 439–490; also, Emerson, pp. 110–111.

During the war, the Smith Act was used only twice, and in neither instance did an appeal reach the Supreme Court. (In one prosecution, a group of Socialist Workers party members were convicted in Minnesota; in the second instance, several persons accused of pro-Nazi sentiments were unsuccessfully tried in Washington, D.C.) After the war, however, the citizens of Western Europe, England, and the United States were confronted with one shock after another as the Soviet Union, a former ally in the battle against Nazi Germany, imposed its authoritarian regime upon the nations of Eastern Europe. As a result, the "Cold War" between Western democracy and communism began. Winston Churchill—in a 1946 speech delivered at Westminster College, Fulton, Missouri—described the tension in memorable language: "From Stettin in the Baltic to Trieste in the Adriatic an iron curtain has descended across the Continent. . . . I do not believe that Soviet Russia desires war. What they desire is the fruits of war and the indefinite expansion of their power and doctrines. . . ."[18] In these words, Churchill identified the central reason for the anti-Communist concern in the United States— the belief that Russia's drive for an "indefinite expansion" of its power and doctrines meant the eventual takeover of America, if not by war then by subversion. With prodding from the House Committee on Un-American Activities (sometimes called the House Un-American Activities Committee, or HUAC), government prosecutors in the Department of Justice began to look for the hub from which the American section of the suspected program of subversion was directed. Soon thereafter they claimed to have found it in the headquarters of the Central Committee of the Communist party in New York.

In July of 1948, Eugene Dennis and ten other members of the Central Committee of the Communist party were indicted in New York under the Smith Act. In a trial that lasted for six months, all were convicted of violating Sections 2 and 3 of the act. The U.S. Court of Appeals upheld the convictions, asserting that ample evidence had been presented during the trial to show that the defendants were engaged in a conspiracy to overthrow the government.[19] Subsequently, the Supreme Court granted judicial review to examine the constitutional issues raised by the convictions. On June 4, 1951, in a 6-to-2 decision (recently appointed Justice Tom C. Clark did not participate), the Court upheld the courts below.

Although six justices voted to uphold the convictions, they did so for three different (yet related) reasons. First, Chief Justice Vinson presented the thinking agreed upon by Justices Reed, Burton, Minton, and himself (thus forming a plurality but not a majority for any one opinion of the Court); second, Justice Frankfurter concurred in the result, but for his own reasons; finally, Justice Jackson concurred, stating an argument that was different from Justice Frankfurter's, although it did share some of the basic doctrine argued by Chief Justice Vinson (i.e., bad tendency). An examination of the three opinions of this "fractured majority" is revealing to the student of Supreme Court decision making.

The chief justice began by summarizing the facts of the case, including the charge that the defendants conspired to organize the Communist party in order to "teach and advocate the overthrow and destruction of the Government of the United States by force and violence" in violation of Sections 2 and 3

[18]Eric F. Goldman, *The Crucial Decade—and After: America, 1945–1960* (New York: Vintage Books, 1960), pp. 37–38.

[19]*United States v. Dennis*, 183 F.2d 201 (2d Cir. 1950).

Dennis v. United States, 341 U.S. 494 (1951)
Decided June 4, 1951

Vote: 6 to 2 for sustaining the conviction of Dennis and his associates.

Plurality Opinion By: Chief Justice Vinson.

Concurring Justices: Reed, Burton, and Minton concur with the chief justice; Frankfurter and Jackson concur with the result, each writing a separate opinion.

Dissenting Justices: Black and Douglas.

Justices Not Participating: Clark.

Summary: Eugene Dennis, secretary general of the Communist party, and ten associates were convicted in *federal* court of violating provisions of the 1940 Smith Act that made it illegal to advocate the overthrow of the government by force and violence, to organize a group to teach such advocacy, or to conspire to violate the Smith Act. In upholding the convictions, Chief Justice Vinson (joined by Justices Reed, Burton, and Minton) said (1) that a difference exists between the *discussion* of revolution and *indoctrination and advocacy* that tend toward achieving a revolution; also, (2) that the "gravity of the evil" presented by communism is so great that it is foolish "to wait until the putsch is about to be executed" before stopping it. The clear-and-present-danger test, though given frequent lip service, is abandoned and the *tendency* doctrine is employed. Justice Frankfurter, concurring, uses *balancing,* asserting that on a scale of values, the speech of Dennis "ranks low." Justice Jackson, concurring, argues a *conspiracy* variation of tendency, saying that if the *end* is punishable, "there is no doubt of the power to punish conspiracy for the purpose" of accomplishing that end. Justices Black and Douglas, in spirited dissent, charge that the record fails to show that the defendants actually advocated any specific or immediate illegal conduct; in other words, say the dissenters, no *clear* and *present* danger was demonstrated.

Rule Established; Significance of Case: This important decision upheld the constitutionality of the Smith Act, asserting that when the *gravity of the evil* is great enough, teachings that tend toward eventual violent revolution may be punished by the government without violating the First Amendment.

of the Smith Act. It is certainly within the power of Congress to legislate against such threats, he added, so that the central question in the case remained "whether the *means* it has employed conflict with the First and Fifth Amendments to the Constitution." He emphasized that the Smith Act allowed the study of ideas about revolution, as in a college course, although it did prohibit the *advocacy* of violent revolution, "the very kind of activity in which the evidence showed these petitioners engaged." Having attempted to separate discussion from advocacy, he then cited the clear-and-present-dan-

ger doctrine, proceeding to interpret it as a kind of tendency rule to be applied when the country is confronted with a great evil. In such instances, he asked, what do the words "clear and present danger" mean?

Chief Justice Vinson *delivered the plurality opinion:*

Obviously, the words cannot mean that before the Government may act, it must wait until the putsch is about to be executed, the plans have been laid and the signal is awaited. If Government is aware that a group aiming at its overthrow is attempting to indoctrinate its members and to commit them to a course whereby they will strike when the leaders feel the circumstances permit, action by the Government is required. . . . In the instant case the trial judge charged the jury that they could not convict unless they found that petitioners intended to overthrow the Government "as speedily as circumstances would permit." This does not mean, and could not properly mean, that they would not strike until there was certainty of success. What was meant was that the revolutionists would strike when they thought the time was ripe. We must therefore reject the contention that success or probability of success is the criterion. . . .

Chief Judge Learned Hand, writing for the majority below, interpreted the phrase as follows: "In each case [courts] must ask whether the gravity of the 'evil,' discounted by its improbability, justifies such invasion of free speech as is necessary to avoid the danger." We adopt this statement of the rule. As articulated by Chief Judge Hand, it is as succinct and inclusive as any other we might devise at this time. It takes into consideration those factors which we deem relevant, and relates their significances. More we cannot expect from words.

Likewise, we are in accord with the court below, which affirmed the trial court's finding that the requisite danger existed. The mere fact that from the period 1945 to 1948 petitioners' activities did not result in an attempt to overthrow the Government by force and violence is of course no answer to the fact that there was a group that was ready to make the attempt. The formation by petitioners of such a highly organized conspiracy, with rigidly disciplined members subject to call when the leaders, these petitioners, felt that the time had come for action, coupled with the inflammable nature of world conditions, similar uprisings in other countries, and the touch-and-go nature of our relations with countries with whom petitioners were in the very least ideologically attuned, convince us that their convictions were justified on this score. . . . If the ingredients of the reaction are present, we cannot bind the Government to wait until the catalyst is added.

Justice Frankfurter concurred in the result, but arrived at his decision to do so by a line of argument different from that stated by the chief justice. To Frankfurter, the weighing of values needed to be added to any degree-of-danger test. This weighing, or *balancing,* of speech against social interests should include factors such as "the relative seriousness of the danger in comparison with the value of the occasion for speech or political activity," or the "specific intent with which the speech or activity is launched."

For Justice Jackson, who concurred in the result, the issue was the right of Congress to punish a *conspiracy.* Argued Justice Jackson: "I do not suggest that Congress could punish conspiracy to advocate something, the doing of which it may not punish. . . . But it is not forbidden to put down force or violence, it is not forbidden to punish its teaching or advocacy, and the end being punishable, there is no doubt of the power to punish conspiracy for the purpose." The First Amendment did not protect Dennis and his associates, he concluded, for "there is no constitutional right to 'gang up' on the Government."

Justices Black and Douglas, the two dissenters, stir memories of the Holmes-Brandeis opinions earlier in the century. Justice Black made two important points in his dissent, urging (1) that Section 3 of the Smith Act, under which the conspiracy convictions were obtained, was an unconstitutional prior restraint upon the freedom to communicate, and (2) that the established clear-and-present-danger test, if applied to the petitioners, would have resulted in an acquittal. He then moved to the conclusion of his argument.

Justice Black, *dissenting:*

. . . The opinions for affirmance indicate that the chief reason for jettisoning the [clear-and-present-danger] rule is the expressed fear that advocacy of Communist doctrine endangers the safety of the Republic. Undoubtedly, a governmental policy of unfettered communication of ideas does entail dangers. To the Founders of this Nation, however, the benefits derived from free expression were worth the risk. They embodied this philosophy in the First Amendment's command that Congress "shall make no law abridging . . . the freedom of speech, or of the press . . . ." I have always believed that the First Amendment is the keystone of our Government, that the freedoms it guarantees provide the best insurance against destruction of all freedom. At least as to speech in the realm of public matters, I believe that the "clear and present danger" test does not "mark the furthermost constitutional boundaries of protected expression" but does "no more than recognize a minimum compulsion of the Bill of Rights."

So long as this Court exercises the power of judicial review of legislation, I cannot agree that the First Amendment permits us to sustain laws suppressing freedom of speech and press on the basis of Congress' or our own notions of mere "reasonableness." Such a doctrine waters down the First Amendment so that it amounts to little more than an admonition to Congress. The Amendment as so construed is not likely to protect any but those "safe" or orthodox views which rarely need its protection. . . .

Public opinion being what it now is, few will protest the conviction of these Communist petitioners. There is hope, however, that in calmer times, when present pressures, passions and fears subside, this or some later Court will restore the First Amendment liberties to the high preferred place where they belong in a free society.

In his dissent, Justice Douglas agreed with Justice Black that the defendants were sentenced to prison for the "crime" of meeting together for the purpose of teaching themselves and others the doctrines of Marx and Lenin—an activity which, he points out, involves speech but *not antisocial conduct*. He de-

veloped this point, then argued that the clear-and-present-danger test should have been applied to Dennis and his codefendants.

Justice Douglas, *dissenting:*

The vice of treating speech as the equivalent of overt acts of a treasonable or seditious character is emphasized by a concurring opinion, which by invoking the law of conspiracy makes speech do service for deeds which are dangerous to society. The doctrine of conspiracy has served divers and oppressive purposes and in its broad reach can be made to do great evil. But never until today has anyone seriously thought that the ancient law of conspiracy could constitutionally be used to turn speech into seditious conduct. Yet that is precisely what is suggested. I repeat that we deal here with speech alone, not with speech plus acts of sabotage or unlawful conduct. Not a single seditious act is charged in the indictment. To make a lawful speech unlawful because two men conceive it is to raise the law of conspiracy to appalling proportions. That course is to make a radical break with the past and to violate one of the cardinal principles of our constitutional scheme.

. . . Free speech—the glory of our system of government—should not be sacrificed on anything less than plain and objective proof of danger that the evil advocated is imminent. On this record no one can say that petitioners and their converts are in such a strategic position as to have even the slightest chance of achieving their aims.

The First Amendment provides that "Congress shall make no law . . . abridging the freedom of speech." The Constitution provides no exception. This does not mean, however, that the Nation need hold its hand until it is in such weakened condition that there is no time to protect itself from incitement to revolution. Seditious conduct can always be punished. But the command of the First Amendment is so clear that we should not allow Congress to call a halt to free speech except in the extreme case of peril from the speech itself. The First Amendment makes confidence in the common

FIGURE 3.4.   JUSTICE HUGO L. BLACK.

FIGURE 3.5.   JUSTICE WILLIAM O. DOUGLAS.

Justice Hugo L. Black and Justice William O. Douglas were the two liberal voices of the U.S. Supreme Court in the post-World War II national security cases. Dissenting from the decision of the majority to sustain the convictions of eleven Communists for sedition in the 1951 case of Dennis v. United States, *both Black and Douglas argued that the First Amendment protected the right of political dissidents, including Eugene Dennis and his associates, to meet, talk, and advocate their views. As Justice Douglas stated, only "when the provocateurs among us move from speech to action" should the government interfere. Justices Black and Douglas were appointed to the Court by President Franklin D. Roosevelt, Black in 1937 and Douglas in 1939. Justice Black served for thirty-four years, retiring because of illness in 1971, the year of his death. Justice Douglas served for thirty-six years, retiring because of poor health in 1975. Douglas died in 1980.*

Both pictures, Library of Congress.

sense of our people and in their maturity of judgment the great postulate of our democracy. Its philosophy is that violence is rarely, if ever, stopped by denying civil liberties to those advocating resort to force. The First Amendment reflects the philosophy of Jefferson "that it is time enough for the rightful purposes of civil government for its officers to interfere when principles break out into overt acts against peace and good order." The political censor has no place in our public debates. Unless and until extreme and necessitous circumstances are shown, our aim should be to keep speech unfettered and to allow the processes of law to be invoked only when the provocateurs among us move from speech to action.

Vishinsky wrote in 1948 in *The Law of the Soviet State,* "In our state, naturally there can be no place for freedom of speech, press, and so on for the foes of socialism."

Our concern should be that we accept no such standard for the United States. Our faith

Yates v. United States, 354 U.S. 298 (1957)
Decided June 17, 1957

Vote: 6 to 1 to remand (i.e., send the case back) to the district court with orders to acquit some of the defendants and retry the others. The district court dismissed the case because prosecutors could not meet the standards of evidence set by the Supreme Court.

Majority Opinion By: Justice Harlan.

Concurring Justices: Chief Justice Warren, Justices Black, Frankfurter, Douglas, and Burton.

Dissenting Justices: Clark.

Justices Not Participating: Brennan and Whittaker (both newly appointed).

Summary: Oleta Yates and thirteen others, all members of the Communist party in California, were convicted in federal court of conspiracy to violate the Smith Act by teaching the necessity of the forcible overthrow of the government. The Supreme Court remanded the convictions, not forthrightly on First Amendment grounds but on the bases that (1) the trial judge had given incorrect instructions to the jury and that (2) the evidence was insufficient. The Court ruled that the trial judge should have distinguished more clearly between the advocacy of *ideas* ("abstract doctrine"), which the Smith Act permits, and the advocacy of *violent revolution* ("unlawful action"), which may be punished. Furthermore, the Court asserted that the evidence submitted in the trial was insufficient to prove that the defendants had actually urged criminal conduct. Justices Black and Douglas concurred in the result, but for a different reason—namely, that the Smith Act itself was unconstitutional.

Rule Established; Significance of Case: This decision clarified the Court's distinction between the advocacy of abstract doctrine, which was legal, and the advocacy of illegal action of the type outlawed by the Smith Act. The difficulty of meeting the standards of evidence under the *Yates* "clarification" resulted in the dismissal of most Smith Act prosecutions that were under way at the time.

should be that our people will never give support to these advocates of revolution, so long as we remain loyal to the purposes for which our Nation was founded.

Following the successful prosecutions in *Dennis,* the U.S. Justice Department proceeded against a number of Communists, indicting them for seditious expression as defined by the Smith Act. The government's efforts all but ceased, however, when in 1957 the Supreme Court *reversed* the conviction of Communist Oleta Yates and thirteen associates in a case arising from a federal district court in California.

A careful reading of the instructions of the trial judge to the jury led the justices of the Supreme Court to conclude that the *Yates* jury could have found the defendants guilty for advocating *ideas* rather than illegal *action.* Because of the uncertainty created by this question, the Court reversed, and in so doing attempted to clarify, the doctrine first articulated in *Dennis.*

Justice Harlan *delivered the opinion of the Court:*

In failing to distinguish between advocacy of forcible overthrow as an abstract doctrine and advocacy of action to that end, the District Court appears to have been led astray by the holding in Dennis that advocacy of violent action to be taken at some future time was enough. . . .   In other words, the District

Court apparently thought that Dennis obliterated the traditional dividing line between advocacy of abstract doctrine and advocacy of action.

. . .The essence of the Dennis holding was that indoctrination of a group in preparation for future violent action, as well as exhortation to immediate action, by advocacy found to be directed to "action for the accomplishment" of forcible overthrow, to violence "as a rule or principle of action," and employing "language of incitement," is not constitutionally protected when the group is of sufficient size and cohesiveness, is sufficiently oriented towards action, and other circumstances are such as reasonably to justify apprehension that action will occur. This is quite a different thing from the view of the District Court here that mere doctrinal justification of forcible overthrow, if engaged in with the intent to accomplish overthrow, is punishable per se under the Smith Act. That sort of advocacy, even though uttered with the hope that it may ultimately lead to violent revolution, is too remote from concrete action to be regarded as the kind of indoctrination preparatory to action which was condemned in Dennis. As one of the concurring opinions in Dennis put it: "Throughout our decisions there has recurred a distinction between the statement of an idea which may prompt its hearers to take unlawful action, and advocacy that such action be taken." There is nothing in Dennis which makes that historic distinction obsolete.

After concluding the explanation of the difference between teaching abstract doctrine and urging illegal conduct, the Court turned its attention to the inadequacy of the evidence in the case. The key question: Did the government's evidence prove the advocacy of illegal *action?*

Justice Harlan *continues for the Court:*

We recognize that distinctions between advocacy or teaching of abstract doctrines, with evil intent, and that which is directed to stirring people to action, are often subtle and difficult to grasp, for in a broad sense, as Mr. Justice Holmes said in his dissenting opinion in *Gitlow:* "Every idea is an incitement." But the very subtlety of these distinctions required the most clear and explicit instructions with reference to them, for they concerned an issue which went to the very heart of the charges against these petitioners. The need for precise and understandable instructions on this issue is further emphasized by the equivocal character of the evidence in this record . . . . Instances of speech that could be considered to amount to "advocacy of action" are so few and far between as to be almost completely overshadowed by the hundreds of instances in the record in which overthrow, if mentioned at all, occurs in the course of doctrinal disputation so remote from action as to be almost wholly lacking in probative value. Vague references to "revolutionary" or "militant" action of an unspecified character, which are found in the evidence, might in addition be given too great weight by the jury in the absence of more precise instructions. Particularly in light of this record, we must regard the trial court's charge in this respect as furnishing wholly inadequate guidance to the jury on this central point in the case. We cannot allow a conviction to stand on such "an equivocal direction to the jury on a basic issue."

In a separate opinion, concurring in part and dissenting in part, Justices Black and Douglas agreed with the result but not with all of the reasoning of the majority in reaching that result. Rather than chip away at the Smith Act, as the Court did by stating and refining definitions and setting out complex standards of evidence, the two liberals on the Court preferred to confront the Smith Act with the First Amendment, directly, and thereby witness the act's demise. As Justice Black asserted, "I would reverse every one of these convictions and direct that all the defendants be acquitted. In my judgment the statutory provisions on which these prosecutions are based abridge freedom of speech, press and assembly in violation of the First Amendment of the United States Constitution."

Even though the Court was unwilling to declare the Smith Act unconstitutional, as urged by Justices Black and Douglas, the standards of evidence agreed upon were too strict for government attorneys who, after *Yates*, had to prove that the accused actually advocated illegal conduct. Consequently, no new Smith Act prosecutions were undertaken following the decision, and except for the case of Junius Scales, all others under way were eventually dropped by the prosecutors or dismissed by the courts.[20] Altogether, 141 persons had been indicted under the Smith Act (primarily for communicating "seditious" opinions), and of that number twenty-nine served time in prison, including those convicted in *Dennis,* seventeen defendants from two trials after *Dennis* (neither of which was granted review by the Supreme Court), and Junius Scales.[21]

Although the 1957 *Yates* decision ended the government's campaign to prosecute the

Communist party under the Smith Act, it did so for a reason *indirectly* related to the First Amendment—namely, the standard for *evidence* that must be met by the government. Twelve years later, however, in the case of Ohio Ku Klux Klan leader Clarence Brandenburg, the Supreme Court was much clearer than before, announcing an *incitement* statement that was even more liberal than previous applications of the clear-and-present-danger test.

In its unanimous per curiam decision, the Supreme Court cited the Ohio Criminal Syndicalism Statute under which Brandenburg was convicted (for advocating the "duty, necessity, or propriety of crime, sabotage, violence, or unlawful methods of terrorism as a means of accomplishing industrial or political reform," and for voluntarily assembling "with any society, group, or assemblage of persons formed to teach or advocate the doctrines of criminal syndicalism"). For making a seditious speech and for assembling with others to advocate sedition, Brandenburg had been fined $1,000 and sentenced to prison for from one to ten years. Referring to the films of the KKK rally made by a local television station, the Supreme Court summarized what took place.

Per Curiam:

One film showed 12 hooded figures, some of whom carried firearms. They were gathered around a large wooden cross, which they burned. No one was present other than the participants and the newsmen who made the film. Most of the words uttered during the scene were incomprehensible when the film was projected, but scattered phrases could be understood that were derogatory of Negroes and, in one instance, of Jews. Another scene on the same film showed the appellant, in Klan regalia, making a speech. The speech, in full, was as follows:

"This is an organizers' meeting. We have had

---

[20]Junius I. Scales of Greensboro, North Carolina, has the distinction of being the only American convicted for violating the membership clause of Section 2 of the Smith Act. In *Scales* v. *United States,* 367 U.S. 203 (1961), the Supreme Court sustained his conviction by a vote of 5 to 4, not because Scales advocated seditious conduct but because he was a member of a group that allegedly did so (the Communist party). In a second membership case decided on the same day, John F. Noto's conviction was unanimously reversed by the Supreme Court because of insufficient evidence in *Noto* v. *United States,* 367 U.S. 290 (1961). On Christmas Eve 1962, after serving six months of his six-year sentence, Scales was released from the federal prison at Lewisburg, Pennsylvania, by President John F. Kennedy in response to a petition signed by a large number of distinguished Americans, including Reinhold Niebuhr, Martin Luther King, Jr., Saul Bellow, A. Philip Randolph, and Paul Green. The *Greensboro Record,* October 11, 1976, p. A-2.

[21]Emerson, p. 124.

LANDMARK CASE
Brandenburg v. Ohio, 395 U.S. 444 (1969)
Decided June 9, 1969

Vote: 9 to 0 for reversal of conviction of Brandenburg.
Majority Opinion By: (per curiam).
Concurring Justices: Chief Justice Warren, Justices Black, Douglas, Harlan, Brennan, Stewart, White, Fortas, and Marshall.
Dissenting Justices: (none)
Justices Not Participating: (none)
Summary: Clarence Brandenburg, a leader in the Ku Klux Klan in Ohio, spoke at a Klan rally in a rural part of the state. His remarks, which included a threat of "revengeance" against the president, the Congress, and the Supreme Court, were recorded on film by a television crew invited by Brandenburg to cover the meeting. The prosecution relied heavily upon the content of the film in securing a conviction under Ohio's Criminal Syndicalism Act, which made it a crime to advocate the use of violence and terrorism to accomplish industrial or political reform. The Supreme Court unanimously reversed the conviction (and in so doing specifically overruled the 1927 *Whitney* decision), stating that the principle of distinguishing between the advocacy of ideas and the advocacy of illegal action developed since *Whitney* (in cases such as *Dennis, Yates,* and *Noto*) made the Ohio Criminal Syndicalism Act unconstitutional, since it failed to make that distinction. Justices Black and Douglas, concurring, go further, arguing that even the clear-and-present-danger test has "no place in the interpretation of the First Amendment."

Rule Established; Significance of Case: This decision is called a landmark because, by requiring the government to prove that the danger presented was *real,* not imaginary, it extends the First Amendment to speech that had not been previously protected. Even threatening speech is protected, said the Court, unless the state can prove that the "advocacy is directed to inciting or producing imminent lawless action and is likely to incite or produce such action." Some scholars describe this as a strict application of the clear-and-present-danger doctrine, even though the words "clear and present danger" are not used by the Court; in fact, it goes beyond past uses of "clear and present danger" and establishes an *incitement* standard.

quite a few members here today which are—we have hundreds, hundreds of members throughout the State of Ohio. I can quote from a newspaper clipping from the Columbus, Ohio *Dispatch,* five weeks ago Sunday morning. The Klan has more members in the State of Ohio than does any other organization. We're not a revengent organization, but if our President, our Congress, our Supreme Court, continues to suppress the white, Caucasian race, it's possible that there might have to be some revengeance taken.

"We are marching on Congress July the Fourth, four hundred thousand strong. From there we are dividing into two groups, one group to march on St. Augustine, Florida, the other group to march into Mississippi. Thank you."

The second film showed six hooded figures one of whom, later identified as the appellant, repeated a speech very similar to that recorded on the first film. The reference to the possibility of "revengeance" was omitted, and one sentence was added: "Personally, I believe the nigger should be returned to Africa, the Jew returned to Israel." Though some of the figures in the films carried weapons, the speaker did not.

FIGURE 3.6. CLARENCE BRANDENBURG. Ohio Ku Klux Klan leader Clarence Brandenburg, whose antigovernment speech delivered during a Klan rally prompted state officials to indict him for violating the Ohio criminal syndicalism law. Brandenburg was convicted in state court and sentenced to serve from one to ten years in prison. Upon appeal, the U.S. Supreme Court unanimously reversed the conviction and in so doing announced the landmark incitement *standard by which seditious speech is currently judged.*
AP/Wide World Photos.

The Court continued by stating that the Ohio law, enacted in 1919, is similar to the California Criminal Syndicalism Statute upheld in the 1927 case of *Whitney* v. *California.* In that decision, the California law was upheld on the "ground that, without more, 'advocating' violent means to effect political and economic change involves such danger to the security of the State that the State may outlaw it." The Court then proceeded to articulate its landmark incitement standard.

Per Curiam, *continued:*

But *Whitney* has been thoroughly discredited by later decisions . . . [which] have fashioned the principle that **the constitutional guarantees of free speech and free press do not permit a State to forbid or proscribe advocacy of the use of force or of law violation except where such advocacy is directed to inciting or producing imminent lawless action and is likely to incite or produce such action.** As we said in *Noto* v. *United States* . . . , "the mere abstract teaching . . . of the moral propriety or even moral

necessity for a resort to force and violence, is not the same as preparing a group for violent action and steeling it to such action." . . . A statute which fails to draw this distinction impermissibly intrudes upon the freedoms guaranteed by the First and Fourteenth Amendments. It sweeps within its condemnation speech which our Constitution has immunized from governmental control. . . .

Measured by this test, Ohio's Criminal Syndicalism Act cannot be sustained. The act punishes persons who "advocate or teach the duty, necessity, or propriety" of violence "as a means of accomplishing industrial or political reform"; or who publish or circulate or display any book or paper containing such advocacy; or who "justify" the commission of violent acts "with intent to exemplify, spread or advocate the propriety of the doctrines of criminal syndicalism"; or who "voluntarily assemble" with a group formed "to teach or advocate the doctrines of criminal syndicalism." Neither the indictment nor the trial judge's instructions to the jury in any way refined the statute's bald definition of the crime in terms of mere advocacy not distinguished from incitement to imminent lawless action.

Accordingly, we are here confronted with a statute which, by its own words and as applied, purports to punish mere advocacy and to forbid, on pain of criminal punishment, assembly with others merely to advocate the described type of action. Such a statute falls within the condemnation of the First and Fourteenth Amendments. The contrary teaching of *Whitney* v. *California* . . . cannot be supported, and that decision is therefore overruled.

Reversed.

The key to the *Brandenburg* decision is the element of *intent*. If expression is judged to represent "talking big" or "blowing off steam" with no serious intent to incite unlawful conduct, or if expression concerns *belief* in some doctrine of violent conduct yet does not attempt to incite to imminent achievement of that conduct, it is protected speech under the First Amendment. As the Court said in the "thesis sentence" of *Brandenburg,* to be punishable the speech must be "directed to inciting or producing imminent lawless action" and it must be "likely to incite or produce such action." America entered the decade of the 1970s with this liberal standard intact, and it was sustained during the 1970s to remain the operational test of the Court. Two post-*Brandenburg* cases illustrate how the Court has applied the incitement doctrine.

In the 1973 case of *Hess* v. *Indiana*, defendant Gregory Hess had been convicted in Bloomington, Indiana, of violating the state's disorderly conduct statute during a student antiwar demonstration when he commented on the activity of the sheriff and his deputies in clearing the street by saying, "We'll take the fucking street later." The Supreme Court reversed the conviction and, in its per curiam opinion, cited *Brandenburg* to conclude that student Hess was not inciting to "imminent lawless action." In a second case, announced about a year after *Hess,* the Supreme Court

ruled that the Communist party of Indiana could have its candidates' names placed on the ballot without having these candidates sign a loyalty oath pledging not to advocate the overthrow of the government by force or violence (strangely, neither the Republican nor Democratic candidates had been asked to sign such an oath). Quoting *Brandenburg,* Justice Brennan delivered the opinion of the Court to the effect that unless the Communist party advocated incitement "producing imminent lawless action," then mere belief in the abstract doctrine of overthrowing the government at some future date was no reason to keep the group off the ballot.[22]

Political Heresy Since 1940 in Brief

The Smith Act cases (particularly *Dennis* and *Yates*) and the *Brandenburg* decision are of vital significance to the development of First Amendment doctrine concerning seditious speech in the United States. A careful reading of these opinions reveals to the student of freedom of speech how Supreme Court doctrine evolves over time, eventually crystallizing in language that says clearly and concisely what some have been urging for years. To review:

1. In the 1951 *Dennis* decision, in which the convictions of eleven Communists were upheld, no clear and present danger was cited and no illegal conduct was proved. Rather, the Court determined that when the "gravity of the evil" faced by the nation was great enough, the government could punish advocacy during its indoctrination phase, before it achieved the status of obvious and immediate danger. Such punishment reverted to the doctrine of bad tendency for support.

[22]*Hess* v. *Indiana*, 414 U.S. 105 (1973); and *Communist Party of Indiana* v. *Whitcomb*, 414 U.S. 441 (1974).

2. In the *Yates* decision of 1957, in which the convictions of fourteen Communists were reversed, the Court attempted to clarify the distinction begun in *Dennis* between the advocacy of ideas, or "abstract doctrine," which the First Amendment protects, and the advocacy of "unlawful action," which it does not. In addition, the Court stressed that the evidence must show that the speakers specifically urged illegal conduct.

3. The clarification of advocacy of "abstract doctrine" versus advocacy of "unlawful action" begun in *Yates* matured in the 1969 *Brandenburg* decision, which resulted in the reversal of Brandenburg's conviction for violating a state sedition law. Here there was no semantic floundering, as had occurred in *Dennis* and, to a lesser extent, in *Yates*. In *Brandenburg* the Court was clear and concise, stating that to be punishable in the future, antigovernment speech must have the clear intent of producing "imminent lawless action" and be "likely to incite or produce such action." Thus, the clear-and-present-danger doctrine argued so passionately by Holmes and Brandeis in the years between the two world wars was, in a sense, reinstated, then immediately surpassed by the announcement of the incitement standard. After *Brandenburg,* to paraphrase the Constitution, "Congress shall make no law abridging antigovernment speech, except for that which is directed to inciting or producing imminent lawless action and is likely to incite or produce such action." This might not be what Jefferson and Madison had in mind, but it would have been good news to Schenck, Frohwerk, Debs, Abrams, Gitlow, and Whitney!

III. POLITICAL HERESY: RELATED TOPICS

In addition to the major issues and cases concerning seditious speech analyzed thus far, a number of subissues have developed over the years. Among those are the seven topics summarized below, which help to complete the picture of attempts by government to constrain "seditious" expression or to compel expressions of patriotism. The topics discussed are (1) threatening the life of the president, (2) the unauthorized naming of intelligence officers and agents, (3) antiwar remarks by an elected official, (4) advising youth against the draft, (5) compelling public school students to salute the flag, (6) preventing political heretics from speaking on state college campuses, and (7) the use of defamation laws to punish those who criticize public officials.

1. Threatening the Life of the President

In a statute approved on February 14, 1917, the Congress made it illegal to "knowingly and willfully" threaten the life of the president of the United States. Since its passage, the law has been amended to include the vice-president, the president-elect, and the vice-president-elect as well as any "other officer next in the order of succession to the office of President of the United States." Violators are subject to a fine of $1,000, imprisonment for up to five years, or both.[23] The law applies whether the threat is delivered by mail or "otherwise," which would include oral communication. The statute has been declared constitutional in several instances, including the case of *Watts* v. *United States.*[24] This 1969 decision concerned an eighteen-year-old black defendant, Robert Watts, who was convicted of threatening the life of President Johnson when, during a civil rights rally on the grounds of the Washington Monument in Washington, D.C., he shouted that he was not going to honor his draft call,

---

[23]18 *U.S. Code* Sec. 871.
[24]394 U.S. 705 (1969).

and "If they ever make me carry a rifle the first man I want to get in my sights is L.B.J." Although the Supreme Court overturned the conviction, since the majority viewed the remark of Watts as hyperbole lacking in intent to carry out the "threat," the Court asserted that "the statute under which petitioner was convicted is constitutional on its face." One should assume, therefore, that expression threatening the life of the president of the United States, or the vice-president or any other officer of government in line for the presidency, is *not* protected by the First Amendment.

2. Unauthorized Naming of Intelligence Officers and Agents

During the 1970s and early 1980s a small number of Americans, including a few who had worked at one time for the Central Intelligence Agency, acted to show their opposition to the secret work of CIA agents abroad by deliberately and systematically publishing the names and locations of agents in the field. Two periodicals that featured this type of information were *Counterspy* and the *Covert Action Information Bulletin*. In 1975, Richard S. Welch, the CIA Station Chief in Athens, Greece, was murdered in front of his home within a month of the time that he was publicly identified, and in 1980 an official of the American Embassy in Kingston, Jamaica, was the object of an attempted assassination within hours of the public announcement by an anti-CIA group that the official worked for the CIA. A number of other assassination attempts against American officials in various parts of the world were attributed, rightly or wrongly, to the publication of the names and locations of alleged secret agents.

In 1980 the Congress began to consider various proposals for protecting the identities of intelligence agents and, after two years of hearings, passed the Intelligence Identities

Protection Act of 1982.[25] This legislation makes it a crime not only for former government officials who had authorized access to classified information to intentionally identify covert agents but also for others to publish the identities of secret agents "in the course of a pattern of activities intended to identify and expose" such agents for the purpose of impairing "the foreign intelligence activities of the United States." Here, authorized access to classified information is *not* a prerequisite to conviction (for which the convicted communicator can be fined up to $15,000, or imprisoned for up to three years, or both). Any person who is in the business of naming the names of covert agents, who dedicates himself or herself to the task of discovering and publishing such names, and who does so with the *intent* of subverting the foreign intelligence activities of the United States is a candidate for indictment under the 1982 law.

The burden of proof upon the government is a heavy one—and deliberately so, as the legislative history of the act demonstrates[26]—in order to protect what Congress perceives as legitimate First Amendment concerns. Meanwhile, until legal challenges and subsequent court decisions determine the constitutionality of the statute, public communicators should know that dedicating oneself to a pattern of "blowing the cover" of secret agents abroad for the purpose of neutralizing the agents or damaging the work of the CIA (or other government agency authorized to collect intelligence in foreign countries) is prohibited by law.

---

[25]Public Law 97–200 (June 23, 1982). In 96 *Statutes at Large* 122–125 (1982). The act is an amendment to Section 2(a) of the National Security Act of 1947, and appears at 50 *U.S. Code* Sec. 421.

[26]See *U.S. Code Congressional and Administrative News,* July 1982, pp. 145–176, for an excellent summary of the legislative history of the bill.

3. Antiwar Comments by an Elected Official

In 1965, while the United States was involved in the Vietnam War, black civil rights leader Julian Bond, who had been elected to the Georgia House of Representatives, publicly endorsed an antiwar statement issued by the Student Nonviolent Coordinating Committee (SNCC), of which he was a member. Among other things, the SNCC document asserted that "We are in sympathy with, and support, the men in this country who are unwilling to respond to a military draft." In endorsing the SNCC position paper, Bond said, "I like to think of myself as a pacifist and one who opposes that war and any other war and [I am] eager and anxious to encourage people not to participate in it for any reason that they choose." The members of the Georgia House of Representatives voted not to seat Bond because his antiwar opinions had given "aid and comfort to the enemies of the United States." Bond took the issue to court, charging that the Georgia legislature had violated his First Amendment rights. When the case reached the Supreme Court in 1966, the High Court agreed and ordered Bond seated in the Georgia House. In its decision, the Court said that the "manifest function of the First Amendment in a representative government requires that legislators be given the widest latitude to express their views on issues of policy."[27]

4. Advising Youth Against the Draft

Both the Espionage Act of 1917 and the Selective Service Act of 1948 make it illegal to advise those eligible for the draft to resist conscription. Although the case of Julian Bond, mentioned above, touches on the issue, it does not confront the matter directly, since Bond did not specifically counsel draft-eligible youth to engage in illegal conduct. Two cases decided prior to *Bond,* however, address the issue in a direct way. In the first instance, a Kansas physician who advised his stepson not to register for the draft was convicted and sent to prison; in the second case, a dean of men at a Mennonite college who had urged students at the college not to register was convicted and imprisoned.[28]

During the Vietnam conflict of the 1960s, numerous antiwar and antidraft statements were issued by opponents of the Vietnam War. Most went unchallenged by the government. However, in 1968 the Justice Department moved against Dr. Benjamin Spock, Rev. William Sloan Coffin, and others for their antidraft advocacy, and the result was a jury verdict of "guilty" of unlawfully counseling draft registrants to refuse or evade military service. The convictions were overturned on appeal, *but not on First Amendment grounds.*[29] From these cases one can conclude that counseling young people to violate the draft law by refusing to register or by evading the draft is expression *not* protected by the First Amendment (although no definitive opinion has yet been forthcoming on the matter from the U.S. Supreme Court).

---

[27]*Bond* v. *Floyd,* 385 U.S. 116 (1966).

[28]The Kansas case is *Warren* v. *United States,* 177 F.2d 596 (10th Cir. 1949); the Supreme Court denied review of this case. The second case is *Gara* v. *United States,* 178 F.2d 38 (6th Cir. 1949), which was allowed to stand because of a tie vote of 4 to 4 by the U.S. Supreme Court, 340 U.S. 857 (1950).

[29]*United States* v. *Spock,* 416 F.2d 165 (1st Cir. 1969). For the law on this issue, see 50 App. *U.S. Code* Sec. 462(a). Also, for a vivid example of the type of antidraft protest of the decade of the 1960s, see "A Call to Resist Illegitimate Authority," an advertisement signed by over three hundred prominent Americans and published in *The New Republic,* October 7, 1967, pp. 34–35, and in *The New York Review of Books,* October 12, 1967, p. 7.

5. Compelling Public School Students to Salute the Flag

In 1943 the Supreme Court ruled that the Barnette children of West Virginia—members of Jehovah's Witnesses, who do not believe in pledging allegiance to the flag of any government—could not be compelled to pledge loyalty to the United States by way of a flag salute. In denying the authority of school officials to require a pledge to the flag, the Court said, "To believe that patriotism will not flourish if patriotic ceremonies are voluntary and spontaneous instead of a compulsory routine is to make an unflattering estimate of the appeal of our institutions to free minds." In strong language, the Court added: "If there is any fixed star in our constitutional constellation, it is that no official, high or petty, can prescribe what shall be orthodox in politics, nationalism, religion, or other matters of opinion or force citizens to confess by work or act their faith therein."[30]

6. Preventing Political Heretics from Speaking on State College Campuses

Early in the 1960s the North Carolina General Assembly approved a bill to prohibit "known communists" or any "known advocate" of the overthrow of the government from speaking on the campuses of state colleges and universities. A few years later, the Mississippi Board of Higher Education passed a regulation that had a purpose similar to that of the North Carolina law, prohibiting any speaker who advocated the violent overthrow of the government from speaking on a state college campus. Federal judges in both states rejected the antisedition rules as unconstitutional. The North Carolina

"Speaker Ban Law" was voided by the U.S. District Court, primarily because of vagueness (what is meant by "known" Communist, or "known" advocate?); however, the First Amendment right of students to hear controversial speakers was mentioned when the Court asserted that "university students should not be insulated from the ideas of extremists . . . ."[31] In the second instance, the Mississippi District Court turned down the regulation of the Board of Higher Education precisely because it conflicted with the First Amendment. Citing *Schenck, Noto, Yates,* and *Brandenburg,* the court declared that in the area of political speech, state college officers may not interfere unless the speaker advocates action that presents a "reasonable apprehension of imminent danger to organized government."[32] In a number of additional cases that developed out of the civil rights and antiwar protests of the 1960s, federal district and circuit courts have been called upon to invoke the First Amendment against state officials who would censor messages of political heresy on state college campuses.[33] Although the issue has not been defined by the U.S. Supreme Court, the decisions of lower federal courts make clear that regulations of prior restraint against political heresy on state college campuses are unconstitutional; also, post-facto punishment should meet the standards set forth in *Yates* and *Brandenburg.*

7. The Criticism of Public Officials

One of the key elements of the English common law of seditious libel was that criticism

---

[30]*West Virginia State Board of Education* v. *Barnette*, 319 U.S. 624 (1943).

[31]*Dickson* v. *Sitterson*, 280 F. Supp. 486 (M.D.N.C. 1968).
[32]*Stacy* v. *Williams*, 306 F. Supp. 963 (N.D. Miss. 1969).
[33]For example, see *Smith* v. *University of Tennessee*, 300 F. Supp. 777 (E.D. Tenn. 1969), and *Brooks* v. *Auburn University*, 412 F.2d 1171 (5th Cir. 1969).

directed at the king or his officers was considered a crime and was subject to severe punishment. Later, with the decline of the power of the monarchy and the rise of democracy, with its elected officials, in both England and America, criticism of individuals in government often combined elements of both private libel and seditious libel, for the person being criticized was at once a private citizen (protected by his state's law of defamation) and a public official (who, by tradition, was protected by the law of sedition, which is severely constrained in the United States by the First Amendment). Public officials in the United States, recognizing the limitations placed upon them by the Constitution, occasionally responded to charges concerning their official conduct by filing suit under state defamation laws. This practice was severely curtailed in 1964, when the U.S. Supreme Court announced its landmark opinion in the case of *New York Times* v. *Sullivan.*[34] Messages critical of government officials are protected by the First Amendment, said the Court, unless the official can prove that the message, *including defamatory falsehoods,* was uttered with "actual malice" (i.e., with knowledge that the content was false or with reckless disregard for the truth). In short, if a critic knows that he or she is lying and maliciously does it anyhow, then the case is actionable; the burden of proof, however, is upon the government officer. Because this rule significantly changed the law of defamation in the United States, it and the cases that grew out of it are analyzed in detail in Chapter 4.

CONCLUSION

Most First Amendment law under which Americans now live has been molded by the

[34]376 U.S. 254 (1964).

U.S. Supreme Court since 1919, and this has occurred to a great extent in decisions concerning seditious libel. The evolution of the Court's views on freedom of speech for political dissent falls generally into two historical periods: (1) from the landmark *Schenck* case of 1919, in which the clear-and-present-danger test was first proposed, to the Smith Act of 1940; and (2) from the Smith Act prosecutions following World War II to the present day. During the first period (1919–1940), the Court announced the new clear-and-present-danger doctrine but continued to decide cases according to the more conservative common-law principle of bad tendency. Meanwhile, Justices Holmes and Brandeis, in a series of influential dissents, urged the Court to be more liberal and to allow antigovernment opinion to be communicated until such time as the government could prove that the speech was producing a danger that was both *clear* and *present.* The conservative majority listened but refused to follow Justices Holmes and Brandeis; in fact, the clear-and-present-danger test was not employed to reverse the conviction of a single political dissident during the years prior to 1940 (although De Jonge went free in 1937, the Court did not cite the clear-and-present-danger doctrine as the reason).

Following the Second World War, during the anti-Communist hysteria of the late 1940s and the 1950s, the Court abandoned its move toward a realistic application of the clear-and-present-danger doctrine, upholding the conviction of Communist Eugene Dennis (1951) on the grounds that his speech *tended* to go beyond mere academic discussion about revolution to reach the point of actual indoctrination and advocacy of forceful overthrow of the government. This distinction between the teaching of "abstract doctrine" and the advocacy of "unlawful action," which was not clearly explained by the Court in *Dennis,* was clarified in the *Yates* decision of 1957, in which the convictions were *reversed* because the evidence submitted by the prosecutors was inadequate to prove that the defendants actually urged their hearers to illegal action. *Yates,* in effect, moved away from bad tendency toward clear and present danger. Finally, in the landmark decision of *Brandenburg* v. *Ohio* (1969), the Court went beyond the clear-and-present-danger doctrine, with which it had been flirting since 1919, to require that before expression can be suppressed, the government must prove that it is directed "to inciting or producing imminent lawless action and is likely to incite or produce such action." Thus, the incitement test of *Brandenburg,* the "liberal child" of clear and present danger, exceeds that which Justices Holmes and Brandeis had urged in the 1920s and 1930s. Under the *Brandenburg* decision, citizens of the United States are currently permitted a greater latitude of political dissent than ever before in the nation's history.

In addition, seven subareas are noted:

1. Threats against the life of the president, vice-president, or any other officer in line to succeed to the presidency are not protected by the First Amendment.

2. The Intelligence Identities Protection Act of 1982 makes it a federal crime for any person to seek out and publish the names of secret agents abroad when such publication is part of a pattern of activities done for the purpose of damaging the nation's foreign intelligence-gathering work.

3. Antiwar remarks by elected representatives are protected by the Constitution and may not be used to deny a seat in the legislature to a representative who so speaks.

4. Speech urging young people to resist the draft during times of national emergency has never been given First Amendment protec-

tion in lower federal courts; the Supreme Court has not ruled in a definitive way on this issue.

5. Public school students may not be compelled to express a message of patriotism in the form of a flag salute.

6. State regulations to prohibit political heretics from speaking on the campuses of tax-supported schools violate the First Amendment (although reasonable time, place, and manner regulations are permitted).

7. Public officials may not use state defamation statutes as a means of retaliation against those who criticize their official conduct, even though the charges against them are false, unless the maligned official can prove that the remarks were made with knowledge of their falsity or with reckless disregard for the truth. (More on this issue in Chapter 4.)

EXERCISES

A. Classroom projects and activities.

  1. Here are three questions phrased for classroom debate:

  a. Resolved, that First Amendment freedoms should be denied to antidemocratic groups.

  b. Resolved, that *absolute* freedom for the advocacy of political opinion should be allowed in the United States.

  c. Resolved, that this class approves the clear-and-present-danger test as the best test for determining the limits of antigovernment speech.

  2. Here are the same three issues phrased for panel or group discussion:

  a. What is the best policy for the government of the United States to have toward the speech of antidemocratic groups?

  b. Should the U.S. Supreme Court interpret the First Amendment so as to permit *absolute* freedom of speech for political advocacy?

c. If freedom of speech is not absolute, what is the preferred test for limiting the communication of political opinion?

3. Invite a local leader in the American Civil Liberties Union (ACLU) to address the class about the Union's current policies concerning political dissent. (Try to secure policy statements in advance; duplicate and give to each member of the class to facilitate discussion.)

4. Have each student prepare a three-minute speech on "My Belief About Freedom of Speech for Political Dissenters." Each talk should be the result of careful thought and clear organization. Set aside a period for the presentation of the short talks; discuss the results.

5. Make photocopies of Justice Holmes's summary of the remarks of Socialist Eugene Debs that resulted in a prison sentence for Debs (the brief opinion can be found in 249 U.S. 211, 1919). Study the content of the speech as reported by Justice Holmes, then discuss whether or not it merited a prison sentence.

6. The "Left Wing Manifesto" that contributed to the conviction of Benjamin Gitlow is published as a footnote to the opinion of the Court in *Gitlow* v. *U.S.*, 268 U.S. 652 (1925). Make photocopies of the manifesto and distribute in class. After study, discuss whether or not the conviction was justified. Should messages such as those contained in the manifesto be permitted today? Would the Supreme Court now permit them under the incitement doctrine of *Brandenburg?*

7. Make photocopies of the antidraft advertisement entitled "A Call to Resist Illegitimate Authority," which was published during the Vietnam War of the 1960s (see *The New Republic,* October 7, 1967, pp. 34–35, or *The New York Review of Books,* October 12, 1967, p. 7). Distribute the document to each member of the class and discuss the message of the advertisement. Should statements such as this be permitted during a time of national emergency? Compare and contrast with the message communicated by *Schenck* (1919).

8. Using your school's library or the library of a local law firm, locate the criminal code of your state and determine whether or not it includes a sedition law (look under "criminal anarchy" and "criminal syndicalism"). If such a law is included, make copies for class distribution. Invite an attorney to discuss the law; based upon the incitement test of *Brandenburg,* do you think that your state's sedition law meets constitutional requirements?

9. Invite a member of your faculty who is a long-time member of the American Association of University Professors (AAUP) to address the class on academic freedom for teachers during the anti-Communist hysteria of the late 1940s and the 1950s (the "McCarthy era"). Ask the faculty member to bring along AAUP position statements which are directed toward the protection of opinions of political heresy, both on campus and off.

10. Check with your college administration concerning your school's regulations governing on-campus speaking by persons from off campus. Do any of the regulations concern the appearance of controversial *political* speakers or the distribution of controversial political literature? Report to the class.

11. Moving ahead to the final part of Chapter 6, study William E. Bailey's essay concerning speech efficacy. Then discuss Bailey's point of view as it might apply to the clear-and-present-danger test and even to the incitement standard of the *Branden-burg* decision. Is either test justified in light of modern communication theory?

B. Topics for research papers or oral reports.

1. From the Espionage Act Arrests of World War I to the Present: A Brief History of the American Civil Liberties Union. (From the reading list, see Reitman's *The Pulse of Freedom* for a start of this topic.)

2. The Palmer Raids and Freedom to Dissent During and After World War I. (This topic concerns the repressive tactics of U.S. Attorney General A. Mitchell Palmer during the period of 1918–1920. For a start, see Reitman and Chafee in the reading list.)

3. State Criminal Anarchy and Criminal Syndicalism Laws Since 1900.

4. The Suppression of Dissent in America During World War I: An Overview.

5. Eugene Debs and the Socialist Party: How and Why Was Their Speech Suppressed?

6. America Attacks the Teachings of Communism: The Suppression of the Communist Message Since 1918.

7. A Study of the Implications of *Gitlow:* The First Amendment Is Applied to the States.

8. Justices Holmes and Brandeis on the First Amendment.

9. Judge Learned Hand and the First Amendment. (Judge Hand served for years on the U.S. Court of Appeals for the Second Circuit; his First Amendment opinions have been influential in American law.)

10. Justice Hugo Black (or Justice William O. Douglas) on "Seditious Speech" and the First Amendment.

11. The Impact of *Brandenburg* on First Amendment Law in the United States.

12. An Examination of Free Speech Issues in the Smith Act Cases of *Scales* (367 U.S. 203, 1961) and *Noto* (367 U.S. 290, 1961).

13. Arguments for and Against Granting Freedom of Speech to Antidemocratic Groups. (From the reading list, see Emerson, Ross and Van Den Haag, Hook, and Barth for a start on this topic.)

14. First Amendment Issues in Advising Youth Against the Draft.

15. Speaker Bans on the Campuses of American Colleges.

16. Dissent in America During Two World Wars: A Comparison and Contrast Between World War I and World War II.

17. Freedom of Speech and Adolf Hitler: Political Dissent in Nazi Germany, 1934–1945.

18. Freedom of Speech in the Soviet Union.

19. The "Warren Court" and the First Amendment. (This topic concerns the 1950s and 1960s, when Chief Justice Earl Warren headed the U.S. Supreme Court.)

20. The Dismissal of Elizabeth Gurley Flynn from the Board of the ACLU: Did the Civil Liberties Union Live Up to Its Own Standards? (This 1940 action of the ACLU concerned admitted Communist Elizabeth Flynn. For a start, see J. W. Patterson's essay in the reading list which follows.)

SELECTED READINGS

Barron, Jerome A., and Dienes, C. Thomas. *Handbook of Free Speech and Free Press.* Boston: Little, Brown, 1979. See chapter 1, "Controlling Speech Content: Clear and Present Danger," pp. 11–31.

Barth, Alan. *The Loyalty of Free Men.* New York: Viking, 1951.

Bosmajian, Haig, comp. *Justice Douglas and Free-*

dom of Speech. Metuchen, N.J.: Scarecrow Press, 1980.

Brown, Cynthia Stokes, ed. *Alexander Meiklejohn: Teacher of Freedom.* Berkeley, Calif.: Meiklejohn Civil Liberties Institute, 1981.

Caute, David. *The Great Fear: The Anti-Communist Purge Under Truman and Eisenhower.* New York: Simon and Schuster, 1978.

Chafee, Zechariah, Jr. *Free Speech in the United States.* Cambridge, Mass.: Harvard University Press, 1941.

Countryman, Vern, ed. *Douglas of the Supreme Court.* Garden City, N.Y.: Doubleday, 1959.

Cox, Archibald. *The Warren Court.* Cambridge, Mass.: Harvard University Press, 1968.

Dennis, Everette, Gillmor, Donald M., and Grey, David L., eds. *Justice Hugo Black and the First Amendment: "'No Law' Means No Law."* Ames, Iowa: Iowa State University Press, 1978.

Dillard, Irving, ed. *One Man's Stand for Freedom: Mr. Justice Black and the Bill of Rights.* New York: Knopf, 1963.

Dunne, Gerald T. *Hugo Black and the Judicial Revolution.* New York: Simon and Schuster, 1977.

Emerson, Thomas I. *The System of Freedom of Expression.* New York: Random House, 1970.

Farber, Daniel A. "National Security, the Right to Travel, and the Court." In *The Supreme Court Review: 1981,* pp. 263–290. Edited by Philip B. Kurland, Gerhard Casper, and Dennis J. Hutchinson. Chicago: University of Chicago Press, 1981.

Griffith, Robert. *The Politics of Fear: Joseph R. McCarthy and the Senate.* Lexington, Ky.: University Press of Kentucky, 1970.

Haiman, Franklyn S. *Speech and Law in a Free Society.* Chicago: University of Chicago Press, 1981. In particular, part 4, "Communication and the Social Order" (composed of chapters 12 and 13).

Hand, Learned. *The Bill of Rights.* Cambridge, Mass.: Harvard University Press, 1958.

Hentoff, Nat. *The First Freedom: The Tumultuous History of Free Speech in America.* New York: Delacorte Press, 1980.

Hook, Sidney. *Paradoxes of Freedom.* Berkeley, Calif.: University of California Press, 1962. (Hook argues that freedom of speech should be allowed for antidemocratic groups.)

Kimball, Clark. "Patriots vs. Dissenters: The Rhetoric of Intimidation in Indiana During the First World War." In *Free Speech Yearbook: 1972,* pp. 49–65. Edited by Thomas L. Tedford. New York: Speech Communication Association, 1973.

Konefsky, Samuel J. *The Legacy of Holmes and Brandeis: A Study in the Influence of Ideas.* New York: Macmillan, 1956.

Lofton, John. *The Press as Guardian of the First Amendment.* Columbia, S.C.: University of South Carolina Press, 1980.

Lower, Frank J. "Julian Bond: A Case Study in a Legislator's Freedom of Speech." In *Free Speech Yearbook: 1974,* pp. 35–44. Edited by Alton Barbour. New York: Speech Communication Association, 1975.

Meiklejohn, Alexander. *Political Freedom: The Constitutional Powers of the People.* New York: Oxford University Press, 1965. (This edition includes Meiklejohn's *Free Speech and Its Relation to Self-Government,* first published in 1948.)

Millis, Walter. "Legacies of the Cold War." In *The Price of Liberty,* pp. 19–44. Edited by Alan Reitman. New York: Norton, 1968.

Mitford, Jessica. *The Trial of Dr. Spock.* New York: Knopf, 1969. (This study is about the conspiracy trial of Dr. Spock and others for speaking against the Vietnam War.)

Murray, Robert K. *Red Scare: A Study in National Hysteria, 1919–1920.* New York: McGraw-Hill, 1964.

Patterson, J. W. "ACLU Limitations on Free Speech: The Case of Elizabeth Flynn." In *Free Speech Yearbook: 1972,* pp. 31–39. Edited by Thomas L. Tedford. New York: Speech Communication Association, 1973.

Preston, William, Jr. *Aliens and Dissenters: Federal Suppression of Radicals, 1903–1933.* Cambridge, Mass.: Harvard University Press, 1963.

Reitman, Alan, ed. *The Pulse of Freedom—American Liberties: 1920–1970's.* New York: Norton, 1975.

Ross, Ralph, and Van Den Haag, Ernest. *The Fabric of Society.* New York: Harcourt, Brace and World, 1957. (The authors argue that freedom of speech should *not* be extended to antidemocratic groups.)

Rovere, Richard H. *Senator Joe McCarthy.* New

York: Harcourt, Brace, Jovanovich, 1959. (Paper edition published by Harper Colophon Books, 1973.)

Siegel, Paul. "Protecting Political Speech: *Brandenburg vs. Ohio* Updated." *Quarterly Journal of Speech* 67 (February 1981): 69–80.

Simmons, Jerold. "The American Civil Liberties Union and the Dies Committee, 1938–1940." *Harvard Civil Rights-Civil Liberties Law Review* 17 (Spring 1982): 183–207.

Strong, Frank R. "Fifty Years of 'Clear and Present Danger': From Schenck to Brandenburg—and Beyond." In *The Supreme Court Review: 1969*, pp. 41–80. Edited by Philip B. Kurland. Chicago: University of Chicago Press, 1969.

CHAPTER 4

Defamation and Invasion of Privacy

*Who steals my purse steals trash; 'tis
something, nothing;
'Twas mine, 'tis his, and has been slave to
thousands;
But he that filches from me my good name
Robs me of that which not enriches him
And makes me poor indeed.*

—*Shakespeare*, Othello, *Act III, Scene iii*

The March 2, 1976, issue of the *National Enquirer,* a tabloid that features bits of "news" and gossip concerning the lives of various political and show-business personalities, printed a short story about actress Carol Burnett claiming that she had behaved in a drunken manner in a Washington, D.C., restaurant. After having a "loud argument" with another diner (former Secretary of State Henry Kissinger), Burnett, the *Enquirer* charged, "traipsed around the place offering everyone a bite of her dessert." In the process, the story continued, she "raised eyebrows" by knocking a glass of wine over and spilling it on a customer, whereupon Burnett "started giggling instead of apologizing." Soon after the article appeared, the actress filed suit under California's defamation law, asking $10 million in damages. Despite the printing of a retraction by the publishers of the *National Enquirer,* Burnett persisted, and early in 1981 her case finally went to trial, resulting in a decision by the jury to award her $1.6 million—$300,000 in general damages and $1.3 million in punitive damages (later reduced by a California judge to $50,000 in general damages and $750,000 in punitive damages; on appeal, the California courts upheld the $50,000 in general damages but further reduced the punitive damages to $150,000).[1] As the publishers of the *National*

Enquirer discovered, stories which injure the reputation of another person are not necessarily protected by the First Amendment.

The historical review of Chapter 1 serves as a reminder that legal protection against defamation is of ancient origin. The Athenians authorized laws against "speaking evil" of the dead and against slandering fellow citizens with "actionable words," which included false charges of murder or of abusing one's parents. The Romans, either by law or by tradition, provided for the punishment of slander under specific conditions, such as defaming a magistrate in a court of law or speaking ill of a person by name from the stage during a dramatic production. In England, the common law of defamation evolved from the ecclesiastical courts to the state courts and prohibited a wide range of speech considered insulting or destructive of one's good name. The British common law then provided the basis for American law on the subject.

The basic idea behind rules of law to punish defamatory expression is a simple one: each person has the right to protect his or her personal reputation against slanderous remarks that destroy the person's standing in the community. The common law proposes that *speech can be called defamatory if it tends to lower a person's reputation before others, cause that person to be shunned, or expose that person to hatred, contempt, or ridicule.* Defamatory statements are of two types: those that are libelous within themselves, called libel per se; and those that are libelous because of the cir-

---

[1]*Burnett* v. *National Enquirer*, 9 Med.L.Rptr. 1921 (1983). The California Court of Appeal did permit Bur-

nett to choose to have a second trial on the question of punitive damages; otherwise, she must accept the reduced amount. The California Supreme Court declined to review this decision, and Burnett has said that she will ask for a new trial rather than accept the reduction in damages. See "News Notes," Med.L.Rptr., January 10, 1984. In mid-February 1984, the U.S. Supreme Court denied certiorari in the case, which had been appealed from the California courts by the *National Enquirer*.

cumstances in which they were spoken, called libel per quod.

Libel per se applies to statements that are defamatory on their face—that is, under the common law they are considered to be intrinsically, automatically destructive of the reputation of the person toward whom they are directed. Such statements are of four types: (1) those accusing another of criminality; (2) those asserting that another has a contagious or offensive disease; (3) those attacking a person's reputation in his or her business, trade, profession, or calling; and (4) those charging another with sexual immorality, particularly if such charges are directed toward a virtuous woman. Examples would be the publication of statements such as "Jane Doe cheats on her income tax" or "John Doe has genital herpes."

Libel per quod ("per quod" is Latin for "whereby") refers to statements alleged to be defamatory because of the context in which they are spoken. The legal principle was explained by the U.S. Court of Appeals for the Sixth Circuit in the 1963 case of *Electric Furnace Corp.* v. *Deering Milliken Research Corp.* as follows: "Where the defamatory nature of the writing does not appear upon the face of the writing, but rather appears only when all of the circumstances are known, it is said to be libel *per quod,* as distinguished from libel *per se* . . . ."[2] Whereas libel per se is, in a sense, obvious, libel per quod is not; extrinsic details must be supplied to demonstrate that libel per quod has occurred. For example, to say that "Jim Smith is perfectly healthy" is certainly not defamatory per se; however, if Smith is accused of defrauding an insurance company by collecting benefits based upon the claim of a job-related disease, the statement that he is "perfectly healthy" when he

is in fact seriously ill can be defamatory per quod.

From the viewpoint of the common law, the *medium* by which an alleged defamation is communicated is an important factor in determining the seriousness of the offense. Before the invention of broadcasting, print was the major means for the widespread distribution and permanent filing of information. Therefore, the English made the dissemination of printed defamation a serious offense and called it *libel*. On the other hand, spoken defamation, which was heard by relatively few persons and was transitory in nature, was classified as a minor offense called *slander*. Needless to say, the invention of radio and television—and the recording of messages on film, voice, and videotape—has neutralized the rationale of the common law for the libel-slander distinction. Nowadays, a defamatory remark broadcast over network television (some suggest that the term "defamacast" be used in such instances) has the potential for reaching millions of persons, yet—since it is oral—it would be classified as slander under a strict reading of the common law. On the other hand, a defamatory memorandum circulated among a dozen or so employees of a company would be considered libel, even though it reached few receivers. By the evolutionary process of judicial interpretation, together with the state-by-state modernizing of defamation statutes (all laws concerning libel and slander are at the *state level* in the United States, there being no federal law of defamation), the common law's outdated distinction between spoken and printed defamation is gradually being revised to reflect more realistically the changes that electronic channels of communication and message storage have created during the twentieth century. In fact, since the American Law Institute took the position in 1977 that defamatory remarks which are broadcast

---

[2]*Electric Furnace Corp.* v. *Deering Milliken Research Corp.*, 352 F.2d 761 (6th Cir. 1963), at 764–765.

should be treated as libel rather than slander, many authorities consider the matter settled.[3] The public communicator would be well advised to assume that in a modern court of law, speech harmful to reputation spoken on either radio or television will be classified as libel.

The main influence of the federal government upon the law of defamation has come from the judicial branch, primarily the U.S. Supreme Court. Throughout the nation's history, the Court has assumed that defamatory speech is not protected by the Constitution, commenting from time to time to this effect. For example, in the 1942 case of *Chaplinsky* v. *New Hampshire* (which concerned profane speech more than slander), Justice Murphy, speaking for the Court, observes that "There are certain well-defined and narrowly limited classes of speech, the prevention and punishment of which have never been thought to raise any constitutional problem. These include . . . the libelous . . . ."[4] Justice Murphy adds that since such utterances "are no essential part of any exposition of ideas," and are of such "slight social value as a step to truth," they simply do not deserve the protection of the Constitution. Insofar as defamatory falsehoods directed at *private citizens* (as contrasted with public officials or public figures) are concerned, the view of Justice Murphy in *Chaplinsky* remains the basic philosophy of the Supreme Court. Persons planning to enter communications-oriented professions, such as journalism, should take note of this fact.

The Supreme Court's philosophy concerning sharp attacks—even, in some instances, defamatory falsehoods—directed toward certain *public persons* (that is, "public officials" and "public figures") is a different matter. In 1964 the Court announced its landmark decision on this subject in the case of *New York Times* v. *Sullivan,* declaring for the first time that in the interest of "robust" and "wide open" debate on public matters, persons in government should accept the fact that "vehement, caustic, and sometimes unpleasantly sharp attacks" are to be expected.[5] In this context, reasoned the Court, even defamatory falsehoods directed at those in public life, especially if the remarks concern their official conduct, ought to be protected by the First Amendment unless the criticized official could meet a new and difficult burden of proof, namely, that the remark was made with "actual malice," that is, with knowledge that it was false, or with reckless disregard for the truth. (The term "actual malice" is used throughout this book as shorthand for the entire test, including knowledge of falsity or reckless disregard for the truth.) This landmark decision demolished much of the framework of the law of libel and slander and opened new directions for litigation, some of which the members of the Supreme Court in 1964 could not have foreseen. In fact, the reverberations from this case are still sounding today. In order to analyze systematically developments of the law concerning defamatory speech, and to include the related issue of invasion of privacy, the following discussion is divided into three parts: (1) the traditional law of defamation prior to *Times-Sullivan* of 1964, (2) the law of defamation after 1964, and (3) speech that invades privacy.[6]

---

[3]American Law Institute, *Restatement of the Law: Torts,* 2nd ed. (St. Paul, Minn.: American Law Institute, 1977). Note: The *Restatement* says that "defamation by any form of communication that has the potentially harmful qualities characteristic of written or printed words is to be treated as libel." Vol. 3, p. 182.

[4]*Chaplinsky* v. *New Hampshire,* 315 U.S. 568 (1942).

[5]*New York Times* v. *Sullivan,* 376 U.S. 254 (1964).

[6]The overview provided in this chapter is not intended to be a "textbook" in law; neither does it attempt

I. SPEECH THAT DEFAMES: THE TRADITIONAL LAW OF LIBEL AND SLANDER BEFORE 1964

Types of Actions: Civil and Criminal

Defamatory falsehoods against private persons are actionable in all fifty states provided that the specific requirements of the law of each state are met (no two states have identical rules on this offense). Defamation statutes are of two types: civil and criminal. Most cases tried today are *civil* ones, in which one citizen sues another over an alleged "wrong." No "crime" is involved, and the damages sought are usually monetary, although in some instances a public apology or retraction is acceptable to the plaintiff. Not all states have *criminal* libel laws, and nowadays those that do rarely invoke them. When they are invoked, they are enforced by the state criminal justice system and are tried in criminal court following the same procedures as are followed in a trial for any other "crime." In theory, conviction could result in a fine, imprisonment, or both.

Under the common law, spoken defamation (slander) was not actionable as criminal libel; however, under certain circumstances, published defamation (libel) was classified as criminal. This was particularly true if the expression in question was interpreted as a form of "verbal assault" that tended to provoke others to anger and a breach of the peace. An example often cited concerns publication of insulting and derogatory remarks concerning a deceased person in such a way as to anger that person's posterity, thus threatening a breach of the peace. In such an instance, the message would be actionable as criminal libel and could result in a jail sentence.

Subjects and Forms of Defamation

As a general rule, the subject of a defamatory statement is another person; however, this need not always be the case. Subjects such as company products, trade labels, and property deeds are mentioned in casebooks on the tort of defamation. For example, false assertions that all soups canned by a certain company contain rodent hairs could be actionable, as could the charge that all lots sold by a given real estate company contain landfill composed of hazardous wastes. A case in point occurred in the summer of 1982, when the Procter & Gamble Company filed defamation suits against several persons, in locations ranging from Florida to New Mexico, claiming damages for libel per se because of "false and malicious" statements made against the company's "Moon and Stars" trademark (see Figure 4.1). According to the company, the defendants had "libeled the character" of Procter & Gamble by charging that the trademark represented satanism and devil worship. Subsequently, most of the cases were dismissed when the defendants apologized and agreed to cease and desist from communicating the defamatory message further.

The form of a defamatory message is usually that which is spoken, as in a public speech, or that which is published in a traditional journalistic medium, such as a newspaper. However, defamation is not limited to these forms. Poems, plays, novels (with real people "thinly disguised" as the characters), photographs, cartoons, paintings, and effigies are among the many forms of defamation ad-

---

to explain how to try a case. Rather, it represents an effort to explain in broad outline some of the basic principles of the common law of defamation and privacy—as interpreted by the U.S. Supreme Court—that place constraints upon certain expression. A communicator who needs legal advice concerning the complexities of the law in a given state should see a good attorney.

*In July of 1982 the Procter & Gamble Company
filed defamation suits against a number of
individuals in several states alleging libel per se
against the "character" of the company and
requesting monetary damages plus injunctive relief
to stop "false and malicious" statements made
against the company's "Moon and Stars"
trademark. The suits were prompted by rumors,
of unknown origin, claiming that the trademark
was a symbol for satanism and devil worship and
that a P&G executive had admitted this during
an appearance on national television. Despite
statements by a number of prominent clergymen,
including Billy Graham and Jerry Falwell, that
the symbol had nothing to do with satanism, and
despite evidence that no P&G executive had ever
discussed satanism on national television, the
rumors persisted until the legal steps taken by the
company were publicized. Inquiries about the
matter, which once exceeded more than twelve
thousand calls per month to company offices,
began to decline soon after the suits were filed, a
sign that "the message was getting through" to
those responsible. P&G's "Moon and Stars"
trademark originated prior to the Civil War and
was first registered with the U.S. Patent Office
in 1882. The thirteen stars commemorate the
original American colonies.*
Trademark used with permission of Procter & Gamble.

judicated in England and the United States.
In a recent case, a jury in New York City
awarded two artists $30,000 each in a libel
decision arising from the public display of a
painting entitled *The Mugging of the Muse* in
which the faces of the two artists were identified in the form of masks worn by the
"muggers." The artists complained, and the
jury agreed, that the painter of the picture
had lessened their reputations before their
peers "because if an artist attacks the muse,
he's killing art."[7]

The Defamation Case

In the case itself, three matters are of particular importance: (1) basic conditions which
must be met, (2) defenses, and (3) damages.
Although these vary in detail from state to

---

[7]*Time,* January 5, 1981, p. 81. (The painting in question is reproduced in color by *Time.*) Note: Politicians

have also sued editorial cartoonists for libel; see Randall
P. Harrison, *The Cartoon: Communication to the Quick*
(Beverly Hills, Calif.: Sage Publications, 1981), e.g., p.
124.

state, students of public communication should be aware of the broad categories when studying a specific statute.

Basic Conditions

Traditionally, the following three basic conditions must be met before a suit for libel is actionable: defamation, publication, and identification. *First,* the message must be perceived as insulting or harmful (i.e., as *defamatory*) among "right-thinking persons." For example, the statement that "John Jones is honest" is not defamatory among "right-thinking persons," although it might be harmful to Jones's reputation if he is a thief and the remark is spoken to a group of fellow thieves (who would be considered "wrong-thinking persons" in this instance). *Second,* the plantiff must show that the alleged libel has actually been communicated to a third party (i.e., that it has been *published*). *Third,* the plaintiff must be *identifiable* as the person defamed. Prior to 1964 and the landmark case of *New York Times* v. *Sullivan* in which the U.S. Supreme Court initiated its continuing review and revision of the law of defamation, if the three conditions listed above were met, libel was *presumed* to have occurred—no fault (such as negligence) on the part of the defendant needed to be proved by the plaintiff.

In the *Times-Sullivan* case of 1964, the Supreme Court added a fourth condition, namely, *fault.* Although this development is explained in more detail later, it must be noted here in order to clearly demonstrate its relationship to the three conditions listed above. The *Times-Sullivan* holding was restricted to a narrow class of plaintiffs—"public officials" and, later, "public figures" as well. These persons in public life, the Court said, must prove a strict standard of fault known as "actual malice," meaning that they had to prove that the defamation was a deliberate and malicious falsehood. No similar re-

quirement was applied to private plaintiffs. But in the 1974 case of *Gertz* v. *Welch* the Supreme Court did include private plaintiffs to this extent: private individuals who sue media defendants (publishers and broadcasters) for defamation must now prove a minimum standard of fault known as "negligence." Currently, therefore, in addition to the three traditional conditions of (1) defamation, (2) publication, and (3) identification, the Supreme Court says that (4) fault must be proved in most defamation cases. The degree of fault varies, however, from simple "negligence" to "actual malice," depending upon the circumstances of the case.

Defenses in Defamation Suits

Three lines of argument are quite common as defenses in slander and libel actions: (1) that the message is true, (2) that the message does not do further harm to a reputation already badly tarnished, and (3) that the message is privileged under state law.[8]

TRUTH. Ella Cooper Thomas, in her handbook *The Law of Libel and Slander,* points out that "there is a popular misconception . . . that if a defamer speaks the truth, he is completely and always exonerated from any liability for his remarks." This is not the case in most of the states, she adds, for many statutes "provide that truth is a defense . . . if it is published with good motives and for justifiable ends only."[9] "Good motives" has been intrepreted to mean that

---

[8]A fourth defense based upon the First Amendment—sometimes described as the "constitutional defense"—was added by the Supreme Court in its 1964 landmark decision in the case of *New York Times* v. *Sullivan.* For the details, see the next main heading of this chapter, "Speech That Defames Public Persons."

[9]Ella Cooper Thomas, *The Law of Libel and Slander,* 2nd ed. (Dobbs Ferry, N.Y.: Oceana Publications, 1963), p. 39.

the critical thought was published without a selfish interest and was intended for the public benefit. This determination is made, of course, by the jury. Although truth is a strong defense and is usually a successful one, communicators should consult the law of the state in which they work to see what qualifications apply.[10]

TARNISHED REPUTATION. A second line of argument available to the defense is that the plaintiff's reputation is already so tarnished that the speech in question could not have harmed it further. For example, the reputation of the "town drunk" cannot be harmed much by a report that he was seen staggering along the street "in a drunken manner" on Saturday night—even if the statement turns out to be in error. This line of defense, while not always successful in winning the case, is often effective in reducing the amount of monetary damages awarded by the jury.

PRIVILEGED COMMUNICATION. A third defense is that the communication is privileged and therefore not actionable under state defamation laws. Two types of privileged speech are recognized by common law tradition, by statute, or by court decisions: those that are *absolute* and those that are *qualified*.

An *absolute privilege* provides complete protection for the message and is extended to certain government officials in the official conduct of their work, such as legislators in

floor debates[11] and judges, attorneys, and witnesses in a trial. In addition, absolute privilege is provided for any thought that is communicated with the permission of the plaintiff (the defendant must prove that this is the case) and to communications between husband and wife.

A *qualified privilege* provides some immunity, but not complete protection, to the communicator. Journalistic reports of legislative activity or of court proceedings have a qualified privilege, as does "fair comment" in the review of artistic productions (books, plays, films, concerts, etc.), scientific theories or discoveries, or commercial products, as in *Consumer Reports*. This privilege of fair comment extends to one's professional opinion of the work, discovery, or product but does not apply to defamatory comments about the artist, scientist, or manufacturer. In addition, the common law right of self-defense has created a qualified privilege of reply "in kind" when one is attacked verbally or is helping defend another person (especially a weak or defenseless one) who has been defamed. In such instances, the reply must be in answer to the original attack and should not be stronger than is proper under the circumstances of the case. For other examples of either absolute or qualified privilege, the reader should examine the laws of the state in which he or she lives.

Damages

Under the common law, the plaintiff who proves libel per se (i.e., convinces the jury of defamation by a communication charging criminality, disease, dishonesty in business or profession, or sexual immorality, etc.) is *pre-*

[10]Justice Powell in his concurring opinion in *Cox* v. *Cohn,* 420 U.S. 469 (1975)—a privacy case discussed later in this chapter—expresses the opinion that the *Gertz* decision of 1974—also discussed later in this chapter—makes truth an absolute defense for defamatory speech that injures the reputation of a private citizen. However, he recognizes that the majority of the Court suggested that the matter is an "open" question. See *Cox* v. *Cohn* at 497–499.

[11]For example, U.S. senators and representatives are protected by Article I, Section 6 of the Constitution, which states that "for any Speech or Debate in either House, they shall not be questioned in any other Place."

sumed to deserve damages. No further proof is needed, although evidence can be produced to show why the amount of damages should be larger than would otherwise be awarded. Ella Cooper Thomas explains the matter by stressing that once libel per se is proved, "Recovery of damages is based on the conclusive legal presumption, which may have no basis in fact, that the plaintiff has sustained an injury to reputation for which he is entitled to recover."[12] In other words, the award of damages follows automatically upon the finding that libel was committed. (This principle of the common law was altered by the U.S. Supreme Court in the 1974 case of *Gertz* v. *Welch;* for details, see Part II of this chapter.) On the other hand, the rules vary from state to state as to whether damages are presumed or must be specifically proved in instances of libel per quod. In some jurisdictions damages are presumed in all cases where libel is proved, whether the libel is per se or per quod; in other jurisdictions presumed damages are permitted only in cases of libel per se, whereas in cases of libel per quod damages must be specifically proved (see discussion of *specific* damages below).

Monetary damages are assessed by the jury, as a rule, and are of three types: specific (also called "special"), general (which includes "presumed"), and punitive. *Specific* (or *special*) damages are those which can be calculated in a fairly precise way, such as the amount of income lost to a defamed business-person by using a comparison to previous sales, or the amount of property remaining unsold after publication of falsehoods about dangerous landfill in a subdivision. (In the Carol Burnett case, mentioned at the beginning of this chapter, no specific damages

were awarded.) *General* damages are more intuitive than are specific damages, for they lack a measurable base for calculation; such damages reflect the jury's subjective opinion of the seriousness of the harm inflicted by the defamatory expression. (In the Burnett decision, the jury awarded $300,000 in general damages, later reduced by a judge to $50,000.) Finally, *punitive* damages are awarded as a form of punishment when the defamation has been particularly malicious and destructive of reputation. (Burnett was given $1.3 million in punitive damages by the jury, later reduced to $150,000.)

The Special Case of Group Libel

During and after World War II, some state legislators, hoping to discourage the kind of tragic racism that destroyed Germany under Adolf Hitler, proposed group libel statutes, and they were adopted in a few states. The concept of group libel is similar to that of the traditional law of slander and libel except that it attempts to punish defamatory speech that undermines the good name of *groups* of people rather than of single individuals. The only time the U.S. Supreme Court ruled on the matter was in 1952 in the case of *Beauharnais* v. *Illinois*. Illinois had a statute making it unlawful for any person to communicate a message portraying "depravity, criminality, unchastity, or lack of virtue of a class of citizens, of any race, color, creed or religion" or which exposed the "citizens of any race, color, creed or religion to contempt, derision, or obloquy or which is productive of breach of the peace or riots." Beauharnais, who was president of an organization calling itself the White Circle League, published and circulated an antiblack leaflet urging city officials to prevent blacks from moving into white neighborhoods. Asserting that such invasions by blacks would "mongrelize" the

[12]Thomas, p. 45.

races, Beauharnais warned that blacks would bring "rapes, robberies, knives, guns and marijuana" into the white sections of the city. The leaflet concluded with an appeal to the reader to join the White Circle League, and an application blank was printed at the bottom.[13] For this, Beauharnais was convicted of violating the state's group libel law and fined $200.

On appeal, the Supreme Court upheld the conviction by a vote of 5 to 4. Justice Frankfurter, speaking for the five-man majority, treated the matter as one of criminal libel, asserting that "if an utterance directed at an individual may be the object of criminal sanctions, we cannot deny to a State power to punish the same utterance directed at a defined group . . . ." Of the four dissenters, Justices Black and Douglas were the most vigorous in stating their objections to the opinion of the Court. Justice Black argued that the decision "degrades First Amendment freedoms," for "the same kind of state law that makes Beauharnais a criminal for advocating segregation in Illinois can be utilized to send people to jail in other states for advocating equality and nonsegregation." He adds: "If there be minority groups who hail this holding as their victory, they might consider the possible relevancy of this ancient remark: 'Another such victory and I am undone.'" Justice Douglas was equally outspoken in his condemnation of the majority's view.

Although the Illinois legislature in later years dropped the group libel statute from the criminal code, some states still have such laws, even though they are not often used. One reason for this neglect is that group defamation laws are of doubtful constitutionality today in light of the 1964 decision of the Supreme Court in *New York Times* v. *Sullivan*, which for the first time brought certain types of defamation under the protection of the Constitution—something that had not occurred in 1952, when *Beauharnais* was decided.[14] Since the Supreme Court has not ruled specifically on the question of group libel since its 1964 landmark decision in *New York Times,* public communicators should consult applicable state law and secure the opinion of an attorney to determine the status of this issue in the state (or states) in which they work.[15]

Private Defamation in Brief

In summary, laws against slander and libel are ancient in origin, serving the purpose of helping to protect an individual's good name from statements that damage reputation, cause the person to be shunned, or expose the person to hatred, contempt, or ridicule. Defamation is of two types: libel per se, consisting of statements which are defamatory on their face (including charges of criminality, dishonesty, disease, or unchastity), and libel per quod, consisting of statements that are not obviously damaging to the reputation (as in libel per se) but are shown to be defamatory within the context in which they were uttered. By tradition, spoken defamation (such as a public speech), being transitory in nature, is a minor offense called *slander;* printed defamation, which is more permanent than the spoken word and therefore is

---

[13]*Beauharnais* v. *Illinois,* 343 U.S. 250 (1952). Note: The Supreme Court decision includes a reproduction of the leaflet distributed by the defendant.

[14]*New York Times* v. *Sullivan,* 376 U.S. 254 (1964); also see *Garrison* v. *Louisiana,* 379 U.S. 64 (1964), which applied the *"New York Times* Doctrine" to criminal libel cases. Both of these cases, as well as others relating to the matter, are discussed in the next part of this chapter.

[15]For a discussion of the issue of group libel, see Thomas I. Emerson, *The System of Freedom of Expression* (New York: Random House, 1970), chapter 10, "Criminal Libel and Group Libel."

assumed to be more harmful, is a serious offense called *libel*. (The advent of broadcasting has severely undermined this distinction, which was inherited from the common law.) The Supreme Court considers properly drawn laws against private defamation to be constitutional, including those extended to company products, trade labels, and deeds to property.

Prior to the *Gertz* decision of 1974, at least three basic conditions had to exist before a defamation suit was actionable: defamation, publication, and identification. This meant that (1) the message must be shown to be damaging to reputation, (2) the alleged libel must be communicated to a third party, and (3) the plaintiff must be identifiable as the person defamed. In *Gertz,* the Supreme Court added a fourth condition that applies when private persons sue media defendants for defamation, namely, (4) *fault.* That is, some degree of negligence on the part of publishers or broadcasters must now be proved. If these conditions are met, the burden of proof then rests with the defendant, who may defend himself or herself by demonstrating (a) that the offending message was true, (b) that it did not do further harm to a reputation already tarnished, or (c) that it was privileged under the law. Damages are of three types: specific/special (out-of-pocket losses), general (damage to reputation and standing in the community), and punitive (intended to punish a malicious libel).

Although group libel laws appear on the statute books of some states, they are rarely enforced and might even be unconstitutional in light of the Supreme Court's decision in the 1964 case of *New York Times* v. *Sullivan* (however, since 1964 the Supreme Court has not officially ruled on this question). In all cases of private defamation, *state* law determines the specifics of the offense, there being no federal law of slander or libel. Communicators should study the laws of the state or states in which they work in order to keep their speech free of actionable defamation.

II. SPEECH THAT DEFAMES PUBLIC PERSONS: LIBEL AND SLANDER AFTER *TIMES-SULLIVAN* OF 1964

The Landmark Case of *New York Times* v. *Sullivan*

As the historical review of Chapters 1 and 2 explains, government officials who over the ages have been criticized for their conduct of public office—whether they held the office of king, member of Parliament, governor of a colony, member of a colonial assembly, or president of the United States (the Sedition Act of 1798)—have attempted to punish the criticizers. When criticisms of those who hold public office are of a defamatory nature—for example, an accusation that a member of Congress is an alcoholic or is dishonest in the conduct of his or her office—the classifications of sedition and defamation *merge* into one message. Since 1917, as the Supreme Court gradually expanded the right of citizens to criticize public policy as well as the persons in government who formulated those policies, public officials have found it less and less effective to try to suppress criticism by shouting "sedition." In response, some people in government have brought court actions against their critics by using state defamation statutes; even when these suits were unsuccessful, they had a "chilling effect" upon the critic, because the cost of mounting a legal defense was too great for some citizens or small newspapers to bear. The issue was addressed by the Supreme Court in 1964 in a case concerning ex-official L. B. Sullivan, who lashed back at his critics

*FIGURE 4.2. JUSTICE WILLIAM J.
BRENNAN, JR., OF THE U.S. SUPREME
COURT.*
*Justice William J. Brennan, Jr., authored the
opinion of the Court in the landmark defamation
decision of* New York Times *v.* Sullivan
*(1964). In this ruling, the Supreme Court
dramatically altered the common law of
defamation by extending the protection of the
First Amendment to defamatory remarks made
about public officials unless those officials could
prove that the remarks were made with "actual
malice"—that is, with knowledge that they were
false or with reckless disregard of the truth.
Justice Brennan was appointed to the bench by
President Dwight D. Eisenhower in 1956.*
The Supreme Court Historical Society.

by using the libel laws of his state, Alabama. In the resulting decision of *New York Times* v. *Sullivan,* the Supreme Court came down on the side of freedom of expression and in so doing radically altered the law of defamation in the United States.

Speaking for a unanimous Supreme Court, Justice Brennan first reviewed the facts of the case. In March of 1960 a group of civil rights activists published a full-page advertisement in the *New York Times* entitled "Heed Their Rising Voices," which began with the statement: "As the whole world knows by now, thousands of Southern Negro students are engaged in widespread non-violent demonstrations in positive affirmation of the right to live in human dignity as guaranteed by the U.S. Constitution and the Bill of Rights." The advertisement went on to charge that the students were "being met by an unprecedented wave of terror," some of which came from police officials in the South, including

those of Montgomery, Alabama. The advertisement was signed by sixty-four persons (some of whom later insisted that they had no knowledge that their names were being used) and was attributed to the "Committee to Defend Martin Luther King and the Struggle for Freedom in the South." Readers were urged to contribute funds to the cause.

After the advertisement had been widely circulated, L. B. Sullivan brought an action for civil libel under Alabama law, alleging that even though he was not named in the *Times* item, he was nevertheless defamed, since, at the time of the incidents described, he had been a commissioner of public affairs in Montgomery and his responsibilities had included supervision of the police who were accused of misconduct. Because there were several errors of fact—that is, "defamatory falsehoods"—in the advertisement, Sullivan argued that he deserved damages. The Montgomery County jury agreed and awarded

LANDMARK CASE
New York Times v. Sullivan, 376 U.S. 254 (1964)
Decided March 9, 1964

Vote: 9 to 0 for reversal of the libel award.

Majority Opinion By: Justice Brennan.

Concurring Justices: Chief Justice Warren, Justices Black, Douglas, Clark, Harlan, Stewart, White, and Goldberg.

Dissenting Justices: (none)

Justices Not Participating: (none)

Summary: On March 29, 1960, a full-page advertisement entitled "Heed Their Rising Voices" was published in the *New York Times* urging support for civil rights activists in the South. Specific reference was made to the misconduct of police in Montgomery, Alabama; this prompted L. B. Sullivan, formerly a commissioner of public affairs in Montgomery whose duties included supervision of the police department, to claim that errors of fact in the advertisement defamed him, even though he was not specifically named. In a suit for civil libel, an Alabama jury awarded Sullivan $500,000 in damages, and the Alabama Supreme Court affirmed. Despite factual errors in the advertisement, the Supreme Court reversed the decision in an opinion that for the first time extended the protection of the Constitution to defamatory speech of a specific type, namely, that which criticized public officials in matters concerning their official conduct. Reasoning that this was more a *sedition* case than it was an action of private libel (Sullivan was objecting to implied criticism of his duties as an officer of the government), the Court unanimously ruled that henceforth legal action by public officials "which encroaches on freedom of utterance under the guise of punishing Libel" would not be tolerated unless the plaintiff assumed the burden of proof to show that the defamation was communicated with "actual malice," which means that the communicator knew that the message was false or recklessly disregarded his or her obligation to discover and publish the truth. (Justices Black, Douglas, and Goldberg wanted to go further; even though they concurred in the majority opinion, they argued that the Constitution granted the press *absolute* protection for speech critical of the government or officials of the government and that not even proof of "actual malice" should alter that unconditional privilege.)

Rule Established; Significance of Case: For the first time, the Supreme Court extended the protection of the First Amendment to a class of defamation—that which is directed at officials of the government. The test established, sometimes called the Times-Sullivan rule (or "actual malice" rule), is that the Constitution "prohibits a public official from recovering damages for a defamatory falsehood relating to his official conduct unless he proves that the statement was made with 'actual malice'— that is, with knowledge that it was false or with reckless disregard of whether it was false or not."

him $500,000, the full amount asked. In reversing the judgment, Justice Brennan stated the central issue of the case: whether the rule of liability for defamation, such as the Alabama statute (and, by implication, the defamation statutes of all states), "as applied to an action brought by a public official against critics of his official conduct, abridges the freedom of speech and of the press that is guaranteed by the First and Fourteenth Amendments."

Justice Brennan *delivered the opinion of the Court:*

Respondent relies heavily, as did the Alabama courts, on statements of this Court to the effect that the Constitution does not protect libelous publications. Those statements do not foreclose our inquiry here. None of the cases sustained the use of libel laws to impose sanctions upon expression critical of the official conduct of public officials. . . . [In past cases] the Court was careful to note that it "retains and exercises authority to nullify action which encroaches on freedom of utterance under the guise of punishing libel"; for "public men, are, as it were, public property," and "discussion cannot be denied and the right, as well as the duty, of criticism must not be stifled." . . . [L]ibel can claim no talismanic immunity from constitutional limitations. It must be measured by standards that satisfy the First Amendment. . . .

Thus we consider this case against the background of a profound national commitment to the principle that debate on public issues should be uninhibited, robust, and wide-open, and that it may well include vehement, caustic, and sometimes unpleasantly sharp attacks on government and public officials. . . . The present advertisement, as an expression of grievance and protest on one of the major public issues of our time, would seem clearly to qualify for the constitutional protection. The question is whether it forfeits that protection by the falsity of some of its factual statements and by its alleged defamation of respondent.

. . . The constitutional protection does not turn upon "the truth, popularity, or social utility of the ideas and beliefs which are offered." . . . As Madison said, "Some degree of abuse is inseparable from the proper use of every thing; and in no instance is this more true than in that of the press." . . . That erroneous statement is inevitable in free debate, and that it must be protected if the freedoms of expression are to have the "breathing space" that they "need . . . to survive" [has been recognized] . . . .

Having laid the groundwork for what was to follow, Justice Brennan turned his attention to the overlap between sedition and defamation in the advertisement published in the *New York Times*. In so doing he underscored the reasoning of the Court that the case should be seen as a matter of sedition in the guise of libel.

Justice Brennan *continued for the Court:*

If neither factual error nor defamatory content suffices to remove the constitutional shield from criticism of official conduct, the combination of the two elements is no less inadequate. This is the lesson to be drawn from the great controversy over the Sedition Act of 1798 . . . which first crystallized a national awareness of the central meaning of the First Amendment. . . .

Although the Sedition Act was never tested in this Court, the attack upon its validity has carried the day in the court of history. Fines levied in its prosecution were repaid by Act of Congress on the ground that it was unconstitutional. . . . [John C.] Calhoun, reporting to the Senate on February 4, 1836, assumed that its invalidity was a matter "which no one now doubts." . . . Jefferson, as President, pardoned those who had been convicted and sentenced under the Act and remitted their fines . . . . The invalidity of the Act has also been assumed by Justices of this Court. . . . These views reflect a broad consensus that the Act, because of the restraint it imposed upon criticism of government and public officials, was inconsistent with the First Amendment.

. . . A rule compelling the critic of official conduct to guarantee the truth of all his factual assertions—and to do so on pain of libel judgments virtually unlimited in amount—leads to a comparable "self-censorship." Allowance of the defense of truth, with the burden of proving it on the defendant, does not mean that only false speech will be deterred. Even courts accepting this defense as an adequate safeguard have recognized the difficulties of adducing legal proofs that the alleged libel was true in all its factual particulars. . . . Under such a rule, would-be critics of official conduct may be deterred from voicing their criticism, even though it is believed to be true and even though it is in fact true, because of doubt whether it can be proved in court or fear of the expense of having to do so. They tend to make only statements which "steer far wider of the unlawful zone." . . . The rule thus dampens the vigor and limits the variety of public debate. It is inconsistent with the First and Fourteenth Amendments.

The constitutional guarantees require, we think, a federal rule that prohibits a public official from recovering damages for a defamatory falsehood relating to his official conduct unless he proves that the statement was made with "actual malice"—that is, with knowledge that it was false or with reckless disregard of whether it was false or not. . . .

Justices Black, Douglas, and Goldberg wanted to go even further, arguing that critics of government should be granted complete immunity from libel suits and that even the permissive "actual malice" rule was too constricting. Justice Black stated this view in a concurring opinion—in which Justice Douglas joined—when he asserted that his vote to reverse was based "on the belief that the First and Fourteenth Amendments not merely 'delimit' a State's power to award damages to 'public officials against critics of their official conduct' but completely prohibit a State from exercising such a power." He added that it was his belief that the U.S. Constitution granted the press "an absolute immunity for criticism of the way public officials do their duty. . . . I regret that the Court has stopped short of this holding . . . ." (Justice Goldberg wrote a separate concurring opinion in which he expressed similar views.)

Eight Issues Growing Out of *Times-Sullivan*

Once the Supreme Court breaks new ground in a landmark ruling, a series of opinions seeking to interpret and refine that ruling seems inevitable. (Readers will recall from Chapter 3 the numerous cases, over a span of fifty years, attempting to interpret and apply the clear-and-present-danger doctrine first announced in the *Schenck* case of 1919.) The process of reinterpreting the common law of defamation began soon after the *Times-Sullivan* decision was announced, and it remains alive today, with no end yet in view. Interestingly, the sedition argument so eloquently stated by Justice Brennan in *Times-Sullivan* soon faded into obscurity as the Court moved further toward trying to harmonize its landmark decision with the common law, the statutes of the various states, and legal precedent. Key issues raised by the entry of the Supreme Court into the "defamation thicket" can be stated in the form of eight central questions, each of which is examined below:

1. Does the *Times-Sullivan* decision, which concerned a case of *civil* libel, also apply to *criminal* libel statutes?
2. Does the *Times-Sullivan* rule requiring proof of "actual malice" apply only to persons in government (e.g., to "public officials"), or does it apply to other classes of public persons?
3. Who is classified as a "public official" or a "public figure," and how far down the hierarchy does the *Times-Sullivan* rule reach?
4. In addition to subjects related to the "official conduct" of a public official, are any matters pertaining to his or her *private* life covered by the *Times-Sullivan* rule?
5. How are the terms "actual malice" and "reckless disregard" to be interpreted and applied in specific cases?
6. Does the *Times-Sullivan* rule apply if the *subject matter* of a dispute is of wide public interest although the parties involved are not public persons?

7. How far can a defamed person go in getting answers to questions (depositions and interrogatories) from a defendant in order to prove "actual malice" in a libel action?

8. Have any cases other than *Times-Sullivan* significantly altered the common law of defamation in recent years?

1. Does the Times-Sullivan *Rule Extend to* Criminal *Libel?*

Eight months following the announcement of the new rules of defamation in *Times-Sullivan,* which was a *civil* libel case, the Supreme Court did extend its ruling to cover criminal libel as well. The decision to do so was in response to an appeal from the conviction of New Orleans District Attorney Garrison for violating the Louisiana criminal libel law when he accused several state court judges of being lazy and inefficient and of interfering with his efforts to enforce the vice laws.[16] In unanimously reversing the conviction of Garrison and declaring the Louisiana criminal libel statute unconstitutional, the Supreme Court announced that its *Times-Sullivan* ruling applied to *both civil and criminal* defamation.

2. Does Times-Sullivan *Apply to Persons Other Than "Public Officials"?*

In 1967 the Supreme Court expanded the reach of the *Times-Sullivan* rule to include "public figures" as well as "public officials," at least insofar as their official or public conduct was concerned. This step was taken in *Curtis Publishing Co.* v. *Butts* which combined two appeals into one opinion. The first concerned an appeal from Wally Butts, athletic director of the University of Georgia; the second concerned retired Army General Edwin Walker, who had won a libel judgment

from the Associated Press.[17] Neither Butts nor Walker were "public officials" in the narrow sense; yet they were "public figures," and for that reason were placed under the *Times-Sullivan* rule.

3. Who Is Classified as a "Public Official" or a "Public Figure," and How Far Down the Hierarchy Does the Times-Sullivan Rule Reach?

There are some persons who clearly belong in the classification "public official" (e.g., elected officers of government) or "public figure" (e.g., the host of a nationally televised talk show), and there are other persons who obviously are *private* citizens and do not fit either "public person" category (e.g., the manager of a small business, a kindergarten teacher, etc.). The problem comes in making judgments about those in between and deciding how far down the hierarchy to go in each case. Determining the plaintiff's classification is of major importance since *Times-Sullivan* and progeny, for if the plaintiff falls into the public official–public figure group, he or she assumes the difficult burden of proving that the defendant was lying and knew it or acted with reckless disregard for the truth (i.e., the "actual malice" standard); on the other hand, if the plaintiff falls into the private citizen category, he or she need only prove the standard of negligence set forth in state law (generally a much easier standard of proof to meet). Public communicators—particularly writers, journalists, and commentators in

[16]*Garrison* v. *Louisiana,* 379 U.S. 64 (1964).

[17]*Curtis Publishing Co.* v. *Butts,* 388 U.S. 130 (1967). Note: By a vote of 5 to 4, the Supreme Court allowed the award of damages to Butts to stand because the Court found the *Saturday Evening Post* grossly negligent in determining the truth of the charge that Butts conspired to "fix" a football game; however, a unanimous Court reversed the libel judgment against the Associated Press, finding that under the pressure of events the error in the AP report on Walker's participation in a riot at the University of Mississippi was an innocent one.

media channels such as publishing and broad-casting—need to be aware of some general guidelines, both stated and implied, set forth by the Supreme Court and, in some instances, by lower federal and state courts, for identifying public officials and public figures.

PROFILE OF A "PUBLIC OFFICIAL." Elect-ed public officials are clearly covered by the *Times-Sullivan* rule; the landmark case itself originated in an action brought by former *elected* Commissioner L. B. Sullivan against the *New York Times.* The question of public officials who are not elected, such as appointed officers or government employees of various types, was addressed by the Supreme Court in a 1966 case in which a former supervisor of a county recreation area (Baer) brought an action for libel against an unpaid journalist (Rosenblatt) who, in a published newspaper column, had questioned the financial integrity of those who administered the recreation area.[18] The trial court found for plaintiff Baer, but the U.S. Supreme Court reversed and remanded for a new trial in which Baer would have to meet the "actual malice" standard of *Times-Sullivan.* In so doing, the Court ruled that "the 'public official' designation applies at the very least to those among the hierarchy of government employees who have, or appear to the public to have, substantial responsibility for or control over the conduct of government affairs." In other words, supervisor Baer was a "public official" in the view of the Supreme Court, and as such assumed the burden to prove "actual malice."

In 1971 the Supreme Court further clarified its definition of "public official" by including *candidates* for public office.[19] In addition to elected persons and candidates, various courts have included judges, police officers, tax assessors, and public school administrators in the "public official" classification.[20] One can assume, therefore, that the term "public official" includes elected officials and candidates for public office and most if not all government employees who have positions of "substantial responsibility" for the conduct of public affairs. Speech concerning the general fitness of the person for office or the person's official conduct of the office is covered by the *Times-Sullivan* rule.

PROFILE OF A "PUBLIC FIGURE." Guidelines by which a public communicator can determine whether or not a nongovernment individual is a public figure are difficult to state. One federal judge has compared attempts at defining "public figure" with "trying to nail a jellyfish to the wall."[21] In *Curtis Publishing Co.* v. *Butts,* mentioned earlier in this chapter, the Supreme Court classified athletic director Wally Butts of the University of Georgia as a "public figure," as well as retired Army General Edwin Walker (who had voluntarily thrust himself into a public controversy). In the 1970 case of *Greenbelt* v. *Bresler,* the Supreme Court said that real estate developer Charles S. Bresler was a public figure in his community because he "was deeply involved in the future development of the city of Greenbelt."[22]

In 1974, with four conservative justices appointed by President Nixon sitting on the Court (Chief Justice Burger and Justices

---

[18]*Rosenblatt* v. *Baer,* 383 U.S. 75 (1966).

[19]In *Monitor Patriot Co.* v. *Roy,* 401 U.S. 265 (1971), in which Alphonse Roy, candidate for the U.S. Senate in New Hampshire, was classified as a "public official" in a defamation action.

[20]See Jerome A. Barron and C. Thomas Dienes, *Handbook of Free Speech and Free Press* (Boston: Little, Brown, 1979), p. 274. Note: For a more detailed discussion of "public officials" and "public figures," read Barron and Dienes, chapter 6, "The Rise of the Public Law of Defamation."

[21]Ibid., p. 276.

[22]*Greenbelt Cooperative Publishing Assoc.* v. *Bresler,* 398 U.S. 6 (1970).

Blackmun, Powell, and Rehnquist), the expansion of the *Times-Sullivan* rule to cover a wider and wider range of "public figures" ceased, and a two-tiered system was put into place in the important case of *Gertz* v. *Welch*.[23] In this decision, Justice Lewis Powell, speaking for the Court, declared that on one level there are some individuals who "occupy positions of such persuasive power and influence that they are deemed public figures for all purposes. More commonly, those classed as public figures have thrust themselves to the forefront of particular public controversies in order to influence the resolution of the issues involved. In either event, they invite attention and comment." Examples of these "full-fledged" public figures include Johnny Carson of television fame and William F. Buckley, Jr., author, columnist, and television personality.[24]

At the second level are those persons who are only temporarily acting as public figures, usually because they voluntarily participate in some public activity or speak out on some public issue of the time. In *Gertz*, Justice Powell speaks of the individual who "voluntarily injects himself or is drawn into a particular public controversy and thereby becomes a public figure for a limited range of issues." In truth, media communicators cannot determine with any degree of accuracy to whom this classification belongs; in a defamation suit, one discovers the classification in a court of law after the judge makes a determination. Barron and Dienes, authors of the authoritative *Handbook of Free Speech and Free Press*, comment that the term "voluntary limited public figure" is so poorly defined by the courts "that it is difficult to identify any of the essential elements to be used in placing a

plaintiff in this category as opposed to the private figure category."[25] Journalists and broadcasters, therefore, should exercise great caution in making this judgment. Here are four instances in which the Supreme Court declared that the plaintiffs were *not* public figures, either full-fledged or limited, for none had voluntarily thrust themselves into the controversy that precipitated the libel action:

a. An attorney employed as counsel in a controversial case does not become a public figure as a result.[26]

b. A prominent socialite who is being sued for divorce by her wealthy husband does not become a public figure, either because of her many local social activities or because her divorce case receives a great deal of press attention.[27]

c. A research scientist who receives a federal grant of funds to assist in his research does not become a public figure as a result.[28]

d. A person once convicted of a crime, even though at the time the trial and conviction attracted considerable media attention, does not retain his or her public figure status forever (otherwise, said the Supreme Court, society would "create an 'open season' for all who sought to defame persons convicted of a crime," even though those persons had been living private lives out of the public spotlight since the serving of a sentence).[29]

4. In Addition to Subjects Related to the "Official Conduct" of a Public Official, Are Any Matters Pertaining to His or Her Private Life Covered by the Times-Sullivan *Rule?*

In the 1971 case of *Monitor Patriot Co.* v. *Roy,* the Supreme Court did include certain

---

[23]*Gertz* v. *Welch,* 418 U.S. 323 (1974). For more on this case, see question 8 below.
[24]See *Carson* v. *Allied News,* 529 F.2d 206 (7th Cir. 1976), and *Buckley* v. *Littel,* 539 F.2d 882 (2nd Cir. 1976).

[25]Barron and Dienes, p. 281.
[26]*Gertz* v. *Welch,* 418 U.S. 323 (1974).
[27]*Time* v. *Firestone,* 424 U.S. 448 (1976).
[28]*Hutchinson* v. *Proxmire,* 443 U.S. 111 (1979).
[29]*Wolston* v. *Reader's Digest Assoc.,* 443 U.S. 157 (1979).

private matters under the "actual malice" standard of *Times-Sullivan*.[30] In this case, the *Concord Monitor* of Concord, New Hampshire, had published a column in which Alphonse Roy, a candidate for the U.S. Senate from New Hampshire, was described as "a former small-time bootlegger." Roy sued for damages and, after finding that the remark concerned the candidate's private life and that as a result the *Times-Sullivan* rule did not apply, the trial court awarded him $20,000. The judgment was affirmed by the New Hampshire Supreme Court. The U.S. Supreme Court reversed and remanded for a new trial, asserting that the *Times-Sullivan* rule "is not rendered inapplicable merely because an official's private reputation, as well as his public reputation, is harmed. The public-official rule protects the paramount public interest in a free flow of information to the people concerning public officials, their servants." The Court then added these key sentences: *"To this end, anything which might touch on an official's fitness for office is relevant. Few personal attributes are more germane to fitness for office than dishonesty, malfeasance, or improper motivation, even though these characteristics may also affect the official's private character."* The ruling applies not only to those already in government but also to candidates for public office, for, said the Court, a candidate "who vaunts his spotless record and sterling integrity cannot convincingly cry 'Foul!' when an opponent or an industrious reporter attempts to demonstrate the contrary."

5. How Are the Terms "Actual Malice" and "Reckless Disregard" to Be Interpreted and Applied in Specific Cases?

Since announcing its decision in *New York Times* v. *Sullivan* in 1964, the Supreme Court

has given some guidance to public communicators about the meaning of "actual malice" and "reckless disregard for the truth." Four decisions are particularly relevant, for they include specific interpretations of the meaning of the language of the "actual malice" test.

First, in the 1967 case of *Curtis Publishing Co.* v. *Butts,* the Court recognized that the *Saturday Evening Post,* a weekly magazine, differed from a wire service such as the Associated Press. In sustaining the judgment against the *Post,* the Court noted that a magazine is not under the same deadline pressures as some other channels of public communication and that for it to publish without properly checking the facts represents "an extreme departure from the standards of investigation and reporting ordinarily adhered to by responsible publishers."[31] In the companion case involving General Walker and the Associated Press, the Court reversed the award to Walker and ruled in favor of the AP, stating that "considering the *necessity for rapid dissemination,* nothing in this series of events gives the slightest hint of a severe departure from accepted publishing standards." [Emphasis supplied.] One can conclude, therefore, that for a book or magazine publisher to rush into print without careful research might be called "reckless disregard for the truth" if a libel action results, whereas for a "hot news" medium such as a wire service, a daily newspaper, or a television news program to do so might not be considered irresponsible. (Of course, communicators in the "hot news" media should at all times exercise the highest standards of accuracy allowed by their medium; this is of special importance when one realizes that the time factor in *Curtis* v. *Butts* is not precise and would be judged on a case-by-case basis.)

---

[30]*Monitor Patriot Co.* v. *Roy,* 401 U.S. 265 (1971).

[31]*Curtis Publishing Co.* v. *Butts,* 388 U.S. 130 (1967).

In a second case, Phil St. Amant was campaigning for public office in Louisiana; in a televised campaign speech, he made charges against his opponent that he believed to be true but which later turned out to be unverified and possibly false.[32] In a defamation action, St. Amant's opponent was awarded damages; on appeal, the U.S. Supreme Court reversed. The Court reasoned that in a heated political campaign some errors of fact were inevitable and that St. Amant did not "knowingly" communicate a falsehood. To meet the *Times-Sullivan* standard, said the Court, "There must be sufficient evidence to permit the conclusion that the defendant in fact entertained serious doubts as to the truth of his publication. Publishing with such doubts shows reckless disregard for truth or falsity and demonstrates actual malice." Since St. Amant believed that his information was true, he was not guilty of "actual malice."

In the third case, *Time* magazine published a news story concerning police brutality that was based upon information in a report of the U.S. Commission on Civil Rights. Some of the information reflected upon police officer Frank Pape, and its accuracy was not confirmed either in the commission's report or by the magazine. In addition, the writer of the piece had neglected to qualify the details with the terms "reportedly" or "alleged."[33] Officer Pape sued, charging reckless disregard for the truth. The Supreme Court ruled in favor of *Time,* however, deciding that since the magazine assumed the truth of the report of the Commission on Civil Rights, "it can hardly be said that *Time* acted in reckless disregard of the truth. Given the ambiguities of the Commission Report as a whole, and the testimony of the *Time* author and researcher, *Time*'s conduct reflected at

most an error of judgment." (The Court goes on to emphasize that nothing in the opinion "is to be understood as making the word 'alleged' a superfluity in published reports of information damaging to reputation. Our decision today is based on the specific facts of this case . . . .")

In the final case, a small daily newspaper in Florida, the Ocala *Star-Banner,* published a story about a candidate for public office in which it confused the candidate, Leonard Damron, with his brother James.[34] (The paper reported that Leonard had been charged with perjury in a federal court, when in fact it was James who had been so charged.) In defense of itself, the newspaper argued that its area editor was new to the job, had never heard of James, and assumed—incorrectly—that the story he was editing referred to the well-known Leonard, who at the time was mayor of the city. The Supreme Court accepted this explanation, ruling the mistake to be an honest one and holding that as such the error did not represent "actual malice" on the part of either the editor or the paper.

What can one conclude about the meaning of the *Times-Sullivan* rule from these cases? Four observations are in order:

a. The terms "actual malice," "knowledge that it was false," and "reckless disregard of whether it was false or not" are clearly intended to discourage the communication of falsehoods that are deliberate or that result from gross negligence.

b. The *intent* of the message source is a key factor in a libel action, for no person can be guilty of "actual malice" who sincerely and with reasonable certainty believed that the message delivered was true.

c. The *time element concerning copy deadlines*

[32]*St. Amant* v. *Thompson*, 390 U.S. 727 (1968).
[33]*Time* v. *Pape*, 401 U.S. 279 (1971).

[34]*Ocala Star-Banner* v. *Damron*, 401 U.S. 295 (1971).

inherent in the medium is a third consideration. Communicators—such as publishers of books and magazines—who do have the time to research a story carefully before publication bear a heavier responsibility for accuracy than do those who—like the reporter for the Associated Press—work under the pressure for the "rapid dissemination" of the news.

d. Finally, all communicators should be careful to *qualify their messages* with terms such as "reportedly" or "allegedly" when the facts are not fully verified. (Qualifying language does not, in itself, mean that the message will be judged nondefamatory, since many factors in addition to this enter into such a determination. However, the use of qualifying language is still recommended, for even if the defendant loses the case, the presence of qualifying terms can mitigate damages.)

6. Does the Times-Sullivan *Rule Apply if the* Subject Matter *of a Dispute Is of Wide Public Interest, Although the Persons Involved Are Neither "Public Officials" Nor "Public Figures"?*

In the 1971 case of *Rosenbloom* v. *Metromedia,* the Supreme Court moved in the direction of extending the *Times-Sullivan* rule to *subjects* of general public interest, even when the persons involved were *private* citizens.[35] In this case, George A. Rosenbloom was a distributor of nudist magazines in the Philadelphia area who, in a regional "obscenity crackdown," was arrested and tried for the dissemination of "obscene" materials. He was found not guilty, the jury determining that his materials did not meet the state's definition of "obscenity." Meanwhile, a local radio station had called Rosenbloom a "smut distributor" and a "girlie book peddler"

without qualifying the charges with terms such as "reportedly" or "allegedly." Rosenbloom sued under the libel laws of Pennsylvania; the jury awarded him $25,000 in general damages and $725,000 in punitive damages. The radio station appealed the verdict.

In a vote of 5 to 3, the U.S. Supreme Court denied private citizen Rosenbloom his damages and in so doing extended the *Times-Sullivan* rule to cover questions of public interest. Among the five-man majority, three justices (Chief Justice Burger and Justices Brennan and Blackmun) formed a plurality to argue that since the controversy was of public interest, the "actual malice" standard should apply. (Justices Black and White concurred in the decision, but for different reasons; the key point here is that only three justices voted for the "public interest" position and that the argument *never* received the support of a majority of the members of the Court.) Justice Brennan, speaking for the plurality, stated: "If a matter is a subject of public or general interest, it cannot suddenly become less so merely because a private individual is involved, or because in some sense the individual did not 'voluntarily' choose to become involved."

The move in the direction of liberalizing the coverage of *Times-Sullivan* came to a jarring halt in 1974 with the Court's opinion in *Gertz* v. *Welch* (for more on this important case, see question 8 below).[36] Here the majority rejected the plurality view of Justice Brennan, Chief Justice Burger, and Justice Blackmun in *Rosenbloom,* reaffirming the pre-*Rosenbloom* requirement that the persons in a defamation action must be public officials or public figures for the *Times-Sullivan* rule to apply; in other words, the "subject of public

---

[35]*Rosenbloom* v. *Metromedia,* 403 U.S. 29 (1971).

[36]*Gertz* v. *Welch,* 418 U.S. 323 (1974).

or general interest" was within itself inadequate to trigger the "actual malice" rule.

Since 1974 the Supreme Court has been firm in its rejection of *Rosenbloom*. Therefore, public communicators should know that even in matters of general public interest, a defamed person need not assume the heavy burden of proving "actual malice" unless he or she is a public official or a public figure as defined by the Court.

7. *How Far Can a Defamed Person Go in Getting Answers to Questions from a Defendant in Order to Prove "Actual Malice"?*

Colonel Anthony Herbert, who in 1969 and 1970 had publicly accused some persons in the military of atrocities during the Vietnam War and had received much media attention as a result, was the subject of an uncomplimentary CBS *60 Minutes* television segment on February 4, 1973. Later, CBS editor Barry Lando, who had supervised the television program on Herbert, authored an article, published in *Atlantic Monthly,* that raised serious questions about some of Herbert's allegations and activities. In response, "public figure" Herbert brought suit for libel against Lando, commentator Mike Wallace (who had participated in the *60 Minutes* program), and the publishers of *Atlantic Monthly.* To help prove that the defendants were guilty of "actual malice," Herbert and his attorneys went through the legal process of "discovery" by asking Lando questions (getting a "deposition"). Lando answered most of the questions but refused, on First Amendment grounds, to answer those concerning his subjective editing of the television program and what went on in his mind as he wrote the article for publication. The U.S. Court of Appeals summarized five questions to which Lando objected:

a. Lando's conclusions during his research and investigations regarding people or leads to be pursued, or not to be pursued, in connection with the story.

b. Lando's conclusions about information provided by interviewees, and his "state of mind" with respect to the veracity of those interviewed.

c. The basis for conclusions where Lando testified that he did reach a conclusion concerning the veracity of persons, information, or events.

d. Conversations between Lando and Mike Wallace about what to include and what to exclude from the *60 Minutes* segment.

e. Lando's intentions as manifested by his decision to include or to exclude certain material.[37]

The judge in the U.S. District Court agreed with Herbert and ordered Lando to answer the questions, but the U.S. Court of Appeals disagreed, coming down on the side of First Amendment protection for Lando in reference to his "state of mind" during editing and writing. The U.S. Supreme Court, however, rejected the view of the court of appeals, agreed with the district court, and ordered Lando to answer the questions in Herbert's deposition. The reason, said the Court, was quite simple—if "actual malice" is to be proved, then "state-of-mind" questions must be answered. "Inevitably," wrote Justice White for the Court, "unless liability is to be completely foreclosed, the thoughts and editorial processes of the alleged defamer would be open to examination." Therefore, public communicators—especially those in the various channels of the mass media—should know that according to the U.S. Supreme Court, the First Amendment does not protect one's subjective thought processes from the discovery process in libel actions.

[37]*Herbert* v. *Lando,* 441 U.S. 153 (1970), at 157, note 2.

8. Have Any Cases Other Than Times-Sullivan *Significantly Altered the Common Law of Defamation in Recent Years?*

The answer to this question is yes, and the case in which the established law of defamation was substantially altered is *Gertz* v. *Welch*—a case previously cited in this chapter (see questions 3 and 6 above). *Gertz* is significant, not only because it changed the ground rules by which states determine liability and damages in defamation cases but also for its detailed explanation of the reasoning of the Court concerning the obligation of government to protect the reputation of the private citizen. Attorney Elmer Gertz of Chicago was the object of a vicious personal attack in the April 1969 issue of *American Opinion,* published by Robert Welch, Inc., as an outlet for the views of the ultraconservative John Birch Society. The attack included the false charges that Gertz had a criminal record, had planned a "frame-up" of the police officer being sued, and was a "Leninist" and a "communist fronter." Although the issues involved were public ones, the Court determined that the person defamed was a private citizen in the specific circumstances of this case, and that a gross injustice would be done to that person's personal and professional reputation if the defamatory falsehood were allowed to stand unpunished. Regardless of one's opinion concerning the relationship of the law of defamation to the First Amendment, a careful reading of *Gertz* is instructive.

After reviewing the facts of the case, Justice Lewis Powell, spokesman for the five-man majority, reviewed previous decisions in similar cases in order to underscore the Court's agreement with the principle that the nation must have "robust" and "wide-open" debate on public issues and that, in the process, some abuses were bound to occur. If unreasonable punishment of error results, he

noted, society will lose the benefit of a vigorous press, for a press intimidated becomes a press overly cautious. Nevertheless, wrote Justice Powell, while protecting the freedom of the press and while encouraging the free press to be bold in its service to society, government must not neglect the "legitimate state interest underlying the law of libel," namely, "compensation of individuals for the harm inflicted on them by defamatory falsehood." He then quoted his Brother, Justice Potter Stewart, in a concurring opinion in the 1966 case of *Rosenblatt* v. *Baer,* in which Justice Stewart argued that the individual's right to the protection of his good name "reflects no more than our basic concept of the essential dignity and worth of every human being—a concept at the root of any decent system of ordered liberty," after which he explained the Court's rationale for distinguishing among public officials, public figures, and private individuals.

Justice Powell *delivered the opinion of the Court:*

The first remedy of any victim of defamation is self-help—using available opportunities to contradict the lie or correct the error and thereby to minimize its adverse impact on reputation. Public officials and public figures usually enjoy significantly greater access to the channels of effective communication and hence have a more realistic opportunity to counteract false statements than private individuals normally enjoy. Private individuals are therefore more vulnerable to injury, and the state interest in protecting them is correspondingly greater.

More important than the likelihood that private individuals will lack effective opportunities for rebuttal, there is a compelling normative consideration underlying the distinction between public and private defamation plaintiffs. An individual who decides to seek governmental office must accept certain necessary consequences of that involvement in public affairs.

Gertz v. Welch, 418 U.S. 323 (1974)
Decided June 25, 1974

Vote: 5 to 4 for reversal of the ruling favoring Welch in the U.S. District Court and in the U.S. Court of Appeals and remanded for a new trial (in other words, the Supreme Court found in favor of Gertz).

Majority Opinion By: Justice Powell.

Concurring Justices: Stewart, Marshall, Blackmun, and Rehnquist.

Dissenting Justices: Chief Justice Burger; Justices Douglas, Brennan, and White.

Justices Not Participating: (none)

Summary: The family of a youth who had been shot and killed by a Chicago policeman engaged the services of attorney Elmer Gertz to bring a civil action for damages against the offending police officer, who had already been convicted of murder in the incident. Subsequently, Robert Welch, Inc., publishers of *American Opinion,* the voice of the John Birch Society, published an article written by Alan Stang in the April 1969 issue of the magazine. In the article, Stang included a number of falsehoods, including the charge that Gertz had a criminal record and that he was a "communist fronter" and a participant in a conspiracy to undermine the authority of the nation's police. Gertz, an expert in libel law, filed suit in federal district court, a procedure permitted by the U.S. Constitution in cases where the parties in an action are from different states (called "diversity of citizenship" in the language of the law).

The trial judge instructed the jury that Gertz was neither a public official nor a public figure and that "actual malice" need not be proved. The jury then found the article in question constituted libel *per se* under Illinois law and awarded $50,000 in damages. Then, upon a posttrial motion by counsel for Welch, Inc., that "actual malice" *should* have been proved, and with an eye on the case of *Rosenbloom* v. *Metromedia* which was before the U.S. Supreme Court (but which had not yet been decided), the judge vacated the verdict of the jury and denied Gertz his damages. The U.S. Court of Appeals affirmed the decision to vacate, citing the by-now-decided *Rosenbloom* case.

On appeal, the U.S. Supreme Court reversed the courts below and remanded the case for another trial. In so doing, the Court rejected the view expressed by the *Rosenbloom* plurality that the *Times-Sullivan* "actual malice" standard of fault be extended to defamation cases in which the subject matter is of general public interest. Instead, the Court drew a pre-*Rosenbloom* line between public persons and private persons, and in the process rewrote the law of defamation as explained below.

Rule Established; Significance of Case: The Court balanced the competing interests of (a) protecting private individuals from libel and (b) protecting the media from excessive monetary awards; in the process, it altered the principle of the common law of defamation that permitted *presumed* damages (those based upon the principle of "strict liability") when libel per se was proved. Specifically, the Court ruled as follows:

1. *Private persons* need more protection from defamation than do public persons and do not, therefore, have to meet the stringent "actual malice" standard of *Times-Sullivan,* even if the subject of the dispute is of general public interest. (Here the Court rejected the argument of the *Rosenbloom* plurality and adhered to the rule set forth in 1964 in *Times-Sullivan.*)

2. *Media defendants* (publishers and broadcasters) merit two *new* rules of protection, as follows: (a) First, "strict liability" is abolished for cases involving media defendants being sued by private individuals; in its place is a requirement that each state establish a *minimum standard of fault* that private plaintiffs must prove, so long as the minimum standard is no less than "negligence" (states may have tougher standards, such as "gross negligence" or even "actual malice," but nothing weaker than "negligence"). (b) Second, damages are hereafter limited to "actual injury" in those

cases where the minimum standard of fault is used; "actual injury" covers the *specific* damages involved, such as out-of-pocket financial loss, plus those *general* damages to reputation (Justice Powell includes "impairment of reputation of standing in the community, personal humiliation, and mental anguish and suffering" in this category) that are proved in court by "competent evidence." Neither *presumed* nor *punitive* damages are allowed any longer except in those instances where the plaintiff proves the most difficult standard of fault—namely, "actual malice."

He runs the risk of closer public scrutiny than might otherwise be the case. . . .

Those classed as public figures stand in a similar position. Hypothetically, it may be possible for someone to become a public figure through no purposeful action of his own, but the instances of truly involuntary public figures must be exceedingly rare. For the most part those who attain this status have assumed roles of especial prominence in the affairs of society. Some occupy positions of such persuasive power and influence that they are deemed public figures for all purposes. More commonly, those classed as public figures have thrust themselves to the forefront of particular public controversies in order to influence the resolution of the issues involved. In either event, they invite attention and comment.

Even if the foregoing generalities do not obtain in every instance, the communications media are entitled to act on the assumption that public officials and public figures have voluntarily exposed themselves to increased risk of injury from defamatory falsehood concerning them. No such assumption is justified with respect to a private individual. He has not accepted public office or assumed an "influential role in ordering society." . . . He has relinquished no part of his interest in the protection of his own good name, and consequently he has a more compelling call on the courts for redress of injury inflicted by defamatory falsehood. Thus, private individuals are not only more vulnerable to injury than public officials and public figures; they are also more deserving of recovery.

Having provided the Court's rationale for distinguishing between public and private persons in defamation actions, Justice Powell then announced the new rules that apply in suits brought by private individuals against media defendants, namely: (a) the rejection of the common-law doctrine of "strict liability" and the substitution of a rule that each state must determine a minimum degree of fault for libel suits, and that this minimum degree be no less than "negligence"; (b) the limitation of damages to "actual injury" in those cases where the minimum degree of fault is employed, thus altering the common law principle of presumed damages. In order to grasp fully the significance of these changes in the common law, one might wish to review the explanations earlier in this chapter of libel per se, the conditions of a defamation case, and the types of damages allowed in the past. In addition, an understanding of the terms "strict liability," "presumed damages," and "fault" is helpful. Each is defined in turn.

STRICT LIABILITY. This term means "liability without fault"; that is, if a person commits an act coming under this rule (such as defaming another) even by accident, or in ignorance, or with good motives, and so on, that person is liable for damages. There is no requirement that any fault—not even simple negligence—be shown; the only proof required is that it meet the conditions set forth by law (defamation, publication, and identification) and that the defendant did it. Of course, liability can be mitigated by an effective defense.

FIGURE 4.3.   JUSTICE LEWIS F. POWELL, JR.

Justice Lewis F. Powell, Jr. (above left), authored the opinion of the Court in the 1974 case of Gertz v. Welch, *the most significant ruling of the Supreme Court in the area of defamation since the* Times-Sullivan *decision of a decade earlier. Chicago Attorney Elmer Gertz (above right) had been falsely accused of being a "Leninist" and a "communist fronter" in a 1969 issue of* American Opinion, *mouthpiece of the John Birch Society. (Alan Stang, author of the attack on Gertz, had announced in his previous writings that the following were also "communist fronters": President John F. Kennedy, Martin Luther King, Jr., Hubert Humphrey, and John Foster Dulles.) When the trial judge denied Gertz his $50,000 damages as awarded by the jury, Gertz appealed and the U.S. Supreme Court agreed with him, ordering a new trial. Following this second trial, the jury awarded Gertz $100,000 for actual injury plus $300,000 in punitive damages. The court of appeals upheld the award, and in February 1983 the U.S. Supreme Court declined to review the case. The victory for Elmer Gertz came after a court battle that lasted almost thirteen years.*

FIGURE 4.4.   ATTORNEY ELMER GERTZ.

Justice Powell was appointed to the U.S. Supreme Court by President Richard Nixon in 1972.

Justice Powell. The Supreme Court Historical Society.

Elmer Gertz. With permission of Elmer Gertz (photo by Gene Lovitz).

PRESUMED DAMAGES.   Under the common law of defamation, the courts presume (i.e., assume without further proof) that if the conditions of the case are met, monetary damages are justified and follow automatically. The jury determines the dollar amount of these presumed damages by making an intuitive estimate of what the amount should be—in other words, the jury guesses. Presumed damages are not the same as general damages but are a subtype of general damage. General damages consist of two types: (1) those *based upon proof,* such as the testimony of witnesses in court, and (2) those that are *presumed,* for which no proof is required.

FAULT. The three degrees of fault that apply to defamation cases are "negligence" (the easiest to prove), "gross negligence" (moderately difficult to prove), and "actual malice" (very difficult to prove).

1. "Negligence" is the failure to do something that reasonable persons in the course of ordinary human affairs would not fail to do; or, put another way, doing something that reasonable or "prudent" persons would not do.

2. "Gross negligence" is more serious than mere "negligence," for it describes intentional failure to do what is reasonable and prudent; the elements of willfulness and wantonness are stronger in this category of fault.

3. "Actual malice" means deliberately, knowingly committing an act that is harmful to another. Applied to defamation it means "slander or libel in the first degree," for it describes the act of communicating a falsehood deliberately—knowing it is false—or doing so with a reckless disregard for the truth.

With the assistance of the explanations above, perhaps the nonlawyer can better understand this bit of legal jargon concerning the common law of defamation prior to the changes initiated by the Supreme Court in 1964: "Under the common law, the plaintiff in a defamation suit acted under the doctrine of *strict liability,* was not required to prove any degree of *fault* against the defendant, and collected *presumed* damages as the jury willed." Note below that the Court described this peculiar combination of rules as "an oddity of tort law."

Justice Powell *continued for the Court:*

The common law of defamation is an oddity of tort law, for it allows recovery of purportedly compensatory damages without evidence of actual loss. Under the traditional rules . . . the existence of injury is presumed from the fact of publication. Juries may award substantial sums as compensation for supposed damage to reputation without any proof that such harm actually occurred. The largely uncontrolled discretion of juries to award damages where there is no loss unnecessarily compounds the potential of any system of liability for defamatory falsehood to inhibit the vigorous exercise of First Amendment freedoms. . . .

We also find no justification for allowing awards of punitive damages against publishers and broadcasters held liable under state-defined standards of liability for defamation. In most jurisdictions jury discretion over the amounts awarded is limited only by the gentle rule that they not be excessive. Consequently, juries assess punitive damages in wholly unpredictable amounts bearing no necessary relation to the actual harm caused. And they remain free to use their discretion selectively to punish expressions of unpopular views. . . . [Hereafter] the private defamation plaintiff who establishes liability under a less demanding standard than that stated by *New York Times* may recover only such damages as are sufficient to compensate him for actual injury.

In addition to affirming the pre-*Rosenbloom* position that private individuals receive more protection from defamation under the law than do public persons, what did the Supreme Court say in *Gertz* which, by way of summary, the public communicator should be aware of? *First,* speakers and writers should recognize that *Gertz* altered several nationally accepted standards of the law of defamation, specifically (a) by requiring each state to establish a minimum liability of "negligence" for a libel action against a media defendant, (b) by limiting damages to "actual injury" in cases where the state's minimum standard is used, and (c) by prohibiting juries from awarding presumed or punitive damages unless the *Times-Sullivan* standard of "actual malice" is met. These requirements are intended, in part, at least, to protect publishers and broadcasters from prohibitively high damage awards. *Second,* since the Court allowed each state to define "negligence" and "actual injury" for itself, there is currently great disparity throughout the United States in how the terms are interpreted and applied.[38] The public communicator should seek the advice of experienced persons in the print and broadcasting media for advice on how to comply with *Gertz* in a given state. Where the content of a story raises serious doubts in the mind of the communicator, the advice of a good libel attorney is needed. *Finally,* while one is cautiously attempting to understand and comply with the various interpretations of *Times-Sullivan,* including *Gertz,* he or she can recall with nostalgia the simple and direct "absolute privilege" for the press urged by the late Justices Hugo Black and William O. Douglas: "We would . . . more faithfully interpret the First Amendment by holding that at the very least it leaves the people and the press free to criticize officials and discuss public affairs with impunity."[39]

Times-Sullivan and Progeny in Brief

In the 1964 case of *New York Times* v. *Sullivan* the Supreme Court of the United States set into motion a revision of the common law of defamation as applied by the various states. Initially, the reasoning of the Court was based upon a sedition argument—that some public officials were attempting to punish criticism of their official conduct by initiating libel actions against their critics. To preserve free and "wide-open debate" on public matters, the Court announced a rule to make it difficult for public officials to recover damages, thereby providing a more complete protection for the press. The *Times-Sullivan* decision altered the common law of defamation in two specific ways. *First,* the doctrine of strict liability was abandoned for those cases in which the plaintiffs were classified as "public officials" (later to include "public figures" as well); in its place the High Court ruled that the strict standard of fault known as "actual malice" must be proved before damages are allowed. *Second,* by basing the decision upon First Amendment grounds the Court added a new defense to the traditional three (truth, tarnished reputation, and privileged communication), namely, the "constitutional defense," so called because it is based upon the federal Constitution.

In a series of cases based upon *Times-Sullivan,* the Supreme Court explained that the "actual malice" rule includes both civil and criminal libel, that it covers public figures and candidates for public office and extends down the hierarchy of government officials to those who have "substantial responsibility for or control over the conduct of government affairs," and that the term "official conduct" includes those matters of an official's private life that touch on his or her fitness for office. Furthermore, the Court refused to expand *Times-Sullivan* to include *subjects* of general public interest where the parties involved are private citizens, and it permitted the process of discovery to cover inquiry into the subjective "state of mind" of a media defendant in matters pertaining to the editorial process (to help a plaintiff show "actual malice").

Finally, in the 1974 case of *Gertz* v. *Welch,* the Supreme Court sought to strike a new balance between the right of a private individual to protect his or her reputation from defamatory falsehoods and the need to pro-

[38]See William O. McCarthy, "How State Courts Have Responded to *Gertz* in Setting Standards of Fault," *Journalism Quarterly* 56 (1979): 531–539 ff.
[39]Concurring opinion in *New York Times* v. *Sullivan,* 376 U.S. 254 (1964), at 296.

vide publishers and broadcasters greater protection from prohibitively expensive damage awards. To try to accomplish this balance, the Court altered the common law in two significant areas. *First,* the doctrine of strict liability no longer applies when a private plaintiff sues a media defendant; rather, a minimum standard of fault no less than "negligence" must now be proved (states may set a standard of fault stiffer than negligence, but nothing weaker than negligence is allowed). *Second,* in those cases where the minimum standard of fault is proved, damages are restricted to "actual injury" (no *presumed* or *punitive* damages are permitted). By "actual injury" the Court meant *specific* damages plus those *general* damages that are proved in court. Plaintiffs who wish to sue for presumed or punitive damages must now meet the strict "actual malice" standard of fault.

III. SPEECH THAT INVADES PRIVACY

Although the U.S. Constitution nowhere explicitly mentions a right of privacy, a judicial concern for certain fundamental privacy rights has developed in the nation during the twentieth century—on the ground, according to some students of the Constitution, that a right of privacy is *implied* in the document by which the nation is governed. Of course, concern for privacy is not entirely a development of the twentieth century; its roots predate the American Constitution and the Bill of Rights and include such matters as protecting a person's home from unreasonable search, objections to forced quartering of troops in a residence, and respect for privacy in matters of religious belief and practice. The specific constraints detailed below, however, are relatively recent developments in the law.

The legal community traces its contemporary views on the right of privacy to an 1890 article written by Samuel Warren and Louis Brandeis (the latter was appointed to the Supreme Court and is noted for his dissents with Justice Holmes in favor of greater freedom of political expression—see Chapter 3).[40] In this influential essay, Warren and Brandeis argued for a common-law right "to be let alone" and in the process articulated a rationale by which constraints have been placed upon expression that invades the individual's personality and seclusion. These controls are similar in many respects to those imposed by the law of defamation and, like slander and libel, are primarily matters of state rather than federal enforcement.

Four Types of Invasion of Privacy

At least four problem areas in the developing law of privacy are of concern to the public communicator: (1) disclosure, (2) false light, (3) appropriation (including right of publicity), and (4) intrusion. Although the first three are clearly issues of speech *content,* the fourth is more a matter of how information is *gathered.* These four privacy torts can be briefly defined as follows:

1. *Disclosure*—publicity about private matters that are of no legitimate concern to the public—such as the details of the sex life of a private individual.

2. *False light*—the publication of falsehoods or distortions of the truth that give the reader or listener an incorrect impression about a

---

[40]Samuel Warren and Louis Brandeis, "The Right to Privacy," *Harvard Law Review* 4 (1890): 193 ff. Note: For a review of the common-law right of privacy in the century preceding the Warren-Brandeis essay, see "The Right of Privacy in Nineteenth Century America," *Harvard Law Review* 94 (June 1981): 1892–1910.

person; for example, the cropping of a photograph of a room full of people to show only two people "whispering" to one another so as to suggest that the photo is of a clandestine meeting of the two.

3. *Appropriation*—the use of a person's name or likeness, or other highly personal material, without that person's permission, usually in the context of commercial exploitation; for example, naming a product after a film star and using the star's picture on the product, all without permission.

4. *Intrusion*—the invasion of a person's private space or "physical solitude" in order to gather information; as by placing hidden cameras or microphones in a private home in order to spy on the inhabitants.

Disclosure of Private Matters

The public disclosure of matters that are private differs from defamation in that in the disclosure issue the message is *true*—it is simply none of the public's business. Three requirements must be met before such communications become actionable as a violation of privacy: (a) the plaintiff must show that the defendant was the one who publicized the matter and that it was communicated "to the world at large" (not to just one or two other persons); (2) the story must relate to the plaintiff's *private* life and not be a matter of public record (see *Cox* v. *Cohn* below); and (3) the account must be offensive to a "reasonable person" and not be of an ordinary, nonoffensive nature (for example, publication of the number of square feet in a person's home would, as a rule, be nonoffensive in nature, whereas publication of that person's toilet habits might very well be highly offensive).

The decision of the Supreme Court in the 1975 case of *Cox Broadcasting Corp.* v. *Cohn* is of particular relevance to the public communicator who is concerned about the matter

of disclosure.[41] In this case, a television reporter in Georgia discovered the name of a young rape-murder victim in the public records and mentioned the victim's name over the air, even though state law prohibited the dissemination of such information. The family sued for invasion of privacy, but the U.S. Supreme Court rejected their plea. Speaking for the Court, Justice White states that the majority is "reluctant to embark on a course that would make public records generally available to the media but forbid their publication if offensive to the sensibilities of the supposed reasonable man. Such a rule would make it very difficult for the media to inform citizens about the public business and yet stay within the law." After emphasizing how such a rule of liability would cause timidity and self-censorship by communicators, Justice White concludes: *"At the very least, the First and Fourteenth Amendments will not allow exposing the press to liability for truthfully publishing information released to the public in official court records.* If there are privacy interests to be protected in judicial proceedings, the States must respond by means which avoid public documentation or other exposure of private information." Consequently, the decision of whether or not to publish information which is "disclosed in public court documents open to public inspection" is left up to the judgment of the publisher or broadcaster.[42]

---

[41]*Cox* v. *Cohn*, 530 U.S. 469 (1975).

[42]A specific application of the *Cox* principle occurred four years later, when the Supreme Court declared unconstitutional a West Virginia statute prohibiting the publication of the name of a juvenile offender even if the name was legally obtained. The reporters for a Charleston newspaper had heard the name over the police radio and subsequently published the information. By a vote of 8 to 0, the Court ruled that a state may not "punish the truthful publication of an alleged juvenile delinquent's name lawfully obtained by a newspaper." *Smith* v. *Daily Mail Publishing Co.*, 443 U.S. 97 (1979).

False-Light Communications

Expression that publicizes private information about an individual in such a way as to present a distortion of the truth so that "reasonable persons" find the account offensive is described as a "false-light" communication. False-light speech is of two types: (1) that which "fictionalizes" the truth by adding details from the imagination of the communicator and (2) that which distorts not with "fictions" but by omissions, slanting, photo cropping, misleading camera angles, and so on. Of course, the two types can be combined in a single story. The first instance in which the U.S. Supreme Court decided an issue concerning a false-light communication was the 1967 case of *Time, Inc.* v. *Hill*.[43] This privacy action began with a real-life incident in which three escaped convicts held the James Hill family hostage for several hours in their home near Philadelphia before releasing them unharmed. The matter was fictionalized in a novel by Joseph Hayes entitled *The Desperate Hours*, later dramatized in a Broadway play of the same title. In its February 28, 1955, issue, *Life* magazine published a picture story entitled "True Crime Inspires Tense Play," in which the real-life incident and the Broadway dramatization were compared and contrasted. The Hill family sued for invasion of privacy under the laws of the State of New York and were awarded $30,000 in damages. On appeal, the Supreme Court set aside the judgment and remanded the case after concluding that the opinion of the Court in *New York Times* v. *Sullivan* was applicable (see part 2 of this chapter) and, since *Life* was not guilty of "actual malice," no damages should be assessed. Justice Brennan, speaking for the Court, states: "We hold that the constitutional protections for speech and press pre-

clude the application of the New York statute to redress false reports of matters of public interest in the absence of proof that the defendant published the report with knowledge of its falsity or in reckless disregard of the truth." In this language the Supreme Court established a *constitutional defense* for false-light privacy actions, for it determined that all plaintiffs, including *private* individuals who bring false-light suits over the communication of matters of "public interest," must prove the "actual malice" degree of fault against the defendant, just as do *public* persons in defamation suits.

That burden of proof was met to the satisfaction of the Supreme Court in a 1974 case in which the *Cleveland Plain Dealer* published a feature story concerning the impact of the death (along with forty-three other persons) of husband and father Melvin Cantrell in the collapse of the Silver Bridge across the Ohio River.[44] The story was based upon interviews conducted and photographs made during a visit to the Cantrell home by the reporter and photographer in the absence of Mrs. Cantrell. After the journalists had talked with the children and taken pictures, the feature—emphasizing the family's poverty, the old clothing worn by the children, and the run-down condition of the house in which the Cantrells lived—was published. Among other things, the story falsely claimed that the mother was present during the interview and photo-taking session. Mrs. Cantrell sued for damages under the false-light theory of privacy, claiming that the many inaccuracies and false statements in the story made the family "objects of pity and ridicule," thereby damaging the members of the family by causing them "to suffer out-

---

[43]*Time, Inc.* v. *Hill*, 385 U.S. 374 (1967).

[44]*Cantrell* v. *Forest City Publishing Co.*, 419 U.S. 245 (1974).

rage, mental distress, shame, and humiliation." The jury agreed and awarded damages. On appeal, the Supreme Court sustained the judgment against the newspaper, the writer, and the photographer because the "calculated falsehoods" in the story cast the family in a false light "through knowing or reckless untruth." In other words, plaintiff Cantrell proved "actual malice" on the part of the defendants.

Some First Amendment scholars are already speculating about whether or not the Supreme Court will continue to require *private* plaintiffs in privacy actions against media defendants on matters of public interest to assume the heavy *Times-Sullivan* burden of proof.[45] For defamation actions, the *Gertz* decision of 1974 (summarized in part 2 of this chapter) removed this requirement for private persons unless presumed or punitive damages are sought. Meanwhile, the Supreme Court has *not* altered the precedent set in *Time, Inc.* v. *Hill,* and public communicators should be aware of that fact as they fashion their speech, so as to tell the truth without casting a fellow citizen in a false light.

Appropriation and Right to Publicity

A third type of speech that illegally invades privacy is one which "appropriates" a person's name or likeness and publicizes it without permission. The origins of this category of privacy action in the United States can be traced to New York, where, in 1902, the Franklin Mills Flour Company used a picture of Abigail Roberson of Albany, New York, in company advertising without her consent. Roberson sued but lost her case because no right of privacy could be found by the courts, either at common law or in state statutes. Public outrage of this finding caused the

New York legislature in 1903 to approve the nation's first appropriation-privacy bill. The focus of this early statute was to prevent the commercial exploitation of a citizen's name or likeness without permission. Other states have followed this precedent, either by statute or common law determinations in the courts.

In 1977 the U.S. Supreme Court ruled in an appropriation case concerning the unauthorized showing of a "human cannonball" act on a television news program.[46] The Great Zacchini was an entertainer whose "cannonball" act was featured at a county fair in Ohio. A reporter for an Ohio television station filmed the entire fifteen-second act and, over the objections of Zacchini, televised it on a news program. Zacchini demanded payment for this unauthorized, public communication of his act; when the company refused, he sued for damages in state court, charging "unlawful appropriation" of his "professional property." The trial court awarded damages, but on appeal the Ohio Supreme Court reversed the judgment on the basis that broadcasters enjoy a constitutional privilege to include matters of public interest in newscasts, a finding that relied heavily upon the reasoning of the U.S. Supreme Court in the 1967 case of *Time* v. *Hill.*

On appeal, the U.S. Supreme Court reversed the Ohio court and reinstated the judgment for damages against the Scripps-Howard Broadcasting Company, thus recognizing Zacchini's ownership rights (the "right to publicity") to his act. Justice White, spokesman for the majority in this decision, pointed out that the "broadcast of a film of [Zacchini's] entire act poses a substantial

---

[45]For example, see Barron and Dienes, pp. 375–384.

[46]*Zacchini* v. *Scripps-Howard Broadcasting Company,* 433 U.S. 562 (1977).

threat to the economic value of that performance. . . . [I]f the public can see the act free on television, it will be less willing to pay to see it at the fair." In addition, Justice White noted, "the broadcast of petitioner's entire performance, unlike the unauthorized use of another's name for purposes of trade or the incidental use of a name or picture by the press, goes to the heart of petitioner's ability to earn a living as an entertainer." Justice White concluded by agreeing that entertainment events under certain circumstances are newsworthy and that the communication of "news" about such events enjoys First Amendment protection. In this specific case, however, the television station was guilty of appropriation. Zacchini did not seek to prevent the broadcast, emphasized Justice White, "he simply wanted to be paid for it." In the process of ruling that the First and Fourteenth Amendments to the Constitution did not protect the showing of Zacchini's entire act on television without compensation, the Supreme Court demonstrated that it accepted the constitutionality of carefully drawn state laws constraining appropriation or right to publicity of a person's name, likeness, or work (such as a complete circus act).

Intrusion

The issue of intrusion concerns conduct more than message content, yet it merits attention at this point in order to complete the overview of the four major privacy torts. Although intrusion cases are relatively uncommon, those that are litigated typically involve a reporter or a photographer who is accused of invading the physical solitude of the plaintiff in the process of gathering information for possible use in a journalistic enterprise. The few cases available for study are at the state or lower federal court levels, there being no definitive U.S. Supreme Court decisions on the subject. Despite this paucity of case

law, it is possible to sketch a general outline of the key issues at stake.

First, the Constitution does not give a reporter the right to violate the ordinary rules of law governing trespass, theft, or the placing of secret surveillance devices. A public communicator who enters private property that is protected by a state's trespass laws or who purloins documents such as a diary or other private papers is guilty of illegal conduct and will find little if any sympathy if he or she pleads a journalistic privilege under the First Amendment as a defense. As U.S. Circuit Judge Shirley Hufstedler said in her opinion against *Life* magazine (whose reporters and photographers used concealed tape recorders and cameras inside a person's home, to which they had gained admission under false pretense): "The First Amendment has never been construed to accord newsmen immunity from torts or crimes committed during the course of newsgathering. The First Amendment is not a license to trespass, to steal, or to intrude by electronic means into the precincts of another's home or office."[47]

Second, reporters and photographers may in general observe, record, and photograph that which occurs in *public places* without running the risk of successful court action as long as the activity does not reach the point of harassment. When one goes too far, even in public places, a suit can result, as freelance photographer Ron Galella discovered when he made a nuisance of himself by constantly following and photographing members of the Kennedy family. In a suit brought by the Kennedys, Galella was enjoined by a federal judge to desist from his aggravating behavior.[48]

---

[47] *Dietemann v. Time,* 449 F.2d 245 (9th Cir. 1971).
[48] *Galella v. Onassis,* 487 F.2d 986 (2d Cir. 1973).

Finally, state laws and court rulings in various jurisdictions vary on a wide range of issues related to intrusion; furthermore, the specific circumstances of a case (such as when the use of a telephoto lens invades privacy and when it does not) provide further variables that make it difficult to provide comprehensive guidelines as to what is allowed and what is not. Two examples illustrate this point. In the first instance, most states do not prohibit a reporter's use of a tape recorder concealed on his or her person (or in a briefcase or purse being held by the reporter); however, as of 1980, thirteen states had outlawed this type of "intrusion."[49] In the second instance, it is usually illegal for a photographer to enter a private home without the consent of the owner to make a photograph, yet the practice can be legal under unusual circumstances. In 1972 a Florida *Times-Union* photographer covering a house fire was invited into the burned home by an investigating officer whose camera was out of film and who needed a photograph to aid him in his work. The reporter cooperated and provided the official with the picture. But when the same picture was published in the *Times-Union,* the owner of the home sued for invasion of privacy. The courts of Florida denied relief to the plaintiff, however, on the grounds that the photographer entered the home with "implied consent," since no person objected to the entry and since it was done at the invitation of investigating officers.[50] As these two examples suggest, the investigative reporter should study case and statute law in the state where he or she works in order to comply with applicable standards.

Defenses in Privacy Actions

The three primary defenses in privacy cases are (1) consent, (2) public interest (newsworthiness), and (3) the U.S. Constitution. A brief examination of each concludes the discussion of invasion of privacy.

Consent

Obviously, if a person consents to the publication of material, that person should not later allege an invasion of privacy on the matter. Public communicators, however, should be aware of at least two matters relating to this defense. First, the burden of proof to show consent is upon the *defendant,* so adequate records and reliable witnesses should be available to prove that consent did indeed occur. Second, the consent given must be as broad as the invasion of privacy that follows. A person who consents to have his photograph used in a sympathetic human interest story in a local newspaper does not at the same time consent to the sensationalized use of that photograph in a nationally distributed "true crime" magazine. In short, public communicators should have an understanding with the party or parties involved about how far the consent agreement reaches.

Public Interest or Newsworthiness

A traditional defense against invasion-of-privacy actions based upon the *disclosure* tort is that the material published was news and that it was published in the public interest. In clear-cut instances, such a defense is usually effective in demolishing a plea for damages.

---

[49]Kent R. Middleton, "Journalists and Tape Recorders: Does Participant Monitoring Invade Privacy?" *COMM/ENT Law Journal* 2 (1980): 299 ff. Note: The thirteen states listed by the author are California, Delaware, Florida, Georgia, Illinois, Maryland, Massachusetts, Michigan, Montana, New Hampshire, Oregon, Pennsylvania, and Washington.

[50]*Florida Publishing Co.* v. *Fletcher,* 340 So.2d 914 (Florida 1977).

For example, a person who is in a bank when a holdup occurs would likely be classified by the courts as an "unwilling actor" in a newsworthy event and be denied damages if he sued a newspaper for reporting his presence, his on-the-spot comments, or a photograph showing him being interviewed by a police officer. On the other hand, this same information published five years later might, in special circumstances, constitute an invasion of privacy, since it is no longer "news." Furthermore, the public-interest defense is a little assistance in cases based upon the torts of intrusion or commercial appropriation.

The Constitutional Defense

The U.S. Supreme Court has provided a constitutional defense in two specific areas of invasion of privacy. *First*, in the 1967 case of *Time* v. *Hill,* the Supreme Court established a First Amendment defense in *false-light* privacy cases that concern a subject of general public interest. In such instances, said the Court—going to its defamation decision in the 1964 case of *New York Times* v. *Sullivan* for guidance—the U.S. Constitution requires a plaintiff, whether a private or a public person, to prove "actual malice" against a defendant. Public communicators should note that the ruling is restricted to newsworthy events and does not cover false-light communications that are not related to a matter of general public interest. *Second,* in the 1975 *disclosure* case of *Cox* v. *Cohn* (which concerned broadcasting of the name of a juvenile rape-murder victim in violation of state law prohibiting such disclosure) the Supreme Court ruled that since the reporters had secured the name from public documents, no damages were permitted. In the words of the Court, "the First and Fourteenth Amendments will not allow exposing the press to liability for truthfully publishing information released to the public in official court records."

Privacy in Brief

In summary, a twentieth-century development in First Amendment law concerns constraints placed upon expression that invades privacy. Either by state statute or common-law determination by the courts, four privacy torts are recognized: (1) *disclosure*—accounts that publicize private matters which "reasonable persons" find offensive; (2) *false light*—accounts that, by the addition of falsehoods or by distortion, present a person in a false light; (3) *appropriation*—accounts that use another person's name or likeness, usually for commercial purposes, without permission, and those that violate a person's "right to publicity" concerning an entertainment act (or similar matters) without permission or compensation; and (4) *intrusion*—the invasion of a person's physical solitude in order to secure information. The three standard defenses in privacy cases are (a) consent, (b) newsworthiness, and (c) the U.S. Constitution.

CONCLUSION

Defamatory speech and that which invades privacy remain outside the protection of the First Amendment. Defamatory speech is that which tends to lower a person's reputation before others, cause that person to be shunned, or expose that person to hatred, contempt, or ridicule. In the United States all defamation laws are at the state level, there being no federal law of slander and libel. Defamation per se (sometimes called intrinsic libel) occurs when a person communicates a critical story to a third party, charging another with criminality, disease, dishonesty, or unchastity; such accusations are libelous on their face. Defamation per quod (sometimes called extrinsic libel) is that speech which is not libelous per se but requires supporting information to demonstrate that in the peculiar circumstances of the case at bar, libel has occurred. To prove a case of defamation, the plaintiff must show four things: (1) that defamation has occurred, (2) that it has been communicated to a third party, (3) that the plaintiff is identifiable as the person defamed, and (4) in most cases, a minimum degree of fault (known as "negligence"), which—since *Gertz* v. *Welch,* discussed further below—must be proved. The four standard defenses are (a) truth, (b) an already tarnished reputation on the part of the plaintiff, (c) privilege, and (d) after the *Times-Sullivan* decision of 1964, the U.S. Constitution. Damages are of three types: *specific*—those that can be calculated in a fairly precise way, such as out-of-pocket losses; *general*—losses that are more intuitive than specific, reflecting the opinion of the jury concerning the degree of damage to reputation; and *punitive*—designed to punish a particularly vicious libel.

The four areas of action for invasion of privacy are (1) disclosure (concerning private matters that are no business of the public), (2) false light (misrepresentation by distortion of the truth), (3) appropriation (use of another's name, likeness, or entertainment act without permission), and (4) intrusion (invasion of physical solitude to gain information). The three standard defenses in privacy suits are (a) consent, (b) newsworthiness, and (c) the U.S. Constitution.

In the 1964 landmark case of *New York Times* v. *Sullivan,* the Supreme Court extended the protection of the First Amendment to defamatory remarks about public officials concerning their official conduct unless the official could prove that the defamatory material was communicated with "actual malice," that is, "with knowledge that it was false or with reckless disregard of whether it was false or not." This was done, the Court

explained, in order to discourage public officials from trying to punish criticism of their official conduct by threatening to sue for libel; the result, the Court declared, ought to be robust and wide-open debate on public issues. Eight issues that flowed from the *Times-Sullivan* decision were developed and clarified in the years after 1964, as follows:

1. The "actual malice" rule applies to both civil and criminal libel.

2. The "actual malice" rule covers both "public officials" and "public figures."

3. "Public officials" are those who are elected to office or who have "substantial responsibility for or control over the conduct of public affairs." "Public figures" are those who "occupy positions of . . . persuasive power and influence" or who voluntarily inject themselves "into a particular public controversy."

4. The private life of a public official is open to criticism insofar as the subject concerns his or her "fitness for office."

5. "Actual malice" cannot occur when a communicator believes that he or she is telling the truth, so *intent* is an important consideration; copy deadlines vary from medium to medium, and thus "hot copy" media such as wire services have more leeway for error under the law than do magazines and books.

6. Private persons caught up in a public issue do not have to prove the "actual malice" standard of fault; the *Times-Sullivan* rule extends only to "public officials" and "public figures," *not* to subject matter of public interest.

7. Plaintiffs may employ the process of discovery to inquire into the "state of mind" of journalists as a story was being written or edited; this knowledge of a communicator's subjective thought processes can be legally requested by one trying to prove "actual malice."

8. The important case of *Gertz* v. *Welch* (1974) determined that private persons bringing libel suits against media defendants (publishers and broadcasters) must prove a minimum degree of fault known as "negligence" and that, when this minimum degree of fault is used, no presumed or punitive damages are allowed; plaintiffs who wish to sue for presumed or punitive damages must prove the tough degree of fault known as "actual malice."

As the public communictor can readily ascertain, the constraints of defamation and privacy law, despite the First Amendment, remain very much alive in the United States. The current conservative composition of the U.S. Supreme Court suggests that these constraints upon expression will persist for many years to come. What, then, should the communicator do in order to "stay out of court"? Here are four recommendations:

1. *Know the law*—Study the laws of the state or states in which you work; get expert legal advice on these laws if necessary.
2. *Consult with colleagues and use employer guides*—Seek advice from experienced journalists; also, study any published guides concerning media liability made available by your employer.
3. *Avoid obvious invitations to trouble*—Most defamation and invasion of privacy cases are avoidable; here are some steps a public communicator can take to anticipate and steer clear of problems:
   a. When a story is critical of a person, check with that individual before publication in order to get his or her point of view.
   b. When a story concerns a technical subject, get the opinion of an independent expert or two before publication.
   c. When a story is based upon legal documents, such as court opinions or briefs, read the entire document carefully before preparing materials based upon it.
   d. When allegations are involved, qualify the language with terms such as "reportedly" or "alleged."
   e. Carefully avoid making "wild charges," or employing name-calling or insulting language in a story.
4. *Be ethical*—The public communicator who is conscientious in his or her efforts to speak truthfully and with fairness will want to confirm all "facts" before publicizing a conclusion; in this and other ways, the speaker or writer can work to meet high standards of individual responsibility in the area of public communication.

EXERCISES

A. Classroom projects and activities.
   1. Here are three questions phrased for classroom debate:
      a. Resolved, that an *absolute* privilege be extended to those critical of public officials in matters concerning their official conduct.
      b. Resolved, that all defamation statutes should be abolished.
      c. Resolved, that the U.S. Constitution does imply a right of privacy.
   2. Here are the same questions phrased for classroom discussion:
      a. Should officials in government ever be allowed to sue for defamation over criticism of their official conduct?
      b. Should all defamation statutes be abolished? What would be the benefits to publishers, broadcasters, and other public communicators? What would be the effects upon those persons, both public and private, who were defamed under a complete-freedom rule?

c. Should the Supreme Court "discover" an "implied right of privacy" in the Constitution? Keep in mind that privacy is not specifically mentioned in the Constitution.

3. Using your college library or the library of a local lawyer, look up and make copies of the defamation and privacy statutes of your state. Distribute the copies to the class for analysis and discussion.

4. Invite a local attorney (or a panel of attorneys) to explain the defamation and privacy laws of your state. In the matter of privacy, make sure to keep the focus upon materials that invade privacy—disclosure, false light, appropriation, and intrusion.

5. Invite an editor of a local newspaper or manager of a local television station (or a panel with representatives from the press, television, and radio) to speak to the class on specific ways by which their medium avoids defamatory stories or those that invade privacy. Ask the speaker (or panel members) about libel insurance. Do they carry such insurance? What do they think of this type of insurance as an answer to libel and privacy actions?

6. Look up the Supreme Court decision in *Beauharnais* v. *Illinois,* 343 U.S. 250 (1952), in which Beauharnais was found "guilty" of defaming a *group* of persons. A copy of the handbill distributed by Beauharnais is included in *U.S. Reports;* make copies of the handbill and distribute in class. Discuss. Should expression of this type be legal?

7. In *Gertz* v. *Welch* (summarized in this chapter), Justice Powell, who delivered the opinion of the Court, questions the practice of awarding *punitive* damages in defamation cases. Should punitive damages ever be awarded or should damages *always* be limited to "actual injury"? Discuss.

8. Ask each student to purchase a copy of the *National Enquirer* or some similar "gossipy" tabloid; study the contents, then report to the class. Let each student summarize (or read aloud) the story which he or she thinks is "the most defamatory" or the "worst invasion of privacy" in the issue purchased. Discuss whether or not the First Amendment should be extended to such publications.

9. Have each student prepare a *brief* (approximately 300-word maximum) statement of opinion concerning whether or not slander and libel should be protected by the First Amendment. These short, tightly reasoned statements could be called "My Opinion Concerning Defamation and Freedom of Speech." Let each student (or selected students) read his or her statement in class. Discuss.

10. In *Cox* v. *Cohn,* the Supreme Court ruled that anything in an official court record—even the names of rape victims—could be published or broadcast without legally invading privacy. Do you think this was a wise move by the Court? Discuss.

11. Keep a scrapbook of newspaper and newsmagazine accounts of defamation and privacy cases during the semester. Near the end of the term, select the case in which you believe the plaintiff was most justified in going to court. Make photocopies of the account of this "worst" instance, distribute to the other members of the class, and discuss. (Note: When clipping, be sure to write the source and the date on each item.)

B. Topics for research papers or oral reports.

1. Government Officials Should Learn to "Take the Heat"—Arguments in Favor of an *Absolute* Privilege for Comment About Public Officials.

2. In Defense of *Times-Sullivan:* Government Officials Need Some Protection from Abuse by the Media.

3. Trusting the Public: The Case for Abolishing *All* Defamation Statutes.

4. The Case *for* Laws Against Slander and Libel.

5. Justice Hugo Black and the Law of Defamation.

6. Group Libel Statutes: Pro and Con. (Examine viewpoints on both sides of the issue.)

7. An Analysis and Criticism of *Criminal* Libel Statutes.

8. Punitive Damages in Defamation Actions: Arguments Pro and Con.

9. A Short History of the Law of Defamation in the United States.

10. A History and Analysis of the Common-Law Distinction Between Slander and Libel (with recommendations for the future).

11. A Short History of the Developing Law of Privacy in the United States. (Be sure to emphasize First Amendment issues in this project.)

12. What Hath *Gertz* Wrought? An Analysis and Criticism of *Gertz* v. *Welch.*

13. Extending the "Actual Malice" Rule to *Subjects* of Public Concern: A Look at Arguments Pro and Con.

14. The Editor's "State of Mind": The Implications of *Herbert* v. *Lando* for Publishers and Broadcasters.

15. Should There Be a *Constitutional* Right of Privacy? Arguments Pro and Con.

16. The Saga of the James Hill Family: A History and Analysis. (Begin with a careful reading of *Time* v. *Hill,* 385 U.S. 374, 1967; examine the novel and the play, both entitled *The Desperate Hours;* read the article in *Life,* "True Crime Inspires Tense Play," in the February 28, 1955 issue, pp. 75–78. Also, study the decisions in the federal district court, as well as the court of appeals.)

17. A Study of the Laws of Your State Concerning Defamation (or Privacy).

18. Alternatives to Tort Actions in Defamation Disputes: A Look at Ways to "Stay out of Court." (Include such proposals as public apologies, retractions, a right of reply, arbitration, etc.)

19. A Study of Strange Ways of Defaming Another. (Include novels, poems, effigies, etc.)

20. Defamation and the First Amendment: My Personal Philosophy. (Or Privacy and the First Amendment.)

SELECTED READINGS

American Law Institute. *Restatement of the Law of Torts.* 2nd ed. Philadelphia: American Law Institute, 1975.

Ashley, Paul. *Say It Safely.* 5th ed. Seattle: University of Washington Press, 1976. (Readable, practical advice for the public communicator.)

Barron, Jerome A., and Dienes, C. Thomas. *Handbook of Free Speech and Free Press.* Boston: Little, Brown, 1979. See chapter 6 on defamation and chapter 7 on privacy.

Cahn, Edmond. "Justice Black and First Amendment 'Absolutes': A Public Interview." *New York University Law Review* 37 (1962): 549 ff.

Comment. "*Edwards v. National Audubon Society, Inc.:* A Constitutional Privilege to Republish Defamation Should Be Rejected." *Hastings Law Journal* 33 (May 1982): 1203–1225.

Coronna, David M. "The Right of Publicity." *Public Relations Journal* 39 (February 1983): 29–31.

Eldredge, Laurence H. "The Spurious Rule of Libel Per Quod." *Harvard Law Review* 79 (1966): 733 ff.

Emerson, Thomas I. "Right of Privacy and Freedom of the Press." *Harvard Civil Rights-Civil Liberties Law Review* 14 (Summer 1979): 329–360.

Emerson, Thomas I. *The System of Freedom of Expression.* New York: Random House, 1970. Especially chapters 10 and 14, which concern libel and privacy.

Franklin, Marc A. "Winners and Losers and Why: A Study of Defamation Litigation." *American Bar Foundation Research Journal* 1980 (Summer 1980): 455–500.

Haiman, Franklyn S. *Speech and Law in a Free Society.* Chicago: University of Chicago Press, 1981. See chapter 3 on defamation and chapter 4 on privacy.

Haiman, Franklyn S. "Speech v. Privacy: Is There a Right Not to Be Spoken To?" *Northwestern University Law Review* 67 (May–June 1972): 153–199.

Hayden, Trudy, and Novik, Jack. *Your Rights to Privacy.* New York: Avon Books, 1980.

Hentoff, Nat. "Free Speech: The Price Is Going Up." *The Progressive,* May 1983, pp. 34–37. (Concerns how libel suits are used to silence critics.)

Hunsaker, David M. "Freedom and Responsibility in First Amendment Theory: Defamation Law and Media Credibility." *Quarterly Journal of Speech* 65 (February 1979): 25–35.

Ingber, Stanley. "Defamation: A Conflict Between Reason and Decency." *Virginia Law Review* 65 (June 1979): 785–858.

Lawhorne, Clifton O. *The Supreme Court and Libel.* Carbondale, Ill.: Southern Illinois University Press, 1981.

McCarthy, William O. "How State Courts Have Responded to *Gertz* in Setting Standards of Fault." *Journalism Quarterly* 56 (1979): 531–539 ff.

McGaffey, Ruth. "Group Libel Revisited." *Quarterly Journal of Speech* 65 (April 1979): 157–170.

Middleton, Kent R. "Journalists and Tape Recorders: Does Participant Monitoring Invade Privacy?" *COMM/ENT Law Journal* 2 (1980): 299 ff.

Minnick, Wayne C. "The United States Supreme Court on Libel." *Quarterly Journal of Speech* 68 (November 1982): 384–396.

Note. "Electronic Surveillance and the Fourth Amendment: The Arrival of Big Brother?" *Hastings Constitutional Law Quarterly* 3 (1976): 261 ff.

Note. "Group Vilification Reconsidered." *Yale Law Journal* 89 (December 1979): 308–332.

Note. "Mediaocracy and Mistrust: Extending *New York Times* Defamation Protection to Nonmedia Defendants." *Harvard Law Review* 95 (June 1982): 1876–1895.

Note. "Privacy in the First Amendment." *Yale Law Journal* 82 (1973): 1462 ff.

Note. "The Right to Privacy in Nineteenth Century America." *Harvard Law Review* 94 (June 1981): 1892–1910.

Note. "Telescopes, Binoculars, and the Fourth Amendment." *Cornell Law Review* 67 (January 1982): 379–395.

Pember, Don R. *Mass Media Law.* 2nd ed. Dubuque, Iowa: William C. Brown, 1981. In particular, chapter 4, "Libel," and chapter 5, "Invasion of Privacy."

Phelps, Robert, and Hamilton, Douglas. *Libel: Rights, Risks, Reponsibilities.* New York: Dover, 1978.

Posner, Richard A. "The Uncertain Protection of Privacy by the Supreme Court." In *The Supreme Court Review: 1979,* pp. 173–216. Edited by Philip B. Kurland and Gerhard Casper. Chicago: University of Chicago Press, 1979.

Prosser, William L. "Privacy." *California Law Review* 48 (1960): 383 ff.

Shattuck, John H. F. *Rights of Privacy.* Skokie, Ill.: National Textbook Co., 1977.

Thomas, Ella Cooper. *The Law of Libel and Slander.* 2nd ed. Dobbs Ferry, N.Y.: Oceana Publications, 1963.

Warren, Samuel, and Brandeis, Louis. "The Right to Privacy." *Harvard Law Review* 4 (1890): 193 ff.

Wilson, Vivian Deborah. "The Law of Libel and the Art of Fiction." *Law and Contemporary Problems* 44 (Autumn 1981): 27–50.

CHAPTER 5

Religio–Moral Heresy: From Blasphemy to Obscenity

"The history of obscenity legislation points . . . to origins in aspirations to holiness and propriety. Laws against obscenity have appeared conjoined and cognate to laws against sacrilege and blasphemy . . . ."

—Louis Henkin, *"Morals and the Constitution: The Sin of Obscenity"*[1]

In 1979 Warner Brothers began the American distribution of the English film *Life of Brian,* produced by the Monty Python comedy group, a British crew known for its zany and "irreverent" humor. *Life of Brian* tells the story of a young man who lived during New Testament times and who was mistaken for the promised Messiah by hundreds of the inhabitants of Jerusalem; Brian's efforts to escape from his admirers and to return to living a normal life provide the situation around which the humor occurs. Although many who saw the film were delighted, describing it as "hilariously funny," others were shocked and even angered by it, calling it "blasphemous," "disgusting," and even "obscene." Efforts were organized in a number of states to prohibit the showing of the film because of its alleged "blasphemous" quality. In South Carolina, U.S. Senator Strom Thurmond used his office to urge the distributors of the film to keep it out of the state (Senator Thurmond, who had not seen the film, later withdrew from the controversy); in Louisiana, at least six theater managers were pressured into canceling the movie; strong protests were launched by conservative religious groups in both Utah and Nebraska (apparently without much success) as well as numerous other locales. In Valdosta, Georgia, *Brian* was closed by court order

when representatives of ten local churches appeared before a Valdosta judge and persuaded him that the movie was obscene because an episode in which Brian appears at a window without clothing violated state law against the "lewd exhibition of genitals."[2] Soon thereafter, the judge (who evidently took the time to view the film) canceled his court order, announced that the movie was not legally obscene, and refused to interfere further in the matter.

The controversy over Monty Python's *Life of Brian* illustrates well the interrelationship between expression classified as blasphemous and that classified as obscene. As the historical survey at the beginning of this book explains, the orgin of the term "obscene libel" in Anglo-American law can be found in the ecclesiastical courts of the Church of England, where—until early in the eighteenth century—all accusations concerning "lewdness," "profanity," "heresy," and 'blasphemy" were adjudicated. The crime of obscenity entered the secular common law in 1727, when a British judge convicted Richard Curl of "reflecting on religion, virtue, and morality" by publishing a naughty story entitled *Venus in the Cloister, or the Nun in Her Smock.* From this specific case the common-law crime of obscenity developed into the elaborate system of constraints upon the communication of ideas about human sexuality which is one of the major concerns of this chapter.

Religio-moral heresy is not limited to the English common-law crimes of blasphemous libel and obscene libel; in fact, at least six overlapping and interacting types of religio-moral heresy can be identified as one examines the issues and cases in Anglo-American ecclesiastical and secular law: (1) false doc-

---

[1] In *Columbia Law Review* 63 (March 1963): 391 ff.

[2] "For the Love of Brian," *Newsletter on Intellectual Freedom,* January 1980, pp. 5 and 20.

trine; (2) irreverent expression; (3) profane and disgusting speech; (4) sexual communications of a sensual and erotic nature; (5) scientific opinion and fact, including both "sex education" data (such as materials on sexual intercourse or birth control) and challenges to church dogma concerning earth and life sciences (such as the "place" of the earth in the universe, the origins of life, and the theory of evolution); and (6) nonconforming views on private morality. As Figure 5.1 explains, these six merge in a variety of combinations; in theory—as the circle in the center of the figure suggests—several categories can be present in a single assertion of opinion. The significant point to keep in mind is that some church authorities in years gone by (and some even today) decided that each of the six forms of expression was heretical. In an historical sense, then, obscenity remains the last religious heresy which the U.S. Supreme Court permits *state authority* to punish by means of the enforcement of secular law, which is generally applicable to all citizens, including consenting adults. Furthermore, an understanding of the history of the issue helps to explain why conservative church leaders and members of "fundamentalist" religious groups are usually at the forefront of "antismut" campaigns, for there have always been those in the established religion who believe that they are justified in suppressing doctrinal error, blasphemy, and "immorality" by means of the civil law.

Confusion concerning the definition of terms, particularly the terms "obscenity" and "pornography," adds another interesting dimension to the study of religio-moral heresy. Although some communicators use the two terms interchangeably, the etymology of the words suggests that this is a development of the last 250 years. It began in the eighteenth century, when English judges began to apply the Latin *obscenus*—meaning "offensive" or "repulsive"—to erotic poems and stories. Contemporary speakers and writers would better reflect the original meanings by restricting their use of the term "obscene" to category 3 of Figure 5.1 (the profane and disgusting), while limiting their use of the term "pornographic" (from the Greek *pornographos,* which literally means "writing about harlots") to category 4 (the sensual and erotic). On the other hand, readers should keep in mind that the legal definition of "obscenity"—which once encompassed categories 3 (the profane and disgusting), 4 (the sensual and erotic), and 5 (scientific information about sex)—has been gradually narrowed over the years to focus primarily upon category 4. This development of the twentieth century was set in motion by the U.S. Supreme Court in the 1896 case of *Swearingen* v. *U.S.,* when the Court overturned the obscenity conviction of Swearingen for using crude language, observing that "obscenity" did not apply to coarse and vulgar language but was a concept reserved for the message "of immorality which has relation to sexual impurity."[3]

Before going into the specific issues and cases that have shaped laws concerning religio-moral heresy in the United States, an elaboration of Figure 5.1 is in order. The reader will note that the figure avoids using labels such as "blasphemy," "obscenity," and "pornography." Rather, an effort is made to point the reader to the *operational definition* underlying each of the categories; to this end the descriptive terms "false doctrine," "irreverence," and so on are employed. The key to the concept is the type of message *behind* the label; once the six different types of messages are understood, the labels can be applied with more precision and the resulting discussion of

---

[3]*Swearingen* v. *U.S.*, 161 U.S. 446 (1896).

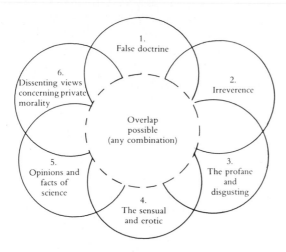

FIGURE 5.1.   *RELIGIO-MORAL HERESY:*
COMPONENTS AND PRIMARY
RELATIONSHIPS.

Development and Examples

1. *False doctrine* (often called religious
   heresy).
   a. The teachings of "pagan" religions.
   b. To the "established church," the
      teachings of Joseph Smith (Mormon).
   c. The agnosticism of Robert Ingersoll;
      the atheism of Madalyn M. O'Hair.
2. *Irreverence* or *impious speech* (often called
   blasphemy or *sacrilege*).
   a. Boccaccio's *Decameron,* for making fun
      of the clergy.
   b. In England, 1977, the *Gay News* was
      fined $1,700 for publishing a poem
      about a Roman centurion who had
      sexual relations with the body of the
      crucified Christ. The charge:
      blasphemy. (*Time,* July 25, 1977, p.
      54.)
   c. To some, the film *Life of Brian* (1979).
3. *Profane and disgusting speech* (cursing;
   "nasty" language; indecency).
   a. The profanity of General Patton in the
      film *Patton.*
   b. The slogan "Fuck the Draft" on the
      jacket worn by Paul Cohen (see
      Chapter 6, "Provocation to Anger").
   c. The language of George Carlin's
      monologue "Filthy Words."

4. *Sexual, sensual, and erotic communications*
   (often called *obscenity* or *pornography*).
   a. John Cleland's *Memoirs of a Woman of*
      Pleasure (Fanny Hill), published in
      England in the 1740s and containing
      no profanity or "four-letter words."
   b. Sensual and explicit descriptions of the
      sex act in modern novels.
   c. Films such as *Deep Throat* and *The*
      Devil in Miss Jones.
5. *Opinions and facts of science* (from sex
   education to the theory of evolution).
   a. Materials on birth control and family
      planning, such as Margaret Sanger's
      Family Limitation and Marie Stopes's
      Married Love and *Contraception.*
   b. Contemporary sex education books,
      such as *Show Me!* and *The Joy of Sex.*
   c. The views of science concerning
      creation and the universe; Darwin's
      Origin of the Species; Sagan's television
      series *Cosmos.*
6. *Dissenting views concerning private morality*
   (presented in a nonerotic way).
   a. Hugh Hefner's "Playboy philosophy,"
      argued over the years in *Playboy.*
   b. The opinion expressed by
      homosexuals that "gay is good."
   c. The viewpoint of some sexologists
      that "masturbation is good for you."

the issues clarified. To that end, the six categories can be further illustrated and explained as follows.

1. *False doctrine* (often called *heresy*). A message of false doctrine teaches an "incorrect" religious belief concerning the basic tenets of the faith. An example of a constraint upon the communication of false doctrine is found in the *General Laws and Liberties of the Massachusetts Colony* of 1646, which provided punishment for any "Christian within this jurisdiction" who denies "the immortality of the soul, or resurrection of the body," or who teaches that any of the books of the Bible are not the "infallible word of God."[4]

2. *Irreverence* (often called *blasphemy* or *sacrilege*). Irreverent expression includes that which reviles or curses the Deity or makes fun of religion. For example, some persons describe the films *Life of Brian* and *Wholly Moses!* as blasphemous because these persons believe that the films make fun of religion. In another instance, a group of Massachusetts citizens was offended when, in 1977, *National Lampoon* published a cartoon showing Mary, the mother of Jesus, being kicked out of her home by her father, thus suggesting that Jesus was born out of wedlock. A criminal proceeding was begun against the magazine under the state's blasphemy statute (which still remains on the law books), but the charge was dismissed by the judge.[5]

3. *Profane and disgusting speech* (historically the term "obscenity" fits here; however, in Anglo-American law the original meaning has been corrupted and "obscenity" has been transferred to category 4). One of the most celebrated examples of this category within recent years occurred in 1973, when comedian George Carlin's satirical monologue "Filthy Words" was broadcast uncut over WBAI, the Pacifica FM radio station in New York City. The monologue, which had been recorded during a live performance in California, concerns seven words that are not allowed on the public airwaves; namely, as Carlin puts it, "shit, piss, fuck, cunt, cocksucker, motherfucker, and tits." These words, says Carlin, "are the ones that will curve your spine, grow hair on your hands, and maybe even bring us, God help us, peace without honor, um, and a bourbon." In the course of the routine, the "forbidden words" are repeated numerous times. For example, Carlin says "shit" more than twenty times within the course of two or three minutes in such "humorous" lines as "You don't know shit from Shinola," and "I don't know whether to shit or wind my watch!" Upon complaint of a citizen, the Federal Communications Commission issued a warning order against the Pacifica station, and the Supreme Court upheld that order in a 1978 opinion. In the course of agreeing that the language used by Carlin was *indecent,* the Supreme Court made it clear that Carlin's monologue was *not* legally obscene.[6]

4. *The sensual and erotic* (often called *obscene* or *pornographic*). Sexual communications expressed in a warm, "sexy" way, employing

---

[4]Leo Pfeffer, *Religious Freedom* (Skokie, Ill.: National Textbook Company, 1977), pp. 5–6. Note: As an additional measure to keep the citizens from heretical temptation, Massachusetts also forbade Jesuits and Quakers from living within its borders.

[5]"Blasphemy," *Newsletter on Intellectual Freedom,* March 1978, pp. 38 and 41. For a thorough survey of blasphemy in Western culture to 1700, see Leonard W. Levy, *Treason Against God: A History of the Offense of Blasphemy* (New York: Schocken Books, 1981).

erotic language or pictorial representations or both, are the focus of this form of religio-moral heresy. Examples include explicit love scenes in literature, photographs of nudes, and sexually explicit paintings, films, and videotapes. Historically, the term "pornography" fits this form of expression; however, as explained above, it has been displaced by the term "obscenity" in Anglo-American law. The "crime of obscenity" concerns expression in this category, although most contemporary prosecutions are limited to *explicit* sexual language and visual images. Examples of this type of expression—although not all are legally obscene today—are the love scenes in D. H. Lawrence's novel *Lady Chatterley's Lover,* the nude scenes in the musical *Hair,* and films such as *Deep Throat, Misty Beethoven, The Greatest Little Cathouse in Las Vegas,* and *Debbie Does Dallas.*

5. *Scientific information and opinion.* This category covers two types of scientific messages: (a) those presenting information about human sexuality, including "sex education" materials on subjects such as intercourse, birth control, pregnancy, venereal diseases, abortion, and so on; and (b) those concerning nonsexual scientific theories about the universe, creation, and evolution. Expression in the first group was the target of an attempt by the U.S. Post Office to prevent the mailing of a Consumer's Union pamphlet entitled *Analysis of Contraceptive Materials* in the late 1930s and early 1940s. Finally, in 1944, the federal courts ordered the postal authorities to cease their efforts to apply the Comstock Act of 1873 to the educational pamphlet.[7] The second group is illustrated by the tribulations of Galileo, who, in the early seventeenth century, questioned the accepted view of the church concerning the nature of the universe. A more recent example is that of teacher John T. Scopes, convicted in 1925 of teaching the theory of evolution in the public schools of Tennessee in violation of a state law prohibiting such instruction (interestingly, the debate over the theory of evolution continues with gusto in some American communities).

6. *Dissenting views concerning private morality* (as a rule, expressed in a nonerotic way). Beliefs about private morality can range from questions about legalized gambling to those concerning drug use, the drinking of alcoholic beverages, or even cheating on an examination. The focus here, of course, is upon sexual morality and includes the advocacy of nonconforming opinions on subjects such as premarital sex, certain "forbidden" sex acts (such as oral sex), masturbation, homosexuality, group sex, and so on. In the past, even opinions favoring the right of divorce or the right of a divorced person to remarry were considered by some authorities of the church to be immoral. Contemporary examples of dissent covered by category 6 include the efforts of gay rights advocates to abolish laws making homosexual conduct a crime, opinions favoring a wide range of sexual experimentation by lovers, and the view that contraceptives should be made readily available to all who want them—even teenagers.

---

[6]*FCC* v. *Pacifica,* 438 U.S. 726 (1978). The monologue is from the album entitled *Occupational Foole,* issued by Little David Records as #LD-1005. For more on this case, see the chapter concerning broadcasting.

[7]"Behind the Reports," *Consumer Reports,* October 1979, p. 562. Note: This issue of *Consumer Reports* includes a lengthy review of condoms; no post office censorship was attempted in 1979.

An examination of how the courts have dealt with efforts to constrain expression based upon the six categories outlined above is now in order. Over the years the judiciary has subsumed the six into four areas of legal concern, as follows: (a) those cases that attend doctrinal error and irreverence (categories 1 and 2); (b) those cases that focus upon the ideas of science about the origins and development of life (category 5); (c) those cases that concern the advocacy of "immoral" ideas (category 6); and (d) those cases that relate to the expression of "sexually immoral" points of view, particularly if the viewpoint is presented in a sensual and erotic manner (categories 3, 4, 5, and 6)—a group blending into what the law classifies as "obscenity." Each of the four groups is now examined in light of the preceding analysis.

I. THE RELIGIO-MORAL HERESY OF BLASPHEMY

The question of teaching religious *doctrine* that is at variance with local majority opinion has rarely been a significant issue at law since the adoption of the Bill of Rights; evidently the Founding Fathers were effective in persuading the American people in general to allow the communication of various biblical interpretations provided that this was done in an "appropriate" and "reverent" manner. But irreverence, usually called "blasphemy" or "sacrilege," is another matter, for it concerns messages perceived as mocking or reviling God, Jesus Christ, or the basic beliefs of the Christian religion. As Chapter 2 recounts, one of the first instances of irreverence to come before the civil courts after the American Revolution was the 1811 case of a Mr. Ruggles, who was convicted in the New York courts of the common-law crime of blasphemy for having said that Jesus was a

"bastard" and his mother a "whore." In the process of convicting Ruggles, the judge announced that the state was not obligated to protect faiths other than Christianity, for other religions, such as those of "Mahomet or of the Grand Lama," are "imposters."[8] A few years later, in 1834, Abner Kneeland was convicted of blasphemy by the courts of Boston for having circulated irreligious remarks in a newspaper.

Not all efforts to prosecute persons for blasphemy ended early in the nation's history. In 1928 a warrant was issued but never served in Massachusetts for the arrest of Horace M. Kallen, a well-known educator, for having uttered the "blasphemous" remark that "If Sacco and Vanzetti were anarchists, so also were Socrates and Jesus Christ." In that same year an atheist missionary was convicted in Arkansas of the crime of "ridiculing the Christian religion" because of the content of the atheist literature he was distributing.[9] And in Massachusetts in 1977 the Senate voted to retain the state's seventeenth-century blasphemy law on the books after religious fundamentalists in the Commonwealth insisted that it not be removed. By a vote of 26 to 13, the senators agreed to keep the following law in the Massachusetts criminal code:

> Whoever wilfully blasphemes the holy name of God by denying, cursing or contumeliously reproaching God, his creation, government or final judging of the world, or by cursing or contumeliously reproaching Jesus Christ or the Holy Ghost, or by cursing or contumeliously reproaching or exposing to contempt and ridicule, the holy word of God contained in the holy scriptures shall be punished by imprison-

[8]Leo Pfeffer, *Church, State and Freedom,* rev. ed. (Boston: Beacon Press, 1967), p. 665.
[9]Ibid., p. 663.

ment in jail for not more than one year or by a fine of not more than $300, and may also be bound to good behavior.[10]

The Supreme Court of the United States has never ruled on an appeal in which the issues of false doctrine or blasphemy have been the central questions at bar. However, the Court has indirectly decided the matter by its findings in the New York film censorship case of *Burstyn* v. *Wilson* (1952). Although the case reached the Court as a challenge to the film censorship laws of the Empire State, the opinion is equally significant to the question of the First Amendment's protection for "irreligious" ideas. Whereas the Court allowed the practice of the prior restraint of movies to continue in effect in New York, it did strike down the specific application of that practice to the film in question. An examination of the religious heresy addressed by the Court in *Burstyn* is revealing.

In November of 1950 the Italian film *The Miracle,* directed by Roberto Rossellini and starring Anna Magnani, was licensed by the New York State Board of Regents for distribution within the state of New York. A public outcry followed immediately because of charges that the Italian-language film, shown with English subtitles, was "sacrilegious." In February of 1951 the regents revoked the license for the film, and a court challenge was the result.

The Miracle, considered by many to be a religious film with a pious message, concerns a simple-minded woman (played by Magnani) who tends goats in the fields near a small Italian village and becomes pregnant by a bearded stranger whom she believes to be St. Joseph. She views her pregnancy as a miraculous gift from God and, upon informing

the citizens of the village of the "miracle," is treated variously with humor, ridicule, and physical torment. To escape her persecutors, the young woman hides in a nearby cave until she is about to give birth. She then slips back into town and into the church, where her baby is born. The film, which lasts forty minutes, ends with the new mother reaching for her "miracle" child while murmuring "My son! My love! My flesh!" The censorship action of the regents was upheld by the courts of the state of New York, but upon appeal it was reversed by the Supreme Court of the United States. In the process of reversing the courts below, the nation's highest tribunal issued a firm and unanimous opinion about state efforts to prohibit or punish irreligious messages.

Justice Clark, speaking for the Court, first reviewed the history of the controversy caused by efforts to show *The Miracle* in the motion picture theaters of the state of New York. In the process, as noted in the summary above, he announced that, effective with this case, the protection of the First Amendment was extended to films, an issue discussed further in Chapter 9 under "prior restraint." He then addressed the issue of blasphemy raised by the film in question.

Justice Clark *delivered the opinion of the Court:*

New York's highest court says there is "nothing mysterious" about the statutory provision applied in this case: "It is simply this: that no religion, as that word is understood by the ordinary, reasonable person, shall be treated with contempt, mockery, scorn and ridicule . . . ." This is far from the kind of narrow exception to freedom of expression which a state may carve out to satisfy the adverse demands of other interests of society. In seeking to apply the broad and all-inclusive definition of "sacrilegious" given by the New York courts, the censor is set adrift upon a boundless sea

---

[10]"Blasphemy," *Newsletter on Intellectual Freedom,* March 1978, p. 38.

FIGURE 5.2. ANNA MAGNANI IN A SCENE FROM THE MIRACLE. *This scene from the Italian film* The Miracle *shows Anna Magnani (center foreground) as the simple-minded peasant woman whose belief that her pregnancy is a miracle calls forth comments of derision and ridicule from fellow villagers. When the film was banned by New York authorities on the grounds of sacrilegiousness, the case was appealed to the U.S. Supreme Court. The Court's unanimous decision of 1952, in the case of* Burstyn v. Wilson, *reversed the ban and asserted that in America the government should not be in the business of suppressing "real or imagined attacks upon a particular religious doctrine."* Bettmann Archive.

amid a myriad of conflicting currents of religious views, with no charts but those provided by the most vocal and powerful orthodoxies. New York cannot vest such unlimited restraining control over motion pictures in a censor. . . . Under such a standard the most careful and tolerant censor would find it virtually impossible to avoid favoring one religion over another, and he would be subject to an inevitable tendency to ban the expression of unpopular sentiments sacred to a religious minority. Application of the "sacrilegious" test, in these or other respects, might raise substantial questions under the First Amendment's guaranty of separate church and state with freedom of worship for all. However, from the standpoint of freedom of speech and the press, it is enough to point out that the state has no legitimate interest in protecting any or all religions from views

distasteful to them which is sufficient to justify prior restraints upon the expression of those views. **It is not the business of government in our nation to suppress real or imagined attacks upon a particular religious doctrine, whether they appear in publications, speeches, or motion pictures.**

Conservative Justice Felix Frankfurter, in a lengthy concurring opinion, was at times even more outspoken than was Justice Clark in asserting that the states had no authority to punish religious dissent by classifying such dissent as "sacrilegious" or "blasphemous." (His survey of the history of blasphemy laws from ancient times to the present and his etymological review are recommended to those who wish to study the issue further.)

Burstyn v. Wilson, 343 U.S. 495 (1952)
Decided May 26, 1952

Vote: 9 to 0 to reverse New York's ban on the showing of *The Miracle.*

Majority Opinion By: Justice Clark.

Concurring Justices: Chief Justice Vinson and Justices Black, Reed, Frankfurter, Douglas, Jackson, Burton, and Minton.

Dissenting Justices: (none)

Justices Not Participating: (none)

Summary: The Italian film *The Miracle,* concerning a simple-minded peasant woman who believes that her illegitimate child was fathered by St. Joseph and that the child is a miraculous gift from God, was licensed by the New York censors in 1950; however, the license was revoked fourteen months later because of charges that the film was "sacrilegious." The courts of New York upheld the revocation, but the U.S. Supreme Court unanimously reversed. While permitting New York's system of film licensing to remain in operation, the Supreme Court ruled that under the U.S. Constitution, states could not censor a communication simply on the ground of its being irreligious (i.e., "blasphemous" or "sacrilegious").

Rule Established; Significance of Case: This case is significant for two reasons. *First,* it makes clear that blasphemy is not a constitutional basis for the suppression of ideas in the United States. *Second,* it explicitly reverses the 1915 decision in *Mutual Film* v. *Ohio Industrial Commission* (which declared that film did not merit the protection of the First Amendment) and announced that "liberty of expression by means of motion pictures is guaranteed" by the Constitution.

Justice Frankfurter concluded his tongue-lashing of the New York authorities by observing that conduct and beliefs "dear to one may seem the rankest 'sacrilege' to another. . . . History does not encourage reliance on the wisdom and moderation of the censor" when the message in question concerns religion. "We not only do not know but cannot know what is condemnable by 'sacrilegious.' And if we cannot tell, how are those to be governed by the [New York statute in question] . . . to tell?"

Although the decision of the Supreme Court in *Burstyn* was determinative in the religio-moral area only in finding prior restraint upon the communication of messages because of alleged sacrilegious content to be unconstitutional, the strong language in the opinions of Justices Clark and Frankfurter suggests that they wished to settle more. As

Leo Pfeffer observes in his authoritative study of church and state in America, the decision in *Burstyn* leaves little doubt that if the issue of blasphemy law were squarely put to the Supreme Court, "it would hold all blasphemy statutes unconstitutional."[11]

II. THE RELIGIO-MORAL HERESY OF DARWINISM

In 1925, in response to the fundamentalist fervor of the 1920s, the Tennessee legislature adopted a statute making it a crime to teach the theory of evolution in the public schools. By so doing, the Tennesseans rekindled in the twentieth century a controversy reminis-

---

[11]Pfeffer, p. 675.

cent of Galileo's tribulations with the Catholic church in the early 1600s as well as those that some scientists had experienced at the hands of various clergymen since that time. Even Thomas Jefferson encountered the issue when, in 1814, he attempted to secure a French scientific treatise concerning the creation of the world from his Philadelphia book agent, only to discover that the book was the object of state censorship. (Jefferson did receive his book, for it was shipped directly to him by the author, M. de Becourt.) Upon learning of the efforts to suppress the treatise, Jefferson wrote the Philadelphia book dealer as follows:

> I am really mortified to be told that, *in the United States of America,* a . . . science book can become a subject of inquiry, and of criminal inquiry too, as an offence against religion; that a question about the sale of a book can be carried before the civil magistrate. Is this then our freedom of religion? and are we to have a censor whose imprimatur shall say what books may be sold, and what we may buy? And who is thus to dogmatize religious opinions for our citizens? Whose foot is to be the measure to which ours are all to be cut or stretched? Is a priest to be our inquisitor, or shall a layman, simple as ourselves, set up his reason as the rule for what we are to read, and what we must believe? It is an insult to our citizens to question whether they are rational beings or not, and blasphemy against religion to suppose it cannot stand the test of truth and reason. If M. de Becourt's book be false in its facts, disprove them; if false in its reasoning, refute it. But, for God's sake, let us freely hear both sides, if we choose. . . .[12]

The 1925 Tennessee antievolution statute, which soon became known as the "monkey law," became the subject of national and international interest when it was enforced to prevent public school biology teacher John T. Scopes from teaching Darwinism to his students. For attempting to communicate the religio-moral heresy of the theory of evolution to those in his classroom, Scopes was indicted and tried in a widely publicized trial, featuring orator William Jennings Bryan for the prosecution and attorney Clarence Darrow for the defense. The case ended with a conviction, and teacher Scopes was fined $100; upon appeal, the Supreme Court of Tennessee upheld the constitutionality of the "monkey law" (the case did not reach the U.S. Supreme Court) but voided the $100 fine on technical grounds. In addition, the Supreme Court of Tennessee announced that for the "peace and dignity of the State" Scopes would not be prosecuted further.[13]

Not to be outdone by their dedicated "brothers and sisters" to the east, a group of antievolution fundamentalists in Arkansas proposed a law similar to the one in Tennessee and managed to get their proposal on the ballot for a statewide referendum in 1928. The Arkansas "monkey law" campaign was waged on simple either-or terms—heaven versus hell, religion versus irreligion, Christians versus sinners. As one procensorship advertisement put it:

> THE BIBLE OR ATHEISM, WHICH? All atheists favor evolution. If you agree with atheism vote against Act No. 1. If you agree with the Bible vote for Act No. 1 . . . . Shall conscientious church members be forced to pay taxes to support teachers to teach evolution which will undermine the faith of their children? The [*Arkan-*

---

[12]Letter to N. G. Dufief, April 19, 1814. Thomas Jefferson, *The Writing of Thomas Jefferson,* ed. Andrew A. Lipscomb and Albert E. Bergh, vol. 14 (Washington, D.C.: The Thomas Jefferson Memorial Association, 1904), pp. 126–129.

[13]*Epperson* v. *Arkansas,* 393 U.S. 97 (1968), at 98, note 2.

sas] *Gazette* said Russian Bolshevists laughed at Tennessee. True, and that sort will laugh at Arkansas. Who cares? Vote FOR ACT NO. 1.[14]

Arkansas's 1928 antievolution law did not meet a court challenge until the mid-1960s, when Susan Epperson, a young biology teacher in the Little Rock, Arkansas, public schools, was provided with a text that included a chapter setting forth the theory that humans evolved from a "lower form of animal." Aware of the 1928 act that forbade any public school teacher "to teach the theory of doctrine that mankind ascended or descended from a lower order of animals," Epperson decided to seek a court determination of the matter so that she and others in her position around the state would know how they stood before the law if they taught from the prescribed textbook (the opinion of Justice Fortas for the U.S. Supreme Court, discussed below, suggests that Epperson *favored* the right of the biologist to teach the theory of evolution in the public schools). The state's chancery court declared the law unconstitutional, but the Arkansas Supreme Court disagreed and reinstated the law on the simple basis that the issue was one of the curriculum and that the state had the right to specify what was to be taught in the public schools. Biologist Epperson then turned to the U.S. Supreme Court.

Justice Abe Fortas authored the opinion of the Court and in the process explained why the antievolution act of 1928 was a violation of the U.S. Constitution. "There is and can be no doubt that the First Amendment does not permit the State to require that teaching and learning must be tailored to the principles or prohibitions of any religious sect or dogma," commented Justice Fortas. "While

study of religions and of the Bible from a literary and historic viewpoint, presented objectively as part of a secular program of education, need not collide with the First Amendment's prohibition," he continued, "the State may not adopt programs or practices in its public schools or colleges which 'aid or oppose' any religion." He then added with emphasis, "This prohibition is absolute. It forbids alike the preference of a religious doctrine or the prohibition of theory which is deemed antagonistic to a particular dogma."

Justice Fortas then cited the dean of the University of Arkansas School of Law to the effect that antievolution laws are founded historically upon the "typical blasphemy statute" and are thus "ideological" in that they attempt by censorship to "punish the presentation of intellectually significant matter which contradicts accepted social, moral or religious ideas."[15] He then reached the conclusion of his argument.

Justice Fortas *delivered the opinion of the Court:*

In the present case, there can be no doubt that Arkansas has sought to prevent its teachers from discussing the theory of evolution because it is contrary to the belief of some that the Book of Genesis must be the exclusive source of doctrine as to the origin of man. No suggestion has been made that Arkansas' law may be justified by considerations of state policy other than the religious views of some of its citizens. It is clear that fundamentalist sectarian conviction was and is the law's reason for existence. Its antecedent, Tennessee's "monkey law," candidly stated its purpose: to make it unlawful "to teach any theory that denies the story of the Divine Creation of man as taught in the Bible, and to teach instead that man has descended from a lower order of animals." Perhaps the sensational publicity attendant upon the *Scopes* trial

[14]Ibid., at 108, note 16.

[15]Ibid., at 107–108, note 15.

Epperson v. Arkansas, 393 U.S. 97 (1968)
Decided November 12, 1968

Vote: 9 to 0 declaring the Arkansas antievolution law unconstitutional.

Majority Opinion By: Justice Fortas.

Concurring Justices: Chief Justice Warren and Justices Black, Douglas, Harlan, Brennan, Stewart, White, and Marshall.

Dissenting Justices: (none)

Justices Not Participating: (none)

Summary: Arkansas' 1928 antievolution law prohibited any teacher in the public schools from teaching the theory that "mankind ascended or descended from a lower order of animals." In 1968, biology teacher Susan Epperson challenged the law in the courts to determine whether or not she could legally use a chapter on evolution in a new biology text prescribed by the school system of Little Rock, Arkansas. The Supreme Court of Arkansas upheld the "monkey law" as a legitimate exercise of the power of the state to determine the public school curriculum; on appeal, the U.S. Supreme Court reversed the Arkansas court and declared the antievolution law unconstitutional as an infringement upon the First Amendment's prohibition concerning statutes which function to establish a particular religion.

Rule Established; Significance of Case: This important decision makes clear that no level of government in the United States has the right to censor the teaching of scientific fact and opinion in tax-supported schools on the basis that the teachings are in conflict with the religious beliefs of the majority in the community. Although the ruling was based primarily upon the establishment clause of the First Amendment, its practical effect is to assure the free-speech rights of teachers and students of science in public institutions of learning.

induced Arkansas to adopt less explicit language. It eliminated Tennessee's reference to "the story of the Divine Creation of man" as taught in the Bible, but there is no doubt that the motivation for the law was the same: to suppress the teaching of a theory which, it was thought, "denied" the divine creation of man.

Arkansas' law cannot be defended as an act of religious neutrality. Arkansas did not seek to excise from the curricula of its schools and universities all discussion of the origin of man. The law's effort was confined to an attempt to blot out a particular theory because of its supposed conflict with the Biblical account, literally read. Plainly, the law is contrary to the mandate of the First, and in violation of the Fourteenth, Amendment to the Constitution.

The judgment of the Supreme Court of Arkansas is *Reversed.*

Having lost the fight to prohibit the communication of scientific viewpoints which they consider to be religious heresy, the anti-evolution censors have recently developed a strategy of *compelled* speech. According to this approach, if the theory of evolution is taught in the schools, equal time must be given to the biblical account of creation as told in the book of Genesis. The label given to the biblical account by those favoring the compelled-speech approach is "creation science." In 1981 and 1982, several state legislatures considered bills to require that "creation science" be taught in all science classes where theories of natural selection and evolution were considered. Arkansas was one state that enacted such a law. The ensuing legal challenge, brought by a number of rep-

FIGURE 5.3.   CHARLES DARWIN.

FIGURE 5.4.   SUSAN EPPERSON.
English naturalist Charles Darwin (above left) started a worldwide controversy over the origin and development of life on earth when he published his Origin of Species *in 1859. The controversy continues in modern times, as Arkansas biology teacher Susan Epperson (above right) discovered when she submitted the state's law against the teaching of evolution to the courts for a determination of its constitutionality. In the 1968 U.S. Supreme Court case of* Epperson v. Arkansas, *the young teacher won a significant victory for academic freedom, for the Court declared the Arkansas statute unconstitutional.*
Darwin, *from* Harper's Weekly, *April 8, 1871.*
Epperson, *the* Arkansas Gazette.

resentatives of various Christian and Jewish organizations who argued that the law required the teaching of religion and was thus unconstitutional, was heard in the U.S. District Court for the Eastern District of Arkansas. Following the trial, District Judge Overton declared the law in violation of the establishment clause of the First Amendment.[16] "The only inference that can be drawn from the circumstances," Judge Overton observed, "is that the statute was passed with the specific purpose of advancing religion." This is especially true, he emphasized, for the "statute lacks legitimate education value because 'creation science' as defined in the statute is simply not science." The "excessive government entanglement with reli-

gion" which is inevitable under the law renders it unconstitutional, he concluded. For the time being, at least, Judge Overton's unequivocal rejection of "creation science" laws seems to have cooled the fervor of those who favor compelled teaching of religion in the science classes of the nation's public schools.

[16]*McLean* v. *Arkansas Board of Education,* 50 *Law Week* 2412 (1982).

Kingsley International Pictures v. Regents, 360 U.S. 684 (1959)
Decided June 29, 1959

Vote: 9 to 0 for reversal of the courts of New York that had sustained the regents; in effect, the film in question must be licensed.

Majority Opinion By: Justice Stewart.

Concurring Justices: Chief Justice Warren and Justices Black, Frankfurter, Douglas, Clark, Harlan, Brennan, and Whittaker.

Dissenting Justices: (none)

Justices Not Participating: (none)

Summary: The licensing board of the state of New York refused a permit for the film *Lady Chatterley's Lover* even though there were no explicit sex scenes in the movie. In support of their decision, the members of the board cited a New York law which made it illegal to show a film "of such a character that its exhibition would tend to corrupt morals . . . or which portrays acts of sexual immorality . . . as desirable, acceptable or proper patterns of behavior." Since there was no "obscenity" in the film, the United States Supreme Court viewed the decision of the licensers as an effort to suppress *ideas* about private morality and thus rejected the censorship effort.

Rule Established; Significance of Case: In this case, the U.S. Supreme Court determined by a unanimous vote that nonconforming points of view concerning private sexual morality are considered protected speech under the Constitution provided that those viewpoints are communicated in a nonobscene way. As Justice Stewart said in his opinion of the Court, the Constitution "protects advocacy of the opinion that adultery may sometimes be proper, no less than advocacy of socialism or the single tax."

III. THE RELIGIO-MORAL HERESY OF "IMMORAL" IDEAS

In 1959, in yet another film censorship case from the state of New York, the U.S. Supreme Court (as in *Burstyn*) unanimously turned back the censors. This case involved a nonobscene film (there were no explicit sex scenes, the love affair being implied but not shown) based upon the D. H. Lawrence novel *Lady Chatterley's Lover.* Because the movie was clear in revealing that an adulterous relationship existed between Lady Chatterley and her gamekeeper, the New York review board refused to issue a license. The legal fight that followed ended up on the nation's court of last resort.

Following his review of the facts of the case, Justice Potter Stewart addressed the central issue raised by this controversy as seen by the justices of the Court—the suppression of *ideas.* At this point, students of the First Amendment should be aware that some censors classify as obscene not only explicit sexual descriptions and pictorial representations but also *ideas and arguments* that do not conform to society's accepted views concerning private sexual conduct. A leading proponent of this school of thought is Ernest Van Den Haag, professor of social philosophy at New York University, who in a 1962 essay defines as *obscene* any "suggestion or argument in favour of heterodox attitudes about sexual matters."[17] The classification

[17]Ernest Van Den Haag, "Quia Ineptum," in *"To Deprave and Corrupt": Original Studies in the Nature and Definition of "Obscenity,"* ed. John Chandos (New York: Association Press, 1962), p. 117.

applies, even though the argument is presented without resort to "four-letter words." It was to this line of reasoning that the Supreme Court spoke in *Kingsley* v. *Regents.*

Justice Stewart *delivered the opinion of the Court:*

What New York has done, therefore, is to prevent the exhibition of a motion picture because that picture advocates an idea—that adultery under certain circumstances may be proper behavior. Yet the First Amendment's basic guarantee is of freedom to advocate ideas. The State, quite simply, has thus struck at the very heart of constitutionally protected liberty.

It is contended that the State's action was justified because the motion picture attractively portrays a relationship which is contrary to the moral standards, the religious precepts, and the legal code of its citizenry. This argument misconceives what it is that the Constitution protects. Its guarantee is not confined to the expression of ideas that are conventional or shared by the majority. It protects advocacy of the opinion that adultery may sometimes be proper, no less than advocacy of socialism or the single tax. And in the realm of ideas it protects expression which is eloquent no less than that which is unconvincing.

Advocacy of conduct proscribed by law is not, as Mr. Justice Brandeis long ago pointed out [in *Whitney* v. *California,* 1927], "a justification for denying free speech where the advocacy falls short of incitement and there is nothing to indicate that the advocacy would be immediately acted on. . . . Among free men, the deterrents ordinarily to be applied to prevent crime are education and punishment for violation of the law, not abridgment of the rights of free speech. . . ."

Blasphemy, Darwinism, and "Immoral" Ideas in Brief

Each of the attempts by powerful forces in society to suppress the religio-moral heresies

considered to this point have been turned back by unanimous votes of the justices of the U.S. Supreme Court. In review, the Court ruled as follows:

1. *Burstyn* v. *Wilson,* 1952 (the effort in New York to prevent the showing of the film *The Miracle* on grounds of false doctrine and blasphemy; see Figure 5.1, categories 1 and 2): the Supreme Court ruled that it is "not the business of government in our nation to suppress real or imagined attacks upon a particular religious doctrine, whether they appear in publications, speeches, or motion pictures."

2. *Epperson* v. *Arkansas,* 1968 (concerning a biology teacher's challenge to an Arkansas law which made it illegal to teach the theory of evolution in tax-supported schools; see Figure 5.1, category 5): the Supreme Court ruled that the Arkansas "monkey law" was an attempt "to blot out a particular theory because of its supposed conflict with the Biblical account, literally read. Plainly, the law is contrary to the mandate of the First . . . Amendment to the Constitution."

3. *Kingsley International Pictures* v. *Regents,* 1959 (another New York film case in which the nonobscene movie version of *Lady Chatterley's Lover* was denied a license because it allegedly portrayed sexual "immorality" in a manner so as to "corrupt morals"; see Figure 5.1, category 6): the Supreme Court firmly rejected the position of the New York authorities, asserting that since the censors were attempting to suppress the *idea* that "adultery under certain circumstances may be proper behavior" and since the "First Amendment's basic guarantee is of freedom to advocate ideas," the State of New York had "quite simply . . . struck at the very heart of constitutionally protected liberty."

Because of these clear-cut decisions of the

Supreme Court, the public communicator in the United States has the constitutional freedom to criticize the religious doctrines and positions of the majority, to teach the theories of science (including various theories of evolution) in tax-supported schools, and to advocate ideas concerning sexual conduct that are at variance with accepted opinions. These viewpoints and criticisms, however, must be communicated in a "nonobscene" way—a constraint that has a particular application to the advocacy of ideas concerning sexual behavior—or else risk prosecution by the state or federal criminal justice systems. Perhaps the church representatives in Valdosta, Georgia, who in 1979 tried to stop the showing of the *Life of Brian* (as discussed at the beginning of this chapter), were aware that charges of blasphemy would not pass constitutional muster because of the court decisions reviewed above. Therefore, the only "actionable" heresy they could urge upon the judge was obscenity. On this basis the film was restrained for a brief period until the judge determined that no obscenity as defined by the U.S. Supreme Court was involved, and the ban was lifted. The church representatives were correct in their central point, however, for obscenity remains an offense at law, First Amendment or no First Amendment—the judges of the United States Supreme Court have told the nation so. As the following analysis illustrates, the unanimity of the judges in defense of freedom of expression in *Burstyn, Epperson,* and *Kingsley* is shattered when the "heresy of obscenity" is at bar.

IV. THE RELIGIO-MORAL HERESY OF "OBSCENITY"

On May 27, 1867, an English metal broker and outspoken anti-Catholic named Henry Scott appealed a conviction from the court of the borough of Wolverhampton, in which he had been found guilty of violating the Obscene Publications Act of 1857 (sometimes called "Lord Campbell's Act," after its author—see Chapter 1) for distributing immoral publications. The material in question was actually an anti-Catholic pamphlet with the weighty title *The Confessional Unmasked; Shewing the Depravity of the Romish Priesthood, the Iniquity of the Confessional, and the Questions Put to Females in Confession* (the pamphlet is usually referred to simply as *The Confessional Unmasked*). As a result of the appeal, Recorder Benjamin Hicklin, whose name the case bears, decided that the pamphlet was not legally obscene because it was intended as an anti-Catholic message; he ordered the publications returned to Scott pending a final decision by the Court of Queen's Bench. Because of the explicit sexual descriptions contained in the pamphlets, however, the Court of Queen's Bench disagreed with Recorder Hicklin and affirmed the trial court's finding that the publications were obscene. In the process of making this determination, Lord Chief Justice Cockburn announced the influential "Hicklin rule": *"The test of obscenity is this, whether the tendency of the matter charged as obscenity is to deprave and corrupt those whose minds are open to such immoral influences, and into whose hands a publication of this sort may fall."*[18] Thus, from a pamphlet that some would describe as "blasphemy" against the Catholic religion came the English definition of obscenity that was eventually adopted by judges in American courts and which was affirmed as the acceptable definition by the U.S. Supreme

---

[18]*Regina* v. *Hicklin* (1868), cited in Haig A. Bosmajian, comp., *Obscenity and Freedom of Expression* (New York: Burt Franklin and Company, 1976), p. 1.

Court in the 1896 decision of *Rosen* v. *United States* (discussed in Chapter 2).

From *Rosen* to *Roth:* The Growing Censorship Debate

In order to follow the major legal developments of the sixty years between the Supreme Court's *Rosen* decision (in which the Hicklin rule was adopted) and the landmark case of *Roth* v. *United States* (1957, in which the Hicklin rule was officially replaced by the *Roth* test), the student of communication rights needs to be familiar with two threads of the controversy, namely: (1) the erosion of the Hicklin rule's influence in American courts and (2) the emerging framework of judicial tests for obscenity, announced by various judges at various judicial levels and in a variety of cases, which provided the philosophical context for the formulation of the *Roth* standard in 1957. Each of these two "threads" is now summarized.

The Erosion of the Hicklin Rule

As a quick analysis of the Hicklin rule reveals, the effect of the test is to make obscene any work that has *isolated passages* which judges or jurors might decide would "deprave" or "corrupt" *a child* ("into whose hands a publication of this sort may fall"). The test does not allow for consideration of the work as a whole; neither does it recognize that some communications not suitable for children might be quite acceptable for an adult audience. Little wonder, then, that early in the twentieth century judges began to question this standard, established in England in 1868. One of those who disagreed with the Hicklin principle was Judge Learned Hand, who, in a 1913 censorship case, observed, "I hope it is not improper for me to say that the [Hicklin] rule as laid down, however consonant it may be with mid-Victorian

morals, does not seem to me to answer to the understanding and morality of the present time, as conveyed by the words, 'obscene, lewd, or lascivious.'" Proceeding to find the materials in question *not* legally obscene, Judge Hand further noted that the Hicklin rule reduced society's "treatment of sex to the standard of a child's library."[19]

In 1933, U.S. District Judge John Woolsey, who obviously agreed with the position of Judge Hand, rejected attempts of U.S. Customs to prohibit the importation of James Joyce's *Ulysses* on obscenity grounds. In ruling that the novel was not legally obscene, Judge Woolsey made three specific changes in the Hicklin rule's definition of obscenity: (1) the materials in question must be judged in their entirety (not by isolated passages); (2) the material must "stir the sex impulses" or "lead to sexually impure and lustful thoughts" (no longer would the terms to "deprave" and "corrupt" morals apply); and (3) the alleged sexual stirrings must be judged according to a "person with average sex instincts" (not the most susceptible person, such as a child).[20] The U.S. Court of Appeals sustained Judge Woolsey's decision and in the process asserted that the Hicklin standard adopted in *Rosen* was no longer an acceptable rule of law, particularly since its application would exclude many of the "great works of literature."[21] In the eyes of numerous jurists, the authority of the Hicklin rule was greatly diminished by the *Ulysses* decisions of 1933 and 1934, even though the case did not reach the Supreme Court. Finally, in the 1957 case of *Butler* v. *Michigan* (which was announced prior to *Roth*), the U.S. Supreme Court unanimously declared a Michigan statute

[19]*United States* v. *Kennerley,* 209 F. 119 (1913).
[20]*United States* v. *One Book Called "Ulysses,"* 5 F. Supp. 182 (S.D.N.Y. 1933).
[21]*United States* v. *Ulysses,* 72 F.2d 705 (1934).

based on the Hicklin rule to be unconstitutional.[22] Justice Frankfurter in his opinion for the Court noted that the Michigan statute banning books "manifestly tending to the corruption of the morals of youth" was too restrictive, for it reduces "the adult population of Michigan to reading only what is fit for children."

The Merging Framework of Judicial Tests: The Foundation Is Laid for Roth

As the Hicklin rule faded into obscurity, a variety of ad hoc censorship rulings were announced in various state and federal courts throughout the nation. But since there was no binding decision forthcoming from the U.S. Supreme Court on the issue, the outcome of the cases depended to a large extent upon the inclinations of the individual judge or judges in the case. In 1942 the Supreme Court did decide an important case that eventually influenced the way in which it defined obscenity. This 1942 decision was not about obscenity but concerned the "fighting words" used by Jehovah's Witness Chaplinsky when he became angry and cursed the police of Rochester, New Hampshire.[23] In upholding the conviction of Chaplinsky, the Supreme Court put into place a two-level standard for judging constitutionally protected expression, which was later to become an important factor in the Court's strategy for dealing with erotic expression. Justice Murphy, speaking for the Court in *Chaplinsky,* announced that there are certain utterances which "are no essential part of any exposition of ideas, and are of such slight social value as a step to truth" that they do not deserve the protection of the Constitution. In-

cluded in this category of *worthless* expression are *obscenity,* profanity, defamation, and insulting or "fighting" words. (No attempt is made by Justice Murphy to define "obscenity" in the *Chaplinsky* decision.) The resulting two levels can be described as follows. At the first level is *worthwhile* expression, which contains ideas and is, therefore, deserving of protection by the First Amendment; at the second level, however, is *worthless* expression—that which, according to the Court, is so useless to society, so lacking in ideas, and so valueless that it simply is not "speech" as the Constitution means the term and is not even tested by the standard judicial tests, such as clear and present danger or balancing. The student should look for the inclusion of this concept in the *Roth* decision, soon to be discussed.

In lower-court cases concerning obscenity, two general points of view were expressed. The *first* was that the "dirt for dirt's sake" and "lustful" appeal of erotic materials provided an adequate basis for censorship—no threat to society need be proved (this merges with the "worthless expression" concept in the two-level theory, for such "dirty expression" supposedly has no value). The *second* point of view demanded more than a showing of appeal to lusts. As Judge Curtis Bok argued in the Pennsylvania state case of *Commonwealth* v. *Gordon* (where he found *Sanctuary, Wild Palms, God's Little Acre, Studs Lonigan,* and other literature *not* obscene), in addition to the calculated excitement of sexual desire, to be legally obscene a communication *must create a danger of incitement to criminal conduct.* Judge Bok, in effect, applied the clear-and-present-danger test to the question, stating that there must be "a reasonable and demonstrable cause to believe that a crime or misdemeanor has been committed or is about to be committed as the perceptible result of the publication and distribution of the writ-

---

[22]*Butler* v. *Michigan,* 352 U.S. 380 (1957).
[23]*Chaplinsky* v. *New Hampshire,* 315 U.S. 568 (1942). Note: For more on this case, see Chapter 6, "Provocation to Anger."

ing in question. . . . The causal connection between the book and the criminal behavior must appear beyond a reasonable doubt."[24]

Lacking a definitive ruling from the United States Supreme Court, disparate and unpredictable standards for determining obscenity were applied by police, prosecutors, judges, and juries in various parts of the country. To illustrate the problem, the following materials were the objects of obscenity prosecutions in the United States between 1934 (when the U.S. Court of Appeals agreed with Judge Woolsey that *Ulysses* was not obscene) and 1957 (the year of the Supreme Court's landmark *Roth* decision): Radclyffe Hall's *The Well of Loneliness,* Henry Miller's *Tropic of Cancer* and *Tropic of Capricorn,* a songbook compiled by Eric Posselt entitled *Give Out: Songs Of, For and By the Men in the Service,* Frank Harris' *My Secret Life,* Edmund Wilson's *Memoirs of Hecate County,* William Faulkner's *Mosquitoes,* Lillian Smith's *Strange Fruit,* Dr. Alan F. Guttmacher's *The Complete Book of Birth Control,* Ernest Hemingway's *To Have and Have Not* and *For Whom the Bell Tolls,* Erskine Caldwell's *Tobacco Road,* Vivian Connell's *The Chinese Room,* and John O'Hara's *Appointment in Samarra.*[25] Obviously, there existed a pressing need for the Supreme Court to clarify the constitutional issues related to censorship, and in 1957—eighty-four years after the passage of the Comstock Act—the Court ruled.

The Landmark Case of *Roth* v. *United States* (1957)

In the mid-1950s Samuel Roth, a New York businessman who published and sold books,

magazines, and photographs, was convicted in a jury trial in the U.S. District Court for the Southern District of New York for mailing obscene circulars and advertising in violation of the federal Comstock Act. His conviction was affirmed by the U.S. Court of Appeals for the Second Circuit, whereupon he appealed to the U.S. Supreme Court, which granted certiorari. Despite the strong suggestion of Circuit Judge Jerome Frank in his reluctant concurring opinion at the appeals level that the time had come for Victorian obscenity laws to be invalidated in the United States, the Supreme Court disagreed and by a vote of 6 to 3 sustained the conviction of Roth.[26] In this decision, which for the first time upheld the constitutionality of the obscenity provisions of the nineteenth-century Comstock Act, the Supreme Court (1) accepted the principle that obscenity was a type of worthless speech and thereby (2) rejected Judge Bok's argument in *Commonwealth* v. *Gordon* (1949) that a clear and present danger must be created by the erotica and that a causal connection to actual criminal *behavior* must be demonstrated. In effect, a value-laden moral approach rather than a degree-of-danger principle was followed.

Justice William Brennan, who had only recently been appointed to the Supreme Court by President Eisenhower and who became the Court's leading spokesman in support of obscenity laws over the next sixteen years (but who early in the 1970s changed his mind and dissented passionately from Chief Justice

---

[24]*Commonwealth* v. *Gordon,* 66 D.&C. 101 (1949).

[25]Ann Lyon Haight and Chandler B. Grannis, *Banned Books: 387* B.C. *to 1978* A.D., 4th ed. (New York: Bowker, 1978), pp. 71 ff.

[26]*Roth* v. *United States* and *Alberts* v. *California,* 354 U.S. 476 (1957) are two appeals combined into one opinion. David S. Alberts had been convicted under the statutes of California for the offense of having obscene books for sale; the U.S. Supreme Court affirmed the conviction of both Roth and Alberts. The present analysis is focused upon *Roth* because it is the federal case in which the Comstock Act was challenged. (Some authorities refer to this case as *Roth-Alberts.*)

FIGURE 5.5. SAMUEL ROTH.
New York publisher Samuel Roth during an appearance before a New York Senate Committee on Juvenile Delinquency in 1955, where he is being queried about the relationship of explicit sexual materials to juvenile delinquency. Two years later Roth's federal conviction for mailing "obscene" circulars in violation of the Comstock Act of 1873 was upheld by the U.S. Supreme Court in the landmark case of Roth v. United States.
UPI/Bettmann Archive.

Burger's procensorship views in the 1973 cases of *Miller* v. *California* and *Paris Adult Theatre I* v. *Slaton),* began by reviewing the facts of the case and by noting the landmark nature of the decision which for the "first time" presented the First Amendment issues raised by obscenity laws "to this Court." He then summarized the history of obscenity legislation in America, observed that blasphemy, profanity, and obscenity were related offenses in the colonies, and admitted that obscenity was not a developed area of the law even at the time of the adoption of the Bill of Rights. Nevertheless, he concluded, the evidence suggested that at the nation's founding, "obscenity . . . was outside the protection intended for speech and press." Justice Brennan then argued his *first* principle supporting censorship, namely, that the purpose of the First Amendment is to protect *ideas,* and that obscenity contains no ideas worth protecting.

Justice Brennan *delivered the opinion of the Court:*

All ideas having even the slightest redeeming social importance—unorthodox ideas, controversial ideas, even ideas hateful to the prevailing climate of opinion—have the full protection of the guarantees, unless excludable because they encroach upon the limited area of more important interests. But implicit in the history of the First Amendment is the rejection of obscenity as utterly without redeeming social importance. . . . This is the same judgment expressed by this Court in *Chaplinsky* v. *New Hampshire* . . . "[that] *the lewd and obscene . . . are no essential part of any exposition of ideas, and are of such slight social value as a step to truth that any benefit that may be derived from them is clearly outweighed by the social interest in order and morality. . . .*" [Emphasis supplied by the Court.]

We hold that obscenity is not within the area of constitutionally protected speech or press.

LANDMARK CASE
Roth v. United States, 354 U.S. 476 (1957)
Decided June 24, 1957

Vote: 6 to 3 to affirm the conviction of Roth.
Majority Opinion By: Justice Brennan.
Concurring Justices: Chief Justice Warren and Justices Frankfurter, Burton, Clark, and Whittaker.
Dissenting Justices: Black, Douglas, and Harlan.
Justices Not Participating: (none)
Summary: Samuel Roth was found guilty by a federal jury in New York of violating the Comstock Act of 1873 by mailing obscene advertising. The court of appeals sustained the conviction, as did the U.S. Supreme Court. In his majority opinion, Justice Brennan recognized that obscenity, blasphemy, and profanity were historically related religio-moral offenses; nevertheless, he ruled, the provisions of the federal law against the mailing of "obscene, lewd, lascivious, or filthy" materials did not violate the First Amendment for two reasons: obscenity is both (1) worthless (citing *Chaplinsky* of 1942 to the effect that obscenity is not essential to the "exposition of ideas") and (2) sexually lewd ("that form of immorality which has relation to sexual impurity and has a tendency to excite lustful thoughts"). In strong dissent, Justices Black and Douglas argued that unless incitement to illegal conduct is proved, the First Amendment protects expression that arouses lustful thoughts as much as it does that which concerns "theology, economics, politics, or any other field."

Rule Established; Significance of Case: This landmark decision determined for the first time in the Court's history that the Comstock Act's obscenity provisions were constitutional. In upholding this federal censorship law of the nineteenth century, the Supreme Court set forth a two-part definition: obscenity is that form of expression which is both (1) *worthless* ("utterly without redeeming social importance") and (2) *sexually lewd,* meaning (a) "whether to the average person" (b) "applying contemporary community standards" (c) "the dominant theme of the material taken as a whole" (d) "appeals to prurient interest."

Justice Brennan then stated that since obscenity is not protected speech, it need not be tested by the clear-and-present-danger test (or, by implication, any other judicial test), for such testing is done only for that expression which is protected by the Constitution. In short, obscenity is so worthless that it does not deserve to be measured by the standards applied to speech containing ideas. He then moved to the *second* part of his argument, namely, that obscene expression is immoral, sexually "impure," and intended to arouse lustful desires in readers or viewers. Therefore, he urged, it is necessary to separate this illegal type of expression from sexual communications that are protected by the First Amendment.

Justice Brennan *continued for the Court:*

However, sex and obscenity are not synonymous. Obscene material is material which deals with sex in a manner appealing to prurient interest. The portrayal of sex, e.g., in art, literature and scientific works, is not itself sufficient reason to deny material the constitutional protection of freedom of speech and press. Sex, a great and mysterious motive force in human life, has indisputably been a subject of absorbing interest to mankind through the ages; it is one of the vital problems of human interest and public concern. . . .

The fundamental freedoms of speech and press have contributed greatly to the development and well-being of our free society and are indispensable to its continued growth. Ceaseless vigilance is the watchword to prevent their erosion by Congress or by the States. . . . It is therefore vital that the standards for judging obscenity safeguard the protection of freedom of speech and press for material which does not treat sex in a manner appealing to prurient interest.

The [Hicklin standard of 1868] . . . allowed material to be judged merely by the effect of an isolated excerpt upon particularly susceptible persons. . . . Some American courts adopted this standard but later decisions have rejected it and substituted this test: **whether to the average person, applying contemporary community standards, the dominant theme of the material taken as a whole appeals to prurient interest.** The Hicklin test, judging obscenity by the effect of isolated passages upon the most susceptible persons, might well encompass material legitimately treating with sex, and so it must be rejected as unconstitutionally restrictive of the freedoms of speech and press. On the other hand, the substituted standard provides safeguards adequate to withstand the charge of constitutional infirmity.

In dissent, Justice Harlan would permit the censorship of obscenity, but not by the federal government; like defamation, he urged, obscenity should be left up to the states to handle. Justices Black and Douglas, on the other hand, took a much stronger position in favor of freedom of speech and in opposition to censorship, and in the first of what became a lengthy record of dissents concerning government's efforts to suppress sexual communications, stated their objections to the opinion of the Court. Two main arguments are set forth by Justice Douglas, with whose dissent Justice Black concurred: (1) the First Amendment nowhere excludes from its protection expression that allegedly stirs "impure thoughts" and (2) "community standards" are not permitted to determine what is protected expression in other fields, such as theology and politics, and therefore should not be allowed to determine what is permissible when the subject of a communication is sex.

Justice Douglas concluded his dissent by urging that government "should be concerned with antisocial conduct, not with utterances." Also, he rejected the Court's weighing of the social value of expression as a way of determining its constitutionality when he stated that the "First Amendment, its prohibition in terms absolute, was designed to preclude courts as well as legislatures from weighing the values of speech against silence. The First Amendment puts free speech in the preferred position." Finally, in a vote of confidence in the ability of each individual citizen to decide for himself or herself concerning matters of moral heresy, he added, "I would give the broad sweep of the First Amendment full support. I have the same confidence in the ability of our people to reject noxious literature as I have in their capacity to sort out the true from the false in theology, economics, politics, or any other field."

Before proceeding to examine the progeny of *Roth* by way of a review of seven major cases over the next fifteen years in which the language of Justice Brennan was "interpreted," "clarified," and "explained," four observations merit attention. These four can be described as (1) the *religio-moral problem,* (2) the *semantic solution* to the problem, (3) the *constitutional basis* for that solution (as argued by Justice Brennan), and (4) a *rhetorical issue* that arises from the Court's approach. Students of the censorship debate should keep these four observations in mind as they continue to analyze the Supreme Court's obscenity rulings.

1. *The religio-moral problem of prohibiting "sinful" expression.* Permeating the controversy over *Roth* and progeny, and including the changes made by the Supreme Court in 1973 under Chief Justice Warren Burger, is the historical fact that civil obscenity laws evolved from the ecclesiastical courts of England to the common law, and from the common law to statute law, eventually to judicial confirmation by judges who were themselves members of the very Judeo-Christian religious tradition they were judging. The matter is pointedly discussed by Justice Thurgood Marshall in his opinion for the Court in 1969 overturning the conviction of a Georgia citizen for possession of erotic films in his home for his own personal use.[27] Observed Justice Marshall, "Georgia asserts the right to protect the individual's mind from the effects of obscenity. We are not certain that this argument amounts to anything more than the assertion that the State has the right to control the moral content of a person's thoughts." In amplification of his opinion, Justice Marshall cites the following paragraph from Louis Henkin's often quoted 1963 essay, first published in the *Columbia Law Review:*

> Communities believe, and act on the belief, that obscenity is immoral, is wrong for the individual, and has no place in a decent society. They believe, too, that adults as well as children are corruptible in morals and character, and that obscenity is a source of corruption that should be eliminated. Obscenity is not suppressed primarily for the protection of others. Much of it is suppressed for the purity of the community and for the salvation and welfare of the "consumer." Obscenity, at bottom, is not crime. Obscenity is a sin.[28]

To a large degree, therefore, the debate was and still is between those who would permit the individual citizen to receive "immoral" viewpoints and to make his or her own moral judgments about those viewpoints and those who believe, rightly or wrongly, that they have both the right and the obligation to use the civil law to enforce private morals and thereby, perhaps, to save men and women from themselves.[29]

2. *The semantic solution to the problem.* The key method by which the Supreme Court attempted in *Roth* to constrain explicitly erotic communications was a semantic one (the same method is followed in *Miller*). By announcing a verbal description (i.e., a definition) of the immorality it sought to punish, the Court evidently hoped to provide judges and juries throughout the nation with clear guidelines for making decisions about "obscene" expression. However, as with any attempt to employ symbols (in this case, words) to represent the subjective, nonverbal perceptions within unique human beings, the hope was not realized, as the variety of views expressed by the members of the Court in censorship decisions over the next fifteen years demonstrates. The issue is broader than whether or not concepts such as "obscenity" or "prurience" can be verbally defined, for it reaches a question raised by semanticists years ago over the adequacy of words to depict abstract personal perceptions accurately. Regardless of the opinion of semanticists, though, there are many who still believe that a verbal statement (whether the Roth test of 1957 or the Miller test of 1973) is clear

[27]*Stanley v. Georgia,* 394 U.S. 557 (1969), at 565.
[28]Ibid., note 8. See footnote 1 at the beginning of this chapter.
[29]A related issue concerns the use of civil law to govern the private sexual conduct of citizens; some view such use of the law as a form of establishment of religion. See Walter Barnett, *Sexual Freedom and the Constitution: An Inquiry Into the Constitutionality of Repressive Sex Laws* (Albuquerque, N.M.: University of New Mexico Press, 1973).

enough for communicators to understand. We may ask: Is it possible to define obscenity so that public communicators will know what is legal and what is not? Many would answer with a firm yes. The debate, in part, then, is a semantic one, for others would just as firmly say no.

3. *The constitutional foundation of the Roth test.* In defense of Justice Brennan's verbal test in *Roth,* one should note that the test's supporters believed that the principle announced was based firmly upon the protection that the First Amendment extends to ideas. Although the intent of the Roth test was to permit government to suppress obscenity, the test made clear that "all ideas having even the slightest redeeming social importance" were protected, even if those ideas were despised by a majority in a community or in the nation. *The burden of proof was upon the prosecution* to show (a) that the material in question was *completely* lacking in ideas ("utterly without redeeming social importance") and (b) that it appealed to the consumer's sexual lusts ("prurient interest"). To meet this burden of proof was difficult, and there was no censorious "reign of terror" under *Roth;* in fact, many classics were liberated from censorship and there was considerable expansion of the freedom to communicate to the general public on matters sexual. Some censorship-minded persons found the rule "too liberal" and yearned for a return to pre-*Roth* control over books, magazines, and films.

So liberating was the "utterly worthless" standard in practice that it became the target of procensorship organizations throughout the country, which urged its elimination. The Supreme Court acceded to this request in the 1973 case of *Miller* v. *California,* substituting the rule that explicit sexual communications could be censored unless the *defendant* could prove that the materials in question had *serious* social value. When the

two tests are compared, perhaps one can better understand what Justice Brennan was attempting to explain in *Roth* and why he believed that his formulation was based upon constitutional principles. An interesting question that the student should consider from time to time while studying the remainder of this chapter is this: Which of the two tests for obscenity—*Roth* of 1957 or *Miller* of 1973—is more firmly grounded in the First Amendment?

4. *A rhetorical issue that emerges from the Supreme Court's obscenity decisions.* Finally, a second look at the *Kingsley* case of 1959 (considered in the previous section of this chapter) raises an interesting rhetorical issue concerning the *means of persuasion.*[30] Why, one might ask, was the film version of *Lady Chatterley's Lover* protected by the Constitution, even though it advocated the idea of adultery, when the same or similar views expressed by Roth were not protected? The critical difference, apparently, was in the *means of persuasion,* for Roth was alleged to have employed frankly erotic language and visual images, whereas the *Lady Chatterley* film did not. By allowing the First Amendment to protect what Thomas Emerson described as "thematic" or "ideological obscenity" in the *Lady Chatterley* film (Figure 5.1, category 6) while refusing to protect the use of persuasive but erotic language and visual imagery (Figure 5.1, overlap of categories 4 and 6) in Roth's materials, the Court seems to imply that the advocacy of "immoral" ideas is protected, but not necessarily when the advocate employs all "available means of persuasion."[31]

---

[30]Recall Aristotle's definition of rhetoric: "So let Rhetoric be defined as the faculty of discovering in the particular case what are the available means of persuasion." *The Rhetoric of Aristotle,* trans. Lane Cooper (New York: Appleton-Century Company, 1932), p. 7.

[31]Thomas I. Emerson, *The System of Freedom of Expression* (New York: Random House, 1970), p. 475.

In short, *if the advocate of "immorality" becomes too effective, he is likely to go to jail.*

The rhetorical issue can be stated in question form, as follows: Why doesn't the Constitution protect the use of explicit sexual materials in support of the advocacy of nonconforming ideas concerning sexual behavior? Or, even more directly: Could it be that "obscenity" and "pornography" are suppressed precisely because they do advocate ideas and reveal some truth of which powerful forces in society disapprove? One who would answer yes to the preceding question is writer and literary critic Susan Sontag, who believes that the explicitly erotic can in its own way be a means of communicating some truth. In her significant essay "The Pornographic Imagination," she argues that those who speak in pornographic terms have something to say that is "worth listening to." She adds:

. . . this spectacularly cramped form of the human imagination has . . . its peculiar access to some truth. And this truth—about sensibility, about sex, about individual personality, about despair, about limits—can be shared when it projects itself into art. . . . That something one might call the poetry of transgression is also knowledge. He who transgresses not only breaks a rule. He goes somewhere that the others are not; and he knows something the others don't know.[32]

In summary, the four questions raised above—which the student of freedom of expression should keep in mind in the ensuing study of censorship decisions—are as follows: (1) Should individual Americans be al-

lowed to receive sexual messages and judge them for themselves (as with politics, theology, philosophy, etc.), or should civil government prohibit such "sinful" messages in order to help save men and women from themselves? (2) Is it possible to define "obscenity" clearly? (3) Which of the two tests for obscenity—*Roth* or *Miller*—is more firmly grounded in the First Amendment? And (4) Should the Constitution protect explicit erotic materials when those materials are judged to be the available means of persuasion in the advocacy of heterodox opinions concerning sexual behavior? It is now appropriate to turn to seven significant decisions of the Supreme Court over the fifteen or so years following *Roth* and prior to the Court's change of direction in the *Miller* decision of 1973. The cases to be examined are: (1) *Jacobellis* v. *Ohio* (1964); (2) *Memoirs* v. *Massachusetts* (1966); (3) *Ginzburg* v. *U.S.* (1966); (4) *Mishkin* v. *N.Y.* (1966); (5) *Redrup* v. *N.Y.* (1967); (6) *Ginsberg* v. *N.Y.* (1968); and (7) *Stanley* v. *Georgia* (1969).

The Progeny of *Roth:* 1957–1973

In his 1872 classic *Through the Looking Glass,* Lewis Carroll writes of Alice's discussion with Humpty Dumpty about the meaning of some of Humpty Dumpty's statements. "When *I* use a word," Humpty Dumpty says to Alice in a scornful tone, "it means just what I choose it to mean—neither more nor less." Reflecting the questionable wisdom of Humpty Dumpty, the U.S. Supreme Court adopted a verbal definition of the abstract concepts of "obscenity" and "prurience" and expected the country to agree that its words meant neither more nor less than the Court intended. Over the next several years, however, the censorship-minded judges of the U.S. Supreme Court learned—much to their consternation—that their definition did not

[32]Susan Sontag, "The Pornographic Imagination," in *Perspectives on Pornography,* ed. Douglas A. Hughes (New York: St. Martin's Press, 1970), p. 167. Originally published in Sontag's *Style of Radical Will* (Farrar, Straus & Giroux, 1966).

take into consideration certain types of sexual expression which had to be judged. Furthermore, they found that they rarely agreed among themselves about the meaning of their own definition.

While analyzing what one writer describes as "The Grapes of Roth,"[33] the student should recall the two requirements of Justice Brennan's test: *first,* that the material be worthless, and *second,* that the material be sexually lewd as determined by the four-part definition, (1) to the average person, (2) applying contemporary community standards, (3) the dominant theme of the material taken as a whole (4) appeals to the prurient interest. A *third* factor now needs to be included in preparation for studying the progeny of *Roth,* namely, a category of *additions* to the original two-part test. The student, in other words, should look for these three developments in the cases below: (a) What changes, if any, are made in the standard of worthlessness? (b) What changes, if any, are made in the four-part definition of sexual lewdness? And (c) what new elements, if any, are added to the original test by the Court? To begin with, the first requirement that the material must be worthless, that is, "utterly without redeeming social value," *was maintained* by the Supreme Court until 1973, when it was discarded by Chief Justice Burger in the *Miller* decision. By the process of elimination, then, the student can focus upon the second and third developments in the seven cases below.

1. *Jacobellis* v. *Ohio,* 378 U.S. 184 (1964).

In this early challenge to the *Roth* standard, the Ohio courts found Cleveland Heights theater manager Nico Jacobellis guilty of possessing and showing an obscene film, *Les Amants* (The Lovers), on the basis that the film's brief, nonexplicit love scene violated state law. Upon appeal, and by a vote of 6 to 3, the U.S. Supreme Court reversed the conviction. In so deciding, the justices revealed clearly the problems inherent in the semantic solution to censoring "obscenity" as adopted in *Roth* seven years earlier, for the six justices forming the majority could not agree upon an opinion of the Court. Justice Brennan's opinion was joined only by Justice Goldberg, Justice Black's opinion was joined by Justice Douglas, Justice White concurred in the judgment but wrote no opinion, and Justice Stewart concurred in a separate opinion.

Justice Brennan's effort to clarify what was meant by the term "contemporary community standards" by arguing that it meant *national,* not local, standards, did not win majority approval (in fact, the term remained unclear until 1973, when, in *Miller* v. *California,* the Court defined it to mean *local* standards). Also, Justice Stewart's observation that he could not define obscenity but "I know it when I see it" became a widely used quotation in the legal profession, following him until the day he announced his retirement from the bench. *Jacobellis* was certainly not an auspicious beginning for the Roth test, for although the test emerged unchanged, it was obvious that the members of the Court could not agree upon what it meant.

On March 21, 1966, the Supreme Court ruled on three appeals (all announced on the same date) and in the process both pleased and disturbed many American citizens. In the *Memoirs* decision, the Court pleased the literary community by freeing John Cleland's *Fanny Hill* from censorship; at the same time, it shocked numerous thoughtful persons in the fields of law and literature by finding publisher Ralph Ginzburg guilty of "pandering," *an offense with which he was never charged.* The Court not only changed its ob-

[33]C. Peter Magrath, "The Obscenity Cases: Grapes of Roth," in *The Supreme Court Review: 1966,* ed. Philip B. Kurland (Chicago: University of Chicago Press, 1966), pp. 7–77.

scenity standard in order to "get Ginzburg" but also, in a separate change of its definition, managed to sustain a lower court's conviction of Mishkin.

2. *Memoirs v. Massachusetts,* 383 U.S. 413 (1966).

John Cleland's novel of 1750, *Memoirs of a Woman of Pleasure* (also known as *Fanny Hill,* after its heroine), was declared obscene under Massachusetts law in a hearing before a single judge in a state court. The Massachusetts judge believed that he had complied with the Roth test by noting that the novel had *minimal* literary value (thus meeting the requirement of worthlessness) and that it was often erotic (thus meeting the second part of the test, prurience). By a vote of 6 to 3, the U.S. Supreme Court reversed, thereby extending the protection of the Constitution to Cleland's underground classic. As in *Jacobellis,* sharp divisions emerged, even among the majority, and no opinion of the Court was announced. Instead, a plurality opinion by Justice Brennan, who was joined by Chief Justice Warren and Justice Fortas, explained that the trial court had not met its burden of proof to show that the literature in question was *utterly* without redeeming social value. In other words, *Fanny Hill* had *some* literary merit and was, therefore, protected under the Roth test. Since there was no evidence in the court record that the book had been sold in a "pandering" manner, it was, when judged simply as a book, not legally obscene. Because of divisions among the majority, *Memoirs* did not alter the Roth test; however, each of the next two cases *did* change the test.

3. *Ginzberg v. United States,* 383 U.S. 463 (1966).

New York publisher Ralph Ginzburg was convicted by a federal judge in a nonjury trial in the eastern district of Pennsylvania of mailing obscene publications in violation of the Comstock Act. Specifically, the conviction was for mailing copies of the magazine *Eros,* a newsletter on sexual topics called *Liaison,* and a book of clinical confessions entitled *The Housewife's Handbook on Selective Promiscuity.* The court of appeals had sustained Ginzburg's conviction, even though none of the magazine's photographs were explicitly sexual and little of the language in any of the three publications consisted of "four-letter words." Without finding the materials in question obscene, the U.S. Supreme Court by a vote of 5 to 4 sustained Ginzburg's conviction—*but for the crime of "pandering"* (i.e., of employing suggestive advertising to promote the sale of the publications), *an offense with which he had not been charged and for which he had not been tried in the district court.*

Speaking for the Court, Justice Brennan explained that there was "abundant evidence to show that each of the accused publications was originated or sold as stock in trade of the sordid business of pandering—'the business of purveying textual or graphic matter openly advertised to appeal to the erotic interest of their customers.'" He pointed out that Ginzburg attempted to mail some of his brochures from the towns of Intercourse and Blue Ball, Pennsylvania, in order to have these postmarks on the front. When this effort was turned back because the towns were too small to handle the volume, Ginzburg mailed the circulars from Middlesex, New Jersey. For this and other reasons, Justice Brennan concluded, the advertising was permeated by "the leer of the sensualist." Following further explication of the concept of pandering, he concluded by adding it to the Roth test, which at this point can be paraphrased as follows: *To be obscene, expression must be utterly worthless and also be of a nature so that to the average person, applying contemporary community standards, the dominant theme of the material taken as a whole appeals to the prurient interest,* **or is advertised as if the material appeals to the prurient interest.**

Strong dissents were penned by Justices Black, Douglas, Harlan, and Stewart, each of whom wrote a separate opinion and each of whom argued that Ginzburg was convicted of a violation that was different from the charge in the trial court. The view of Justice Potter Stewart is particularly thoughtful.

Justice Stewart, *dissenting:*

Censorship reflects a society's lack of confidence in itself. It is a hallmark of an authoritarian regime. Long ago those who wrote our First Amendment charted a different course. They believed a society can be truly strong only when it is truly free. In the realm of expression they put their faith, for better or for worse, in the enlightened choice of the people, free from the interference of a policeman's intrusive thumb or a judge's heavy hand. So it is that the Constitution protects coarse expression as well as refined, and vulgarity no less than elegance. A book worthless to me may convey something of value to my neighbor. In the free society to which our Constitution has committed us, it is for each to choose for himself. . . .

The Court today appears to concede that the materials Ginzburg mailed were themselves protected by the First Amendment. But, the Court says, Ginzburg can still be sentenced to five years in prison for mailing them. Why? Because, says the Court, he was guilty of "commercial exploitation," of "pandering," and of "titillation." **But Ginzburg was not charged with "commercial exploitation"; he was not charged with "pandering"; he was not charged with "titillation." Therefore, to affirm his conviction now on any of those grounds, even if otherwise valid, is to deny him due process of law. . . .**

For me, however, there is another aspect of the Court's opinion in this case that is even more regrettable. Today the Court assumes the power to deny Ralph Ginzburg the protection of the First Amendment because it disapproves of his "sordid business." That is a power the Court does not possess. For the First Amendment protects us all with an even hand. It ap-

plies to Ralph Ginzburg with no less completeness and force than to G. P. Putnam's Sons. In upholding and enforcing the Bill of Rights, this Court has no power to pick or to choose. When we lose sight of that fixed star of constitutional adjudication, we lose our way. For then we forsake a government of law and are left with government by Big Brother.

I dissent.

4. *Mishkin* v. *New York,* 383 U.S. 502 (1966).

The third decision handed down on March 21, 1966, concerned the conviction of another New York publisher whose name was Mishkin and whose stock in trade consisted of inexpensive paperback books that emphasized what many would describe as "abnormal" sexual behavior such as sadomasochism, fetishism, and homosexuality. (The content of the books was not explicitly sexual in its language or graphics; in the words of Justice Stewart, these books were "not hard-core pornography.") Among the seventy-two titles from the defendant's book list, as appended to the Court's opinion, are the following: *Her Highness, Mistress of Leather, The Whipping Chorus Girls, Cult of the Spankers, Bound in Rubber, Screaming Flesh, Swish Bottom, The Strap Returns, Stud Broad,* and *Queen Bee.* By a vote of 6 to 3, the Supreme Court upheld Mishkin's conviction for trafficking in obscenity in violation of the laws of the state of New York and in so ruling *changed* the Roth test in order to reach the materials in question.

The change, explained by Justice Brennan in his opinion of the Court, concerned the phrase "average person" in the four-part test of prurience. Mishkin's basic defense was that his books were not obscene as that term was defined in *Roth.* As Justice Brennan stated,

appellant's sole contention regarding the nature of the material is that some of the books involved in this prosecution, those depicting various deviant sexual practices, such as flagellation, fetishism, and lesbianism, do not satisfy the prurient-appeal requirement because they do not appeal to a prurient interest of the "average person" in sex, that *"instead of stimulating the erotic, they disgust and sicken."* [Emphasis supplied.]

In other words, no *average* person would find these books sexually stimulating! As peculiar as the argument appears upon first consideration, it certainly has considerable truth on its side; what Mishkin had done was to question the semantic approach of the Court and to demonstrate the inadequacy of that approach. The Court was not deterred, however, for it simply changed the Roth test (again). Justice Brennan accomplished this by announcing, "We adjust the prurient-appeal requirement to social realities by permitting the appeal of this type of material to be assessed in terms of the sexual interests of its intended and probable recipient group." Consequently, the Roth test, with the *Ginzburg* and *Mishkin* "adjustments" incorporated, can be paraphrased as follows: *To be obscene, the expression must be utterly worthless and also be of a nature so that to the average person* **or its intended and probable recipient group,** *applying contemporary community standards, the dominant theme of the material taken as a whole appeals to the prurient interest or is advertised as if the material appeals to the prurient interest.*

Among the opinions of the three dissenters—Justices Black, Douglas, and Stewart—that of Justice Black is noteworthy, for in it he charged that the majority on the Court had begun to function as a "national board of censors over speech and press." This charge was to appear from time to time in the future opinions by this outspoken defender of the First Amendment.

Justice Black, *dissenting:*

I would reverse this conviction. The three-

year sentence imposed on Mishkin and the five-year sentence imposed on Ginzburg for expressing views about sex are minor in comparison with those more lengthy sentences that are inexorably bound to follow in state and federal courts as pressures and prejudices increase and grow more powerful, which of course they will. . . . The only practical answer to these concededly almost unanswerable problems is, I think, **for this Court to decline to act as a national board of censors over speech and press but instead to stick to its clearly authorized constitutional duty to adjudicate cases over things and conduct. . . .** I think the Founders of our Nation in adopting the First Amendment meant precisely that the Federal Government should pass "no law" regulating speech and press but should confine its legislation to the regulation of conduct. So too, that policy of the First Amendment made applicable to the States by the Fourteenth, leaves the States vast power to regulate conduct but no power at all, in my judgment, to make the expression of views a crime.

The national censorship controversy became more heated as a result of the decisions of the Supreme Court in the three cases just reviewed—*Memoirs*, *Ginzburg*, and *Mishkin*. On the one hand, those who favored the suppression of the moral heresy of obscenity were appalled that the novel *Fanny Hill* could now be purchased at the local drugstore; on the other hand, civil libertarians were outraged at what they believed to be a grossly unfair ruling in Ralph Ginzburg's case (and to a lesser extent in that of Mishkin). Among the proposals which emerged from the debate were these: (a) adults should be allowed to read and view any erotic materials they wished as long as the material was not available to juveniles (the "adults only" argument) and (b) to receive erotic materials, the adults should be *consenting,* for no invasion of privacy should be allowed where erotic materials were "thrust" upon unwilling receivers (the privacy argument). Both of these ideas were given some credence in the next obscenity pronouncement of the Court.

5. *Redrup* v. *New York,* 386 U.S. 767 (1967).

In 1967 the Supreme Court ruled on three cases combined into one opinion—*Redrup* v. *New York* plus related cases from the states of Kentucky and Arkansas—because of the similarity of the issues involved. In all three, the courts below had rendered verdicts of guilty for the sale of obscene books and magazines under state law, even though the materials were not explicit "hard-core pornography." Included in the convictions were the paperback books *Lust Pool* and *Shame Agent* and the magazines *High Heels, Spree, Swank, Gent, Bachelor, Modern Man, Cavalcade, Ace,* and *Sir* (all of which featured pinup pictures of scantily clad females revealing bare bosoms and buttocks but showing no explicit sexual activity). Again, the members of the Court were so sharply divided that they could not reach agreement adequate to produce a signed majority opinion. Therefore, by a 7-to-2 vote, the Court reversed, announcing its decision per curiam.

Among the several reasons mentioned by the Court for reversing the obscenity findings of the courts below, three are emphasized: (a) there was no evidence that any of the materials had been sold to juveniles, (b) in none of the cases had the publications been thrust upon unwilling recipients, and (c) no pandering of the type condemned in the *Ginzburg* decision was involved. After mentioning several other points of view, ranging from the full-protection position of Justices Black and Douglas to the worthless-prurience position of Justice Brennan, the Court concluded: "Whichever of these constitutional views is brought to bear upon the cases before us, it is clear that the judgments cannot stand." Stated another way, the Court said that although the justices could not agree

on the main reasons for doing so, they reversed the convictions anyway.

Although the lack of consensus meant that *Redrup* did not further alter the Roth test (as amended in *Ginzburg* and *Mishkin*), the decision did suggest that the Court was moving toward approval of a "consenting adults" interpretation of the First Amendment that would restrict the punishment of erotic expression to those cases involving juveniles or the invasion of privacy. But this was only a hint and it never became the law of the land, despite further moves in that direction in the next two decisions on the subject. (The movement in *Redrup* was stopped cold in 1973 by the opinions of the Court in *Miller* v. *California* and *Paris Adult Theatre I* v. *Slaton.*)

On the national political scene, in the year following *Redrup,* Richard Nixon was elected president of the United States on a strong law-and-order platform that included promises to put a stop to the "moral decay" of the nation (and that meant a crackdown on obscenity and a promise to appoint conservative judges with "old-fashioned values" to the Supreme Court). The work of the President's Commission on Obscenity and Pornography was under way, having been authorized by Congress in 1967, while Lyndon Johnson was president; and the Danish Parliament's total abolition of censorship for adults was being celebrated by artists, publishers, and movie producers as the wave of the future. The film *Deep Throat* was released to the delight of some but to the outrage of others; soon thereafter *The Devil in Miss Jones* began its underground tour of the "midnight movie—for adults only" set. Chief Justice Earl Warren retired from the bench; to replace him, President Nixon appointed law-and-order judge Warren Burger, who soon let it be known that he approved of a strong censorship policy for explicit sexual communications. The final two cases reviewed below, therefore, represent a kind of farewell nudge by moderate-to-liberal justices on the High Court in the direction of freedom from censorship for consenting adults.

6. *Ginsberg* v. *New York,* 390 U.S. 629 (1968).

Sam Ginsberg and his wife operated Sam's Stationery and Luncheonette in Bellmore, Long Island, New York. This small retail business served meals and sold various items, including "girlie" magazines (showing pinup pictures, bare breasts and buttocks, but no explicit sexual photographs). A sixteen-year-old youth was asked by his mother, who was deliberately trying to show that juveniles could purchase girlie books at Sam's, to enter the establishment and buy some of the items. The youth did so, paid for two, and turned them over to his mother, who informed the police of the transaction. Sam Ginsberg was arrested and later convicted of violating the New York Penal Law, which prohibited dissemination of "harmful materials" to minors. He was given a suspended sentence by the judge; but because the conviction put him in danger of losing his retail license, he appealed.

The U.S. Supreme Court by a vote of 6 to 3 sustained Ginsberg's conviction by announcing that the New York law concerning the exposure of minors to "harmful material" was constitutional. Justice Brennan, in his opinion of the Court, stated that it was "constitutionally permissible" for the state of New York to "accord minors under 17 a more restricted right than that assured to adults . . . ." Viewed in the context of the preceding cases, the *Ginsberg* holding was seen by many observers to be a preparatory step by the Court in the direction of a consenting-adults rule on the subject of obscenity, for the result of this case was to make clear that states could adopt constitutionally

sound laws to prohibit the sale of erotica to minors. Although *Ginsberg* did not further alter the Roth test, it did give weight to the *Redrup* suggestion that special rules could be set for juveniles.

7. *Stanley* v. *Georgia,* 394 U.S. 557 (1969).

In 1969 the Supreme Court announced one of its most widely praised opinions concerning the religio-moral heresy of obscenity. In this case of *Stanley* v. *Georgia,* the police, armed with a warrant specifying that they were looking for gambling paraphernalia, searched the home of defendant Stanley; they found little evidence of illegal gambling but did discover in a desk drawer three reels of 8mm film. Upon viewing the films, the police declared them obscene and charged Stanley with the possession of obscene matter in violation of a Georgia law *that made such private possession a crime.* The Supreme Court of Georgia affirmed the conviction.

Upon appeal, a unanimous U.S. Supreme Court reversed the conviction and declared the Georgia law (and others similar to it in various states) to be unconstititional. Although Justices Brennan, Stewart, and White limited their vote to the Fourth Amendment violation of improper search and seizure, the other six justices were outspoken in their defense of the right of the *privacy* of the home. An indignant Justice Thurgood Marshall, speaking for the Court, focused upon the issue in a way that sets this case apart from the six preceding ones.

Justice Marshall *delivered the opinion of the Court:*

"The makers of our Constitution undertook to secure conditions favorable to the pursuit of happiness. . . . They sought to protect Americans in their beliefs, their thoughts, their emotions and their sensations. They conferred, as against the Government, the right to be let alone—the most comprehensive of rights and the right most valued by civilized man. . . ."

These are the rights that appellant is asserting in the case before us. He is asserting the right to read or observe what he pleases—the right to satisfy his intellectual and emotional needs in the privacy of his own home. He is asserting the right to be free from state inquiry into the contents of his library. . . . **Whatever may be the justifications for other statutes regulating obscenity, we do not think they reach into the privacy of one's own home. If the First Amendment means anything, it means that a State has no business telling a man, sitting alone in his own house, what books he may read or what films he may watch. Our whole constitutional heritage rebels at the thought of giving government the power to control men's minds.**

And yet, in the face of these traditional notions of individual liberty, Georgia asserts the right to protect the individual's mind from the effects of obscenity. We are not certain that this argument amounts to anything more than the assertion that the State has the right to control the moral content of a person's thoughts. To some, this may be a noble purpose, but it is wholly inconsistent with the philosophy of the First Amendment. . . .

We hold that the First and Fourteenth Amendments prohibit making mere private possession of obscene material a crime. . . .

Although *Stanley* did not alter the basic provisions of the Roth test as amended over the years, it did *add* to it the provision that once a consumer gets the erotica home, he or she may enjoy it in private with impunity. The Roth test, as explained in the Court's decision in *Stanley* v. *Georgia,* can now be summarized as follows: *To be obscene, the expression must be utterly worthless and also be of a nature so that the average person or its intended and probable recipient group, applying contemporary community standards, the dominant theme of the material taken as a whole appeals to the prurient interest or is advertised as if the material ap-*

peals to the prurient interest; **also, government may not punish any citizen for the mere private possession of obscenity in the home for his or her own personal use.**

Over the next two years some lower-court judges reasoned that if it was legal to peruse explicit sexual materials in the privacy of one's home, it must be legal to sell it to consenting adults who intended to enjoy it in private. Others accepted the argument that it was permissible to mail erotica to consenting adults and even that an "adults only" theater was an extension of a citizen's personal privacy, as explained in *Stanley,* and was therefore protected from government censorship. This line of reasoning, however, was rejected by the U.S. Supreme Court in the 1971 case of *United States* v. *Reidel* (which concerned Reidel's mailing of an explicitly sexual publication entitled *The True Facts About Imported Pornography*).[34] In *Reidel,* the underlying doctrine of which was reaffirmed two years later in the five cases decided by the Court on June 21, 1973, the Court decided by a vote of 7 to 2 (Justices Black and Douglas dissenting) that the Comstock Act prohibited the sale of explicit erotica to consenting adults, and that the *Stanley* decision was limited to the privacy of one's home and did not allow for the commercial distribution and sale to citizens, even if they intended to take it straight home for their own personal use. This interpretation of *Stanley* remains the Supreme Court's view.

On September 30, 1970, the Commission on Obscenity and Pornography submitted its *Report* to the President and the Congress, only to have its work immediately condemned by both.[35] The commission recom-

---

[34]*United States* v. *Reidel,* 402 U.S. 351 (1971).
[35]*The Report of the Commission on Obscenity and Pornography* (Washington, D.C.: U.S. Government Printing Office, 1970).

mended that censorship be ended for consenting adults but that it be continued for juveniles, and it provided a considerable amount of empirical evidence in support of its findings. Model legislation for the implementation of the *Report*'s recommendations was also included. What the commission members did not realize, evidently, was the depth of the religio-moral attitude which formed the societal support for obscenity laws and which, as word spread of the "libertine" proposals in the *Report,* was to emerge with evangelical fervor in opposition to the commission's findings.[36] Without taking the time to study the *Report* or to consult the technical data upon which its conclusions were built, the U.S. Senate, with only five members in dissent, voted to condemn it. A few days later, President Nixon announced that "So long as I am in the White House, there will be no relaxation of the national effort to control and eliminate smut from our national life. . . . American morality is not to be trifled with. The Commission . . . has performed a disservice and I totally reject its report."[37]

In support of his viewpoint on censorship, President Nixon had already begun to act by appointing conservative judges to the High Court in fulfillment of a campaign promise to reverse the "liberal" trends of the preceding years. As Chief Justice Earl Warren and Justices Fortas, Black, and Harlan retired, they were replaced by Chief Justice Warren Burger and Justices Blackmun, Powell, and Rehnquist. The direction of the Court's movement toward the abolition of censorship for consenting adults was about to be challenged. But before examining the outcome of that challenge, a look back is in order.

Roth and Progeny in Brief

In 1957 the U.S. Supreme Court in *Roth* v. *United States* announced its landmark decision upholding the constitutionality of the antiobscenity provisions of the Comstock Act, which made it a crime to mail "obscene, lewd, lascivious, or filthy" materials. *Without* finding that explicit sexual expression created any kind of clear and present danger to society, the Court declared that the Constitution did not protect obscene speech because such expression was both worthless and prurient. With finality, the Court rejected the old Hicklin rule inherited from English law and substituted a new test, which became known as the Roth test: obscene speech is that which is (1) utterly worthless and (2) at the same time is sexually lewd, meaning that (a) to the average person, (b) applying contemporary community standards, (c) the dominant theme of the material taken as a whole (d) appeals to the prurient interest. Between the years of 1957 and 1973, the Court attempted to explain what it meant in *Roth,* mainly in these seven cases:

1. *Jacobellis* v. *Ohio,* 1964 (an Ohio theater manager was found guilty in state courts of showing the film *Les Amants,* which, because of a brief love scene, was declared obscene). In overturning the conviction of Jacobellis,

---

[36]There were outspoken dissenters among the members of the commission, also, including clergymen Morton A. Hill and Winfrey C. Link. In addition, Charles H. Keating, Jr.—an active leader in the national censorship organization Citizens for Decent Literature (CDL, now renamed Citizens for Decency Under Law), who had been appointed to the commission by President Nixon following the resignation of one of its original members—objected in prose that exemplifies the religio-moral nature of the issue: "For those who believe in God, in His absolute supremacy as the Creator and Lawgiver of life, in the dignity and destiny which He has conferred upon the human person, in the moral code that governs sexual activity—for those who believe in these 'things,' no argument against pornography should be necessary." Ibid., p. 515.

[37]*New York Times,* October 25, 1970, p. 71.

the Supreme Court did not change the Roth test; but it did demonstrate the difficulty of agreeing upon what was meant by "obscenity," since no opinion of the Court was forthcoming (only plurality and individual opinions resulted).

2. *Memoirs* v. *Massachusetts,* 1966 (concerning state censorship of John Cleland's 1750 novel, *Memoirs of a Woman of Pleasure,* also known as *Fanny Hill*). The U.S. Supreme Court reversed the court below and declared that *Fanny Hill* was protected by the Constitution because it had *some* literary value.

3. *Ginzburg* v. *United States,* 1966 (publisher Ralph Ginzburg had been found guilty in federal court of mailing obscene publications, including *Eros, Liaison,* and a book entitled *The Housewife's Handbook on Selective Promiscuity*). The Supreme Court sustained Ginzburg's conviction without ever ruling on the obscenity of the materials he mailed; rather, the Court found Ginzburg guilty of "pandering" (an offense with which he had never been charged)—that is, of advertising his materials in such a way as to "appeal to the erotic interest" of his potential customers. Consequently, the crime of pandering was appended to the Roth test.

4. *Mishkin* v. *New York,* 1966 (concerning a conviction for selling obscene books dealing with abnormal sexual behavior, such as sadomasochism and fetishism). Mishkin argued that as defined in *Roth,* his materials were not legally obscene since they did not appeal to the "average person" but to sex deviates (the "average person," said Mishkin, would find his books disgusting rather than prurient). The Supreme Court upheld Mishkin's conviction, and in so doing changed the Roth test by adding to the "average person" this phrase: or to the "intended and probable recipient group."

5. *Redrup* v. *New York,* 1967 (concerning convictions in New York, Kentucky, and Arkansas for the sale of girlie magazines of a nonexplicit nature). The Supreme Court reversed the convictions, and in the process took a step in the direction of a consenting-adults view on obscenity by noting that in none of the cases at bar was there any evidence of sale to juveniles, of thrusting of sexual materials upon unwilling recipients, or of pandering.

6. *Ginsberg* v. *New York,* 1968 (Sam Ginsberg, proprietor of a stationery and luncheonette establishment, sold girlie magazines to a juvenile). The Supreme Court sustained the conviction and thereby upheld New York's law prohibiting the sale of erotic materials to minors.

7. *Stanley* v. *Georgia,* 1969 (while searching for gambling paraphernalia in Stanley's home, the police found three reels of 8mm "stag" film). The conviction for private possession of erotic materials was overturned by the Supreme Court in a unanimous vote, primarily on the basis that the Georgia law was an unconstitutional invasion of privacy. Said the Court, "a State has no business telling a man, sitting alone in his own house, what books he may read or what films he may watch." This ruling was restricted to private possession for personal use and did not extend to commercial dissemination of explicit sexual materials.

After *Stanley,* the Roth test as altered over the years can be summarized as follows: *to be obscene, the expression must be (1) utterly worthless and also (2) of a sexually lewd nature, so that (a) to the average person or its intended and probable recipient group, (b) applying contemporary community standards, (c) the dominant theme of the material taken as a whole (d) appeals to the prurient interest or is advertised as if the material appeals to the prurient interest. Furthermore, government may not punish a citizen for the mere private possession of erotica for his or her own per-*

sonal use. The Supreme Court's move in the direction of a consenting-adults policy was given support in 1970 by the *Report of the Commission on Obscenity and Pornography,* which proposed legislation to abolish censorship for adults. However, the *Report* was promptly condemned by the U.S. Senate, President Nixon, and numerous religious leaders throughout the nation, and its legislative recommendations were rejected by the Congress. Meanwhile, at the Supreme Court, a significant philosophical shift was under way that would soon affect the outcome of a variety of First Amendment appeals. In the area of obscenity, five decisions were announced in June of 1973, dramatically revealing where the now altered Court stood on the question of censorship for the religio-moral offense of obscenity.

Obscenity Redefined and Censorship Reconfirmed: *Miller* v. *California* and Four Companion Cases of June 21, 1973

Following the Supreme Court's recess in the summer of 1971, Chief Justice Warren Burger, acting in his capacity as Court administrator, held in abeyance the various obscenity appeals to which the justices granted review. This highly irregular procedure, which effectively prevented a final determination of the cases until the chief justice was ready for such determination, continued throughout 1972 and into 1973—until President Nixon had named two more justices to the Court, making a total of four appointed by his administration. Counting on the support of one or two holdovers from previous years, the chief justice was now ready to allow a vote on the accumulated cases.[38] The five cases held by Chief Justice Warren

[38]See "Giant Step Backward," *The Nation,* July 16, 1973, p. 37.

Burger until June of 1973, by which time he had his majority of five votes (the four Nixon appointees were joined by only one holdover—Justice Byron White, who was appointed in 1962 and has a consistent record of conservative votes on First Amendment issues), together with a brief summary of each, is given below. Afterward, a more detailed analysis is presented. Readers should note that none of the convictions was reversed but that *all were vacated and remanded* (i.e., sent back) to the lower courts for reconsideration in light of the new tests for obscenity articulated primarily in the *Miller* decision.

1. *Miller* v. *California,* 413 U.S. 15 (1973). Marvin Miller was convicted of violating the California obscenity statute for distributing advertising brochures that contained pictures of explicit sexual activity.

2. *Paris Adult Theatre I* v. *Slaton,* 413 U.S. 49 (1973). A state case in which the Supreme Court of Georgia held that two commercial films shown to adults only were obscene "hard-core pornography," even though the sex acts were simulated.

3. *Kaplan* v. *California,* 413 U.S. 115 (1973). Murray Kaplan, proprietor of an "adult" bookstore, was convicted of violating the California obscenity statute for selling a plain-covered, unillustrated book which contained numerous verbal descriptions of the sex act.

4. *United States* v. *12 200-Ft. Reels of Super 8mm. Film,* 413 U.S. 123 (1973). The defendant was attempting to bring explicit sex materials from Mexico to the United States for his own personal use but was prohibited by the customs service under the 19 *U.S. Code* Sec. 1305.

5. *United States* v. *Orito,* 413 U.S. 139 (1973). George J. Orito shipped by common carrier (the airlines) eighty-three reels of explicit sex film and was charged with violating

FIGURE 5.6 THE "MILLER COURT" OF 1973. *The U.S. Supreme Court in 1973, at the time of the procensorship decision in* Miller v. California *and companion cases. The names of the five who composed the majority are in boldface type; all names are given from left to right. Front row, seated: Justice Potter Stewart, Justice William O. Douglas,* **Chief Justice Warren Burger,** *Justice William Brennan, and* **Justice Byron R. White.** *Back row, standing* **Justice Lewis F. Powell, Jr.,** *Justice Thurgood Marshall,* **Justice Harry Blackmun,** *and* **Justice William Rehnquist.** *Library of Congress.*

18 *U.S. Code* Sec. 1462, which prohibits the interstate transportation of obscene matter.

An examination of the major changes in the Supreme Court's obscenity standards as announced in *Miller* and the other four cases is now in order. The majority opinions are considered as a group, since the five decisions blend together into one "big opinion" with several subparts. Then the dissents are considered as a group for the same reason.

Chief Justice Burger, after reviewing the facts of the case, noted the semantic problem in obscenity law when he observed that, except for the initial formulation of the Roth test, "no majority of the Court has at any given time been able to agree on a standard to determine what constitutes obscene, pornographic material . . . . We have seen 'a variety of views among the members of the Court unmatched in any other course of constitutional adjudication.'" He added, "This is not remarkable, for in the area of freedom of speech and press the courts must always remain sensitive to any infringement on genuinely serious literary, artistic, political, or scientific expression.[39] This is an area in which there are few eternal verities." After explaining that one of the cornerstones of the new test is the requirement that states must spell out in *specific terms* the type of conduct that, when described or depicted in an erotic way, will make the expression obscene (thereby avoiding the charge of vagueness so often

[39]Neither here nor in later cases does the Court include "religious" or "educational" expression, serious or otherwise, in its obscenity standard.

Miller v. California, 413 U.S. 15 (1973)
Decided June 21, 1973

Vote: 5 to 4 to vacate and remand the conviction of Miller (i.e., to send it back to the California courts for reconsideration in light of the revised definition of obscenity set forth in this case).

Majority Opinion By: Chief Justice Burger.

Concurring Justices: White, Blackmun, Powell, and Rehnquist.

Dissenting Justices: Douglas, Brennan, Stewart, and Marshall.

Justices Not Participating: (none)

Summary: Defendant Marvin Miller had been convicted in a jury trial in a state court of disseminating advertising brochures containing explicit sexual illustrations. The conviction was obtained under the state's obscenity law after the trial judge had instructed the jury to evaluate the prurience of the materials according to *state* rather than national standards. When the state courts of appeal sustained the conviction, Miller appealed to the U.S. Supreme Court. Chief Justice Warren Burger used this case as a means of revising the Roth test of 1957 in order to make it easier for states to prosecute obscenity cases successfully.

Rule Established; Significance of Case: Chief Justice Burger changed the Roth test by discarding the "utterly worthless" requirement and defining "contemporary community standards" to mean state or local standards—not necessarily national ones. He also added a requirement that state laws must be clear and specific in describing the type of sexual conduct covered by obscenity legislation. The new test is as follows: (1) whether the average person, applying contemporary standards of the *state or local community,* would find that the work, taken as a whole, appeals to the prurient interest; (2) whether the work depicts or describes in a patently offensive way *sexual conduct specifically defined by the applicable state law; and (3) whether the work lacks serious* literary, artistic, political, or scientific value (sometimes called the "SLAPS test" for *Serious Literary, Artistic, Political, or Scientific value).*

leveled at *Roth* and progeny), the chief justice proceeded to develop his substitute for *Roth.*

Chief Justice Burger *delivered the opinion of the Court:*

The basic guidelines for the trier of fact must be: (a) whether "the average person, applying contemporary community standards" would find that the work, taken as a whole, appeals to the prurient interest, . . . (b) whether the work depicts or describes, in a patently offensive way, sexual conduct specifically defined by the applicable state law, and (c) whether the work, taken as a whole, lacks serious literary, artistic, political, or scientific value. We do not adopt as a constitutional standard the *"utterly without redeeming social value"* test. . . . If a state law that regulates obscene material is thus limited, as written or construed, the First Amendment values applicable to the States through the Fourteenth Amendment are adequately protected by the ultimate power of appellate courts to conduct an independent review of constitutional claims when necessary. . . .

We emphasize that it is not our function to propose regulatory schemes for the States. That must await their concrete legislative efforts. It is possible, however, to give a few plain examples of what a state statute could define for regulation under the second part (b) of the standard announced [above] . . . :

(a) Patently offensive representations or descriptions of ultimate sexual acts, normal or perverted, actual or simulated.

(b) Patently offensive representations or descriptions of masturbation, excretory functions, and lewd exhibition of the genitals.

Sex and nudity may not be exploited without limit by films or pictures exhibited or sold in places of public accommodation any more than live sex and nudity can be exhibited or sold without limit in such public places. At a minimum prurient, patently offensive depiction or description of sexual conduct must have serious literary, artistic, political, or scientific value to merit First Amendment protection. . . . For example, medical books for the education of physicians and related personnel necessarily use graphic illustrations and descriptions of human anatomy. In resolving the inevitably sensitive questions of fact and law, we must continue to rely on the jury system, accompanied by the safeguards that judges, rules of evidence, presumption of innocence and other protective features provide, as we do with rape, murder and a host of other offenses against society and its individual members.

The chief justice then turned his attention to the issue of national versus local standards for the determination of prurience. Although he recognized that the nation has a national Constitution whose "fundamental First Amendment limitations on the powers of the States do not vary from community to community," he nevertheless announced that this does not apply to the question of what is meant by "prurient interest" or "patently offensive." To require a national standard for obscenity cases, he argued, "would be an exercise in futility." Therefore, "It is neither realistic nor constitutionally sound to read the First Amendment as requiring that the people of Maine or Mississippi accept public depiction of conduct found tolerable in Las Vegas, or New York City. . . . People in different States vary in their tastes and attitudes, and this diversity is not to be strangled by the absolutism of imposed uniformity."[40]

Chief Justice Burger then concluded his

procensorship argument by stating that "to equate the free and robust exchange of ideas and political debate with commercial exploitation of obscene material demeans the grand conception of the First Amendment and its high purposes in the historic struggle for freedom." To this end, he added, "we (a) reaffirm the *Roth* holding that obscene material is not protected by the First Amendment, (b) hold that such material can be regulated by the States . . . without a showing that the material is 'utterly' without redeeming social value,' and (c) hold that obscenity is to be determined by applying 'contemporary community standards,' . . . not 'national standards.'"

Paris Adult Theatre I *v.* Slaton

Following *Miller,* Chief Justice Burger turned his attention to a film case from Georgia in which two sexy but nonexplicit movies, *Magic Mirror* and *It All Comes Out in the End,* were declared obscene by the Georgia Supreme Court and therefore suppressible under state law. The films had been shown in the Paris Adult Theatre I of Atlanta to consenting adults only. Key issues raised by the case included (1) the rights of consenting adults, (2) the prosecution's burden of proof, (3) the lack of evidence to demonstrate a harmful effect upon society, and (4) ways in which state law may differ from the holdings of the Supreme Court on obscenity matters. The quesions, and Chief Justice Burger's answers for the Court in *Paris Adult Theatre I* v. *Slaton,* are as follows:

1. *Do consenting adults have a constitutional right of privacy to make their own choices about the religio-moral heresy of obscenity (especially when there is no "pandering," no thrusting upon*

---

[40]This view is described as "local option on the First Amendment" by one communication scholar. See Ruth McGaffey, "Local Option on the First Amendment," in

Free Speech Yearbook: 1974, ed. Alton Barbour (New York: Speech Communication Association, 1975), pp. 11–17.

unwilling receivers, and no involvement of juveniles)? To this question the chief justice replied, "We categorically disapprove the theory . . . that obscene, pornographic films acquire constitutional immunity from state regulation simply because they are exhibited for consenting adults only."

2. *Must the prosecution assume the burden of proof to show that the materials are obscene by presenting "expert" affirmative evidence to that end?* The chief justice said no, there was no error in the trial just because the prosecution failed "to require 'expert' affirmative evidence that the materials were obscene. . . . The films, obviously, are the best evidence of what they represent." This viewpoint, which is reinforced in the *Kaplan* decision, *shifts the burden of proof* to the defendant to prove that the materials have serious value or are not obscene for some other reason. In effect, accused materials are "guilty" until proved "innocent."

3. *Is censorship permissible in view of the lack of scientific evidence to show that explicit sexual materials cause antisocial conduct on the part of those who peruse them?* Yes, such censorship is permissible, said the chief justice, for even though "there is no conclusive proof of a connection between antisocial behavior and obscene material, the legislature of Georgia could quite reasonably determine that such a connection does or might exist. . . . From the beginning of civilized societies, legislators and judges have acted on *various unprovable assumptions*."[41] [Emphasis supplied.]

[41]For a further look at this interesting statement, see Thomas L. Tedford, "Unprovable Assumptions? The Reasons and Empirical Evidence of Twelve Who Favor Censorship," in *Free Speech Yearbook: 1978,* ed. Gregg Phifer (Falls Church, Va.: Speech Communication Association, 1979), pp. 156–161. The study reveals a number of reasons given by the censors for suppressing erotica, but *none* of the reasons is supported by any empirical evidence whatsoever.

4. *In what ways, if any, may state laws in the future differ from the standards set forth here and in the other four cases?* The chief justice affirmed that state laws may be more liberal, but not more restrictive, than the standards being announced. "The States," he noted, "may follow . . . a 'laissez faire' policy and drop all controls on commercialized obscenity, if that is what they prefer," but they need not do so since "we hold that the States have a legitimate interest in regulating commerce in obscene material and in regulating exhibition of obscene material in places of public accommodation, including so-called 'adult' theatres from which minors are excluded."

Kaplan *v*. California

The third case, *Kaplan* v. *California,* reaffirmed decisions made in the first two cases, namely, that state or local standards could be used to decide the matter of prurience, that limiting the sale of sexual materials to consenting adults did not result in constitutional protection, and that the prosecution did not err when it failed to call "expert" witnesses to testify as to the worthlessness and prurience of the work in question. One new issue did emerge, however, for the book was not illustrated, and the argument was made by the defendant that only *graphic* sexual depictions should be found legally obscene. Not so, said the chief justice in rejecting the argument, for when the Court "declared that obscenity is not a form of expression protected by the First Amendment, no distinction was made as to the medium of the expression. . . . Obscenity can . . . manifest itself in conduct, in the pictorial representation of conduct, or in *the written and oral description* of conduct." [Emphasis supplied.]

United States *v*. 12 200–Ft. Reels of Super 8mm. Film

In the fourth case, an American citizen

named Paladini tried to bring some sexually explicit films, slides, photos, and printed materials from Mexico through U.S. Customs to the United States, arguing at the customs checkpoint that the materials were for his personal, private use. When the customs inspectors refused entry, Paladini sought court relief, and the federal district court, citing *Stanley* v. *Georgia,* ordered the materials returned to the claimant. The U.S. Supreme Court disagreed and upheld the constitutionality of the import restriction as per 19 *U.S. Code* Sec. 1305. Chief Justice Burger stated:

> We are not disposed to extend the . . . holding of *Stanley* to permit importation of admittedly obscene materials simply because they are imported for private use only. . . . We have already indicated that the protected right to possess obscene material in the privacy of one's home does not give rise to a correlative right to have someone sell or give it to others. . . . It follows that *Stanley* does not permit one to go abroad and bring such material into the country for private purposes.

United States *v.* Orito

The final case concerned the shipment of explicit sexual materials in interstate commerce by a common carrier (not the U.S. mails) such as an express company, an airline, or a bus. Such interstate shipment is a crime under 18 *U.S. Code* Sec. 1462, as George J. Orito discovered when he was arrested for shipping sex films by commercial airline from San Francisco to Milwaukee, Wisconsin. Before the district court, Orito claimed a privacy right and also argued that the statute in question was overbroad for not distinguishing between "public" and "nonpublic" means of transportation. Agreeing with Orito, the district court dismissed the case, declared the federal statute involved to be unconstitutional, and affirmed that non-

public transportation of obscene materials was protected by the Constitution.

The U.S. Supreme Court disagreed, however, and reinstated the indictment. In his opinion for the Court, Chief Justice Burger asserted that the right to privacy was strictly limited to one's home, that the federal law in question was not too broad, and that it was not a violation of the Constitution for the Congress to prohibit the interstate shipment of explicit sexual materials, even if they are intended for the recipient's private use. The combined effect of *Orito* and the case immediately preceding, concerning Paladini's attempt to bring erotic materials through customs, is that *neither importation nor interstate shipment* of obscene materials is legal.

Justices Douglas and Brennan in Dissent

Justices Douglas, Brennan, Stewart, and Marshall dissented from the opinion of the Court in each of the cases, making the vote 5 to 4 in all five decisions. However only Justices Brennan and Douglas announced dissenting opinions, for the others concurred without comment in the published views of Justice Brennan in each instance. Justice Douglas began his rebuttal in the *Miller* case by emphasizing his deep conviction, often stated during his years on the Court, that the First Amendment allowed no exception for the explicit sexual expression that legislatures and the courts classify as obscene. At the time of the adoption of the Bill of Rights, he pointed out, "there was no recognized exception to the free press . . . which treated 'obscene' publications differently from other types of papers, magazines, and books." He also decried the Court's action in allowing Miller to be punished under a definition of obscenity that was not in effect at the time of his arrest (as was done to Ginzburg and Mishkin in 1966) and for failing to recognize the futility of trying to censor where the subjective "tastes and standards of literature" were involved.

Without conceding his First Amendment argument, Justice Douglas then urged the adoption of a minimal "fairness" procedure that would at least provide "fair warning" to public communicators that certain messages presented by certain means were considered obscene, and therefore illegal, in the local community. In other words, Justice Douglas argued that if society must censor, the procedure used should be such that communicators will *clearly* know what is illegal. The way to accomplish this, he proposed, is by the civil adversary hearing which, without criminal penalty, would label materials as obscene and give the communicator the right to withdraw the material from distribution prior to criminal sanction.[42]

Justice Douglas then emphasized that no "captive audience" problem occurred in any of the five censorship cases, for no citizen was "being compelled to look or to listen." Then, with rare feeling and passion—qualities of argument on behalf of the First Amendment that have been almost totally missing from the Court since the retirements of Justices Hugo L. Black and William O. Douglas—he concluded that the decisions of the day were nothing less than a "radical break with the traditions of a free society."

Justice Douglas, *dissenting:*

. . . The First Amendment was not fashioned as a vehicle for dispensing tranquilizers to the people. Its prime function was to keep debate

open to "offensive" as well as to "staid" people. The tendency throughout history has been to subdue the individual and to exalt the power of government. The use of the standard "offensive" gives authority to government that cuts the very vitals out of the First Amendment. As is intimated by the Court's opinion, the materials before us may be garbage. But so is much of what is said in political campaigns, in the daily press, on TV or over the radio. . . .

We deal with highly emotional, not rational, questions. To many the Song of Solomon is obscene. I do not think we, the judges, were ever given the constitutional power to make definitions of obscenity. If it is to be defined, let the people debate and decide by a constitutional amendment what they want to ban as obscene and what standards they want the legislatures and the courts to apply. Perhaps the people will decide that the path towards a mature, integrated society requires that all ideas competing for acceptance must have no censor. Perhaps they will decide otherwise. Whatever the choice, the courts will have some guidelines. Now we have none except our own predilections.

To the surprise of many Court observers, Justice William Brennan, the leading procensorship spokesman for the Court since 1957, announced in his dissent in *Paris Adult Theatre* (his key rebuttal to the Court's opinion in all five cases) that he had changed his mind concerning the best way to handle the obscenity quandary. Justice Brennan began by stating that he was "convinced that the approach initiated 15 years ago in *Roth* . . . , and culminating in the Court's decision today, cannot bring stability to this area of the law without jeopardizing fundamental values, and . . . that the time has come to make a significant departure from that approach." Without delivering any "ringing defense" of freedom of expression, Justice Brennan built his proposals upon a utilitarian foundation— the *Roth* approach had not worked; therefore,

---

[42]Chief Justice Burger rejected this proposal in 1973, and the Court continues to refuse to require a civil adversary hearing in obscenity cases. States are free to do so, however, and a number have put this idea into effect, including Arkansas, Louisiana, Massachusetts, North Carolina, North Dakota, Vermont, and Wisconsin. Information from the amicus curiae brief filed by the Association of American Publishers in the case of *Smith* v. *United States,* 431 U.S. 291 (1977).

a new approach was called for. His lengthy dissent and the detailed arguments presented in it can be summarized in outline form as follows:

1. *The inherent weaknesses of* Roth *are continued in* Miller. Justice Brennan argued that the Court had been "unable to provide 'sensitive tools' to separate obscenity from other sexually oriented but constitutionally protected speech, so that efforts to suppress the former do not spill over into the suppression of the latter." He added that in *Miller* "a majority of the Court offers a slightly altered formulation of the basic *Roth* test, while leaving entirely unchanged the underlying approach." Observing that the approach of the past cannot be reconciled with fundamental First Amendment principles, Justice Brennan admitted,

I am reluctantly forced to the conclusion that none of the available formulas, including the one announced today, can reduce the vagueness to a tolerable level. . . . Any effort to draw a constitutionally acceptable boundary on state power must resort to such indefinite concepts as "prurient interest," "patent offensiveness," "serious literary value," and the like. The meaning of these concepts necessarily varies with the experience, outlook, and even the idiosyncracies of the person defining them. . . .[43]

2. *There are three special problems with the new formula:*

a. *Fair notice.* Even the most "painstaking efforts to determine in advance whether certain sexually oriented expression is obscene must inevitably prove

unavailing," noted Justice Brennan, adding that the "resulting level of uncertainty is utterly intolerable, not alone because it makes 'bookselling a hazardous profession,' . . . but as well because it invites arbitrary and erratic enforcement of the law."

b. *Chilling effect.* The vagueness of the concept of obscenity has a "chilling effect" upon the exercise of First Amendment freedoms.

c. *Institutional stress.* Based upon his fifteen years of experience, Justice Brennan emphasized that the Court's censorship efforts place heavy stress upon the institutions of law enforcement and the courts, for "one cannot say with certainty that material is obscene until at least five members of this Court, applying inevitably obscure standards, have pronounced it so."[44]

3. *There are four "unsatisfactory" alternatives:*

a. *Prohibit all depictions of sex.* While such an approach would provide fair notice, Justice Brennan observed, it must be rejected as "appallingly overbroad," for it would permit "the suppression of a vast range of literary, scientific, and artistic masterpieces. Neither the First Amendment nor any free community could possibly tolerate such a standard."

b. *Try to define the meaning of "obscenity."* This is the current approach, used in *Roth* and continued in *Miller*. It has not worked, nor will it, Justice Brennan

[43]A similar view was expressed in different words by Justice William O. Douglas in 1968: "Censors are, of course, propelled by their own neuroses. That is why a universally accepted definition of obscenity is impossible. Any definition is indeed highly subjective, turning on the neurosis of the censor." Dissenting opinion in *Ginsberg* v. *New York*, 390 U.S. 629 (1968).

[44]Justice Brennan was proved right on this point soon after the Miller test was announced. Later in 1973, Georgia attempted to ban the film *Carnal Knowledge,* a standard Hollywood release (starring Jack Nicholson and Candice Bergen) voted one of the ten best films produced in 1971. The U.S. Supreme Court had to reverse the courts of Georgia, doing so in *Jenkins* v. *Georgia*, 418 U.S. 153 (1974). For more, see the next section, "Progeny of *Miller*."

reemphasized, after which he criticized the chief justice's "Miller test" by pointing out that it "necessarily assumes that some works will be deemed obscene—even though they clearly have *some* social value—because the State was able to prove that the value, measured by some unspecified standard, was not sufficiently 'serious' to warrant constitutional protection. The result," he argued, "is nothing less than a rejection of the fundamental First Amendment premises and rationale of the *Roth* opinion and an invitation to widespread suppression of sexually oriented speech." In a final sentence Justice Brennan noted a historical fact: *"Before today, the protections of the First Amendment have never been thought limited to expressions of serious literary or political value."* [Emphasis supplied.]

c. *The Court could withdraw and turn the issue over to local juries.* This simply would not fit with the Constitution, Justice Brennan asserted, for "the first Amendment requires an independent review by appellate courts of the constitutional fact of obscenity. That result is required by principles applicable to the obscenity issue no less than to any other area involving free expression . . . or other constitutional right."

d. *Extend First Amendment protection to explicit sexual communications.* "Finally," Justice Brennan stated, "I have considered the view, urged so forcefully since 1957 by our Brothers Black and Douglas, that the First Amendment bars the suppression of any sexually oriented expression. That position," he notes,

would effect a sharp reduction . . . of the uncertainty that surrounds our current approach. Nevertheless, I am convinced that it would achieve that desirable goal only by stripping the

States of power to an extent that cannot be justified by the commands of the Constitution, at least so long as there is available an alternative approach that strikes a better balance between the guarantee of free expression and the States' legitimate interests.[45]

4. *A new solution is called for under a doctrine of privacy: allow consenting adults to make their own choices.* "In short," concluded Justice Brennan,

while I cannot say that the interests of the State—apart from the question of juveniles and unconsenting adults—are trivial or nonexistent, I am compelled to conclude that these interests cannot justify the substantial damage to constitutional rights and to this Nation's judicial machinery that inevitably results from state efforts to bar the distribution even of unprotected material to consenting adults. . . .

I would hold, therefore, that at least in the absence of distribution to juveniles or obtrusive exposure to unconsenting adults, the First and Fourteenth Amendments prohibit the state and federal governments from attempting wholly to suppress sexually oriented materials on the basis of their allegedly "obscene" contents.

Justice Brennan's change of view concerning the Supreme Court's policy on censorship was too late. By the time he reached the conclusion that the Constitution did grant to adult citizens of the United States the right to decide for themselves about sexual communications—even explicitly "sinful" ones—he had too few votes on the Court to make the

---

[45]In other words, Justice Brennan rejected the First Amendment argument that all "sexually oriented expression" was protected speech. Evidently he believed that this would lead to an undermining of state efforts to prohibit dissemination to juveniles and to nonconsenting adults. He opted instead for a *privacy* approach that would leave intact controls upon sale or distribution to minors and to those adults who do not want to receive explicit sexual messages. Even this compromise position was rejected by the Court.

consenting-adults interpretation of the Constitution the law of the land. However, his dissenting opinion in *Paris Adult Theatre* remains one of the best arguments against censorship to emerge from Supreme Court debates on the subject.

Before we examine the Court's efforts to explain its new rules—under "Progeny of *Miller*," which follows—a summary of the standards announced in the five opinions of June 21, 1973, is needed. *First,* the Supreme Court redefined obscenity in these words: "(a) whether 'the average person, applying contemporary community standards' would find that the work, taken as a whole, appeals to the prurient interest, . . . (b) whether the work depicts or describes, in a patently offensive way, sexual conduct specifically defined by the applicable state law, and (c) whether the work, taken as a whole, lacks serious literary, artistic, political, or scientific value." *Second,* the Court made it clear that (a) the term "contemporary community standards" meant *state or local* standards; (b) consenting adults do *not* have the right to receive or view explicit sexual materials outside the home; (c) prosecutors no longer have to prove that the material at bar is without value, thus shifting the burden of proof to the defendant to show that the material does have serious value; (d) this is done while admitting that scientific evidence does not support the claim that society needs censorship; (e) state laws may be more liberal than the standards set by the Supreme Court; (f) unillustrated materials consisting of *words only* come under obscenity law just as do graphic materials; (g) no constitutional right exists to import explicit sexual materials (not even for use in the privacy of one's own home); and (h) the interstate shipment of obscene materials by common carrier is illegal. *Third,* the five opinions by Chief Justice Burger left at least three previous obscenity rulings in force: (a) pandering remains illegal, as set forth in *Ginzburg* v. *United States* (1966); (b) the terms "or its intended and probable recipient group" remain a part of the "average person" clarification of the Court, as set forth in *Mishkin* v. *New York* (1966); and (c) states may continue to have special statutes aimed at preventing the dissemination of sexual materials to minors, as announced in *Ginsberg* v. *New York* (1968).

The Progeny of *Miller*

The opinions announced by Chief Justice Burger in June of 1973 were met with shouts of "hallelujah" from those who favored the use of civil law to suppress the religio-moral offense of obscenity, whereas those same opinions were met with cries of "repression" from civil libertarians—including many publishers, booksellers, filmmakers, librarians, and teachers—who correctly predicted that the rulings would influence local officials in areas beyond "adult" bookstores and "adult" theaters. Only three months after the chief justice reconfirmed censorship, the American Library Association reported (and continues to report to the present day in its bimonthly *Newsletter on Intellectual Freedom*) that not only materials such as *Deep Throat* were under renewed attack but also public school libraries, city and county libraries, and nonobscene regular cinema productions such as *Last Tango in Paris.* In Jacksonville, Florida, a member of the city council asked the state attorney to investigate the Jacksonville Public Library for illegal materials (the council member was upset over the presence of Mickey Spillane's novel *The Erection Set* on the shelves), and in Macon, Georgia, the mayor ordered the county schools to "purge library shelves of objectionable literature" or face the prospect of police action.[46]

---

[46]"In the Court's Wake . . . ," *Newsletter on Intellectual Freedom,* September 1973, pp. 98 ff.

Interpretations from the Supreme Court were not long in coming. In some instances the Court's ruling put an abrupt end to certain local censorship efforts (as in the case of the film *Carnal Knowledge,* discussed below), whereas in others the Court sustained such efforts (as in *Ward* v. *Illinois,* also discussed below). An examination of the Court's adjustments and "clarifications" of *Miller* plus rulings in cognate areas of the law can be summarized according to three groupings. *First* are those standard "obscenity" decisions in which the content of expression is central (four decisions); *second* are those cases that pertain to special time, place, manner, and "nuisance" approaches to regulation of erotic expression (three decisions); and *finally,* the Supreme Court's landmark decision in the field of child pornography, announced in 1982.

Four Content-Centered Cases

1. *Jenkins* v. *Georgia,* 418 U.S. 153 (1974). A jury in Dougherty County, Georgia, had found the award-winning movie *Carnal Knowledge,* starring Jack Nicholson and Candice Bergen, obscene under state law, and the Georgia Supreme Court had sustained the verdict. By a unanimous vote, the U.S. Supreme Court reversed the courts below. Justice Rehnquist, in his opinion of the Court, let it be known that the Supreme Court was not trying to constrain serious films, even when such films include some nudity and imply that sexual conduct is occurring. The film *Carnal Knowledge* does not treat sex in a "patently offensive" manner, he asserted, for there is "no exhibition whatever of the actors' genitals, lewd or otherwise, during the [sex] scenes." Also, Justice Rehnquist added, even though there were "occasional scenes of nudity . . . [this] alone is not enough to make material legally obscene under the *Miller* standards." (The ruling sent a message to prosecutors throughout the na-

tion that only "hard-core" erotica was to be censored, and in most cases legal moves against films such as *Last Tango in Paris* were discontinued.)

Justice Rehnquist also attempted to explain what the Court meant by the term "contemporary community standards" in its Miller test. While restating that judges and juries were not required to use "national standards" in obscenity cases, he stated that it was up to the legislatures of the various states to decide whether to use *local* standards (i.e., those of the forum community from which the jury is drawn) or *statewide* standards.[47]

2. *Smith* v. *United States,* 431 U.S. 291 (1977). By a vote of 5 to 4, the Supreme Court upheld the conviction of Jerry Lee Smith for mailing explicit erotic materials to a consenting adult who had requested them (but who turned out to be a federal postal inspector), even though the materials did not leave the state of Iowa, which had a liberal consenting-adults statute in effect at the time. In other words, Smith mailed the erotica from one part of Iowa to another and was convicted for it even though the material mailed was legal under state law. Never mind, said the Court, the mails come under the federal Comstock Act and cannot be used to transport obscenity under any circumstances. Public communicators should note this ruling carefully, for it—like another

---

[47]In fact, states may specify national standards if they wish. *Miller,* as it turns out, permits a choice, and state law may name (1) local, (2) statewide, or (3) national standards in obscenity statutes. See Jerome A. Barron and C. Thomas Dienes, *Handbook of Free Speech and Free Press* (Boston: Little, Brown 1979), p. 626. Furthermore, jury members are permitted to "guess" what the local or state standards are, since there is no requirement for the introduction of empirical evidence concerning current attitudes in the geographical area specified by state law. For more, see Marc B. Glassman, "Community Standards of Patent Offensiveness: Public Opinion Data and Obscenity Law," *Public Opinion Quarterly* 42 (1978): 161–170.

mails-use case decided three years earlier[48]— makes clear that mailing explicit sexual materials remains a *federal* crime, regardless of local or state laws.

3. *Ward* v. *Illinois,* 431 U.S. 767 (1977). Ward's appeal from an obscenity conviction in Illinois raises a question similar to that raised by Mishkin in 1966, for both claimed that the language of the law under which they were convicted was not clear and specific in its application to their books and magazines. Ward was convicted under the Illinois obscenity law for selling the magazines *Bizarre World* and *Illustrated Case Histories—A Study in Sado-Masochism.* After the Illinois Supreme Court sustained the conviction, Ward appealed to the U.S. Supreme Court, emphasizing in his brief that the Illinois statute under which he had been charged did not conform to that part of the three-part *Miller* standard requiring that the work in question depict or describe "in a patently offensive way, sexual conduct *specifically defined by the applicable state law."* [Emphasis supplied.] Ward was correct in his argument, for the Illinois law did not mention, much less "specifically define," sadomasochistic erotica. As Justice White cited in his opinion of the Court, the law stated: "A thing is obscene if, considered as a whole, its predominant appeal is to prurient interest, that is, a shameful or morbid interest in nudity, sex or excretion, and if it goes substantially beyond customary limits of candor in description or representation of such matters."

By a vote of 5 to 4, the Burger Court affirmed, thereby continuing the practice employed in the 1966 cases of *Ginzburg* and *Mishkin* of formulating post facto redefinitions of "obscenity" that are, in turn, used to justify the decision to sustain the conviction. Justice White, speaking for the Court in *Ward,* observed that even though the Illinois statute did not specifically describe the materials sold by the defendant, Ward should have known from previous rulings of the Illinois Supreme Court that sadomasochistic materials were illegal in the state. Furthermore, Justice White asserted, "there was no suggestion in *Miller* that we intended to extend constitutional protection to [this] . . . kind of flagellatory material . . . ." In short, the U.S. Supreme Court held that even though the statute was not specific, Ward *should have known* that it was meant to cover his materials, that the Illinois Supreme Court had said as much in years gone by, and that the Supreme Court never intended to extend protection to such stuff.

Justice John Paul Stevens, with whom Justices Brennan, Stewart, and Marshall joined, dissenting, perceptively analyzed the self-inflicted wound that the majority gave to its own test, so recently announced, by reasoning as it did in *Ward.* Justice Stevens observed, "Today, the Court silently abandons one of the cornerstones of the Miller test announced so forcefully" in 1973. He then quoted from the *Miller* decision, which set forth the following requirement:

Under the holdings announced today, no one will be subject to prosecution for the sale or exposure of obscene materials unless these materials depict or describe patently offensive " hard core" sexual conduct specifically defined by the regulating state law, as written or construed. We are satisfied that these specific prerequisites will provide fair notice to a dealer in such materials that his public and commercial activities may bring prosecution.

---

[48]*Hamling* v. *United States,* 418 U.S. 87 (1974). Hamling sold an illustrated version of the *Report of the Commission on Obscenity and Pornography,* and although the jury could not agree that the illustrated *Report* was obscene, it did find the brochure advertising the product to be obscene.

Justice Stevens then noted that more than fifty obscenity cases were sent back to the lower courts following the 1973 reformulations in order to give defendants in those cases the "benefit" of this aspect of *Miller*. He explained further.

Justice Stevens, dissenting:

Many state courts, taking *Miller* at face value, invalidated or substantially limited their obscenity laws. Others, like Illinois, did "little more than pay lip service to the specificity requirement in *Miller*." . . . Like most pre-*Miller* obscenity statutes, the Illinois statute contained open-ended terms broad enough to prohibit the distribution of any material making an "appeal . . . to prurient interest." In its post-*Miller* opinions, the Illinois Supreme Court has made it clear that the statute covers all of the *Miller* examples. It has not, however, stated that the statute is limited to those examples, or to any other specifically defined category.

Nevertheless, this Court affirms the conviction in this Illinois case on two theories. The first is that this particular defendant had notice that the State considered these materials obscene, because prior Illinois cases had upheld obscenity convictions concerning similar material. . . . The Court's second theory is that, in any event, the Illinois statute is sufficiently specific to satisfy *Miller*. Although the statute does not contain an "exhaustive list" of specific examples . . . it passes muster because it contains a generic reference to "the *kinds* of sexual conduct which may not be represented or depicted under the obscenity laws . . . ." To hold that the list need not be exhaustive is to hold that a person can be prosecuted although the materials he sells are not specifically described in the list. [In *Miller*] . . . the Court promised that "no one" could be so prosecuted. . . .

One of the strongest arguments against regulating obscenity through criminal law is the inherent vagueness of the obscenity concept. The specificity requirement as described in *Miller* held out the promise of a principled effort to respond to that argu- **ment. By abandoning that effort today, the Court withdraws the cornerstone of the *Miller* structure and, undoubtedly, hastens its ultimate downfall.** Although the decision is therefore a mixed blessing, I nevertheless respectfully dissent.

Before the *Ward* decision was announced, the second part of the Miller test required that the judge or jury member in an obscenity proceeding to decide "whether the work depicts or describes, in a patently offensive way, sexual conduct specifically defined by the applicable state law." After *Ward*, this part of the Miller standard can be paraphrased to read as follows: whether the work depicts or describes, in a patently offensive way, sexual conduct which is specifically defined *or which one believes was intended to be defined* by the applicable state law." (Students of the First Amendment should note that in this case, as with *Ginzburg* and *Mishkin*, the U.S. Supreme Court reflects the view of Lewis Carroll's Humpty Dumpty as adapted to the topic under discussion: "When we judges of the High Court define 'obscenity,' it means just what we choose it to mean—neither more nor less.")

4. *Pinkus* v. *United States,* 436 U.S. 293 (1978). In this federal case, Pinkus had been convicted of violating the Comstock Act by sending obscene materials through the mail. At the conclusion of the trial, the judge instructed the jury that the first part of the Miller test, which says "the average person, applying contemporary community standards," should include everyone from "the community as a whole, young and old, educated and uneducated, the religious and irreligious, men, women, and *children,* from all walks of life." [Emphasis supplied.] Holding that the inclusion of children in the instructions was a major error, the U.S. Supreme Court reversed the conviction, thereby not-

ing that to include minors would substantially weaken the "average person" requirement. As a consequence of this decision, the term "average person" is interpreted to mean *adult* persons and to exclude juveniles.[49] In a related matter, the Supreme Court did express its approval of the trial judge's view that the pandering doctrine, as announced in the 1966 *Ginzburg* case, was still in force and could be a factor in determining guilt.

Time, Place, Manner, and "Nuisance"
Controls: Three Cases

1. *Erzoznik* v. *Jacksonville,* 422 U.S. 205 (1975). In 1975 the Supreme Court heard a case in which Jacksonville, Florida, had tried to enforce a public nuisance ordinance against a drive-in theater whose screen could be seen from nearby streets. The ordinance made it a nuisance to show "any motion picture, slide, or other exhibit in which the male or female bare buttocks, human female bare breasts, or human bare pubic areas are shown, if such motion picture, slide or other exhibit is visible from any public street or public place." The Court struck down the ordinance for being too broad, emphasizing that "all nudity cannot be deemed obscene." Furthermore, the Court noted that the law was not directed specifically at explicit sexual activity and as written would even prohibit the showing of "a picture of a baby's buttocks." Over the protests of Chief Justice Burger and Justices Rehnquist and White, the Court majority made it clear that obscenity laws must be more narrowly drawn than was the Jacksonville ordinance.

2. *Young* v. *American Mini-Theatres,* 427 U.S. 50 (1976). The *Young* case concerned Detroit's attempt to zone a "skid row" section of the city so as to prevent the accumulation of "adult" bookstores, theaters, pool halls, bars, and so on in one area. The ordinance sought to disperse "adult" establishments by prohibiting them within 500 feet of a residential area or within 1,000 feet of each other. By a vote of 5 to 4, the U.S. Supreme Court sustained the Detroit law, even though in prior cases issues of place of expression required a content-neutral decision—that is, one that was not based upon the message being communicated. (As readers have no doubt noted, where the "sin" of obscenity is concerned, judges do not hesitate to create exceptions to precedent.) Consequently, it is now permissible for municipalities to use a form of zoning control to keep adult establishments dispersed.

3. *Vance* v. *Universal Amusement,* 455 U.S. 308 (1980). Two Texas "public nuisance" statutes, one approved in 1952 and the other in 1978, combined to make it possible for a state judge to *close* a bookstore or theater that had been found guilty of disseminating obscenity in the past, thereby enforcing a prior restraint upon the dissemination of *all* types of material in the future, including books, magazines, and films fully protected by the Constitution. A three-judge federal district court in Texas found the laws unconstitutional because they functioned as a form of prior restraint upon the right to communicate. Citing *Near* v. *Minnesota,* the landmark case of 1931 that prohibits prior restraint except in the most unusual circumstances (for more, see Chapter 9 on prior restraint and free press-fair trial), the district court characterized the Texas approach as a "heavy hand" upon freedom of speech. In its per curiam opinion, which represented the view of only five justices, the Supreme Court upheld the view of the district court and thus denied states the right to practice prior restraint un-

---

[49]To have ruled otherwise would have been a throwback to the Hicklin rule of the nineteenth century, which had been thoroughly discredited in the United States (and in England) during the twentieth century.

der the guise of "nuisance" proceedings. Among the four dissenters (Chief Justice Burger and Justices Powell, White, and Rehnquist), Justice White in an opinion joined by Justice Rehnquist expressed a willingness to allow states greater leeway in the use of "nuisance abatement" court orders in obscenity cases than *Vance* permitted. Also, some public officials have evidently not studied the *Vance* decision carefully, for new state efforts at prior restraint in obscenity matters emerge annually.[50] Students of the First Amendment should stay alert to this issue, for it is likely to be adjudicated further in the years ahead.

Child Pornography: The Landmark Ruling of New York v. Ferber *(1982)*

In 1977 the legislature of the State of New York enacted a child pornography statute that made it a felony to use a juvenile under the age of sixteen in a sexual performance, actual or simulated, for the preparation or dissemination of visual materials such as films, photographs, plays, dances, or "any other visual presentation exhibited before an audience." The statute listed a variety of proscribed sexual activities, ranging from regular intercourse to bestiality, and explained that the prohibition was absolute, even if the expression that resulted from the sexual use of a minor was not legally obscene (i.e., had serious social value). In short, the law placed a flat ban upon the use of minors in sexual performances. Soon after the law was enacted, Paul Ira Ferber was arrested in his adult bookstore and charged with violating the child pornography law by selling films which showed children masturbating.

The resulting litigation led to a landmark ruling by the U.S. Supreme Court.

Justice White, in his opinion of the Court (joined by Chief Justice Burger and Justices Powell, Rehnquist, and O'Connor),[51] cited five reasons for establishing child pornography as a new form of expression which is not protected by the Constitution. The five are as follows:

1. The constraint is needed in order to safeguard the physical and emotional well-being of minors. This judgment "easily passes muster under the First Amendment."

2. Sexual abuse of children occurs, even when the material being prepared has some serious value. Therefore, the Miller standard for testing obscenity is not a satisfactory solution to the problem. "It is irrelevant to the child [who has been abused] whether or not the material . . . has a literary, artistic, political, or scientific value."

3. Constraints upon advertising and selling child pornography will help remove the economic motive for manufacturing and disseminating this kind of material and thus help combat the problem of sexual abuse of children.

4. The use of juveniles in the preparation of serious works concerning sex is rarely, if ever, necessary. Other means of portrayal can be employed, such as using a model of legal age who looks younger.

5. This content-based constraint is consistent with earlier decisions of the Court in First Amendment matters. The balancing of the "evil to be restricted" against the "expressive interests" supports the censorship of

---

[50]See, for example, Chris Finan, " 'Obscene Nuisance' Laws: Their Fate in 1982 and Prospects for 1983," *Newsletter on Intellectual Freedom,* May 1983, pp. 35 ff.

[51]Without comment, Justice Blackmun concurred in the result; also, Justices Brennan, Marshall, and Stevens concurred in the judgment, stating their reservations in separate opinions. Justice O'Connor also filed a separate, concurring opinion.

LANDMARK CASE
New York v. Ferber, 458 U.S. 747 (1982)
Decided July 2, 1982

Vote: 9 to 0 to uphold New York's law prohibiting the production or dissemination of child pornography (even if the material in question is not legally obscene).

Majority Opinion By: Justice White.

Concurring Justices: Chief Justice Burger and Justices Brennan, Marshall, Blackmun, Powell, Rehnquist, Stevens, and O'Connor.

Dissenting Justices: (none)

Justices Not Participating: (none)

Summary: Paul Ira Ferber, proprietor of a Manhattan adult bookstore, was convicted of disseminating child pornography under a 1977 New York statute making it a crime to produce or disseminate sexually explicit films or photographs involving children or to use children in live sexual performances regardless of whether or not the material or performance in question was legally obscene. The jury in the case did not find the films sold by Ferber (which showed young boys masturbating) obscene under the law, but the jury did convict Ferber under the child pornography statute that did not require proof of obscenity. Following a series of appeals, the U.S. Supreme Court upheld the constitutionality of the New York statute under which the conviction was obtained, stressing that, on balance, the need to protect the physical and psychological well being of children far outweighed any societal interest in actually employing children in the production of *visual* materials involving explicit sexual activity.

Rule Established; Significance of Case: Child pornography in which juveniles are actually employed in the preparation of explicitly sexual materials of a *visual* nature is outside the protection of the Constitution—along with obscenity, the defamation of private persons, and the use of language that incites to violence. This decision does not alter the Miller test for obscenity; however, it does establish a new category of prohibited expression—child pornography—and a new reason for censorship—to protect the mental and physical well being of minors.

child pornography, for when material such as that singled out by the New York statute "bears so heavily and pervasively on the welfare of children engaged in its production, we think the balance of competing interests is clearly struck and that it is permissible to consider these materials as without the protection of the First Amendment."

The First Amendment implications of the *Ferber* decision became apparent almost immediately. Within a few days after the Court ruled, St. Martin's Press withdrew the sex education manual *Show Me!* from distribution in the United States because the book included several photographs of nude children as illustrations of child sexual behavior. Fur-

thermore, when a bill based upon the New York law was submitted to the North Carolina General Assembly in 1983, the drafters of the legislation observed that no exceptions for serious scientific or literary value were provided. This would mean, the bill's supporters said, that materials such as the Brooke Shields film *Blue Lagoon* would likely be banned in North Carolina in the future (because Shields was only fifteen years of age when the simulated love scenes in the movie were filmed).

The combined problems of foolishness on the part of the censors and overbreadth in the laws governing child pornography present serious issues to the student of freedom of expression. Justice O'Connor recognized some of these issues when she noted in her concurring opinion in *Ferber:*

> For example, clinical pictures of adolescent sexuality, such as those that might appear in medical textbooks, might not involve the type of sexual exploitation and abuse targeted by New York's statute. . . .Similarly, pictures of children engaged in rites widely approved by their cultures, such as those that might appear in issues of *National Geographic,* might not trigger the compelling interest identified by the Court.

If the past is any guide to what contemporary and future censors will attempt to suppress, readers can expect that, sooner or later, the concerns expressed by Justice O'Connor—and related issues as well—will work their way to the Court, and that *Ferber* will be "refined" and "clarified."

Miller and Progeny in Brief

On June 21, 1973, Chief Justice Warren Burger, joined by Justices White, Blackmun, Powell, and Rehnquist, discarded much of the Roth test of 1957 and redefined the religio-moral offense of obscenity in the case of *Miller* v. *California* and four companion cases. The Miller test announced that day said that obscenity was to be determined as follows:

> (a) whether "the average person, applying contemporary community standards" would find that the work, taken as a whole, appeals to the prurient interest, . . . (b) whether the work depicts or describes, in a patently offensive way, sexual conduct specifically defined by the applicable state law, and (c) whether the work, taken as a whole, lacks serious literary, artistic, political, or scientific value.

At the same time the Court made it clear that it intended to delegate to state authorities the primary responsibility for deciding obscenity matters in the future, that local and state standards of offensiveness would prevail, and that the accused had the burden of proof to show that the material in question had serious value.

Inevitably, however, a few cases from the lower courts were reviewed by the Supreme Court, and just as *Roth* (1957) had been interpreted by its "progeny," so was *Miller* (1973) interpreted over the years. Consequently, the current test of obscenity, based upon the Miller standard as explained by the Court, and including those precedents of *Roth* and progeny which were retained in 1973, can be paraphrased as follows: *to be obscene, the expression must be (1) to the average adult person or its intended or probable recipient group, applying contemporary standards of the local community (unless state or national standards are specified by state law) the work taken as a whole, appeals to the prurient interest or is advertised as if it appeals to the prurient interest; (2) whether the work depicts or describes, in a patently offensive way, sexual conduct specifically defined by applicable state law, or which the judge or member of the jury believes was intended to be included in the definition even though no exhaustive list is supplied; and (3) whether the work, taken as a whole, lacks serious literary, artistic, political, or scientific value* (the last phrase has been described as the "SLAPS test" for Serious Literary, Artistic, Political, or Scientific value). Related and subordinate rules include:

1. Consenting adults do not have a privacy right to receive obscene materials (*Paris Adult Theatre I* v. *Slaton* and *U.S.* v. *12 200 Ft. Reels of Super 8mm Film,* both 1973).

2. It remains illegal to import obscenity, to ship it by common carrier from state to state, or to send it through the mails (*U.S.* v. *12 200-Ft. Reels* and *U.S.* v. *Orito,* both 1973; also *Smith* v. *U.S.,* 1977).

3. Nudity and obscenity are not the same,

and broadly written laws that prohibit all depictions of nudity in public displays violate the Constitution (*Erzoznik* v. *Jacksonville,* 1975).

4. The use of zoning ordinances to disperse adult entertainment establishments, including theaters and bookstores, does not violate the Constitution (*Young* v. *American Mini-Theatres,* 1976).

5. "Nuisance" abatement statutes permitting the *closing* of bookstores and theaters that have disseminated obscene materials in the past are unconstitutional, for such laws function as a form of prior restraint upon future communications, including those protected by the First Amendment (*Vance* v. *Universal Amusement,* 1980).

6. A flat prohibition upon the use of minors for the preparation or presentation of visual materials involving explicit sexual activity even if the resulting expression is not legally obscene is permissible under the Constitution (*New York* v. *Ferber,* 1982).

CONCLUSION

At least six clearly defined religio-moral offenses of belief and expression emerge from Anglo-American history: teaching false doctrine, blasphemy, profane and disgusting speech, explicit erotic expression, certain opinions and facts of science, and dissenting views concerning private morality. These six (as shown by Figure 5.1) have merged over the years into four religio-moral issues which have become the subjects of First Amendment rulings by the U.S. Supreme Court: (1) blasphemy, (2) the scientific claims of Darwinism, (3) the advocacy of "immoral" ideas, and (4) the communication of sensual and erotic thoughts (called "obscenity" by the law). The Supreme Court has rejected the attempts of the states to suppress the communication of ideas that fall in the first three categories but has permitted—and continues to permit—both state and federal governments to censor the fourth. The result, in summary form, is as follows:

1. In the 1952 case of *Burstyn* v. *Wilson,* in which New York tried to prevent the showing of the film *The Miracle* on grounds of sacrilege, the High Court ruled that it is "not the business of government in our nation to suppress real or imagined attacks upon a particular religious doctrine, whether they appear in publications, speeches, or motion pictures."

2. In the 1968 case of *Epperson* v. *Arkansas,* in which Arkansas attempted to prohibit the teaching of Darwin's theory of evolution in the public schools, the Court ruled that the statute in question was an effort "to blot out a particular theory because of its supposed conflict with the Biblical account, literally read. Plainly, the law is contrary to the mandate of the First . . . Amendment to the Constitution."

3. In the 1959 case of *Kingsley International Pictures* v. *Regents,* in which New York refused a license to the nonobscene movie version of *Lady Chatterley's Lover* because it portrayed sexual "immorality" so as to "corrupt morals," the Supreme Court ordered the license granted. In so deciding, the Court noted that the Empire State censors were obviously attempting to suppress the *idea* that "adultery under certain circumstances may be proper behavior," and since the Constitution protects the right to express ideas, New York had "quite simply . . . struck at the very heart of constitutionally protected liberty."

Because of the Court's position on the three topics above, laws are unconstitutional that prohibit or punish advocacy of minority opinion concerning religious beliefs (including blasphemy), scientific views (including Darwinism), and personal morality (including sexual conduct) provided the ideas are presented in a nonobscene manner. The requirement to avoid explicit sexual imagery (i.e., "obscenity") is particularly limiting on the third category, which deals with the advocacy of "immoral" conduct, since erotic language and graphics can be effective in the support of such ideas. However, on the question of First Amendment protection for obscene expression, the Supreme Court has consistently said no, although it continues to have difficulty defining what it means by "obscenity."

4. The continuing saga of the effort of the U.S. Supreme Court to explain its position on the religio-moral heresy of obscenity can be summarized in three phases: (a) from *Rosen* to *Roth*, (b) from *Roth* to *Miller*, and (c) from *Miller* to the present time.

a. *From* Rosen *to* Roth *(1896 to 1957)*. In 1896 the Supreme Court announced in *Rosen* v. *United States* that it was adopting the English Hicklin rule, articulated by Lord Cockburn in the 1868 case of *Regina* v. *Hicklin* as the definition of obscenity to be followed in American courts. Under this rule the *"test of obscenity is this, whether the tendency of the matter charged as obscenity is to deprave and corrupt those whose minds are open to such immoral influences, and into whose hands a publication of this sort may fall."* During the first half of the twentieth century, this definition was rejected by a number of influential federal judges in the United States for being too restrictive, so that by the 1950s little remained of the rule announced in *Rosen*. In 1957 the Supreme Court moved to bring things up to date.

b. *From* Roth *to* Miller *(1957–1973)*. In the landmark decision of *Roth* v. *United States* (1957), the Supreme Court upheld the constitutionality of the obscenity provisions of the Comstock Act of 1873, which make it a crime to mail messages considered to be "obscene, lewd, lascivious, or filthy." In this ruling, the Court threw out the old Hicklin rule and defined obscenity as that expression which is both *worthless* (i.e., utterly lacking in redeeming social value) and *sexually lewd*—meaning that which *(1) to the average person, (2) applying contemporary community standards, (3) the dominant theme of the material taken as a whole (4) appeals to prurient interest.*

In seven key cases between 1957 and 1970, the Supreme Court attempted to interpret, explain, clarify, and justify its Roth test, so that eventually the concise *worthless-lewd* standard took on large proportions. In paraphrase, the Roth formula as adjusted by the seven cases from *Jacobellis* (1964) through *Stanley* (1969) can be stated as follows: *to be obscene, the expression must be (1) utterly worthless, and also (2) be of a nature so that (a) to the average person or its intended and probable recipient group, (b) applying contemporary community standards, (c) the dominant theme of the material taken as a whole (d) appeals to the prurient interest, or is advertised as if the material appeals to the prurient interest. Furthermore, government may not punish a citizen for the mere private possession of obscenity at home for his or her own personal use.*

c. *From* Miller *(1973) to date*. Following the appointment of four conservative justices to the Supreme Court by President Nixon, the Court's definition of obscenity was once again revised—this time by the new chief justice, Warren Burger. In a series of five opinions, all announced on June 21, 1973, the four Nixon appointees, joined only by Justice White from among the "holdovers" on the bench, rewrote the law of obscenity. In the case of *Miller* v. *California* a three-part test was articulated: *"(a) whether 'the average person, applying contemporary community standards' would find that the work, taken as a whole, ap-*

peals to the prurient interest, . . . (b) whether the work depicts or describes, in a patently offensive way, sexual conduct specifically defined by the applicable state law, and (c) whether the work, taken as a whole, lacks serious literary, artistic, political, or scientific value" [i.e., the SLAPS test].

In a number of obscenity cases reviewed by the Supreme Court since 1973, the language of the Miller test has been interpreted, "clarified," and adjusted so that the current definition of the religio-moral crime of obscenity can be paraphrased as follows: *to be obscene, the expression must be (1) to the average adult person or its intended or probable recipient group, applying contemporary standards of the local community (unless state or national standards are specified by state law) the work taken as a whole, appeals to the prurient interest or is advertised as if it appeals to the prurient interest; (2) whether the work depicts or describes, in a patently offensive way, sexual conduct specifically defined by applicable state law, or which those judging the material believe was intended to be included in the state's definition even though no exhaustive list is supplied; and (3) whether the work, taken as a whole, lacks serious literary, artistic, political, or scientific value.* Furthermore, since 1973 the Supreme Court has made it clear that (1) consenting adults do not have a right of privacy to receive obscene materials; (2) importing, mailing, or shipping obscene materials by common carrier in interstate commerce remain illegal; (3) nudity and obscenity are not synonymous, and broadly worded laws that prohibit all depictions of nudity are unconstitutional; (4) dispersing adult establishments by zoning does not necessarily violate the Constitution; (5) states may not practice prior restraint upon adult bookstores and theaters by closing the business under "nuisance abatement" laws; and (6) child pornography statutes that prohibit the use of minors for the preparation or pre-

sentation of visual materials involving simulated or explicit sexual activity, even if the resulting expression is not legally obscene, are constitutional.

Finally, the student of the First Amendment, using the information in this chapter as a guide, can observe the difference between the time and effort spent trying to suppress the "sin" of erotic speech and the effort spent on the other "sins"—blasphemy, the theories of science concerning the origins and development of life, and the advocacy of "immoral" ideas. Obviously, the abolition of censorship saves government tremendous amounts of time and money, for litigation is for the most part, simply ended. One might ask, therefore: Is continued censorship of sexual materials worth the effort? Also, the student of freedom of speech should continue to seek informed answers to the four questions which were raised earlier in the chapter following the discussion of *Roth* v. *United States,* namely:

1. Should adult citizens be permitted to receive explicit sexual messages and judge them for themselves, or should the state continue to censor "sinful" messages in order to help save men and women from themselves?

2. Is it possible to clearly define what is meant by "obscenity"?

3. Which test for obscenity—Roth or Miller—is more firmly grounded in the First Amendment?

4. Should the First Amendment protect explicit sexual materials—even those now considered legally obscene—when those materials are judged by the speaker to be the available means of persuasion in the advocacy of heterodox views concerning sexual behavior?

Whatever determination the U.S. Supreme Court and other concerned parties—including Congress, the state legislatures, and ulti-

FIGURE 5.7. *THE* ROTH *AND* MILLER *DEFINITIONS OF "OBSCENITY" AT A GLANCE.★*

The Roth Test of 1957	The Miller Test of 1973
To be legally obscene, the material in question must meet two standards:	*To be legally obscene, the material in question must meet three standards:*
1. first, the material must be completely worthless (i.e., "utterly without redeeming social importance"); also . . .	*1. first, the material must be* lacking in serious literary, artistic, political, or scientific value *(known as the "SLAPS test"); also . . .*

2. second, the material must be sexually lewd, *defined as that which*
    a. to the average person,
    b. applying contemporary community standards,
    c. the dominant theme of the material taken as a whole
    d. appeals to the prurient interest.
	2. second, the material must be sexually lewd, *now defined as that which*
	    a. to the average person,
	    b. applying the standards of the state or local community,
	    c. the work taken as a whole
	    d. appeals to the prurient interest; also . . .

	3. third, whether the work depicts or describes, in a patently offensive way, sexual conduct *specifically defined by the applicable state law.*

★*Note: For the sake of simplicity, the various adjustments in both tests, as set forth in the progeny of* Roth *and* Miller, *are not included above; also, the actual order of points employed by Chief Justice Burger in his statement of the Miller test is changed to match the Roth column.*

mately the people of the nation—make of the controversy in the future, one central fact of history stands out, namely: *obscenity is the last religio-moral heresy to be suppressed by civil authority in the United States.* In this sense, then, obscenity prosecutions raise issues not only of the censorship of expression but also of government support of an establishment of religion, both of which activities are addressed by the U.S. Constitution in these words: *"Congress shall make no law respecting an establishment of religion, or prohibiting the free exercise thereof; or abridging the freedom of speech, or of the press; or the right of the people peaceably to assemble, and to petition the Government for a redress of grievances."*

EXERCISES

A. Classroom projects and activities.

1. Here are three questions phrased for classroom debate:

a. Resolved, that "creation science" should be taught along with the theory of evolution in public school biology classes.

b. Resolved, that from the standpoint of the law, the terms "obscenity" and "pornography" are impossible to define clearly.

c. Resolved, that all censorship for *consenting adults* should be abolished in the United States.

2. Here are the same three questions phrased for discussion:

a. Should "creation science" be a *required* part of the biology curriculum in the public schools?

b. Is it possible to phrase a clear, legal definition of the terms "obscenity" and "pornography"? If so, state your preference of a clear definition. If not, why is it impossible?

c. Should a consenting-adults policy toward obscenity be adopted in the United States? (Note again the dissent of Justice William Brennan in the 1973 case of *Paris Adult Theatre.*)

3. Two of the four basic questions raised in this chapter are included in the topics above (definition of terms and the matter of consenting adults); here are the other two phrased for class discussion:

a. Which test for obscenity—*Roth* or *Miller*—is more firmly grounded in the First Amendment?

b. Should the First Amendment protect explicit sexual materials when those materials are judged by the speaker to be the "available means of persuasion" in the advocacy of heterodox views about sexual conduct?

4. Look up the obscenity statutes of your state, make copies for each student, and distribute. Discuss. Does your state's censorship law describe in specific detail the kinds of sexual conduct considered obscene (as requested in *Miller*), or is it a generally "open-ended" law, similar to the one of Illinois (as in *Ward* v. *Illinois*)? Is your state's law clear, so that all can easily understand what is legal and what is not?

5. Have each student in the class write a model obscenity statute that is based upon the standards announced by the Supreme Court in *Miller* v. *California* (1973) and that provides for constraints upon obscenity, even for consenting adults. The model statute should be *clear.* Share the results with the class.

6. Invite an anticensorship spokesman (such as a member of the American Civil Liberties Union) and a procensorship spokesperson (such as a member of the Moral Majority or Citizens for Decency Under Law) to the class for an exchange of views. The format could be either that of a debate or of a symposium-forum. Prepare in advance some hard questions to ask the speakers on both sides of the issue.

7. Have each student prepare a short paper of 500 to 600 words (or a short talk of from three to five minutes in length) on the subject: "Explicit Sexual Materials: Where I Would Draw the Line." The instructor can select several papers representing different points of view to be read to the class (or, in the case of speeches, permit as many talks as time allows).

8. Invite a librarian (or a panel of librarians) from your local public library to discuss policies concerning materials selection and circulation, with particular attention to how explicit sexual materials are handled. Does the library make any distinction between what is suitable for minors and what is suitable for adults? What controversies over obscenity have occurred? How did the library deal with the controversy?

9. Designate one class period for hearing the views of creative artists on the subject of obscenity and censorship. Invite a panel to include representatives from the fields of literature, drama, art, film, and dance. Ask each panel member to prepare in advance a one-page summary of where they would draw the line in the presentation of explicit sexual material in their field. If possible, make copies and distribute the summaries to members of the class in advance of the meeting (or at the beginning of the meeting).

10. Try to locate copies of Ralph Ginzburg's ill-fated magazine *Eros* for examination in class. Four issues of the magazine were forthcoming in 1962 before the federal government ended its publication by moving against the publisher for violation of the Comstock Act. After examining the exhibits, discuss whether members of the class consider the magazines obscene. Should Ginzburg (or anyone else) have been charged with obscenity for mailing these materials to consenting adults?

11. If your community permits "adult" bookstores, consider arranging a class tour of one or more of the establishments. (An advance notice to the bookstore manager should be considered, as should state laws on age restrictions.) Afterward, discuss the reactions of class members to the tour, then take a vote on whether or not members of the class believe such "adults only" outlets should be permitted by law.

B. Topics for research papers or oral reports.

1. A Short History of the Suppression of Literature for *Moral Reasons* in the United States.

2. A Study of the Censorship of James Joyce's *Ulysses.*

3. The Strange Case of Ralph Ginzburg: An Analysis of the "Pandering" Conviction of 1966.

4. The Reaction of America's Religious Community to the Publication of the Kinsey Reports (*Sexual Behavior in the Human Male,* 1948; and *Sexual Behavior in the Human Female,* 1953).

5. Theories for Controlling "Obscenity": A Survey and Analysis of Leading Proposals.

6. Justices Hugo L. Black and William O. Douglas on the Censorship of Sex.

7. The Scopes Trial of 1925: A Study in Religious Heresy.

8. The Contemporary "Creation Science" Debate: A Study of Compelled Speech in the Science Classroom.

9. The Religio-Moral Heresy of Feminists Marie Stopes and Margaret Sanger.

10. The Semantics of Censorship: An Analysis of Various Attempts to Define "Obscenity" and "Pornography."

11. A Brief History of Efforts to Suppress Blasphemy in the United States.

12. The Abolition of Censorship for Adults in Denmark: What Has Been the Result?

13. What Do We Know for Sure About the Relationship of Explicit Sexual Materials to Antisocial Behavior?

14. What Do We Know for Sure About the Effect of Explicit Sexual Materials upon Juveniles?

15. Therapeutic Uses of "Obscene" Materials: Is There a Positive Side?

16. Censorship Organizations in America: Who Are They and What Do They Stand For?

17. Should Pornography Be Censored as an Affront to the Dignity of Women? An Analysis of the Issues and Arguments Raised by "Women Against Pornography."

18. Censorship in the Mother Country: How Do the English Handle the Obscenity Issue?

19. Current Federal Laws Controlling the Dissemintion of Obscenity: What Are They and How Are They Enforced?

20. A Short History of Obscenity Legislation in the State of ——————. (A good law library in the state to be studied is essential here.)

21. Sex Education in America: A Study of a Continuing Moral Issue.

22. A Study of the Censorship of the Works of George Bernard Shaw for Religio-Moral Heresy. (Include a careful reading of Shaw's famous rebuttal, written as the Preface to his 1909 play *The Shewing-Up of Blanco Posnet.*)

23. "How to Talk Dirty and Go to Jail!":
A Study of the Trials and Tribulations of
the Late Lenny Bruce.

24. An Analysis of the Minority Opinions to the *Report of the Commission on Obscenity and Pornography.*

25. A Study of First Amendment Implications of the Supreme Court's 1982
"Child Pornography" Decision *(New York
v. Ferber).*

SELECTED READINGS

Barron, Jerome A., and Dienes, C. Thomas.
Handbook of Free Speech and Free Press. Boston:
Little, Brown, 1979. (Chapter 10, on obscen-
ity.)

Berns, Walter. *Freedom, Virtue and the First Amendment.* Baton Rouge, La.: Louisiana State University Press, 1957.

Bosmajian, Haig A., comp. *Obscenity and Freedom
of Expression.* New York: Burt Franklin and
Co., 1976. (Excellent collection of court cases
on the subject, from *Regina* v. *Hicklin* of 1868
through *Miller* of 1973.)

Boyer, Paul S. *Purity in Print: The Vice-Society
Movement and Book Censorship in America.* New
York: Scribner's, 1968.

Byerly, Greg, and Rubin, Rick. *Pornography, the
Conflict Over Sexually Explicit Materials in the
United States: An Annotated Bibliography.* New
York: Garland, 1980.

Chandos, John, ed. *"To Deprave and Corrupt":
Original Studies in the Nature and Definition of
"Obscenity."* New York: Association Press,
1962.

Cline, Victor B., ed. *Where Do You Draw the Line?*
Provo, Utah: Brigham Young University
Press, 1974. (Essays which, in general, reflect a
procensorship point of view.)

Clor, Harry M. *Obscenity and Public Morality: Censorship in a Liberal Society.* Chicago: University
of Chicago Press, 1969. (Clor argues that obscenity can be defined and should be censored.)

Craig, Alec. *Suppressed Books: A History of the
Conception of Literary Obscenity.* Cleveland:
World, 1963.

Crowther, Bosley. "The Strange Case of 'The
Miracle.'" *Atlantic Monthly,* April 1951, pp. 35
ff.

Devlin, Patrick. *The Enforcement of Morals.* London: Oxford University Press, 1965.

Emerson, Thomas I. *The System of Freedom of
Expression.* New York: Random House, 1970.
(See Chapter 13, on obscenity.)

Ernst, Morris L., and Schwartz, Alan U. *Censorship: The Search for the Obscene.* New York:
Macmillan, 1964.

Gardiner, Harold G. *Catholic Viewpoint on Censorship.* Garden City, N.Y.: Doubleday, 1958.
(Presents a procensorship argument.)

Goldstein, Michael, and Kant, Harold. *Pornography and Sexual Deviance.* Berkeley, Calif.: University of California Press, 1973.

Gordon, George N. *Erotic Communications: Studies
in Sex, Sin and Censorship.* New York: Hastings
House, 1980.

Haiman, Franklyn S. *Speech and Law in a Free Society.* Chicago: University of Chicago Press,
1981. (Chapter 9, "Debasing Attitudes and Values.")

Hart, Harold H., ed. *Censorship: For and Against.*
New York: Hart, 1971.

Hentoff, Nat. *The First Freedom.* New York: Delacorte Press, 1980. (Part V, "Freedom of—and
from—Religion under the First Amendment";
also chapter 24, pp. 283–299, which concerns
obscenity.)

Holbrook, David, ed. *The Case Against Pornography.* LaSalle, Ill.: The Library Press, 1973.

Hughes, Douglas A., ed. *Perspectives on Pornography.* New York: St. Martin's Press, 1970.

Kalven, Harry, Jr. "The Metaphysics of the Law
of Obscenity." In *The Supreme Court Review:
1960,* pp. 1–45. Edited by Philip B. Kurland.
Chicago: University of Chicago Press, 1960.

Kamp, John. "Obscenity and the Supreme Court:
A Communication Approach to a Persistent Ju-
dicial Problem." *Communications and the Law* 2
(Summer 1980): 1–42.

Levy, Leonard W. *Treason Against God: A History
of the Offense of Blasphemy.* New York:
Schocken Books, 1981.

Marcus, Steven. *The Other Victorians: A Study of
Sexuality and Pornography in Mid-Nineteenth-Cen-

tury England. New York: Basic Books, 1966.

Obeler, Eli M. *The Fear of the Word: Censorship and Sex.* Metuchen, N.J.: Scarecrow Press, 1974.

Paul, James C. N., and Schwartz, Murray L. *Federal Censorship: Obscenity in the Mail.* New York: The Free Press of Glencoe, 1961.

Pember, Don. *Mass Media Law.* 2nd ed. Dubuque, Iowa: Wm. C. Brown, 1981. (Chapter 9, "Obscenity, Pornography, and Other Dirty Words.")

Pfeffer, Leo. *Church, State, and Freedom.* Rev. ed. Boston: Beacon Press, 1967. (For Pfeffer's discussion of blasphemy, including his analysis of the controversy over *The Miracle,* see pp. 663–675.)

Pfeffer, Leo. *God, Caesar, and the Constitution.* Boston: Beacon Press, 1975.

Pfeffer, Leo. *Religious Freedom.* Skokie, Ill.: National Textbook Co., 1977.

Putnam, George H. *The Censorship of the Church of Rome.* New York: Putnam's, 1906.

Rembar, Charles. *The End of Obscenity.* New York: Random House, 1968.

The Report of the Commission on Obscenity and Pornography. Washington, D.C.: U.S. Government Printing Office, 1970. (Note: the technical reports which supplement and support the commission's *Report* are available in many libraries.)

Rist, Ray C., ed. *The Pornography Controversy.* New Brunswick, N.J.: Transaction Books, 1975.

Schauer, Frederick F. *The Law of Obscenity.* Washington, D.C.: Bureau of National Affairs, 1976.

Scott, George Ryler. *"Into Whose Hands": An Examination of Obscene Libel in Its Legal, Sociological and Literary Aspects.* London: Gerald G. Swan, 1945.

Sharp, Donald B., ed. *Commentaries on Obscenity.* Metuchen, N.J.: The Scarecrow Press, 1970. (This collection gives particular attention to the case of Ralph Ginzburg in 1966.)

Ten, C. L. "Blasphemy and Obscenity." *British Journal of Law and Society* 5 (Summer 1978): 89–96.

Thomas, Donald. *A Long Time Burning: The History of Literary Censorship in England.* New York: Praeger, 1969.

Zurcher, Louis A., Jr., and Kirkpatrick, George. *Citizens for Decency: Anti-Pornography Crusades as Status Defense.* Austin, Tex.: University of Texas Press, 1976.

CHAPTER 6

Provocation to Anger

"Besides actual breaches of the peace, any thing that tends to provoke or excite others to break it, is an offence of the same denomination. Therefore challenges to fight, *either by word or letter, or to be the bearer of such challenge, are punishable by fine and imprisonment, according to the circumstances of the offence."*

—*William Blackstone (1769)*[1]

On April 26, 1938, Jehovah's Witness Newton Cantwell and his two sons, Jesse and Russell, were knocking on doors and talking to people on the street of a Catholic neighborhood in New Haven, Connecticut, seeking financial support for and converts to their religion. Each carried books, pamphlets, a phonograph, and phonograph records, which they offered to play for those who would grant them permission. At least one of the records contained a strong anti-Catholic message urging the listener to purchase the book *Enemies,* one of the items the Cantwells had for sale. Son Jesse persuaded two Catholic men to listen to the *Enemies* recording, including its attack upon "all organized religious systems as instruments of Satan," with particular emphasis upon the evil influence of the Catholic religion.

The message so angered the men that one threatened to strike Jesse and the other told him to leave or he would throw him "off the street." Young Cantwell quickly but peaceably packed his materials and left. Later, the Cantwells were arrested and charged with violating a state law that required solicitors to obtain permission before attempting to collect funds for a religious cause and for the common-law offense of disturbing the peace.

They were convicted in trial court and the state courts—including the Supreme Court of Connecticut—sustained the convictions. The Cantwells then appealed to the U.S. Supreme Court on the ground that the convictions violated the First and Fourteenth Amendments to the Constitution.[2]

The *Cantwell* case, which is discussed further below, illustrates well the issue of speech that provokes others to anger, the punishment of which has been recognized for centuries under the common law. However, exactly how the common-law doctrine was to function under the First Amendment was not decided by the U.S. Supreme Court until the *Chaplinsky* decision of 1942. Furthermore, *Cantwell, Chaplinsky,* and other provocation-to-anger cases to be studied here are relevant to questions of "speech efficacy" raised by William Bailey in his 1980 essay entitled "The Supreme Court and Communication Theory," a major portion of which is reprinted at the conclusion of this chapter.[3] Whereas the courts have with regularity viewed speech as having the power to "get at" auditors without their consent, thus causing listeners to believe or do things they otherwise would not believe or do (such as start a fight), Bailey points out that contemporary communication theory questions this view. In order to present the key issues on the subject, this chapter is organized under these two headings: (1) "Issues and Cases of Provocation to Anger" and (2) "Does Speech Have the Capacity to Incite? An Examination of the Reasoning of the Court" (Bailey's essay).

---

[1]William Blackstone, *Commentaries on the Laws of England,* vol. 4 (Oxford: Clarendon Press, 1769), p. 149.

[2]*Cantwell* v. *Connecticut,* 310 U.S. 296 (1940).

[3]William Bailey, "The Supreme Court and Communication Theory: Contrasting Models of Speech Efficacy," in *Free Speech Yearbook: 1980,* ed. Peter E. Kane (Annandale, Va.: Speech Communication Association, 1981), pp. 1–15.

I. ISSUES AND CASES OF PROVOCATION TO ANGER

Although the Bible, in Proverbs 15:1, asserts that "A soft answer turneth away wrath: but grievous words stir up anger," communicators are not always mindful of this advice—or, if they are, they do not heed it. Because speech sometimes provokes listeners to anger, thus creating a disturbance of the peace, the common law, as noted above, recognizes the right of government to intervene in certain volatile situations. As Supreme Court Justice Roberts stated in his opinion for the Court in *Cantwell,* "The state of Connecticut has an obvious interest in the preservation and protection of peace and good order within her borders." Before addressing the charge that the Cantwells disturbed the peace, however, Justice Roberts announced that Connecticut's "prior restraint" licensing statute was unconstitutional because it gave state officials too much discretion over who would be permitted to solicit funds for religious causes. He then turned to the second issue, which concerned Jesse Cantwell and the provocative opinions communicated by way of "victrola."

Justice Roberts reviewed the facts of the case, including the information that the two men who were offended by the anti-Catholic record first gave their permission for Jesse to play the phonograph, that nowhere did the evidence show that the defendant "intended to insult or affront the hearers," and that as soon as the auditors showed their anger—as one witness testified—young Cantwell took "the victrola and he went." Cantwell's conduct, therefore, observed the judge, "did not amount to a breach of the peace." But what about the opinion expressed? Even though the defendant conducted himself in a peaceful manner, could not the message itself be the cause of a breach of the peace? "One may

. . . be guilty of the offense," Justice Roberts continued, "if he . . . makes statements likely to provoke violence and disturbance of good order." Then, in a key phrase—which in the *Chaplinsky* decision of two years later was amplified into the more elaborate "fighting-words" doctrine—Justice Roberts asserted: "Resort to epithets or personal abuse is not in any proper sense communication of information or opinion safeguarded by the Constitution, and its punishment as a criminal act would raise no question under that instrument." Jesse Cantwell did not go this far, the justice ruled in reversing the conviction, pointing out that "in the instant case no assault or threatening of bodily harm, no truculent bearing, no intentional discourtesy, no personal abuse" was proved. Instead, he concluded, "we find only an effort to persuade a willing listener to buy a book or to contribute money in the interest of what Cantwell, however misguided others may think him, conceived to be true religion." The Cantwells went home, free.

The "Fighting Words" of Chaplinsky (1942)

The next Jehovah's Witness to come before the High Court for provoking another to anger was neither as discreet in his choice of language nor as fortunate in the outcome of his appeal as were the Cantwells. Walter Chaplinsky was distributing Jehovah's Witness materials on the streets of Rochester, New Hampshire. In the process, he greatly irritated a number of citizens by telling them that he was preaching the "true facts of the Bible" and that all organized religion was a "racket." A disturbance ensued, and a city traffic officer asked Chaplinsky to go with him to the police station. On the way, communicator Chaplinsky and the officer encountered Rochester City Marshal Bowering,

LANDMARK CASE
Chaplinsky v. New Hampshire, 315 U.S. 568 (1942)
Decided March 9, 1942

Vote: 9 to 0 for sustaining the conviction of Chaplinsky.

Majority Opinion By: Justice Murphy.

Concurring Justices: Chief Justice Stone and Justices Roberts, Black, Reed, Frankfurter, Douglas, Byrnes, and Jackson.

Dissenting Justices: (none)

Justices Not Participating: (none)

Summary: Walter Chaplinsky, a Jehovah's Witness, created a disturbance on the streets of Rochester, New Hampshire, while distributing the literature of his sect and, in the process, telling those he approached that organized religion was a "racket." While being taken to the police station, Chaplinsky allegedly said to the city marshal, "You are a God damned racketeer" and "a damned Fascist and the whole government of Rochester are Fascists or agents of Fascists." For this, Chaplinsky was convicted of violating the public laws of New Hampshire, which prohibit the speaking of "any offensive, derisive or annoying word to any other person who is lawfully in any street or other public place." Upon appeal, the U.S. Supreme Court unanimously affirmed Chaplinsky's conviction, rejecting the argument that his language in this case was protected by the Constitution. Instead, the Supreme Court announced that words likely to "inflict injury" upon the listener or "incite an immediate breach of the peace" are not within the First Amendment's range of protected communication.

Rule Established; Significance of Case: This landmark decision divides expression into two categories: (1) that which has social value as a step to truth (i.e., *worthwhile* speech) and (2) that which has no social value as a step to truth (i.e., *worthless* speech). The second part of this worthwhile/worthless dichotomy, states the Court, includes not only insulting or "fighting words" but also language that is lewd, obscene, profane, and libelous. (Thus, *Chaplinsky* throws a very large net that reaches beyond fighting words and for that reason is influential in several areas of First Amendment law, such as obscenity law and the law of defamation.) The Court divides the "fighting-words" category in two subparts, to cover language which by its very utterance (1) inflicts injury upon the listener *or* (2) tends "to incite an immediate breach of the peace." Put another way, the *Chaplinsky* definition of "fighting words" reaches both *foul language* in general (which does not provoke a fight) as well as *fight-provoking words.*

who was rushing to the scene, having been told that a riot was under way. In the ensuing verbal exchange between Marshal Bowering and Chaplinsky, "insulting" words were spoken. Jehovah's Witness Chaplinsky, in a lapse of piety, angrily accused the city marshal of being a "God damned racketeer," whereupon Bowering arrested the profane prophet.

After reviewing the facts of the case, Justice Murphy cited the New Hampshire law under which Chaplinsky was convicted: "No person shall address any offensive, derisive or annoying word to any other person who is lawfully in any street or other public place, nor call him by any offensive or derisive name, nor make any noise or exclamation in his presence and hearing with intent to deride, offend or annoy him, or to prevent him from pursuing his lawful business or occupation." After describing the language allegedly used by the defendant, Justice Murphy

FIGURE 6.1. JUSTICE FRANK MURPHY
OF THE U.S. SUPREME COURT.
Justice Frank Murphy authored the opinion of a
unanimous Court in the 1942 landmark decision
of Chaplinsky v. New Hampshire upholding
the conviction of Walter Chaplinsky for uttering
"fighting words" to a New Hampshire police
officer. Because Chaplinsky's language was both
worthless and likely to incite a breach of the
peace, wrote Justice Murphy, it was not protected
by the Constitution. Justice Murphy was
appointed to the Supreme Court by President
Franklin D. Roosevelt in 1940 and served for
nine years until his death in 1949.
Library of Congress.

reached the heart of the Court's rationale.

Justice Murphy delivered the opinion of the Court:

Allowing the broadest scope to the language and purpose of the [First and] Fourteenth Amendment[s], it is well understood that the right of free speech is not absolute at all times and under all circumstances. There are certain well-defined and narrowly limited classes of speech, the prevention and punishment of which have never been thought to raise any Constitutional problem. **These include the lewd and obscene, the profane, the libelous, and the insulting or "fighting" words— those which by their very utterance [1] inflict injury or [2] tend to incite an immediate breach of the peace. It has been well observed that such utterances are no essential part of any exposition of ideas, and are of such slight social value as a step to truth that any benefit that may be derived from them is clearly outweighted by the social interest in order and morality.** . . .

Agreeing with the New Hampshire courts that the statute under which Chaplinsky was convicted was not overbroad and had been carefully intrepreted to punish language that would likely "cause an average addressee to fight," Justice Murphy concluded that such laws did not unreasonably impinge upon the privilege of free speech. The fighting-words doctrine was thus put in place without a dissenting vote, despite the presence of Justices Black and Douglas on the bench.[4]

[4]Why Justices Black and Douglas concurred in *Chaplinsky* remains a mystery. Years after the decision was announced, Professor Franklyn S. Haiman of the School of Speech, Northwestern University, tactfully inquired of Justice Black concerning why there was no dissent in *Chaplinsky*. In his reply of January 7, 1964, Justice Black wrote: "I have just received your letter asking why there was no dissent in the case of *Chaplinsky* v. *New Hampshire,* 315 U.S. 568. Besides the fact that the case was decided twenty-two years ago, it would hardly be proper for me to discuss reasons that may have been responsible for the decision. I suppose you will just have to guess." Cited in Franklyn S. Haiman, *Freedom of Speech* (Skokie, Ill.: National Textbook Company, 1976), p. 91.

Before turning to the series of cases which over the years revised, refined, and eventually limited the sweep of *Chaplinsky,* the student should pause to contemplate some of the implications of Justice Murphy's opinion of the Court. Although the case began when one man publicly "cussed out" another, the Supreme Court, for reasons forever sealed "in the bosom of the judges" sitting at the time, went beyond a narrow holding on the specific facts of the case to articulate what one leading First Amendment scholar has described as a broad, two-level theory of freedom of speech.[5] In an abbreviated, outline form, the two-level concept, with the *Chaplinsky* categories included, looks like this:

I. *Level one—worthwhile speech:* that expression which has social value as a step to truth and which, therefore, merits the protection of the First Amendment (e.g., the reporting of the news, newspaper editorials and opinion columns, speeches on social issues, debates during a political campaign, etc., all helping to "make the voters wise").

II. *Level two—worthless speech:* that expression which has little, if any, social value as a step to truth and which, therefore, is not deserving of First Amendment protection (i.e., is not "speech" in the sense that the Constitution uses the term); this level includes the following:

A. The lewd, obscene, and profane.

B. Slander and libel.

C. Insulting or "fighting words," defined in *Chaplinsky* as:

1. Offensive language (even if it does not provoke a fight); this part of the definition was eventually discarded by the Court.

2. Fight-provoking language that tends to incite violence; this part of the definition has been retained by the Court.

Students of the First Amendment can use this outline as a point of reference in discussing the two-level theory or in applying the theory to various areas of the law. Furthermore, under topic II, item C in the outline, students can note how subsequent decisions—particularly *Cohen* v. *California* (1971) and *Gooding* v. *Wilson* (1972)—discard part 1 of the definition but retain part 2, which concerns direct confrontation likely to incite an addressee to violence.

Terminiello Goes Free (1949)

Seven years after *Chaplinsky,* the Supreme Court announced its opinion in another case concerning provocation to anger, with quite different results for the defendant. Father Arthur Terminiello, an outspoken anti-Semitic, racist Catholic priest from Alabama who was on suspension by his bishop, was brought to Chicago at the invitation of right-wing extremist Gerald L. K. Smith and a group calling itself the Christian Veterans of America. Terminiello's speech attracted a capacity crowd of over eight hundred supporters to the auditorium, plus between a thousand and fifteen hundred angry protesters who gathered outside. Bricks, rocks, bottles, ice picks, and other objects were thrown at the auditorium and at the police who were attempting to protect those inside. Numerous windows were broken as Terminiello delivered his message (in which he called those outside "slimy scum," and condemned the "Communistic Zionistic" Jews of America, evoking cries of "Kill the Jews" and "dirty kikes"

[5]Harry Kalven, Jr., "Metaphysics of the Law of Obscenity," in *The Supreme Court Review: 1960,* ed. Philip B. Kurland (Chicago: University of Chicago Press, 1960), pp. 1 ff.

FIGURE 6.2. FATHER ARTHUR TERMINIELLO AND GERALD L. K. SMITH. *Father Arthur Terminiello (on left) with Gerald L. K. Smith in March of 1946. The photograph was made a few days after Terminiello had been tried and convicted in a Chicago court for disorderly conduct based upon his delivery of a racist, anti-Jewish speech in a Chicago auditorium. Terminiello's appearance in the Windy City was sponsored by Gerald L. K. Smith and a group calling itself the Christian Veterans of America. The conviction was appealed, eventually reaching the U.S. Supreme Court, which ruled in Terminiello's favor in 1949.*
UPI/Bettmann Archive.

from his listeners). The police finally arrested Terminiello, charging him with violation of a Chicago ordinance providing that "all persons who shall make, aid, countenance or assist in making any improper noise, riot, disturbance, breach of the peace or diversion tending to a breach of the peace" shall be guilty of disorderly conduct.[6] Terminiello was convicted, and the Illinois courts upheld his conviction.

On appeal, the U.S. Supreme Court, in an opinion written by Justice Douglas, reversed Terminiello's conviction by a vote of 5 to 4. The reason, explained Justice Douglas, was *the overly broad way in which the trial judge instructed the jury concerning the meaning of the* term "breach of the peace" in the Chicago ordinance. He stated that by defining the term in an expansive way to include speech that "stirs the public to anger, invites dispute, brings about a condition of unrest, or creates a disturbance," the trial court erred; therefore, the conviction must be reversed.

Justice Douglas *delivered the opinion of the Court:*

The vitality of civil and political institutions in our society depends on free discussion. As Chief Justice Hughes wrote in *De Jonge v. Oregon*, . . . it is only through free debate and free exchange of ideas that government remains responsive to the will of the people and peaceful change is effected. The right to speak freely and to promote diversity of ideas and programs is therefore one of the chief distinctions that sets us apart from totalitarian regimes.

[6] *Terminiello* v. *Chicago*, 337 U.S. 1 (1949).

Accordingly a function of free speech under our system of government is to invite dispute. It may indeed best serve its high purpose when it induces a condition of unrest, creates dissatisfaction with conditions as they are, or even stirs people to anger. Speech is often provocative and challenging. It may strike at prejudices and preconceptions and have profound unsettling effects as it presses for acceptance of an idea. That is why freedom of speech, though not absolute, . . . is nevertheless protected against censorship or punishment, unless shown likely to produce a clear and present danger of a serious substantive evil that rises far above public inconvenience, annoyance, or unrest. . . . There is no room under our Constitution for a more restrictive view. For the alternative would lead to standardization of ideas either by legislatures, courts, or dominant political or community groups.

The ordinance as construed by the trial court seriously invaded this province. It permitted conviction of petitioner if his speech stirred people to anger, invited public dispute, or brought about a condition of unrest. A conviction resting on any of those grounds may not stand.

Despite the strong objections of the dissenters (Justice Jackson is particularly outspoken, accusing the majority of being too idealistic and of being in danger of walking "into a well from looking at the stars"), the conviction of the shrill Terminiello was overturned—even though he was a party to a much more serious incident than was Chaplinsky. Students of the First Amendment should note that *Terminiello* nicely illustrates how trial errors or other technical details can influence the outcome of a case upon appeal. Such knowledge should reinforce the habit of studying a decision carefully before forming a firm opinion about it (or before communicating the results to others).

Feiner Goes to Jail (1951)

At about 6:30 P.M. on March 8, 1949, two months before the Supreme Court announced its findings in *Terminiello,* college student Irving Feiner mounted a wooden box on a public sidewalk in Syracuse, New York, and, using a loudspeaker system attached to a nearby automobile, began speaking to a small group of persons. His message included an appeal for the blacks in his racially mixed audience, which soon grew in number to about seventy-five persons, to revolt against racist oppression in the United States. In the course of his speech, Feiner made a number of "provocative" remarks; these included a description of the mayor of Syracuse as a "champagne-sipping bum" and derogatory comments about President Harry Truman and the American Legion. Several in the crowd became restless and began to push and shove; there was hostile murmuring and milling around. Two police officers who were present sensed a growing danger of violence, and one of them twice asked Feiner to stop speaking so that the crowd could be peaceably dispersed. When the speaker refused, he was asked a third time to stop, after which he was arrested and charged with violating a New York disorderly conduct law. The bill of particulars charged that the young advocate had ignored and refused "to heed and obey reasonable police orders issued at the time and place mentioned in the information to regulate and control said crowd and to prevent a breach or breaches of the peace and to prevent injury to pedestrians attempting to use said walk, and being forced into the highway adjacent to the place in question, and prevent injury to the public generally."[7] Feiner was convicted and sen-

---

[7]*Feiner v. New York,* 340 U.S. 315 (1951).

tenced to thirty days in jail; the courts of the state of New York sustained his conviction.

The case was then appealed to the U.S. Supreme Court, which agreed with the courts below and *upheld* the conviction. In so doing, Chief Justice Vinson, speaking for the six-man majority, asserted that Feiner's message had created a clear and present danger and that, under the circumstances, the speaker should have obeyed the request of the police officers to stop while things were still peaceful. "It is one thing to say that the police cannot be used as an instrument for the suppression of unpopular views," wrote the Chief Justice,

and another to say that, when as here the speaker passes the bounds of argument or persuasion and undertakes incitement to riot, they are powerless to prevent a breach of the peace. . . . The findings of the state courts as to the existing situation and the imminence of greater disorder coupled with petitioner's deliberate defiance of the police officers convince us that we should not reverse this conviction in the name of free speech.

In outspoken disagreement, Justices Black and Douglas (with whom Justice Minton concurred) objected to the reasoning of the majority. Justice Black was particularly forthright in arguing that the police should protect the speaker, not arrest him, when listeners are provoked to anger.

Justice Black, *dissenting:*

The Court's opinion apparently rests on this reasoning: The policeman, under the circumstances detailed, could reasonably conclude that serious fighting or even riot was imminent; therefore he could stop petitioner's speech to prevent a breach of peace; accordingly, it was "disorderly conduct" for petitioner to continue speaking in disobedience of the officer's request. As to the existence of a dangerous situation on the street corner, it seems far-fetched to suggest that the "facts" show any imminent threat of riot or uncontrollable disorder. It is neither unusual nor unexpected that some people at public street meetings mutter, mill about, push, shove, or disagree, even violently, with the speaker. Indeed, it is rare where controversial topics are discussed that an outdoor crowd does not do some or all of these things. Nor does one isolated threat to assault the speaker forebode disorder. . . .

Moreover, assuming that the "facts" did indicate a critical situation, I reject the implication of the Court's opinion that the police had no obligation to protect petitioner's constitutional right to talk. The police of course have power to prevent breaches of the peace. **But if, in the name of preserving order, they ever can interfere with a lawful public speaker, they first must make all reasonable efforts to protect him.** Here the policeman did not even pretend to try to protect petitioner. According to the officers' testimony, the crowd was restless but there is no showing of any attempt to quiet it; pedestrians were forced to walk into the street, but there was no effort to clear a path on the sidewalk; one person threatened to assault petitioner but the officers did nothing to discourage this when even a word might have sufficed. **Their duty was to protect petitioner's right to talk, even to the extent of arresting the man who threatened to interfere. Instead, they shirked that duty and acted only to suppress the right to speak.**[8]

Justice Black concluded by arguing that "a man making a lawful address is certainly not required to be silent merely because an officer

[8]The issue addressed by Justice Black is sometimes called the "heckler's veto," in reference to how hecklers in an audience can effectively stop a speech by creating a disturbance. Sometimes the hecklers are so effective that the *speaker* is arrested for disturbing the peace. For an analysis of the problem in reference to a specific situation, see Franklyn S. Haiman, "Nazis in Skokie: Anatomy of the Heckler's Veto," in *Free Speech Yearbook: 1978,* ed. Gregg Phifer (Falls Church, Va.: Speech Communication Association, 1978), pp. 11–16.

directs it. . . . I understand that people in authoritarian countries must obey arbitrary orders. I had hoped that there was no such duty in the United States."

An overview of the four cases examined thus far reveals the following sequence in the development of the Supreme Court's view concerning provocation to anger:

1. In *Cantwell* v. *Connecticut* (1940), the Court ruled that resort to personal abuse directed at another is not protected speech under the Constitution. (The Cantwells, who played an anti-Catholic message on a phonograph, were set free because they had not resorted to epithets or personal abuse.)

2. In *Chaplinsky* v. *New Hampshire* (1942), the Court announced its landmark fighting-words doctrine—an elaboration of the reasoning expressed in *Cantwell*—which asserts that the Constitution does not protect language that, by its very utterance, (1) inflicts injury upon the sensibilities of others *or* (2) tends "to incite an immediate breach of the peace." (Chaplinsky, who had called the city marshal a "God damned racketeer," had his conviction upheld by the Supreme Court.)

3. In *Terminiello* v. *Chicago* (1949), the Court ruled that overbroad interpretations of laws governing prohibited speech so as to reach protected speech can result in the reversal of a conviction obtained under such an expansive definition. (Terminiello, who had inflamed his listeners and thus helped fuel a dangerous situation, had his conviction reversed because the instructions to the jury by the trial judge were overly broad.)

4. Finally, in *Feiner* v. *New York* (1951), the Court ruled that speech that exceeds the "bounds of argument or persuasion" and creates a clear and present danger of inciting to riot is not protected by the Constitution. (Feiner, who made a speech on a public street, had refused to cooperate with police who asked him to stop speaking as a means of preserving the peace; the Supreme Court sustained his conviction.)

The principles from these four cases can be combined to say that by the early 1950s the Supreme Court had determined that "fighting words" which are likely to offend the sensibilities of auditors or are addressed to another in such a way as to provoke that person to violence, and public speeches that reach the point of creating a clear and present danger of violence, are *not* protected by the Constitution. Furthermore, in the trial of free-speech cases, applicable statutes must be narrowly defined so that protected speech is not mixed with unprotected speech to form the basis for a conviction.

During the next twenty years, especially in the 1960s, when civil rights protests and anti-Vietnam War dissent occurred with great frequency, the Supreme Court ruled on numerous First Amendment issues. In most cases, however, the issue of provocation to anger was subordinated to situational factors, such as time, place, and manner of protest. For this reason, the development of much First Amendment law during the 1960s is found in Chapter 8, "Time, Place, Manner, and Institutional Constraints." In 1971, however, the first of several provocative "four-letter word" cases reached the Supreme Court, with results that deserve close scrutiny by students of free speech, for, among other things, the Court's decisions greatly contracted the scope of the "fighting-words" doctrine announced in the 1942 *Chaplinsky* case. The first of the appeals originated near the end of the "decade of dissent" when, in 1968, a war protester quietly walked into a public building wearing a jacket upon which was printed a jarring message. The protester's arrest because of that message led to a long journey through the nation's courts.

Cohen's Jacket (1971)

On April 26, 1968, a young man named Paul Robert Cohen walked into the Los Angeles County Courthouse wearing a jacket bearing the words "Fuck the Draft" plainly visible for all to see. The California courts made a point of noting for the record that there were women and children in the corridor where Cohen stood and where he was soon arrested, as if to suggest that the presence of females and juveniles made Cohen's message even more offensive than it might otherwise have been. There was no evidence that the defendant said anything or created any disturbance prior to his arrest or that he made any threats or committed any acts of violence when approached by the police. The trial court found the choice of words so outrageous, however, that it ruled Cohen guilty of "offensive conduct" and sentenced him to jail. Thus began the saga of Cohen's jacket.

In a novel reversal of roles, conservative Justice John M. Harlan authored the majority opinion accepting Cohen's First Amendment argument, whereas liberal Justice Hugo Black—whose belief in the appropriateness of manner and place of communication was offended in this instance—voted with the dissenters. Following a review of the facts of the case, Justice Harlan pointed out that the law under which the conviction was obtained (1) covered the entire state (not just public buildings, such as courthouses); (2) that it concerned neither lewd, erotic speech (obscenity) nor "fighting words" (i.e., did not consist of "those personally abusive epithets which, when addressed to the ordinary citizen, are, as a matter of common knowledge, inherently likely to provoke violent reaction"); and (3) that those who were in the corridor where Cohen stood were not captives to his message, for they could either leave or simply look away (in other words, there was no

intolerable invasion of privacy). The central issue, then, was not obscenity, not fighting words, and not invasion of privacy but "whether California can excise, as 'offensive conduct,' one particular scurrilous epithet from the public discourse, either upon the theory of the court below that its use is inherently likely to cause violent reaction or upon a more general assertion that the States, acting as guardians of public morality, may properly remove this offensive word from the public vocabulary." He then spoke on behalf of freedom of expression.

Justice Harlan *delivered the opinion of the Court:*

. . . The constitutional right of free expression is powerful medicine in a society as diverse and populous as ours. It is designed and intended to remove governmental restraints from the arena of public discussion, putting the decision as to what views shall be voiced largely into the hands of each of us, in the hope that use of such freedom will ultimately produce a more capable citizenry and more perfect polity and in the belief that no other approach would comport with the premise of individual dignity and choice upon which our political system rests. . . .

To many, the immediate consequence of this freedom may often appear to be only verbal tumult, discord, and even offensive utterance. These are, however, within established limits, in truth necessary side effects of the broader enduring values which the process of open debate permits us to achieve. That the air may at times seem filled with verbal cacophony is, in this sense not a sign of weakness but of strength. We cannot lose sight of the fact that, in what otherwise might seem a trifling and annoying instance of individual distasteful abuse of a privilege, these fundamental societal values are truly implicated. That is why "[w]holly neutral futilities . . . come under the protection of free speech as fully as do Keats' poems or Donne's sermons," . . . any why "so long as the means

Cohen v. California, 403 U.S. 15 (1971)
Decided June 7, 1971

Vote: 5 to 4 for reversal of Cohen's conviction.

Majority Opinion By: Justice Harlan.

Concurring Justices: Douglas, Brennan, Stewart, and Marshall.

Dissenting Justices: Chief Justice Burger and Justices Black, White, and Blackmun.

Justices Not Participating: (none)

Summary: Paul Robert Cohen was arrested in the Los Angeles County Courthouse in the spring of 1968 for knowingly wearing a jacket upon which the words "Fuck the Draft" were plainly visible. Although the defendant explained that the message on his jacket was an attempt by him to express his opposition to the war in Vietnam, he was, nevertheless, charged with violating a California law that prohibits "maliciously and willfully disturb[ing] the peace or quiet of any neighborhood or person . . . by . . . offensive *conduct*." [Emphasis supplied.] The facts showed that Cohen was not loud or threatening during the incident and that no person threatened him because of the message on his garment. Despite these findings, the trial court found him guilty and sentenced young Cohen to thirty days in jail. On appeal, the U.S. Supreme Court reversed and in so doing addressed at length the important constitutional issue raised by the case, namely, the punishment of shocking *words only* by the procedure of classifying them as "conduct," even though the language in question is legally neither "obscene" nor composed of "fighting words." Expression of this type is protected by the Constitution for three reasons: (1) it is not possible to articulate a principle by which citizens will know which words are permissible and which are not; (2) much provocative language does serve the function of communicating both ideas and emotions; and (3) when the state attempts to prohibit certain words, it inevitably creates "a substantial risk of suppressing ideas."

Rule Established; Significance of Case: Shocking language that is not legally obscene (i.e., is not "erotic") and not directed at an individual hearer in such a way as to provoke a person to violence is protected by the Constitution from abridgement by the states. By so ruling, the Court narrowed the definition of "fighting words" stated in *Chaplinsky* to words which actually are directed to another in such a way as to create a danger of breach of the peace. Furthermore, this unusual decision is of great importance to students of human communication, for it recognizes that even shocking language, such as "Fuck the Draft," can serve a dual communication function: the *cognitive* in which ideas are expressed and the *emotive* in which deep personal emotions are expressed. As Justice Harlan's majority opinion states, "We cannot sanction the view that the Constitution, while solicitous of the cognitive content of individual speech, has little or no regard for that emotive function which, practically speaking, may often be the more important element of the overall message sought to be communicated."

are peaceful, the communication need not meet standards of acceptability."

Justice Harlan then set out the three main reasons for reversing the conviction of Cohen. *First*, government is not capable of setting forth a clear principle by which certain words will be allowed and others disal-lowed. *Second*, language such as that used by Cohen has important emotive content (more on this below). *Finally*, forbidding certain words creates a serious risk that protected ideas will be suppressed. On his second point, which is of particular interest to public communicators, Justice Harlan wrote of the dual function of communication.

Justice Harlan *continued for the Court:*

Additionally, we cannot overlook the fact, because it is well illustrated by the episode involved here, that much linguistic expression serves a dual communicative function: it conveys not only ideas capable of relatively precise, detached explication, but otherwise inexpressible emotions as well. In fact, words are often chosen as much for their emotive as their cognitive force. **We cannot sanction the view that the Constitution, while solicitous of the cognitive content of individual speech, has little or no regard for that emotive function which, practically speaking, may often be the more important element of the overall message sought to be communicated.** Indeed, as Mr. Justice Frankfurter has said, "[O]ne of the prerogatives of American citizenship is the right to criticize public men and measures—and that means not only informed and responsible criticism but the freedom to speak foolishly and without moderation."

Finally, three of the dissenters in a short opinion written by Justice Blackmun and joined by Chief Justice Burger and Justice Black (Justice White dissented, but not for the reason stated here) asserted that "Cohen's absurd and immature antic . . . was mainly conduct and little speech." In addition, they argued that the "fighting-words" doctrine of *Chaplinsky* applied to Cohen (even though, in fact, no threatening confrontation with another person took place) and that the majority's "agonizing First Amendment values seems misplaced and unnecessary." This objection by a minority of justices persists in the next group of provocation-to-anger cases to reach the Court.

Gooding v. Wilson (1972) and Progeny

On August 18, 1966, Johnny C. Wilson and other anti-Vietnam War activists attempted to stop the processing of new military recruits by blocking the entrance to an army office building in Atlanta, Georgia. In a scuffle that followed when police moved in to clear the door, Wilson said to one officer, "White son of a bitch, I'll kill you," and to a second officer, "You son of a bitch, if you ever put hands on me again, I'll cut you all to pieces." Wilson was arrested, tried, and convicted of violating a Georgia statute providing that any "person who shall, without provocation, use to or of another, and in his presence . . . opprobrious words or abusive language, tending to cause a breach of the peace . . . shall be guilty of a misdemeanor."[9]

On appeal, the U.S. District Court for the Northern District of Georgia set aside the conviction on the ground that the state law was vague and overbroad. The court of appeals agreed with the district court, as did the U.S. Supreme Court by a vote of 5 to 2 (Justices Black and Harlan had recently retired from the bench, and newly appointed Justices Powell and Rehnquist took no part in the *Gooding* decision).[10]

Justice Brennan delivered the opinion of the Court with an emphasis upon how terms such as "opprobrious words" and "abusive language" must be narrowly defined and applied by state judges so as not to suppress protected speech. He observed that the fighting-words doctrine of *Chaplinsky* did not reach all words found offensive by society but was strictly limited to language that had *"a direct tendency to cause acts of violence by the person to whom, individually, the remark is addressed."* Only when the words in question plainly tended to incite an *individual* addressee

---

[9]*Gooding* v. *Wilson,* 405 U.S. 518 (1972).
[10]Note: Justice Hugo L. Black retired from the Court in 1971 because of illness; he died of that illness soon thereafter.

to a breach of the peace, Justice Brennan emphasized, do they meet the First Amendment standard determined in *Chaplinsky*. Because the Georgia Supreme Court had failed over the years to interpret the statute in question narrowly, as required by *Chaplinsky*—permitting such words as "You swore a lie," and "God damn you, why don't you get out of the road?" to be tried under the statute—the law *as construed* by the Georgia Supreme Court was unconstitutional.

When this case is combined with *Cohen* v. *California,* two requirements of the U.S. Supreme Court for an objectionable-language statute to pass constitutional muster can be identified: namely, the law in question must be restricted to language (1) spoken to another person in a face-to-face confrontation (2) which is likely to incite an immediate breach of the peace. Put another way, fighting-words laws may no longer be employed broadly to punish cursing, the use of four-letter words, and similar types of language that would probably offend the "sensibilities" of many persons. As attorney Mark C. Rutzick put it in his study of the evolution of the fighting-words doctrine, the Court in *Cohen* and *Gooding* has narrowed the *Chaplinsky* definition of offensive language "and has chosen to draw the line of constitutional protection around every reaction but one—that of physical violence. Furthermore, it has established its unwillingness to assume the likelihood of physical violence in any context other than face-to-face confrontations. In so doing," Rutzick concludes, "the Court has adopted a rule highly protective of free speech."[11]

In several cases subsequent to *Gooding,* the Court has returned to the lower courts for reconsideration those fighting-words appeals which might have been decided by the trial court on grounds inconsistent with *Cohen* and *Gooding*. In one such decision, *Lewis* v. *City of New Orleans,* the High Court remanded a Louisiana state court conviction of Mallie Lewis for cursing a police officer who was in the process of arresting her son. The city ordinance under which the conviction was obtained stated that "It shall be unlawful and a breach of the peace for any person wantonly to curse or revile or to use obscene or opprobrious language toward or with reference to any member of the city police while in the actual performance of his duty."[12] When, after reconsideration, the state court *sustained* the conviction, the Supreme Court in the second appeal of the same case reversed the state court and declared the New Orleans ordinance under which the conviction was obtained to be unconstitutional. In a concurring opinion that implicitly recognizes that the total communication situation—particularly the nature of the receiver of the message—should be considered by the Court in determining communication efficacy, Justice Powell stated the view that police officers should be trained to control their anger when they are the objects of verbal abuse. "A properly trained officer," wrote Justice Powell, "may reasonably be expected to 'exercise a higher degree of restraint' than the average citizen, and thus be less likely to respond belligerently to 'fighting words.' "[13]

In addition to the *Lewis* appeals, the U.S. Supreme Court since 1972 has vacated and remanded a number of additional fighting-words cases for reconsideration in light of the

---

[11]Mark C. Rutzick, "Offensive Language and the Evolution of First Amendment Protection," *Harvard Civil Rights–Civil Liberties Law Review* 9 (January 1974): 27.

[12]*Lewis* v. *City of New Orleans* (I), 408 U.S. 913 (1972). Note: A second appeal of this conviction reached the Supreme Court in 1974; the cases are sometimes referred to as *Lewis* (I) and *Lewis* (II).

[13]*Lewis* v. *City of New Orleans* (II), 415 U.S. 130 (1974).

narrow holdings of *Cohen* and *Gooding.*[14] These decisions taken as a group have provoked vigorous dissents from conservatives on the Court—led by Chief Justice Burger and Justice Rehnquist—who argue that the states should be permitted to punish foul language in general as well as words spoken to another in a fight-provoking manner. As those who voted with the majority in *Cohen* and *Gooding* retire from the bench, a shift to the conservative position remains a possibility. Students of the First Amendment should watch developments closely.

Provocation to Anger in Brief

In the 1942 landmark decision of *Chaplinsky* v. *New Hampshire,* the U.S. Supreme Court declared that "the lewd and obscene, the profane, the libelous, and the insulting or 'fighting' words . . . are no essential part of any exposition of ideas, and are of such slight social value as a step to truth" that they may be abridged by the states without violating the First Amendment. Implied in the opinion of the Court is the concept of two types of expression: (1) that which is *worthwhile,* and protected, and (2) that which is *worthless* (such as "fighting words"), and unprotected. Some First Amendment scholars have called this a "two-level theory," noting that whatever the Court defines into the *worthless* level is not "speech" as the Constitution uses the term and may, therefore, be proscribed. In *Chaplinsky,* the Court went beyond the specific issue of insulting language which was raised by the facts of the case to announce that the *worthless* category also included language that was "obscene" and "libelous."

[14]These include *Rosenfeld* v. *New Jersey,* 408 U.S. 901 (1972); *Brown* v. *Oklahoma,* 408 U.S. 914 (1972); *Lucas* v. *Arkansas,* 416 U.S. 919 (1972); *Kelly* v. *Ohio,* 416 U.S. 923 (1974); and *Karlan* v. *Cincinnati* with *Rosen* v. *California,* 416 U.S. 924 (1974).

The fighting-words doctrine itself, as announced in *Chaplinsky,* was defined to cover two forms of expression, namely: (1) that which by its "very utterance" tends to inflict injury upon the sensibilities of listeners and (2) that which tends to "incite an immediate breach of the peace." Since 1942 the Supreme Court has gradually been restricting the scope of the fighting-words rule, a process that can be explained in two points. *First,* laws punishing language that provokes to anger must be narrowly drawn and narrowly construed by trial judges so as not to mix protected speech with the "fighting words" that are unprotected. Statutes written or interpreted in such a way as to punish protected expression (such as punishing speech that "invites dispute" or brings about "a condition of unrest"—both being protected by the Constitution, as per *Terminiello*) while trying to "get at" unprotected expression will likely be declared unconstitutional by the Court. *Second,* the *Cohen* and *Gooding* decisions have rejected the first part of the *Chaplinsky* definition (i.e., words that offend the sensibilities of hearers), thereby sharply limiting the reach of the fighting-words rule to language uttered in a face-to-face confrontation between speaker and addressee and spoken in a threatening or inciting manner likely to create a breach of the peace. In short, only those words that meet a localized clear-and-present-danger test are currently abridgeable under the fighting-words rule.

Finally, the narrowness of the opinions of the Court in *Cohen* and *Gooding* has not "set well" with conservative justices, who would prefer to allow states to punish not only that language likely to provoke a fight but also offensive language in general. Evidently, some justices of the U.S. Supreme Court would prefer to see the full two-part *Chaplinsky* definition of "fighting words" restored. Students of the First Amendment should observe closely how new appointees to the U.S. Supreme Court vote in the future in cases concerning this area of the law, yet to be *definitively* settled.

II. DOES SPEECH HAVE THE CAPACITY TO INCITE? AN EXAMINATION OF THE REASONING OF THE COURT (AN ESSAY BY WILLIAM E. BAILEY)

At the foundation of much legislation and many court decisions concerning speech that allegedly creates a clear and present danger, whether to national security or to the tranquillity of the local community, is the assumption that certain words communicated in certain ways cause those who hear or read the message to behave in a predictable, antisocial way. Is this assumption sound? Professor of communication William E. Bailey of the University of Arizona investigates the question in light of contemporary communication theory, with interesting results.

Bailey considers two types of communication situations: *first,* those in which the speaker has a goal in mind that he or she urges upon a sympathetic audience (e.g., an anarchist attempting to incite an assembly of fellow anarchists) and, *second,* those in which the listeners are hostile and a negative reaction that is not necessarily sought by the speaker is provoked (e.g., "fighting-words" cases, such as Chaplinsky cursing a police officer). The student should review Chapter 3, "Political Heresy," for an overview of cases in the first group, as well as the provocation-to-anger cases of the present chapter, for an overview of important examples of the second group. Key sections of Bailey's essay concerning the power of speech to incite audiences are given below as a means of encouraging the student of free speech to consider the soundness of past decisions of the Supreme Court concerning communication efficacy. While studying Bailey's argument, readers might also ask whether or not "defamatory" speech really has the capacity to destroy reputations and whether or not "obscene" speech really has the capacity to make audiences behave in an "immoral" way.

CONCLUSION

In *Chaplinsky* v. *New Hampshire,* a landmark decision of 1942, the U.S. Supreme Court announced a two-part "fighting-words" doctrine that excluded from constitutional protection (1) speech which by its "very utterance" tends to inflict injury upon the sensibilities of auditors as well as (2) speech that tends to "incite an immediate breach of the peace." Over the years, the Court has refined the *Chaplinsky* rule by dropping the first part (offending sensibilities) to sustain only the second. Consequently, the "fighting words" now excluded from First Amendment protection are limited to those spoken in a face-to-face confrontation between speaker and hearer so as to create a clear and present danger of a breach of the peace.

Professor of communication William E. Bailey argues that in both national security and "fighting-words" cases, the reasoning of the Supreme Court concerning the power of speech to incite an audience is not supported by contemporary empirical research. The key error of the Court has been generally to ignore the part played by the *audience* as an essential factor in determining speech efficacy (speech lacks the capacity to make an audience behave a certain way against its will). Should the Court take a scientific view of the matter, Bailey concludes, "the abridgment of free speech by incitement prosecution would end."

"THE SUPREME COURT AND COMMUNICATION THEORY: CONTRASTING MODELS OF SPEECH EFFICACY," BY WILLIAM E. BAILEY[15]

Chafee wrote some years ago that the "real issue in every free speech controversy is . . . whether the state can punish all words which have some tendency, however remote, to bring about acts in violation of law, or only words which directly incite to acts in violations of law."[1] Thus the question of incitement readily reduces to a question of causal relationships between the speech and the violation of law. Chafee marked off the free speech boundary by postulating a series of statements that ranged from disapproval of war to direct advocacy of resisting induction, and a series of audiences that ranged from women in an old women's home to inductees starting for a training camp: "Somewhere in such a range of circumstances is the point where direct causation begins and speech becomes punishable as incitement under the ordinary standards of statutory construction and the ordinary policy of free speech . . . ."[2]

In this view, what must be determined is the real or probable efficacy of the speech in a given set of circumstances and with a given audience. But we may note now for later reference that the concern with the audience is with its direct involvement in the issues, and not with its attitudes or predisposition toward the issues. And another assumption of this view needs explicit statement: the law against incitement is not arbitrary; advocacy of acts in violation of law is a positive harm in that it brings about, causes, the unlawful acts, and it is this harm that justifies the abridgment of free speech. If the laws were arbitrary, if speech caused no harm, presumably incitement laws would be unconstitutional.

The Supreme Court's Mechanistic Model

A central problem for this view of incitement is that causation is not observable but is an inference of relationships between or among phenomena. In an ordinary mechanical sequence of effects—say, one man pulling the trigger of a loaded gun pointed at another man—the sequence follows patterns of physical law. The chain of effects is empirically demonstrable, repeatable, and is of unquestionable harm to the man shot. But suppose bullets were no more harmful than water from a water pistol unless the person shot, for some reason, wanted them to be lethal. The law would take a much different position on the harm of shooting a man because the volition of the man shot would be the critical factor. This situation, while not wholly parallel with the speech situation, illustrates something of the problem of free speech prosecution: a speech is not "shot" at a man with the kind of predictable effects which characterize a gunshot, and to a considerable

[1]Zechariah Chafee, *Free Speech in the United States* (Cambridge, 1941), p. 23. [Note the numbering of footnotes corresponds to those used by Bailey, as does style of documentation. When text is elided, so are footnotes that correspond to the omitted material.]
[2]*Ibid.,* p. 48.

[15]This essay was originally published in the *Free Speech Yearbook: 1980* (Annandale, Va.: Speech Communication Association, 1981). It received the H. A. Wichelns Memorial Award for the most significant contribution to the *Yearbook* for 1980. The introduction and final third of the essay are reprinted here in their entirety; however, the discussion of national security and provocation-to-anger cases is elided. The reader is referred to Chapter 3 and the present chapter for coverage of most of the elided material. The headings have all been *added* to facilitate reader location of key concepts. Selections from the original essay are reprinted here with the permission of the author and of the Speech Communication Association.

degree because the efficacy of the speech is extremely dependent upon the volition of the audience. Traditionally, the situation that follows a speech is taken as the measure of the effect of the speech, but in part this is an instance of the *post hoc* fallacy in classic form; the response made to a speech by an audience may be a more accurate measure of the predisposition of the audience than the power of the speaker to persuade. The speech act to a considerable degree serves as an occasion for the audience to manifest their convictions; most often the audience probably hears a speaker with which it is already in agreement, but some members of the audience may be there to heckle and disagree. In sum, the efficacy of a speech or speaker is very difficult to demonstrate.

Aspects of speech efficacy assuredly tend to follow certain patterns of probability, but the variables are so plentiful and so complex that it is doubtful the cause-effect relationships of the speech act can ever be shown to approach the regularity of mechanical cause-effect relationships.

This essay will argue that the Supreme Court has, like Chafee, assumed a very mechanistic model of speech efficacy: it will (1) attempt to illustrate the origin and nature of the model expressed in selected Court decisions; (2) attempt to present a typical, empirical model of speech efficacy; (3) attempt to relate the significance of the empirical model to free speech prosecution. In brief, the contention to be supported is that the Court has both over-determined and over-estimated the efficacy of the speech act because of an inadequate model of the communication process. This essay will concern itself with Court decisions that are primarily applications or derivations of the "clear and present danger" test,[3] but the study is relevant to any test that assumes speech efficacy. The intention is to illustrate factors relevant to the Court's model, or concept, of speech efficacy, and not to account for either the development or abandonment of the clear and present danger test. Whatever contentions may be subsequently made concern only the pragmatics of the Court's view, and surely will not be mistaken for arguments of constitutional law. When the Court considers questions of probability or clear and present danger, it enters the realm of pragmatics, and it seems reasonable to suggest that when the Court's pragmatic assumptions fail to accord with contemporary knowledge, they should be revised or abandoned.

• • •

[*At this point, Bailey discusses several sedition and criminal anarchy cases that reached the U.S. Supreme Court in the years between World War I and the beginning of World War II; his purpose is to illustrate the nation's fear of the speech of political dissenters. His discussion includes* Schenck v. United States *(1919),* Abrams v. United States *(1919),* Gitlow v. United States *(1925), and* Whitney v. California *(1927). He then surveys the post-World War II cases, including* Dennis v. United States *(1951),* Yates v. United States *(1957), and* Brandenburg v.

---

[3]The clear and present danger test makes most obvious assumptions concerning speech efficacy. Its current viability has been called into question. See Harry Kalven, "The *New York Times* Case: A Note on 'The Central Meaning of the First Amendment,' " *The Supreme Court Review*, 1964, pp. 191–221; for a rather brief contrary opinion flavored by international implications see William van Alstyne, "The First Amendment and the Suppression of Warmongering Propaganda in the United States: Comment and Footnotes," *Law and Contemporary Problems: International Control of Propaganda*, XXXI (Summer 1966), fn. 56, pp. 546–47. The concern of this essay is only with the test's propensity for forcing the Court to state causal relationships between speech and illegal acts.

Continued

"THE SUPREME COURT AND COMMUNICATION THEORY: CONTRASTING MODELS OF SPEECH EFFICACY," BY WILLIAM E. BAILEY (Continued)

Ohio (1969). These examples, Bailey argues, illustrate the Supreme Court's use of the mechanistic model of speech efficacy, which leads one to assume that speech has the inherent capacity to create a danger or to produce an otherwise harmful effect.

Next, Bailey examines leading cases of the U.S. Supreme Court that concern provocation to anger, including Cantwell v. Connecticut (1940), Chaplinsky v. New Hampshire (1942), Terminiello v. Chicago (1949), Feiner v. New York (1951), Cohen v. California (1971), and Gooding v. Wilson (1972). Even with the narrow limits placed upon "fighting words" by the Supreme Court in the Cohen and Gooding cases, Bailey argues that the Court has not yet recognized the citizen's capacity "to walk away from 'fighting words,' to resist incitements to breaches of the peace or other illegal acts." In short, the Court has not adequately considered the audience as a causal factor in the speech situation.

He continues as follows.]

• • •

Before moving to the next section, a summary here may be helpful. The early free speech cases occurred during a period of time when society was frightened virtually to hysteria by the threat of propaganda. It was, and still is, feared that the persuader could "get at" an audience without its consent. Especially suspect were the emotional appeals that could cause men to act irrationally. In this view, speech is a direct instrumentality that compels behavior, and the flow of influence is unidirectional, from the speaker to the audience. This view of speech is inherent to the rationale behind prosecution of incitement and has manifested itself in the opinions of the Court.

The Empirical Model of Speech Efficacy

This section will be devoted to the presentation of a reasonably typical empirical model of speech efficacy. Rather than attempt to integrate individual experiments or theories, the presentation will draw upon summary opinions of scholars and researchers making comment upon such broad areas of study as propaganda and public opinion. There is no intent to present a thorough, scholarly survey, but only to present as clearly as possible in the least amount of space the contemporary view of speech efficacy based upon empirical research.

The Mechanistic (Social) and Empirical (Scientific) Models Compared

At the outset it seems advantageous to contrast the model discussed in the prior section with the model to be presented in this section. Professor Bauer accomplishes the contrast with considerable efficiency:

The *social model* of communication is a model of one-way influence in which the communicator presumably has power and "does something to the audience," with or without its consent. This model of communication emphasizes the exploitation of man by man . . . . In fact, however, the history of communication research seems to offer more support for a different model.

The *scientific model* of communication more accurately reflects what is known from communication research. It views communication as a two-way transaction between communicator and audience in which each party is engaged in problem solving, and in which each party both gives and gets something.[65]

The transactional aspect of the model is important. As Professor Bauer points out, in the latter model we are led to look not only for the influence of the speaker upon the audience, but as well "for the audience's effect upon the communicator."[66] Bauer feels that "perhaps the most important implication of the transaction is that when we try to change others we get changed ourselves."[67] The social model has been wholly abandoned and the emphasis is upon constructing a model adequate to the transactional elements of the communication process.[68] There is no question that the speech situation is effective in changing attitudes of behavior; however, the efficacy depends to a significant degree upon the audience.[69] Both the hidden and overt persuader are far less powerful than previously thought. The study of propaganda has brought forth considerable information on this point.

A common and significant insistence of propaganda studies is that decided differences in both kind and efficacy of propaganda exist between democratic and totalitarian societies. Qualter points out that the greater power of the totalitarian propaganda does not derive from superior techniques but from a monopoly control over the means of propaganda and the use of force to exclude rival propaganda; this fact leads him to conclude that in a genuine democracy there will be the greatest possible free competition among the propagandists for a variety of causes:

> This competition is desireable, not only to prevent the emergence of a totalitarian monopoly . . . but also because the fillip of new, controversial ideas is in itself a stimulating educating force . . . . Rival propaganda campaigns are one of the most important forces for provoking individual thinking on any issue. Now, although a democratic government may give a lead to public opinion . . . it is not part of its function to determine the religious, philosophic, economic, social, or purely eccentric beliefs of its people. The government is not the guardian of the public conscience and has no authority to object to the faith of any of its citizens or to their desire to convert others to that faith.[70]

Qualter goes on to point out that the average propagandist in a democracy may have ambitions of "moulding a public mind to his own design," but the competition forces his propaganda to take on an educational function, about which the audience makes up its own mind: "The propaganda makes the people aware of the issues to be considered, but it seems to have less effect than once imagined in determining how people will react to

---

[65]Raymond A. Bauer in *The Obstinate Audience*, Donald E. Payne, ed. (a seminar sponsored and published by the Foundation for Research on Human Behavior: Ann Arbor, 1965), p. 1. [Note: the material elided from Bailey's article is documented with footnotes 4 through 64, which are also elided.]

[66]*Ibid.*, p. 10.

[67]*Ibid.*, p. 11.

[68]So much has been published on this point that a reference is arbitrary. Of several excellent works, *The Process and Effects of Mass Communication*, Wilbur Schramm, ed. (Urbana, 1957) is one of the best. See especially Schramm's article, "How Communication Works," pp. 3–36.

[69]Joseph T. Klapper, "The Comparative Effects of the Various Media," in Schramm, pp. 102–103.

[70]Terence H. Qualter, *Propaganda and Psychological Warfare* (New York, 1962), pp. 4–6.

Continued

"THE SUPREME COURT AND COMMUNICATION THEORY: CONTRASTING MODELS OF SPEECH EFFICACY," BY WILLIAM E. BAILEY (Continued)

these issues."[71] Similarly, Klapper points out that "The condition believed to render persuasion most effective is [a] monopoly propaganda position. In the United States, such a position can be achieved only by persuasion for attitudes which already enjoy almost universal sanction."[72]

George A. Miller finds that the "power of the propaganda campaign is not as alarming as it might seem on first consideration. People seek out and believe what they want to believe, and they let themselves be pushed in the way they want to go."[73] Roger Brown concludes that the power of propaganda has been "oversold,"[74] and that fear in this country of Russian propaganda that appears to hold the Russians in its grip fails to recognize the difference between the monopoly situation in Russia and the competitive situation in the United States.[75] Roger Brown makes a very significant point on speech efficacy when he states, "Speech is not directly instrumental, it does not compel action. The consent of the audience is won by convincing them that the recommended action is in their own best interests."[76]

J. A. C. Brown concludes:

> . . . it would appear that the main lesson to be drawn from our present study of propaganda is how very resistant people are to messages that fail to fit into their own picture of the world and their own objective circumstances, how they deliberately (if unconsciously) seek out only those views which agree with their own.[77]

J. A. C. Brown makes a quite ironic point: he argues that in their study of Gallup polls and motivation research to find out what the people really think, the "would-be brainwashers of Western democracies are being brainwashed"; only in the Communist "people's democracies" are the brainwashers "performing their proper function."[78]

Berelson writing on public opinion and communication provides from that point of view a close parallel with the opinions already expressed:

> The point is that the nature of one's audience places certain limits upon what one can say to it—and still have an audience . . . .
> It is important to take account of this direction in the flow of influence between communication and public opinion in order to appreciate the reciprocal nature of that influence, i.e., to recognize that it is not all a one way process. It is also important to note that the total effect of this reciprocal process is probably to stabilize and "conservatize" opinion since ideologies are constantly in process of reinforcement thereby. The over-all picture then, is that of like begetting like begetting like.[79]

---

[71]Ibid., p. 153.

[72]Joseph T. Klapper, "Mass Media and Persuasion," in Schramm, pp. 317–18.

[73]George A. Miller, Language and Communication (New York, 1951), p. 269.

[74]Roger Brown, Words and Things (New York, 1958), p. 302.

[75]Ibid., p. 339.

[76]Ibid., p. 340.

[77]J. A. C. Brown, Techniques of Persuasion (London, 1963), p. 309.

[78]Ibid., pp. 310–311.

[79]Bernard Berelson, "Communication and Public Opinion," in Schramm, p. 345.

It is clear that the efficacy of the persuader has been in the past over-estimated and that a considerably greater danger may attach to limiting speech significantly than to giving it free rein. One of the most relevant statements with regard to policy concerning free speech was made by Daniel Katz, commenting on the study of attitudes. Katz defines two streams of thought that have been traditionally held and that assume contrasting models.[80] On the one hand is the tradition that assumes an irrational model and holds that men are very limited in powers of reason, reflection, discrimination, self insight and memory, and that "Whatever mental capacities people do possess are easily overwhelmed by emotional forces and appeals to self-interest and vanity."[81] In the second tradition, a rational model is invoked. This model assumes that man "seeks understanding . . . , consistently attempts to make sense of the world about him, that he possesses discriminating and reasoning powers . . . and that he is capable of self-criticism and self-insight. It relies heavily upon getting adequate information to people."[82] Both of these viewpoints have been supported by research, and Katz concludes:

> Now either school of thought can point to evidence which supports its assumptions, and can make fairly damaging criticism of its opponent . . . .
> The conflict between the rationality and irrationality models was saved from becoming a worthless debate because of the experimentation and research suggested by these models . . . . In general, the irrational approach was at its best where the situation imposed heavy restrictions upon search behavior and response alternatives . . . . On the other hand, where the individual can have more adequate commerce with the relevant environmental setting, where he has time to obtain more feedback from his reality testing, and where he has a number of realistic choices, his behavior will reflect the use of his rational faculties.[83]

The import of this position is clear: if irrationality is the desired end for man, restrict his access to communication, effect a persuasive monopoly; if rationality is the desired end, give him free access to all possible views and advocacies, make a persuasive monopoly impossible. But the primary force of the arguments of this section should be directed against the concept of incitement. It should be evident that the Court has assumed wrongly that the speaker is *the* causative agent in the speech situation, and it is this unwarranted assumption that modern communication research most strongly rejects.

The Empirical Model Applied to Free-Speech Decisions

This section will conclude the essay with an attempt to sharpen the relationship and significance of the empirical model to free speech prosecution. To that end a very contemporary complaint about the lack of empirical analysis on the part of the Court is relevant. In his free speech arguments relating to black power advocacy Paul Harris contends, "The clear and present danger test sidesteps the question whether or not there was a real causal connection [between advocacy and violence] by requiring only that

[80]Daniel Katz, "The Functional Approach to the Study of Attitudes," *Reader in Public Opinion and Communication*, Bernard Berelson and Morris Janowitz, eds. (New York, 1966), pp. 51–52.
[81]*Ibid.*, p. 52.
[82]*Ibid.*
[83]*Ibid.*, pp. 52–53.

Continued

"THE SUPREME COURT AND COMMUNICATION THEORY: CONTRASTING MODELS OF SPEECH EFFICACY," BY WILLIAM E. BAILEY (Continued)

reasonable men agree that the advocacy could have caused the violence."[84] Harris continues:

> The Court has never made a full empirical analysis of the advocate's relationship to the expected danger. It may be that the judicial process is not adequate to make these kinds of determinations. But if the Court is committed to a formula which requires determinations as to when there is an actual danger and as to the likelihood [of] speech causing action, then its refusal to attempt empirical answers to these issues results in vague notions of danger and causality determining the scope of free speech.[85]

The arguments of this essay support the contentions of Harris but point in a direction other than empirical determination by the Court of individual speech efficacy. As Harris intimates, the judicial process does not seem adequate to make such determinations. Nor does it need to. The empirical model is a generalization of empirical findings with regard to speech efficacy. If the Court were guided by such a model in its deliberations, it could not affirm incitement convictions but would hold that too many variables enter to allow the conviction and that no audience can be compelled by words to commit acts they do not want to commit.

The major function of the empirical model of communication in free speech prosecution would be the correction it would make of the older model's over-estimation and over-determination of the efficacy of a speaker or a speech. Correction would be accomplished primarily through the model's inclusion of the audience as a definite and possibly determinant factor in speech efficacy, and this inclusion renders the causal factors traditionally assigned to the speaker possibilities rather than certainties. The empirical model, if incitement prosecution could be contemplated under its auspices, could as easily lead to prosecution of an audience for incitement of a speaker as the reverse. But in fact, the model destroys the concept of incitement.

The significance of the empirical model is that it wholly denies the notion of inherent efficacy which was the enabling assumption of the Espionage Act convictions. Guided by such a model the Court could not assume that words "by their very nature" or "by their very utterance" have any efficacy, because the efficacy of the words is dependent upon the audience hearing them. In brief, guided by the empirical model the Court would hold the position that the speech act is at least as much determined in its efficacy by the mind of the listener as by anything the speaker may do.

It is plain then, that should the Court adopt an empirical view of speech efficacy, the abridgment of free speech by incitement prosecution would end. "Reasonable men" could not agree that an advocacy could cause violence in the absence of a predisposition toward violence on the part of the audience. And assuming such a predisposition could be demonstrated, "reasonable men" would not agree that the speaker's contribution could be separated from the audience's contribution.

At this point some objections may be considered. One objection might be to the

[84]Paul Harris, "Black Power Advocacy: Criminal Anarchy or Free Speech," *California Law Review* 56 (May, 1968), p. 732.
[85]*Ibid.*, p. 734.

general tenor of an argument against incitement prosecution: why should advocacy in violation of law receive First Amendment protection? This question reflects an increasingly popular attitude, and since the Court's decisions have affirmed incitement convictions, the burden of proof seems to rest on the libertarian. But the easy assertion that freedoms are not absolute is not a rationale for limiting those freedoms in the absence of a clearly defined harm. The arguments of this essay have raised substantive questions concerning the pragmatics of the Court's assumptions relating to incitement. If incitement convictions cannot be upheld by the Court upon an empirical, factual basis, surely everyone would agree the very notion of incitement is one that the judicial process is better off without. It is not necessary for one to approve of the radical's method or message to see the injustice of prosecution or conviction based upon erroneous premises. The fore-going arguments attack the basis of incitement prosecutions: the assumption that incitement has inherent efficacy and therefore causes violation of the law. If it cannot be maintained that speech is the direct instrument of violation of law, the argued need for abridgment of First Amendment protections by incitement statutes is without substance.

It may be objected that "incitement" is used in this essay in a far stronger sense than it has in legal usage, where it means only to "urge," "stimulate," or "advocate," and not at all "to compel by a speech." Citations from the Court opinions given above manifest assumptions of inherent efficacy that argue to the contrary. Besides, if "urging," "stimulating," or "advocating" where not deemed highly effective in causing the proscribed act, if "incitement" does not in meaning approach "compelling speech," then why should it be prosecuted?

The assumption of a rational audience may be considered excessively idealistic, but that has already been answered in part, above, by Katz. The counter-assumption, that man is irrational, carries its own condemnation: how does he who asserts man's irrationality exempt himself and his statement? Most probably he does not mean *all* men, and when pressed will reveal the elitist assumption of irrational masses. But the questions of whether or not the masses are rational must assume the masses have free access to opinion and information.

Finally, whether or not men are rational, or have free will, the law obviously assumes they do, and it makes each man responsible for his individual acts. Even the most hardy opponent of the arguments offered here against incitement prosecution must surely concede that it is inconsistent for the law to assume individual responsibility, but yet punish a speaker for what an audience did, or might have done, as if the speaker were some warlock or wizard who could deprive the individual of his reason and autonomy. Future generations may well look back upon the speech prosecutions of this age with the same feelings we experience when we contemplate the earlier period of our history when men burned witches.

EXERCISES

A. Classroom projects and activities.

1. Here are three propositions phrased for debate:

a. Resolved, that Paul Robert Cohen should have been punished for the public display of vulgar language.

b. Resolved, that the original two-part *Chaplinsky* definition of "fighting words" to include offensive language in general should be reinstated by the U.S. Supreme Court.

c. Resolved, that this class agrees with the late Justice Hugo Black that the speech of Irving Feiner should have been fully protected under the Constitution.

2. Here are the same three questions phrased for discussion:

a. Should the courts extend the protection of the First Amendment to language such as "Fuck the Draft," as was done in the case of *Cohen* v. *California*?

b. Should offensive language in general be protected by the First Amendment or should such language be constrained under law, as is face-to-face speech that provokes to a breach of the peace?

c. Was the Supreme Court correct in upholding the conviction of Irving Feiner? Should police protect the speaker from a hostile audience, or should the speaker be removed from the scene and prosecuted as the agent who caused the audience to become hostile?

3. Examine the ordinances of your town and the statutes of your state to determine what restrictions, if any, are placed upon the use of "vulgar," "profane," "lewd," or "fighting" words in public. Report your findings to the class. Discuss.

4. Interview a police officer (or several) or have two or three officers visit the class to discuss their views about being subjected to verbal abuse while performing official duties. Do they receive special training to prepare them for verbal assaults? Do they agree or disagree with Justice Lewis Powell (see *Lewis* v. *New Orleans,* 1974) that a "properly trained officer may reasonably be expected to 'exercise a higher degree of restraint' than the average citizen, and thus be less likely to respond belligerently to 'fighting words'"?

5. Invite a professor of communication theory (or a panel of experts) to critique William E. Bailey's essay "The Supreme Court and Communication Theory," part of which appears in this chapter. Discuss with the professor or the panel whether or not offensive language can communicate ideas. Is such language ever the *best* way by which to communicate an idea? Is it ever *essential*?

6. Have a class discussion of the conclusions of William E. Bailey concerning "speech efficacy" in provocation-to-anger cases. Should the U.S. Supreme Court adopt the view espoused by Bailey? To what extent has the Supreme Court, in national security and "fighting-words" rulings, been *scientific*?

7. Discuss the following statement from Franklyn S. Haiman, professor of speech at Northwestern University: "How it can seriously be argued that calling a policeman a 'Fascist,' or school board members 'motherfuckers,' is without ideational content escapes me completely. Indeed I would suggest that it is precisely the ideational content that makes the listener so angry." In Haiman's *Speech and Law in a Free Society* (Chicago: University of Chicago Press, 1981), p. 133.

8. Discuss the view of Thomas I. Emerson that speakers who provoke an audience to anger should be allowed to continue to speak, for there "should be no such doctrine as protective custody or protective silencing in American law." In Emerson's *The System of Freedom of Freedom of Expression* (New York: Random House, 1970), p. 339.

9. Abstract the lengthy and vigorous dissent of Justice Robert H. Jackson in *Terminiello* v. *Chicago,* 337 U.S. 1 (1949), at 13–37. Make copies of your summary, distribute them to the class, and discuss. Ask the class's opinion of Jackson's closing statement protesting the freeing of Terminiello: "In the long run, maintenance of free speech will be more endangered if the population can have no protection from the abuses which lead to violence. . . . The choice is not between order and liberty. It is between liberty with order and anarchy without either. There is danger that, if the Court does not temper its doctrinaire logic with a little practical wisdom, it will convert the constitutional Bill of Rights into a suicide pact."

10. Discuss the following statement made by Justice Harlan in his opinion of the Court in *Cohen* v. *California:* ". . . much linguistic expression serves a dual communicative function: it conveys not only ideas capable of relatively precise, detached explication, but otherwise inexpressible emotions as well. In fact, words are often chosen as much for their emotive as their cognitive force. We cannot sanction the view that the Constitution, while solicitous of the cognitive content of individual speech, has little or no regard for that emotive function which, practically speaking, may often be the more important element of the overall message sought to be communicated."

11. Have each member of the class draft an "ideal" statute for the control of "fighting words" as narrowed by the Supreme Court in the cases of *Cohen* and *Gooding;* each person should make photocopies of his or her draft for class distribution and discussion. By class vote, select the best proposed statute (or the top three) and submit to a local attorney for a critique.

B. Topics for research papers or oral reports.

1. The Influence of *Chaplinsky* v. *New Hampshire* (1942) on Supreme Court Decisions Since 1942.

2. Who Created the *Real* Danger? A Comparison and Contrast of the Cases of *Terminiello* and *Feiner.*

3. An In-Depth Analysis of the Implications of the Opinion of the Court in *Cohen* v. *California.*

4. A Historical Survey of Legal Constraints on "Offensive" Language, with a Proposal for the Future.

5. Jehovah's Witnesses and the First Amendment: A Survey of One Group's Impact on Freedom of Speech in America.

6. The Two-Level Theory of Freedom of Speech: How Valid Is It? (Begin with a reading of the article of Harry Kalven, Jr., from the list of recommended sources at the end of the chapter.)

7. An Argument in Favor of Total Abolition of Legal Constraints on *All Types* of "Fighting Words."

8. Who Were Gerald L. K. Smith and Arthur Terminiello? A Closer Look at Two American Extremists.

9. How Various Scholars of First Amendment Theory Would Deal with Provocation to Anger. (Examine the points of view of leading thinkers, such as Alexander Meiklejohn, Zechariah Chafee, Thomas I. Emerson, and Franklyn S. Haiman.)

10. Even if Permitted, Should Offensive Language Be Employed by the Public Communicator? An Examination of Ethical Issues in Speech That Provokes to Anger.

SELECTED READINGS

(Note: A number of related readings are given at the conclusion of Chapter 8, "Time, Place, Manner, and Institutional Constraints.")

Barker, Lucius J., and Barker, Twiley W. "The Case of an Unpopular Student: *Feiner v. New*

York, 340 U.S. 315 (1951)." In *Freedoms, Courts, Politics: Studies in Civil Liberties.* Englewood Cliffs, N.J.: Prentice-Hall, 1965, pp. 42–59. Reprinted in Haig A. Bosmajian, ed., *The Principles and Practice of Freedom of Speech.* New York: Houghton Mifflin, 1971, pp. 192–209.

Barron, Jerome A., and Dienes, C. Thomas. *Handbook of Free Speech and Free Press.* Boston: Little, Brown, 1979. See chapter 3, "Speech in the Local Forum."

Berns, Walter. *The First Amendment and the Future of American Democracy.* New York: Basic Books, 1976. In particular, chapter 5, pp. 190–205, "Vulgar Speech and Public Good."

Delgado, Richard. "Words That Wound: A Tort Action for Racial Insults, Epithets, and Name-Calling." *Harvard Civil Rights–Civil Liberties Law Review* 17 (Spring 1982): 133–181.

Farber, D. A. "Civilizing Public Discourse: An Essay on Professor Bickel, Justice Harlan, and the Enduring Significance of *Cohen v. California.*" *Duke Law Journal* 1980 (April 1980): 283–303.

Gard, Stephen. "Fighting Words as Free Speech." *Washington University Law Quarterly* 58 (1980): 531–581.

Haiman, Franklyn S. *Speech and Law in a Free Society.* Chicago: University of Chicago Press, 1981. Especially Chapter 2, "What Is Speech?" and Chapter 7, "Symbolic Battery."

Kalven, Harry, Jr. "Metaphysics of the Law of Obscenity." *The Supreme Court Review: 1960,* pp. 1 ff. Edited by Philip B. Kurland. Chicago: University of Chicago Press, 1960. (Note: in this essay Kalven explains his view of the two-level theory of free speech that can be traced to the 1942 *Chaplinsky* decision on "fighting words.")

Note: "Fighting Words Doctrine—Is There a Clear and Present Danger to the Standard?" *Dickinson Law Review* 84 (Fall 1979): 75–96.

Note. "Hostile Audience Confrontations: Police Conduct and First Amendment Rights." *Michigan Law Review* 75 (1976): 180 ff.

Rothwell, J. Dan. "Verbal Obscenity: Time for Second Thoughts." *Western Speech* 35 (Fall 1971): 231–242.

Rutzick, Mark C. "Offensive Language and the Evolution of First Amendment Protection." *Harvard Civil Rights–Civil Liberties Law Review* 9 (January 1974): 1–28.

CHAPTER 7

Commercial Speech

"Commercial advertising might well be called the stepchild of the first amendment. . . . [Yet] advertising is a medium of information and persuasion, providing much of the day-to-day 'education' of the American public and facilitating the flexible allocation of resources necessary to a free enterprise economy. Neither profit motivation nor desire to influence private economic decisions necessarily distinguishes the peddler from the preacher, the publisher, or the politician."

—*Harvard Law Review* (1967)[1]

In 1969 the U.S. Congress approved the Public Health Cigarette Smoking Act, Section 6 of which provided that after January 1, 1971, "it shall be unlawful to advertise cigarettes on any medium of electronic communication subject to the jurisdiction of the Federal [Communications] Commission." As the deadline approached for the act to take effect, six radio stations joined in a legal challenge to its anticigarette provisions, arguing that Section 6 violated both the First and Fifth Amendments to the Constitution.[2]

By a vote of 2 to 1, a three-judge district court for the District of Columbia upheld the censorship provisions of the statute, asserting that it "is established that product advertising is less vigorously protected than other forms of speech." In support of this "established" position, the majority stated further that broadcasters "have lost no right to speak—they have only lost an ability to collect revenue from others for broadcasting their commercial messages." On appeal, the U.S. Supreme Court, without opinion, affirmed the decision below.[3]

The reluctance of the courts to extend First Amendment protection to commercial expression during the first three-quarters of the twentieth century reflects at least two sociopolitical attitudes of Americans toward advertising. *First,* there exists a profound distrust of commercial messages because of the numerous examples of exaggeration and outright falsehood exposed over the years. No doubt, revelations of deceptive advertising have caused many individuals to place commercial speech near the bottom of the scale of First Amendment values, and this attitude has been reflected by the courts. *Second,* a number of influential First Amendment scholars, notable among whom is Alexander Meiklejohn, have urged that commercial expression is less deserving of constitutional protection than is political speech, because "mere advertising" is not essential to the process of self-government. In other words, commercial speech—like defamation and profanity—is of little social value as a "step to truth" and therefore deserves less protection.

The first concern—exaggeration, "puffery," and the making of false claims—has been recognized for centuries. In 1779 British playwright Richard Brinsley Sheridan satirized the advertiser's art in *The Critic.* In Act I, Scene 2, he has the character Puff address characters Sneer and Dangle on the subject:

[1]"Developments in the Law: Deceptive Advertising," *Harvard Law Review* 80 (1967): 1027. Note: this entire issue, composed of pp. 1005–1163 of vol. 80, is devoted to the subject of advertising and the law.

[2]*Capitol Broadcasting Co.* v. *Mitchell,* 333 F. Supp. 583 (D.C.D.C. 1971). The Fifth Amendment argument charged that since some media could continue to advertise cigarettes while broadcasters could not, an "arbitrary and invidious" distinction had been drawn by the Congress, thus violating the due process clause of the Constitution. The courts rejected this argument, just as they did the one based on the First Amendment.

[3]*Capitol Broadcasting Co.* v. *Acting Attorney General,* 405 U.S. 1000 (1972).

FIGURE 7.1. *ADVERTISEMENT FOR DR. SCOTT'S ELECTRIC CORSET.*
This advertisement typifies the quackery of the late nineteenth and early twentieth centuries, prior to the establishment of the Food and Drug Administration and the Federal Trade Commission.
Harper's Weekly, *January 7, 1882.*

"I make no Secret of the trade I follow . . . . I am Sir—a Practitioner in Panegyric—or to speak more Plainly—a Professor of the Art of Puffing, at your service or anybody else's." Puff then brags about how he has assisted his clients:

> . . . 'twas I first enrich'd their style—'twas I first taught them to crowd their Advertisements with panegyrical superlatives, each epithet rising above the other . . . . From me they learned to inlay their Phraseology with variegated Chips of Exotic metaphor: . . . yes Sir by me they were instructed to . . . raise upstart oaks where there never had been an Acorn . . .

or fix the temple of Hygeia in the fens of Lincolnshire![4]

During the nineteenth and early twentieth centuries—before the passage of strong truth-in-advertising legislation and the establishment of governmental enforcement agencies such as the Federal Trade Commission (FTC)—American consumers were subjected to some advertising campaigns the "panegyrical superlatives" of which make contemporary claims for mouthwash, perfume, and

[4]In *The Major Dramas of Richard Brinsley Sheridan,* ed. George H. Nettleton (Boston: Ginn, 1906), pp. 234–236.

shaving lotion seem mild by comparison. Among the peculiar products hawked in the nineteenth century were Dr. Scott's Electric Corset (see Figure 7.1) and Hostetter's Celebrated Stomach Bitters (a 94-proof compound that supposedly cured whatever ailed the purchaser).[5]

The second attitude—that commercial speech is of less social value as a step to truth than is political speech, and therefore merits less constitutional protection—was widely accepted in the legal community during the first two hundred years of the nation's history. A typical twentieth-century statement of this point of view appears in the writings of constitutional theorist Alexander Meiklejohn, who argued that the First Amendment was intended primarily to protect expression essential to self-government. Because commercial speech was not a necessary part of the democratic process, he reasoned, it could be constrained by law. Meiklejohn observed, for example, that the "constitutional status of a merchant advertising his wares" or of a "paid lobbyist fighting for the advantage of his client is utterly different from that of a citizen who is planning for the general welfare."[6]

Meiklejohn's thinking about commercial expression was certainly in harmony with legal precedent, even that of relatively recent times. Since the establishment of the Federal Trade Commission in 1914, both Congress and the U.S. Supreme Court have treated advertising and related matters of commercial communication as issues of business and property law rather than as important questions of freedom of speech. During the 1970s, following the appointment of four new justices to the bench by President Richard M. Nixon, the Supreme Court changed its view, dramatically altering precedent by extending constitutional protection for the first time to certain categories of advertising. The analysis of developments in the area of commercial speech is presented below according to two main topics: (1) a look at the past, emphasizing the constraints upon communication exercised by governmental administrative agencies (the FTC in particular), and (2) constitutional issues, with an emphasis upon recent decisions of the U.S. Supreme Court.

I. FEDERAL ADMINISTRATIVE AGENCIES AND COMMERCIAL SPEECH

Prior to the entry of the federal government in the field of policing false and misleading advertising, the consumer had to rely upon common-law remedies (such as civil suits under tort law), voluntary industry codes, and various state laws for assistance in responding to dishonest claims by business and industry. The common-law remedy of bringing suit against an offending advertiser was generally ineffective, because of both the expense entailed and the difficulty of establishing one's claims in a system weighted in favor of the companies. Furthermore, voluntary industry codes had little influence upon those dishonest firms that did not subscribe to them, and in many instances state laws were either nonexistent or too weak to be of much help.

Between 1900 and 1912 a number of newspapers and magazines published exposés of useless "medicines" and the false claims made for them; the American Medical Association

---

[5]See Stewart H. Holbrook, *The Golden Age of Quackery* (New York: Macmillan, 1959); and Ernest S. Turner, *The Shocking History of Advertising* (New York: Dutton, 1953).

[6]Alexander Meiklejohn, *Free Speech and Its Relation to Self-Government.* Collected with additional Meiklejohn papers in *Political Freedom: The Constitutional Powers of the People* (New York: Harper & Row, 1960). Citation above from the paperbound reissue by Oxford University Press, 1965, p. 37.

joined in the educational effort by publishing its own reports concerning various patent medicines and health-improvement devices. Public opinion was aroused, and corrective legislation was demanded.[7] In response, *Printer's Ink,* the trade publication of the advertising industry, proposed a model state law which made it a misdemeanor for an advertisement to contain "any assertion, representation or statement of fact which is untrue, deceptive or misleading."[8] Although forty-four states eventually adopted the *Printer's Ink* statute, much dishonesty in advertising continued because of the inconsistent enforcement of the law from state to state. Before long, the U.S. Congress intervened.

The discussion of federal activity in constraining deceptive commercial messages is presented below in two parts. First, the work of the FTC—the most active of the various federal agencies in the truth-in-advertising field—is detailed; second, the assistance provided by other federal agencies is briefly summarized. (These agencies include the Food and Drug Administration, the Federal Communications Commission, the Securities and Exchange Commission, and the U.S. Postal Service.)

The Federal Trade Commission

History and Development of the FTC

In 1914, in a move strongly supported by President Woodrow Wilson, the U.S. Congress passed the Federal Trade Commission Act, thereby establishing the FTC. Originally, the agency was intended to help en-

force antitrust laws, particularly those involving "unfair methods of competition in commerce." Although there was no mention of false advertising in the original statute, the members of the commission interpreted the language of the law broadly to include false and misleading advertising. As might be expected, the work of the new agency was soon challenged in the courts.

The first case to reach the U.S. Supreme Court concerning the authority of the FTC to move against deceptive advertising resulted in a victory for the commission. In 1922 the Supreme Court ruled in the case of *FTC* v. *Winsted Hosiery Co.* that the commission had acted legally to cite Winsted for dishonest advertising based upon the practice of the company to label its products "woolen" when, in fact, they were less than 10 percent wool.[9] Over the next nine years, from 1922 to 1931, the courts upheld twenty-two of twenty-nine FTC orders concerning false advertising. Then as now, the First Amendment was no barrier to judicial holdings that deception in commercial advertising could be constrained by law.

A setback for the FTC occurred in 1931, when the Supreme Court curtailed the agency's activity on behalf of consumers. The Court ruled in the case of *FTC* v. *Raladam Co.* that the 1914 statute establishing the commission restricted its work to matters of unfair *business* competition and did not otherwise provide for consumer protection.[10] In other words, the Court interpreted the language of the law narrowly, deciding that since consumers were not specifically mentioned, the work of the FTC was restricted to "competition in commerce." Soon thereafter, discussions began in the Congress about how best to reverse the effect of *Rala-*

---

[7]Earl W. Kintner, *A Primer on the Law of Deceptive Practices* (New York: Macmillan, 1971), pp. 5–14. One of the most influential series of articles was written by Samuel Hopkins Adams and published in *Collier's* in 1906.

[8]Ibid., p. 480.

[9]*FTC* v. *Winsted Hosiery Co.,* 258 U.S. 483 (1922).

[10]*FTC* v. *Raladam Co.,* 283 U.S. 643 (1931).

dam with legislation. The result, several years later, was the Wheeler-Lea Amendment of 1938, which added the words "unfair or deceptive acts or practices in commerce" to the law, thereby explicitly authorizing the FTC to act for the benefit of the public in general.

The consumer protection authority of the FTC was again strengthened with the passage of the Magnuson-Moss Act of 1975. Subsequently, the enforcement zeal of some officers of the commission so offended many manufacturers and advertisers that a countermovement was started to work for legislation to restrict the power of the agency. This effort, added to a national conservative political shift in the late 1970s, resulted in yet another assessment of FTC authority, and in 1980 the Congress acted to curtail the FTC. Despite the 1980 legislation, the fundamental authority of the commission to police false and deceptive advertising remains intact.

The FTC's Basic Rules for Commercial Advertising

The Federal Trade Commission expects advertising to be truthful; claims made in commercial messages should be provable by the objective standards of science. In interpreting the central standard of truthfulness, the following general rules are applied (each has been sustained at one time or another by the courts). According to the FTC, an advertisement is false or deceptive:

1. If it has a tendency to deceive (no actual deception need be proved).
2. If it misrepresents a product, even though the advertiser is not aware that the claim is false or has no intent to deceive.
3. If it presents the literal truth in such a way as to leave a false impression, thus leading the consumer to a false conclusion (in other words, literal truth is not enough—the conclusion it leads one to draw must also be true).

4. If it is ambiguous and can be interpreted in a false or misleading way.[11]

The FTC has developed a variety of rules, procedures, and applications based upon the standards of truthfulness listed above. Those concerning puffery, testimonials, and specific dishonest procedures are illustrative.

"Puffery" is a term used to describe abstract claims and assertions of opinion that are difficult if not impossible to test empirically. Examples of puffery include suggestions that certain types of lotions make one irresistible to the opposite sex or that a particular automobile is "the best looking machine in town." As the reader can imagine, checking a factual claim concerning the gasoline mileage for an automobile is easier to do, and produces more concrete conclusions, than trying to determine whether or not the car in question is "the best looking machine in town." Both state and federal consumer-protection agencies permit a good deal of puffery in advertising, if for no other reason than expediency, for to do otherwise would consume most of the resources of the agency in unproductive areas of investigation. The basic test for puffery adopted by the FTC is whether or not average consumers would recognize the claim for the advertised product or service as hyperbole or would be deceived by it.[12] This test permits the commission to constrain extreme instances of exaggeration while conserving resources for the more productive work of policing the factual claims of advertisers.

---

[11]Kintner, pp. 30–31. Supporting court decisions include *FTC v. Standard Education Society,* 302 U.S. 112 (1937), a pro-FTC decision authored by Justice Hugo Black, a strong defender of the First Amendment; *DDD Corp. v. FTC,* 125 F. 2d 679 (7th Cir. 1942); *Bockenstette v. FTC,* 134 F.2d 369 (10th Cir. 1943); and *FTC v. Mary Carter Paint Co.,* 382 U.S. 46 (1965).

[12]See *Western Radio Corp. v. FTC,* 339 F.2d 937 (1965), in which this standard is articulated.

Testimonials are permitted under FTC rules and are evaluated by a policy adopted by the commission in 1975. Among the standards that apply to advertising employing testimony are the following: the person testifying must be an actual user of the product, must have some expertise that qualifies him or her to make claims for the product or service, must adhere to the same basic standards of truth generally applied to other types of advertising, must not be an actor pretending to be an ordinary consumer, and must reveal any personal financial interest in the product (such as part ownership of the company) that he or she might have.

A number of *specific dishonest procedures* are forbidden by the FTC. Examples include price deceptions (claiming that the advertised price is a special sale price when it is not, or saying that the price has been "cut in half" when it has not, etc.) and bait-and-switch advertising in which the consumer is lured into the store with the promise of a bargain, only to be subjected to high-pressure selling for higher-priced merchandise because the "bargain" is "sold out," or of such a shoddy quality as to be undesirable.

FTC Enforcement Procedures

The FTC works with manufacturers and advertisers to avoid legal confrontation whenever possible. This is done in three ways. First, *industry guides* that interpret the rules of the commission are available to the public for study. Second, *advisory opinions* are issued in response to specific questions from industry concerning the legality of a proposed action, such as an advertising campaign. Finally, newly developed *trade regulation rules* are published in advance to give industry an opportunity to comment before the proposals are put into effect. If, despite these efforts, a conflict occurs, the commission moves to enforce its decisions.

The FTC exercises two general types of enforcement powers: (1) publicity and negotiation (the latter includes voluntary compliance agreements and consent orders) and (2) legal proceedings. In the first type, the commission often pressures an offending company into stopping false or misleading advertising by launching a publicity campaign calling attention to the dishonest message being communicated. Also, through out-of-court settlements (called voluntary agreements or consent orders), the commission secures a program of compliance from an erring firm without incurring the time and expense of court proceedings. If the offending advertiser does not settle the matter in response to the various out-of-court negotiations available, the FTC is empowered to move to the second step in enforcement—legal proceedings—and to issue a cease-and-desist order or its variation, the corrective advertising order.[13]

A cease-and-desist order, which is similar to an injunction, remains in effect indefinitely unless appealed within sixty days to the U.S. Court of Appeals. The advertiser who fails to comply with such an order risks stiff civil fines—up to $10,000 per day for each offense. The corrective advertising requirement, used only occasionally by the FTC, appears as a subsection of a regular cease-and-desist order; it states that a company must spend a percentage of its advertising budget (usually from 15 to 25 percent) for a specified period of time (such as one year) to pay for "corrective" messages informing the public of past misinformation in the company's advertising. Both types of FTC orders

---

[13]Furthermore, an extreme remedy was authorized by Congress in the Trans-Alaska Pipeline Authorization Act of 1973. It enables the FTC to request an injunction from the federal court and thus to *stop* an advertisement that violates the law.

are illustrated in the following section. The Colgate-Palmolive "Rapid Shave" case is an example of a standard stop order, and the Warner-Lambert "Listerine" decision exemplifies the corrective advertising approach.

The FTC at Work: Two Cases

CASE 1: THE RAPID SHAVE DECEPTION. In December of 1961 the FTC issued a cease-and-desist order against the Colgate-Palmolive Company on the grounds that three television commercials promoting a product called Rapid Shave were "false and deceptive." The commercials, all prepared by the advertising agency of Ted Bates and Company, claimed that Rapid Shave "outshaves them all" because of its "super-moisturizing power," which could even soften sandpaper so effectively that the sand could easily be shaved off. It was "apply . . . soak . . . and off in a stroke," said the announcer, as the television viewer watched what appeared to be sandpaper being shaved clean by a razor immediately after an application of Rapid Shave.

What the viewer was seeing, however, was not an actual demonstration but a mock-up consisting of Plexiglas to which loose sand had been applied. Even though the FTC examiner found that Rapid Shave made it possible to shave sandpaper after about *eighty minutes* of soaking, the commission decided that the commercial was misleading to the consumer because the Plexiglas-and-loose-sand substitute for real sandpaper was *not* disclosed to the television viewer, thereby making it appear that the sandpaper was shaved immediately after an application of the cream.

Following protracted hearings, which included a circuit court of appeals decision that the original FTC order was too broad in that it seemed to make all simulations by advertis-

ers illegal, the commission rewrote its cease-and-desist order to focus more precisely on the case in question, reissuing the revised "final order" in 1963. Colgate-Palmolive's appeal eventually reached the U.S. Supreme Court, and in 1965 the Court issued its opinion, siding with the FTC. Although the Supreme Court declined to forbid all simulations in product advertising (some are not misleading but are simply a convenience in preparing the commercial), it did uphold constraints upon those which lead the consumer to make false inferences, such as the conclusion by television viewers that "they are seeing the test, experiment or demonstration for themselves, when they are not because of undisclosed use of mock-ups."[14]

CASE 2: CORRECTIVE ADVERTISING FOR LISTERINE. Listerine antiseptic mouthwash has been on the market in the United States since 1879; during this time, its formula has not changed. From the outset the product has been represented as being beneficial in the treatment and prevention of colds, cold symptoms, and sore throats. Beginning in 1921 the makers of Listerine began to make specific claims for cold-prevention and related benefits in direct advertising to the consumer. In 1972 the FTC initiated a proceeding against Warner-Lambert Company, the manufacturers of Listerine, to determine whether or not the product actually accomplished what the advertising claimed. After a series of scientific tests and after hearing considerable expert testimony, the commission reached these six conclusions: (1) the ingredients in Listerine were not strong enough to

---

[14]*FTC* v. *Colgate-Palmolive Co.,* 380 U.S. 374 (1965), at 386. Note: For an interesting essay concerning this case, see Daniel Seligman, "The Great Sandpaper Shave: A Real-Life Story of Truth in Advertising," *Fortune,* December 1964, pp. 131–133 ff.

have any therapeutic effect; (2) gargling did not distribute the liquid to the critical areas of the body as claimed; (3) the liquid could not penetrate the tissue cells of the body, even if it did reach the critical areas; (4) the "scientific" studies used by the company to support its claims were not reliable; (5) killing germs in the mouth "by the millions," as claimed in the advertising, had no medical significance to the treatment of colds or sore throats; and (6) specifically, Listerine had "no significant beneficial effect on the symptoms of sore throat."[15]

On the basis of the six conclusions just cited, the commission issued a three-part cease-and-desist order, the first two parts of which required Warner-Lambert to stop claiming that Listerine would prevent, cure, or have any "significant beneficial effect" on colds or sore throats or their symptoms. The third part of the order—the corrective advertising section—required the company to spend the substantial sum of *$10 million* to publicize the following message: "Contrary to prior advertising, Listerine will not help prevent colds or sore throats or lessen their severity."[16] The federal court of appeals upheld the FTC order with one exception: the phrase "contrary to prior advertising" was deleted as punitive in nature and not essential to the informative thrust of the corrective message. Furthermore, said the court of appeals, the commission's order did not violate the Constitution, for the First Amendment presented "no obstacle" to the regulation of

false or deceptive commercial speech by the government. The court of appeals even went as far as to state its approval of the FTC's "entirely reasonable" corrective advertising standard, which it included in its opinion, as follows:

> If a deceptive advertisement has played a substantial role in creating or reinforcing in the public's mind a false and material belief which lives on after the false advertising ceases, there is clear and continuing injury to competition and to the consuming public as consumers continue to make purchasing decisions based on the false belief. Since this injury cannot be averted by merely requiring respondent to cease disseminating the advertisement, we may appropriately order respondent to take affirmative action designed to terminate the otherwise continuing ill effects of the advertisement.[17]

Stung by the decision of the court of appeals in favor of the FTC, the manufacturers of Listerine appealed to the U.S. Supreme Court, which denied review and thereby refused to interfere with the enforcement of the commission's order.[18]

Other Federal Administrative Agencies and Commercial Speech

In addition to the Federal Trade Commission, which is the most active federal agency enforcing truth-in-advertising laws, a number of other federal agencies are involved in the administration of controls upon commercial expression. Among these, four are particularly important because of the duties assigned to them by the Congress. These are the Food and Drug Administration (FDA),

---

[15]*Warner-Lambert Company* v. *FTC,* 562 F.2d 749 (1977).

[16]The FTC began using corrective advertising orders in the early 1970s. Other instances include *In Re. ITT Continental Baking Company,* 79 F.T.C. 248 (1971), concerning the weight-reduction claims for Profile Bread; and *Ocean Spray Cranberries, Inc.,* 70 F.T.C. 975 (1972), concerning the claims of caloric value for cranberry juice.

[17]*Warner-Lambert Company* v. *FTC,* 562 F.2d 749 (1977), at 762.

[18]*Warner-Lambert Company* v. *FTC, cert. denied,* 436 U.S. 950 (1978).

the Federal Communications Commission (FCC), the Securities and Exchange Commission (SEC), and the U.S. Postal Service. A brief explanation of the responsibilities of each is appropriate at this point.

The Food and Drug Administration

The FDA was established by Congress in 1906, thus predating the formation of the FTC by eight years. The 1906 law charged the FDA with policing foods, drugs, medicines, and liquors that were mislabeled or adulterated (however, no authority for the supervision of advertising was included in this early law). Over the years, various amendments to the pure food and drug laws and to the statutes governing the work of the FTC have resulted in some overlapping of responsibilities between the FDA and the FTC. The two agencies have developed a general division of responsibility which assigns the FDA the task of policing product *labeling* and the FTC the task of supervising product *advertising*. In this regard, students of freedom of speech should note that the Constitution does not protect false or misleading information either on the label or in the advertising.[19]

The Federal Communications Commission

Among its various duties, the FCC, established by act of Congress in 1934, is charged with the granting of licenses to radio and television stations based upon the applicant's proposals for serving "the public interest, convenience, or necessity." Although the FCC may exercise no prior restraint upon what a station chooses to communicate over the air, it can exact post facto punishment for violations of law or of broadcast regulations

(punishment may vary from a warning to an outright revocation of a license). The examination of a station's record upon application for a license renewal includes a review of its commercial advertising, and—because of this and other powers granted to it—the FCC has considerable influence over the content of commercial messages on radio and television.

The FCC's authority in the area of commercial advertising was invoked in a concrete way in the late 1960s, when the commission granted antismoking advocates a "significant amount" of free time to answer procigarette radio and television commercials. The narrow ruling was restricted to advertising for cigarettes and was based upon the FCC's Fairness Doctrine, which requires balanced coverage by broadcasters of controversial issues of public importance. In the legal challenge that followed the commission's decision, the federal circuit court sided with the FCC, noted that commercial speech has traditionally received less protection under the Constitution than political speech, and ruled that the requirement for a "significant amount" of free time to answer cigarette commercials did not violate the First Amendment.[20]

In 1969, as noted at the opening of this chapter, Congress went even further than the FCC in the cigarette-smoking controversy by legislating a ban upon the airing of procigarette commercials. The censorship of these commercials, which became effective on January 1, 1971, was sustained by the U.S. Supreme Court.[21] As the reader can easily sur-

---

[19]For more on the complexities of overlapping responsibilities between the FDA and the FTC, see Kintner, chapter 22, "Food, Drugs, Cosmetics, and Devices."

[20]*Banzhaf* v. *FCC,* 405 F.2d 1082 (D.C. Cir. 1968); *cert. denied* without comment, 296 U.S. 842 (1969). Note: Chief Judge Bazelon, in his opinion for the circuit court, asserted that "cigarette commercials . . . are at best a negligible 'part of any exposition of ideas, and are of . . . slight social value as a step to truth.'"

[21]*Capitol Broadcasting Co.* v. *Acting Attorney General,* 405 U.S. 1000 (1972).

mise from the brief discussion above, the FCC, by virtue of commission-developed regulations (such as the Fairness Doctrine) or by explicit legislative authority (such as the Public Health Cigarette Smoking Act), exercises significant power over the broadcasting of commercial messages in the United States.

The Securities and Exchange Commission

Just as the FTC is empowered to enforce truth in advertising for a wide range of commercial products, the SEC is authorized to police false and deceptive advertising for securities, such as stocks and bonds. This authority is derived from federal laws that were passed, in the early 1930s, in response to widespread dishonesty in the securities business in the years preceding the stock market crash of 1929.[22] Before the sale of a security can proceed, complete accurate information about it must be filed with the SEC. The advertising for the sale of the security must be truthful, or its offering can be terminated by an SEC "stop order." In addition, it is illegal to use the mails to falsely advertise stocks and bonds, and any consumer who has been victimized by deceitful information concerning a security is authorized by law to bring suit for damages.

The U.S. Postal Service

The authority of the U.S. Postal Service to assist in the policing of false advertising for securities, as noted immediately above, is not the only way in which the post office constrains communication. A number of federal

obscenity statutes focus upon the dissemination of erotic materials through the mail (see Chapter 5, "Religio-Moral Heresy," for a full development of this area of the law). Furthermore, the postal service is empowered to deter false advertising—particularly as it relates to mail-order businesses—to the point of halting delivery of orders addressed to a dishonest business. The postal service can even impound suspected materials sent through the mails. Finally, the service can bring criminal charges against those suspected of mail fraud; a conviction can result in a fine of up to $1,000, a prison term of up to five years, or both.[23]

Federal Agencies and Commercial Speech in Brief

The constitutional right of Congress, and of the various administrative agencies created by Congress, to regulate commercial advertising appears to be firmly implanted in the law of the United States. The principle was clearly put in the mid-1950s when E. F. Drew and Company challenged the authority of the FTC to regulate the advertising of oleomargarine. In upholding the FTC, the federal court of appeals stated "that Congress can prohibit or control misleading advertising . . . without deprivation of First Amendment rights. There is no constitutional right to disseminate false or misleading advertisements."[24]

The Federal Trade Commission, established by Congress in 1914, is the most active federal agency in policing commercial advertising. The basic policy of the FTC is that commercial messages should be truthful and

---

[22]For the Securities Act of 1933, and the Securities Exchange Act of 1934, as amended over the years, see 15 *U.S. Code Annotated* Secs. 77 and 78. An interesting account of many of the abuses these statutes were designed to prevent is in Gordon Thomas and Max Morgan-Witts, *The Day the Bubble Burst: A Social History of the Wall Street Crash of 1929* (Garden City, N.Y.: Doubleday, 1979).

[23]See 39 *U.S. Code Annotated* Sec. 3003, and 18 *U.S. Code Annotated* Sec. 1341.

[24]*E. F. Drew and Co.* v. *FTC*, 235 F.2d 735 (2d Cir. 1956), at 739–40; *cert. denied*, 352 U.S. 969 (1957).

should be provable by the objective standards of science. To enforce its decisions, the FTC can use various out-of-court procedures (such as publicity, voluntary compliance agreements, and consent orders) or apply such strong measures as the issuance of a cease-and-desist order, a variation of which is the corrective advertising order.

Other federal agencies that have responsibilities in specific areas of commercial expression include the Food and Drug Administration (labeling of food and drugs), the Federal Communications Commission (broadcast advertising), the Securities and Exchange Commission (advertising for stocks and bonds), and the U.S. Postal Service (mail fraud). The focus of most of the constraints applied by these agencies, including the FTC, is *dishonest* advertising. But what about *honest* advertising—that commercial speech which involves no false or misleading information? In short, to what extent does the First Amendment protect *truthful* commercial expression? An examination of this question—long neglected by the federal courts until the Supreme Court's 1942 *Chrestensen* decision (discussed below)—is now in order, for there have been several significant court decisions concerning it within recent years.

II. COMMERCIAL SPEECH AND THE CONSTITUTION

Commercial Speech Excluded from the Constitution

In 1940 F. J. Chrestensen, owner of an old U.S. Navy submarine that he exhibited at various waterfront locales for an admission fee, docked on the East River in New York City and began to distribute handbills advertising his novel enterprise. Little did Chrestensen realize that he was about to become a leading participant in a First Amendment controversy, the result of which would determine the constitutional status of commercial advertising for many years to come. That is what happened, however, when New York City authorities moved to enforce a section of the city's sanitary code forbidding the distribution on the streets of handbills, cards, and circulars of a purely commercial nature but permitting handbills of a political or public information nature to be distributed. Denied permission to give out his handbills, Chrestensen had a two-faced sheet printed, one side of which featured his commercial message for visits to the submarine and the other a message of political protest concerning his treatment by New York authorities. The police were not amused, and the two-faced handbill was also prohibited. The stubborn showman then secured an injunction against enforcement of the ordinance from the federal district court, whereupon Police Commissioner Lewis J. Valentine appealed the district court's decision. When the federal court of appeals agreed with the district court, Commissioner Valentine carried his case to the U.S. Supreme Court, urging that contrary to Chrestensen's free-speech claim, the First Amendment did not protect commercial expression.

In ensuing years, the *Chrestensen* doctrine prevailed, and commercial speech was considered outside the umbrella of First Amendment protection. For example, when an Alexandria, Louisiana, ordinance prohibiting the door-to-door canvassing of private homes was challenged in the early 1950s, the Supreme Court upheld the law (even though its prohibitions included solicitation for magazines, the contents of which might be protected by the Constitution). In so ruling, the High Court noted that canvassing was commercial in nature and that the First Amendment did not protect "solicitors for gadgets

Valentine v. Chrestensen, 316 U.S. 52 (1942)
Decided April 13, 1942

Vote: 9 to 0 to uphold the constitutionality of the New York City ordinance (the courts below were reversed, and the injunction set aside).

Majority Opinion By: Justice Roberts.

Concurring Justices: Chief Justice Stone and Justices Black, Reed, Frankfurter, Douglas, Murphy, Byrnes, and Jackson.

Dissenting Justices: (none)

Justices Not Participating: (none)

Summary: Businessman F. J. Chrestensen, attempting to evade a New York City ordinance forbidding the distribution of *commercial* handbills (but permitting *political* ones), prepared a two-faced handbill, one side of which featured a commercial message and the other a message of political protest. When New York authorities classified the two-faced leaflet as *commercial* and warned against its distribution on the streets, Chrestensen entered federal court to challenge the rule. The federal district court issued an injunction, thus halting enforcement of the ordinance; the court of appeals sustained the district court. The U.S. Supreme Court, however, agreed with the New York authorities that the handbill was commercial and proceeded to reverse the courts below.

Rule Established; Significance of Case: The Supreme Court ruled that whereas it was clear that the streets could be used "for the exercise of the freedom of communicating information and disseminating opinion," it was equally clear that the Constitution granted no such privilege to "purely commercial advertising." Commercial speech, the Court concluded for the first time in its history, could be regulated by act of the legislature without violating the First Amendment—a determination that was applied as the "law of the land" for almost one-third of a century. (The concurrence of Justices Black and Douglas in the opinion of the Court is revealing of their attitude toward commercial expression. Seventeen years later, in a concurring opinion in *Cammarano* v. *U.S.,* 358 U.S. 498 (1959), at 514, Justice Douglas wrote that the *Chrestensen* ruling was "casual, almost offhand. And it has not survived reflection.")

or brushes."[25] By the 1960s, however, signs of erosion of the commercial speech doctrine began to appear.

A significant exception to *Chrestensen* was articulated by the Supreme Court in the 1964 case of *New York Times* v. *Sullivan,* in which a paid political advertisement was given constitutional protection (for more on the *Times-Sullivan* case, see Chapter 4, "Defamation and Invasion of Privacy").[26] True, the *Times* advertisement in question announced political information and opinion rather than an appeal for the purchase of some commercial product or service (this political-content vs. commercial-content dichotomy was stated by the Court to help justify its conclusion in the case)—yet was not the example in question, at base, a type of commercial speech? This question gave rise to others, such as: What was meant by the term "commercial speech"? Had the Court been clear about

[25]*Breard* v. *Alexandria,* 341 U.S. 622 (1951). Note: Both Justices Black and Douglas dissented from this decision, arguing that the inclusion of magazine soliciting in the ordinance violated the liberty of speech guaranteed by the Constitution.

[26]*New York Times* v. *Sullivan,* 376 U.S. 254 (1964).

when "commercial speech" was protected by the Constitution and when it was not? If a paid political advertisement was protected by the Constitution even when it included some false statements, why should not paid commercial advertising be protected when it communicated truthful information concerning a product or a service that was quite legal?

The 1973 case of *Pittsburgh Press* v. *Pittsburgh Commission on Human Relations* revealed that the Court was no longer satisfied with the commercial speech doctrine as set forth in *Chrestensen*.[27] In the Pittsburgh case, the Supreme Court upheld a city ordinance prohibiting the publication of classified advertising for employment according to sex-designated columns. A major reason for this ruling, said the Court, was that sex discrimination in employment was not legal; therefore advertisements for "male help wanted" and "female help wanted" were proposals for an *illegal* commercial activity. Furthermore, the Court implied that some degree of First Amendment protection for the advertisements might have been considered if the ads had been for a *legal* commercial transaction rather than for an illegal one.

Barron and Dienes, in their *Handbook of Free Speech and Free Press,* comment that *Pittsburgh Press* is "perhaps the last Supreme Court case resting on the original understanding of the commercial speech doctrine . . . . [In this decision] the Court indicated some degree of discomfort with respect to applying the doctrine. This reluctance was a harbinger of things to come."[28] Those who interpreted *Pittsburgh Press* as a sign of immi-

nent change proved correct when, in 1975, the High Court began to address a number of commercial speech issues that had been "swept under the rug" by *Chrestensen.*

Let Commercial Speech Flow "Cleanly" and "Freely": The Old Doctrine Reconsidered

Two cases concerning the freedom to advertise reached the Supreme Court shortly after the *Pittsburgh Press* decision, thus providing the Court with opportunities to initiate an expansion of First Amendment rights for commercial expression. The first challenged a Virginia statute making it illegal to advertise abortion services; the second challenged another Virginia statute making it a matter of "unprofessional conduct" for a pharmacist to advertise the prices of prescription drugs. A close look at each decision is needed, for they mark a dramatic shift in the Court's commercial speech doctrine.

The February 8, 1971, issue of the *Virginia Weekly,* a newspaper published in Charlottesville that focused upon student readers at the University of Virginia, carried an advertisement for an abortion referral service in New York City, headlined: "UNWANTED PREGNANCY, LET US HELP YOU." The ad went on to say that "Abortions are now legal in New York," and that there "are no residency requirements." Strict confidentiality was assured, and the address and phone numbers of the Women's Pavilion referral service were given.[29]

Soon after the advertisement appeared, Jeffrey C. Bigelow, managing editor of the *Virginia Weekly,* was charged with violating a state law making it illegal to publish advertising for abortion services. Bigelow was con-

[27]*Pittsburgh Press* v. *Pittsburgh Commission on Human Relations,* 413 U.S. 376 (1973).

[28]Jerome A. Barron and C. Thomas Dienes, *Handbook of Free Speech and Free Press* (Boston: Little, Brown, 1979), p. 160.

[29]*Bigelow* v. *Virginia,* 421 U.S. 809 (1975), at 812.

Bigelow v. Virginia, *421 U.S. 809 (1975)*
Decided June 16, 1975

Vote: 7 to 2 to reverse the conviction of Bigelow (which had been sustained by the Virginia Supreme Court).

Majority Opinion By: Justice Blackmun.

Concurring Justices: Chief Justice Burger and Justices Douglas, Brennan, Stewart, Marshall, and Powell.

Dissenting Justices: Rehnquist and White.

Justices Not Participating: (none)

Summary: In February of 1971 the Charlottesville *Virginia Weekly* published an abortion services advertisement of the Women's Pavilion of New York City. The listing pointed out that abortions were legal in New York City and that low-cost services were available in accredited hospitals and clinics. For making contact, an address and two telephone numbers were included. Three months later Jeffrey C. Bigelow, managing editor of the *Virginia Weekly,* was charged, tried, and convicted of a misdemeanor under state law that made it illegal to advertise abortion service information. The state circuit court upheld the conviction, as did the Virginia Supreme Court, which noted that since the message in question was of a "purely commercial nature," the First Amendment did not apply. Editor Bigelow then appealed to the U.S. Supreme Court, which reversed his conviction, asserting that the advertisement that had created the controversy "contained factual material of clear 'public interest.' Portions of its message . . . involve the exercise of the freedom of communicating information and disseminating opinion."

Rule Established; Significance of Case: This important decision altered the commercial speech doctrine established by *Chrestensen* in 1942. While it did not extend constitutional protection to all commercial messages (such as those that are deceptive or which promote illegality), it made clear that truthful advertising conveying facts and information "of potential interest and value" to the general public merits considerable First Amendment protection.

victed in state court and his appeal eventually reached the U.S. Supreme Court—with interesting results, not only for the editor but also for the commercial speech doctrine itself.

Over the protests of Justices Rehnquist and White, who argued in their dissenting opinion that states should be permitted to regulate commercial advertising, as they had done in the past, Justice Blackmun observed that the advertisement in question communicated important information "not only to readers possibly in need of the services offered, but also to those with a general curiosity about, or genuine interest in, the subject matter of the law of another State and its development, and to readers seeking reform in Virginia."

He then made official the Court's break with the past.

Justice Blackmun *delivered the opinion of the Court:*

We conclude, therefore, that the Virginia courts erred in their assumptions that advertising, as such, was entitled to no First Amendment protection and that appellant Bigelow had no legitimate First Amendment interest. . . .

Advertising, like all public expression, may be subject to reasonable regulation that serves a legitimate public interest. . . . To the extent that commercial activity is subject to regulation, the relationship of speech to that activity may be one factor, among others, to be considered in weighing the First Amendment interest against the governmental interest alleged. Advertising is not thereby stripped of all First Amendment protection. The relationship of speech to the marketplace of products or of services does not make it valueless in the marketplace of ideas. . . .

If application of this statute were upheld . . . , Virginia might exert the power sought here over a wide variety of national publications or interstate newspapers carrying advertisements similar to the one that appeared in Bigelow's newspaper or containing articles on the general subject matter to which the advertisement referred. Other States might do the same. The burdens thereby imposed on publications would impair, perhaps severely, their proper functioning. . . .

We conclude that Virginia could not apply [its statute] . . . to appellant's publication of the advertisement in question without unconstitutionally infringing upon his First Amendment rights. The judgment of the Supreme Court of Virginia is therefore reversed.

A year following *Bigelow,* in a challenge to another Virginia statute, the Supreme Court emphasized its departure from *Chrestensen* and developed its new commercial speech doctrine more fully. The controversy this time concerned whether or not pharmacists should be permitted to advertise the prices of prescription drugs. The Virginia statute, supported by the Virginia State Board of Pharmacy, said no. The U.S. Supreme Court, with only Justice Rehnquist dissenting, disagreed.

Justice Blackmun, who emerged as the chief spokesman for the majority in the reformulation of the Court's commercial speech doctrine, noted that the Virginia State Board of Pharmacy—appellants in the case—"contend that the advertisement of prescription drug prices is outside the protection of the First Amendment because it is 'commercial speech.' " He agreed that the argument reflected a view once subscribed to by the

Court. Citing both *Valentine* v. *Chrestensen* and *Breard* v. *Alexandria* as examples of the application of the doctrine in years gone by, Justice Blackmun emphasized that in 1975 "in *Bigelow v. Virginia,* the notion of unprotected 'commercial speech' all but passed from the scene." He then developed two main reasons for extending the First Amendment to advertising: *consumer* interest and *social* interest.

Justice Blackmun *delivered the opinion of the Court:*

As to the particular consumer's interest in the free flow of commercial information, that interest may be as keen, if not keener by far, than his interest in the day's most urgent political debate. Appellee's case in this respect is a convincing one. Those whom the suppression of prescription drug price information hits the hardest are the poor, the sick, and particularly the aged. A disproportionate amount of their income tends to be spent on prescription drugs; yet they are the least able to learn by shopping from pharmacist to pharmacist, where their scarce dollars are best spent. When drug prices vary as strikingly as they do, information as to who is charging what becomes more than a convenience. It could mean the alleviation of physical pain or the enjoyment of basic necessities.

[Concerning the social interest, advertising] . . . however tasteless and excessive it sometimes may seem, is nonetheless dissemination of information as to who is producing and selling what product, for what reason, and at what price. So long as we preserve a predominantly free enterprise economy, the allocation of our resources in large measure will be made through numerous private economic decisions. It is a matter of public interest that those decisions, in the aggregate, be intelligent and well informed. To this end, the free flow of commercial information is indispensable. And if it is indispensable to the proper allocation of resources in a free enterprise, it is also indispensable to the formation of intelligent opinions as to how that system ought to be regulated or altered. Therefore, even if the First Amendment

FIGURE 7.2. JUSTICE HARRY
BLACKMUN OF THE U.S.
SUPREME COURT.
*Justice Harry Blackmun was spokesman for the
Supreme Court in several important decisions of
the 1970s that extended the protection of the First
Amendment to certain types of commercial speech.
The Constitution protects advertising that
communicates to the general public "truthful
information about entirely lawful activity,"
Justice Blackmun asserted in the case of* Virginia
State Board of Pharmacy *v.* Virginia
Citizens Council *(1976); however, he and
others on the Supreme Court have made clear
that the federal government and the states may
continue to police false or misleading advertising
or advertising for illegal products or services.
Justice Blackmun was appointed to the Supreme
Court by President Richard Nixon in 1970.*
The Supreme Court Historical Society.

were thought to be primarily an instrument to
enlighten public decision-making in a democracy, we could not say that the free flow of information does not serve that goal.

Justice Blackmun continued by asserting
that reasonable constraints of time, place, and
manner could still be applied to commercial
speech, as could controls over deceptive advertising or that which promoted an illegal
product or service. "The First Amendment,
as we construe it today," he stressed, "does
not prohibit the State from insuring that *the
stream of commercial information flows cleanly as
well as freely*." (Emphasis supplied.) He then
concluded as follows: "What is at issue is
whether a State may completely suppress the
dissemination of concededly truthful information about entirely lawful activity, fearful
of that information's effect upon its dissemi-
nators and its recipients. Reserving other
questions [such as advertising by lawyers and

physicians], we conclude that the answer to
this one is in the negative."

The New Commercial Speech Doctrine Expanded and Refined: The Progeny of *Bigelow* and *Virginia State Board of Pharmacy*

When the Supreme Court strikes out in a
new direction on a First Amendment issue,
questions immediately arise as to how far the
Court will go and how the new doctrine will
be refined and applied (recall the continuing
saga of trying to define "obscenity" since the
1957 *Roth* decision, as well as a variety of rulings trying to explain *New York Times* v. *Sullivan* of 1964 and *Gertz* of 1974—both in the
area of defamation). As Justice Blackmun anticipated in *Virginia State Board of Pharmacy*,
one unanswered question concerned constitutional protection for advertising by those in
the professions, particularly lawyers and doc-

Va. State Board of Pharmacy v. Va. Citizens Consumer Council, 425 U.S. 748 (1976)
Decided May 24, 1976

Vote: 7 to 1 in favor of declaring the state law unconstitutional (the Virginia statute made it a matter of "unprofessional conduct" for a pharmacist to advertise drug prices).

Majority Opinion By: Justice Blackmun.

Concurring Justices: Chief Justice Burger and Justices Brennan, Stewart, White, Marshall, and Powell.

Dissenting Justices: Rehnquist.

Justices Not Participating: Stevens.

Summary: A Virginia consumer organization sued to invalidate the state law which made the advertising of prescription drug prices by licensed pharmacists a matter of "unprofessional conduct." A three-judge federal district court declared the law unconstitutional, and the U.S. Supreme Court affirmed this decision. Writing for the Court, Justice Blackmun explicitly approved of the regulation of false and deceptive advertising as well as advertising for illegal products and services. He then stated two main reasons for extending First Amendment protection to truthful, legal commercial speech: (1) such advertising often includes information that consumers need to know in order to make wise choices and (2) in a free enterprise system, freedom for commercial messages is needed in order that the public in general can have the information needed to form "intelligent opinions as to how that system ought to be regulated or altered."

Rule Established; Significance of Case: Building upon the *Bigelow* decision of the preceding year, this decision confirms the Court's view that the old commercial speech doctrine no longer holds and that the protection of the First Amendment applies to that commercial expression which disseminates to the general public "truthful information about entirely lawful activity." Significantly, the opinion emphasizes the right of the public to *receive* commercial messages.

tors. This issue, and related ones, were quick to reach the courts and to rise to the level of Supreme Court review. In order to examine developments in an orderly fashion, the progeny of the new doctrine are discussed according to the following three topics: (1) advertising by the professions, (2) commercial speech rights of corporations, and (3) miscellaneous decisions concerning products and services.

Advertising of Professional Services

For years it has been the custom of a number of state, regional, and national professional bodies, such as state bar associations and various medical groups, to prohibit advertising—other than, for example, to an-

nounce the opening of an office or the listing of a telephone number—by their members. The no-advertising rule was especially strict as applied to attorneys and physicians. Early in 1976, Arizona attorneys John R. Bates and Van O'Steen, who were attempting to keep open their "legal clinic" in Phoenix, decided that it was essential to their survival to advertise their basic services and modest fees. Consequently, they published an advertisement concerning their law practice in the February 22, 1976, edition of the *Arizona Republic,* a daily newspaper in Phoenix.

The Bates and O'Steen advertisement was conservative, for it listed only basic information about certain services and the cost of each. No claims, extravagant or otherwise, were made concerning the quality of the services offered. Despite this, the State Bar of Arizona entered the Arizona Supreme Court, which was responsible for enforcing certain bar regulations in the state, to have Bates and O'Steen disciplined for violating state bar rules. The Arizona Supreme Court rejected the First Amendment claims of the young attorneys and agreed to disciplinary action. Bates and O'Steen then appealed to the U.S. Supreme Court.

Justice Blackmun, in his opinion of the Court, accepted the First Amendment arguments of Bates and O'Steen, ruling that just as *Virginia State Board of Pharmacy* had granted pharmacists the right to advertise their prescription prices, so should attorneys be allowed to advertise their services and prices.[30] Emphasizing, as the Court had in the past, that constraints were still permissible when deception and illegality were at bar, and that law associations could still supervise advertisements in which "misstatements . . . quite inappropriate in legal advertising" were involved, Justice Blackmun concluded as follows: "The constitutional issue in this case is only whether the State may prevent publication in a newspaper of appellants' truthful advertisement concerning the availability and terms of routine legal services. We rule simply that the flow of such information may not be restrained, and we therefore hold the present application of the disciplinary rule against appellants to be violative of the First Amendment."

In May of 1978 the Supreme Court announced its opinion in a second case concerning commercial speech by attorneys. In *Ohralik* v. *Ohio State Bar Association,* attorney Albert Ohralik had been disciplined by the Ohio State Bar for in-person solicitation via phone and personal visits to potential clients who had been involved in an automobile accident.[31] When called to question for direct solicitation of legal business, Ohralik argued that his activities were protected by the First and Fourteenth Amendments to the U.S. Constitution. The Supreme Court disagreed and upheld the disciplinary moves of the Ohio State Bar. In an opinion by Justice Powell, the Court made clear that the application of the First Amendment to straightforward, informative advertising, as in the *Bates* case, did not mean that in-person solicitation was covered by the rule. Wrote Justice Powell:

> The solicitation of business by a lawyer through direct, in-person communication with the prospective client has long been viewed as inconsistent with the profession's ideal of the attorney-client relationship . . . . The substantive evils of solicitation have been stated over the years in sweeping terms; stirring up litigation, assertion of fraudulent claims, debasing the legal profession, and potential harm to the solicited client in the form of overreaching, overcharging, underrepresentation, and misrepresentation. . . . We hold that the application of [the Ohio Bar's] Disciplinary Rules . . . to appellant does not offend the Constitution.

In a third case, the Supreme Court ruled in 1982 on a matter that began soon after its *Bates* decision of 1977 making truthful, informative advertising by attorneys a form of protected expression under the Constitution.

---

[30]*Bates* v. *State Bar of Arizona,* 433 U.S. 350 (1977). Note: Briefs of amici curiae urging the Supreme Court to affirm the Arizona ruling and deny First Amendment protection to advertising by attorneys were filed by numerous professional organizations, including the American Bar Association, the American Dental Association, the American Optometric Association, the American Veterinary Medical Association, the Maryland State Bar Association, and the Virginia State Bar Association. See footnote at 352.

[31]*Ohralik* v. *Ohio State Bar Association,* 436 U.S. 447 (1978).

Following *Bates,* the Committee on Professional Ethics and Responsibility of the Supreme Court of Missouri had prepared highly specific standards to govern lawyer advertising within the state of Missouri. The rules did permit some advertising by attorneys but limited it to specified categories of information, going so far as to state the *exact language* that must be used. When a St. Louis attorney, identified in court records only as R. M. J., announced the opening of his practice, he employed language slightly different from that prescribed by the Missouri rules (for example, he used "Real Estate" rather than the court-approved term "Property Law"); he then mailed announcement cards to individuals other than those on the court-approved list (the rules restricted such mailings to "lawyers, clients, former clients, personal friends, and relatives"). As a result, the ethics committee objected and took R. M. J. to court. The charge? Unprofessional conduct. When the Supreme Court of Missouri upheld the rules under which the nonconforming barrister was charged and issued a stern reprimand, attorney R. M. J. appealed on constitutional grounds to the U.S. Supreme Court.[32]

In an opinion written by Justice Powell, a unanimous Court determined that the Missouri regulations as applied to the commercial messages of attorney R. M. J. were much too restrictive. Whereas professional standards for lawyer advertising were certainly permissible, such standards must be reasonable in order to be constitutional; the Missouri rules, in short, went too far.

Justice Powell *delivered the opinion of the Court:*

> In sum, none of the . . . restrictions . . . upon appellant's First Amendment rights can be

sustained in the circumstances of this case. There is no finding that appellant's speech was misleading. . . . We emphasize, as we have throughout the opinion, that the States retain the authority to regulate advertising that is inherently misleading or that has proven to be misleading in practice. There may be other substantial State interests as well that will support carefully drawn restrictions. But although the States may regulate commercial speech, the First and Fourteenth Amendments require that they do so with care and in a manner no more extensive than reasonably necessary to further substantial interests. The absolute prohibition on appellant's speech, in the absence of a finding that his speech was misleading, does not meet these requirements.

Accordingly, the judgment of the Supreme Court of Missouri is *reversed.*

The fourth and final decision of the Supreme Court to be considered here concerns advertising by physicians. In 1979 the FTC issued a cease-and-desist order against the American Medical Association (AMA) requiring it to permit doctors to advertise their services, compete for business, and enter into nontraditional financial arrangements for the practice of medicine. The FTC moved as it did not only to make it possible for physicians to advertise their services but also to legitimize physician-organization contracts (such as between a doctor and a union, or a clinic), including competitive bidding for those contracts. In 1980 the U.S. Court of Appeals for the Second Circuit sided with the FTC, thereby sustaining the order against the AMA.[33] Among other things, the decision by the court of appeals said that medical associations such as the AMA *are* subject to FTC regulation, that past policies of the AMA did have an anticompetitive purpose and effect, and that the FTC order did not

---

[32]*In re R.M.J.,* 455 U.S. 191 (1982).

[33]*AMA* v. *FTC,* 638 F.2d 443 (2d Cir. 1980).

violate the First Amendment rights of the medical association.

In March of 1982 the U.S. Supreme Court, in an even division of 4 to 4 (Justice Blackmun did not participate in the decision), let the ruling of the court of appeals stand in the case of *AMA v. FTC;* however, as students of the Court are aware, the tie vote did not establish precedent concerning the issues at bar.[34] One can infer, however, that as long as physicians advertise in a conservative, truthful, and informative way—following the same standards set forth by the Court in reference to advertising by attorneys—their commercial expression is protected by the First Amendment. In addition, one can reasonably assume that the Court's rulings extend to persons in professions other than law and medicine.

The First Amendment Rights of Corporations

In 1978 the U.S. Supreme Court expanded its commercial speech doctrine to include the right of corporations to express their viewpoints on public issues. In the case of *First National Bank of Boston v. Bellotti,* and by a vote of 5 to 4, the Court invalidated a Massachusetts statute prohibiting business corporations from making contributions or expenditures "for the purpose of . . . influencing or affecting the vote on any question submitted to the voters, other than one materially affecting any of the property, business, or assets of the corporation."[35] The case began when a group of banks, businesses, and corporations including the First National Bank of Boston challenged the statute in question because of their desire to spend funds to publicize their opposition to a proposed constitutional amendment that would allow Mas-

sachusetts to have a graduated income tax (subsequently, the proposed amendment was defeated at the polls). The Massachusetts Supreme Judicial Court upheld the constitutionality of the challenged law, citing two main reasons: (1) the First Amendment is designed to protect the *individual citizen* as a participant in the affairs of government and, other than the corporate press, does not apply to businesses whose wealth and power would give them an unfair advantage in public debate; (2) the statute protects the rights of those corporation shareholders whose views differ from those of management and who would be forced to help finance the communication of political ideas with which they disagreed.

On appeal, the U.S. Supreme Court reversed the court below. In declaring the Massachusetts statute unconstitutional, Justice Powell, who authored the majority opinion, noted the position taken by the Court two years earlier in *Virginia State Board of Pharmacy,* namely, that the "free flow of commercial information" is protected by the Constitution. Observing that the Court was not attempting to mark the "outer boundaries" of the free-speech rights of corporations and that it was not at this time attempting to determine "whether corporations have the full measure of rights that individuals enjoy under the First Amendment," he emphasized that the flow of information in this instance concerned a public question and that the First Amendment was intended to protect a full and free discussion of such issues.

Justice Powell *delivered the opinion of the Court:*

. . . If the speakers here were not corporations, no one would suggest that the State could silence their proposed speech. It is the type of speech indispensable to decision-making in a democracy, and this is no less true because the speech comes from a corporation rather than an

---

[34]*AMA v. FTC,* 455 U.S. 676 (1982).

[35]*First National Bank of Boston v. Bellotti,* 435 U.S. 765 (1978).

individual. The inherent worth of the speech in terms of its capacity for informing the public does not depend upon the identity of its source, whether corporation, association, union, or individual.

Yet appellee suggests that First Amendment rights generally have been afforded only to corporations engaged in the communications business or through which individuals express themselves. . . . But the press does not have a monopoly on either the First Amendment or the ability to enlighten. Similarly, the Court's decisions involving corporations in the business of communication or entertainment are based not only on the role of the First Amendment in fostering individual self-expression, but also on its role in affording the public access to discussion, debate, and the dissemination of information and ideas. Even decisions seemingly based exclusively on the individual's right to express himself acknowledge that the expression may contribute to society's edification. . . . A commercial advertisement is Constitutionally protected not so much because it pertains to the seller's business as because it furthers the societal interest in the "free flow of commercial information."

On June 20, 1980, two years after its significant decision in *First National Bank of Boston,* the U.S. Supreme Court announced its findings in two additional commercial speech cases; in so doing, it clarified (to a degree) and strengthened its position in favor of First Amendment rights for corporations. By coincidence, both cases involved efforts by utility companies in New York to obtain the lifting of communication restrictions that had been imposed by the Public Service Commission of that state. In the first case, *Consolidated Edison Company* v. *Public Service Commission,* the issue was over the refusal of the commission to permit the company to enclose political messages as inserts in monthly bills (the contested insert was entitled "Independence Is Still a Goal, and Nuclear Power

Is Needed To Win the Battle"); in the second instance, *Central Hudson Gas and Electric* v. *Public Service Commission,* the controversy concerned the authority of the commission to assist the cause of energy conservation by forbidding the utilities to run advertising that promotes energy use.[36]

In the *Consolidated Edison* case, the New York Public Service Commission had decided that utility customers who received bills containing inserts were a "captive audience of diverse views who should not be subjected to the utility's beliefs." Therefore, said the commission, utility companies could not include bill inserts that express "their opinions or viewpoints on controversial issues of public policy." Not so, said Justice Powell, writing for the U.S. Supreme Court, for the Constitution protected the message which the company was trying to communicate, and—as affirmed in *First National Bank of Boston*—the right to communicate to the public "does not depend upon the identity of its source, whether corporation, association, union, or individual." And what of the captive-audience argument advanced by the commission? "The customer of Consolidated Edison," answered Justice Powell, "may escape exposure to objectionable material simply by transferring the bill insert from envelope to wastebasket." He then summarized the opinion of the Court as follows: "The Commission's suppression of bill inserts that discuss controversial issues of public policy directly infringes the freedom of speech protected by the First and Fourteenth Amendments. The state action is neither a valid time, place, or manner restriction, nor a permissible subject-matter regulation, nor a narrowly drawn prohibition justified by a com-

[36]*Consolidated Edison Company* v. *Public Service Commission,* 447 U.S. 530 (1980); and *Central Hudson Gas and Electric* v. *Public Service Commission,* 447 U.S. 557 (1980).

pelling state interest. Accordingly, the regulation is invalid."

And what of the Public Service Commission's well-intentioned policy, addressed by the Court in *Central Hudson Gas and Electric,* to help conserve energy by prohibiting all advertising that promoted the use of electricity? That, too, was unconstitutional, said Justice Powell, writing for the majority, for the prohibition failed to meet a four-part test that had grown out of *First National Bank of Boston,* namely, (1) the commercial message in question must be truthful and be concerned with lawful activity; (2) the governmental interest in constraining a truthful, legal commercial message must be substantial; (3) the regulation placed upon the message must advance the governmental interest that is asserted; and (4) the regulation must not be more extensive than is needed to achieve its goal.[37] The commission's order was not constitutional, stated Justice Powell, primarily because it violated the fourth element of the test. That is, the absolute ban imposed by the commission went too far, since it even forbade the advertising of energy conservation products and services (such as the heat pump and the use of supplementary electrical power to back up solar-power systems). In sum, the regulation was more extensive "than is necessary to serve the state interest."[38]

Thus, by the beginning of the 1980s, cor-porate expression was beginning to enjoy a degree of legal protection that it had not had before. Although the boundaries of this newly defined freedom are not as great as are the boundaries for individual speech and liberty of the press, they are certainly greater than ever before in the nation's history. In the years ahead, students of freedom of expression should note with interest how the High Court continues to refine its standards for applying the First Amendment to corporate speech.

Other Commercial Speech Decisions

In four other cases the Supreme Court has addressed issues of commercial speech and the First Amendment. Two of the cases concerned health service controversies, whereas the other two concerned local attempts to regulate commercial signs. In the health service area, the Court struck down a New York law that made it a crime not only for any person to distribute contraceptives to a minor under sixteen years of age but also for anyone, including licensed pharmacists, to advertise or display contraceptives.[39] In the second health-services decision, the Court found to be constitutional a Texas statute prohibiting the practice of optometry under a trade name (the law was a consumer protection measure that had the effect of requiring optometrists to use their given names in advertising, thereby enabling consumers to know which doctor they were reading or hearing about). Since the Texas law did not result in suppressing knowledge of prices or services or otherwise keep needed information from the public, the Court ruled that it

---

[37]*Central Hudson Gas and Electric* v. *Public Service Commission,* at 566.

[38]Justice Powell also made clear that the Court still had reservations about extending full First Amendment protection to commercial speech. He observed that the Court continued to recognize a "commonsense" difference between commercial speech and "other varieties of speech," then added that the Constitution "accords a lesser protection to commercial speech than to other consitutionally guaranteed expression. . . . The protection available for particular commercial expression turns on the nature both of the expression and of the governmental interest served by its regulations." Ibid., pp. 562–563.

[39]*Carey* v. *Population Services International,* 431 U.S. 678 (1977). Note: Population Services, a North Carolina firm that advertised and sold contraceptives through the mail, brought the action challenging the New York statute. The Court's decision means that it is now legal to both advertise and ship contraceptives through the mail.

was not a violation of the First Amendment.[40]

The two cases involving commercial signs presented a contrast between signboards small and large. In the first instance, the township of Willingboro, New Jersey, attempted to discourage the flight of white homeowners from racially integrated neighborhoods by banning "For Sale" and "Sold" real estate signs from residential yards, but the Supreme Court ruled the township's ordinance unconstitutional. Citing its decision in *Virginia State Board of Pharmacy,* the Court declared that such signs facilitated "the flow of truthful and legitimate commercial information," and that, therefore, Willingboro's move to prohibit them was "constitutionally infirm."[41] In the second case, the Court invalidated a San Diego, California, ordinance banning all billboards, except those that fell within certain specific categories (such as temporary political campaign signs and government signs). Although the goals of the city—such as eliminating traffic hazards and improving the overall appearance—were commendable, the ordinance was, nevertheless, unconstitutional. Why? The Court could not agree on a majority opinion, but four justices in a plurality opinion reasoned that the law was discriminatory, since it did allow on-site commercial billboards but prohibited all others, including those for noncommercial messages. In a concurring opinion, Justices Brennan and Blackmun expressed the view that the total ban was simply too broad.[42]

Dissenting Views Concerning Freedom for Commercial Speech

The commercial speech rulings of the Su-preme Court starting with *Bigelow* in 1975 have stirred considerable controversy among First Amendment scholars. Two essays typical of those expressing reservations about constitutional protection for commercial advertising are summarized below, so as to provide the reader with information concerning significant dissenting points of view.

First, in a 1979 article, law professors Thomas H. Jackson and John C. Jeffries, Jr., argue that the *Bigelow-Virginia State Board of Pharmacy* decisions were mistakes and that the expansion of constitutional rights for commercial speech should be "cut short."[43] The authors base their thinking on the principle that the First Amendment should serve two main values: (1) effective self-government and (2) individual self-fulfillment through free expression. "Neither value," they add, "is implicated by governmental regulation of commercial speech." They state further: "Measured in terms of traditional first amendment principles, commercial speech is remarkable for its insignificance. It neither contributes to self-government nor nurtures the realization of the individual personality. Thus, although business advertising may play an important role in ordering the marketplace, it falls outside the accepted reasons for protecting the freedom of speech."[44] Jackson and Jeffries conclude that the reasons given by the Burger Court for protecting "good" commercial speech are simply not adequate to support the major "doctrinal innovation" that results; consequently, the commercial speech cases since *Bigelow* represent a "misuse of the first amendment and a departure from the principles that should

---

[40]*Friedman* v. *Rogers,* 440 U.S. 1 (1979).

[41]*Linmark Associates* v. *Township of Willingboro,* 431 U.S. 85 (1977).

[42]*Metromedia* v. *San Diego,* 453 U.S. 490 (1981).

[43]Thomas H. Jackson and John C. Jeffries, Jr., "Commercial Speech: Economic Due Process and the First Amendment," *Virginia Law Review* 65 (February 1979): 1–41.

[44]Ibid., p. 14.

govern the exercise of judicial review in a representative democracy."[45]

Second, in an essay entitled "For Sale: Freedom of Speech," practicing attorney Charles Rembar argues that the commercial speech decisions of the Burger Court since 1975 will have the effect of granting wider access to the marketplace of ideas for the *wealthy*—such as businesses and corporations—while limiting that access for the *poor,* who cannot afford to advertise their views.[46] He proceeds to tie the various commercial speech decisions of the 1970s to the Supreme Court's ruling in the case of *Buckley* v. *Valeo* (1976), in which the Court invalidated that section of the 1974 Federal Election Campaign Act that, in the name of making elections fairer by equalizing expenditures, limited overall political campaign spending.[47] In this case the Court ruled that financial restrictions upon campaigning are unconstitutional because the "First Amendment's protection against governmental abridgment of free expression cannot properly be made to depend on a person's financial ability to engage in public discussion." In other words, Rembar charges, the Court held "in essence, that spending money is a form of speech."[48] He concludes his attack upon the Court's commercial speech decisions of recent years by reminding his readers that the expression "marketplace of ideas" is a metaphor only, and that the Court should not take it so literally:

> . . . We are more or less committed to a capitalistic system in our economy. But this does

not mean that the use of capital should determine First Amendment rights. A literal marketplace of ideas, anarchic except for the iron rule of money, contradicts the First Amendment. If all the stalls are occupied by the few merchants rich enough to rent them, we cannot have the free and multifarious offerings that the metaphor suggests. We have instead, a few super-supermarkets, and here and there a lonely peddler who cannot possibly compete.

Let us not, by faddish extensions of meaning, make First Amendment guarantees seem silly. Let us not get free private enterprise confused with free expression.[49]

Commercial Speech and the Constitution in Brief

In the 1942 case of *Valentine* v. *Chrestensen,* a unanimous Supreme Court ruled for the first time that the Constitution did not protect "purely commercial advertising" and that commercial speech, therefore, could be regulated by the legislature without offending the First Amendment. This decision established a precedent that was followed for thirty-three years (although it began to erode in the 1960s, particularly with the Court's 1964 decision in the case of *New York Times* v. *Sullivan*). The old commercial speech doctrine announced in *Chrestensen* was dramatically altered in the mid-1970s by the decision of the Supreme Court in two instances: *Bigelow* v. *Virginia* (1975), which extended the First Amendment to a commercial advertisement for an abortion referral service, and *Virginia State Board of Pharmacy* (1976), which determined that the Constitution protected the advertising of prescription drug prices by pharmacists. The effect of these two decisions was to provide *some* First Amendment protection for truthful commercial advertis-

---

[45]Ibid., pp. 40–41.
[46]Charles Rembar, "For Sale: Freedom of Speech," *The Atlantic,* March 1981, pp. 25–32.
[47]*Buckley* v. *Valeo,* 424 U.S. 1 (1976). Note: The Court did uphold some portions of the 1974 act, including limitations on individual contributions to a candidate.
[48]Rembar, p. 29.

[49]Ibid., p. 32.

ing for legal products and services; however, the Court explained that the degree of protection for commercial communication was not as great as for the speech of individuals or for speech which is essential to democratic government. In support of its change in direction, the Court asserted two main arguments: (1) truthful advertising of legal products and services includes information that consumers need to know in order to make wise choices and (2) in a system of free enterprise, the public needs to hear commercial messages of various types in order to be fully informed before participating in the development of policy at all levels of government concerning the regulation of commerce.

In later decisions, the Supreme Court balanced competing interests to conclude (1) that the advertising of basic services and prices by professionals, such as lawyers and doctors, was protected by the First Amendment; (2) that corporations had some First Amendment rights to communicate their views to the public; and (3) that a variety of other prohibitions placed upon commercial expression—ranging from laws banning the advertising of contraceptives to ordinances prohibiting all billboards (with specified exceptions) within a municipality—were unconstitutional. Furthermore, the Court clarified its position about the types of regulation it would permit, namely, legislatures could control commercial expression that was false, misleading, or concerned illegal products or services; reasonable constraints of time, place, and manner were said to be constitutional.

Finally, the Court's shift on the issue of freedom for commercial speech did not go unchallenged. In addition to the views of various dissenting justices of the Court, a number of legal scholars objected to the inclusion of commercial speech beneath the protective umbrella of the First Amendment. The ar-

guments of legal scholars who doubt the wisdom of the Court's rulings in *Bigelow, Virginia State Board of Pharmacy,* and progeny include the following: (1) the First Amendment should be restricted to speech which serves the purposes of self-government and individual self-fulfillment, and commercial speech does neither; (2) that the Court has by its decisions given too much power to the wealthy, who can now "buy" freedom of speech through advertising, thus denying the poor and not-so-wealthy equal access to the "marketplace of ideas." (The student of the First Amendment should keep a close watch on developments in this area of the law; since the issue of constitutional protection for commercial speech is still in its "formative stage," further clarification and refinement are inevitable.)

CONCLUSION

During the first decade of the twentieth century, a number of American newspapers and magazines published exposés concerning false and misleading advertising for various "medicines" and health devices, thus marshaling public opinion and pressuring the Congress to legislate some type of control upon commercial speech. In response, Congress acted in 1906 by establishing the Food and Drug Administration (FDA) to police the mislabeling and adulteration of foods, drugs, medicines, and liquors. In 1914 Congress acted again, authorizing the establishment of the Federal Trade Commission (FTC), thus strengthening the authority of the federal government to punish dishonest advertising. The FTC has been the most active federal regulatory agency in the arena of policing commercial expression, enforcing a basic policy that requires advertising to be truthful—including the standard that advertising claims must be provable by the objective standards of science. In general, the courts have upheld the power of the FTC to regulate commercial speech, beginning with the 1922 case of *FTC* v. *Winsted Hosiery Company,* in which the U.S. Supreme Court ruled in favor of the commission's efforts to enforce truth-in-advertising regulations against a hosiery manufacturer. Enforcement procedures of the FTC are of two types: out-of-court moves (publicity pressures, voluntary compliance, and consent decrees) and hard-line legal action when persuasion is ineffective (mainly cease-and-desist orders). Some overlapping of effort in the enforcing of proconsumer legislation exists not only between the FDA (which stresses truth in labeling) and the FTC (which stresses truth in advertising) but also between and among other federal regulatory agencies such as the Federal Communications Commission (FCC; broadcast advertising), the Securities and Exchange Commission (SEC; advertising of stocks and bonds), and the U.S. Postal Service (mail fraud).

The question of the First Amendment's application to commercial speech was generally ignored by the courts during the first forty years of the twentieth century; when the issue was raised in the 1942 case of *Valentine* v. *Chrestensen,* the Supreme Court curtly dispensed with it by announcing that there was no constitutional protection for "purely commercial advertising." The *Chrestensen* precedent was followed until the mid-1960s, when it began to erode, particularly following the Supreme Court's decision in the 1964 case of *New York Times* v. *Sullivan;* in the decade following *Times-Sullivan,* the question of constitutional protection for commercial speech ripened for sweeping reexamination. In two important decisions, the 1975 case of *Bigelow* v. *Virginia* (which extended protection to an advertisement for an abortion referral service) and the 1976 case of *Virginia*

State Board of Pharmacy v. *Virginia Citizens Consumer Council* (which announced that the advertising of prescription drug prices was a form of protected speech), the Supreme Court overruled the *Chrestensen* doctrine and rewrote the law concerning commercial expression. The essentials of the new rulings: (1) generally speaking, truthful advertising for legal products and services is protected by the Constitution because (a) the public needs the free flow of commercial information in order to make wise consumer choices and (b) such information is important in informing the public about matters which affect the free enterprise system and governmental policy concerning it; (2) however, the legislatures—state and federal—are still permitted to control false and deceptive advertising as well as advertising for illegal products and services. The current philosophy of the U.S. Supreme Court was encapsulated by Justice Blackmun in a comment made in his majority opinion in *Virginia State Board of Pharmacy:* "The First Amendment . . . does not prohibit the State from insuring that the stream of commercial information flows cleanly as well as freely."

EXERCISES

A. Classroom projects and activities.
1. Here are three questions phrased for classroom debate:
a. Resolved, that this class agrees with the view of Alexander Meiklejohn that commercial speech is less deserving of constitutional protection than is speech concerning self-government.
b. Resolved, that commercial broadcasters should be granted the same degree of freedom as print media to communicate truthful advertising for legal products and services to the general public.
c. Resolved, that the *corrective advertising*

authority of the Federal Trade Commission should be abolished.

2. Here are the same three questions phrased for discussion:

a. Following a careful study of Alexander Meiklejohn's theory of free speech (see Selected Readings, which follow), discuss his distinction between "public" and "private" speech. Does it follow that commercial advertising (classified as "private speech" by Meiklejohn) deserves less protection than speech concerning self-government?

b. Should broadcasters be permitted the same freedom to advertise truthfully for any legal product or service as are newspapers and magazines? What about advertising for cigarettes? "Hard" liquors? Contraceptives?

c. Should the Federal Trade Commission be permitted to compel companies to spend funds on corrective advertising (as in the Listerine case)? Shouldn't a straightforward cease-and-desist order be sufficient?

3. Discuss the quotation with which this chapter begins, namely: ". . . advertising is a medium of information and persuasion, providing much of the day-to-day 'education' of the American public and facilitating the flexible allocation of resources necessary to a free enterprise economy. Neither profit motivation nor desire to influence private economic decisions necessarily distinguishes the peddler from the preacher, the publisher, or the politician." *Harvard Law Review* 80 (1967): 1027.

4. Write to the consumer-protection division of the office of attorney general in your state, asking for policy statements and regulations concerning truth in advertising that are currently being enforced. Distribute photocopies to the class and discuss.

5. Secure from local newspapers and broadcasters copies of voluntary industry codes or locally formulated codes concerning truth in advertising. Make photocopies and distribute to the class for evaluation and discussion.

6. Arrange for a panel of local radio, television, and newspaper officials to visit your class to discuss the question of government-enforced versus voluntary codes for consumer protection in the area of advertising. Be sure to ask the broadcasters their opinion about the federal ban on cigarette advertising on the airwaves.

7. Assign each student the task of finding and bringing to class (a photocopy will do) a commercial advertisement that the student believes to be false, deceptive, or "puffed" in its claims. Let each student explain his or her analysis of the advertisement, then let the class discuss whether or not such commercial messages deserve the protection of the First Amendment.

8. Assign each student the task of finding a "false" or "deceptive" claim by a minister (as in a radio or television sermon) or a politician (as in a speech or a campaign pamphlet). Discuss in class what would happen to such communicators if they were required to meet the same truth standards as are commercial advertisers.

9. Invite a faculty member who is knowledgeable on the subject of subliminal communication to speak to the class on the subject, including the area of subliminal advertising. Should *truthful* subliminal advertising be permitted? Should such advertising be protected by the First Amendment?

10. Discuss these contrasting views. With which do you agree? Why?

a. In the *Virginia State Board of Pharmacy* decision, Justice Blackmun argues in his opinion of the Court that in a free enterprise economy "the free flow of commercial information is indispensable," not only for the wise allocation of resources but also to assist in the "formation of intelligent opinions as to how that system ought to be regulated or altered" (i.e., for the purpose of self-government).

b. In contrast, Jackson and Jeffries, whose reservations concerning speech are presented near the end of the chapter, believe that commercial speech "neither contributes to self-government nor nurtures the realization of the individual personality."

11. Charles Rembar also has reservations about extending the First Amendment to commercial speech (see the discussion of Rembar's views near the end of the chapter). He fears that the wealthy will have an unfair advantage in the "marketplace of ideas" because of recent Supreme Court decisions concerning commercial expression. Rembar asserts: "If all the stalls [in the marketplace] are occupied by the few merchants rich enough to rent them, we cannot have the free . . . offerings that the metaphor suggests. We have instead a few super-supermarkets, and here and there a lonely peddler who cannot possibly compete." Discuss.

B. Topics for research papers or oral reports.

1. A Short History of Advertising Scams and Quackery in the United States.

2. A Survey of Voluntary Industry Codes Governing Truth in Advertising. (Include both print and broadcast media or divide into two topics—print and broadcasting—and assign to two students.)

3. The Federal Trade Commission: A History and Analysis of Its Work in the Matter of False and Deceptive Advertising.

4. A Defense (or a Critique) of Alexander Meiklejohn's Two-Level Theory of Free Speech. (Emphasize the application of his theory to commercial speech.)

5. A Survey and Analysis of Arguments in Opposition to Extending First Amendment Protection to Commercial Speech (or, an Analysis of Arguments in Favor).

6. Subliminal Advertising and the First Amendment: An Analysis with a Proposed Solution. (Let the student propose what he or she thinks should be done in this area.)

7. A Survey of the Regulation of Commercial Speech by Federal Agencies Other than the Federal Trade Commission.

8. A Study of the Regulation of Commercial Speech by State Officials in (Your State).

9. The FTC's Effort to Regulate Television Advertising Directed at Children: A Study in Corporate and Congressional Backlash.

10. Applying the FTC's Standards of Truth to Political and Religious Speech: What If?

SELECTED READINGS

Baker, Samm S. *The Permissible Lie: The Inside Truth About Advertising.* Cleveland: World Publishing, 1968.

Buston, Edward. *Promise Them Anything: The Inside Story of the Madison Avenue Power Struggle.* New York: Stein and Day, 1972.

"Developments in the Law: Deceptive Advertising." *Harvard Law Review* 80 (1967): 1005–1163. (The entire issue concerns advertising.)

DeVore, P. Cameron, and Nelson, Marshall J. "Commercial Speech and Paid Access to the Press." *The Hastings Law Journal* 26 (January 1975): 745–775.

Haiman, Franklyn S. *Speech and Law in a Free Society.* Chicago: University of Chicago Press, 1981. Especially chapter 10, "Lies and Misrepresentations."

Holbrook, Stewart H. *The Golden Age of Quackery.* New York: Macmillan, 1959.

Hyman, Allen, and Johnson, M. Bruce, eds. *Ad-

vertising and Free Speech. Lexington, Mass.: Heath, 1977.

Jackson, Thomas H., and Jeffries, John C., Jr. "Commercial Speech: Economic Due Process and the First Amendment." *Virginia Law Review* 65 (February 1979): 1–41.

Kintner, Earl W. *A Primer on the Law of Deceptive Practices: A Guide for the Businessman*. New York: Macmillan, 1971.

Meiklejohn, Alexander. *Political Freedom: The Constitutional Powers of the People*. New York: Oxford University Press, 1965. (See pp. 34–38, for Meiklejohn's two-level theory of free speech.)

Note. "Electric and Gas Utility Advertising: The First Amendment Legacy of *Central Hudson*." *Washington University Law Quarterly* 60 (Summer 1983): 459–505.

Note. "Two-Track Model of First Amendment Adjudication After *Consolidated Edison Co. v. Public Service Commission*." *Boston University Law Review* 62 (January 1982): 215–256.

Posner, Richard A. *Regulation of Advertising by the FTC*. Washington, D.C.: American Enterprise Institute for Public Policy Research, 1973. (A concise explanation of the working of the FTC.)

Preston, Ivan L. *The Great American Blow-up: Puf-*

fery in Advertising and Selling. Madison, Wis.: University of Wisconsin Press, 1975.

Redish, Martin. "The First Amendment in the Marketplace: Commercial Speech and the Values of Free Expression." *George Washington Law Review* 39 (1971): 429 ff.

Reich, Robert B. "Preventing Deception in Commercial Speech." *New York University Law Review* 54 (October 1979): 775–805.

Rembar, Charles. "For Sale: Freedom of Speech." *Atlantic,* March 1981, pp. 25–32.

Rohrer, Daniel M. *Mass Media, Freedom of Speech, and Advertising*. Dubuque, Iowa: Kendall/Hunt, 1979.

Scharlott, Bradford W. "The First Amendment Protection of Advertising in the Mass Media." *Communications and the Law* 2 (Summer 1980): 43–58.

Schiro, Richard. "Commercial Speech: The Demise of a Chimera." In *The Supreme Court Review: 1976,* pp. 45–98. Edited by Philip B. Kurland. Chicago: University of Chicago Press, 1976.

Shaw, B. "Corporate Speech in the Marketplace of Ideas." *Journal of Corporation Law* 7 (Winter 1982): 265–283.

Turner, Ernest S. *The Shocking History of Advertising*. New York: Dutton, 1953.

Part III

SPECIAL ISSUES

CHAPTER 8
Time, Place, Manner, and Institutional
Constraints

CHAPTER 9
Two Interlocking Topics: Prior
Restraint and Free Press–Fair Trial

CHAPTER 10
Technology and Free Speech—Part I:
Copyright

CHAPTER 11
Technology and Free Speech—Part II:
From Loudspeakers to Broadcasting
and Access Theory

CHAPTER 8

Time, Place, Manner, and Institutional Constraints

"Wherever the title of streets and parks may rest, they have immemorially been held in trust for the use of the public and, time out of mind, have been used for purposes of assembly, communicating thought between citizens, and discussing public questions."

—Justice Owen J. Roberts in Hague v. CIO *(1939)*

On May 10, 1897, the U.S. Supreme Court announced its decision in the case of *Davis* v. *Massachusetts,* upholding the conviction of William F. Davis, a minister, for preaching in a public area of Boston known as "the Common" without a permit from the mayor, as was required by law.[1] For his offense, Davis had been fined and ordered to pay court costs. The Supreme Judicial Court of Massachusetts had affirmed the conviction.

In the process of ruling for the state and against Davis, the U.S. Supreme Court articulated a position concerning the use of public places for speech purposes which was to govern issues and cases of time, place, and manner of expression for more than four decades. In his opinion of the Court, Justice Edward D. White held that since government had legal title to parks, streets, and similar public places, it could control those places as it saw fit. In Justice White's words, "For the legislature absolutely or conditionally to forbid public speaking in a highway or public park is no more an infringement of the rights of a member of the public than for the owner of a private house to forbid it in his house." The Constitution was not offended by the arrest and conviction of the minister, Justice White

[1]*Davis* v. *Massachusetts*, 167 U.S. 43 (1897).

added, for he had "no right . . . to use the Common except in such mode and subject to such regulations as the legislature in its wisdom may have deemed proper to prescribe."

Besides its historical significance, the Boston Common case—the name by which *Davis* v. *Massachusetts* is often called—presents the basic question to be discussed in this chapter, namely: What regulations of time, place, and manner of expression may government and private enterprise enforce without violating the Constitution's free speech guarantees? In general, constraints of time, place, and manner are content-neutral—that is, they are exercised because of situational factors that are apart from the ideas to be presented; also, they apply to all messages equally. In the Boston Common case, the minister was convicted not because his sermon was seditious, defamatory, blasphemous, or obscene but because he spoke in a *place* where the law said he could not speak without a permit.

Two hypothetical examples are useful in further illustrating the subject. First, the constraint of *time* would be a key factor in a city's decision to grant a parade permit for use of a major street during a time of day when traffic was light but to deny the parade sponsors the use of that street during the evening rush hour. And a constraint of *manner* can be illustrated by a policy allowing members of a striking hospital union quietly to pass out leaflets in front of the hospital but not to use a loudspeaker in that same location.

In addition to the standard issues of time, place, and manner, two related topics are included in this chapter: (1) special issues, such as the concept of "speech plus" and its application to symbolic expression and labor picketing, and (2) institutional constraints, summarizing the application of the First Amendment to prisons, the military, and public schools and colleges.

I. TRADITIONAL ISSUES OF TIME, PLACE, AND MANNER

At the outset, the student of the First Amendment should be aware that considerable overlapping exists between issues of time, place, and manner and the topic of prior restraint. This is particularly true in those instances where local authorities use the tactic of permit denial as a means of prohibiting communication activities of various types, such as the distribution of leaflets or the holding of a march or demonstration. Although issues and cases of prior restraint are considered primarily in Chapter 9, some of the same cases are also essential to the present discussion. For example, the 1939 permit-leafletting decision of *Schneider* v. *State* is referred to both here and in Chapter 9.[2] The analysis of traditional time, place, and manner constraints is discussed below according to two developments: (1) cases between 1939 and 1943 in which the Boston Common decision of 1897 was rejected and a theory articulated by the Supreme Court for opening streets and parks for the expression of opinion and (2) cases from 1943 to the present in which the Court has developed and refined its theory of constitutional protection for expression in the public forum, on both *publicly* and *privately* owned property.

Boston Common Rejected: A Theory Is Born for Free Speech Rights in Public Places

The question of the use of streets, parks, and similar public places for the expression of opinion was reopened by the U.S. Supreme Court in 1939, forty-two years after the Boston Common decision. The issue reached the Court after the Congress of Industrial Orga-

nizations (CIO) challenged the constitutionality of an ordinance of Jersey City, New Jersey, requiring a permit for all public meetings in the streets and other public places. Mayor Frank "I Am the Law" Hague of Jersey City had used the ordinance in question, additional ordinances and state laws, and the powers of his office to prevent labor organizers and their sympathizers from speaking in Jersey City. Zechariah Chafee, Jr., in his study *Free Speech in the United States,* observes that under Mayor Hague's orders police seized prospective speakers disapproved by the mayor and his powerful supporters and put them on ferryboats bound for New York City.[3] When the CIO challenged his authority, Mayor Hague argued that the Boston Common decision of 1897 gave the city unlimited discretion over the use of public places. The federal district court disagreed and declared the ordinance unconstitutional, after which the court of appeals affirmed. Mayor Hague then appealed to the U.S. Supreme Court.

As will become apparent in the survey of related issues and cases subsequent to *Hague,* the plurality opinion of Justice Roberts illustrates well the way in which a thoughtful position articulated by a minority of justices can over the years become the accepted view of the Court. In his argument, Justice Roberts neither flatly rejected the Boston Common decision (it concerned a different ordinance and was based upon different circumstances) nor attempted to expand dramatically the reach of the First Amendment. Instead, he urged that, in place of *Davis* v. *Massachusetts,* an historical principle of the use of public places ought to be applied in the present dispute.

---

[2]*Schneider* v. *State,* 308 U.S. 147 (1939).

[3]Zechariah Chafee, Jr., *Free Speech in the United States* (Cambridge, Mass.: Harvard University Press, 1971), p. 410.

LANDMARK CASE
Hague v. CIO, 307 U.S. 496 (1939)
Decided June 5, 1939

Vote: 5 to 2 declaring unconstitutional the Jersey City, New Jersey, ordinance requiring a permit for any assembly in or upon the public streets, parks, or buildings of the city.

Plurality Opinion By: Justice Owen J. Roberts.

Concurring Justices: Chief Justice Hughes and Justice Black concurring in Justice Roberts's plurality and opinion; Justice Stone, with whose opinion Justice Reed concurred.

Dissenting Justices: McReynolds and Butler.

Justices Not Participating: Frankfurter and Douglas (both had only recently been appointed to the Supreme Court).

Summary: Mayor Frank Hague of Jersey City, New Jersey, using the authority of a city ordinance that required a permit for any meeting in public places, prevented labor organizers from holding public meetings in the city by denying permits for such activities. When challenged by the CIO in federal court, Mayor Hague relied upon the Boston Common case of 1897 that, he argued, gave the city absolute discretion over the use of public places. The Supreme Court disagreed, with five justices upholding the judgment of the courts below that the ordinance was unconstitutional. The five could not agree upon a single opinion, however, so that a plurality opinion representing the views of three justices and a second opinion representing the views of two justices were announced in support of the result. The plurality view of Justice Roberts has emerged as the more influential of the two opinions announced by those who composed the majority—indeed, it has become the guiding philosophy of the Court in deciding similar cases since 1939.

Rule Established; Significance of Case: This is classified as a landmark case because in it the Supreme Court ruled for the first time that the Constitution required that streets, parks, and similar public places be open for "assembly, communicating thought between citizens, and discussing public questions." Such use may be *regulated,* said the Court, but it may not be prohibited.

Justice Roberts *delivered the plurality opinion:*

We have no occasion to determine whether, on the facts disclosed, the Davis Case was rightly decided, but we cannot agree that it rules the instant case. **Wherever the title of streets and parks may rest, they have immemorially been held in trust for the use of the public and, time out of mind, have been used for purposes of assembly, communicating thought between citizens, and discussing public questions. Such use of the streets and public places has, from ancient times, been a part of the privileges, immunities, rights, and liberties of citizens.**

The privilege of a citizen of the United States to use the streets and parks for communication of views on national questions may be regulated in the interest of all; it is not absolute, but relative, and must be exercised in subordination to the general comfort and convenience, and in consonance with peace and good order; but it must not, in the guise of regulation, be abridged or denied.

In November of 1939, five months after rebuffing Mayor Hague's heavy-handed effort to control public communication in Jersey City, the Supreme Court added considerable weight to the plurality view of Justice

FIGURE 8.1.   MAYOR FRANK HAGUE OF JERSEY CITY, NEW JERSEY.

FIGURE 8.2.   JUSTICE OWEN J. ROBERTS OF THE U.S. SUPREME COURT.
Mayor Frank "I Am the Law" Hague of Jersey City, New Jersey (above left), whose repressive measures in the 1930s against speakers with whom he disagreed resulted in the landmark Supreme Court decision of Hague v. CIO *(1939), opening up the streets, sidewalks, and similar public places in the nation's towns and cities for First Amendment purposes. According to Zechariah Chafee, Jr., author of* Free Speech in the United States, *speakers denied the right to express their views publicly in Hague's "closed city" included Roger Baldwin of the American Civil Liberties Union, Norman Thomas of the Socialist party, and W. M. Callahan, editor of* The Catholic Worker. *The plurality opinion of Justice Owen J. Roberts of the U.S. Supreme Court (above right) in the* Hague *case has become the accepted view of the courts concerning the use of public places for the expression of opinion. Justice Roberts was appointed to the Supreme Court by President Herbert Hoover and served there for the years 1930–1945.*
Library of Congress.

Roberts as set forth in the *Hague* decision. In the case of *Schneider* v. *State,* the Court declared unconstitutional the ordinances of four cities which, in one form or another, prohibited the distribution of all types of handbills on the public streets.[4] By a vote of 8 to 1, and in a majority opinion authored by Justice Roberts, the Court gave its support to the open-streets argument tentatively set out in *Hague.*

Justice Roberts *delivered the opinion of the Court:*

Municipal authorities, as trustees for the public, have the duty to keep their communities' streets open and available for movement of peo-

[4]*Schneider* v. *State,* 308 U.S. 147 (1939). One city, Irvington, New Jersey, would allow distribution of handbills provided a written permit was secured in advance from the chief of police.

ple and property, the primary purpose to which the streets are dedicated. So long as legislation to this end does not abridge the constitutional liberty of one rightfully upon the street to impart information through speech or the distribution of literature, it may lawfully regulate the conduct of those using the streets. For example, a person could not exercise this liberty by taking his stand in the middle of a crowded street, contrary to traffic regulations, and maintain his position to the stoppage of all traffic; a group of distributors could not insist upon a constitutional right to form a cordon across the street and to allow no pedestrian to pass who did not accept a tendered leaflet . . . . Prohibition of such conduct would not abridge the constitutional liberty since such activity bears no necessary relationship to the freedom to speak, write, print or distribute information or opinion.

The matter of *regulation* of the use of public places for communication purposes, mentioned but not developed in the *Hague* and *Schneider* decisions, reached the High Court in 1941 in a case involving the right of New Hampshire cities to require a permit for a parade and to charge a fee to cover expenses incurred by the government in maintaining public order incident to the event. In *Cox* v. *New Hampshire,* the U.S. Supreme Court upheld the constitutionality of both the permit and fee provisions of the law as construed by the state courts.[5]

The controversy began in Manchester, New Hampshire, when a group of Jehovah's Witnesses (including Walter Chaplinsky, whose name joined legal history the following year in the landmark "fighting

---

[5]*Cox* v. *New Hampshire,* 312 U.S. 569 (1941). Note: This is not to say that the question of fees was clearly settled by this decision. Civil libertarians generally oppose the imposition of fees, including the requirement for insurance, upon those who would exercise their constitutional rights. Over the years the courts have been equivocal on the issue.

words" decision of *Chaplinsky* v. *New Hampshire,* discussed in detail in Chapter 6) paraded without a permit even though they knew that state law required one. When the issue reached the U.S. Supreme Court, the justices were unanimous in rebuffing the marchers and sustaining the New Hampshire statute.

Chief Justice Hughes *delivered the opinion of the Court:*

[The New Hampshire Supreme Court narrowly interpreted the objective of the statute] . . . and defined the duty of the licensing authority and the rights of the appellants to a license for their parade, **with regard only to considerations of time, place and manner so as to conserve the public convenience.** The obvious advantage of requiring application for a permit was noted as giving the public authorities notice in advance so as to afford opportunity for proper policing. And the court further observed that, in fixing time and place, the license served "to prevent confusion by overlapping parades or processions, to secure convenient use of streets by other travelers, and to minimize the risk of disorder." **But the court held that the licensing board was not vested with arbitrary power or an unfettered discretion; that its discretion must be exercised with "uniformity of method of treatment upon the facts of each application, free from improper or inappropriate considerations and from unfair discrimination;"** that a "systematic, consistent and just order of treatment, with reference to the convenience of public use of the highways, is the statutory mandate." . . .

There remains the question of license fees which, as the court said, had a permissible range from $300 to a nominal amount. The court construed the Act as requiring "a reasonable fixing of the amount of the fee." . . . The fee was held to be "not a revenue tax, but one to meet the expense incident to the administration of the Act and to the maintenance of public order in the matter licensed." There is nothing contrary to the Constitution in the charge of a fee limited to the purpose stated. . . .

Having ruled in favor of the regulated use of public places for speech purposes in *Hague, Schneider,* and *Cox,* it remained for the U.S. Supreme Court to explicitly reject the Boston Common decision of 1897. This it did in the 1943 case of *Jamison* v. *Texas* in which Dallas authorities cited *Davis* to support their absolute ban upon the distribution of handbills on the city streets.[6] Justice Hugo Black delivered the opinion of a unanimous Court (Justice Rutledge not participating); after noting the argument of the Dallas authorities, Justice Black cited *Hague* v. *CIO, Schneider* v. *State,* and *Cox* v. *New Hampshire* to conclude that the rule announced in *Davis* v. *Massachusetts* "has been directly rejected by this Court." Thus was the death blow rendered to *Davis* and the position of Justice Owen J. Roberts as first announced in *Hague* confirmed by the nation's highest tribunal.

In summary, the basic philosophy of the U.S. Supreme Court concerning the use of the streets, parks, and similar public places for the communication of opinion developed in five steps:

1. In *Davis* v. *Massachusetts* (1897), the Court cited the principle of property rights to uphold a Massachusetts statute permitting municipalities to close public places to speech activities. Since the city had title to the streets and parks, said the Court, it could exercise absolute control over their use.
2. In *Hague* v. *CIO* (1939), the Court turned from the *Davis* position and, in a landmark ruling, opened up the streets and parks for purposes of "assembly, communicating thought between citizens, and discussing public questions." Such use could be

[6]*Jamison* v. *Texas,* 318 U.S. 418 (1943).

regulated, said the Court, but not prohibited.

3. In *Schneider* v. *State* (1939), decided several months after *Hague,* the Court expanded and strengthened the "open forum" position that was tentatively set out in the plurality opinion of Justice Owen J. Roberts in *Hague* v. *CIO.* In *Schneider,* eight justices concurred with the position that municipal authorities could regulate but not "abridge the constitutional liberty of one rightfully upon the street to impart information through speech or the distribution of literature."

4. In *Cox* v. *New Hampshire* (1941), the Court addressed the issue of *regulation* of the public forum by upholding the constitutionality of a parade permit-and-expense-fee statute that provided for reasonable time, place, and manner regulations for the "public convenience" and was administered without discretion.

5. In *Jamison* v. *Texas* (1943), Justice Hugo L. Black delivered the opinion of a unanimous Court to forthrightly reject the property rights position of *Davis,* thereby confirming the open forum view announced by the Court in *Hague* v. *CIO.*

The philosophy developed in the last four cases summarized above remains the basic position of the Supreme Court. In sum, the Court formulated between 1939 and 1943— and continues to support—*the general principle that the Constitution requires that streets, parks, and similar public places must be open for purposes of communication, although the use of these public areas may be regulated in a nondiscriminatory manner in order to assure the public convenience and good order.* As with other areas of constitutional theory and practice, however, the general principle of speech in the public forum has required periodic reexamination and clarification. The ways in which the Supreme Court and, in some instances, the lower federal courts have interpreted and applied the above-stated theory of time, place, and manner over the years since 1943 is the subject of the section to follow.

The Theory of the Open Forum Developed and Refined

Issues and cases of time, place, and manner of expression have arisen to the Supreme Court primarily from two points of origin: those that question the use of *public property* and those that concern First Amendment rights on *private property*. The discussion below is based upon these two categories.

Freedom of Expression on Public Property

Within the framework of the principles set forth above, the U.S. Supreme Court has generally held to the position that time, place, and manner regulations must (1) be clear and narrowly drawn and (2) be administered in a content-free and nondiscretionary manner.[7] For example, questions of *vagueness and overbreadth* were central to a 1969 decision of the Supreme Court reversing the conviction of civil rights leader Fred Shuttlesworth for parading in Birmingham, Alabama, without a permit as was required by law. The Birmingham ordinance in question lacked clarity and precision, said the Court, and therefore failed the test of constitutionality. The ordinance gave complete authority to the city commission to grant a permit "unless in its judgment the public welfare, peace, safety, health, decency, good order, morals or convenience require that it be refused." The law did not define these terms but left it

up to the subjective opinion of each commissioner to interpret them as he or she pleased; thus, it was unconstitutional, for it lacked "narrow, objective and definite standards to guide the licensing authority."[8]

A case involving both *content-centered discretion* by New York City authorities and *vagueness* in the law was decided by the Supreme Court in 1951, when it reversed the conviction of Carl J. Kunz, a Baptist minister, for preaching in a public place without a permit.[9] Kunz, whose initial permit had expired, applied for a renewal, was denied, and proceeded to speak anyhow. The justices of the U.S. Supreme Court, in both majority and dissenting opinions, noted that Kunz had a record of ridiculing other religions—Catholics and Jews in particular (he called Catholicism a "religion of the devil" and asserted that Jews were "Christ-killers")—and that numerous complaints had been lodged with the authorities concerning remarks he had made. However, since no disorderly conduct or breach of the peace was involved, the Court, by a vote of 8 to 1, determined that the ordinance as applied was an unconstitutional prior restraint upon the minister. Concluded Chief Justice Vinson in his opinion of the Court: "It is sufficient to say that New York cannot vest restraining control over the right to speak on religious subjects in an administrative official where there are no appropriate standards to guide his action."

At this point it will be helpful to examine a number of typical cases in order to further illustrate the variety of factors involved in deciding issues of time, place, and manner. The reader looking for the threads of consistency of legal principles in the examples summa-

---

[7]The Supreme Court established the requirement for nondiscretionary administration of permit ordinances in *Lovell* v. *Griffin,* 303 U.S. 444 (1938), a case discussed more fully under "prior restraint" in the following chapter.

[8]*Shuttlesworth* v. *Birmingham* (II), 394 U.S. 147 (1969). Not to be confused with *Shuttlesworth* v. *Birmingham* (I), 373 U.S. 262 (1963), which involved the same parties but addressed different issues.

[9]*Kunz* v. *New York,* 340 U.S. 290 (1951).

rized below should remember that (1) the *circumstances* vary from case to case and (2) the federal, state, and municipal *statutes* by which the circumstances are judged also vary. With these two variables in mind, the reader can proceed to a review of concrete examples in two categories: (1) expression in the public forum protected by the Constitution and (2) expression in the public forum not protected by the Constitution.

TIME, PLACE, AND MANNER PROTECTED BY THE FIRST AMENDMENT.

1. **Open areas near where the legislature meets.** *Edwards* v. *South Carolina* (1963). In March of 1961 a group of 187 black high school and college students held a peaceful civil rights demonstration in an open area of the South Carolina State House grounds to protest racial discrimination in the state. The demonstration, which was conducted while the legislature was in session, was broken up by police, who arrested the students, charging them with the common-law crime of breach of the peace. They were convicted of this "crime," and the South Carolina Supreme Court upheld the convictions. On appeal, the U.S. Supreme Court, by a vote of 8 to 1, reversed the courts below, and in an eloquent opinion by Justice Potter Stewart asserted that the South Carolina authorities had infringed the students' "constitutionally protected rights of free speech, free assembly, and freedom to petition for redress of their grievances."[10] Justice Stewart continued: *"The circumstances of this case reflect an exercise of these basic constitutional rights in their most pristine and classic form.* The petitioners felt aggrieved by laws of South Carolina which allegedly 'prohibited Negro privileges in this State.' They peaceably assembled at the site of the State Government and there peaceably expressed their grievances 'to the citizens of South Carolina, along with the Legislative Bodies of South Carolina.' " Such expression is essential to a democracy, Justice Stewart concluded, for it "is a fundamental principle of our constitutional system."

2. **Marching and demonstrating on the streets (by an unpopular political party).** *Collin* v. *Smith* (1978). When in 1976 and 1977 the National Socialist (Nazi) party of America and its leader, Frank Collin, attempted to demonstrate in the heavily Jewish community of Skokie, Illinois (a Chicago suburb), Skokie's village officials quickly passed three ordinances to prevent the demonstrations. The ordinances consisted of (1) a comprehensive parade permit regulation that applied to assemblies of more than fifty persons anywhere in town and required permit applicants to secure liability and property damage insurance totaling $350,000; (2) a prohibition upon the dissemination of material that incites racial or religious hatred, with intent to incite such hatred; and (3) a prohibition upon the wearing of military-style uniforms by members of political parties during a demonstration. When party leader Frank Collin applied for a parade permit for use on July 4, 1977 (to march in front of the Village Hall, with party members wearing Nazi uniforms complete with swastikas), the application was denied. Collin then sought relief in the federal courts.

In deciding the controversial case, U.S. District Judge Bernard M. Decker issued a lengthy opinion covering a variety of free-speech issues raised by the parties to the dispute and concluding that all three ordinances were unconstitutional.[11] In reference to the

[10]*Edwards* v. *South Carolina,* 372 U.S. 229 (1962).

[11]*Collin* v. *Smith,* 447 F. Supp. 676 (N.D. Ill. 1978); affirmed by the Court of Appeals, 478 F.2d 1197 (7th Cir. 1978). On appeal, the U.S. Supreme Court denied review, 439 U.S. 916 (1978).

use of public places for the expression of opinion, Judge Decker emphasized in his argument that the ordinances in question were not content-neutral, nondiscretionary regulations of time, place, and manner. Rather, the three ordinances were deliberately drafted and written into law for the purpose of suppressing a hated idea. This underlying reason for declaring the ordinances unconstitutional was buttressed by the judge's specific findings that: (1) the first ordinance had an excessive insurance requirement and also established permit standards imposing a system of prior restraint upon applicants; (2) the language of the second ordinance—which prohibited the distribution of materials promoting "hatred against persons by reason of their race, national origin, or religion"—was vague and overbroad; and (3) the third ordinance, which forbade the wearing of military-style uniforms, was an attempt to ban a repugnant symbol and was, therefore, "clearly unconstitutional." Judge Decker concluded his opinion with his philosophical observation: "The ability of American society to tolerate the advocacy even of the hateful doctrines espoused by the plaintiffs without abandoning its commitment to freedom of speech and assembly is perhaps the best protection we have against the establishment of any Nazi-type regime in this country."[12]

3. **Passenger areas of an airport terminal.** *Chicago Area Military Project* v. *City of Chicago* (1975) and *International Society for*

Krishna Consciousness v. *Rochford* (1977). In response to a 1975 federal court decision that had permitted a nonprofit organization from Chicago to distribute its newspapers in O'Hare Airport,[13] airport officials drafted a new set of regulations that required a daily permit for the passing out of literature or soliciting of donations and which flatly forbade the selling of "anything for commercial purposes" except by licensed airport vendors. The Society of Krishna Consciousness objected, claiming that the strict regulations violated their First Amendment rights to spread religious truth "through solicitation of contributions, dissemination of religious tracts, and sale of religious materials." District Judge George N. Leighton agreed and enjoined authorities from enforcing the new requirements.[14] The regulations in question, observed Judge Leighton, were "vague and uncertain" and "utterly lacking in standards that can guide airport officials in making decisions which may manifest the censor's heavy hand on the freedom of religion, of thought, speech, and the press." What can one conclude from the two airport decisions? Although neither occurred at the Supreme Court level, both give strong support to the principle that passenger terminals, including those for buses and trains, are appropriate places for the reasonable exercise of First Amendment rights.

[12]After winning its legal battle, the National Socialist party decided not to march in Skokie after all. The case did serve sharply to divide civil libertarians throughout the country, however, many of whom were critical of the American Civil Liberties Union for representing the National Socialist party in the litigation. For more on the controversy, see Aryeh Neier, *Defending My Enemy: American Nazis, the Skokie Case, and the Risks of Freedom* (New York: Dutton, 1979); also, David Hamlin, *The Nazi/Skokie Conflict: A Civil Liberties Battle* (Boston: Beacon Press, 1980).

[13]*Chicago Area Military Project* v. *City of Chicago,* 508 F.2d 921 (7th Cir. 1975).
[14]*International Society for Krishna Consciousness* v. *Rochford,* 425 F. Supp. 734 (1977). James R. Rochford, who is named in the action, was superintendent of the Chicago Police Department. Note: Four years later, and concerning different circumstances, the Supreme Court upheld the authority of Minnesota State Fair officials to require Krishna and other groups to solicit funds, sell items, or pass out literature on the fairgrounds from assigned booths that were allocated on a first-come, first-served basis. See *Heffron* v. *International Society for Krishna Consciousness,* 452 U.S. 640 (1981).

TIME, PLACE, AND MANNER NOT PRO-
TECTED BY THE FIRST AMENDMENT.

1. **Demonstrations near a courthouse.**

Cox v. *Louisiana* (II) (1965) and *United States* v. *Grace* (1983). In 1965 the U.S. Supreme Court announced its decisions in two cases involving the same parties and related issues. In *Cox* v. *Louisiana* (I), the Court reversed the convictions of a group of civil rights demonstrators who had conducted a protest near a Baton Rouge courthouse because the breach-of-the-peace and obstructing-public-passages statutes under which the convictions were obtained were found to be unconstitutionally vague and overbroad as construed by the Louisiana courts.[15] The second case, however, concerned a different issue raised by the same incident, namely, the conviction of Cox and others under a Louisiana law that *prohibited picketing or parading near a courthouse* "with the intent of interfering with, obstructing, or impeding the administration of justice, or with the intent of influencing any judge, juror, witness, or court officer, in the discharge of his duty . . . ." Although the Court overturned the convictions under this statute (it had been improperly applied by the local police, who had early in the demonstration informed Cox that he was *not* too close to the courthouse), it did *uphold the constitutionality of it.* Such narrowly drawn laws, said the Court, serve as safeguards against the disruption of trials or the intimidation of persons involved in the judicial process.[16]

The courthouse chickens "came home to roost" eighteen years later when the question of peacefully demonstrating on the public sidewalks that surround the U.S. Supreme Court building in Washington, D.C., was

decided by the Court. Title 40 of the *U.S. Code,* Section 13k, prohibits the "display [of] any flag, banner, or device designed or adapted to bring into public notice any party, organization, or movement" inside the Supreme Court building or on its grounds, including the public sidewalks around the building. Thaddeus Zywicki, who had on several occasions been stopped by police from leafletting on the sidewalk around the building, and Mary Grace, who was ordered by police to move when she stood on the sidewalk in front of the Supreme Court displaying a large sign upon which was written the text of the First Amendment, challenged the law in federal court. In 1983 a unanimous Supreme Court (Justices Marshall and Stevens concurring in the result but dissenting in part in separate opinions) declared the law *as applied to the sidewalks* to be unconstitutional; however, the Court left open the questions of use of the grounds within the boundaries of the sidewalks and the interior of the building itself.[17] Justice White, in his opinion of the Court, observed that absolute prohibitions upon a particular type of expression "will be upheld only if narrowly drawn to accomplish a compelling governmental interest." Since the sidewalks in question were much like those in any other part of the city, concluded Justice White, and since the use of them did not interfere with the peace and tranquillity of the Court, it followed that no compelling government interest was served by the regulation. Consequently, persons who wish to do so may now exercise First Amendment rights on the public sidewalks around the structure which houses the U.S. Supreme Court.

Finally, the *Grace* decision does not alter Title 18 of the *U.S. Code,* Section 1507,

---

[15]*Cox* v. *Louisiana* (I), 379 U.S. 536 (1965).
[16]*Cox* v. *Louisiana* (II), 379 U.S. 559 (1965).

[17]*United States* v. *Grace,* 51 *Law Week* 4444 (1983).

which—much like the Louisiana statute sustained in *Cox* (II)—prohibits demonstrators from interfering with the administration of justice by picketing, parading, and using a sound truck in a disturbing manner near a United States courthouse. The signal from the Court seem to be this: a courthouse, particularly during the time of a trial, is *not* an appropriate place for a demonstration— especially a noisy one or one involving a large number of persons. In short, the *Grace* decision appears to have left undisturbed the position of the Court as set out in *Cox* (II), that narrowly drawn statutes to prevent marching, picketing, or demonstrating near a courthouse do not "infringe upon the constitutionally protected rights of free speech and free assembly."[18]

2. **Demonstrations on the grounds of a jailhouse.** *Adderley* v. *Florida* (1966). In the mid-1960s, and in connection with civil rights protests in Tallahassee, Florida, Harriett Louise Adderley and about two hundred other demonstrators entered the grounds of the jail of Leon County, Florida, to show their disapproval of the arrest earlier in the day of other civil rights protesters who were being held in the jail. The entry upon the jailhouse grounds was done without permission and came as a surprise to the officers inside. Adderley and thirty-one of her colleagues were arrested and charged with violating a Florida trespass statute. Upon conviction and after having that conviction upheld by the Florida courts, Adderley and her associates appealed to the U.S. Supreme Court. By a vote of 5 to 4, the Court sustained the convictions.[19] Justice Black, who argued often during the civil rights demonstrations of the 1960s that speakers and demonstrators do not have a right to express their views

"whenever and however and wherever they please,"[20] delivered the opinion of the Court. Contrasting this case with *Edwards* (which occurred on the South Carolina State Capitol grounds), Justice Black summarized the issue as he saw it: "Traditionally, state capitol grounds are open to the public. Jails, built for security purposes, are not." One can conclude from this decision that the grounds of jails and prisons are inappropriate places for protest demonstrations.

3. **Blocking the entrance to government property.** *Cameron* v. *Johnson* (1968). In response to the many civil rights protests that were occurring across the state, the Mississippi legislature in 1964 enacted a statute that prohibited marchers and demonstrators from obstructing the entrance to "any public premises, State property, county or municipal courthouses, city halls, office buildings, jails, or other public buildings or property" of the various governmental units of the state of Mississippi. When a group of civil rights activists convicted under this law appealed their convictions, the U.S. Supreme Court, by a vote of 7 to 2, upheld the law.[21] The statute is neither vague nor overbroad, declared Justice Brennan in his opinion of the Court, adding: "All that it prohibits is the obstruction of or unreasonable interference with ingress and egress to and from public buildings, including courthouses, and with traffic on the streets or sidewalks adjacent to those buildings." In this decision the Supreme Court made it very clear that blocking driveways and doors to buildings, or blocking the sidewalks and streets around those buildings, is not "expression" protected by the Constitution.

4. **Making disturbing noises near a school while it is in session.** *Grayned* v.

---

[18]*Cox* v. *Louisiana* (II), at 563.
[19]*Adderley* v. *Florida*, 385 U.S. 39 (1966).

[20]Ibid., at 48.
[21]*Cameron* v. *Johnson*, 390 U.S. 611 (1968).

Rockford (1972). In April of 1969 a number of black students together with family members and friends demonstrated near a Rockford, Illinois, high school in support of their efforts to get black students on the cheerleading squad as well as more black teachers and counselors in the school. The protest was carried out in violation of two city ordinances, the first of which prohibited picketing and demonstrating near a school during school hours (except for labor picketing at any school involved in a labor dispute) and the second of which forbade the making of a "noise or diversion" near a school while it was in session. The demonstrators were convicted of violating both laws, and their appeal eventually reached the U.S. Supreme Court.[22] The Court unanimously found the antipicketing law unconstitutional (because it permitted labor pickets but not others, it violated the equal protection clause of the Constitution); but by a vote of 8 to 1—with only Justice Douglas dissenting—it sustained the antinoise ordinance. Speaking for the majority, Justice Marshall authored an opinion which gives some excellent guidance to public communicators who might have occasion to contemplate what is and is not permissible in the public forum.

Justice Marshall *delivered the opinion of the Court:*

Clearly, government has no power to restrict such activity [as marches and demonstrations] because of its message. Our cases make equally clear, however, that reasonable "time, place and manner" regulations may be necessary to further significant governmental interests, and are permitted. For example, two parades cannot march on the same street simultaneously, and government may allow only one. . . . A demonstration or parade on a large street during rush hour might put an intolerable burden on the essential flow of traffic, and for that reason could be prohibited. . . . If overamplified loudspeakers assault the citizenry, government may turn them down. . . . Subject to such reasonable regulation, however, peaceful demonstrations in public places are protected by the First Amendment. Of course, where demonstrations turn violent, they lose their protected quality as expression under the First Amendment.

The nature of a place, "the pattern of its normal activities, dictate the kinds of regulations of time, place, and manner that are reasonable." Although a silent vigil may not unduly interfere with a public library, . . . making a speech in the reading room almost certainly would. That same speech should be perfectly appropriate in a park. **The crucial question is whether the manner of expression is basically incompatible with the normal activity of a particular place at a particular time. Our cases make clear that in assessing the reasonableness of a regulation, we must weigh heavily the fact that communication is involved; the regulation must be narrowly tailored to further the State's legitimate interest.** Access to the "streets, sidewalks, parks, and other similar public places . . . for the purpose of exercising [First Amendment rights] cannot constitutionally be denied broadly . . . ." Free expression "must not, in the guise of regulation, be abridged or denied."

Justice Marshall concluded that in "light of these general principles" the Rockford antinoise ordinance protecting schools during school hours did not violate the First Amendment. From this decision one can infer that narrowly drawn laws against excessive noise near certain other types of public buildings— hospitals, for example—would likewise be found constitutional.

5. **Political advertising inside or upon the vehicles of a city's rapid transit system.** *Lehman* v. *Shaker Heights* (1974). When

[22]*Grayned* v. *Rockford*, 408 U.S. 104 (1972).

Harry J. Lehman, candidate for state office in 1970, applied for advertising space (car cards) inside the vehicles of the Shaker Heights, Ohio, transit system, he was informed that city policy allowed commercial advertising but not political and public-issue advertising in or upon transit system vehicles. Claiming a violation of his First Amendment rights, Lehman challenged the rule in the courts and lost. The U.S. Supreme Court, by a vote of 5 to 4, ruled that the city's policy, which had been in effect for twenty-six years and was administered without discretion, did not violate the Constitution.[23] Justice Blackmun, in his plurality opinion representing the views of four justices, explained: "No First Amendment forum is here to be found. The city consciously has limited access to its transit system advertising space in order to minimize chances of abuse," including the appearance of political favoritism and the imposing of political or public-issue messages upon a captive audience. The fifth vote was provided by Justice Douglas, who, in concurring in the result, argued that passengers in a public transit vehicle composed a captive audience whose privacy should be respected. One can conclude, therefore, that unless and until the Supreme Court takes a different position on the matter, advertising spaces of various sorts under the supervision of government-run transit systems are commercial-type enterprises not automatically open to First Amendment claims. Of course, one can also conclude that units of government may open transit system advertising to political messages if they wish, provided that applications for such space are handled in a nondiscriminatory manner.

6. **On a military base.** *Greer* v. *Spock* (1976). Fort Dix, New Jersey, a U.S. Army post, has for years enforced regulations against partisan political speaking and demonstrating on the base and the distribution of printed materials of any type without a permit from the base commander. The regulations, according to the court record, have been applied in a nondiscriminatory manner to all who inquired or applied for a permit. In 1972 a number of political candidates who were denied permission to speak on the grounds of Fort Dix submitted the regulations to a court test. In 1976 the U.S. Supreme Court decided the issue, ruling in favor of the military authorities by a vote of 6 to 2 (Justice Stevens did not participate in the decision).[24] Justice Potter Stewart delivered the opinion of the Court to emphasize that people do not have a constitutional right to express their views "whenever and however, and wherever they please." He concluded that because it is "the business of a military installation like Fort Dix to train soldiers, not to provide a public forum," there was no constitutional right to enter such an installation for communication purposes. One can conclude, therefore, that just as *Adderley* v. *Florida* (1966) determined that jailhouse grounds were not proper locations for a demonstration, military installations are not proper places for unregulated speaking, demonstrating, and leafletting.[25]

---

[23]*Lehman* v. *Shaker Heights,* 418 U.S. 298 (1974).

[24]*Greer* v. *Spock,* 424 U.S. 828 (1976).

[25]Note: This decision contrasts with *Flower* v. *United States,* 407 U.S. 197 (1972), because the Supreme Court perceived significant differences in circumstances. In *Flower,* the Court permitted leafletting on an open street that was within the limits of Fort Sam Houston, San Antonio, Texas, because the street was used by the public like any other street in the city—it was, in fact, an "important public artery" upon which between 15,000 and 17,000 vehicles per day traveled. "Under such circumstances," said the Court, "the military has abandoned any claim that it has special interests in who walks, talks, or distributes leaflets on the avenue." For more, see Justice Brennan's dissent in *Greer* v. *Spock,* in which he argues that Fort Dix, like Fort Sam Houston, is an open base to civilian traffic (a major state highway traverses the reservation) and that it should have been more open than it was to "traffic in ideas."

7. **On the streets and sidewalks of residential areas.** *Carey* v. *Brown* (1980). Picketing in a residential neighborhood raises not only the standard time, place, and manner issues of freedom of expression versus public order and convenience but also the significant issue of the privacy of a person's home. Justice Hugo L. Black (whose view was joined by William O. Douglas) underscored the matter in his concurring opinion in a 1969 case involving the picketing of a residence.[26] "I believe that the homes of men," stressed Justice Black, "sometimes the last citadel of the tired, the weary, and the sick, can be protected by government from noisy, marching, tramping, threatening picketers and demonstrators bent on filling the minds of men, women, and children with fears of the unknown." For many years the High Court has skirted the question of First Amendment protection for residential picketing, even though about one-third of the states and numerous municipalities have laws regulating such activity.[27] During the 1970s, however, the Court strongly hinted that it sympathized with Justice Black's point of view. For example, it let stand a court of appeals decision upholding the constitutionality of an ordinance of the city of Artesia, New Mexico, which flatly forbade any person to picket "before or about the residence or dwelling of any individual."[28]

Although the Supreme Court has not yet confronted the question directly, it telegraphed a clear signal about its view in the 1980 case of *Carey* v. *Brown*.[29] Here the Court declared unconstitutional an Illinois law that allowed peaceful labor picketing of a dwelling but prohibited other types of residential picketing. Speaking for the Court, Justice Brennan cited the statute's distinction based upon content (the message of labor was permitted and other messages were denied) to find the law in violation of the due process clause of the Fourteenth Amendment. This was not to imply, Justice Brennan added, "that residential picketing is beyond the reach of uniform and nondiscriminatory regulation," for government may protect the tranquillity of homes, just as it can protect the peace and quiet of "courts, libraries, schools, and hospitals." In other words, a flat prohibition upon all forms of residential picketing is likely to be found constitutional by the U.S. Supreme Court.

The preceding overview of time, place, and manner of expression on public property can be summarized in two points. *First,* the federal courts have affirmed the right of persons to express themselves in a peaceful way (1) in open areas near the seat of the legislature; (2) on the public streets, sidewalks, and in the parks of a city; and (3) in the passenger areas of transportation terminals. *Second,* the courts have permitted governmental units to constrain the freedom of expression when the expression occurs (1) near a courthouse, (2) on the grounds of a jail, (3) in a manner that results in the blocking of entrances to government buildings, (4) in a disturbingly loud way near a school while that school is in session, (5) by way of posters and cards in or on the vehicles of a government-operated transit system, (6) on a military base, and (7) in a residential area. But what happens to a person's right of free speech when he or she steps off of the street or sidewalk onto *private*

---

[26]*Gregory* v. *Chicago*, 394 U.S. 111 (1969), decided without addressing the question of picketing in a residential area. Gregory's conviction for leading a march to the home of Chicago's Mayor Daley was overturned for other reasons, including overbroad instructions to the jury by the trial judge.

[27]See generally, Comment, "Picketers at the Doorstep," *Harvard Civil Rights–Civil Liberties Law Review* 9 (January 1974): 95–123, especially 103.

[28]*Garcia* v. *Gray*, 507 F.2d 539 (10th Cir. 1974); *cert. denied*, 421 U.S. 971 (1975).

[29]*Carey* v. *Brown*, 447 U.S. 455 (1980)

property—such as the parking lot of a shopping center? An examination of the issue of First Amendment rights on private property is now in order.

Freedom of Expression on Private Property

The issue of a communicator's First Amendment rights on private property has been addressed by the U.S. Supreme Court primarily in three contexts: on the grounds of private homes, on the streets of company-owned towns, and on the privately owned parking lots and walkways surrounding modern shopping centers. The shopping center question has emerged as a particularly important (and troublesome) one, for in many communities suburban shopping centers and malls have largely replaced downtown areas as centers of consumer commerce and have thus become privately owned replacements for what was a significant public forum of yesteryear. In order to survey the subject of free speech on private property, the section to follow is organized according to the three topics mentioned above, namely, First Amendment rights (1) on residential property, (2) on the property of company towns, and (3) on the grounds of shopping centers.

FREEDOM OF SPEECH ON RESIDENTIAL PROPERTY. As noted earlier in this chapter, the U.S. Supreme Court has indirectly supported the position that marches, picketing, and similar forms of expression upon the *public streets and sidewalks* of a residential neighborhood may be flatly prohibited by narrowly drawn statutes. However, when a communicator steps upon the residential property, different legal precedents apply. For example, the Supreme Court has ruled that municipalities may regulate *commercial* solicitation of homes—even to the point of prohibiting such solicitation except with the prior consent of the occupier—if they wish, but that absolute prohibitions upon *noncommercial* solicitation and distribution of printed materials, as by religious or political groups, violate the First Amendment.[30]

The rules can change once again if the home one seeks to reach is within an apartment complex or, by extension of the principle, within an apartment house with visitor controls. In 1948 the U.S. Supreme Court let stand a New York ruling that upheld the right of the owner of a large apartment complex to ban from the premises all who wished to canvass, solicit, or distribute literature.[31] As one can surmise, regular residential neighborhoods remain more open for First Amendment purposes than do apartment houses and complexes where rules of selective entrance are enforced.

Finally, in a recent decision, the Court ruled that home letter boxes are not a public forum and may not be used for the deposit of unstamped messages in violation of federal law. By act of Congress, letter boxes are reserved for the deposit of mail carried by the U.S. Postal Service and remain so restricted by a 7-to-2 vote of the Supreme Court.[32]

In short, as the Supreme Court said in 1976, "door-to-door canvassing and solicitation are [not] immune from regulation under the State's police power, whether the purpose of the regulation is to protect from danger or to protect the peaceful enjoyment of the

[30]The regulation of commercial solicitation was sustained in *Breard* v. *City of Alexandria,* 341 U.S. 622 (1951); the prohibition upon noncommercial expression at residences was overturned in *Martin* v. *City of Struthers,* 319 U.S. 141 (1943).

[31]*Watchtower Bible and Tract Society* v. *Metropolitan Life Insurance Co.,* 297 N.Y. 339, 79 N.E.2d 433; *cert. denied,* 335 U.S. 886 (1948).

[32]*U.S. Postal Service* v. *Greenburgh Civic Associations,* 453 U.S. 114 (1981), upholding the constitutionality of Title 18 of the *U.S. Code,* Section 1725.

home."[33] Although precise rules are difficult to state in advance because of the unpredictable variety in the circumstances which can attend a residential solicitation case, the courts have made these points: (1) *commercial* solicitation, except with the prior consent of the occupier of the home, can be flatly prohibited; (2) *noncommercial* canvassing, such as that done by religious or political groups, may be regulated but not flatly prohibited in regular residential areas; (3) all solicitation can be banned from apartment houses and apartment complexes by the owners of the property; and (4) home mailboxes are reserved for use by the U.S. Postal Service and do not represent a "public forum" for the deposit of unstamped materials.

FREEDOM OF SPEECH IN COMPANY TOWNS. In the mid-1940s Jehovah's Witness Grace Marsh entered the town of Chickasaw, Alabama, a suburb of Mobile entirely owned by the Gulf Shipbuilding Corporation, to distribute religious literature on the streets. Although the town was 100 percent privately owned, from its streets and sidewalks to its buildings (both residential and commercial), it functioned much like any other town. It even included a post office, near which Marsh stood as she began to pass out her materials. When the deputy sheriff, an employee of the Gulf Shipbuilding Corporation, told Marsh to stop leafletting because of company regulations against solicitation of any kind without a permit (he also informed her that she would *not* be granted a permit), Marsh disobeyed the order and continued her activity. She was then arrested and charged under state law with trespass upon private property. Upon conviction and after the state courts of appeal had sustained that conviction, Marsh petitioned the U.S. Supreme Court, claiming that her constitutional rights of freedom of speech and religion had been violated. The Court granted the appeal.

By a vote of 5 to 3 (Justice Jackson did not participate in the decision), the Supreme Court reversed the conviction of Marsh.[34] Speaking for the majority, Justice Black balanced the scales in favor of First Amendment rights over property rights as far as company towns are concerned.

Justice Black *delivered the opinion of the Court:*

. . . Whether a corporation or a municipality owns or possesses the town the public in either case has an identical interest in the functioning of the community in such manner that the channels of communication remain free. As we have heretofore stated, the town of Chickasaw does not function differently from any other town. The "business block" serves as the community shopping center and is freely accessible and open to the people in the area and those passing through. The managers appointed by the corporation cannot curtail the liberty of press and religion of these people consistently with the purposes of the Constitutional guarantees, and a state statute, as the one here involved, which enforces such action by criminally punishing those who attempt to distribute religious literature clearly violates the First and Fourteenth Amendments to the Constitution.

FREEDOM OF SPEECH IN PRIVATELY OWNED SHOPPING CENTERS. The rapid rise and fall of First Amendment rights on the property of privately owned shopping centers has developed in four steps, each of which being one in "a tortured line of

---

[33]*Hynes* v. *Mayor and Council of the Borough of Oradell,* 425 U.S. 610 (1976). Here the Court overturned the borough's ordinance for regulation of expression in residential neighborhoods because of vagueness.

[34]*Marsh* v. *Alabama,* 326 U.S. 501 (1946).

cases"[35] decided by the Supreme Court since 1968. Each case is considered briefly below.

1. Picketing of a supermarket in a labor dispute is permitted. *Amalgamated Food Employees Union* v. *Logan Valley Plaza* (1968).

The question of First Amendment rights on the private property of shopping centers was first addressed by the Supreme Court in a case involving a labor dispute between a union and a supermarket in the Logan Valley Mall, near Altoona, Pennsylvania.[36] When the state courts, at the request of the owners of the shopping center, enjoined the union from picketing on the property of the mall, the union appealed to the U.S. Supreme Court and won. By a vote of 6 to 3 and in an opinion by Justice Marshall, the Court—relying heavily upon its decision in *Marsh* v. *Alabama* (the 1946 company town decision discussed above)—determined that the Logan Valley Mall was "the functional equivalent of a 'business block' and for First Amendment purposes must be treated in substantially the same manner." The union picketers were permitted to return to the outside area near the supermarket to resume their peaceful activity.

In dissent, Justice Black (Justices Harlan and White also wrote dissenting opinions), who had authored the opinion of the Court in *Marsh* opening up the company town to the exercise of First Amendment rights, objected that "I can find very little resemblance between the shopping center involved in this case and Chickasaw, Alabama." In strong language accusing the majority of permitting

trespass and the confiscation of property, Justice Black concluded that in the case at bar private ownership of property weighed more heavily than First Amendment rights. "These pickets do have a constitutional right to speak," he said, but the shopping center is not obligated by the Constitution "to furnish them a place to do so on its property."

2. The distribution of handbills is not permitted inside an enclosed mall. *Lloyd Corp.* v. *Tanner* (1972).

By 1972 Chief Justice Earl Warren and Justice Abe Fortas, both of whom had voted with the majority in the *Logan Valley* case, had retired from the Court and had been replaced by conservative justices appointed by President Nixon.[37] Therefore, when the case of *Lloyd Corp.* v. *Tanner,* concerning the right of individuals peacefully to distribute anti-Vietnam War handbills *inside* an enclosed mall, reached the Supreme Court, the parties to the handbill case faced a Court considerably changed since *Logan Valley* was decided in 1968. In *Lloyd,* by a vote of 5 to 4 and in an opinion of the Court authored by recently appointed Justice Lewis Powell, the Supreme Court ruled that the Constitution does not give communicators the right to distribute handbills inside a private mall which has rules against such activity.[38] Justice Powell distinguished this case from the *Logan Valley* decision by noting that the earlier case allowed picketing related to a

[35]Jerome A. Barron and C. Thomas Dienes, *Handbook of Free Speech and Free Press* (Boston: Little, Brown, 1979), p. 105.

[36]*Amalgamated Food Employees Union* v. *Logan Valley Plaza,* 391 U.S. 308 (1968). The Logan Valley Mall was owned by a company known as Logan Valley Plaza, Inc., which explains the discrepancy in names.

[37]In addition to Chief Justice Warren and Justice Fortas, Justices Black and Harlan had also retired from the bench, allowing President Nixon to appoint four new members to the Court between 1968 and 1972. The four new appointees—Chief Justice Burger and Justices Blackmun, Powell, and Rehnquist—have consistently favored property rights over free-speech rights in shopping center cases.

[38]*Lloyd Corp.* v. *Tanner,* 407 U.S. 551 (1972). Voting with Powell were Chief Justice Burger and Justices White, Blackmun, and Rehnquist. Justice Marshall's dissent was joined by Justices Douglas, Brennan, and Stewart.

specific store in the shopping center, whereas the present case concerned handbills on a public issue that was not tied to the operation of the mall. In addition, the enclosed mall in question was surrounded by public sidewalks and streets that provided ample alternate space for the leafletters to use in the distribution of their materials. In brief, Justice Powell argued, the circumstances of the two cases were not the same. But he did not stop there. Justice Powell then argued for a narrowing of free-speech rights on private property by quoting from Justice Black's dissent in *Logan Valley* and by observing that the First Amendment constrains the hand of *government* but as a rule not the "action by the owner of private property." He concluded: "We hold that there has been no such dedication of Lloyd's privately owned and operated shopping center to public use as to entitle respondents to exercise therein the asserted First Amendment rights."

3. **The constitutional right of free speech on the property of a privately owned shopping center is rejected.** *Hudgens* v. *NLRB* (1976). In March of 1976 the Supreme Court completed the move away from First Amendment protection for the expression of opinion in private shopping centers, which it had begun in the 1972 *Lloyd* decision. In *Hudgens* v. *NLRB* and by a vote of 6 to 2 (Justice Stevens did not participate), the Court declared that the Constitution did *not* grant union members the right to picket a retail store in a mall. In the process, the Court reversed its *Logan Valley* ruling of 1968.[39] Observing that "the rationale of *Logan Valley* did not survive the Court's decision in the *Lloyd* case," the Court ruled that

"the ultimate holding in *Lloyd* amounted to a total rejection of the holding in *Logan Valley.*" It follows, therefore, the Court concluded, "that if the respondents in the *Lloyd* case did not have a First Amendment right to enter the shopping center to distribute handbills concerning Vietnam, then the pickets in the present case did not have a First Amendment right to enter this shopping center for the purpose of advertising their strike against the Butler Shoe Co." Despite the strong dissenting opinion of Justice Marshall, joined by Justice Brennan, that the decision was in error because "the shopping center owner has assumed the traditional role of the state in its control of historical First Amendment forums" such as sidewalks, streets, and similar public places, the present conservative majority of the Supreme Court is unlikely to make substantial changes in its "closed forum" ruling of *Hudgens*. Therefore, public communicators should be aware that according to the Supreme Court of the United States, persons do not have a constitutional right to speak, demonstrate, picket, distribute handbills, etc., on the property of privately owned shopping centers without the permission of the owners. Unless, that is, the would-be shopping center communicator lives in California or some other state where the right of free speech in shopping centers is assured by *state* law, as the fourth and final case explains.

4. **States may open shopping centers for purposes of speech and petition if they wish.** *Pruneyard Shopping Center* v. *Robins* (1980). Although the Supreme Court announced in 1976 that the Constitution does not guarantee access to the property of private shopping centers for free-speech purposes, what about the authority of states to guarantee that access? May a state, acting under its own laws, open shopping centers to reasonable and peaceful expressions of opinion without violating the constitutional rights

---

[39]*Hudgens* v. *NLRB,* 424 U.S. 507 (1976). This case concerned the efforts of union members to picket the Butler Shoe Company retail store in the North DeKalb Shopping Center near Atlanta, Georgia.

of the property owner? In answer to this question, the Court has said yes. In 1980, and by a unanimous vote, the U.S. Supreme Court affirmed a ruling of the California Supreme Court, which had construed the Constitution of the State of California so as to require access to shopping centers for the exercise of the rights of expression and petition.[40] In upholding the decision of the California court, the Supreme Court of the United States said: "We conclude that neither appellants' federally recognized property rights nor their First Amendment rights have been infringed by the California Supreme Court's decision recognizing a right of appellees to exercise state-protected rights of expression and petition on appellants' property."[41]

The shifting and backtracking of the Supreme Court in the shopping center cases has resulted in considerable criticism from the legal profession. Not only does the sequence of events reveal a certain fickleness on the part of the Court as an institution but also—as one critic put it in response to *Lloyd Corp.* v. *Tanner,* the anti-handbilling decision—the Court's approach "indicates an unwillingness" on the part of the justices "to deal with some new and basic changes in American economic life caused by the modern mall shopping center."[42] No doubt there will be further clarifications and adjustments by the High Court in the years ahead in this controversial area of the law. Meanwhile, one who has a clear vision of what he believes the First Amendment should protect is Franklyn S. Haiman, professor of communication studies at Northwestern University, who, in *Speech and Law in a Free Society,* advocates a position at variance with the current holding of the U.S. Supreme Court. Haiman would apply the company town principle of *Marsh* to large shopping centers because of the "preferred position" of the First Amendment in the hierarchy of the nation's constitutional values. "It is but a small intrusion on their property rights," he argues, "to ask such property owners to accommodate nondisruptive, albeit unwelcome, communication as the price of their doing business on such a grand scale with so many members of the public."[43]

Traditional Issues of Time, Place, and Manner in Brief

In the landmark decision of *Hague* v. *CIO* (1939), the U.S. Supreme Court "opened up" the public streets, sidewalks, and parks to those who wished to use such places for the expression of opinion. States and cities may regulate these public forums, said the Court, but may not close them to use by public communicators. In the years following the *Hague* decision, the Court has refined, explained, and clarified the free-speech rights of persons who wish to use the public forum as applied to both *public* and *private* property.

Where *public* property is concerned, the

[40]*Pruneyard Shopping Center* v. *Robins,* 447 U.S. 74 (1980). Here, a group of high school students were told by the owners of the shopping center that they could not pass out leaflets and secure petitions on a public issue about which the students were concerned.

[41]A result different from that reached in California was announced by the conservative justices of the North Carolina Supreme Court in *State* v. *Felmet,* 302 N.C. 173, 273 S.E.2d 708 (1981). By a unanimous vote the judges construed the North Carolina Constitution so as to *deny* a legal right of access to private shopping centers for purposes of expression and petition. For a sharp criticism of this decision, see Note, "Constitutional Law—*State* v. *Felmet:* The Extent of Free Speech Rights on Private Property Under the North Carolina Constitution," *North Carolina Law Review* 61 (October 1982): 157–166.

[42]Note, "*Lloyd Corp.* v. *Tanner:* The Demise of *Logan Valley* and the Disguise of *Marsh,*" *Georgia Law Journal* 61 (1973): 1217.

[43]Franklyn S. Haiman, *Speech and Law in a Free Society* (Chicago: University of Chicago Press, 1981), p. 326.

regulation of marches and parades may include a permit system (administered equally to all) and controls upon the time and location of the activity. Some locations are more appropriate for the exercise of First Amendment rights than are others. Besides streets, sidewalks, and parks, the Supreme Court has held that open areas near where the legislature meets are logical and proper places for peaceful demonstrations to petition for redress of grievances; also, that passenger areas of airports (and, by extension, bus and train depots) may not be closed to solicitation and the distribution of literature. On the other hand, the Supreme Court has ruled that certain locations—such as courthouses (especially during a trial), jailhouse grounds, military bases, and in some circumstances even the sidewalks and streets of residential neighborhoods—are dedicated to uses incompatible with the open forum; therefore expression in such locations may be tightly restricted or even flatly prohibited. Furthermore, the Court has determined that the Constitution does not guarantee a person access to advertising space (posters or car cards) in or on the vehicles of a public transit system, nor does it protect noisy demonstrations near schools and hospitals (or in similar quiet zones) or the blocking of entrances to buildings by demonstrators. The Court's general rule was well stated by Justice Marshall in *Grayned* v. *Rockford* (1972): "*The crucial question is whether the manner of expression is basically incompatible with the normal activity of a particular place at a particular time.*"

The public forum contracts considerably when the would-be communicator steps onto *private* property. Although residential property may not, as a rule, be completely closed to noncommercial expression, it may be closed to commercial solicitation by narrowly drawn ordinance. Mailboxes are restricted to the deposit of stamped mail delivered by the U.S. Postal Service and are not available for free use by others who would deposit their messages therein. Company towns must open their sidewalks and streets for First Amendment purposes in the same way that regular municipalities do. However, the federal Constitution does not give one the right to picket, solicit, or distribute literature without permission on the property of a privately owned shopping center, although a state constitution may confer such a right.

II. SPECIAL ISSUES OF FREE SPEECH IN THE PUBLIC FORUM

In addition to the basic principles of free speech in the public forum, discussed above, at least two additional topics merit attention in order to help complete the presentation of the subject of this chapter. The *first* is the concept of "speech plus," including how the concept helps explain the position of the courts toward both symbolic expression and labor picketing; the *second* concerns two unusual forms of protected expression, namely, the solicitation of legal business and the economic boycott.

The Concept of "Speech Plus"

"Speech plus" is a term employed by some First Amendment scholars to describe the distinction made by the courts between "pure speech" (i.e., verbal expression, as in a traditional public speech or a newspaper editorial) and speech conjoined with conduct (as in marching in front of an army recruitment office chanting "no more war," the marching being the "plus" in the matter).[44] The con-

---

[44]See, generally, Harry Kalven, Jr., "The Concept of the Public Forum: *Cox* v. *Louisiana*," in *The Supreme Court Review: 1965*, ed. Philip B. Kurland (Chicago: University of Chicago Press, 1965), pp. 1–32.

duct in the "speech plus" equation can vary from the basic physical activity of parading, picketing, or demonstrating to the more symbolic conduct of flag burning, draft-card burning, or even pouring human blood upon the files of a local draft board. Simply put, "speech plus" is shorthand for *speech interwoven with action* (for this reason, the concept is also called the "speech–action dichotomy" for some commentators). Furthermore, a basic tenet of "speech plus" is that the "plus" (conduct) receives less protection under the First Amendment than does "speech."

The Supreme Court's position on speech versus conduct seems to have originated in the 1940s in various labor union cases involving picketing. In one such case, Justice Black—a leading supporter of the distinction between speech and action—wrote for the Court: "But it has never been deemed an abridgement of freedom of speech or press to make a course of conduct illegal merely because the conduct was in part initiated, evidenced, or carried out by means of language, either spoken, written, or printed."[45] This concept was given strong support by Justice Goldberg in a 1965 civil rights demonstration case (black demonstrators near a courthouse in Baton Rouge, Louisiana), when he announced in his opinion of the Court: "We emphatically reject the notion . . . that the First and Fourteenth Amendments afford the same kind of freedom to those who would communicate ideas by conduct such as patrolling, marching, and picketing on streets and highways, as these amendments afford to those who communicate ideas by pure speech."[46] In subsequent years, the Supreme Court on a number of occasions has cited with approval Justice Goldberg's "pure speech" versus conduct position, thereby making the speech–action dichotomy an element of judicial decision making with which all students of the First Amendment should be familiar.[47]

The speech–action dichotomy expounded by Justice Goldberg in *Cox* v. *Louisiana* has been sharply criticized by a number of constitutional scholars. For example, both Harry Kalven, Jr., and Thomas I. Emerson find the concept lacking in precision of definition and therefore a threat to legitimate rights of petition and assembly. "I would suggest," notes Kalven, "that all speech is necessarily 'speech plus.' If it is oral, it is noise and may interrupt someone else; if it is written, it may be litter." In similar vein, Emerson observes that the Court's analysis is both "confusing and destructive of First Amendment rights" because it provides "no functional basis for deciding what is 'pure speech' and what is other 'conduct,' or for differentiating between the kind of protection that should be extended to one but not the other."[48] The criticisms of Kalven, Emerson, and others are also applicable to some cases of symbolic expression where the Court employs the speech–action dichotomy in its reasoning. For an examination of this and other issues concerning constitutional protection for symbolic communication, it is now appropriate to turn to that subject.

Symbolic Expression

Symbolic expression can be thought of as a special *manner* of communication which is nonverbal in nature and ranges from the pas-

---

[45]*Giboney* v. *Empire Storage and Ice Co.*, 336 U.S. 490 (1949), at 502.

[46]*Cox* v. *Louisiana* (I), 379 U.S. 536 (1965), at 555.

[47]The speech–action dichotomy has been cited most often by the Court in cases involving picketing and demonstrations, e.g., *Walker* v. *Birmingham*, 388 U.S. 307 (1967), at 316; *Cameron* v. *Johnson*, 390 U.S. 611 (1968), at 617; and *Amalgamated Food Employees Union* v. *Logan Valley Plaza*, 391 U.S. 308 (1968), at 315–316.

[48]Kalven, p. 23. Also, Thomas I. Emerson, *The System of Freedom of Expression* (New York: Random House, 1970), pp. 297–298.

sive display of a symbol (such as a flag decal on a window) to symbolic conduct (i.e., "speech plus," such as burning a flag or stripping nude to protest laws against nude swimming on a public beach). Its forms are numerous, including activities as disparate as KKK cross burnings, Fourth of July parades, guerrilla theater, the releasing of doves by peace groups, or the burning of a copy of the Constitution to protest some government action. Because the forms and variations are almost limitless, the effort to develop a clear, workable philosophy of symbolic communication under law is compounded. In fact, the formulation of a comprehensive legal theory in this area remains a challenge to both legal and communication scholars.[49] Be that as it may, there have been developments in the courts that provide a basis for study, analysis, and theorizing in the years ahead. These developments are summarized below according to a four-part division: (1) leading cases on issues other than flag desecration, (2) the issue of flag desecration, (3) the wearing of a military uniform of the U.S. Armed Forces in a dramatic production, and (4) personal appearance (hair length, beards, dress, etc.) as a form of nonverbal communication.

LEADING CASES OF SYMBOLIC EXPRESSION. One of the first cases concerning symbolic expression considered by the U.S. Supreme Court reached it in 1931, when the Court overturned the conviction in the state courts of California of Yetta Stromberg, a member of the Young Communist League, for leading a group of young people in raising and saluting a Russian flag.[50] The conviction was obtained under a state law that inherently recognized the communicative element of a flag as a symbol by making it a felony to, among other things, "display a red flag and banner in a public place and in a meeting place as a sign, symbol and emblem of opposition to organized government." The U.S. Supreme Court found this language unconstitutionally vague and reversed the courts below. Although there is little amplification of the subject of symbolic expression in the opinion of the Court, the flag is recognized as a symbol that could function as a part of the "political discussion" of a free society.[51]

A dozen years after *Stromberg*, the High Court again had occasion to recognize the element of communication inherent in nonverbal symbols when it declared unconstitutional the compulsory flag salute of the public schools of West Virginia.[52] This time, however, the subject of symbolic expression was more fully explicated.

Justice Jackson *delivered the opinion of the Court:*

There is no doubt that, in connection with the pledges, the flag salute is a form of utterance. Symbolism is a primitive but effective way of communicating ideas. The use of an emblem or flag to symbolize some system, idea, institution, or personality, is a short cut from mind to mind. Causes and nations, political parties, lodges and ecclesiastical groups seek to

[49]For example, see, generally, Barron and Dienes, chapter 5, "Symbolic Speech"; also, Franklyn S. Haiman, "Nonverbal Communication and the First Amendment: The Rhetoric of the Streets Revisited," *Quarterly Journal of Speech* 68 (November 1982): 371–383.

[50]*Stromberg* v. *California,* 283 U.S. 359 (1931).

[51]In the Nazi-Skokie controversy discussed earlier in this chapter, the federal district court cited *Stromberg* and other cases to strike down as unconstitutional the Skokie, Illinois, ordinance against the wearing of military-type uniforms and regalia in marches and demonstrations. The Court ruled that even the hated symbols of the Nazis were forms of symbolic political speech protected by the First Amendment. *Collin* v. *Smith,* 447 F. Supp. 676 (N.D. Ill. 1978), at 700.

[52]*West Virginia State Board of Education* v. *Barnette,* 319 U.S. 624 (1943).

knit the loyalty of their followings to a flag or banner, a color or design. The State announces rank, function, and authority through crowns and maces, uniforms and black robes; the church speaks through the Cross, the Crucifix, the altar and shrine, and clerical raiment. Symbols of State often convey political ideas just as religious symbols come to convey theological ones. Associated with many of these symbols are appropriate gestures of acceptance or respect: a salute, a bowed or bared head, a bended knee. A person gets from a symbol the meaning he puts into it, and what is one man's comfort and inspiration is another's jest and scorn . . . .

Because the flag stood for an idea, and compelling a flag salute was to force a person symbolically to show support for that idea, the state regulation must fall. "If there is any fixed star in our constitutional constellation," concluded Justice Jackson for the Court, "it is that no official, high or petty, can prescribe what shall be orthodox in politics, nationalism, religion, or other matters of opinion or force citizens to confess by word *or act* their faith therein." (Emphasis supplied.)

A third highly significant case in the development of legal precedent concerning symbolic expression is one that concerns draft-card burning during the protests of the 1960s against the war in Vietnam. Here, David Paul O'Brien was convicted in federal district court of burning his registration certificate in violation of a 1965 federal law making it illegal to forge, alter, knowingly destroy, or knowingly mutilate the document. Although the federal circuit court of appeals reversed the conviction on First Amendment grounds, accepting O'Brien's argument that his act was symbolic expression protected by the Constitution, the Supreme Court disagreed and, with only Justice Douglas in dissent, reinstated the conviction.[53]

[53]*United States* v. *O'Brien*, 391 U.S. 367 (1968).

The Court, in an opinion by Chief Justice Warren, weighed the "speech" element of O'Brien's act against the "plus" element of burning a registration certificate in violation of federal law and came down on the side of protecting government documents from deliberate destruction. The law in question, wrote the Chief Justice, "no more abridges free speech on its face than a motor vehicle law prohibiting the destruction of drivers' licenses, or a tax law prohibiting the destruction of books and records." He then addressed the argument of O'Brien that his conduct was protected by the First Amendment because it was done to demonstrate "against the war and against the draft."

Chief Justice Warren *delivered the opinion of the Court:*

We cannot accept the view that an apparently limitless variety of conduct can be labeled "speech" whenever the person engaging in the conduct intends thereby to express an idea. However, even on the assumption that the alleged communicative element in O'Brien's conduct is sufficient to bring into play the First Amendment, it does not necessarily follow that the destruction of a registration certificate is constitutionally protected activity. This Court has held that when "speech" and "nonspeech" elements are combined in the same course of conduct, a sufficiently important governmental interest in regulating the nonspeech element can justify incidental limitations on First Amendment freedoms. . . .

And what are the specific governmental interests in the draft card requirement? The Chief Justice argued for at least four, as follows:

1. The card serves as proof that the person described on it has registered for the draft.
2. The card contains information which

facilitates communication between the registrant and the local draft board.

3. The card contains reminders concerning change of address and other changes in status of which the registrant needs to be aware.

4. The regulation against mutilation of certificates helps avoid the misuse of draft cards by those who would alter or forge them.

For these reasons, concluded Chief Justice Warren, "a sufficient governmental interest" in protecting draft cards from mutilation or destruction "has been shown to justify O'Brien's conviction." (Following this ruling, many antiwar protesters burned *photocopies* of their certificates, an act that was not illegal under the statute used to convict O'Brien provided the real draft card was retained unaltered.)

The fourth and final case to be considered here concerns a protest against the Vietnam War that employed a different means of symbolic expression than O'Brien's. In this instance, three schoolchildren wore black armbands to classes as a way of showing their disapproval of American involvement in Vietnam. Upon being suspended by school authorities, the young protesters went to court, eventually winning their case before the nation's highest tribunal.[54] In upholding the First Amendment right of the children symbolically (and quietly, there being no disruption of classroom activity) to express themselves, the Court by a vote of 7 to 2 (Justices Black and Harlan dissenting), and in an opinion by Justice Fortas, recognized the communicative element in the armbands. As Justice Fortas observed, the armbands were

"closely akin to 'pure speech' which . . . is entitled to comprehensive protection under the First Amendment." He concluded that for the students to wear a small band of black cloth as a way of expressing "disapproval of the Vietnam hostilities" was a form of expression protected by the Constitution.

Based upon the four cases just discussed, what can the student of the First Amendment conclude concerning constitutional protection for symbolic expression? A short review of the cases is helpful in deciding:

1. *Stromberg* v. *California* (1931), in which the Supreme Court overturned a state conviction for raising and saluting a Russian flag and in the process recognized that flags function as symbols for ideas and as such can be a part of the political discussion of a democratic society.

2. *West Virginia State Board of Education* v. *Barnette* (1943), in which the Supreme Court declared unconstitutional a state rule that public school students pledge allegiance to the American flag each day. In this decision the Court expanded its recognition of the pervasiveness of symbolic expression in society, adding: "Symbolism is a primitive but effective way of communicating ideas. The use of an emblem or flag to symbolize some system, idea, institution, or personality is a shortcut from mind to mind."

3. *United States* v. *O'Brien* (1968), in which the Supreme Court upheld O'Brien's conviction for burning his draft card in violation of federal law. On balance, ruled the Court, the "nonspeech" element of burning an important government document weighed more heavily on the scale than did the "speech" element claimed by O'Brien, who said he burned the document in order to express his disapproval of the war in Vietnam. When a "sufficiently important governmental interest in regulating the nonspeech element"

---

[54]*Tinker* v. *Des Moines School District*, 393 U.S. 503 (1969). Note: This case is discussed in more detail later in this chapter under the heading "First Amendment Rights in the Schools."

is present in symbolic conduct, such an interest "can justify incidental limitations on First Amendment freedoms."

4. *Tinker* v. *Des Moines School District* (1969), in which the Supreme Court ruled that the Tinker children could attend classes while wearing black armbands to symbolize their disapproval of the war in Vietnam. The armband, said the Court, was closely akin to "pure speech," which is entitled to "comprehensive protection under the First Amendment."

At least two conclusions can be drawn from the Supreme Court's decisions in the four cases summarized above. *First,* the Court does recognize nonverbal communication as a form of speech protected by the Constitution; however, it has never said—not even in *Tinker*—that symbolic expression receives the same degree of First Amendment protection as does verbal expression. *Second,* one can infer that passive symbolic expression which is similar to "pure speech" (a black armband, for example) will receive a greater degree of protection by the courts than will symbolic *conduct.* Recall that even the liberal Warren Court of 1968 was unwilling to classify O'Brien's draft-card burning as symbolic expression worthy of the constitutional shield. Because the composition of the Supreme Court today is much more conservative than it was in the Warren era, the Court is likely in the future to give even less weight than did the *O'Brien* Court to First Amendment arguments in symbolic-conduct cases. Briefly put in terms of the "speech plus" concept, the more "plus" to the symbolic expression, the less protection the Constitution provides.

FLAG BURNING AND DESECRATION.   Near the beginning of the current century a brand of bottled beer offered for sale in Nebraska carried on its label a representation of the American flag. Incensed, state officials moved to stop the sale of the product; they did so under a flag desecration provision of the Nebraska Constitution that forbade the emblematic use of the national flag to advertise any product offered for sale. In upholding Nebraska's law, the U.S. Supreme Court commended the state's effort to teach patriotism by protecting the flag from abuse. Observed the Court: "To every true American the flag is the symbol of the nation's power—the emblem of freedom in its truest, best sense. It is not extravagant to say that to all lovers of the country it signifies government resting on the consent of the governed; liberty regulated by law; the protection of the weak against the strong; security against the exercise of arbitrary power; and absolute safety for free institutions against foreign aggression."[55] However, as the decision made abundantly clear, the liberties symbolized by the flag did not include the freedom to sell beer in bottles upon which a picture of the flag appeared!

The inherent tension between the First Amendment's protection for the expression of opinion and the censorship imposed upon symbolic speech by state and federal flag-desecration laws is reflected in a series of opinions from the Supreme Court in which the issues are more often than not decided indirectly and upon the narrowest of grounds. In fact, the Supreme Court has thus far avoided a clear-cut, determinative ruling on the issue of flag desecration even when given the opportunity to do so. This does not mean that one cannot predict with accuracy the legal outcome of certain uses of the flag; it does mean, however, that comprehensive guidelines are missing and that flag alteration, des-

[55]*Halter* v. *Nebraska,* 205 U.S. 34 (1907).

ecration, or abuse remain high-risk ventures. The statements of the Supreme Court in recent years on the subject of flag desecration are summarized below according to a five-step chronological development.

1. **Speaking defiant, contemptuous words about the flag is expression protected by the Constitution.** *Street* v. *New York* (1969). On June 6, 1966, Sidney Street, a black resident of Brooklyn, New York, heard over the radio that civil rights activist James Meredith, the first black to attend the University of Mississippi, had been wounded by a sniper's bullet in Mississippi. In disgust, Street took his American flag outside, walked to a nearby intersection, set it afire, and tossed it to the pavement. The police who were called to the scene overheard Street, who readily admitted his deed, shout to a small crowd that "We don't need no damn flag," and "If they let that happen to Meredith, we don't need an American flag." Symbol-burner Street was arrested, tried, and convicted in state court for violating a New York statute making it illegal to publicly "mutilate, deface, defile, or defy, trample upon or cast contempt upon, *either by words or act*" any flag of the United States. (Emphasis supplied.) The state courts of appeal sustained the conviction.

In his appeal to the Supreme Court, Street's attorneys (he was defended by the New York Civil Liberties Union) asked the justices to confront the act of flag burning directly and to find that it was a form of symbolic expression protected by the First Amendment. Instead, the Court reversed the conviction *without ever reaching the issue of flag burning.*[56] By a vote of 5 to 4 in an opinion of

the court authored by Justice Harlan, the majority reasoned that because the New York law made it illegal to show contempt for the flag by either *words* or by act, it was theoretically possible that Street had been found guilty because of his disrespectful language rather than for burning the flag—the trial record did not distinguish the two. Therefore, concluded the Court, the conviction could not stand, for the "right to differ as to things that touch the heart of the existing order" encompasses the "freedom to express publicly one's opinions about our flag, including those opinions which are defiant or contemptuous." Having thus reversed the conviction on these grounds, the Court found it unnecessary to consider other issues raised by the case. Street went home knowing that the Constitution protected his right to abuse the flag verbally but not whether it protected his right to burn the flag as an expression of political protest.

Before moving to a consideration of the next case, a word about the dissenters in the *Street* decision is in order. The four dissenters consisted of conservative Justice White, moderate Chief Justice Warren, and liberal Justices Black and Fortas. Each in a separate opinion made it clear that he believed that laws against flag desecration were constitutional and that Street's conviction should have been sustained. The position of Chief Justice Earl Warren is typical: "I believe that the States and the Federal Government do have the power to protect the flag from acts of desecration and disgrace." Rarely (if ever) does one encounter an opinion of a justice of the U.S. Supreme Court that is clearly at odds with this position. The point is that, in general, even moderate and liberal jurists have shown little inclination to extend the protection of the First Amendment to flag mutilation or burning as forms of symbolic expression. All students of free speech should

---

[56]*Street* v. *New York*, 394 U.S. 576 (1969). For an interesting discussion of this case and related issues of symbolic expression, see Haiman, *Speech and Law in a Free Society,* pp. 26–38.

understand this fact of life as they consider further the issue of flag desecration.

2. **The Supreme Court divides 4 to 4 on the issue of making sculpturelike constructions of the flag.** *Radich* v. *New York* (1971). In 1966, to protest the war in Vietnam, New York City art gallery proprietor Stephen Radich displayed several works of artist Marc Morrell consisting of thirteen constructions shaped and formed from Vietcong, Russian, Nazi, and American flags. Among the items on exhibit were at least three made from or using American flags—a gun caisson form wrapped in a flag, a flag stuffed in the shape of a human form hanging from a noose, and an erect penis shape wrapped in a flag. A policeman who saw the exhibit arrested gallery operator Radich, who was tried and convicted of violating New York's flag desecration law. When the state's highest court upheld the conviction, Radich appealed to the U.S. Supreme Court which, without announcing any opinions, let the conviction stand on a split vote of 4 to 4 (Justice Douglas did not participate in the decision).[57] Later, Radich persuaded a federal district court to hear the case (arguing successfully that the tie vote of the Supreme Court had not settled the matter) and won an acquittal on First Amendment grounds.[58] Would-be "flag artists" should realize, however, that the U.S. Supreme Court has never so ruled and that the likelihood that the Court as presently constituted would agree with the ultimate disposition of Radich's case is, to say the least, slight.

3. **Conviction for wearing a small flag sewn to the seat of the pants is overturned on grounds of vagueness in the law.** *Smith* v. *Goguen* (1973). Early in 1970 Valarie Goguen, who had been wearing a small cloth flag sewed to the rear of his blue jeans, was arrested, tried, and convicted of violating the Massachusetts flag desecration statute. The state law under which the conviction was obtained provided that "Whoever publicly mutilates, tramples upon, defaces or *treats contemptuously* the flag of the United States . . . where such flag is public or private property" is in violation of the law. (Emphasis supplied.) A federal district court reversed the conviction on the due process bases of vagueness and overbreadth in the law, and the federal court of appeals affirmed this ruling. Without reaching the question of overbreadth, the Supreme Court agreed with the court below on vagueness grounds alone. The question of symbolic expression was not a factor in the decision.[59]

By a vote of 6 to 3, in an opinion of the Court written by Justice Powell (Chief Justice Burger and Justices Blackmun and Rehnquist dissenting), the Supreme Court decided that the phrase "treats contemptuously" in the state law was unconstitutionally vague. As Justice Powell wrote: "The statutory language under which Goguen was charged . . . fails to draw reasonably clear lines between the kinds of nonceremonial treatment that are criminal and those that are not. Due process requires that all 'be informed as to what the State commands or forbids' . . . and that 'men of common intelligence' not be forced to guess at the meaning of the criminal law." Because it was not clear in a day of "relaxed clothing styles" that wearing a flag on the seat of the pants was necessarily an act of contempt, the law as applied to Goguen's case did not meet the standards of the Constitution.

[57] *Radich* v. *New York,* 401 U.S. 531 (1971).
[58] *U.S. ex rel. Radich* v. *Criminal Court of New York,* 385 F. Supp. 165 (1974).

[59] *Smith* v. *Goguen,* 415 U.S. 566 (1974). Note: Appellant Smith was the sheriff of Worcester County, Massachusetts, where Goguen's arrest occurred.

4. **Displaying a flag upside down with a peace symbol taped upon it in order to communicate a message of political protest is expression protected by the First Amendment.** *Spence* v. *Washington* (1974). In May of 1970, college student Spence of Seattle, Washington, used removable black tape to affix a peace symbol to each side of his American flag; then he hung it upside down from a window in his apartment as a way of protesting the war in Vietnam and the shooting of students by national guardsmen at Kent State University. For this he was arrested, tried, and convicted of violating a state law forbidding "improper use" of the American flag; however, he was not charged under Washington's flag desecration statute. The supreme court of the state of Washington sustained the conviction.

On appeal, the U.S. Supreme Court reversed; in the process, it addressed the issue of *using,* but without mutilation or destruction, an American flag as a means of symbolic expression. In a per curiam opinion (Chief Justice Burger and Justices White and Rehnquist dissenting) the Court agreed that young Spence was indeed expressing an opinion by displaying the flag as he did and that there was in this instance no overriding state interest in preventing him from so using the flag.[60] Four factors justified the reversal, said the Court: (1) the flag was privately owned (mishandling a flag that is public property would be different); (2) Spence displayed the flag on private property (there was

no trespass); (3) there was no breach of the peace; and (4) appellant Spence did engage in a "form of communication," namely, he wanted others to know of his belief that "America stood for peace." Concerning this final element, the Court stated further: "It may be noted . . . that this was not an act of mindless nihilism. Rather, it was a pointed expression of anguish by appellant about the then-current domestic and foreign affairs of his government. An intent to convey a particularized message was present, and in the surrounding circumstances the likelihood was great that the message would be understood by those who viewed it." Finally, the Court emphasized that Spence was not charged with desecration, disfiguring, or destroying the flag. Rather, "He displayed it as a flag of his country in a way closely analogous to the manner in which flags have always been used to convey ideas. Moreover, his message was direct, likely to be understood, and within the contours of the First Amendment."

5. **Flag burning as a form of symbolic expression is not protected by the Constitution.** *Kime* v. *United States* (1982). After deciding *Spence* v. *Washington* in 1974, the U.S. Supreme Court returned to the states (remanded) a number of flag cases to be reconsidered in light of the Court's rulings in *Smith* v. *Goguen* (1973) and *Spence.* Among these were two flag burning cases, one from Illinois and the other from Iowa, in which the state courts had found the defendants guilty of violating state laws against flag desecration.[61] After reconsideration, both the Illinois and Iowa courts again ruled that flag burning was a violation of state law and that the state laws in question did not offend the federal Constitution. The defendants in the Iowa case again appealed to the U.S. Su-

[60]*Spence* v. *Washington,* 418 U.S. 405 (1974). Note: A few days later, the Supreme Court affirmed a federal circuit court opinion that a New York law prohibiting the placing of any design on an American flag was void for vagueness and overbreadth. State officials had employed the law against the display of car windshield decals showing a peace symbol with a flaglike stars and stripes background; see *Cahn* v. *Long Island Vietnam Moratorium Committee,* 418 U.S. 906 (1974). The Circuit Court decision is found at 437 F.2d 344 (2d Cir. 1970).

[61]*Sutherland* v. *Illinois* and *Farrell* v. *Iowa,* both remanded at 418 U.S. 907 (1974).

FIGURE 8.3. TERESA KIME BURNING AN AMERICAN FLAG.

Teresa Kime of the Revolutionary Communist party burns an American flag as an act of political protest on the sidewalk in front of the federal building in Greensboro, North Carolina, on March 27, 1980. The flames were set by her fellow party member Donald Bonwell, who does not appear in the photograph. The other demonstrators in the picture, holding red flags and party literature, are also party members. For the act pictured here, Kime and Bonwell were arrested, tried, and convicted of violating a federal flag desecration law. Both served time in federal prison for their conduct.

The Greensboro News and Record.

preme Court, which denied review for lack of a "substantial federal question."[62] The Court's message, although indirect, was clear, namely, that flag burning as a means of nonverbal communication was not protected by the Constitution.

Two who did not get the message were Teresa Kime and Donald Bonwell, members of the Revolutionary Communist party, who burned a privately owned American flag on March 27, 1980, during a peaceful political demonstration on the sidewalk in front of the federal courthouse in Greensboro, North Carolina. Both Kime and Bonwell announced that the burning was done as an act of political protest and a means of advertising an upcoming political rally of the party. The two were charged by the U.S. attorney in Greensboro of violating a 1968 federal statute providing that "Whoever knowingly casts contempt upon any flag of the United States by publicly mutilating, defacing, defiling, burning, or trampling upon it shall be fined not more than $1,000 or imprisoned for not more than a year, or both."[63] Kime and Bonwell were tried by jury before a United States

[62]The state rehearings are *People* v. *Sutherland,* 29 Ill. App.3d 199, 329 N.E.2d 820 (1975); and *State* v. *Farrell,* 223 N.W.2d 270 (Iowa 1974). The U.S. Supreme Court denied review to *Farrell* at 421 U.S. 1007 (1975).

[63]18 *U.S. Code* Sec. 700. Note: The law was passed by Congress in response to numerous reports of flag desecration by opponents of the war in Vietnam during the 1960s, the "decade of dissent."

magistrate, found guilty of casting contempt upon the flag, and each sentenced to eight months in prison.[64] The federal district court upheld the convictions, as did the federal circuit court of appeals. With only Justice Brennan voting to hear the appeal, the U.S. Supreme Court denied review.[65] Upon learning of the Court's refusal to grant certiorari, the *Greensboro Daily News,* whose editorial offices are only two blocks away from where Kime and Bonwell burned the flag, expressed its disagreement with the outcome of the case: "Across the land the flag is honored and well-kept. That a few rag-tag radicals would destroy a flag in public does nothing to diminish what the flag stands for. It is curious that the high court's decision in effect protects only the symbol of the country—the flag—and not the essence of it—freedom and free speech. Curious, and regrettable."[66]

In summary, although the U.S. Supreme Court has ruled that speaking "defiant and contemptuous" words about the flag is expression protected by the First Amendment (*Street,* 1969) and although the Court has reversed convictions in at least two instances (*Spence* and *Cahn,* both 1974) in which the flag was used as a visual background for a peace symbol, the Court has made it "perfectly clear" that it does not view the mutilation or destruction of the flag to be symbolic expression deserving of the protective umbrella of the Constitution. Despite arguments to the contrary by a number of legal scholars who believe that in certain circumstances flag mutilation or burning can be a form of nonverbal communication deserving of First Amendment protection,[67] the conservative view as articulated in the dissent of Justice William Rehnquist in the 1974 case of *Smith* v. *Goguen* seems to represent the current philosophy of the Court concerning desecration of the flag. Justice Rehnquist mentions the "deep emotional feelings" aroused by the flag in "a large part of our citizenry," adding that the national symbol "is not merely cloth dyed red, white, and blue, but also the one visible manifestation of two hundred years of nationhood . . . ." It is proper, he concludes, that persons be "prohibited from impairing the physical integrity of a unique national symbol which has been given content by generations of . . . our forebears . . . ."[68] Things have not changed much since 1907, when the U.S. Supreme Court, in upholding Nebraska's right to prohibit the use of a flag symbol on a bottle of beer, said: "For that flag every true American has not simply an appreciation, but a deep affection. . . . Hence, it has often occurred that insults to a flag have been the cause of war, and indignities put upon it, in the presence of those who revere it, have often been resented and sometimes punished on the spot."[69]

---

[64]On November 17, 1982, after the U.S. Supreme Court refused to review the conviction, Kime and Bonwell reported to federal authorities to begin serving their sentences. Both were released from federal prison in May of 1983 after serving six months of their eight-month sentences. Telephone interview with attorney John R. Kernodle, Jr., counsel to the defendants, Greensboro, North Carolina, July 11, 1983.

[65]*Kime* v. *United States, cert. denied,* 51 *Law Week* 3301 (1982). Justice Brennan entered a vigorous dissent from denial of certiorari, arguing that the Court should hear the case because of the elements of communication in the political act of Kime and Bonwell in burning the flag. "I feel sure," said Justice Brennan, that in light of earlier decisions concerning the flag, "the Court would be persuaded after briefing and oral argument that petitioners' convictions violate their First Amendment rights . . . ."

[66]"Waving a Red Flag," editorial in the *Greensboro Daily News,* October 23, 1982, p. A-12.

[67]For example, see Emerson, pp. 87–88; and Haiman, "Nonverbal Communication and the First Amendment," p. 378.

[68]*Smith* v. *Goguen,* 415 U.S. 566 (1974), at 602–604.

[69]*Halter* v. *Nebraska,* 205 U.S. 34 (1907), at 41.

WEARING A U.S. MILITARY UNIFORM IN A DRAMATIC PRODUCTION. In December of 1967 Daniel Jay Schacht and two other persons performed an antiwar "street theater" skit in front of the Armed Forces Induction Center in Houston, Texas. Schacht, who acted the part of an American soldier, wore an army uniform as a costume to symbolize the presence of the U.S. military in Vietnam. For this he was arrested, tried, and convicted of violating federal laws against the unauthorized wearing of a military uniform and the use of a uniform in a theatrical production that "tends to discredit" the armed forces.[70] The U.S. Supreme Court unanimously reversed the conviction, ruling that (1) the Constitution protected amateur actors performing street theater as well as professional actors in more sophisticated facilities and (2) skits and plays critical of the armed forces are as fully protected by the First Amendment as those that are favorable.[71] After emphasizing its first point concerning the rights of amateurs to perform theater on the street, the Court developed its second argument.

Justice Black *delivered the opinion of the Court:*

In the present case Schacht was free to participate in any skit at the demonstration that praised the Army, but under the [law] . . . he could be convicted of a federal offense if his portrayal attacked the Army instead of praising it. In light of our earlier finding that the skit . . . was a "theatrical production" within the meaning of [the law], . . . it follows that his conviction can be sustained only if he can be punished for speaking out against the role of our Army and our country in Vietnam. Clearly punishment for this reason would be an unconstitutional abridgment of freedom of speech. The final clause of [section] 772(f), which leaves Americans free to praise the war in Vietnam but can send persons like Schacht to prison for opposing it, cannot survive in a country which has the First Amendment. . . .

HAIR LENGTH AND DRESS STYLES AS FORMS OF SYMBOLIC EXPRESSION. During the 1960s and early 1970s a number of students entered the courts to challenge the right of authorities in public schools and colleges to regulate hair length and style of dress. Choices in these matters should not be subject to government control, so the students argued, for one's personal appearance was a form of symbolic expression (or a matter of personal liberty or privacy) protected by the Constitution. The result is a continuing division among the twelve circuits of the federal courts of appeal, for some circuits have discovered constitutional issues whereas others have not. Because the U.S. Supreme Court over the years has refused to grant review to student dress code appeals, the degree of constitutional protection a student has in regard to personal appearance depends upon where the student lives. The situation can be summarized in three points.

First, not all hair and dress cases raise First Amendment issues. Some persons wear their hair or dress as they do out of simple personal preference, not because they are attempting to express themselves symbolically. Legal efforts against hair and dress codes in instances where no communicative intent is present would likely focus upon other constitutional rights, such as personal liberty or privacy. On the other hand, a number of

---

[70]18 *U.S. Code* Sec. 702 makes it a crime to wear without authorization any armed forces uniform; 10 *U.S. Code* Sec. 772(f) granted an exception for actors in theatrical productions provided "the portrayal does not tend to discredit" the armed forces. (Notice how the second statute functions in a way similar to a flag desecration law; both punish those who make use of a national symbol, whether flag or military uniform, so as to cast contempt upon it.)

[71]*Schacht* v. *United States,* 398 U.S. 58 (1970).

judges have ruled that hair and dress styles do contain elements of nonverbal communication about the wearer's viewpoint concerning preference for elegance or simplicity, orthodoxy or unorthodoxy, conformity or nonconformity, and so on.[72]

Second, the federal circuit courts of appeal have split into two groups in the debate over extending constitutional protection to students in matters of hair length and style of dress. In 1977 the American Civil Liberties Union reported this division on a state by state basis, particularly as it applies to hair length regulations:

Group I—states in those federal circuits holding that rules on hair length are unconstitutional unless the school assumes the burden of proof to show that the style in question is disruptive of the educational process: Arkansas, Connecticut, Idaho, Illinois, Indiana, Iowa, Maine, [Maryland,] Massachusetts, Minnesota, Missouri, Nebraska, New Hampshire, New Jersey, New York, North Carolina, North Dakota, Rhode Island, South Carolina, South Dakota, Vermont, Virginia, West Virginia, and Wisconsin.

Group II—states in those federal circuits holding that the Constitution does not protect the length of a student's hair, thus permitting school authorities to enforce those regulations they feel are needed: Alabama, Alaska, Arizona, California, Colorado, Florida, Georgia, Hawaii, Kansas, Kentucky, Louisiana, Michigan, Mississippi, Montana, Nevada, New Mexico, Ohio, Oklahoma, Oregon, Tennessee, Texas, Utah, Washington, and Wyoming.[73]

Third, the U.S. Supreme Court shows no inclination to grant review to personal-appearance cases concerning schools and colleges in order to establish a uniform, national standard on the subject.[74] The individual caught up in a controversy over hair length or dress style in the schools would be wise, therefore, to seek the advice of an attorney about the best way to proceed in the state in which the case originated.

Before proceeding to the "speech plus" topic of labor picketing, it is appropriate to briefly restate the key points from each of the four headings in the present section on symbolic expression. *First,* nonverbal communication has been given some constitutional protection by the courts, but not as much as has verbal expression ("pure speech"). The more action or conduct ("speech plus") present in the nonverbal communication, the less protection the effort is likely to receive (e.g., the quiet wearing of a black armband received more protection under the First Amendment than did the active burning of a draft card). *Second,* flag mutilation or destruction is not protected by the Constitution, even when it is done as an act of political protest. One may speak contemptuous words to the flag or carefully use it as background

---

[72]For example, see the dissent of Judge Wisdom in *Karr* v. *Schmidt,* 460 F.2d 609 (1972), in which the fifteen judges of the fifth circuit sitting *en banc* (i.e., hearing the case as a group) voted 8 to 7 to reject a First Amendment argument concerning hair length. Here, Judge Wisdom argues that a person's hairstyle is "one aspect of the manner in which we hold ourselves out to the rest of the world."

[73]Alan H. Levine and Eve Cary, *The Rights of Students,* rev. ed. (New York: Avon Books, 1977), p. 48. Note: Inexplicably, the ACLU list omits the states of Delaware and Pennsylvania, and the District of Columbia. Maryland, also omitted, belongs in Group I, along with her sister states of the Fourth Circuit—North Carolina, South Carolina, Virginia, and West Virginia.

[74]In 1973 the Supreme Court even denied review to the appeal of three Pawnee Indian children who had been suspended from the public schools in Oklahoma for wearing their hair in long braids, as was traditional with members of their tribe. *Rider* v. *Board of Education,* 414 U.S. 1097 (1973).

for visual illustrations such as a peace symbol, but one must not desecrate it. *Third, actors* may wear a military uniform as a costume for skits or plays, even if the theatrical event in question is critical of the military or of the government. *Fourth,* the U.S. Supreme Court has refused to decide for the nation as a whole whether or not there are elements of freedom of expression in the way public school and college students wear their hair or clothing. The lower courts have split on the issue, so that in some states students have a degree of protection whereas in others they do not.

Labor Picketing

During the nineteenth century and for the first several decades of the twentieth century, labor picketing was considered an illegal practice under the common law of England, a position generally adopted by judges in the United States. The rationale for this viewpoint was based upon the antimonopoly laws that were directed against "merchants' combinations"; if merchants cannot cooperate so as to create a monopoly, so reasoned the judges, then workers should not be able to conspire in "workers' combinations" so as to bring pressure upon a business. Even today, the courts in some parts of the United States continue to reflect the common-law tradition of cool reserve—and in some instances show outright hostility—toward union activity, including picketing.[75]

Organized labor was finally given legal recognition and protection in the United States when in 1935, as part of the New Deal program of President Franklin D. Roosevelt, Congress enacted the National Labor Rela-

tions Act (NLRA).[76] This landmark legislation not only extended the right of collective bargaining to organized labor but also established the National Labor Relations Board (NLRB) to hear complaints concerning unfair labor practices as defined by the law. In this way did union activity, including picketing, become regulated by an agency of the federal government. (Recall that commercial advertising is similarly regulated by the Federal Trade Commission, and that broadcasting is supervised by the Federal Communications Commission.) Those interested in the complexities of the NLRA, including its sections concerning picketing, are referred to the act itself and to various specialized studies of labor law in the United States.[77]

The U.S. Supreme Court has responded to First Amendment issues concerning labor picketing by the assertion of three important principles. *First,* the Court has ruled that labor picketing is deserving of some First Amendment protection and, therefore, cannot be absolutely prohibited.[78] *Second,* the Court has applied a "speech plus" doctrine to the issue, generally accepting the view of the common law that picketing in labor–management disputes has many "plus" factors, including tendencies to violence, to coercive conduct and to irrational, emotional responses from those who are parties to a dispute.[79] Consequently, the High Court has

---

[75]See, generally, Note, "Peaceful Labor Picketing and the First Amendment," *Columbia Law Review* 82 (November 1982): 1469–1497.

[76]The NLRA, sometimes called the Wagner Act, as amended over the years, can be found at 29 *U.S. Code* Secs. 151–169.

[77]For example, 29 *U.S. Code* Secs. 157 and 158 spell out some of the permissible forms of picketing and some that are considered to be unfair labor practices. Also, as an example of one of many specialized essays on labor law and free speech, see C. L. Mack and R. L. Lieberwitz, "Secondary Consumer Picketing: The First Amendment Questions Remain," *Mercer Law Review* 32 (Spring 1981): 815–831.

[78]In *Thornhill* v. *Alabama,* 310 U.S. 88 (1940).

[79]For example, see the opinion of the Court in *Hughes* v. *Superior Court,* 339 U.S. 460 (1950).

held that while picketing cannot be prohibited, it can be *regulated.*

Third, and finally, the Supreme Court has been firm over the years in denying organized labor any First Amendment right to picket on behalf of an unlawful objective. The *unlawful objective* doctrine was forcefully stated by Justice Black in his opinion of the Court in the case of *Giboney* v. *Empire Storage and Ice Company,* in which the union was attempting to prevent the company from selling ice wholesale to nonunion peddlers. If agreed to by the company, this policy would have been a violation of the antitrust laws of the State of Missouri.[80] In rejecting the union's position, Justice Black ruled that it was constitutional to apply Missouri's antitrust laws to labor unions in this specific case and that the First Amendment did not protect picketing by the union to further an illegal end, namely, an agreement with the ice company to sell to union members only. In the words of Justice Black: "It rarely has been suggested that the constitutional freedom for speech and press extends its immunity to speech or writing used as an integral part of conduct in violation of a valid criminal statute. We reject the contention now." To interpret the First Amendment otherwise, he added, "would make it practically impossible ever to enforce laws against agreements in restraint of trade as well as many other agreements and conspiracies deemed injurious to society."

In summary, under laws both state and federal, labor picketing is classified as a special form of expressive conduct that is subject to supervision by the government. The U.S. Supreme Court, while holding that labor picketing is protected by the First Amendment, has applied the concept of "speech plus" to the activity, thereby extending less protection to it than to "pure speech." Among other things, the Court has held that unions may be prohibited from picketing on behalf of an unlawful objective without violating the free-speech rights of the picketers.

Two Unusual Means of Expression: Solicitation of Legal Business and the Economic Boycott

Two special means of expression—by litigation and by economic boycott—have been recognized by the U.S. Supreme Court as forms of communication deserving of First Amendment protection. Interestingly, each of the two Court rulings which established the special protections summarized below began as civil rights controversies, the first in Virginia in 1956 and the second in Mississippi in 1966.

In the case of *NAACP* v. *Button,* the Supreme Court declared unconstitutional a Virginia statute passed by the legislature in 1956 as part of a package of "states' rights," antidesegregation legislation. The statute in question redefined the law against unlawful solicitation of legal business so as to proscribe the work of the National Association for the Advancement of Colored People and its Defense Fund within the State of Virginia.[81] In declaring the statute unconstitutional, the Supreme Court by a vote of 6 to 3, in a majority opinion authored by Justice Brennan, asserted that the type of activity engaged in by the

---

[80]*Giboney* v. *Empire Storage and Ice Company,* 336 U.S. 490 (1949).

[81]*NAACP* v. *Button,* 371 U.S. 415 (1963). Note: The common law identifies three forms of improper solicitation of legal business, namely, *barratry* (maliciously exciting an argument in order to promote legal action), *champerty* (wherein a stranger to a dispute profits from it by offering to finance it or carry it on), and *maintenance* (the unauthorized interference in a suit by one who has no legitimate interest in it, as by providing funds or advice to one side or the other).

NAACP's Defense Fund was protected by the federal Constitution against state interference. The objectives of the NAACP, observed Justice Brennan, differed from those in which private disputes are resolved; rather, the NAACP was interested in "achieving the lawful objectives of equality of treatment . . . for the members of the Negro community in this country. It is thus a form of political expression." Therefore, Justice Brennan reasoned, litigation in these circumstances is protected by the first Amendment, for it "may well be the sole practicable avenue open to a minority to petition for redress of grievances." In other words, under certain circumstances court action is a form of free speech.

The second case began in 1966 after white elected officials of Claiborne County, Mississippi, refused to respond in a constructive way to demands by blacks for racial equality and integration, thus stirring black leaders, in a meeting sponsored by the NAACP, to launch an economic boycott of white merchants in the area. Three years later, as the boycott continued, several white merchants sued the NAACP and other sponsors of the protest movement for monetary damages to compensate for losses incurred as a result of the boycott. The Mississippi trial court agreed with the merchants and awarded damages over the objections of the defendants that their activities, including the boycott, were forms of political expression protected by the Constitution. On appeal, the Mississippi Supreme Court sustained the award of damages, although it did not agree with all of the findings of the trial court.

In 1982 the U.S. Supreme Court unanimously reversed the courts below (Justice Marshall took no part in the decision) and, in an opinion authored by Justice Stevens, ruled that the nonviolent aspects of the appellants' activities—including those of speech, assembly, petition, and association—were protected by the First Amendment.[82] As for the boycott itself, Justice Stevens wrote: "In sum, the boycott clearly involved constitutionally protected activity. . . . Through speech, assembly, and petition—rather than through riot or revolution—petitioners sought to change a social order that had consistently treated them as second-class citizens." Later, in reference to the right of a state to supervise economic activity within its borders, Justice Stevens observed: "The right of the States to regulate economic activity could not justify a complete prohibition against a nonviolent, politically-motivated boycott designed to force governmental and economic change and to effectuate rights guaranteed by the Constitution itself." In other words, in certain circumstances even an economic boycott is a form of expression protected by the First Amendment.

Special Issues in Brief

In summary, two special issues of free speech in the public forum are surveyed above, namely, (1) "speech plus," including its application to issues of symbolic expression and labor picketing, and (2) two unusual means of communication—by litigation and by economic boycott. Concerning the *first* of these, the U.S. Supreme Court has established a speech–action dichotomy that it describes as "pure speech" (speaking which is not conjoined with action) and "speech plus" (expression conjoined with action). The point of the dichotomy is to provide a rationale for extending more First Amendment protection to some types of expression than to others (the closer to "pure speech," the more protection the communication receives, whereas

---

[82]*NAACP* v. *Claiborne Hardware,* 458 U.S. 886 (1982).

the more "plus" present in the expression, the less protection the communication receives). This concept helps explain the Court's approach to symbolic speech and labor picketing, as follows.

Symbolic communication has been recognized by the courts as speech deserving of First Amendment protection, although symbolic expression generally receives less recognition than does verbal expression. Furthermore, the doctrine of "speech plus" applies to nonverbal communication in much the same way that it applies to other types of expression, for the more the nonverbal communication is conjoined with action, the less constitutional protection it receives. Concerning three specific subissues, the courts have determined that (1) flag desecration is not expression protected by the Constitution, (2) actors may wear military uniforms as costumes in theatrical productions even when the production is critical of the government or of the military, and (3) hair length and style of dress as forms of symbolic expression may or may not receive a degree of constitutional protection, depending upon the decision of the federal circuit court of appeals which has jurisdiction over the state in which one resides (because the U.S. Supreme Court refuses to hear appeals in hair and dress cases, the divergent conclusions of the circuit courts apply; some circuits recognize elements of expression in hair length and style of dress and others do not).

Labor picketing is a form of communication which, although it is protected by the First Amendment and may not be absolutely prohibited, comes under special statutory and administrative regulations because of its unique nature. In general, the courts have agreed with the principle that industrial picketing is more than "regular speech" and have applied the doctrine of "speech plus" to the activity. One of the key constraints applied—

and one that has been sustained by the U.S. Supreme Court—is that picketing done on behalf of an *unlawful objective* may be enjoined without violating the constitutional rights of the picketers.

Second, in two civil rights decisions, the U.S. Supreme Court extended the protection of the First Amendment to special programs of the National Association for the Advancement of Colored People. In *NAACP* v. *Button* (1963), the Court determined that the litigatory work, including the solicitation of clients, by the association was a form of expression protected by the Constitution. And in *NAACP* v. *Claiborne Hardware* (1982), the Court ruled that an economic boycott organized and carried out by blacks in a county of Mississippi as a form of protest against discriminatory policies by the county's white power structure was likewise protected expression under the Constitution.

III. INSTITUTIONAL CONSTRAINTS: FREEDOM OF SPEECH IN PRISONS, THE MILITARY, AND THE SCHOOLS

To this point, the survey of constraints of time, place, and manner upon freedom of expression has been concerned with public communication in society at large. When the subject of freedom of speech is examined within the context of an institution, however, one inevitably finds that additional controls are layered upon those that apply to society in general. Therefore it is reasonable to assume from the outset that those who attempt to express themselves (or exercise other constitutional rights) within the framework of an institution will confront more roadblocks than do those who attempt to express themselves outside of the institutional context. An examination of three important areas of institutional control in the United States—prisons, the military, and the schools—illustrate the problem. Such a consideration is appropriate here, for institutional expression comes under special "situational" constraints which resemble in principle controls of time, *place,* and manner. As the reader will observe, the three institutions are arranged in order from the *most* restrictive (the prisons) to the *least* restrictive (the schools).

First Amendment Rights of Prisoners

Prior to the 1960s the U.S. Supreme Court generally refused to grant review to appeals from prisoners in civil liberties cases, deferring instead to prison authorities, who were permitted to establish whatever regulations they felt were necessary to control the inmate population. This hands-off attitude by the courts began to change during the 1960s, when the Court began to cautiously grant certiorari in cases where the justices perceived some serious violation of basic civil liberties.[83] By the mid-1970s the old hands-off attitude had clearly been replaced by a "hands-on" policy, not only by the Supreme Court but also by the lower federal courts, which had followed the lead of the court above. In the arena of freedom of speech and association for prisoners, four issues addressed by the federal courts since 1974 merit review, as follows: (1) the censorship of prisoners' mail, (2) media access to prisons, (3) prisoners' rights of association, and (4) the censorship of prison newspapers.

---

[83]See "A Review of Prisoners' Rights Under the First, Fifth, and Eighth Amendments," *Duquesne Law Review* 18 (Spring 1980): 684–685. One of the first grants of certiorari went to *Cooper* v. *Pate,* 378 U.S. 546 (1964), where the Court ruled against prison authorities who were showing a preference for one religion over another.

The Censorship of Prisoners' Mail

In the 1974 case of *Procunier* v. *Martinez,* the U.S. Supreme Court unanimously declared unconstitutional on grounds of vagueness the mail censorship regulations of the California Department of Corrections that proscribed correspondence in which prisoners "unduly complain," "magnify grievances," or express "inflammatory political, racial, religious or other views or beliefs."[84] While recognizing that prison officials have a right to check prisoners' mail for messages affecting prison security, such as a discussion of an escape plan, the Supreme Court, in an opinion written by Justice Powell, established two standards for measuring the constitutionality of prison mail regulations. *First,* the regulation "must further an important or substantial governmental interest unrelated to the suppression of expression" such as the interests of security, order, and rehabilitation. Censorship of mail "simply to eliminate unflattering or unwelcome opinions" is not permitted. *Second,* "the limitation of First Amendment freedoms must be no greater than is necessary or essential to the protection of the particular governmental interest involved"—in short, the rule must not sweep too broadly. The net result of the decision is to recognize that prisoners do have a First Amendment right to uncensored communication by mail but that this right is considerably less than it is for society at large.

Two years later, the Court of Appeals for the Eighth Circuit cited *Procunier* to allow South Dakota prison officials to ban receipt by inmates of mail containing explicit sexual materials. South Dakota had claimed that the censorship was justified by the government interest of *rehabilitation,* and the Circuit Court accepted this argument. The U.S. Supreme Court denied review.[85]

---

[84]*Procunier* v. *Martinez,* 416 U.S. 396 (1974).

[85]*Carpenter* v. *South Dakota,* 536 F.2d 759 (8th Cir. 1976), *cert. denied,* 431 U.S. 931 (1977).

Media Access to Prisons

Three questions concerning media access to prisons and prisoners have been addressed by the Supreme Court, namely: (1) Does the First Amendment give *prisoners* a right to individual, face-to-face interviews with reporters? (2) Does the First Amendment give *reporters* the right to have face-to-face interviews with inmates selected by the reporters? (3) Does the First Amendment give media representatives the right to enter prisons upon demand for the purpose of inspecting, photographing, and reporting on conditions in the prisons? In answer to each question, the Supreme Court has said no, ruling that as long as alternate means of communication with the public are available to prisoners (such as the mails or by visitation), there exists no constitutional right of access to the press for individual interviews, and, conversely, media representatives have no greater privilege of access to the prisons than do members of the general public.[86]

Prisoners' Rights of Association

In 1977 the U.S. Supreme Court decided a case concerning the First Amendment rights of prisoners to form an organization and to promote it by meetings and by the use of the mails.[87] In response to the formation of a so-ciety of prisoners within the state's prison system, the North Carolina Department of Correction had adopted regulations that (1) prohibited inmates from soliciting other inmates for membership, (2) barred all meetings of the group, and (3) denied bulk mailing of union materials addressed to other prisoners. Although a three-judge federal district court found merit in the prisoners' First Amendment arguments and granted limited injunctive relief, the U.S. Supreme Court ruled otherwise, reversed the district court's injunction, and sustained the regulations. By a vote of 7 to 2, in an opinion by Justice Rehnquist, the Court held that when the rights of prisoners were balanced against the legitimate needs and purposes of the prison system, the regulations were reasonable. The rules were, said Justice Rehnquist, consistent with the status of prisoners and appropriate to the operational needs of the prison to control group meetings and organizational activity on behalf of order and security. Referring to the Court's 1974 decision in *Pell*, Justice Rehnquist emphasized that an inmate retains "those First Amendment rights that are not inconsistent with his status as a prisoner or with the legitimate penological objectives of the corrections system."[88] In a nutshell, forming and promoting an organization of prison inmates is *not* one of the First Amendment rights that prisoners retain.

The Censorship of Prison Newspapers

Although the U.S. Supreme Court has not announced an opinion addressing directly the question of content-based censorship of prisoner-published newspapers, the lower federal courts have ruled on the matter on several occasions. One of the most significant of these rulings occurred in *Pittman* v. *Hutto*, de-

---

[86]The first two questions were given a negative answer by the Court in *Pell* v. *Procunier*, 417 U.S. 817 (1974), and *Saxbe* v. *Washington Post*, 417 U.S. 843 (1974), both announced on the same day. The third question concerning the investigation of prison conditions was answered in *Houchins* v. *KQED*, 438 U.S. 1 (1978). Among other things, the Court in *Houchins* pointed to the existence of official investigatory bodies to keep a check on prison conditions, thereby dminishing the need for special access by the press.

[87]*Jones* v. *North Carolina Prisoners' Labor Union*, 433 U.S. 119 (1977). The organization was not a "labor union" in the usual sense but an association formed to urge improvements in the prison system.

[88]*Pell* v. *Procunier*, 417 U.S. 817 (1974), at 822.

cided in 1979 by the U.S. Court of Appeals for the Fourth Circuit.[89] Here an issue of the magazine *FYSK* (an acronym for "Facts You Should Know"), published by inmates of the Virginia prison system since 1973, was suppressed in late 1977 because the authorities disapproved of the contents. In response to a legal challenge mounted by the inmate editors, prison officials successfully argued that the action was taken in keeping with the legitimate need to run a prison safely. Relying upon the Supreme Court's decision in *Jones v. North Carolina Prisoners' Labor Union* to the effect that correction officials need considerable leeway in running a prison, the circuit court allowed the ban to stand.

Although the lower courts sometimes disagree about which side in a prison censorship dispute has the greater burden of proof, content-based censorship of inmate publications, while frowned upon, is permitted under the principles articulated by the Supreme Court in *Procunier, Pell,* and *Jones.* In short, if it can be shown that a specific ban is made necessary by the legitimate goals of security, good order, and rehabilitation inherent in prison life, the ban is likely to be sustained.[90]

In summary, whereas prisoners do retain some First Amendment rights, those rights may be restricted by prison authorities when it can be shown that the restrictions further an important government interest in security, order, or rehabilitation. This principle has been applied in at least four important areas. *First,* prisoner mail may not be censored under broadly sweeping regulations that sustain no legitimate government interest; however, mail censorship is permissible when it is justified by the security and rehabilitation needs of the prison. *Second,* prisoners have no constitutional right of access to the media, and the media have no special right of access to individual prisoners or to the prison itself. *Third,* prisoners have no constitutional right to organize and promote a prisoners' society, to hold meetings of a society, or to send out bulk mailings to other prisoners on behalf of a society. *Fourth,* and finally, the censorship of prison newspapers, while not applauded with any enthusiasm by the federal courts, is permitted if prison officials demonstrate that a particular ban is needed as a matter of security, good order, or rehabilitation. In a word, jailed persons have some First Amendment rights—but not many!

First Amendment Rights of the Military

In his opinion of the Court upholding the constitutionality of the U.S. Army's conviction of Captain Howard Levy for speaking against the war in Vietnam, Justice William Rehnquist observed that "the military is, by necessity, a specialized society separate from civilian society." The basic difference between military and civilian communities, he added, is that "it is the primary business of armies and navies to fight or be ready to fight wars should the occasion arise." Consequently, he continued, the rights of armed forces personnel "must perforce be conditioned to meet certain overriding demands of discipline and duty."[91]

The legal foundation for enforcing the "overriding demands of discipline and duty" in the armed forces can be found in the Uniform Code of Military Justice (UCMJ), the directives of the Department of Defense, the regulations of the branches of the service, and the specific orders of local commanders of

---

[89]*Pittman* v. *Hutto*, 594 F.2d 407 (4th Cir. 1979).

[90]See, generally, Note: "The First Amendment Rights of Prison Newspaper Editors," *Virginia Law Review* 65 (December 1979): 1485–1498.

[91]*Parker* v. *Levy*, 417 U.S. 733 (1974), at 743–744.

military bases and of various theaters of operation.[92] These, in turn, are derived from over two centuries of United States military "common law," the roots of which go back to early codes of British military discipline.[93] One result is that the guarantees of the First Amendment, which apply directly and with such great strength to civilians, are drastically diluted by the UCMJ and the directives of the Department of Defense and the subordinate units of the armed forces. For example, the Defense Department's *Guideline for Handling Dissident and Protest Activities Among Members of the Armed Forces* reads in part:

> It is the mission of the Department of Defense to safeguard the security of the United States. The service member's right of expression should be preserved to the maximum extent possible, consistent with good order and discipline and the national security. On the other hand, no Commander should be indifferent to conduct which, if allowed to proceed unchecked, would destroy the effectiveness of his unit. The proper balancing of these interests will depend largely upon the calm and prudent judgment of the responsible Commander.[94]

The inclination of the federal courts to strike the balance in favor of military regulation rather than free speech is clear. Key issues and cases since the late 1960s illustrate this procontrol point of view, especially as it affects the rights of military personnel in three areas of communication: (1) to speak words of criticism about the military or the government, (2) to collect signatures on a petition while on a military base, and (3) to distribute printed materials and hold public meetings on a military base.

Criticism of the Military or of Government Policy

In 1966, during the Vietnam War, the U.S. Army moved against Captain Howard Levy, an Army physician stationed at Fort Jackson, South Carolina, for uttering antiwar statements which, it was charged, promoted "disloyalty and disaffection among the troops" and represented "conduct unbecoming an officer and a gentleman"—both activities being proscribed by the UCMJ. Among other things, Captain Levy was charged with having said that the "United States is wrong in being involved in the Vietnam War. I would refuse to go to Vietnam if ordered to do so." Also, that "Special Forces personnel are liars and thieves and killers of peasants and murderers of women and children." Levy was convicted in a military court-martial and, when the military courts of appeal sustained the conviction, appealed to the federal courts. Although the federal district court let the conviction stand, the court of appeals reversed, finding the language of the UCMJ under which Levy was charged to be unconstitutional on grounds of *vagueness*.

The U.S. Supreme Court, by a vote of 6 to 2 (Justice Marshall did not participate in the case), reinstated the conviction, thus assuring the military authorities that great leeway would be permitted in the way the language of the UCMJ was interpreted and applied.[95] In words reminiscent of those employed by the Court in the prison cases discussed earlier, Justice Rehnquist in his majority opinion justified the reversal by saying,

[92]The Uniform Code of Military Justice can be found at 10 *U.S. Code* Secs. 933 and 934.
[93]For a brief summary of the military traditions bearing upon dissent, see *Parker v. Levy*, 417 U.S. 733 (1974), at 743–749.
[94]Department of Defense Directive No. 1325.6, adopted September 12, 1969. Cited in Comment, "Freedom of Expression in the Military: *Brown v. Glines*," *New York Law School Law Review* 26 (1981): 1152, note 125.

[95]*Parker v. Levy*, 417 U.S. 733 (1974).

among other things: "While the members of the military are not excluded from the protection granted by the First Amendment, the different character of the military community and of the military mission requires a different application of those protections. The fundamental necessity for obedience, and the consequent necessity for imposition of discipline, may render permissible within the military that which would be constitutionally impermissible outside it."

Three weeks after deciding the fate of Captain Levy, the High Court upheld the military's conviction of enlisted man Mark Avrech, who, while on active duty in Vietnam, prepared to circulate an antiwar statement that included remarks such as "What are we, cannon fodder or human beings?" and "The United States has no business over here." For his attempt Avrech was convicted under the UCMJ for promoting "disloyalty and disaffection among the troops" and was demoted in rank and ordered to forfeit three months' pay. Citing *Parker* v. *Levy* as controlling the present case, the Supreme Court let the decision of the court-martial stand.[96]

Petitioning for Redress of Grievances

While on active duty in California, Captain Albert Glines, a member of the U.S. Air Force Reserve, drafted a petition to the Secretary of Defense and to several members of Congress protesting Air Force grooming standards. Glines, who initially sought signatures from service personnel while away from the military base, gave copies of the document to a sergeant on Guam during a training mission there. The sergeant, in turn, collected several signatures without leaving the Guam installation but was soon stopped under the following regulation: "No member

of the Air Force will distribute or post any printed or written material other than publications of an official governmental agency or base regulated activity within any Air Force installation without permission of the commander or his designee." For giving the petition to the sergeant, Glines was removed from active duty, whereupon he brought suit in federal court charging that (1) the regulation was a form of prior restraint prohibited by the First Amendment and (2) the regulation as enforced was a violation of Title 10 of the *U.S. Code,* Section 1034, which guarantees the right of any person in the military to communicate with Congress "unless the communication is unlawful or violates a regulation necessary to the security of the United States." The federal district court agreed with Glines's arguments, declaring the regulations invalid on their face, and the court of appeals affirmed.

The Department of Defense then appealed to the U.S. Supreme Court, which, by a vote of 5 to 3 (Justice Marshall did not participate) and over the vigorous dissents of Justices Brennan and Stewart as well as a brief but pointed dissent by Justice Stevens, reversed the courts below.[97] In rejecting Glines's First Amendment argument, Justice Powell in his opinion of the Court cited *Parker* v. *Levy,* discussed above, to stress that the military is different from civilian society and that special controls are necessary in order to maintain the morale and discipline of the troops. For this reason, the prior-permission regulation protected an important governmental interest unrelated to the suppression of free speech and was, therefore, constitutional. Likewise, the second argument that Title 10 of the *U.S.*

---

[96]*Secretary of the Navy* v. *Avrech,* 418 U.S. 676 (1974). Note: Although *Avrech* was argued before the Supreme Court before *Levy,* *Levy* was decided first.

[97]*Brown* v. *Glines,* 444 U.S. 348 (1980). Note: Earlier, a similar result was reached by the court of appeals in *Carlson* v. *Schlesinger,* 511 F.2d 1327 (1975), denying military personnel the right to circulate a petition in a combat zone (Vietnam). Glines's petition, however, was circulated in a time of peace and on American territory.

Code, Section 1034, should be interpreted to protect not only individual letters to Congress but also group petitions was rejected by Justice Powell. Interpreting the statute narrowly, Justice Powell applied it to individual communication only. Consequently, while members of the military retained their legal right to communicate *individually* with members of Congress, they were informed in no uncertain terms that this right did not extend to group petitions circulated on military bases. Prior restraint had carried the day.[98]

Distributing Materials and Holding Meetings on a Military Base

In 1969 U.S. District Judge Donald Russell of the District of South Carolina ruled that the regulations of Fort Jackson, South Carolina—which required permission from the post commander prior to the distribution of printed materials on the post or for the conduct of public, open meetings on the post— were constitutional.[99] The issue arose over the efforts of a number of servicemen to secure permission for open meetings on the base to discuss America's involvement in Vietnam, and the denial of that permission by the post commander on the grounds of "a clear danger to military loyalty, discipline or morale" of the military personnel at Fort Jackson. (The commander's decision was not without some basis in fact, for an unofficial on-base discussion held earlier had broken up in fighting among those in attendance.) The court of appeals sustained the decision of the district court, and the U.S. Supreme Court denied review.

Nothing has occurred since *Dash* to justify any hope that the federal courts have changed their minds on the subject of on-base prior restraints. In fact, a year after denying review to the *Dash* appeal, the Supreme Court turned down an appeal from a decision of a lower court allowing a post commander to prohibit the on-base circulation of an "underground newspaper" that he determined to be a detriment to morale and discipline.[100] The subsequent decisions of the Court in *Parker* v. *Levy* (1974) and *Brown* v. *Glines* (1980), both discussed above, dramatically illustrate a trend toward tightening rather than liberalizing constraints upon freedom of expression in the military. One can reasonably conclude, therefore, that in the foreseeable future the federal courts will not intervene to expand the free-speech rights of the military personnel, whether the issue is over (1) "subversive" comments directed toward the military as in *Levy,* (2) the circulation of a petition on a military base as in *Glines,* or (3) the distribution of printed materials or the holding of public meetings on a military post without first securing permission as in *Dash.* The philosophy of the courts on the issue is well reflected by Justice Rehnquist in his majority opinion in *Levy:* "An army is not a deliberative body. It is the executive arm. Its law is that of obedience." The military, he adds, is "a society apart."[101]

First Amendment Rights in the Schools

The final institutional setting to be examined through the lens of the First Amendment is that which exists in the nation's public schools and colleges. Of necessity, the emphasis must be upon communication rights in

[98]In *Secretary of the Navy* v. *Huff,* 444 U.S. 453 (1980), decided on the same day as *Glines,* the Court applied its findings in *Glines* to *Huff* in order to uphold the right of the Navy and Marine Corps to require military personnel on overseas bases to obtain permission in advance of circulating petitions within a base.

[99]*Dash* v. *Commanding General,* 307 F. Supp. 849 (D.S.C. 1969), affirmed on appeal, 429 F.2d 427 (4th Cir. 1970), *cert. denied,* 401 U.S. 981 (1971).

[100]*Schneider* v. *Laird,* 453 F.2d 345 (10th Cir. 1972), *cert. denied,* 407 U.S. 914 (1972).

[101]*Parker* v. *Levy,* 417 U.S. 733 (1974), at 143–144; in part, quoting from *Orloff* v. *Willoughby,* 345 U.S. 83 (1953).

public institutions, for the courts have held that, in general, private schools (i.e., those not tax-supported and not publicly owned and operated) are exempt from the civil liberties requirements of state and federal constitutions.[102] The review of relevant issues and cases is organized according to four main topics: (1) the First Amendment rights of teachers, (2) the First Amendment rights of students, (3) the censorship of school library books, and (4) the student press.

The First Amendment Rights of Teachers

The U.S. Supreme Court has ruled on the First Amendment rights of teachers in two important cases, the first concerning mandatory loyalty oaths (*Keyishian* v. *Board of Regents,* 1967) and the second the right of a teacher to publicly criticize the school board (*Pickering* v. *Board of Education,* 1968). In the *Keyishian* controversy, which concerned a loyalty oath established by the state of New York, teachers were required to certify that they were not and never had been Communists, that they did not favor the overthrow of the government by unlawful means, and that they had not communicated "seditious" opinions to others either by utterance or by the distribution of printed matter. By a vote of 5 to 4, in an opinion authored by Justice Brennan, the U.S. Supreme Court declared the New York oath unconstitutional on the grounds of vagueness and overbreadth.[103] (In this regard, readers should be aware that the Supreme Court has been willing, as a rule, to let stand those types of loyalty oaths which require a simple *affirmation* of support for the

state and federal constitutions; whereas the Court has, as a rule, struck down as unconstitutional *negative* oaths—that is, disclaimers and "test" oaths—which require a person to swear that he or she is not a member of a subversive organization and does not believe in certain subversive ideas listed in the oath.[104] Obviously, the oath at bar in *Keyishian* was of the negative type disapproved by the Court.)

Furthermore, Justice Brennan announced the rejection of the position, once sanctioned by the Court,[105] that teachers and other public employees might have to surrender certain generally held constitutional rights, such as belonging to a "subversive" organization, in order to remain public employees. This was no longer true, said Justice Brennan, for case law over the years had changed the old rule to this: "Mere knowing membership without a specific intent to further the unlawful aims of an organization is not a constitutionally adequate basis for exclusion from such positions as those held by appellants."

Finally, although this decision did not establish academic freedom as a constitutional right, it came as close to accomplishing that purpose as has any Supreme Court opinion either before or since. Justice Brennan's ringing defense of intellectual freedom in the classroom remains one of the enduring components of the *Keyishian* decision.

Justice Brennan *delivered the opinion of the Court:*

> Our Nation is deeply committed to safeguarding academic freedom, which is of transcendent value to all of us and not merely to the

---

[102]See George E. Stevens, "Contract Law, State Constitutions and Freedom of Expression in Private Schools," *Journalism Quarterly* 58 (Winter 1981): 613–617 ff. For a specific case, see *Braden* v. *University of Pittsburgh,* 552 F.2d 948 (3rd Cir. 1977), including references to similar cases.

[103]*Keyishian* v. *Board of Regents,* 385 U.S. 589 (1967).

[104]For example, the simple oath of affirmation was sustained in *Knight* v. *Board of Regents,* 390 U.S. 36 (1968), whereas a complicated negative oath was struck down for vagueness in *Baggett* v. *Bullitt,* 377 U.S. 360 (1964).

[105]In *Adler* v. *Board of Education,* 342 U.S. 485 (1952).

teachers concerned. That freedom is therefore a special concern of the First Amendment, which does not tolerate laws that cast a pall of orthodoxy over the classroom. "The vigilant protection of constitutional freedoms is nowhere more vital than in the community of American schools." . . . The classroom is peculiarly the "marketplace of ideas." The Nation's future depends upon leaders trained through wide exposure to that robust exchange of ideas which discovers truth "out of a multitude of tongues, rather than through any kind of authoritative selection."

In the second Supreme Court decision concerning the free speech rights of teachers, Marvin L. Pickering, a public school instructor in Will County, Illinois, had been dismissed from his job by the board of education for writing a letter critical of board policy which was published in the letters column of a local newspaper. Among other things, charged the board, Pickering did not get his facts straight, and for this and related reasons the letter was "detrimental to the best interests of the schools."[106] The U.S. Supreme Court unanimously rejected the position of the board and, in an opinion authored by Justice Marshall, ruled in favor of the right of a teacher to participate in public debate like any other citizen, even when the issue concerns the schools in which the teacher works. Justice Marshall concluded, "We hold that, in a case such as this, absent proof of false statements knowingly or recklessly made by him, a teacher's exercise of his right to speak on issues of public importance may not furnish the basis for his dismissal from public employment."

In a broader sense, *Pickering* established the First Amendment right of all public employees to participate in public debates about public issues without being fired for that participation. However, the decision did not specifically address the question of the rights of public employees to communicate with others at work concerning on-the-job controversies. That question did reach the Supreme Court in 1983 in the case of *Connick* v. *Myers,* in which the Court reached a conclusion that contrasts sharply with that laid down in *Pickering* concerning the right of employees to participate in debates on public issues.[107] When Sheila Myers, an assistant district attorney in New Orleans, circulated a critical questionnaire concerning office grievances and morale to fifteen other assistant district attorneys of Orleans Parish, she was dismissed from her job by her superior, District Attorney Harry Connick, allegedly for causing a "mini-insurrection" within the office. Her arguments in a suit seeking reinstatement on First Amendment grounds were rejected by the U.S. Supreme Court. By a vote of 5 to 4, in an opinion by Justice White, the Court held that the issues in this case differed significantly from the public debate matter at bar in *Pickering*. The questionnaire circulated by Myers, said Justice White, concerned an "employee grievance" rather than a public issue, and the manner in which it was done might be reasonably expected to "disrupt the office," undermine the authority of the district attorney, and "destroy close working relationships." Therefore, Justice White concluded, "Myers' discharge . . . did not offend the First Amendment." Consequently, teachers in public schools and colleges can conclude that their speech concerning what the Supreme Court considers an "employee grievance" receives little, if any, constitutional protection, although teachers continue to be protected under *Pickering*

[106]*Pickering* v. *Board of Education,* 391 U.S. 563 (1968).

[107]*Connick* v. *Myers,* 51 *Law Week* 4436 (1983).

when they participate in public debate on what the Court considers to be a public issue. Or, as Justice White put it, "Our holding today is grounded in our long-standing recognition that the First Amendment's primary aim is the full protection of speech upon issues of public concern," a position that should not be confused with "the attempt to constitutionalize the employee grievance that we see presented here."

In summary, three points concerning the First Amendment rights of teachers stand out. In *Keyishian*, in addition to invalidating a complex negative loyalty oath for teachers in New York, the Supreme Court announced (1) that teachers and other public employees may not be required to forfeit their constitutional rights, such as the right of association, in order to hold public jobs, and (2) that academic freedom in the classroom is "a special concern of the First Amendment." (3) Furthermore, the Court ruled in *Pickering* (1968) that teachers in public educational institutions have the same rights as other citizens to participate in debate on public issues; however, in *Connick* (1983) the Court refused to extend constitutional protection to the speech of public employees—including teachers—that concerns "employee grievances." (For guidance on the distinction between a public issue and an employee grievance, the student of the First Amendment is referred to the wisdom of the Court in *Connick* v. *Myers*.)

The First Amendment Rights of Students

The U.S. Supreme Court has ruled on the free speech rights of students in three significant cases beginning in the late 1960s, namely, (1) an issue concerning First Amendment rights of elementary and secondary pupils (*Tinker* v. *Des Moines Independent Community School District,* 1969); (2) an issue concerning the right of college students to form an on-campus organization of which the school's administration disapproved

(*Healy* v. *James,* 1972); and (3) another concerning the right of officially registered student groups to conduct religious meetings on the campus of a state university (*Widmar* v. *Vincent,* 1981). The first and most important of the three is the case of the Tinker children in Des Moines, Iowa, whose attempt to wear black armbands to school to protest American involvement in Vietnam triggered a landmark decision extending the protection of the First Amendment to the public schools of the United States. As the summary and discussion below demonstrate, the school board's effort at censorship resulted in a dramatic ruling with profound implications not only for the schools of Des Moines, Iowa, but for public schools nationwide.

Justice Fortas in his opinion of the Court emphasized that wearing a black armband is a form of symbolic expression "within the Free Speech Clause of the First Amendment," that such symbolic expression is "closely akin to 'pure speech,' " and that neither students nor teachers "shed their constitutional rights to freedom of speech or expression at the schoolhouse gate." So long as the conduct was not disruptive of school activities and discipline and did not substantially interfere with the rights of other students—and there was no evidence that the Tinkers had done any of these things—the expression was protected. Then, in a highly significant and oft-quoted paragraph, Justice Fortas broke new constitutional ground.

Justice Fortas *delivered the opinion of the Court:*

In our system, state-operated schools may not be enclaves of totalitarianism. School officials do not possess absolute authority over their students. Students in school as well as out of school are "persons" under our Constitution. They are possessed of fundamental rights which the State must respect, just as they themselves must respect their obligations to the State. In

LANDMARK CASE
Tinker v. Des Moines Independent Community School District, 393 U.S. 503 (1969)
Decided February 24, 1969

Vote: 7 to 2 to allow the nondisruptive wearing of black armbands at school as a symbolic means of communicating an antiwar message, and at the same time extending the protection of the First Amendment to public school students.

Majority Opinion By: Justice Fortas.

Concurring Justices: Chief Justice Warren and Justices Douglas, Brennan, Stewart, White, and Marshall.

Dissenting Justices: Black and Harlan.

Justices Not Participating: (none)

Summary: In December of 1965 John and Mary Beth Tinker and their friend Christopher Eckhardt, all students in the junior and senior high schools of Des Moines, Iowa, wore black armbands to school to protest American involvement in Vietnam, an action that violated a recently adopted school board policy against such expression. For this the three were suspended, whereupon they sought relief in the federal courts. Although both the federal district court and the court of appeals ruled in favor of the school authorities and dismissed the complaint, the U.S. Supreme Court reversed the courts below and remanded the case for further hearings consistent with the First Amendment rights of students as set forth by Justice Fortas in his opinion of the Court. Among other things, Justice Fortas observed that the wearing of black armbands was a form of symbolic expression involving "direct, primary First Amendment rights akin to 'pure speech.' "

Rule Established; Significance of Case: In this landmark decision the Supreme Court held for the first time that elementary and secondary school students had basic free-speech rights while attending school and that authorities could interfere with the exercise of these rights only for good reason, such as to prevent disruption of the educational enterprise. (There was no evidence that the Tinker children or young Eckhardt had been disruptive by the quiet, unobtrusive wearing of black armbands.) As Justice Fortas said in announcing the *Tinker* rule, whereas students had First Amendment rights, "conduct by the student, in class or out of it, which for any reason—whether it stems from time, place, or type of behavior—materially disrupts classwork or involves substantial disorder or invasion of the rights of others is, of course, not immunized by the constitutional guarantee of freedom of speech."

our system, students may not be regarded as closed-circuit recipients of only that which the State chooses to communicate. They may not be confined to the expression of these sentiments that are officially approved. **In the absence of a specific showing of constitutionally valid reasons to regulate their speech, students are entitled to freedom of expression of their views.** . . .

Three years later the Supreme Court quoted from the *Tinker* landmark, as well as from *Keyishian*, to decide that the president

of Central Connecticut State College (CCSC) had violated the First Amendment rights of a student group by refusing to grant that group official recognition because he disagreed with its purposes and goals.[108] The controversy began in the fall of 1969, when several CCSC students attempted to form a local chapter of Students for a Democratic Society (SDS), a move vetoed by President James of CCSC despite a favorable recommendation by the

[108]*Healy v. James*, 408 U.S. 169 (1972).

312 · SPECIAL ISSUES

appropriate faculty committee and a public disavowal by the petitioning students of any close affiliation with the national SDS (which Dr. James had condemned as being prone to disruption and violence).

In response to a suit brought by the rejected students, the Supreme Court unanimously disagreed with the position taken by the college administration. In an opinion by Justice Powell, the Court, in effect, ruled that the SDS chapter should be officially recognized. After emphasizing that the action of the administration was a form of prior restraint upon the First Amendment rights of the students, Justice Powell stated: "The College, acting here as the instrumentality of the State, may not restrict speech or association simply because it finds the views expressed by any group to be abhorrent." As long as the student organization abides by "reasonable campus rules," does not "interrupt classes, or substantially interfere with the opportunity of other students to obtain an education," it deserves treatment equal to that given campus organizations in general.

The third decision of the U.S. Supreme Court to be considered here originated in 1977 on the campus of the University of Missouri at Kansas City, when the administration notified Cornerstone, a registered student religious organization, that it could no longer meet on the campus. The reason? On-campus meetings by religious groups, said the administration (reflecting a decision of the board of curators), violated the establishment of religion clause of the Constitution. Not so, ruled the U.S. Supreme Court, as long as a policy of *equal access* to campus facilities is applied to all registered student groups.[109]

By a vote of 8 to 1 (with only Justice White in dissent), in an opinion by Justice Powell, the Supreme Court decreed that the policy of denying equal access to campus facilities for meetings by registered student religious organizations was a content-based restriction in violation of the free speech clause of the First Amendment. As Justice Powell put it: "Here the University of Missouri has discriminated against student groups and speakers based on their desire to use a generally open forum to engage in religious worship and discussion. These are forms of speech and association protected by the First Amendment." Since an equal-access policy was not in violation of the Court's long-established three-point test for cases concerning separation of church and state,[110] it was not only permissible under the Constitution to allow the meetings but also a violation of the free speech rights of the students not to do so.

In summary, the Supreme Court in the landmark case of *Tinker* v. *Des Moines Independent Community School District* (1969) extended the protection of the First Amendment to students in the public elementary and secondary schools of the United States. However, the free-speech rights of students are conditioned on the rule that the exercise of those rights not disrupt the educational process of the institution. The *Tinker* principles were restated and reinforced in the 1972 case of *Healy* v. *James,* when the Supreme Court ruled that college student groups applying for official campus recognition cannot be denied that recognition simply because the administration disagrees with the purposes and goals of the petitioning organization. As long as the group is not disruptive of the ed-

---

[109]*Widmar* v. *Vincent,* 454 U.S. 263 (1981).

[110]The test: the government policy in question (1) must have a secular purpose, (2) its primary effect must be neither to advance nor inhibit religion, and (3) it must not promote "excessive government entanglement" with religion.

ucational mission of the school and abides by reasonable campus regulations that are applicable to all, it deserves official status under the First Amendment principles of free speech and association. Finally, in *Widmar* v. *Vincent* (1981) the Court held that registered student religious groups had a First Amendment right of equal access to campus facilities and that on-campus religious meetings by these registered organizations did not violate the establishment clause of the Constitution.

The Censorship of School Library Books

As Chapter 5 of this text explains, the federal courts have rejected as unconstitutional state laws that attempted to impose religious beliefs upon the public school science curriculum by prohibiting the teaching of the theory of evolution or by mandating the teaching of "creation science."[111] Also, as is discussed in Chapter 3, the federal courts have rejected as unconstitutional laws in both North Carolina and Mississippi that forbade Communists and other "subversives" from speaking on state college campuses.[112] However, it was not until 1982, in the case of *Island Trees Union Free School District* v. *Pico*, that the Supreme Court of the United States addressed the issue of the authority of a school board to remove from a public school library certain books of which the majority of the board disapproved.[113]

The *Island Trees* controversy began in the fall of 1975, when the local board of education, responding to a demand from a coalition of conservative parents, removed nine "objectionable" books from the high school and junior high school libraries. The nine titles, which the board later characterized as "anti-American, anti-Christian, anti-Semitic, and just plain filthy," are as follows: *Slaughterhouse-Five*, by Kurt Vonnegut; *The Naked Ape*, by Desmond Morris; *Down These Mean Streets*, by Piri Thomas; *Best Short Stories by Negro Writers*, edited by Langston Hughes; *Go Ask Alice* and *A Hero Ain't Nothin' But a Sandwich*, by Alice Childress; *Soul on Ice*, by Eldridge Cleaver; *A Reader for Writers*, edited by Jerome Archer; and *The Fixer*, by Bernard Malamud. In response, Island Trees High School student Steven Pico and four other students sued to have the books returned to the shelves, claiming that by removing them the board had violated the students' First Amendment rights. By a vote of 5 to 4, a sharply divided Supreme Court returned the case to the district court for further trial proceedings to determine the underlying motives of the school board in removing the books— an action regarded by the counsel of the Association of American Publishers Freedom to Read Committee as a "significant victory for the proponents of a vigorous First Amendment and of the freedom to read."[114]

In analyzing this decision, students of the First Amendment need to be aware that it was *not* about the school curriculum, textbook selection, required readings in the classroom, or library acquisitions; rather, it focused narrowly upon the removal of books *once they had been purchased and placed in circulation*. The basic assumption of the majority

---

[111]The antievolution law of Arkansas was declared unconstitutional in *Epperson* v. *Arkansas*, 393 U.S. 97 (1968); a later attempt to compel the teaching of the biblical account of creation in the public school science classes of Arkansas was ruled unconstitutional by the U.S. District Court for the Eastern District of Arkansas in *McLean* v. *Arkansas Board of Education*, 50 *Law Week* 2412 (1982).

[112]The North Carolina decision is *Dickson* v. *Sitterson*, 280 F. Supp. 486 (M.D.N.C. 1968); the Mississippi case is *Stacy* v. *Williams*, 306 F. Supp. 963 (N.D. Miss. 1969).

[113]*Island Trees Union Free School District* v. *Pico*, 457 U.S. 853 (1982). Note: The case is sometimes listed simply as *Island Trees* v. *Pico*.

[114]R. Bruce Rich, "The Supreme Court's Decision in *Island Trees*," *Newsletter on Intellectual Freedom*, September 1982, pp. 149 ff.

FIGURE 8.4.   STEVEN PICO AND
MEMBERS OF THE ISLAND TREES
SCHOOL BOARD ON THE STEPS OF THE
U.S. SUPREME COURT BUILDING.
Steven Pico, in the foreground, and the members
of the Island Trees School Board, of New York's
Island Trees Union Free School District No. 26,
stand on the steps of the U.S. Supreme Court
building on March 2, 1982, the day of oral
arguments in the public school library censorship
case of Island Trees v. Pico (1982). The case
began in 1975 when five public school students,
including Pico, challenged the right of the school
board to remove books from school library shelves
on the grounds that the books were "anti-
American, anti-Christian, anti-Semitic, and just
plain filthy."
Newsday.

of Supreme Court justices seems to be that the First Amendment places restrictions upon the discretion of a school board to remove books from the shelves of a school library; therefore, the reasons for the removal of any book must be made clear before the constitutionality of the action can be ascertained. Because the Island Trees School Board had never adequately explained why it removed the books, the U.S. Supreme Court returned the case to the trial court to give the board an opportunity to justify its decision. Faced with the prospect of having to prove that its book banning was for reasons which met the standards of the federal Constitution, the board opted instead to return all nine works to the shelves.[115] Although there are many unanswered questions in the Supreme Court's

narrow ruling (e.g., exactly what First Amendment standards must be met before a school board can remove books from the library?), the decision does appear to have cooled the fervor of would-be censors on the various school boards of the nation who must now prove in open court that their reasons for censoring a library book are constitutional.

The Student Press

First Amendment activism by student editors and journalists came of age in America during the 1960s, that remarkable "decade of dissent" which led to the establishment of so many legal precedents favorable to the liberties of speech and the press. The principles enunciated by Justice Fortas in his opinion of the Court in the *Tinker* decision of 1969 typify the extent of the Court's acceptance of the right of students to express themselves: "First

[115]Reported in the *Newsletter on Intellectual Freedom*, March 1983, p. 36.

Amendment rights, applied in light of the special characteristics of the school environment, are available to teachers and students. It can hardly be argued that either students or teachers shed their constitutional rights to freedom of speech or expression at the schoolhouse gate."[116] Thus encouraged, student editors increasingly went to court to fight for their First Amendment rights rather than submit to arbitrary administrative censorship. Consequently, students have won a considerable degree of constitutional protection for their on-campus journalistic enterprises, as summarized in the three points below.

First, the courts have held that although a school is not required to publish a student newspaper, once a newspaper (or similar publication, such as a literary magazine) is established, it is protected by the Constitution and cannot be arbitrarily censored, shut down, or its student editors dismissed. In other words, administrative controls must be exercised according to First Amendment standards.[117]

Second, even independent publications such as "underground" newspapers edited and printed by students off campus and distributed on campus are protected by the First Amendment. In an important case, Barbara Papish, a graduate student at the University of Missouri and editor of the independent newspaper *Free Press,* was expelled from school because of administrative disapproval of the contents of her paper (among other things, she was accused of publishing "indecency" because of a political cartoon showing a police officer raping the Statue of Liberty). Papish won her case before the U.S. Su-

preme Court, which ordered her reinstated after finding that the cartoon was not legally obscene and that the *Free Press* did not disrupt the educational mission of the university.[118]

Third, because the U.S. Supreme Court has never ruled on the issue of the extent of First Amendment protection for school-sponsored publications (the *Papish* case discussed above concerned an independent, off-campus paper), the degree of constitutional protection for student publications depends upon the rulings of the federal circuit court of appeals which has jurisdiction over the state in which the material is published. Only in the First Circuit (encompassing Maine, Massachusetts, New Hampshire, Rhode Island, and Puerto Rico) and the Seventh Circuit (encompassing Illinois, Indiana, and Wisconsin) have *full First Amendment rights* been granted to the student press. In all other circuits, administrators and faculty supervisors have more control over what does into publication than is permitted in the First and Seventh Circuits.

Yet, even in those states where the judges have been unwilling to extend full First Amendment rights to the student press, certain procedural safeguards have been formulated to protect students from arbitrary censorship or punishment. In an analysis published in *The High School Journal* in 1983, Harvard doctoral candidate Deni Elliott studied leading student press decisions of the various circuits to determine what procedural regulations had been put in place.[119] The result is a list of five standards that, when viewed as a group, provide a useful guide for

[116]*Tinker* v. *Des Moines Independent Community School District,* 393 U.S. 503 (1969), at 506.
[117]For example, see *Joyner* v. *Whiting,* 477 F.2d 456 (4th Cir. 1973), and *Schiff* v. *Williams,* 519 F.2d 257 (5th Cir. 1975).

[118]*Papish* v. *University of Missouri Curators,* 410 U.S. 667 (1973); for a case with a similar result at the high school level, see *Fujishima* v. *Board of Education,* 460 F.2d 1355 (1972).
[119]Deni Elliott, "Student Press Rights and Tort Liability: A Conflict," *The High School Journal* 66 (April–May 1983): 207–214.

both students and administrators who wish to devise a set of campus regulations providing for prior review of the contents of student publications. A system of prior review, based upon decisions of various federal circuit courts of appeal, requires the school to specify *in advance* (1) the manner of submission of materials for review, (2) exactly who is to receive and review the materials, (3) a definite short time period for consideration of the submission, (4) the procedure for a student appeal, and (5) in *specific* terms, what is not allowed for publication (the most difficult of the five standards to meet).[120]

Briefly put, both on-campus "official" student publications and off-campus independent student publications are protected by the Constitution. However, because the Supreme Court has never issued a determinative ruling on the extent of First Amendment protection for school-sponsored newspapers, the degree of free speech enjoyed by student editors and journalists depends upon the decisions of the federal circuit court of appeals (and in some instances, the appropriate district court) which has jurisdiction over the locale where the paper is published. Whereas the First and Seventh Circuits have extended full First Amendment rights to the student press, the other circuits have not, having opted for a greater degree of administrative control over the student press than is permitted in the First and Seventh Circuits. The advice of a good attorney is helpful in determining exactly what standards apply in a given locale.[121]

[120]Ibid., p. 210. Note: All five standards are not required in all circuits, although it is safe to assume that most do apply. Those who anticipate a campus censorship problem would do well to secure competent legal advice concerning the federal standards in effect in the circuit where the paper is published.

[121]For an excellent overview of the area, including summaries of a variety of lower-court decisions, consult Wayne Overbeck and Rick D. Pullen, *Major Principles of Media Law* (New York: Holt, 1982), chapter 14, "Freedom of the Student Press."

Institutional Constraints in Brief

The survey just completed covers constraints placed upon freedom of expression in three institutions: the prisons, the military, and the schools. In the *first* group, prisoners do retain some First Amendment rights, but not many, since the courts generally defer to the claims of prison officials for constraints upon expression that are perceived as essential to the security, disciplinary, and rehabilitation needs of the institution. Four areas of control are basic: (1) prisoner mail, while not subject to arbitrary censorship, may be censored for reasons of security and rehabilitation; (2) prisoners have no constitutional right of direct access to the media, and reporters have no constitutional right of access to prisons (other than that available to the general public); (3) prisoners have no First Amendment right of association to form and promote organizations or to hold organizational meetings; and (4) the censorship of prison newspapers is permitted in those instances where the authorities demonstrate a threat to the security and good order of the institution.

In the *second* group, the military, freedom of expression is subject to constraints which military commanders and the courts believe are necessary to permit the armed forces to accomplish their assigned task, namely, to fight the nation's wars. Consequently, the courts have described the military as a "society apart," and have ruled that those in the armed forces do *not* have a First Amendment right (a) to speak subversively so as to threaten military discipline and morale (*Parker* v. *Levy,* 1974), (b) to circulate petitions on a military base without first securing permission from the post commander (*Brown* v. *Glines,* 1980), or (c) to distribute printed materials or hold public meetings on a military base without permission (*Dash* v. *Commanding General,* 1971).

In the *third* group, comprising public educational institutions, both faculty and students retain their First Amendment rights while at school. (1) On campus, teachers have a right to teach their subject and students have a right to express themselves in ways that do not disrupt the educational process (as announced in the landmark case of *Tinker* v. *Des Moines Independent Community School District,* 1969). (2) Teachers have a right to participate in debate on public issues without being dismissed from their jobs, even when the subject of that debate is a matter of school board policy; however, expression concerning on-the-job "employee grievances" does not enjoy the protection of the Constitution. (3) A college administration cannot deny official recognition to a student group simply because it disapproves of that group's purposes and goals. (4) Also, a registered student group may hold meetings for religious purposes on the campus of a state college without violating the constitutional principle of separation of church and state. (5) School boards may not exercise arbitrary censorship over the holdings of a school library but must give constitutionally sound reasons for the removal of any book that is already on the shelves. Finally, (6) the degree of First Amendment protection for student newspapers depends upon the decisions of the particular federal circuit court of appeals which has jurisdiction in the case. Whereas the First and Seventh Circuits have given full First Amendment rights to school-sponsored publications, the other federal circuits have not. Specific standards for a given circuit can be discovered by consulting a good attorney.

CONCLUSION

In the 1939 landmark decision of *Hague* v. *CIO,* the U.S. Supreme Court announced that public streets, sidewalks, parks, and similar public places must be open for purposes of communication. The use of these public places may be regulated by reasonable and nondiscretionary rules of time, place, and manner; however, such areas may not be absolutely closed to would-be communicators. Permissible rules include nondiscriminatory issuance of parade permits and even the charging of reasonable cleanup fees for large public marches and demonstrations. Certain areas, such as passenger terminals or open spaces near where a legislative body meets, are more appropriate for use for speech purposes than are other places, such as courthouses (especially during a trial), jailhouse grounds, and the property of a military base. The guiding philosophy developed by the Supreme Court over the years was well put by Justice Marshall in the 1972 case of *Grayned* v. *Rockford: "The crucial question is whether the manner of expression is basically incompatible with the normal activity of a particular place at a particular time."*

When the property in question is *private* rather than public, the rights of would-be communicators to use that property for speech purposes is greatly narrowed. The Court has ruled that privately owned shopping centers and malls are not required to be open for purposes of public communication under the federal Constitution, although they may be opened under state law without necessarily violating the rights of the owners. Private apartment houses and apartment complexes may be closed completely to solicitation of all types; however, regular residential areas are more readily accessible as a general rule, especially for noncommercial solicitation. Finally, one's private letter box is not an extension of the public forum and may not be used for the deposit of unstamped messages.

In addition to the general principles concerning expression on public and private property, as enumerated above, two special issues are surveyed: "speech plus" and its application to symbolic expression and labor picketing; and communication by litigation and by economic boycott. *First,* the Supreme Court has formulated a distinction between "pure speech" and "speech plus," which is sometimes described as the speech–action dichotomy, extending more First Amendment protection to expression classified as "pure speech" than to speech conjoined with action (i.e., "speech plus"). The rule is that the more "plus" (action, or conduct) present in the expression, the less First Amendment protection the expression is likely to receive. (a) Whereas the courts have recognized that symbolic expression is a form of speech protected by the Constitution, symbolic speech is generally seen as a form of "speech plus" deserving of less protection than is given to "pure speech." In this regard, symbolic expression that involves desecration or destruction of the flag is not protected by the Constitution, although the wearing of a military uniform by an actor in a theatrical production is a form of protected expression. Also, hair length and style of dress as forms of symbolic expression have never been given the protection of the First Amendment by the U.S. Supreme Court, although some lower courts have done so. (b) Labor picketing receives some First Amendment protection and may not be absolutely prohibited. However, such picketing is considered a form of "speech plus" by the courts, which permit its strict regulation under special rules and statutes, such as the National Labor Relations Act. *Second,* in *NAACP* v. *Button* (1963), the Supreme Court determined that in certain circumstances court action, including the solicitation of clients, was a form of expression protected by the Constitution; likewise, in *NAACP* v. *Claiborne Hardware* (1982), the Court held that an economic boycott carried out as a form of political protest was expression deserving of the constitutional shield.

Finally, the survey in this chapter includes constraints upon freedom of expression in three institutions: the prisons, the military, and the schools. To begin with, *prisoners* do have some First Amendment rights; however, those rights must yield to the security, disciplinary, and rehabilitation requirements of the prison. Consequently, prisoners' mail may not be arbitrarily censored, but it may be censored for reasons of security or rehabilitation. Furthermore, prisoners do not have a constitutional right of access to the media, and reporters do not have a special right of access to prisons. Prisoners do not have a right to form organizations and hold meetings, and prison newspapers may be censored in specific instances where it can be shown that the censorship is justified by the demands of prison life (i.e., for reasons of security, good order, and rehabilitation).

The free speech rights of those in the *military* must yield to the mission of the armed forces, which is to obey orders and, when necessary, to fight the nation's wars. Although military personnel do have First Amendment rights that protect them against arbitrary censorship, those rights do *not* include (1) freedom of speech to criticize military or government policy so as to undermind the morale of the troops, (2) freedom to circulate petitions on a military base except with prior consent from the commander, or (3) the freedom to distribute printed materials or hold public meetings on a military base except by permission of the commander.

Finally, both *faculty and students* in public schools and colleges retain First Amendment rights while on the campus. As the Supreme Court said in the 1969 landmark case of *Tinker* v. *Des Moines Independent Community School District,* "It can hardly be argued that either students or teachers shed their constitutional rights to freedom of speech or expression at the schoolhouse gate." The basic guideline to emerge from *Tinker* is that the exercise of First Amendment rights by students while in school must not be disruptive of the educational process. In subsequent decisions the Supreme Court has ruled that teachers may participate in public debate on public issues—including decisions of the school board—without being disciplined by the board for making statements of which board members disapprove. However, this protection does not extend to speech concerning on-the-job "employee grievances." Also, a college administration may not deny official recognition to a student organization simply because the administration disagrees with the purposes and goals of the petitioning group; registered student groups may hold meetings for religious purposes on state college campuses without violating the establishment clause of the First Amendment; and school boards must give constitutionally sound reasons before removing books from the shelves of a school library. Finally, because the Supreme Court has not decided the matter for the nation at large, the degree of First Amendment protection enjoyed by student editors and journalists of school-sponsored publications varies from locale to locale, depending upon the decisions of the lower federal courts which have jurisdiction over a given state.

EXERCISES

A. Classroom projects and activities.
   1. Here are three questions phrased for classroom debate:
      a. Resolved, that privately owned shopping centers and malls should be "opened up" for the exercise of First Amendment rights.
      b. Resolved, that flag desecration statutes should be declared unconstitutional.
      c. Resolved, that school-sponsored newspapers in public secondary schools and colleges should have the same First Amendment rights as does the nation's press at large.
   2. Here are the same three questions phrased for class discussion:
      a. Should privately owned shopping centers and malls be required to provide access for the exercise of communication rights? If so, what regulations should be enforced to prevent communicators from interfering with the business of the shopping center?
      b. Should mutilating or burning an American flag as an act of symbolic protest be protected by the First Amendment?
      c. Should school-sponsored newspapers (and other publications) in public schools and colleges be as fully protected by the First Amendment as is the nation's commercial press? (If not, what regulations should be announced in advance to students and faculty who work on sponsored publications?)
   3. Locate and make copies of the laws of your state and city that set forth regulations of time, place, and manner concerning parades, demonstrations, marches, and so on as well as solicitation in residential areas. Pay particular attention to permit requirements. Distribute copies of the laws to the class and discuss. What changes, if any, does the class think should be made in the laws?
   4. Locate the flag desecration statute or statutes of your state, make copies, and distribute to the class for discussion. What changes, if any, does the class think should be made in the laws concerning the flag?
   5. Divide the class into as many subcommittees as necessary to check on the rules of the various large shopping centers and malls in your community concerning the use of the property for communication

purposes. Secure copies of the rules in print and make copies for the class. Discuss the results. If time permits, invite a manager of a shopping center to visit the class to explain the rules and justify them.

6. Make copies of the "1940 Statement of Principles on Academic Freedom and Tenure" of the American Association of University Professors (AAUP) and distribute to the class for study and discussion. The statement should be available from the officers of the local chapter of the AAUP, or it can be found on pages 33–39 of the *Handbook* of the AAUP, edited by Louis Joughin (see the reading list at the end of this chapter). Invite an active member of the AAUP on your campus to visit the class to explain the association's position concerning freedom of speech for both faculty and students in institutions of higher learning.

7. If your school is located near a unit of the state prison system, invite the director of the unit (or a staff member designated by the director) to visit the class to explain the prison's regulations concerning the communication rights of prisoners. Ask the speaker to bring a copy of the official rules governing mail controls, prisoner meetings, the publication of newspapers by prisoners, and so on.

8. Should students in the public schools who consider their hairstyles and mode of dress to be forms of symbolic expression be permitted to dress as they please or wear hairstyles of their own choosing while attending classes? Where would you draw the line? Discuss.

9. Discuss the following quotation from the dissent of Justice Brennan in the military free-speech case of *Brown* v. *Glines*, 444 U.S. 348 (1980), where the U.S. Supreme Court upheld the authority of the military to prohibit the circulation of peti-

tions on a military base. Justice Brennan argued that ". . . the Court has been deluded into unquestioning acceptance of the very flawed assumption that discipline and morale are enhanced by restricting peaceful communication of various viewpoints. Properly regulated as to time, place, and manner, petitioning provides a useful outlet for airing complaints and opinions that are held as strongly by citizens in uniform as by the rest of society. The forced absence of peaceful expression only creates the illusion of good order; underlying dissension remains to flow into the more dangerous channels of incitement and disobedience. In that sense, military efficiency is only disserved when First Amendment rights are devalued."

10. Discuss the following statement from the dissent of Justice Brennan (joined by Justices Marshall, Blackmun, and Stevens) in *Connick* v. *Myers,* 51 *Law Week* 4436 (1983), in which the Supreme Court ruled that on-the-job grievances of public employees did not represent speech protected by the First Amendment. Justice Brennan wrote: "The Court's decision today [permitting Myers to be fired] inevitably will deter public employees from making critical statements about the manner in which government agencies are operated for fear that doing so will provoke their dismissal. As a result, the public will be deprived of valuable information with which to evaluate the performance of elected officials. Because protecting the dissemination of such information is an essential function of the First Amendment, I dissent."

11. Under what circumstances, if any, and according to what standards, should a school board be permitted to remove books or other materials from the shelves of a public school library? (Be sure to review the case of *Island Trees* v. *Pico,* 50

Law Week 4831, 1982, in reference to this question.)

B. Topics for research papers or oral reports.

1. Justice Hugo Black and the Issues of Time, Place, and Manner.

2. Mayor Frank "I Am the Law" Hague and Political Dissent in Jersey City, New Jersey.

3. An Analysis of the Strengths and Weaknesses of the Supreme Court's "Speech Plus" Doctrine.

4. The Case for Greater Freedom for Labor Picketing Under the First Amendment (or, a Defense of Current Law Constraining Labor Picketing).

5. Expression in Privately Owned Shopping Centers: A Proposal for Accommodation with the First Amendment.

6. An Analysis of Problems in the Development of a Comprehensive Theory of Constitutional Protection for Symbolic Expression.

7. The Case Against Flag Desecration Laws (or a Defense of Those Laws).

8. An In-Depth Study of the Attempt by Nazis to Demonstrate in Skokie, Illinois, in the Late 1970s.

9. An In-Depth Study of Problems of Free Speech in the Prison Environment.

10. Free Speech in the Military: The Case for Greater Liberty (or a Defense of Current Constraints).

11. A Short History of Academic Freedom in the United States.

12. Academic Freedom *Should* Be a Constitutional Right: An Argument.

13. Current Trends in the Censorship of Books and Other Materials in the Nation's Public Schools.

14. The American Library Association: Defender of the Right to Read.

15. An Examination of Arguments *in Favor* of the Censorship of Texts and Library Books in the Nation's Public Schools.

16. The Great Loyalty-Oath Binge in America Following World War II.

17. Free Speech in the Public Forum During the 1960s: A Survey of the Warren Court on Issues of Time, Place, and Manner.

18. Free Speech in the Public Forum During the 1970s: A Survey of the Burger Court on Issues of Time, Place, and Manner (if space permits, you might wish to include the 1980s as well).

19. Freedom of Speech in the Workplace After *Connick* v. *Myers* (1983): A Survey of the Literature on an Important Case.

20. Academic Freedom in Nazi Germany (or in the Soviet Union or some other repressive society, past or present).

SELECTED READINGS

Readings Concerning Time, Place, and Manner

Barron, Jerome A., and Dienes, C. Thomas. *Handbook of Free Speech and Free Press*. Boston: Little, Brown, 1979. (Especially chapters 3 and 5.)

Bosmajian, Haig A., comp. *Dissent: Symbolic Behavior and Rhetorical Strategies*. Boston: Allyn and Bacon, 1972.

Comment. "Flag Desecration: A Case Study of the Roles of Categorizing and Balancing in First Amendment Analysis." *Harvard Law Review* 88 (1975): 1482–1508.

Comment. "*Hudgens* v. *NLRB,* A Final Definition of the Public Forum?" *Wake Forest Law Review* 13 (1977): 139 ff.

Comment. "Picketers at the Doorstep." *Harvard Civil Rights–Civil Liberties Law Review* 9 (January 1974): 95–123.

Dorsen, Norman, and Gora, Joel. "Free Speech, Property, and the Burger Court: Old Values, New Balances." In *The Supreme Court Review: 1982*, pp. 195–241. Edited by Philip B. Kurland, Gerhard Casper, and Dennis J. Hutchinson. Chicago: University of Chicago Press, 1982.

Haiman, Franklyn S. "Nazis in Skokie: Anatomy of the Heckler's Veto." In *Free Speech Yearbook: 1978*, pp. 11–16. Edited by Gregg Phifer. Falls Church, Va.: Speech Communication Association, 1978.

Haiman, Franklyn S. "Nonverbal Communication and the First Amendment: The Rhetoric of the Streets Revisited." *Quarterly Journal of Speech* 68 (November 1982): 371–383.

Haiman, Franklyn S. "The Rhetoric of the Streets: Some Legal and Ethical Considerations." *Quarterly Journal of Speech* 53 (April 1967): 99–114.

Haiman, Franklyn S. *Speech and Law in a Free Society*. Chicago: University of Chicago Press, 1981. (Especially chapters 2, 5, and 7.)

Hamlin, David. *The Nazi–Skokie Conflict: A Civil Liberties Battle*. Boston: Beacon Press, 1980.

Kalven, Harry, Jr. "The Concept of the Public Forum: *Cox* v. *Louisiana*." In *The Supreme Court Review: 1965*, pp. 1–32. Edited by Philip B. Kurland. Chicago: University of Chicago Press, 1965.

Mack, C. L., and Lieberwitz, R. L. "Secondary Consumer Picketing: The First Amendment Questions Remain." *Mercer Law Review* 32 (Spring 1981): 815–831.

Neier, Aryeh. *Defending My Enemy: American Nazis, the Skokie Case, and the Risks of Freedom*. New York: Dutton, 1979.

Nimmer, Melville B. "The Meaning of Symbolic Speech Under the First Amendment." *UCLA Law Review* 21 (October 1973): 29–62.

Note. "Constitutional Law—*State* v. *Felmet*: The Extent of Free Speech Rights on Private Property Under the North Carolina Constitution." *North Carolina Law Review* 61 (October 1982): 157–166.

Note. "The Invisible Hand and the Clenched Fist: Is There a Safe Way to Picket Under the First Amendment?" *Hastings Law Journal* 26 (September 1974): 167–189.

Note. "*Lloyd Corp.* v. *Tanner*: The Demise of *Logan Valley* and the Disguise of *Marsh*." *Georgia Law Journal* 61 (1973): 1187 ff.

Note. "Peaceful Labor Picketing and the First Amendment." *Columbia Law Review* 82 (November 1982): 1469–1497.

Note. "Private Abridgement of Speech and the State Constitutions." *Yale Law Journal* 90 (1980): 165 ff.

Note. "Symbolic Conduct." *Columbia Law Review* 68 (1968): 1091 ff.

Pollitt, Daniel H. "Haircuts and School Expulsions." In *Free Speech Yearbook: 1970*, pp. 82–94. Edited by Thomas L. Tedford. New York: Speech Communication Association, 1970.

Pope, James G. "Free Speech Rights of Union Officials Under the Labor–Management Reporting and Disclosure Act." *Harvard Civil Rights–Civil Liberties Law Review* 18 (Summer 1983): 525–584.

Rabinowitz, Mark. "Nazis in Skokie: Fighting Words or Heckler's Veto?" *DePaul Law Review* 28 (1979): 259–287.

Spelfogel, E. J. "Private Property Picketing." *Labor Law Journal* 33 (October 1982): 659–667.

Stone, Geoffrey R. "Fora Americana: Speech in Public Places." In *The Supreme Court Review: 1974*, pp. 233–280. Edited by Philip B. Kurland. Chicago: University of Chicago Press, 1975.

Institutional Constraints: Prisons, Military, and Schools

Comment. "The Constitutional Rights of Students at Center Stage: Freedom of Speech in School-Sponsored Plays." *Buffalo Law Review* 31 (Spring 1982): 547 ff.

Comment. "Freedom of Expression in the Military: *Brown* v. *Glines*." *New York Law School Law Review* 26 (1981): 1135–1154.

Comment. "Freedom of Speech and Assembly—Prisoners' Rights." *New York Law School Law Review* 24 (1978): 290–301.

Comment. "Free Speech and the Armed Forces: The Case Against Judicial Deference." *New York University Law Review* 53 (November 1978): 1102–1123.

Comment. "Student First Amendment Rights in the Public School Setting: A Topic of Increased Litigation." *American Journal of Trial Advocacy* 6 (Summer 1982): 163–182.

Comment. "What Are the Limits to a School Board's Authority to Remove Books from School Library Shelves? *Pico* v. *Board of Education, Island Trees Union Free School District No.*

26." *Wisconsin Law Review* 1982 (1982): 417–471.

Day, Louis A. "The High School Press and the First Amendment: A Summary of Principles." In *Free Speech Yearbook: 1978*, pp. 92–97. Edited by Gregg Phifer. Falls Church, Va.: Speech Communication Association, 1978.

Elliott, Deni. "Student Press Rights and Tort Liability: A Conflict." *The High School Journal* 66 (April–May 1983): 207–214.

Jenkinson, Edward B. *Censors in the Classroom: The Mind Benders*. Carbondale, Ill.: Southern Illinois University Press, 1979.

Joughin, Louis, ed. *Academic Freedom and Tenure: A Handbook of the American Association of University Professors*. Madison, Wis.: University of Wisconsin Press, 1967.

Leverson, Leonard G. "Constitutional Limits on the Power to Restrict Access to Prisons: An Historical Re-Examination." *Harvard Civil Rights–Civil Liberties Law Review* 18 (Summer 1983): 409–455.

Levine, Alan H., and Cary, Eve. *The Rights of Students*. Rev. ed. New York: Avon Books, 1977. (An ACLU Handbook.)

Metzger, Walter P. *The Constitutional Status of Academic Freedom*. New York: Arno Press, 1977.

Note. "First Amendment Interest, Balancing—Behind Bars?" *University of Miami Law Review* 33 (March 1979): 680–691.

Note. "First Amendment Mailing Rights of Parolees and Prison Inmates: A Higher Standard of Judicial Protection." *University of San Francisco Law Review* 13 (Summer 1979): 913–944.

Note. "First Amendment Rights of Prison Newspaper Editors." *Virginia Law Review* 65 (December 1979): 1485–1498.

Note. "Review of Prisoners' Rights Under the First, Fifth, and Eighth Amendments." *Duquesne Law Review* 18 (Spring 1980): 683–704.

Oboler, Eli M., ed. *Censorship and Education*. New York: H. W. Wilson, 1982.

Oboler, Eli M. *Defending Intellectual Freedom: The Library and the Censor*. Westport, Conn.: Greenwood Press, 1980.

O'Neil, Robert M. *Classrooms in the Crossfire: The Rights and Interests of Students, Parents, Teachers, Administrators, Librarians and the Community*. Bloomington, Ind.: Indiana University Press, 1981.

Overbeck, Wayne, and Pullen, Rick D. *Major Principles of Media Law*. New York: Holt, 1982. (Especially chapter 14, "Freedom of the Student Press.")

Rivkin, Robert S., and Stichman, Barton F. *The Rights of Military Personnel*. Rev. ed. New York: Avon Books, 1977. (An ACLU Handbook.)

Rubin, David. *The Rights of Teachers*. New York: Avon Books, 1968. (An ACLU Handbook.)

Rudovsky, David, et al. *The Rights of Prisoners*. Rev. ed. New York: Bantam Books, 1983. (An ACLU Handbook.)

Stevens, George E. "Contract Law, State Constitutions and Freedom of Expression in Private Schools." *Journalism Quarterly* 58 (Winter 1981): 613–617 ff.

CHAPTER 9

TWO INTERLOCKING TOPICS: PRIOR RESTRAINT AND FREE PRESS–FAIR TRIAL

"The exceptional nature of its limitations places in a strong light the general conception that liberty of the press, historically considered and taken up by the Federal Constitution, has meant, principally, although not exclusively, immunity from previous restraints or censorship."

—*Chief Justice Charles Evans Hughes in* Near v. Minnesota *(1931)*

On Friday, January 14, 1983, U.S. District Judge Adrian Duplantier of New Orleans issued a prior restraint order against the CBS program *60 Minutes* prohibiting the airing of a story entitled "Who Killed Officer Neupert?" planned for Sunday evening, January 16, 1983. He took this step after CBS refused to comply with an earlier order that a copy of the script be submitted for review. Why did Judge Duplantier take such drastic action? Because attorneys for seven New Orleans police officers, whose upcoming trial on charges of violating the civil rights of several blacks during their investigation of Neupert's death, persuaded him that the *60 Minutes* report would prejudice the public against the officers, thus making it difficult to get a fair-minded jury. Throughout the weekend of January 15 and 16, 1983, the nation's journalists alerted their hearers, viewers, and readers to the censorship effort with broadcast accounts and newspaper stories bearing headlines such as "JUDGE BLOCKS '60 MINUTES' REPORT."[1]

CBS immediately appealed the decision of Judge Duplantier, and in a rapid series of legal actions on Saturday and Sunday, the U.S. Court of Appeals for the Fifth Circuit overturned all of Duplantier's prior restraint or-

[1]*Greensboro Daily News,* January 15, 1983, p. A-2.

ders. When no justice of the U.S. Supreme Court would intervene to change the decision of the Circuit Court, attorneys for the officers gave up. On Sunday evening, January 16, 1983, "Who Killed Officer Neupert?" was broadcast on *60 Minutes* as originally scheduled.

Although this attempt at prior restraint was settled with a victory for freedom of the press, the controversy it evoked illustrates well the tension existing between two rights that are both guaranteed by the Constitution, namely, the right of public communicators to report the news (including that which concerns impending trials) and the right of an accused person or persons to a fair trial (including the empaneling of an impartial jury). In short, the *60 Minutes* issue of mid-January 1983 illustrates both of the main topics that are the focus of this chapter: prior restraint and free press-fair trial. In order to cover the two areas—and in the process illuminate the legal precedents which guided the court of appeals in its decision to overturn Judge Duplantier's prior restraint orders in the *60 Minutes* case discussed above—the chapter is divided into two main parts: *first,* issues and cases concerning prior restraint and, *second,* issues and cases of free press versus fair trial.

I. PRIOR RESTRAINT

Early in 1950, film censor Lloyd Binford of Memphis, Tennessee, following his standard procedure of previewing each film that was to be shown publicly within the city limits, declared that the 1934 production *Imitation of Life,* starring Fredi Washington and Louise Beavers, could not be shown in Memphis. (The film concerns the decision of a young woman to pass across the color line from black to white.) When asked his reason for prohibiting the showing of the film, censor

Binford replied that it was because the film represented "the worst case of racial equality" he had ever seen![2] Similar examples of the prior restraint of films have arisen in the country for half a century, for the Supreme Court has permitted film censorship boards to function (to protect the "public morality") almost since the beginning of the commercial film industry.

The practice of prior restraint of communication predates the invention of motion pictures, of course, going back at least to the licensing system established in England in the early part of the sixteenth century (see Chapter 1). So distasteful was the licensing process to believers in freedom of expression that any form of it, even today, evokes feelings of distrust on the part of many citizens, legislators, and jurists in both England and the United States. In addition, the subjects of prior restraint activity go beyond the concerns of film review boards (which usually focused upon the sexual, although matters of sacrilege as well as racial matters were included at times) to topics of national security, defamation of public officials, and fair trial for one accused of a crime. At least two recent developments have given fresh life to prior restraint activity in the United States: first, the development of weapons of mass destruction and attempts by some persons to publish allegedly secret information about those weapons and, second, decisions by trial judges to try to "gag" the press so that a fair trial for the defendant will be protected from prejudicial publicity. In order to examine the prior restraint issue in an organized way, the discussion to follow is organized around five key topics: (1) basic issues growing out of the 1931 landmark case of *Near* v. *Minnesota,* (2) film review boards, (3) national security, (4) the duty to obey prior restraint statutes and court orders, and (5) a preview of the question of judge-issued "gag orders" (a transition to the next unit).

While studying the issues and cases of prior restraint cited below, the student of public communication should keep in mind that prior restraint illustrates the principle of *gatekeeping* in its most pristine form. The concept of gatekeeping is explained by B. Aubrey Fisher, professor of communications, as follows: "Like a gate on the channel, the intermediary gatekeeper allows some messages to get through and bars others."[3] In the arena of First Amendment law, the gatekeeping process is at work in prior restraint cases because certain opinions are prevented from reaching certain audiences by means of statutory constraints or court orders (i.e., government controls) applied to the channel by which the message is to be communicated. Readers should look for these channel controls in the issues and cases that follow; such controls can be found in cases concerning handbills and leaflets, newspapers, broadcasting, magazines, books, and films. Furthermore, in almost all instances, the control upon the channel was applied to stop a message of which the gatekeeper disapproved (the possible exception occurs in *Schneider* v. *State* of 1939 where claims of antilitter protection were made).

---

[2]Nickie Fleener, " 'The Worst Case of Racial Equality He Ever Saw': The Supreme Court, Motion Picture Censorship, and the Color Line," in *Free Speech Yearbook: 1979,* ed. Peter E. Kane (Falls Church, Va.: Speech Communication Association, 1979), p. 1.

[3]B. Aubrey Fisher, *Perspectives on Human Communication* (New York: Macmillan, 1978), p. 119; see especially pp. 118–122. The concept of gatekeeping is attributed to Kurt Lewin, *Field Theory in Social Science* (New York: Harper & Row, 1951), and to Lewin's earlier writings. See also David White, "The 'Gate Keeper': A Case Study in the Selection of News," *Journalism Quarterly* 27 (1950): 383–390; and Westley and McClean, "A Conceptual Model for Communication Research," *Journalism Quarterly* 34 (1957): 31–38.

LANDMARK CASE
Near v. Minnesota, 283 U.S. 697 (1931)
Decided June 1, 1931

Vote: 5 to 4 declaring the Minnesota prior restraint statute unconstitutional.
Majority Opinion By: Chief Justice Hughes.
Concurring Justices: Holmes, Brandeis, Stone, and Roberts.
Dissenting Justices: Van Devanter, McReynolds, Sutherland, and Butler.
Justices Not Participating: (none)

Summary: In the fall of 1927, Minnesota scandal-sheet publisher J. M. Near, in several issues of *The Saturday Press,* made numerous anti-Semitic remarks, including the charge that Jewish gangsters controlled gambling, bootlegging, and racketeering in Minneapolis and that local police officials (whom he named) were cooperating with the "gangsters" and were receiving "graft." In response, the offended officials invoked Minnesota's unique prior restraint law and secured a court order prohibiting further publication of any issues of *The Saturday Press* because of its "malicious, scandalous, and defamatory" content. The Minnesota Supreme Court upheld the court order and the statute under which it was issued. The U.S. Supreme Court, however, reversed the court below, holding the Minnesota gag law to be a violation of the Constitution. In so ruling, the Supreme Court asserted that although liberty of speech and press is "not an absolute right," prior restraint has been generally rejected in England and the United States as a means of dealing with threatening or irresponsible speech. The proper course for the Minneapolis officials to follow, the Court implied, was to bring suit under the defamation laws which "remain available and unaffected" by the decision.

Rule Established; Significance of Case: Because prior restraint is such an extreme remedy for abuses of freedom of expression, the U.S. Constitution prohibits the practice except in rare instances (such as time of war, to maintain public decency, or to protect a community from incitement to violence). The proper course of action for those who believe that the press has acted illegally is to apply post facto punishment, using appropriate and valid laws.

Basic Issues of Prior Restraint

During 1925 the Minnesota legislature approved a prior restraint law that attracted the concern of publishers throughout the nation. The statute stated that any publisher or distributor of any "obscene, lewd and lascivious" publication or of any "malicious, scandalous and defamatory" publication was "guilty of a nuisance" and could be stopped by court order from further publication or distribution of the newspaper, magazine, or other periodical. This law was tested two years after its passage when Minneapolis publisher J. M. Near, whose "scandal sheet"

The Saturday Press offended a number of public officials by accusing them of being involved with "Jewish gangsters" in the control of organized crime in the city and county. The angered officials secured an injunction under the 1925 law to prohibit publisher Near from printing and distributing any *future* issues of *The Saturday Press.* The opinion of the U.S. Supreme Court in this prior restraint case became a landmark in First Amendment law.

Chief Justice Hughes, after reviewing the facts of the case, agreed with the plaintiffs that "liberty of speech and of the press is not an absolute right, and the state may punish its abuse." The question in this instance, however, was whether or not the Minnesota gag law went too far in providing for punishment of an alleged "abuse." The chief justice then made four significant observations concerning the statute in question. *First,* the Minnesota law "is not aimed at the redress of individual or private wrongs. Remedies for libel remain available and unaffected." *Second,* the law "is directed not simply at the circulation of scandalous and defamatory statements with regard to *private* citizens, but at the continued publication by newspapers and periodicals of charges against *public officers* of corruption, malfeasance in office, or serious neglect of duty." (Emphasis supplied. Obviously, the Court is suspicious of efforts by government officials to suppress criticism of their official conduct—a suspicion that eventually led to the announcement of the "actual malice" rule in the 1964 case of *New York Times* v. *Sullivan,* discussed in Chapter 4, on defamation.) *Third,* the object of the statute "is not punishment, in the ordinary sense, but suppression of the offending newspaper or periodical." And *fourth,* the statute "not only operates to suppress the offending newspaper or periodical but to put the publisher under an effective censorship. . . . Whether he would be permitted again to publish matter deemed to be derogatory to the same or other public officers would depend upon the [state] court's ruling."

Chief Justice Hughes then summarized some general principles about when prior restraint would be permissible, including the following circumstances: when the nation is at war ("No one would question but that a government might prevent . . . the publication of the sailing dates of transports or the number and location of troops"), to protect the public decency against "obscenity," or to preserve the "security of the community life . . . against incitements to acts of violence . . . ." But these were *not* the questions in this case, he pointed out, as he continued his argument against prior restraint.

Chief Justice Hughes *delivered the opinion of the Court:*

The exceptional nature of its limitations places in a strong light the general conception that liberty of the press, historically considered and taken up by the Federal Constitution, has meant, principally, although not exclusively, immunity from previous restraints or censorship. The conception of the liberty of the press in this country had broadened with the exigencies of the colonial period and with the efforts to secure freedom from oppressive administration. That liberty was especially cherished for the immunity it afforded from previous restraint of the publication of censure of public officers and charges of official misconduct. . . .

The fact that for approximately one hundred and fifty years there has been almost an entire absence of attempts to impose previous restraints upon publications relating to the malfeasance of public officers is significant of the deep-seated conviction that such restraints would violate constitutional right. Public officers, whose character and conduct remain open to debate and free discussion in the press, find their remedies for false accusations in actions under libel laws providing for redress and punishment, and not in proceedings to restrain the publication of newspapers and periodicals. . . .

The importance of this immunity has not lessened. While reckless assaults upon public men, and efforts to bring obloquy upon those who are endeavoring faithfully to discharge official duties, exert a baleful influence and deserve the severest condemnation in public opinion, it cannot be said that this abuse is greater, and it is believed to be less, than that which characterized the period in which our institutions took shape. . . . **The fact that the liberty of the press may be abused by miscreant purveyors of scandal does not make any the less necessary the immunity of the press from previous restraint in dealing with official misconduct. Subsequent punishment for such abuses as may exist is the**

FIGURE 9.1. *CHIEF JUSTICE CHARLES EVANS HUGHES OF THE U.S. SUPREME COURT.*
Chief Justice Hughes was the author of the opinion of the Court in the 1931 landmark decision of Near *v.* Minnesota. *Here the Court ruled for the first time that, under the Constitution, prior restraint of communication was impermissible except in exceptional circumstances, as for reasons of national security, to maintain "public decency," or to preserve the community from a breach of the peace. Chief Justice Hughes was first appointed to the Supreme Court by President William Howard Taft; he served as an associate justice from 1910 to 1916, when he resigned from the bench to run for the office of president of the United States on the Republican ticket (he was defeated by President Woodrow Wilson, who was reelected to his second term in 1916). Hughes was reappointed to the Court as chief justice by President Herbert Hoover in 1930, serving in that capacity until his retirement in 1941.*
Library of Congress.

appropriate remedy, consistent with constitutional privilege.

In general, the principles set out by Chief Justice Hughes in *Near* have been adhered to since 1931 in those cases which are not matters of public decency, national security, or fair trial.[4] *One group* of cases growing out of *Near* concerns local ordinances that require advance permission for the distribution of handbills or leaflets, whether as a litter-control measure, as an attempt to suppress speech content, or for some other reason. The *second group* of cases concerns the content

of mass media channels, such as books, newspapers, or broadcasts. Each group is considered below.

Controls on the Distribution of Handbills and Leaflets

In 1938 the appeal of Alma Lovell, a Jehovah's Witness convicted of passing out religious literature without a permit on the streets of Griffin, Georgia, reached the U.S. Supreme Court. Lovell, who insisted that she was giving out tracts, pamphlets, and magazines because she had been sent "by Jehovah to do His work" and thus needed no permit, was convicted of violating a town ordinance providing that the written permission of Griffin's city manager was needed *before* any person could distribute "circulars, hand-

---

[4]Arbitrariness and discrimination in the granting of permits for the use of public facilities, or for parades and similar public demonstrations, can serve as a form of prior restraint. For an examination of this problem, see Chapter 8, time, place, and manner.

books, advertising, or literature of any kind," even if the material was free, "within the limits of the City."[5] Lovell had been fined $50 and in default of payment had been sentenced to jail for fifty days for attempting to communicate her beliefs. Chief Justice Hughes delivered the unanimous opinion of the Court in reversing Lovell's conviction, emphasizing the broad sweep of the ordinance in question. The law was not limited to the distribution of obscene literature but encompassed *all* literature; also, it did not restrict dissemination on the basis of reasonable time or place regulations but was "comprehensive with respect to the method of distribution." In a word, the law was invalid for *overbreadth.* After hinting that a more narrowly drawn ordinance might have been given a friendlier reception by the Court, the chief justice denounced the law in question as being "invalid on its face," for it struck "at the very foundation of the freedom of the press by subjecting it to license and censorship." Before concluding, Chief Justice Hughes also made it clear that the Constitution protects pamphlets and leaflets, just as it does other means of communication. Such has been our history, he adds, "as the pamphlets of Thomas Paine and others . . . abundantly attest."

A year following *Lovell,* in a decision that combined the appeals of four related cases into one opinion, the Supreme Court struck down as unconstitutional the ordinances of three cities—Los Angeles, Milwaukee, and Worcester (Massachusetts)—that prohibited the distribution of handbills on the public streets because of the litter created by such activity. Also struck down was the ordinance of a fourth city, Irvington, New Jersey, which was much broader than the others in that it prohibited not only street distribution

but also door-to-door solicitation and similar activities unless a permit had been secured in advance.[6] By applying an ad hoc balancing test together with an implied argument based upon the doctrine of less drastic means, Justice Roberts delivered the opinion of the Court to the effect that (1) First Amendment freedoms weighed much heavier in the balance than litter-free thoroughfares and (2) that other means should be used to prevent littering. On the second point, Justice Roberts cogently observes, "There are obvious methods of preventing littering. Amongst these is the punishment of those who actually throw papers on the streets."

The no-prior-restraint principles of *Near,* as developed in *Lovell* and *Schneider,* were affirmed once again as recently as 1971 in a leaflet-restraint attempt that originated in 1967 in the Austin neighborhood of Chicago.[7] The Organization for a Better Austin, a group formed to stabilize the racial ratio in the area by opposing blockbusting tactics employed by certain realtors, distributed a leaflet in which real estate broker Jerome M. Keefe was criticized for his "panic-peddling" methods. Among other things, the Better Austin group published Keefe's home telephone number and urged people to phone Keefe (who lived nearby in Westchester, Illinois), protest his tactics, and ask him to sign an agreement that he would desist from such methods in the future. The leaflets were distributed peacefully in several locations in the city of Westchester.

Realtor Keefe, angered by these activities, secured a court order against the Better Austin group that enjoined its members from "passing out pamphlets, leaflets or literature of any kind, and from picketing, anywhere in the City of Westchester, Illinois." The Il-

[5]*Lovell* v. *Griffin,* 303 U.S. 444 (1938).

[6]*Schneider* v. *State,* 308 U.S. 147 (1939).
[7]*Organization for a Better Austin* v. *Keefe,* 402 U.S. 415 (1971).

linois courts granted and sustained the injunction on the grounds that the Austin association was violating Keefe's privacy, and damaging his reputation.

The U.S. Supreme Court, in an 8-to-1 decision authored by Chief Justice Burger (Justice Harlan dissenting), struck down the Illinois court order on First Amendment grounds. Citing *Near, Lovell, Schneider,* and similar cases, Chief Justice Burger observed that "any prior restraint on expression comes to this Court with a 'heavy presumption' against its constitutional validity," and that this burden was not met by Keefe. While the Court recognized that its prohibition upon prior restraint is not absolute and implied that the privacy of the home might in certain circumstances need the drastic remedy of prior restraint to protect the household from an unwarranted invasion of its privacy, such was not the case at bar. Here, Keefe was objecting to the criticism of his *business* practices and to the distribution of pamphlets to the public about those practices. Calling this an invasion of privacy, concluded the chief justice, "is not sufficient to support an injunction against peaceful distribution of informational literature of the nature revealed by this record."

Controls on the Media: Books, Newspapers, and Broadcasts

Most efforts at prior restraint exercised against the mass media have concerned issues of public decency, national security, or fair trial and are, therefore—with the exception of the one "public decency" case listed below—considered elsewhere in this or another chapter under appropriate headings. At least one public decency case plus three others concerning issues other than national security or fair trial are germane to the present discussion. The first concerned the efforts of the Rhode Island Commission to Encourage Morality in Youth, created by the Rhode Island legislature in 1956 and charged with educating the public about immoral literature and recommending appropriate prosecutions in the area of obscenity. Although the commission had no enforcement powers, it pressured book distributors to drop "objectional" books from their lists, thus establishing a form of prior restraint in the state. In 1963 the U.S. Supreme Court declared this system of extralegal activity unconstitutional.[8] Speaking for the Court, Justice Brennan observed that Rhode Island's attempts to pressure book distributors to cooperate were carried out without judicial supervision, and without adequate standards of what constituted an objectionable publication. "What Rhode Island has done, in fact," Justice Brennan said, "has been to subject the distribution of publications to a system of prior administrative restraints, since the Commission is not a judicial body and its decisions to list particular publications as objectionable do not follow judicial determinations that such publications may lawfully be banned." He concluded that the "procedures of the Commission are radically deficient," and that the system of "informal censorship" which it practiced was unconstitutional.

The second case developed out of a challenge to the Alabama Corrupt Practices Act, which, in the interest of fair and orderly elections, prohibited all election-day editorials (for the reason that such editorials were unfair because there was no time for a reply). In 1962 James E. Mills, editor of the Birmingham *Post-Herald,* violated this prior restraint law by publishing an editorial on election day. For this he was convicted in the courts of Alabama. On appeal, the U.S. Supreme Court reversed Mills's conviction and declared the Alabama statute unconstitutional.[9]

---

[8]*Bantam Books* v. *Sullivan,* 372 U.S. 58 (1963).
[9]*Mills* v. *Alabama,* 384 U.S. 214 (1966).

Justice Hugo Black delivered the opinion of the Court, pointing out that the Alabama law in question

> silences the press at a time when it can be most effective. It is difficult to conceive of a more obvious and flagrant abridgment of the constitutionally guaranteed freedom of the press. . . . We hold that no test of reasonableness can save a state law from invalidation as a violation of the First Amendment when that law makes it a crime for a newspaper editor to do no more than urge people to vote one way or another in a publicly held election.

In the third case, the Supreme Court upheld the legality of a Pittsburgh Human Relations Ordinance which authorized the city's Commission on Human Relations to issue cease-and-desist orders against discriminatory hiring practices. When the commission exercised its authority by ordering the *Pittsburgh Press* to stop carrying "help wanted" advertisements according to sex-designated columns, the newspaper took the commission to court. Because (1) the order concerned commercial speech (which in the past had been excluded from the protection of the First Amendment), (2) the kind of discriminatory employment practice once advertised in the sex-designated columns was made illegal by a city ordinance, and (3) the constraint under review did not reach editorial messages and news coverage in the newspaper, the antidiscrimination order did not weigh heavily as a free-speech issue. Therefore, said the Court, this type of prior restraint upon the classified advertisements in a newspaper was not a violation of the First Amendment.[10]

The fourth and final media case to be considered here reached the U.S. Supreme Court from Georgia and concerned a state law making it a misdemeanor to publish or broadcast the name or identity of any rape victim, even when the same was a matter of public record.[11] When a television reporter discovered the name of a rape-murder victim in the public records and announced his findings over the air, he ran afoul of the Georgia statute and was sued by the family of the named victim. In the legal proceedings that followed, the Georgia Supreme Court upheld the law as constitutional. The U.S. Supreme Court disagreed, reversed the court below, and pronounced the Georgia statute invalid. "At the very least," wrote Justice White for the majority, "the First and Fourteenth Amendments will not allow exposing the press to liability for truthfully publishing information released to the public in official court records."

From the cases noted above concerning both handbills and mass media channels of expression, the public communicator should be aware of the following points:

1. Government may not use broadly drawn permit systems as a means of prohibiting the distribution of all handbills, leaflets, and so on; ordinances prohibiting the distribution of all kinds of literature at all times and places and by any manner are invalid for overbreadth (*Lovell* v. *Griffin*, 1938).

2. Government may not exercise prior restraint upon the public distribution of handbills and leaflets as a means of keeping the streets clear of litter (*Schneider* v. *State,* 1939).

3. The use of a prior restraint court order broadly prohibiting the distribution of leaflets or literature "of any kind," plus denying the right to picket "anywhere" in the city in order to protest the business practices of a real-

---

[10]*Pittsburgh Press Company* v. *Pittsburgh Commission on Human Relations,* 413 U.S. 376 (1973).

[11]*Cox Broadcasting Corp.* v. *Cohn,* 420 U.S. 469 (1975). This case is discussed further in Chapter 4 on defamation and privacy, under the heading concerning "Disclosure of Private Matters," p. 135.

tor, was declared unconstitutional by the U.S. Supreme Court even though the leaflets in question published the realtor's home telephone number. While not ruling out completely the possibility that prior restraint might be justified in some instances to protect the privacy of the home, the Court found that the plaintiff had not met the heavy burden of proof required to justify the censorship of messages critical of his business practices (*Organization for a Better Austin* v. *Keefe,* 1971).

4. For a state to act through an administrative body, such as Rhode Island's Commission to Encourage Morality in Youth, to pressure book distributors to remove "objectionable" books from their lists without stating specific standards for the meaning of "objectionable" and without judicial determination that the materials in question may be lawfully banned, is an unconstitutional prior restraint upon freedom of speech (*Bantam Books* v. *Sullivan,* 1963).

5. Government may not prohibit the publication of election-day editorials, not even in the name of fair and orderly elections (*Mills* v. *Alabama,* 1966).

6. An ordinance that prohibited newspapers in the city of Pittsburgh from publishing help-wanted advertisements according to sex-designated columns was allowed to stand as constitutional, even though the newspaper argued that the prohibition was a form of prior restraint upon the press (*Pittsburgh Press Company* v. *Pittsburgh Commission on Human Relations,* 1973).

7. State laws prohibiting media reports of the names of crime victims that are matters of public record are unconstitutional (*Cox Broadcasting* v. *Cohn,* 1975).

With the single exception of the ordinance prohibiting discriminatory "help wanted" advertisements in sex-designated columns, the U.S. Supreme Court has, in the cases reviewed thus far, denied state and local gov-

ernments the option of prior restraint "gate-keeping" as a means of control upon public communication. The firm stand of the Supreme Court against most attempts at prior restraint has not been sustained, however, when sexually oriented messages considered by some to be detrimental to the "public morality" have been at bar (the case of *Bantam Books* v. *Sullivan,* discussed above, notwithstanding). When the subject of the expression is sex, the rules are often changed—as the next topic demonstrates.

Film Review Boards, "Public Decency," and Prior Restraint

Until recent years when national security and fair-trial controversies have provided the major battlegrounds for debates over prior restraint, the focus has been upon stopping the dissemination of "immoral" ideas, particularly if those ideas were communicated by means of film. The censorship of messages of "sexual immorality"—usually categorized as obscene by lawmakers, judges, and would-be censors—has not been limited to films, of course. The U.S. Customs office has often prohibited the importation of materials deemed obscene, and still practices this form of prior restraint with the approval of Congress and the U.S. Supreme Court; furthermore, the postal service has from time to time attempted prior restraint upon "immoral" materials, as in the 1946 instance of *Hannegan* v. *Esquire,*[12] when the postmaster general ordered a stop to the mailing of an issue of *Esquire* which he believed to be "morally improper" (a unanimous Supreme Court struck down the postmaster's order).

However, a kind of dread of the communicative power of the channel of film seems to have pervaded the thinking of the American judiciary in the past and to an extent con-

[12]327 U.S. 146 (1964).

tinues to the present time, for the judges of America by and large have been willing to single out "immoral" films as representing a combination of content and channel that justifies the exercise of strict gatekeeping by means of administrative licensing—that is, by film review boards. This deep distrust of the medium of film was openly voiced by Justice Clark in the 1952 case of *Burstyn* v. *Wilson,* discussed further below, in which he noted that many persons believe "that motion pictures possess *a greater capacity for evil,* particularly among the youth of a community, than other modes of expression." (Emphasis supplied.)

One consequence of this policy has been the censorship of film-communicated points of view that did not raise questions of public decency but offended the censors for other reasons. As mentioned earlier in this discussion, *Imitation of Life* was denied a permit in Memphis because of its treatment of racial matters; in like manner, Memphis gatekeeper-censor Lloyd Binford—who ran a one-man film licensing bureau for years and banned the showing of numerous nonsexual films because of their treatment of sensitive social issues—prohibited the screening of *The Southerner* because its depiction of tenant farmers "reflected upon the South." Maryland banned a documentary about Poland because "it failed to present a true picture of modern Poland" and also excised a scene from *Joan of Arc* in which Joan cried, "Oh, God, why hast thou forsaken me?" Ohio and Kansas regularly censored the showing of prolabor films, and in Chicago, a permit was denied to a newsreel showing Chicago policemen shooting at labor pickets (censorship in the Windy City was done by the office of the commissioner of police).[13]

[13]The examples given here are only a partial listing from the dissent of Chief Justice Earl Warren (joined by Justices Black, Douglas, and Brennan) in *Times Film Corporation* v. *Chicago,* 365 U.S. 43 (1961).

The attitude of the U.S. Supreme Court toward the medium of film during the twentieth century can be compared to the attitude of the English authorities of both church and state toward the revolutionary channel of print during the sixteenth and seventeenth centuries. Just as licensing of the press was practiced in the mother country for many years, so was the licensing of films allowed in the United States, despite the command of the First Amendment. To begin with, in 1915 the Supreme Court glanced at the upstart channel of film, promptly declared it to be a commercial medium (the Court opined that movies were a bit like circuses), and simply excluded it from contention as a protected means of communicating serious ideas. The case was *Mutual Film* v. *Ohio,* and the author of the Court's opinion was Justice Joseph McKenna, who stated that "the exhibition of moving pictures is a business, pure and simple, originated and conducted for profit, like other spectacles, not to be regarded . . . as part of the press of the country or as organs of public opinions."[14]

By casting the technology of film into the constitutional outer darkness of "nonspeech," the Supreme Court left the medium and *the messages communicated by that medium* to the mercies of state and local gatekeepers for thirty-seven years—from 1915 until 1952. During this time, prior restraint of movies was considered to be of no great concern to the federal courts. The beginning of the end for film review boards began in 1952, when the Supreme Court unanimously rejected New York's attempt to ban the showing of the film *The Miracle* because state censors considered it irreligious. In this decision of *Burstyn* v. *Wilson,* the Court explicitly rejected the commercial speech rationale of

[14]*Mutual Film Corporation* v. *Industrial Commission of Ohio,* 236 U.S. 230 (1915).

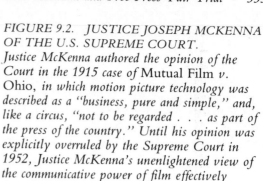

FIGURE 9.2. JUSTICE JOSEPH MCKENNA OF THE U.S. SUPREME COURT.
Justice McKenna authored the opinion of the Court in the 1915 case of Mutual Film v. Ohio, *in which motion picture technology was described as a "business, pure and simple," and, like a circus, "not to be regarded . . . as part of the press of the country." Until his opinion was explicitly overruled by the Supreme Court in 1952, Justice McKenna's unenlightened view of the communicative power of film effectively denied First Amendment protection to the new medium—for a total of thirty-seven years. Justice McKenna was appointed to the Court by President William McKinley in 1898 and served until 1925.*
Library of Congress.

Mutual Film and announced that "expression by means of motion pictures is included within the free speech and free press guarantee of the First and Fourteenth Amendments."[15] This change meant, among other things, that the question of the constitutionality of prior restraint of films—an issue not addressed in *Burstyn*—began to "ripen" for review.

Nine years after *Burstyn,* the Court reviewed an appeal that began as a deliberate challenge by the Times Film Corporation to Chicago's censorship law and, by implication, to all prior restraint statutes applying to films. Times Film applied for a license to show the nonobscene *Don Juan,* a movie based on Mozart's opera *Don Giovanni,* but refused to submit a copy of the film with the application, as was required by the ordinance. The corporation's questioning of prior restraint upon films lost by one vote when it reached the Supreme Court, for in a decision of 5 to 4, the nation's highest tribunal *upheld* the constitutionality of film licensing. Justice Tom C. Clark delivered the opinion of the Court by reaffirming the view of *Near* v. *Minnesota* (1931) that prior restraint upon messages considered indecent or dangerous to the community or nation did not necessarily violate the First Amendment.[16] However, no specific standards for judging the legality of film review laws were announced in this opinion.

Procedural safeguards for film licensing were not long in coming. In 1965, following

[15]*Burstyn* v. *Wilson,* 343 U.S. 495 (1952). Note: For more on this case, see Chapter 5, "Religio-Moral Heresy."

[16]*Times Film Corporation* v. *Chicago,* 365 U.S. 43 (1961). Joining with Justice Clark to sustain film censorship were Justices Frankfurter, Harlan, Whittaker, and Stewart.

the four-year hiatus in the wake of *Times Film,* the case of *Freedman* v. *Maryland* was decided by the Supreme Court. Here, theater owner Ronald Freedman questioned the specific provisions of the Maryland prior restraint statute, arguing that the law as written and enforced violated the Constitution because it unduly constrained *protected* expression. The Supreme Court agreed, threw out the Maryland statute, and announced that in the future all film permit systems must comply with these three standards: (1) the burden of proof is upon the censor to show that the film is "unprotected expression"; (2) censorship boards must expedite their business and either issue a license or go to court to restrain the showing of a film "within a specified brief period"; and finally (3) provision must be made for prompt judicial review.[17] With these requirements in place, film licensing systems around the nation began to collapse. Whereas in the past, in many locales, the burden of proof had been upon the film distributors to show that the movie was legal, that burden was shifted to the censors to show that the film in question was illegal. Also, the pressures for a prompt judicial determination plus the intervention of independent-thinking judges who had to pass on the censor's decision were more than some film review boards could deal with. The systems of Pennsylvania, Oklahoma, North Carolina, Tennessee, Ohio, Georgia, Maryland, and of numerous localities either died or were drastically curtailed.[18] One state that continued its efforts to censor films was Maryland, which rewrote its licensing statute to comply with the *Freedman* requirements. Among

other things, the revised law provided that a film must be either licensed or declared obscene within a maximum of fifteen days. This narrowly drawn law was affirmed as constitutional by the federal courts,[19] and the Maryland Film Censor Board, the last licensing body to operate in the United States, went about its business until 1981, when its authority expired under Maryland's "sunset law" and was not renewed by the state legislature.[20] Thus did the prior restraint of films come to an end in America—not because of an outspoken Supreme Court but because the people of Maryland no longer supported the idea that gatekeeper-censors ought to choose their films for them.

In review, the prior restraint of films in the United States developed and died in four steps. *First,* in *Mutual Film* v. *Ohio* (1915), the Supreme Court refused to extend First Amendment protection to films because the new medium was viewed as one of commercial entertainment only. *Second,* in *Burstyn* v. *Wilson* (1952) the Court reversed its *Mutual Film* decision and granted First Amendment protection to ideas communicated by motion pictures (it did not remove film licensing, however). *Third,* in *Times Film* v. *Chicago* (1961), the Court ruled by a vote of 5-to-4 that film licensing did not violate the Constitution. *Fourth,* in *Freedman* v. *Maryland* (1965), the Court said that even though film licensing was constitutional, certain procedural safeguards were mandatory—namely, that (1) the censors had the burden to prove the film illegal, (2) film licensing must be expedited, and (3) provision must be made for prompt judicial review. Most censorship

---

[17]*Freedman* v. *Maryland,* 380 U.S. 51 (1965).

[18]See Donald M. Gillmor and Jerome A. Barron, *Mass Communication Law: Cases and Comment,* 3rd ed. (St. Paul, Minn.: West, 1979), p. 559. Also, Don R. Pember, *Mass Media Law,* 2nd ed. (Dubuque, Iowa: Wm. C. Brown, 1981), p. 378.

[19]*Star* v. *Preller,* 419 U.S. 955 (1974), sustained the federal courts below, which had declared the revised statute constitutional.

[20]"Sun Sets on Maryland Censor Board," *Newsletter on Intellectual Freedom,* July 1981, p. 111.

boards collapsed in the wake of this decision.

Public communicators should keep in mind that although film licensing died a natural death with the 1981 expiration of the Maryland Film Censor Board, it could be resurrected if public support were again generated for such a system. Since the U.S. Supreme Court has been unwilling to outlaw prior restraint of movies, the matter now rests with the state and local public opinion of the citizenry.

Prior Restraint on National Security Grounds

Although there is some disagreement among legal scholars as to precisely what the Founding Fathers believed about freedom of expression, there is little if any disagreement that many of the problems faced by the nation today are more threatening than were those that existed in the late eighteenth century. No lawmaker who voted to ratify the Bill of Rights could have foreseen a system of communication by which the name, location, and photograph of a secret agent could be instantaneously communicated from country to country or of the communication of messages containing secret information about the making of missiles, nuclear warheads, or deadly germs for use in biological warfare. As the dangers to the nation change and become more serious, so do attempts at censorship increase. Since the early 1970s, three issues have fueled the public debate over prior restraint: (1) the unauthorized publication of military secrets in 1971 (the "Pentagon Papers" case), (2) the attempted publication of an article on how to make an H-bomb in 1979 (the *Progressive* case), and (3) moves by the federal government to prevent ex-CIA agents from publishing books about their secret work without advanced permission from the CIA (the *Marchetti* case of 1972

and the *Snepp* case of 1980). A brief examination of each issue is in order.

The "Pentagon Papers"

Although *Near* v. *Minnesota* (1931) had declared that prior restraint might be permissible on national security grounds in rare circumstances, the government did not attempt to test the matter until forty years later when, in 1971, it tried to stop publication of the "Pentagon Papers." In fact, in the entire history of the United States, *the government had never used the federal courts as a tool for preventing the publication of a message until the 1971 "Pentagon Papers" case developed.* At the time of the controversy, the war in Vietnam was under way, Richard Nixon was president of the United States, and John Mitchell was his attorney general. The spark was struck in the summer of 1971 by war-opponent Daniel Ellsberg, a scientist who had worked for the government on a secret history of the Vietnam conflict, when he allegedly gave copies of his manuscript to both the *New York Times* and the *Washington Post* as an antiwar gesture. When the newspapers began to print in serialized form Ellsberg's "History of the United States Decision-Making Process on Vietnam Policy," the Justice Department went to court to request a restraining order against further publication. The argument used was national security.

In New York, a newly appointed federal district judge, Murray Gurfein, granted the government's request for a temporary restraining order, thus stopping the *New York Times* from publishing any further installments. A few days later Judge Gurfein refused to grant the government's request for a permanent injunction to restrain further publication. The U.S. Court of Appeals for the Second Circuit then reversed this decision, ordering further hearings in the district court to permit the government to develop its arguments for censorship. Meanwhile, said the court of appeals, the restraint on publication was to be continued.

In Washington, D.C., the district court rejected the government's request for a restraint upon the *Washington Post*. The government appealed, but the Court of Appeals for the District of Columbia also turned down the request for prior restraint. With conflicting decisions in the two circuits before them and because of the critical First Amendment issues involved, the Supreme Court granted immediate review and postponed its summer recess in order to resolve the first such dispute in American history.[21]

Rarely has the nation's highest court had such an opportunity to defend the First Amendment with arguments at once reasoned and eloquent and rarely has the Court rendered a decision so fractured and so lacking in guidance for the future. By a 6-to-3 vote, in a brief per curiam opinion, the Court dissolved the restraining order and permitted the continued publication of the "Pentagon Papers." Those who voted with the majority were Justices Black, Douglas, Brennan, Stewart, White, and Marshall. Those in dissent were the two Nixon appointees sitting at the time—Chief Justice Burger and Justice Blackmun—and Justice Harlan. The abrupt per curiam opinion (202 words, minus case references) provided only one reason for striking down the restraining order, namely, that the government had not met its burden of proof to show the justification for prior restraint in this case (according to precedent, in First Amendment controversies the *doctrine*

of preferred freedoms shifts the burden of proof to the government in cases such as this). Each justice then stated his view of the matter, with the result that nine separate opinions were issued. Among the six-man majority, only Justices Black and Douglas took a strong "absolutist" position against prior restraint of the media (public communicators should bear in mind that both of these opponents of prior restraint are deceased and that no current member of the Supreme Court is as committed to the absolutist position as were Justices Black and Douglas). The other four qualified their arguments to agree that prior restraint was permissible in certain circumstances but not in this one.

In dissent, Chief Justice Burger and Justices Harlan and Blackmun objected to the haste with which the Court had acted, stating that ample facts had not been made available to the Court for a wise national security determination to be made. All three let it be known, however, that they sympathized with the executive branch's need to keep sensitive documents secret. As Justice Harlan stated, "I would continue the restraints on publication. I cannot believe that the doctrine prohibiting prior restraints reaches to the point of preventing courts from maintaining the status quo long enough to act responsibly in matters of such national importance as those involved here." As the press rooms of the *Times* and the *Post* began to hum to the lifting of the censorship order, the journalists of America pondered with grave concern the fact that for fifteen days the "free press" of the nation had been prevented from publishing an important document and for their troubles were given an inconclusive and uninspiring "burden of proof" opinion by a sharply divided Supreme Court. There was relief, but no great rejoicing, in the editorial offices of America's publishers and broadcasters.

[21]*New York Times* v. *United States* and *United States* v. *Washington Post*, 403 U.S. 713 (1971). Note: As readers of the early chapters will recall, during the Civil War both North and South practiced prior restraint from time to time, but not by court order. When it happened, it was by executive or military order and usually consisted of simply shutting down a newspaper for a time.

The H-Bomb Recipe and The Progressive

Early in 1979 *The Progressive* magazine, a small political journal founded in 1909 by Wisconsin's Robert M. LaFollette as the voice of the Progressive movement, announced that in its April issue it would publish an article on the making of an H-bomb written by freelance journalist Howard Morland. The reason for doing this, said the editors of the journal, was to give the public information it needed to make judgments concerning issues related to nuclear weapons—a classic "make-the-voter-wise" position. The author of the article as well as the magazine's editors claimed that the content came from various unclassified sources and that no real secrets were to be revealed. The U.S. government, which had been alerted to the article by a scientist who was checking its accuracy at the request of the magazine, disagreed. Citing the Atomic Energy Act's prohibitions upon communicating "restricted data"[22] and on behalf of the Departments of Defense, State, Energy, and Justice, the government moved into federal district court to stop publication on national security grounds. Federal Judge Robert W. Warren, siding with the government, issued a temporary restraining order against publication and, on March 26, 1979, converted that order into a preliminary injunction against *The Progressive*.[23] In so doing, Judge Warren stated that whereas a "mistake in ruling against *The Progressive* will seriously infringe cherished First Amendment rights," a mistake "in ruling against the United States could pave the way for thermonuclear annihilation for us all." (A more clear-cut example of the doctrin of balancing at work is difficult to find.) Then quoting *Near* v. *Minnesota,* he concluded that the "publication of the technical

information on the hydrogen bomb contained in the article is analogous to publication of troop movements or locations in time of war and falls within the extremely narrow exception of the rule against prior restraint." Thus, for the second time within a decade, the "free press" of America was subjected to censorship.[24]

The Progressive promptly announced its intent to appeal the prior restraint order to the court of appeals and then to the U.S. Supreme Court if necessary. A hearing was soon scheduled for early September of 1979 in the Court of Appeals for the Seventh Circuit (Chicago). Meanwhile, journalist Morland, the editors of *The Progressive,* and others knowledgeable in the field of nuclear physics pointed to items already in print that contained much of the "secret" information the government was trying to suppress. Among the items mentioned was an essay in the 1979 edition of the *World Book Encyclopedia* entitled "How the Hydrogen Bomb Works" and an article by scientist Edward Teller on the subject in the *Encyclopedia Americana.* At about the same time, Californian Charles Hansen, another freelance writer, using material available to the public, put together a piece similar to Morland's, and the *Peninsula Times-Tribune* of Palo Alto, California, published some of Hansen's report. As the government rushed to stop this second "leak of secret information," a third writer, Jerry Fass, submitted a story on the subject to the *Milwaukee Sentinel.* On September 16, 1979, the *Press Connection* of Madison, Wisconsin, published much of the Hansen material, after which the *Chicago Tribune* threatened to do the same. At this point the

---

[22]42 *U.S. Code* Secs. 2011 ff., at Sec. 2274.
[23]*U.S.* v. *Progressive,* 467 F. Supp. 990 (1979).

[24]For a summary of the controversy, see Gregg Phifer, "H-Bomb 'Secrets' and the *Progressive,*" in *Free Speech Yearbook: 1980,* ed. Peter E. Kane (Annandale, Va.: Speech Communication Association, 1980), pp. 99–114.

FIGURE 9.3. *FRONT COVER OF* THE PROGRESSIVE *FOR NOVEMBER 1979, WHEN THE CONTROVERSIAL H-BOMB ESSAY WAS FINALLY PUBLISHED.*

FIGURE 9.4. *HOWARD MORLAND, AUTHOR OF THE H-BOMB ESSAY.*
A national security concern over the plans of The Progressive *to print Howard Morland's article "The H-Bomb Secret: To Know How Is to Ask Why," led the U.S. government to try to stop publication of the piece. At the request of the government, U.S. District Judge Robert W. Warren issued a preliminary injunction against publication, the first such example of prior restraint by injunction in American history (the "Pentagon Papers" case of 1971 involved a temporary restraining order but not an injunction). Eventually, the government dropped its case and the magazine proceeded to publish the essay. Howard Morland works in Washington, D.C., where he is affiliated with the Coalition for a New Foreign and Military Policy.*

government gave up and dropped its case against *The Progressive.*

As with the "Pentagon Papers" of 1971, there was no great satisfaction for either side in the outcome of the case. The magazine had been prevented from publishing an article for a period of six months; many in the media who opposed prior restraint privately condemned *The Progressive* for what they considered to be irresponsible journalism; few if any public communicators expressed a strong faith that freedom of expression in America would be strengthened if the case were finally decided by the U.S. Supreme Court. In fact, many people in the media who carefully re-read the nine opinions in the 1971 "Pentagon Papers" case and who noted the absence of Justices Black and Douglas from the bench in 1979 expressed relief that the case was *not* appealed to the Supreme Court. That fact, in itself, deserves the contemplation of students of freedom of expression.

Government Secrecy Contracts and Directives

A third type of national security controversy arose in the early 1970s when Victor Marchetti, a former CIA employee, and John D. Marks, a former State Department employee, announced their intention to write a book, to be published by Knopf, entitled *The CIA and the Cult of Intelligence.* Although both Marchetti and Marks had voluntarily signed secrecy agreements as a condition of their government employment, both expressed an unwillingness to abide by the agreements insofar as the content of their book was concerned. The government went to court and secured an injunction against publication until the manuscript had been purged of classified information;[25] the Supreme Court sustained the prior restraint order by denying review. In a subsequent case based upon the same controversy, the federal court of appeals allowed the government to delete a number of passages from the manuscript prior to publication, and the Supreme Court agreed to this move by denying review.[26] Throughout the controversy the federal courts treated the matter as a *contractual* dispute, thereby avoiding the First Amendment issues raised. The book was eventually published by Knopf with numerous blank spaces to indicate the deletions ordered by the government and agreed to by the courts. Furthermore, Marchetti was *permanently enjoined* from discussing his work with the CIA without prior approval from the director of the agency.

The issue raised by Marchetti and Marks in 1972 reached the U.S. Supreme Court in the 1980 case of *Snepp* v. *United States,* in which the Court announced that secrecy agreements were indeed binding and that the First Amendment could not save expression which came under valid secrecy contracts. In 1968 Frank W. Snepp accepted employment with the CIA and at that time signed a secrecy contract with the government. When he left the agency in 1976, he signed a second document called a "termination secrecy agreement" in which he reaffirmed his obligation never to reveal "any classified information, or any information concerning intelligence or CIA that has not been made public by CIA . . . without the express written consent of the Director of Central Intelligence or his representative." Later, without agency clearing, Snepp published a book, entitled *Decent Interval,* concerning the work of the CIA in South Vietnam.

The government sued ex-agent Snepp for breach of contract, and won.[27] At the district court level, the government asked for (1) a declaration that Snepp was guilty of breach of contract, (2) an injunction to prohibit Snepp from future publication about the CIA unless the material was first cleared, and (3) the establishment of a constructive trust for the government's benefit into which all profits from the book were to be channeled. The district judge granted these three requests, even though there was no evidence that any secret information had been revealed. The U.S. Supreme Court, in a per curiam opin-

---

[25]*United States* v. *Marchetti,* 466 F.2d 1309 (4th Cir. 1972).

[26]*Knopf* v. *Colby,* 509 F.2d 1362 (4th Cir. 1975).

[27]*Snepp* v. *United States,* 444 U.S. 507 (1980).

ion expressing the views of Chief Justice Burger and Justices Stewart, White, Blackmun, Powell, and Rehnquist, sustained the decision of the federal district court. In August of 1980 Snepp began to pay the government what he had earned from the book; all future profits will also go to the government. Although prior restraint per se had not occurred, the decision in fact has a brisk chilling effect upon those who, in the future, might be tempted to publish in violation of their agreements; in addition, Snepp was enjoined from communicating further about his CIA work without clearance and thus lives under a prior restraint order. Public communicators should note, therefore, that according to the U.S. Supreme Court, secrecy contracts with the government are binding despite the First Amendment to the Constitution.[28]

In what was described as a "Draconian gag order" by the American Civil Liberties Union, President Ronald Reagan on March 11, 1983, carried the prior restraint principle of *Snepp* a large step further by issuing his Directive on Safeguarding National Security Information. This executive order required all federal employees who had access to classified information to sign a secrecy agreement as a condition of employment. The ACLU reported that the rule applied to over 100,000 people, including "every senior official in the Departments of State and Defense, all members of the National Security Council

staff, many senior White House officials and all senior military and foreign service offices." Alarmed, Congress acted to delay enforcement of the directive and, in February 1984, President Reagan suspended efforts by his administration to implement the prior restraint features of the executive order.[29] The question of how to protect classified information remains under discussion, however, and students of freedom of speech should be alert to further developments.

The Duty to Obey

In this chapter and the one immediately preceding (see the sections on time, place, and manner), the question of whether or not to obey a law or a court order that constrains expression has been raised a number of times although not discussed at any length. The U.S. Supreme Court has addressed the issue in three types of situations, each of which merits review: (1) when communicators disobey a *statute* they believe to be invalid on its face, (2) when communicators disobey a valid statute *administered* in an unconstitutional way, and (3) when communicators disobey a *court order*. Each is summarized below.

Laws That Are Invalid on Their Face
The first case to be mentioned is discussed earlier in the present chapter and concerns the refusal of Jehovah's Witness Alma Lovell to obey an ordinance of Griffin, Georgia, requiring written permission from the city manager before any person could distribute

---

[28]Ironically, Admiral Stansfield Turner—who, as director of the CIA under President Jimmy Carter, initiated the civil prosecution of Snepp over *Decent Interval*—ran afoul of his own regulations in 1983 when he sought clearance for his book about intelligence gathering. In response to Turner's request for clearance to publish, the CIA's Publications Review Board (which had been established by Turner) examined the manuscript and ordered a number of deletions on grounds of national security. "Keeping the Company's Secrets: The Censors Turn on a Former CIA Director," *Time*, May 30, 1983, p. 19.

[29]The ACLU statement appears in *Free Speech, 1984: The Rise of Government Controls on Information, Debate and Association* (New York: American Civil Liberties Union, 1983), pp. 14–15. The full text of the directive is found in 9 Med.L.Rptr. 1759 (1983). An account of the decision to suspend certain parts of the order is reported in "Canceled Order: Big Brother Backs Down," *Time*, February 27, 1984, p. 26.

literature "of any kind" within the city limits. The Supreme Court unanimously reversed Lovell's conviction because the ordinance was invalid on its face.[30] Similar rulings have been announced by the Supreme Court in other cases, such as *Kunz v. New York,* in which a minister preached without a required permit, and whose conviction was overturned because the ordinance in question was unconstitutional;[31] *Mills v. Alabama,* in which a newspaper editor who was convicted of violating a state law that prohibited the publication of political editorials on election day was cleared by the Supreme Court because the law under which the conviction was obtained was unconstitutional;[32] and *Shuttlesworth v. Birmingham,* in which civil rights leader Fred Shuttlesworth had his conviction for parading without a permit reversed because the city ordinance he disobeyed was unconstitutional.[33] In *Shuttlesworth,* the Court specifically emphasized that its decisions "have made clear that a person faced with such an unconstitutional licensing law may ignore it, and engage with impunity in the exercise of the right of free expression for which the law purports to require a license."[34]

Therefore, one can conclude that in those instances when an invalid statute is used to try to stop or punish expression protected by the First Amendment, that statute may be ignored or disobeyed with a minimum of risk. However, this is not to say that no risk attends such an act of disobedience. First of all, expensive and time-consuming litigation

might be necessary before the defendant in the case is cleared. And second, one always assumes *some* degree of risk in disobeying a law believed to be invalid, for the courts might not agree that the statute in question is "invalid on its face" and might for one reason or another uphold its constitutionality. It would be wise to secure the counsel of a good attorney before making the judgment to disobey a law one believes to be invalid.

Valid Laws Administered in an Unconstitutional Way

The second principle is illustrated by the case of *Poulos v. New Hampshire* in which Jehovah's Witness Poulos requested a license to conduct religious services in a city park of Portsmouth, New Hampshire, only to be turned down by those charged with administering the licensing ordinance. In defiance of this administrative decision, Poulos conducted religious services, as planned, for which he was convicted of violating the law in question. When the case reached the U.S. Supreme Court, the justices upheld the conviction of Poulos saying that the law itself was constitutional but that its reasonable, nondiscriminatory standards had not been followed by city authorities. Rather than disobey this valid law, said the Court, Poulos should have taken the city to court to compel obedience to the ordinance. Put another way, if the ordinance had been properly enforced, a license would have been issued to Poulos, and the way to challenge such incorrect decisions by government officials is to go to court. Although delay is "unfortunate" in such circumstances, said the Court, "the expense and annoyance of litigation is a price citizens must pay for life in an orderly society where the rights of the First Amendment have a real and abiding meaning."[35]

---

[30]*Lovell v. Griffin,* 303 U.S. 444 (1938).

[31]*Kunz v. New York,* 340 U.S. 290 (1951); for more, see Chapter 8.

[32]*Mills v. Alabama,* 384 U.S. 214 (1966), discussed earlier in the present chapter under the heading of "Controls on the Media."

[33]*Shuttlesworth v. Birmingham* (II), 394 U.S. 147 (1969); for more see Chapter 8.

[34]Ibid., at 151.

[35]*Poulos v. New Hampshire,* 345 U.S. 395 (1953), at 409.

Court Orders That Constrain Free Speech

Finally, the Supreme Court has been unwilling to extend the principle of the right to disobey an invalid statute to those cases when would-be communicators have disobeyed court orders they felt were improper or unjust. In the instance of *Walker* v. *Birmingham,* a group of civil rights demonstrators who had marched in Birmingham, Alabama, on Good Friday and Easter Sunday, 1963, in defiance of a temporary injunction of a state court ordering them not to march, had their convictions upheld in a 5 to 4 decision of the U.S. Supreme Court. In his opinion of the Court, Justice Stewart emphasized that it was an established rule of law that the proper way to challenge a questionable court order was through the judicial process. In the "fair administration of justice," wrote Justice Stewart, "no man can be judge in his own case, however exalted his station, however righteous his motives, and irrespective of his race, color, politics, or religion." Then, concluding with a viewpoint similar to that expressed by the Court in the 1953 *Poulos* decision, Justice Stewart said: "One may sympathize with the petitioners' impatient commitment to their cause. But respect for judicial process is a small price to pay for the civilizing hand of law, which alone can give abiding meaning to constitutional freedom."[36]

---

[36]*Walker* v. *Birmingham,* 388 U.S. 307 (1967), at 320–321. Note: The injunction issued by the Alabama judge was an ex parte injunction, meaning that it was done at the request of only one of the parties to the dispute—the City of Birmingham (hence, "ex parte": concerning one side of the case; on behalf of one party only). In other words, the civil rights marchers were not consulted by the judge before he issued the order. A year following *Walker,* the use of ex parte injunctions in First Amendment cases was strongly criticized by the Supreme Court when it overturned such an injunction in *Carroll* v. *Princess Anne County,* 393 U.S. 175 (1968). In *Carroll,* however, the defendants had not disobeyed the order but had subjected it to judicial review.

Briefly put, communicators should be aware of what the U.S. Supreme Court has said about the duty to obey statutes, administrative decisions, and court orders imposing a prior restraint upon expression. The least risk occurs in disobeying an invalid statute; however, if the law is valid but improperly administered, the approved procedure is to take the appropriate government officials to court—not to defy their ruling. Finally, if a court order is believed to be unconstitutional, the proper procedure is to obey it while subjecting it to judicial review. Recall that this is what both the *New York Times* and *The Progressive* did when named in prior restraint court orders.[37]

Judge-Issued Gag Orders: A Transition to Free Press and Fair Trial

Although the landmark case concerning prior restraint (*Near* v. *Minnesota,* 1931) defines three exceptional circumstances that might justify some form of censorship—public decency, national security, and preserving the peace of the community—no mention is made of the question of prior restraint of the press as a means of assuring a fair trial. Yet within recent years the subject of judge-issued gag orders intended to keep prejudicial information from potential jurors has developed into a significant First Amendment debate among judges, prosecutors, defense attorneys, and representatives of the media. Because this matter concerns both prior restraint and free press–fair trial, it is the first order of business in the final unit of this chapter. One can note at this point, however, that gag orders *have* been issued by trial judges, and the result has been another type

---

[37]For an example of this principle at work in the context of news gathering in a courtroom, see the discussion of the Dickinson rule later in this chapter.

of prior restraint upon public communicators. Following the summary below, the Supreme Court's decisions concerning attempts by trial judges to restrain the media in the name of fair trial will be examined, as will other issues of free press and fair trial.

Prior Restraint in Brief

In the 1931 landmark case *Near* v. *Minnesota,* the U.S. Supreme Court declared Minnesota's gag law to be a violation of the First Amendment, thereby affirming that prior restraint gatekeeping was not permitted under the Constitution except in exceptional circumstances (e.g., in matters of public decency, national security, and preserving the peace of the community). In other instances, said the Court, the appropriate remedy was post facto punishment using appropriate and valid laws. Later, *Near* was interpreted so as to declare unconstitutional an ordinance prohibiting all public distribution of literature without a permit (*Lovell* v. *Griffin*), prior restraint upon all leaflets and handbills in the name of preventing litter (*Schneider* v. *State*), and an injunction against the distribution of a handbill that was critical of an Illinois realtor (*Austin* v. *Keefe*). In addition, Rhode Island's extralegal "pressure tactic" to get book distributors to remove objectionable literature from their lists without clear standards of what was meant by "objectionable" and without judicial supervision was rejected as an unconstitutional prior restraint by the Court (*Bantam Books* v. *Sullivan*), an Alabama law that made it illegal to publish editorials on election day was declared unconstitutional (*Mills* v. *Alabama*), as was also a Georgia law forbidding the publication of the names of rape victims even though the names were a matter of public record (*Cox* v. *Cohn*).

To protect the "public decency," the Su-

preme Court upheld the constitutionality of film licensing boards (*Times Film* v. *Chicago*), although three basic procedural safeguards were required starting in 1965 (*Freedman* v. *Maryland*): (1) the burden of proving the film illegal rested upon the censors; (2) the license must be granted or denied within a definite, brief time period; and (3) provision must be made for prompt judicial review. Most film censorship boards died under the weight of trying to comply with the Court's three standards, yet the Supreme Court has never outlawed film licensing per se. (The licensing board of Maryland, the nation's final functioning film censorship body, ceased to exist in 1981, when the state legislature refused to renew its statutory authority.)

In national security matters, the Supreme Court struck down a restraining order against the publication of the classified "Pentagon Papers" in 1971 (*New York Times* v. *U.S.*), although its brief per curiam opinion broke no dramatic First Amendment ground; in fact, the individual opinions of the nine justices revealed a badly fractured Court. The government's effort to restrain *The Progressive* magazine from publishing a story about the H-bomb was successful for six months during 1979, but the case was finally dropped when several papers published similar H-bomb stories (the *Progressive* case did not reach the Supreme Court). Furthermore, the Court has clearly affirmed that those who sign secrecy agreements with the CIA or other branch of government are bound by those agreements, and may not successfully employ the First Amendment to avoid the constraints placed upon them by secrecy contracts (*Snepp* v. *U.S.*).

Finally, concerning the duty to obey a law, administrative decision, or court order imposing prior restraint upon communication, the Supreme Court has said: (a) one may ignore a statute that is "invalid on its face" (the risk being that one is not always certain that the courts will agree that the law in question really is invalid); (b) one should obey an incorrect administrative decision based upon a valid law while challenging that decision in court; and (c) court orders—even when one is certain that they are wrong—should be obeyed while they are being subjected to orderly judicial review.

II. FREE PRESS–FAIR TRIAL AND THE FIRST AMENDMENT

As the reader knows by now, judges often weigh major constitutional principles on the "scales of justice" in order to arrive at a decision in a case. A classic example of this method of deciding occurs in the weighing of the principle of a free press against that of a fair trial. Both are guaranteed by the Constitution, yet from time to time they appear incompatible and the judiciary is called upon to settle the matter. Developments in the continuing conflict between a free press and the guarantee of a fair trial are summarized below according to three topics: (1) prejudicial pretrial publicity and the issue of prior restraint; (2) access to the courtroom by the general public and by journalists; and (3) related issues, including television in the courtroom, reporter's privilege of confidentiality of sources, and police searches of newsrooms.

Prejudicial Publicity and Judge-Issued Gag Orders: The Issue of Prior Restraint

The question of prejudicial publicity that might influence those called upon to serve as jurors in a criminal trial has been of increasing concern to the judiciary since 1961, when the Supreme Court reversed the conviction of Leslie "Mad Dog" Irvin, who had been convicted of murder and sentenced to death in Indiana. Irvin claimed, and the Supreme Court agreed, that extensive press coverage of a prejudicial nature kept him from receiving a fair trial in the locale where the trial was held.[38] Five years later the Supreme Court reversed the murder conviction of Dr. Sam Sheppard, who had been convicted of murdering his pregnant wife, agreeing with the defendant's argument that "massive, pervasive and prejudicial publicity" had prevented him from getting a fair trial.[39] Needless to say, trial judges took notice of these developments, and some of them eventually concluded that they would be justified in the use of prior restraint orders in certain instances in order to assure the accused of a fair trial. The tactic surfaced in 1972 in a federal courtroom in Baton Rouge, Louisiana.

The Dickinson Rule Is Established

Following a preliminary hearing on the proper way to proceed with a murder threat case, a federal judge in Baton Rouge ordered the press not to publish any testimony taken in the courtroom for fear of prejudicing the case if and when it came to trial. Two reporters for the local newspapers, Gibbs Adams and Larry Dickinson, disobeyed the order, believing it to be unconstitutional, and published a story about the hearing. In response, the trial judge found them in criminal contempt and fined them $300 each. On appeal, the Circuit Court held (1) that the judge's gag order was, indeed, unconstitutional, but (2) that the injunction *should have been obeyed* until invalidated by the appeals court. In other words, the proper course of action was for the reporters to challenge the gag order but to obey it until it was struck down. As the Court of Appeals said in *Dick-*

---

[38]*Irvin* v. *Dowd*, 366 U.S. 717 (1961).
[39]*Sheppard* v. *Maxwell*, 384 U.S. 333 (1966).

inson, the order "must be obeyed until reversed by orderly review."[40] Thereby was established the "Dickinson rule," and public communicators should take note of it. Unless they wish to pay a fine or go to jail, journalists should abide by a federal restrictive order until it is evaluated by the court above; even if the order itself is overruled, acts of violation that took place while it was in effect will, in all probability, be punished and the punishment be allowed to stand. Reporters Adams and Dickinson had to pay their fines, even though they were correct in their opinion that the prior restraint order was a violation of the Constitution.[41]

Nebraska Press Association v. Stuart *(1976)*

The question of judge-imposed gag orders reached the U.S. Supreme Court in 1976, and the unanimous decision of the Court was a significant—although not an absolute—victory for opponents of prior restraint. The case concerned a gag order issued by a Nebraska trial judge, later revised but kept in place by a district court and by the Nebraska Supreme Court. It began with the arrest of Erwin Charles Simants for suspicion of murder in the deaths of six members of a Nebraska farm family. Following the arrest and at the request of both the county attorney and Simants's attorney, the county court judge issued a restrictive order that, among other things, forbade reporters and others who attended a scheduled preliminary hearing from releasing for "public dissemination in any form or manner whatsoever any testimony given or evidence adduced."[42] During the hearing, which was open to the public, reporters heard witnesses testify that they had been present when Simants confessed to the murders. Chafing under an order which prevented representatives of the media from telling the general public what had transpired in *open court,* the Nebraska Press Association appealed first to the district court and then to the Nebraska Supreme Court, both of which kept the gag order in effect, although both changed some of the specifics of the order.

The U.S. Supreme Court unanimously reversed the court below and in so doing declared that only in rare and truly exceptional circumstances could gag orders meet constitutional muster. Chief Justice Burger delivered the opinion of the Court, agreeing with the 1931 landmark decision of *Near* v. *Minnesota* that persons who urged the use of prior restraint bore a heavy burden of proof, since the presumption rested with those who opposed it. Only when a clear and present danger to a fair trial was proved would a gag order be justified, and the Nebraska authorities had not so proved. In ruling to overturn the decision of the court below, Chief Justice Burger stated five points of analysis that subsequently have served as guidelines for trial judges:

1. Restrictive orders must be supported with evidence to show that they are essential to a fair trial; no such proof was submitted in the *Nebraska* case. In fact, the details of this particular case were widely circulated by in-

---

[40]*United States* v. *Dickinson,* 465 F.2d 496 (5th Cir. 1972). Note: The Court of Appeals relied upon the decision of the Supreme Court in *Walker* v. *City of Birmingham,* 388 U.S. 307 (1967), in which civil rights marchers ignored a court order not to march and demonstrated anyhow. The Supreme Court ruled in *Walker* that court orders should be obeyed until either struck down or sustained upon appeal, even if this means that a planned civil rights demonstration cannot legally occur. See the heading "The Duty to Obey" earlier in this chapter.

[41]Note: The *Dickinson* decision applies to federal courts, but not necessarily to the states. The rule varies at the state level, depending upon state law and the decisions of state courts. So far, the issue is one which each state is allowed to decide for itself. See Marc A. Franklin, *The First Amendment and the Fourth Estate* (Mineola, N.Y.: The Foundation Press, 1981), pp. 366–368.

[42]*Nebraska Press Association* v. *Stuart,* 427 U.S. 539 (1976).

dividual citizens in the sparsely populated county even without media coverage, suggesting that under the circumstances the gag order served no essential purpose.

2. Less drastic means should be employed whenever possible, such as (a) changing the location of the trial, (b) delaying the trial "to allow public attention to subside," (c) being particularly careful in the selection of a jury, and (d) the issuing of clear and emphatic instructions to the jury by the trial judge.

3. Another alternative, supported by "professional studies," is for "trial courts in appropriate cases" to limit what the "contending lawyers, the police, and witnesses may say to anyone," rather than to restrict the media. (These constraints upon the *sources* of information have become known as "secrecy orders" and since *Nebraska–Stuart* have been used in a number of cases.)

4. The *Nebraska* restrictive orders violated a basic principle established in the 1966 case of *Sheppard* v. *Maxwell,* that the press may not be constrained "from reporting events that transpire in the courtroom." Once the public hearing had been held, wrote Chief Justice Burger, "what transpired there could not be subject to prior restraint."

5. Finally, the *Nebraska* injunctions were "too vague and too broad to survive the scrutiny" of the Supreme Court.

The burden of proof placed upon trial courts by *Nebraska–Stuart* is so heavy that in most if not all cases since 1976 in which trial courts have tried to impose prior restraint upon the media to protect the fair trial process, appellate courts have disagreed with the trial judge and overturned the gag order.[43]

---

[43]See Don R. Pember, *Mass Media Law,* 2nd ed. (Dubuque, Iowa: Wm. C. Brown, 1981), pp. 332–333. Citing studies to support his conclusion, Pember states: "In establishing strict guidelines against the so-called gag order, the high Court effectively put an end to its widespread use."

The outcome can be compared to what happened following the issuing of strict procedural rules for film censorship in *Freedman* v. *Maryland* (1965)—the burden was simply too heavy for the censors to bear and film licensing eventually died. It did not take as long for gag orders to die, however; the blow for freedom to communicate struck by *Nebraska–Stuart* was swift and effective.

Public communicators should note at least two fundamental points that emerge from *Dickinson* and *Nebraska–Stuart. First,* the events and testimony occurring in open court may not be subjected to prior restraint—at least not for long; this point of law is explicitly underscored by Chief Justice Burger in his opinion in the *Nebraska* case. *Second,* if a federal judge—or a state judge in a state which has adopted the Dickinson rule—issues a restrictive order that a reporter or other person believes to be unconstitutional, that individual should obey the injunction until it is reversed (or sustained) by orderly judicial review. (In other words, the "gatekeeping" judge should be obeyed even while the reporter challenges the shut gate.)

Attempts by trial judges to protect the events in their courtrooms from pretrial publicity that might prejudice the fair trial process did not come to an end with the *Nebraska–Stuart* decision. No sooner had the impact of Chief Justice Burger's opinion filtered down to the trial courts than some judges began to consider another approach—simply closing the hearing or the trial to the public. Having settled the question of prior restraint, the Court was next asked to examine the access issue.

The Right of Access to the Courtroom

In 1979 the Supreme Court, by a 5-to-4 decision, upheld an action by New York Judge DePasquale to close a preliminary hearing in a murder case that held the potential for considerable pretrial publicity over involuntary statements the defendants had allegedly given the police. The move to bar the public came at the request of the defense counsel and had the strong support of defendants Kyle Greathouse and David Jones. In sustaining Judge DePasquale's decision, Supreme Court Justice Potter Stewart stated in his opinion for the Court that "The Constitution nowhere mentions any right of access to a criminal trial on the part of the public; its guarantee . . . is personal to the accused."[44] Joining with Justice Stewart were Chief Justice Burger and Justices Powell, Rehnquist, and Stevens (all of whom except Stevens wrote separate opinions).

In strong dissent, and arguing that the Sixth Amendment guaranteed a *public* trial (and that this included preliminary hearings) as a safeguard to both society and to the accused, were Justices Brennan, White, Marshall, and Blackmun. The general disarray of the Court in this decision sent confusing signals to the nation's courtrooms, and—even though *Gannett* was limited to preliminary hearings—a number of judges moved to close their courtrooms for the main trials as well. As William Linsley, professor of speech communication at the University of Houston, reports in the 1980 *Free Speech Yearbook,* this decision "clarified little as judges across the country in more than thirty trials, bolstered by what they thought the *Gannett* decision meant, barred the press and the public."[45]

The question of the public's right to attend a criminal trial was addressed by the Supreme Court a year following the confusing *Gannett* decision, and this time the Court was much clearer concerning its position as well as more protective of the First Amendment rights of the public and the press. The case was on appeal from a murder trial in Virginia, where the judge had closed the trial to the public. Despite protests of the media, including representatives of Richmond Newspapers, Inc., the trial was completed with the public excluded and the defendant found not guilty. When asked to review the case, the justices of the U.S. Supreme Court immediately saw it as a means of clarifying *Gannett*. On July 2, 1980, the Court announced its decision; by a 7-to-1 vote, the justices affirmed that trials must be open to the public.[46]

Chief Justice Burger delivered the opinion of the Court and in so doing noted that the *Gannett* decision of 1979 concerned preliminary hearings, not trials, and for that reason was not altered by the present decision of *Richmond Newspapers.* However, when access to the trial itself is the question before the Court, the rules change, and the public must be admitted. After reviewing the history of the Anglo-American trial system, and emphasizing the common law tradition of *public* criminal trials, the chief justice turned to the First Amendment issues raised by the case:

> The Bill of Rights was enacted against the backdrop of the long history of trials being presumptively open. . . . In guaranteeing freedoms such as those of speech and press, the First Amendment can be read as protecting the right of everyone to attend trials so as to give meaning to those explicit guarantees. . . . Free speech carries with it some freedom to listen. "In a variety of contexts this Court has referred to a First Amendment right to 'receive information and ideas.'" . . . What this means in

[44]*Gannett Company v. DePasquale,* 443 U.S. 368 (1979).

[45]William A. Linsley, "The Supreme Court and the First Amendment: 1979–1980," in *Free Speech Yearbook: 1980,* ed. Peter E. Kane (Annandale, Va.: Speech Communication Association, 1981), pp. 68–69.

[46]*Richmond Newspapers, Inc.* v. *Virginia,* 448 U.S. 555 (1980). Note: Justice Rehnquist was the only dissenter; Justice Powell did not take part in the decision.

the context of trials is that the First Amendment guarantees of speech and press, standing alone, prohibit government from summarily closing courtroom doors which had long been open to the public at the time that Amendment was adopted. . . .

It is not crucial whether we describe this right to attend criminal trials to hear, see, and communicate observations concerning them as a "right of access," . . . or a "right to gather information," for we have recognized that "without some protection for seeking out the news, freedom of the press could be eviscerated." . . . The explicit, guaranteed rights to speak and to publish concerning what takes place at a trial would lose much meaning if access to observe the trial could, as it was here, be foreclosed arbitrarily.

Two reservations should be noted concerning the Court's opinion in the *Richmond Newspapers* case. *First,* by not reversing the 1979 *Gannett* decision, which permitted the closing of a preliminary hearing, the Court left in place its rule that access to a pretrial hearing could be denied if the judge believed that the subsequent publicity might taint the jury pool (i.e., create a strong bias in the community from which the jury would be drawn, thus undermining the Constitution's guarantee of a fair trial). *Second,* Chief Justice Burger's opinion in the *Richmond Newspapers* case does not assert an absolute right of access by the public to criminal trials. In his concluding words, the Chief Justice qualified his opinion to suggest that an exception could occur; he made it clear, however, that any judge who decided to close a trial to the public bore a heavy burden of proof. Such a move must be shown to be a "last resort" to insure fairness to the accused.

The victory for access to criminal trials was confirmed two years later in *Globe Newspaper Co.* v. *Superior Court,* when the U.S. Supreme Court ruled unconstitutional on First Amendment grounds a Massachusetts statute that *required* trial judges in cases concerning certain sexual offenses to close the courtroom to the press and the general public during the testimony of victims under the age of eighteen.[47] By a vote of 6 to 3, the Supreme Court threw out the state law. Justice Brennan, writing for the majority, emphasized that the statute in question made it mandatory that trials be closed under the specified circumstances rather than to allow for consideration of a motion to close based upon the special circumstances of a given case. This general approach of the state of Massachusetts swept too broadly and thus conflicted with a fundamental purpose of the First Amendment, namely, "to protect the free discussion of governmental affairs." True, as announced in *Richmond Newspapers,* the right of access to criminal trials is not absolute; however, exceptions must be individually made with those making the request assuming a heavy burden of proof to justify such drastic action. Only in this way, Justice Brennan concluded, can trial courts meet the requirement of the First Amendment for access to government activities so that the public can be informed.

Related Issues of Freedom of the Press

In concluding this discussion of fundamental issues of free press and fair trial, three related topics are worthy of mention: the use of television in the courtroom, reporter's privilege, and the search of newsrooms by police. Although these issues are not as central to the fair trial matter as are some others, they are, nevertheless, important—particularly to those students who are planning careers in journalism or law.

[47]*Globe Newspaper Co.* v. *Superior Court,* 457 U.S. 596 (1982).

Television in the Courtroom

The question of allowing the channel of television to be used in the courtroom in order to inform the general public of local judicial events has been warmly debated in recent years. Objections to permitting "new gadgets" into the courtroom go back at least to the mid-1930s trial of Bruno Hauptmann for the kidnapping and murder of the Lindbergh infant. Many observers at that trial came away with the conviction that the circuslike atmosphere, abetted by cameras in the courtroom, prevented the defendant from receiving a fair trial. In direct response to the events of the Hauptmann trial, the American Bar Association announced a rule (now numbered as Canon 35) prohibiting cameras, radio, and television in the courtroom. Adherence to the ABA's rule is voluntary, however, and for years the states of Colorado and Texas refused to comply.

In its first opinion concerning the employment of television in the courtroom, the U.S. Supreme Court in 1965 overturned the conviction of financier Billie Sol Estes, whose Texas trial for fraud had been partly televised. The 5-to-4 opinion upsetting the conviction of Estes asserted that, as handled in this specific case, the televising of two days of a preliminary hearing probably prejudiced the jurors in the trial which followed.[48] In addition, said the Court, the presence of the television camera during a trial could have a negative influence upon the witnesses, the trial judge, and the defendant himself. Although the decision did not explicitly forbid the future use of television, it certainly had a decade-long chilling effect upon experimentation with the new medium.

By the late 1970s the chill of *Estes* had begun to dissipate, as over half of the states were experimenting with quietly operated, unobtrusive television cameras in the courtroom. In one of those states, Florida, where only the assent of the judge is needed for a trial to be televised, criminal proceedings against two former police officers charged with burglary were shown on television after the judge agreed to the proposal. Following their conviction in this trial, the defendants appealed to the U.S. Supreme Court, arguing that the presence of television had denied them a fair trial. The Court rejected their argument and upheld their convictions, noting that the defendants had failed to show that the use of television "compromised the ability of the particular jury that heard the case to adjudicate fairly."[49] Furthermore, the Court said that the *Estes* decision of 1965 did not mean that television was barred "in all cases and under all circumstances" from the courtroom. The Court declined, however, to announce a First Amendment right of access by television to a trial—there was no extension of *Richmond Newspapers* forthcoming in *Chandler.* One should note that those states which are either experimenting with or allowing on a regular basis the use of television in the courtroom are free to continue after *Chandler,* and it can be predicted with some certainty that the use of television in the courtroom will be a matter of growing importance to public communicators in the years ahead.

Reporter's Privilege: Keeping Sources Confidential

In 1972 the U.S. Supreme Court stunned the journalists of America by ruling that they could not claim either an absolute or a qualified privilege under the Constitution to remain silent about confidential news sources when called to testify before a grand jury. In

---

[48]*Estes* v. *Texas,* 381 U.S. 532 (1965).

[49]*Chandler* v. *Florida,* 449 U.S. 560 (1981).

the case of *Branzburg* v. *Hayes,* which consolidated three appeals into one opinion, a sharply divided Court, by a 5-to-4 vote, balanced the competing interests of the reporters and the state's investigators, coming down on the side of the state.[50] As Justice White stated in his opinion for the Court, "We are asked to create another [privilege] by interpreting the First Amendment to grant newsmen a testimonial privilege that other citizens do not enjoy. This we decline to do."

The case arose over the refusal of three reporters from different states and in unrelated cases to testify in criminal investigations before grand juries concerning matters about which each had publicly reported. The decision of the Supreme Court did not concern the notes, tapes, or other "raw materials" of these reporters, but it did seek answers to questions about alleged crimes. As Justice White wrote, the issue in *Branzburg* was "whether a newspaper reporter who has published articles about an organization can, under the First Amendment, properly refuse to appear before a grand jury investigating possible crimes by members of that organization who have been quoted in the published articles." (Although television is not mentioned, it is covered by this decision; one of the three appellants, Paul Pappas, worked for a television station.) The answer, as already noted, is that the First Amendment does not entitle newspeople to so refuse.

Three significant developments concerning the issue of the confidentiality of a reporter's sources have emerged since *Branzburg* and should be noted by those in fields of public communication:

1. As usual, most interpretations of the decision have occurred as specific cases arise in the lower courts; many lower courts have found the standards advocated by Justice Stewart in his dissent in *Branzburg* (in which he was joined by Justices Brennan, Douglas, and Marshall) to be useful guidelines. In many instances, in fact, Justice Stewart's three standards have been adopted. As he argued, when "a reporter is asked to appear before a grand jury and reveal confidences, I would hold that the government must (1) show that there is probable cause to believe that the newsman has information which is clearly relevant to a specific probable violation of law; (2) demonstrate that the information sought cannot be obtained by alternative means less destructive of First Amendment rights; and (3) demonstrate a compelling and overriding interest in the information." Those courts which follow these three requirements have extended some degree of protection to reporters.

2. Although *Branzburg* concerns the grand jury process, its principles also reach both criminal and civil trials. Judges in trial courts have generally been more willing to protect the reporter's confidence in civil cases than in criminal ones. In criminal cases where reporters are called upon to testify, the three-part test urged by Justice Stewart is often applied.[51]

3. Finally, although many have urged Congress to pass a national newsperson's

---

[50]*Branzburg* v. *Hayes, In Re Pappas,* and *U.S.* v. *Caldwell,* 408 U.S. 665 (1972). The five-man majority consisted of Justice White, who delivered the opinion of the Court, Chief Justice Burger, and Justices Rehnquist, Blackmun, and Powell. In strong dissent were Justices Douglas, Brennan, Stewart, and Marshall.

[51]For more on this complex development of the law, see Jerome A. Barron and C. Thomas Dienes, *Handbook of Free Speech and Free Press* (Boston: Little, Brown, 1979), pp. 424–474. For an example of a court decision concerning a state shield law, see *Austin* v. *Memphis Publishing,* a decision of the Tennessee Supreme Court reported in 9 Med.L.Rptr. 2070 (1983). For an essay arguing that statutes that create special privileges for the press are not needed, see Robert G. Dixon, Jr., "The Constitution Is Shield Enough for Newsmen," *American Bar Association Journal* 60 (June 1974): 707 ff.

privilege law or even one that applies only to the federal courts, Congress has so far not acted on the idea. More than half the states, however, have revised their journalist's shield laws since *Branzburg.* Reporters and others interested in this complicated and varied (from state to state) area of the law should take the brief discussion here as introductory only, keep up with developments, and be familiar with the specifics of the law in the state or states in which they work.[52]

Police Searches of Newsrooms

In April of 1971 police searched the offices of the *Stanford Daily,* Stanford University's student newspaper, trying to find photographs made by the paper's staff that would help police identify persons who had taken part in a campus riot on the previous day. The officers did have a warrant permitting them to look for "negatives and photographs and films" related to the violence in question. Four officers conducted the search, which included the paper's photographic laboratories. In the process, no locked drawers or locked rooms were opened. The search proved fruitless and no material was taken from the premises.

Later, the staff of the *Stanford Daily* sued Palo Alto Police Chief Zurcher, the district attorney, and others involved in the episode, charging violation of rights under the First, Fourth, and Fourteenth Amendments. The U.S. Supreme Court rejected the claims of the *Stanford Daily* staff and ruled, in effect, that journalists had no special rights to protect them from properly drawn search warrants and were to be treated like any other citizen in the matter.[53] Justice White, speaking for the Court (which rejected the newspaper's claim by a 5-to-3 vote, in which Justice Brennan did not participate), noted that even though there was no question of criminality on the part of the paper's staff and no criminal was alleged to be on the premises, there was "reasonable cause to believe that the specific 'things' to be searched for [i.e., photographs of the rioters] and seized are located on the property to which entry is sought." Therefore, wrote Justice White, "it is untenable to conclude that property may not be searched unless its occupant is reasonably suspected of crime and is subject to arrest." Newsroom searches are rare, he further observed, and adequate safeguards are already built into the Constitution as administered by the nation's magistrates. Justice White concluded his opinion by agreeing that the legislature may, if it wishes, provide special protection to the media for possible search warrant abuses, but that the Court will not intervene to do so.

Rarely has a Supreme Court decision been so roundly condemned by the nation's publishers and broadcasters as was *Zurcher* v. *Stanford Daily.* In some newsrooms, photograph files and other records were systematically destroyed, and new policies for the immediate destruction of photographs, films, and notes deemed unnecessary to the story at hand were put into place. Some journalists charged that the police were simply too lazy or inefficient to do their own investigative work and that, by the abuse of search war-

---

[52]Neither the Stewart test nor the state shield law saved the *New York Times* and its reporter Byron Farber in a 1978 New Jersey case in which Farber and the *Times* were ordered to give confidential documents to the court concerning news stories published in the *Times* that led to a murder indictment and a trial. Farber claimed confidentiality and refused to produce the documents; the *Times* supported him. Reporter Farber spent forty days in jail for contempt, and the newspaper was fined heavily. *In Re Farber,* 394 A.2d 330 (N.J. 1978). Note: The documents were never produced; in 1982 New Jersey Governor Brendan Byrne pardoned both the *New York Times* and Byron Farber.

[53]*Zurcher* v. *Stanford Daily,* 436 U.S. 547 (1978).

rants, they were hoping to get the media to "do their work for them." So heated was the issue that Congress acted to diminish the effects of the decision by legislation. In 1980 the Congress approved and President Jimmy Carter signed the Privacy Protection Act to prohibit searches of journalists for documentary materials connected with their work except in unusual circumstances, such as (1) to prevent death or injury to persons, (2) to prevent documents from being destroyed, (3) when a subpoena has been ineffective in securing appropriate documents, and (4) if and when the journalist himself or herself is believed to be a party to the crime under investigation.[54]

Public communicators should note that *subpoenas* may still be issued for documents in the possession of journalists. There is less objection to the subpoena process since it is slower, allows time for negotiation and arbitration, and may even be challenged in court. It is the "surprise search" by warrant to which persons in the media strongly objected.

Free Press–Fair Trial in Brief

The conflict between the rights of a free press and the rights of an accused person to a fair trial has created some significant clashes within recent years. *First,* the use of gag orders by judges to prevent pretrial publicity from influencing potential jurors has been struck down by the Supreme Court as unconstitutional in most circumstances. How-

ever, according to the Dickinson rule, reporters who wish to avoid a contempt citation should obey a restrictive order even while they are challenging it on constitutional grounds. In addition, the reporting of events that transpire in open court may not be prohibited by a judge-issued prior restraint decree except in the most unusual of circumstances. *Second,* the public does have access to the courtroom and may not be excluded except in rare circumstances; there is less right of access to preliminary hearings, but in most cases these, too, should be open. *Finally,* the quiet and unobtrusive use of television in the courtroom is permissible in state courts if the states wish to allow it; reporters do *not* have a special privilege of keeping their sources confidential from grand jury inquiry (or even from criminal or civil trial testimony in some cases); and the Constitution does *not* prohibit the police from searching newsrooms with a properly drawn search warrant (although Congress has passed special legislation to limit this process and to provide for the use of a subpoena as a less drastic alternative to a warrant).

CONCLUSION

1. *Prior restraint* (the landmark case being *Near* v. *Minnesota,* 1931). Efforts to constrain expression by the imposition of prior restraint are illegal in most instances, the exceptions being (a) to protect the public decency, (b) to assure the national security, and (c) to prevent a breach of the peace. The U.S. Supreme Court has developed its prior restraint doctrine over the years by declaring unconstitutional: (1) a city ordinance whose broad sweep prohibited the public distribution of all literature in the city without written permission from the town's manager (*Lovell* v. *Griffin,* 1938); (2) city ordinances

---

[54]The Privacy Protection Act can be found in 94 *Statutes at Large* 1879. In a related issue, the Supreme Court in 1978 refused to review a decision of a federal circuit court that the records of a reporter's long distance telephone calls could be subpoenaed from the telephone company without the reporter being notified. See *Reporters Committee for Freedom of the Press* v. *A. T. and T.,* 593 F.2d 1030 (D.C. Cir. 1978).

which prohibited all handbill distribution as a means of keeping the streets free of litter (*Schneider* v. *State,* 1939); (3) a broad injunction against the distribution of a handbill critical of the business practices of an Illinois realtor (*Austin* v. *Keefe,* 1971); (4) the prior restraint "pressure tactics" of Rhode Island to prevent the distribution of "objectionable" books in a system that lacked clear standards and had no judicial supervision (*Bantam Books* v. *Sullivan,* 1963); (5) an Alabama law making it illegal to publish editorials on election day (*Mills* v. *Alabama,* 1966); and a Georgia law prohibiting the publication of the names of rape victims, including names that were a matter of public record (*Cox* v. *Cohn,* 1974).

The prior restraint of film, however, has been permitted by the Supreme Court, which in *Times Film Corp.* v. *Chicago* (1961) upheld the constitutionality of film licensing to "protect the public decency." Later, in *Freedman* v. *Maryland* (1965), the Court announced three procedural safeguards that had to be followed by film review boards: (1) the censors had the burden of proof to show that the film was illegal; (2) the license must be granted or denied within a definite, short period of time; and (3) provisions must be made for prompt judicial review. Under these Court-imposed standards, the prior restraint of films was greatly curtailed and eventually died out.

Prior restraint for national security reasons was not permitted by the Supreme Court in 1971, when the government attempted to prevent the publication of the "Pentagon Papers." In a second case, the government's effort to censor *The Progressive*'s H-bomb story in 1979 was finally withdrawn after several newspapers published articles containing information similar to that in the restrained *Progressive* piece. Third, attempts by ex-government agents to publish information about their classified activities, even though they had signed secrecy agreements concerning these activities, were rebuffed by the judiciary. The secrecy contract is legal, said the courts, and the First Amendment does not change that fact. Those who have signed valid secrecy agreements, therefore, must secure clearance for the publication of information concerning their former work with the government.

And what of one's duty to obey statutes, administrative decisions, or court orders that impose prior restraint upon the sending of messages? The Supreme Court has ruled that one may ignore a statute if it is "invalid on its face" (although in many cases one cannot be sure that the courts will agree that the law is invalid, thus some degree of risk is present); however, in those instances when the law itself is valid but is improperly applied by government officials, the proper procedure is to obey the administrative decision while taking the issue to court. Finally, court orders which communicators believe to be unconstitutional prior restraints upon expression should be obeyed while subjecting them to judicial review.

2. *Free press—fair trial.* Judge-issued gag orders to prevent pretrial publicity from prejudicing potential jurors are, in almost all instances, unconstitutional (*Nebraska Press Association* v. *Stuart,* 1976). Also, courtrooms must be open to the public for criminal trials, for the public has a right to know what is communicated in open court (*Richmond Newspapers* v. *Virginia,* 1980; and *Globe Newspaper Co.* v. *Superior Court,* 1982). Prior restraint orders to gag the press or to close a trial to the public bear a heavy burden of proof, since the presumption of constitutionality is on the side of a free press and an open trial. The medium of television may be employed in the courtroom to communicate the events of a trial to the general public without necessarily denying the defendants a fair trial.

And in related matters, the Supreme Court has ruled that the Constitution confers no special privilege upon journalists either to refuse to testify before a grand jury about stories they have published or to prevent police from searching newsrooms under the authority of a search warrant (the Congress has narrowed the instances in which a search warrant may be used for newsroom search).

EXERCISES

A. Classroom projects and activities.

1. Here are three propositions phrased for debate:

a. Resolved, that this class agrees with the efforts of the government to prevent the publication of an H-bomb recipe by *The Progressive*.

b. Resolved, that prior restraint upon the media should *never* be permitted in cases of conflict between free press and fair trial.

c. Resolved, that shield laws are needed to protect the confidential sources of journalists. (The affirmative should outline an ideal shield law and defend it.)

2. Here are the same three questions phrased for discussion:

a. Under what circumstances, if any, would the government be justified in exercising prior restraint in order to protect national security or the safety of the citizenry?

b. Is the state ever justified in exercising prior restraint upon the press in order to assure a fair trial? (Compare the American system with that of the British.)

c. Do journalists need shield laws to provide them with a privilege of keeping their sources confidential? If so, what would an ideal shield law cover?

3. Invite a judge and an attorney to speak to the class about problems related to the televising of criminal trials. What is the policy of your state? What are the advantages and the disadvantages of the use of television in the courtroom?

4. Invite a local investigative reporter (or a panel of reporters) to discuss the issues raised by this chapter, with emphasis upon (a) access to the courtroom and (b) keeping sources confidential. Does the reporter favor a shield law to protect confidential sources? Discuss.

5. Secure reprints of *The Progessive*'s H-bomb story for each member of the class (write for availability and bulk prices to *The Progressive*, 408 W. Gorham St., Madison, WI 53703). Study the article plus the additional materials on the case that are included in the reprint; discuss in class. Take a class vote on whether or not the article should have been censored.

6. Discuss the Dickinson rule from the 1972 case of *U.S.* v. *Dickinson*, in which the federal court of appeals held that a gag order should be obeyed while it is being challenged in the courts. Does not this rule delay "hot news," so that it might no longer be news by the time the appeal is heard and decided? Should the Dickinson rule be changed?

7. Have each student in the class prepare a list of no more than ten subjects (ranked from most important to least important) that he or she believes represents or could represent a clear and present danger to national security and about which prior restraint might be justified. Make copies for distribution and exchange lists. Discuss the results.

8. In the CIA secrecy cases, the courts restricted themselves to the issue of abiding by the terms of a contract. Discuss this in class. Should the courts have gone further to include the First Amendment implications of such secrecy agreements? Take a class vote on the outcome of both the *Marchetti* and *Snepp* cases. (Allow advocates to speak on the side they believe in prior to the vote.)

9. In the 1966 case of *Mills* v. *Alabama,* the Supreme Court struck down a "fair campaign practices" statute which prohibited "last-minute" editorials on election day. Was the action of the Court wise? What other methods can be used to combat last-minute charges that permit no time for rebuttal? Discuss.

10. In the case of *Burstyn* v. *Wilson* (1952), Justice Clark asserted that film was a special medium that required a special censorship because "motion pictures possess a greater capacity for evil . . . than other modes of expression." Was he correct, or not? What scientific evidence does he cite? Discuss.

11. Does your state provide a shield law by which reporters are granted a privilege of keeping their sources confidential? Examine the statutes of your state and report back to the class.

B. Topics for research papers or oral reports.

1. A History of the Practice of Prior Restraint in England (or in America).

2. Chief Justice Charles Evans Hughes and the First Amendment.

3. Sensational Trials in American History: Has the Press Been Responsible in Its Coverage?

4. Television in the Courtroom: Implications for the Future.

5. The Case *for* Prior Restraint for National Security Purposes.

6. Prior Restraint to Assure a Fair Trial: The British System.

7. Fear of New Channels: An Examination of the Reluctance of the Courts to Accept New Technology.

8. Censorship (Prior Restraint) of Films in America for Reasons Other Than "Obscenity."

9. Should *The Progressive* Have Been Permitted to Publish Its H-Bomb Story? A Case Study.

10. The CIA Secrecy Cases *(Marchetti* and *Snepp):* An In-Depth Analysis.

11. The Debate over "Gag Orders" Issued by Trial Judges: Arguments Pro and Con.

12. Television in the Courtroom: An Analysis of Cases Since *Rideau* v. *Louisiana* (373 U.S. 723, 1963).

13. Reporter's Privilege: The Consequences of *Branzburg* v. *Hayes* (1972).

14. From Supreme Court Decision to Congressional Response: A Study of the Case of Police Searches of Newsrooms *(Zurcher* v. *Stanford Daily,* 1978).

15. Freedom of Speech versus the Contempt Power of the Courts: A Conflict Under Law.

16. Do Journalists Need Shield Laws? An Analysis.

17. "Gatekeeper" Theory and Prior Restraint in American Law.

18. Journalism Ethics and Trial Reportage: The Theory and the Practice.

19. Prior Restraint Tribulations of American Films Prior to 1950.

20. A History of the Struggle for *Open Trials* in England and America.

SELECTED READINGS

General Sources and Sources on Prior Restraint

Barnett, Stephen R. "The Puzzle of Prior Restraint." *Stanford Law Review* 29 (Fall 1977): 539–560.

Barron, Jerome A., and Dienes, C. Thomas. *Handbook of Free Speech and Free Press.* Boston: Little, Brown, 1979.

Comment. "National Security and the First Amendment: The CIA in the Marketplace of Ideas." *Harvard Civil Rights–Civil Liberties Law Review* 14 (Fall 1979): 655–709.

DeGrazia, Edward, and Newman, Roger K. *Banned Films: Movies, Censors and the First Amendment.* New York: Bowker, 1982.

Fleener, Nickie. "'The Worst Case of Racial Equality He Ever Saw': The Supreme Court, Motion Picture Censorship, and the Color Line." In *Free Speech Yearbook: 1979,* pp. 1–15. Edited by Peter E. Kane. Falls Church, Va.: Speech Communication Association, 1979.

Franklin, Marc A. *The First Amendment and the Fourth Estate.* 2nd ed. Mineola, N.Y.: The Foundation Press, 1981.

Friedman, Robert. "The United States v. *The Progressive.*" *Columbia Journalism Review* 18 (July–August 1979): 27–35.

Friendly, Fred W. *Minnesota Rag.* New York: Random House, 1981. (Concerns the landmark case of *Near* v. *Minnesota.*)

Goldfarb, Ronald. *The Contempt Power.* New York: Columbia University Press, 1963.

Haiman, Franklyn S. *Speech and Law in a Free Society.* Chicago: University of Chicago Press, 1981.

Huffman, John L., and Trauth, Denise M. "Freedom of the Press: An Eroding Legal Concept." In *Free Speech Yearbook: 1979,* pp. 58–66. Edited by Peter E. Kane. Falls Church, Va.: Speech Communication Association, 1980.

Hunter, Howard O. "Toward a Better Understanding of the Prior Restraint Doctrine: A Reply to Professor Mayton." *Cornell Law Review* 67 (January 1982): 283–296.

Litwack, Thomas R. "The Doctrine of Prior Restraint." *Harvard Civil Rights–Civil Liberties Law Review* 12 (Summer 1977): 519–558.

Mayton, William T. "Toward a Theory of First Amendment Process: Injunctions of Speech, Subsequent Punishment, and the Costs of the Prior Restraint Doctrine." *Cornell Law Review* 67 (January 1982): 245–282.

Medow, Jonathan. "The First Amendment and the Secrecy State: *Snepp* v. *United States.*" *University of Pennsylvania Law Review* 130 (April 1982): 775 ff.

Moffett, Meri West. "Open Secrets: Protecting the Identity of the CIA's Intelligence Gatherers in a First Amendment Society." *Hastings Law Journal* 32 (July 1981): 1723–1775.

Morland, Howard. *The Secret That Exploded.* New York: Random House, 1981. (Morland's account of *The Progressive* censorship case.)

Murphy, William P. "The Prior Restraint Doctrine and the Supreme Court: A Reevalution." *Notre Dame Lawyer* 51 (July 1976): 898–918.

Nelson, Harold L., and Teeter, Dwight L., Jr. *Law of Mass Communications.* 4th ed. Mineola, N.Y.: Foundation Press, 1982.

Note. "Journalists' View of *The Progressive* Case: A Look at the Press, Prior Restraint, and the First Amendment from the Pentagon Papers to the Future." *Ohio State Law Journal* 41 (1980): 1165–1205.

Oakes, James L. "The Doctrine of Prior Restraint Since the Pentagon Papers." *University of Michigan Journal of Law Reform* 15 (Spring 1982): 479 ff.

Overbeck, Wayne, and Pullen, Rick D. *Major Principles of Media Law.* New York: Holt, 1982.

Pember, Don R. *Mass Media Law.* 3rd ed. Dubuque, Iowa: Wm. C. Brown, 1984.

Phifer, Gregg. "H-Bomb 'Secrets' and the *Progressive.*" In *Free Speech Yearbook: 1980,* pp. 99–114. Edited by Peter E. Kane. Annandale, Va.: Speech Communication Association, 1981.

Shapiro, Martin, ed. *The Pentagon Papers and the Courts.* San Francisco: Chandler, 1972.

"Symposium: *Near* v. *Minnesota,* 50th Anniversary." *Minnesota Law Review* 66 (November 1981): 1–208.

Ungar, Sanford J. *The Papers and the Papers: An Account of the Legal and Political Battle Over the Pentagon Papers.* New York: Dutton, 1972.

Sources on Free Press-Fair Trial

Barber, Susanna R. "*Chandler* v. *Florida:* The Supreme Court's Reluctance to Endorse Televised Trials." *Southern Speech Communication Journal* 48 (Summer 1983): 323–339.

Brennan, William J. "Why Protect the Press?" *Columbia Journalism Review* 18 (January–February 1980): 59–62.

"First and Fourth Amendments Do Not Prohibit

Use of Search Warrants Against Newspapers." *Tulane Law Review* 53 (June 1979): 1513–1523.

Lewis, Anthony. "A Public Right to Know About Public Institutions: The First Amendment as Sword." In *The Supreme Court Review: 1980,* pp. 1–25. Edited by Philip B. Kurland and Gerhard Casper. Chicago: University of Chicago Press, 1981.

Marcus, Paul. "The Media in the Courtroom: Attending, Reporting, Televising Criminal Cases." *Indiana Law Journal* 57 (1981–82): 235 ff.

Nesson, Charles R., and Koblenz, Andrew D. "The Image of Justice: *Chandler* v. *Florida.*" *Harvard Civil Rights-Civil Liberties Law Review* 16 (Fall 1981): 405–413.

"Rights of Sources—The Critical Element in the Clash Over Reporter's Privilege." *Yale Law Journal* 88 (May 1979): 1202–1217.

Rubin, David M. "Reporters, Keep Out!" *Columbia Journalism Review* 17 (March–April 1979): 47–58.

Stephenson, D. G., Jr. "Fair Trial-Free Press: Rights in Continuing Conflict." *Brooklyn Law Review* 46 (Fall 1979): 39–66.

Towers, Wayne M. "Empirical Research and Some Major Supreme Court Decisions on Free Press/Fair Trial Conflicts." In *Free Speech Yearbook: 1978,* pp. 60–67. Edited by Gregg Phifer. Falls Church, Va.: Speech Communication Association, 1979.

"*Zurcher* v. *Stanford Daily:* The Legislative Debate." *Harvard Journal on Legislation* 17 (Winter 1980): 152–194.

CHAPTER 10

Technology and Free Speech—Part I: Copyright

"Things are in the saddle,
And ride mankind."

—*Ralph Waldo Emerson,* Ode to W. H. Channing

In the year 1620 Sir Francis Bacon published his important work *Novum Organum,* in which he asserted (in Aphorism 129) that "We should note the force, effect, and consequences of inventions which are nowhere more conspicuous than in those three which were unknown to the ancients, namely, printing, gunpowder, and the compass. For these three have changed the appearance and state of the whole world." Surely Bacon was correct in his assessment, particularly concerning the first of the three, printing. Not only did printing accelerate religious, social, and political change by facilitating the rapid dissemination of ideas which challenged the old order of things, but also additional problems created by the technology itself emerged almost at once. For example, copyright—established in England by royal decree in 1557—is one of the most enduring constraints upon the freedom to communicate to be born out of print technology.

Centuries later, print was supplemented by the marvels of electronic communication, including the telegraph, telephone, radio, motion pictures, loudspeakers, television, and so on. The chapter that follows addresses free-speech issues created by contemporary technology—broadcasting in particular—whereas the present chapter examines the communication constraint of copyright. Following the historical summary, the discussion of copyright is presented below according to two main topics: (1) the basics of U.S. copyright law and (2) First Amendment issues inherent in copyright law.

The invention of the printing press by Johann Gutenberg in 1450 marked the begin-

ning of the influence of technology on the issue of freedom of expression, for, as Chapter 1 explains, the primary methods of communication before printing were the human voice and manuscripts laboriously copied by hand. Neither of these pre-Gutenberg channels was capable of reaching mass audiences. Printing changed matters irrevocably, however, for the press made it possible to produce books, pamphlets, and broadsides in large numbers for the first time in history—a fact not lost upon the clergy and kings of the sixteenth century. The frantic efforts of King Henry VIII and the English clergy to control the upstart press resulted in a system of prior restraint known as licensing and soon led to the establishment of England's first copyright regulation, a royal decree issued by Henry's Catholic daughter Mary during her brief reign. The chronology of events leading to the system of Anglo-American copyright law currently in effect can be summarized in eight steps. (For more on the points below, see Chapters 1 and 2.)

1. In 1557 Queen Mary I, daughter of Henry VIII, announced the grant of the first printer's monopoly in English history. This was done by royal decree, not by act of Parliament, and was issued to the private Stationers' Company, the London-based guild of printers, bookbinders, and booksellers, in exchange for the company's support in suppressing "seditious" and "blasphemous" materials. Consequently, the Stationers' Company exercised a "perpetual lease" upon most materials published in England, including such items as maps and legal documents, for almost 150 years. It is important to note that this first grant of a form of copyright was to printers and booksellers, *not* to authors.

2. In 1559 Queen Elizabeth, who ascended to the throne upon the death of her half-sister Mary in 1558, reconfirmed the

FIGURE 10.1.
GUTENBERG'S FIRST
PROOF.
*Johann Gutenberg's invention of
printing with movable type, in
1450, was of major importance
in the history of communication.
The resulting technology of the
printing press for the first time
made it easy to disseminate
minority opinion to the general
populace, much to the grief of
established systems of
government and religion. In
addition, printing gave birth to
the enduring law of copyright.
This sketch appears in an essay
on early printing published in*
Harper's Magazine, *September
1855.*

perpetual lease Mary had granted to the Stationers' Company (again, this was done as a form of payment to the company for its help in suppressing unlicensed printing).

3. In 1694 the copyright monopoly granted by royal decree to the Stationers' expired when Parliament, rebelling against the practice of prior restraint, refused to renew the licensing system. Almost immediately chaos developed in the publishing industry, since no decree or statute governed who had the right to print what.

4. In 1710 the Statute of Anne, England's first *parliamentary* copyright statute, went into effect. Because of the enormous financial stakes involved in how the language of the Statute of Anne was to be interpreted and applied, heated argument raged among writers, publishers, and those in the legal profession, until the House of Lords ruled on the matter.

5. In 1774 the House of Lords gave a landmark interpretation to the Statute of Anne, declaring that copyright was an au-

thor's right, not a publisher's right as it had been under the royal decrees, and that the protection of copyright was for a limited period of time as set by act of Parliament (initially for fourteen years, renewable for a second term of fourteen years, after which the material entered the public domain). This ruling rejected the old concept of a perpetual lease upon protected materials and eventually became a principle of American copyright law.

6. In 1788 the U.S. Constitution was ratified, thus making the copyright clause of Article I, Section 8:8 the "law of the land." This part of the Constitution does not employ the word "copyright" but does provide the basis for it in the following language: "Congress shall have Power . . . To promote the Progress of Science and useful Arts, by securing for limited Times to Authors and Inventors the exclusive Right to their respective Writings and Discoveries."

7. In 1790 the U.S. Congress approved

the first federal copyright statute, providing protection for writings, maps, charts, and similar materials for a term of fourteen years, renewable for an additional and final term of fourteen years.

8. In 1834 the federal copyright law, as amended by Congress in 1831 (the amendment added "musical composition" to the list of materials protected and lengthened the initial term of protection from fourteen to twenty-eight years, while leaving the length of the second term at fourteen years), was given its landmark interpretation by the U.S. Supreme Court. In this case of *Wheaton* v. *Peters,* the Court upheld the authority of Congress under the Constitution to *create* copyright regulations by statute—in other words, the Court said that copyright in the United States is what Congress says it is, not what tradition or Anglo-American case law (common law) prior to 1834 said it was.[1] The effect of the judgment was to affirm the decision of Congress that copyright to published works in the United States was a monopoly grant to the author for a set period of time. Apparently these early debates, both in the legislature and in the courts, did not generate much if any concern over the inherent tension between copyright monopoly and freedom of speech.

I. GENERAL PRINCIPLES OF U.S. COPYRIGHT LAW

With legal precedent firmly in place following *Wheaton* v. *Peters,* the federal copyright statute has been substantially revised three times: in 1870, in 1909, and most recently in 1976. The revision of 1870 added to the list of protected works such things as plays, photographs, engravings, paintings, and drawings. The revision of 1909 extended the term of *renewal* from fourteen to twenty-eight years, thereby providing authors with a maximum period of protection of fifty-six years. This was the rule until the Copyright Act of 1976 became effective on January 1, 1978, at which time the term was changed to the life of the author plus fifty years, a standard generally used throughout the world. (For anonymous works or works done for hire, the length of copyright under the new law is seventy-five years.)[2] There is no provision for renewal in the Copyright Act of 1976 once the designated terms have expired.

The U.S. Copyright Office defines copyright as a "form of protection given by the laws of the United States to the authors of 'original works of authorship' such as literary, dramatic, musical, artistic, and certain other intellectual works."[3] The 1976 statute generally gives the copyright owner exclusive rights "to do and to authorize" (1) the reproduction of protected work in copies or phonorecords; (2) the preparation of derivative works based upon the copyrighted work; (3) the distribution of copies of the work to the public for sale or other transfer of ownership or by rental, lease, or lending; (4) the public performance of copyrighted works such as plays, musicals, and motion pictures; and (5) the public display of copyrighted works such as paintings, sculptures, or individual images from motion pictures, dramatic productions, or other audiovisual work.

---

[1] *Wheaton* v. *Peters,* 33 U.S. 591 (1834). For a detailed analysis of the complexities of this case, see Lyman Ray Patterson, *Copyright in Historical Perspective* (Nashville, Tenn.: Vanderbilt University Press, 1968).

[2] The current law is found in 17 *U.S. Code* Secs. 101–810 (1976), where it is codified as an appendix to title 17 of the *Code.* Also, it is found in 90 *Statutes at Large* 2541 ff.

[3] U.S. Copyright Office, *The Nuts and Bolts of Copyright,* Circular R-1 (Washington, D.C.: U.S. Government Printing Office, 1980), p. 3.

What Can and Cannot Be Copyrighted

Under the 1976 statute, copyright protection exists automatically—even without official registration with the U.S. Copyright Office—for both unpublished and published "original works of authorship" after they are created, that is, when they become fixed in a *tangible form of expression.* (There are obvious advantages to official registration, however, for the public record established by registration is necessary for most infringement suits.) Copyrightable works include such things as literature, music, drama, pantomimes, choreography, photographs, graphics, sculptures, motion pictures, speeches, sound recordings, computer programs, maps, blueprints, etc.[4] Even video game formats, including the program as manufactured in the game's circuit board, are protected by copyright according to a 1983 decision of the U.S. Court of Appeals for the Seventh Circuit.[5]

Some materials are not eligible for protection under the copyright law. According to the U.S. Copyright Office, these include the following:

Works that have *not* been fixed in a tangible form of expression. For example: choreographic works which have not been notated or recorded, or improvisational speeches or performances that have not been written or recorded.

Titles, names, short phrases, and slogans; familiar symbols or designs; mere variations of typographic ornamentation, lettering, or coloring; mere listings of ingredients or contents.

Ideas, procedures, methods, systems, processes, concepts, principles, discoveries, or devices, as distinguished from a description, explanation, or illustration.

Works consisting entirely of information that is common property and containing no original authorship. For example: standard calendars, height and weight charts, tape measures and rules, schedules of sporting events, and lists or tables taken from public documents or other common sources.[6]

Fair Use

The right of fair use of copyrighted materials has been recognized by the courts for many years; however, it was not incorporated into the *U.S. Code* until 1976, when Congress explicitly included the principles of fair use in the new law. According to Section 107 of the current statute, "the fair use of a copyrighted work . . . for purposes such as criticism, comment, news, reporting, teaching (including multiple copies for classroom use), scholarship, or research, is not an infringement of copyright."[7] The statute then sets out four factors derived from American case law which must be considered when making a fair-use determination. These four factors should be considered as parts of a whole, for they interact with each other to give general guidance to authors and editors—and judges—when questions of unauthorized use of copyrighted materials are decided.

[4]Public speakers should note that copyright protection does exist for addresses fixed in tangible form, and although infringement suits concerning public speeches are rare, some are of record. For example, a federal injunction was issued in 1963 against a recording firm that had issued an unauthorized edition of Martin Luther King's "I Have a Dream" speech while King was in the process of securing a copyright so that income from use of the speech would support the work of the Southern Christian Leadership Conference. See *King* v. *Mister Maestro,* 224 F. Supp. 101 (S.D.N.Y. 1963).

[5]*Midway* v. *Arctic International,* 9 Med.L.Rptr. 1605 (1983).

[6]*The Nuts and Bolts of Copyright,* p. 4.

[7]For an excellent summary of fair-use guidelines applicable to educational institutions, see J. Jeffery Auer, "The Rules of Copyright for Students, Writers, and Teachers," *Communication Education* 30 (July 1981): 245–255. Auer reports, for example, that for multiple copies for classroom use, the instructor should make only one copy per student and that each copy must carry a notice of the copyright.

1. *The purpose and character of the use, including whether such use is of a commercial nature or is for nonprofit educational purposes.* This factor, which suggests that nonprofit, educational use is "fairer" in the eyes of the law than is for-profit commercial use, protects the reasonable use of copyrighted material for purposes such as criticism, scholarship, teaching, news reporting, and so on.

2. *The nature of the copyrighted work.* Some works "invite" a degree of fair use that others do not. For example, reference works such as dictionaries or encyclopedias, as well as public speeches, collected documents of public officials, and similar "quotable" sources, are natural candidates for fair use. On the other hand, specialized short pieces and unpublished letters, poems, musical lyrics, and similar materials are of a different nature and do not "invite" use in the way that a reference work does.

3. *The amount and substantiality of the portion used in relation to the copyrighted work as a whole.* For copyright permission purposes, a direct quotation of 100 words from a lengthy book differs from a quotation of the same length from a short essay. Although the Copyright Act does not spell out specific page-length maximums, it does recognize this principle of proportion. To comply, publishing companies, employing a "common sense" rule of what is permitted, do spell out word maximums for their authors. For example, an examination of contemporary authors' manuals from three American publishers revealed a range of 50 to 150 words without permission from a periodical and of 200 to 400 words without permission from a book.[8] Furthermore, any commercial use of even so much as a single line from a poem, play, or musical lyric requires a per-

mission, as does the reproduction of tables, diagrams, illustrations, cartoons, photographs, maps, and the like.

4. *The effect of the use upon the potential market for or value of the copyrighted work.* This factor is of major importance in fair-use determination, for if the unauthorized use diminishes the commercial value of the original work in a significant way, it is more likely to be classified as an infringement than otherwise. The central principle focuses upon the degree to which the use supplants the usual market for the original material.

Works Done for Hire and the Transfer of Ownership

The author–creator of a work initially owns all rights to the work or creation unless the work is done "for hire." Section 101 of the Copyright Act states that any work is defined as "work made for hire" if it is (1) "prepared by an employee within the scope of his or her employment," or (2) if by written agreement between author and publisher the material is "specially ordered or commissioned for use as a contribution to a collective work, as a part of a motion picture or other audiovisual work, as a translation, as a supplementary work, as a compilation, as an instructional text, as a test, as answer material for a test, or as an atlas." In short, one's employer or the publishing company with which one signs a "for hire" contract owns the copyright to works done for hire.

The copyright belongs to the author–creator in works other than those done for hire. Under provisions of the 1976 act, those authors who create independently may sell all rights to a work or only limited rights—such as permission for one-time use—whichever best suits the needs of the author. For example, the writer of a short story may transfer the ownership (i.e., sell or give away a per-

[8]The manuals consulted were from Random House, Harper & Row, and Kendall/Hunt.

mission) of his or her copyright to a magazine for one-time publication; later, if some editor wishes to include that short story in an anthology or if a film company wishes to make a motion picture based upon the story, the author is free to negotiate a second contract—or, for that matter, even a third and a fourth—for the use of the same material. According to Section 201 of the new copyright law, only when an author has signed a *written* contract which specifically states that he or she transfers complete ownership of copyright does that author give up all future rights to the work in question. For this and other reasons, the Copyright Act of 1976 is often described as "the author's friend."

Additional Information Concerning Copyright

The U.S. Copyright Office of the Library of Congress publishes a number of brochures that are helpful to the individual interested in further details about the 1976 statute. For information on how to apply for a copyright, for example, consult Circular R-1, *The Nuts and Bolts of Copyright,* or write to the U.S. Copyright Office (c/o Library of Congress, Washington, D.C. 20559). Many research libraries have a file on the circulars from the copyright office, and time can be saved by finding the materials locally rather than writing for them. Also, a list of sources concerning copyright is provided at the conclusion of this chapter.

II. COPYRIGHT LAW AND THE FIRST AMENDMENT

In March of 1970 law professor Melville B. Nimmer, an authority on the law of copyright, noted in a lecture to the Copyright Society of the U.S.A. that the Constitution contains a "largely ignored paradox, requiring exploration." This paradox begins with the First Amendment which asserts that "Congress shall make no law . . . abridging the freedom of speech, or of the press," and moves directly to the copyright laws, which in fact do constrain free speech and free press. Nimmer asked his audience: "Does not the Copyright Act fly directly in the face of the command [of the First Amendment]? Is it not precisely a 'law' made by Congress which abridges the 'freedom of speech' and 'of the press' in that it punishes expressions by speech and press when such expressions consist of the unauthorized use of material protected by copyright?"[9] In this way Nimmer focused the spotlight on a First Amendment issue that had been generally neglected by the courts and by legal scholars over the years.

The questions raised by Nimmer and others,[10] when added to the national debate of the late 1960s and early 1970s over how to revise the copyright law (culminating in the approval by Congress of the Copyright Act of 1976), have sparked a growing body of literature on the subject. In addition, at least one federal district court decision of the 1970s is on record as recognizing a First Amendment defense against alleged copyright infringement.[11] In order to analyze systematically the basic issues raised by the "constitutional paradox" of copyright law versus freedom of speech, the following discussion is organized according to three main topics:

[9]Melville B. Nimmer, "Does Copyright Abridge the First Amendment Guarantees of Free Speech and Press?" *UCLA Law Review* 17 (1969–70): 1181.

[10]For example, see Paul Goldstein, "Copyright and the First Amendment," *Columbia Law Review* 70 (1970): 983–1057.

[11]The case, discussed in more detail later in the chapter, is *Triangle Publications* v. *Knight-Ridder Newspapers,* 445 F. Supp. 875 (S.D. Fla. 1978); it was affirmed on appeal, but not on First Amendment grounds, 626 F.2d 1171 (5th Cir. 1980).

(1) areas of harmony and support between copyright and free speech, (2) areas of tension between the two, and (3) cases of the First Amendment defense in copyright infringement suits (including *Triangle Publications* v. *Knight-Ridder Newspapers,* the only successful use of that defense in American jurisprudence).

Areas of Harmony and Support

Generally speaking, copyright serves to promote freedom of expression by encouraging authors to create books, plays, films, etc., assuring these authors of some monetary reward for their labors by guaranteeing a temporary monopoly in the sale and use of their work. Put another way, without the financial incentive provided by copyright, many authors would not create (some simply could not afford to live without the income from their royalties), and society would suffer because of the absence of a thriving community of creative artists. As law professor Paul Goldstein observes, the "rewards of political expression are essentially political, and the only stimulus required to induce political speech is an audience capable of political action." On the other hand, the rewards of artistic expression are monetary and "the artist seeks cash instead of votes." Goldstein concludes: "Copyright, by providing the economic incentive to the production of artistic expression, theoretically assures that the range of subject matter disseminated will include that which is prompted by profit considerations and will not be left merely to the chance of political motivation."[12]

In addition to promoting freedom of expression by providing a financial incentive to the author, as noted above, American

[12]Goldstein, p. 990.

copyright law accommodates the principle of freedom of expression in at least four specific ways: by restricting the grant to certain persons and for a limited period of time, by providing for fair use, by supporting the idea–expression dichotomy, and by permitting the copyright office to administer a "content free" system. Each of these four policies merits a brief explanation.

1. *Restrictions upon grantee and upon time.* By restricting the grant of copyright to the author–creator, and by adding a time limitation upon the monopoly, the law narrows the scope of copyright and guarantees that all materials will eventually fall into the public domain. When this is compared to the first printer's monopoly—a "perpetual lease" given by Queen Mary I to London's Stationers' Company in 1557—its significance becomes apparent.

2. *Fair use.* As discussed above, the Copyright Act of 1976 explicitly recognizes the principles of fair use that have developed in American common law over the years. By permitting considerable "fair use of a copyrighted work," the Congress moved a step toward freedom of speech when it approved the 1976 revision of the statute.

3. *The idea–expression dichotomy.* Authors may copyright their unique manner of expressing an idea, but they may not copyright the idea itself. This important principle is summarized by Celia Goldwag in her Note concerning "Copyright Infringement and the First Amendment," as follows:

The distinction that copyright draws between ideas and the expression of ideas is a . . . useful device for accommodating first amendment interests. A basic premise of copyright is that only the expressions of ideas are copyrightable; the ideas themselves, however original, remain in the public domain. Thus, any number of copyrights may be obtained for material that expresses the same idea, as long as each piece qualifies as an original work.[13]

4. *Content-free administration.* As a general rule, copyright is granted routinely to authors who follow the specified procedures set out by the U.S. Copyright Office—the office makes no judgment concerning either the quality of the work submitted or the religio-moral or political orthodoxy of the content of the work. To the extent that this content-free policy is adhered to, the administrators of the law advance the cause of free speech. Although denial of copyright to a work because of alleged "illegal content" is infrequent, it has occurred even though the federal copyright law does not require such a determination.[14] Attorney Norman A. Palumbo, Jr., in his historical survey of the issue, cites a number of instances of government refusal to grant a copyright to certain works deemed defamatory, blasphemous, or obscene.[15] Examples of the latter category include the denial of copyright in 1867 to a play in which women appeared on the stage in flesh-colored tights (the court stated that it had little interest in protecting a work which called for a scene showing "women 'lying about loose' "); a copyright refusal in 1898 to the song *Dora Dean* because of the "obscene" line "She's the hottest thing you ever seen"; and the attempted denial of copyright to the popular song of the late 1940s, *Rum and Coca-Cola* (an Andrews Sisters recording), because the lyrics allegedly hinted at prostitution ("immoral" hint or not, the federal courts eventually ordered that *Rum and Coca-Cola* be granted a copyright).[16]

In 1980 the issue was evidently put to rest—for the time being, at least—in favor of a content-free policy when the U.S. Supreme Court refused to review a decision of the U.S. Court of Appeals for the Fifth Circuit in which the "adult film" *Behind the Green Door* (which includes numerous explicit sex scenes) was allowed to keep its copyright. The court of appeals had reversed a decision of a federal district court that the film forfeited its claim to copyright because of its allegedly obscene content, and in so ruling the court of appeals stated: "In our view, the absence of content restrictions on copyrightability indicates that Congress has decided that the constitutional goal of encouraging creativity would not be best served if an author had to concern himself not only with the marketability of his work but also with the judgment of government officials regarding the worth of the work."[17]

Areas of Tension

Other than the general inherent tension between copyright and freedom of expression, at least three specific areas of strain have received attention in cases and comment during recent years. These three, each of which is

---

[13]Note, "Copyright Infringement and the First Amendment," *Columbia Law Review* 79 (March 1979): 323.

[14]In contrast, federal law does specify that trademarks and trade names may not be "immoral, deceptive or scandalous." See 15 *U.S. Code* Sec. 1052(a). A case in point occurred in 1971 when the trademark office refused to approve the trade name "Booby Trap" for a line of brassieres, arguing that such a name would offend the propriety and morality of the public. See *U.S. Patents Quarterly* 171 (1971): 443.

[15]Norman A. Palumbo, Jr., "Obscenity and Copyright: An Illustrious Past and Future?" *South Texas Law Journal* 22 (1982): 87–101.

[16]See Palumbo, pp. 94–96. The "flesh-colored tights" case is *Martinetti* v. *Maguire*, 16 F. Cas. 920 (C.C. Cal. 1867), case no. 9,174; the *Dora Dean* controversy is recorded in *Broder* v. *Zend Mauvais Music Co.*, 88 F. 74 (C.C.N.D. Cal., 1898); and the *Rum and Coca-Cola* case is *Khan* v. *Leo Feist, Inc.*, 70 F. Supp. 450 (S.D.N.Y., 1947), affirmed at 164 F.2d 188 (2d Cir., 1947).

[17]*Mitchell Brothers Film Group* v. *Cinema Adult Theatre*, 604 F.2d 852 (5th Cir. 1979), *cert. denied*, 445 U.S. 917 (1980).

discussed briefly below, are as follows: (1) attempts to use copyright as a means of censorship, (2) the problem created when idea and expression cannot be separated, and (3) the chilling effect created by the tedious, time-consuming task of securing permissions.

1. *Using copyright to attempt censorship.* Occasionally some copyright holder will attempt to suppress a critical message by manipulating the copyright law. A clear-cut instance occurred in the early 1960s, when Random House announced its plans to publish an unauthorized biography of wealthy recluse Howard Hughes, only to be confronted with a concerted effort by Hughes to buy up rights to much of the source material employed in the biography and thus suppress the book by denying Random House permission to use it. To accomplish this, Hughes created a special corporation, Rosemont Enterprises, through which he purchased rights to a series of *Look* magazine articles about himself which were used extensively in the biography. When Random House refused to bow to pressure, Hughes-owned Rosemont Enterprises sued for copyright infringement.[18]

The Second Circuit Court of Appeals, recognizing the deviousness of the scheme by noting that Hughes came to the bench with "unclean hands" in this action, rejected the position of Rosemont Enterprises and ruled in favor of Random House. The court of appeals, while alluding to the First Amendment, employed a rationale that combined fair use and public interest to decide the case. Observing that in suits such as this one the "spirit" of the First Amendment applied to copyright, the Court ruled that it was appropriate to "subordinate the copyright holder's interest in a maximum financial return to the greater public interest in the development of art, science and industry." The U.S. Supreme Court denied review, thus allowing the decision of the circuit court to stand. The decision in *Rosemont* clearly signals those who might attempt to use the copyright statutes as a means of deliberate censorship that the courts are likely to reject such efforts by the would-be censors.

2. *When idea and expression cannot be separated.* In certain instances, *ideas* (which cannot be copyrighted) can be communicated effectively only by the use of copyrighted expression. Although the problem usually concerns graphic works, it sometimes does involve unillustrated written materials as well. This inherent weakness in the idea–expression dichotomy was discussed by copyright authority Nimmer in his address to the Copyright Society of the U.S.A. (noted earlier). Nimmer employed an example of the photographs of the Mai Lai massacre perpetrated upon Vietnamese civilians by American soldiers during the war in Vietnam. He observed: "Here is an instance where the visual impact of a graphic work made a unique contribution to an enlightened democratic dialogue. No amount of words describing the 'idea' of the massacre could substitute for the public insight gained through the photographs. The photographic expression, not merely the idea, became essential if the public was to fully understand what occurred in that tragic episode." Nimmer concluded that in those rare instances when the expression of the news photograph was essential to the effective communication of an idea, "the speech interest outweighs the copyright interest." However, he would not extend the First Amendment exception to graphics other than those narrowly and carefully defined as "news photographs."[19] Two court cases serve to further illustrate the controversy.

---

[18]*Rosemont Enterprises* v. *Random House,* 366 F.2d 303 (2d Cir. 1966), *cert. denied,* 385 U.S. 1009 (1967).

[19]Nimmer, pp. 1197–1199.

A 1968 case concerned an infringement suit brought by Time, Inc., against Bernard Geis Associates over the unauthorized use by Geis of selected frames from a Time-owned film of the assassination of President John F. Kennedy. The author of the book published by Geis had made selective use of the copyrighted film in order to try to prove his theory that more than one person was involved in the shooting of the president. The federal district court held for Geis on the grounds that the photos were fairly used since they were essential to the development of the author's theory. In other words, the copyrighted expression (the film) could not be separated from the author's ideas (the theory espoused).[20]

The second case concerned writing—not film, photographs, or other graphics. An infringement suit was brought against author Louis Nizer for his unauthorized use of the letters of Julius and Ethel Rosenberg in his story of the Rosenberg case, *The Implosion Conspiracy.* The letters, published twenty years earlier in a work entitled *The Death House Letters,* were essential, Nizer argued, for the communication of his ideas. The district court agreed with this argument, noting that "the obvious device of not quoting [the letters] directly" would have weakened the author's efforts to convey his ideas about the Rosenbergs "fully and accurately."[21] Even though the district court's decision was overturned upon appeal,[22] University of Nebraska law professor Robert C. Denicola says that the district court's opinion does address "precisely the right question: Can the right to free speech be adequately protected by free access to ideas, or do special circumstances require the freedom to use expression as well?"[23] To answer the question, Denicola reaches a conclusion similar to that of Nimmer, namely, that in those few instances when access to a particular *expression* is necessary for the effective communication of an *idea,* a First Amendment privilege should be recognized for that access. Leonard W. Wang, in his comment in the *Wisconsin Law Review,* proposes a two-point test which, he argues, would accommodate both copyright and speech interests. Says Wang: "In order to protect first amendment interests, unconsented use of copyrighted material should be permitted (1) if the defendant, while perpetrating the alleged copyright infringement, is engaged in expression protected by the first amendment, and (2) if the defendant's expression could not be effectively made without using the unique mode of expression embodied in the copyrighted work."[24] Time will tell whether or not the courts (or the Congress by way of an amendment to the copyright statute) adopt the approach argued by legal scholars such as Nimmer, Denicola, and Wang.

3. *The chilling effect of securing permissions.* Anyone who has pursued the task of arranging for the use of copyrighted material in a book, film, or other creative work knows the frustration of trying to locate the copyright holder, securing an agreement on royalty fees, and getting the legal papers signed and returned in time for publication. Whereas many copyright owners respond to inquiries

---

[20]*Time* v. *Geis,* 293 F. Supp. 130 (S.D.N.Y. 1968).

[21]*Meeropol* v. *Nizer,* 417 F. Supp. 1201 (S.D.N.Y. 1976), at 1212.

[22]560 F.2d 1061 (2d Cir. 1977), *cert. denied,* 434 U.S. 1013 (1978).

[23]Robert C. Denicola, "Copyright and Free Speech: Constitutional Limitations on the Protection of Expression," *California Law Review* 67 (March 1979): 283–316, at p. 308.

[24]Comment, "The First Amendment Exception to Copyright: A Proposed Test," *Wisconsin Law Review* (1977): 1158–1192.

in a prompt, businesslike manner, others are slow or simply do not bother to respond at all. In particular, the individual author who is attempting without professional assistance to secure authorizations for the use of protected materials often faces a time-consuming task in researching the address of the copyright holder, making inquiries concerning fees, following through with permissions forms, and so on. To the extent that this effort discourages an author and results in the omission of important content from a work, it can be said to have a chilling effect upon the exercise of freedom of speech.

An interesting solution to the chilling effect problem is proposed by Professor Paul Goldstein of the State University of New York at Buffalo. Goldstein recommends that a national clearinghouse for copyrighted materials be established, similar to that of the American Society of Composers, Authors and Publishers (ASCAP), which has for a number of years efficiently licensed a majority of America's copyrighted musical works. Like ASCAP, the proposed clearinghouse would be open to all, be content-free and nondiscriminatory in its administration, and would provide a system of reasonable royalty fees that would be efficiently collected and dispersed to the copyright holders. Goldstein observes that the ASCAP system, with its more than 15,000 writer and publisher members, licenses about three-fourths of the nation's copyrighted popular and classical music, and that it does this in a manner which is a great convenience to would-be users of the music it controls. By extending the ASCAP model to written works and other forms of copyrighted expression, Goldstein concludes that access would be facilitated, thereby promoting freedom of speech.[25]

The First Amendment Defense in Copyright Infringement Suits

On November 13, 1977, the *Miami Herald* launched a promotional campaign for its new television supplement—a campaign of comparison advertising that featured both print and television graphics showing the difference in size between the *Miami Herald*'s publication and the widely read *TV Guide* (see Figure 10.2). The publishers of *TV Guide* were not amused and sought a federal injunction to stop the newspaper from using a copy of their magazine in the campaign of comparison. To the surprise of most observers, including copyright attorneys and professors of copyright and First Amendment law from California to New York, Federal District Judge James L. King denied the injunction on First Amendment grounds. Asserting that the doctrine of fair use did not help the defendants in this case, Judge King ruled, nevertheless, for the *Miami Herald* by deciding that the commercial speech doctrine which had recently been announced by the U.S. Supreme Court in *Bates* v. *Arizona* (the lawyer advertising decision discussed in Chapter 7) did in this instance provide a rationale for the unauthorized use of copyrighted material. Quoting from *Bates,* the judge observed that advertising "serves to inform the public of the availability, nature, and prices of products and services" and that such commercial messages serve "individual and societal interests in assuring informed and reliable decisionmaking." Therefore, Judge King concluded, the use of the cover of an issue of *TV Guide* in the case at bar "is in harmony with the fundamental objectives of free speech and free enterprise in a free society."[26]

Subsequently, the Fifth Circuit Court of

[25]Goldstein, pp. 1047–1057.

[26]*Triangle Publications* v. *Knight-Ridder Newspapers,* 445 F. Supp. 875 (S.D. Fla. 1978); the Supreme Court case

**The Herald's new TV Book.
It's a little bit bigger
and a little bit better.**

The TV Book. At no extra cost in Sunday's Miami Herald.

FIGURE 10.2.   THE MIAMI HERALD'S *CONTROVERSIAL ADVERTISEMENT. This advertisement from the* Miami Herald *of November 13, 1977, compared the size of the newspaper's new television supplement with that of* TV Guide, *thus sparking a suit for copyright infringement from the magazine because its cover was used without permission. The federal district court upheld the* Herald'*s use of the cover of* TV Guide *on First Amendment grounds, the first such ruling of record. The federal circuit court of appeals agreed with the result of the district court, but on fair-use rather than First Amendment grounds. There the matter rested—and the district court's decision stands alone, to date, as an example of the successful use of a First Amendment defense in copyright infringement litigation.*

Reproduced with permission of the Miami Herald.

Appeals unanimously affirmed the judgment of the district court, but on grounds of *fair use*—and without reaching the First Amendment issue raised by Judge King.[27] Circuit Judge John R. Brown concurred in the result but dissented over the unwillingness of the

other two members of the panel to address the First Amendment defense—a defense that Judge Brown would like to reject. "Even where, as here, the idea and the expression are wedded in graphic form," Judge Brown argued, "I believe that the First Amendment will rarely prevail over a copyright interest." However, Judge Tate, a second member of the appeals panel, urged in a concurring opinion that the First Amendment option be kept open for the future, when a more appropriate case comes before the bench. Said Judge Tate: "In my view, under limited circumstances, a First Amendment privilege

is *Bates* v. *Arizona,* 433 U.S. 350 (1977). Among those who disagree with the First Amendment rationale of the district court in the *TV Guide* case: Denicola, p. 306; Celia Goldwag in her note, "Copyright Infringement and the First Amendment," p. 327; and Peter E. Hans in his note, "Constitutional Law—Commercial Speech—Copyright and the First Amendment," *Wisconsin Law Review* (1979): 242–266.

[27]*Triangle Publications* v. *Knight-Ridder Newspapers,* 626 F.2d 1171 (5th Cir. 1980).

may, and *should* exist where utilization of the copyrighted expression is necessary for the purpose of conveying thoughts or expressions." He concluded that in the eventuality that the Court were someday to be "squarely faced with the attempted prohibition of a use of copyrighted expression not protected by fair use but necessary for the adequate expression of thought," it would then be appropriate to consider the "sensitive First Amendment issue concerning fundamental values of a free society." Thus was born the common-law doctrine of a First Amendment defense for certain types of copyright infringement cases, a doctrine that has thus far generated little enthusiasm among authors— or among federal judges.

A second case of recent times to raise important questions of First Amendment as well as fair-use privileges in the unauthorized publication of copyrighted material began in March of 1979, when an unnamed source gave to the editor of *The Nation,* a weekly magazine of political opinion, a draft of former President Gerald Ford's memoirs. The manuscript was scheduled for publication by Harper & Row and the Reader's Digest Association under the title of *A Time to Heal;* also, *Time* magazine had arranged to serialize portions of the manuscript for a fee of $25,000, half of which had been paid in advance. On the grounds that the Ford memoirs, even though copyrighted, were newsworthy, *The Nation* in its issue of April 9, 1979, published portions of the material in a three-page article of about 2,250 words, most of which was paraphrased from the original. In fact, only 300 words of direct quotations were taken from the approximately 200,000 words of the book. Upon learning of the unauthorized publication by *The Nation, Time* canceled its serialization agreement, thereby causing a financial loss of the $12,500 still due the copyright holders on the original con-

tract. In response, Harper & Row and the Reader's Digest Association brought suit for copyright infringement in the U.S. District Court for the Southern District of New York.

Despite the claim of Nation Enterprises that its use of the Ford material was privileged for reasons of (1) fair use, (2) the presence of an abundance of noncopyrightable information (such as statements from public documents), and (3) the First Amendment, the trial court was not persuaded. U.S. District Judge Richard Owen ruled for the copyright holders, arguing that *The Nation* had taken "what was essentially the heart of the book," published it for profit, and had thereby "diminished the value of the copyright." Such use, concluded Judge Owen, was neither free speech as intended by the First Amendment nor fair use as described by the federal copyright laws.[28]

On appeal, by a vote of 2 to 1, the U.S. Court of Appeals for the Second Circuit reversed the district court primarily upon fair-use grounds—but fair use within the context of First Amendment values. Writing for the majority, Circuit Judge Irving Kaufman stressed the factual, historical nature of the account published by *The Nation.* Even though the account consisted of a great deal of paraphrasing, such paraphrasing of factual material—much of it already on the public record—was protected by the First Amendment. As Judge Kaufman put it, there exists a "need to strike a definitional balance between the First Amendment and the Copyright Act by permitting the free communication of facts while still protecting an author's expression." He continued:

A construction of the [Copyright] Act insisting it is impermissible copying to paraphrase

[28]*Harper & Row* v. *Nation Enterprises,* 557 F. Supp. 1067 (1983).

discrete facts ignores the unambiguous legislative history which establishes that "information" is not protected. . . . Were information copyrightable . . . , the Act would clash with the First Amendment on every occasion in which an author chose to put in his own words facts which had already been described by another writer. . . .

Nowhere could the need to construe the concept of copyrightability in accord with First Amendment freedoms be more important than in the instant case. Here we are presented with an article describing political events of major significance, involving a former President of the United States. The paraphrasings concern the very essence of news and of history. In such works, courts have carefully confined that troublesome concept "expression" to its barest elements—the ordering and choice of the words themselves. . . . Were "expression" in this context given a broader terrain, an individual could be the owner of an important political event merely by being the first to depict that event in words.[29]

Judge Kaufman then concluded that within the context of First Amendment values discussed above, the doctrine of fair use applied to the magazine article in question. This was especially so in light of the article's presentation of "factual information of great public import," accomplished with the use of only 300 copyrighted words from the original 200,000-word manuscript. Judge Kaufman added:

> Where information concerning important matters of state is accompanied by a minimal borrowing of expression, the economic impact of which is dubious at best, the copyright holder's monopoly must not be permitted to prevail over a journalist's communication. To decide otherwise would be to ignore those values of free expression which have traditionally been

accommodated by the statute's "fair use" provisions. . . . We conclude, accordingly, that there was a "fair use" of copyrighted material in this case.

CONCLUSION

Copyright, which originated in sixteenth-century England as a royal grant of perpetual monopoly to the *publisher,* has been changed over the years in both England and the United States to a statutory grant for a specified, limited period of time to the *author.* Article I, Section 8:8 of the Constitution gives Congress the power to legislate in the area of copyright, and the U.S. Supreme Court has upheld that congressional authority. The regulations currently in effect come from the Copyright Act of 1976 which, among other things, states that a work is protected for the life of the author plus fifty years.

Although inherent tensions exist between copyright monopoly and the First Amendment's guarantee of freedom of speech and press, copyright does promote freedom of expression by giving authors a monetary incentive to create. Without such an incentive, much creative thinking would simply never be expressed in a communicable form and society would suffer as a result. Furthermore, copyright regulations harmonize with the principle of freedom of expression in at least four ways: (1) by restricting the grant to authors and for a limited period of time, (2) by providing for fair use, (3) by supporting the idea–expression dichotomy, and (4) by the Copyright Office policy of "content-free" administration of the law. On the other hand, at least three significant areas of tension exist between copyright and the First Amendment: (1) attempts by some to use copyright as a means of censorship, (2) the

---

[29]*Harper & Row* v. *Nation Enterprises,* 9 Med.L.Rptr. 2489 (1983), at 2495.

problem created when idea and expression cannot be separated, and (3) the chilling effect of the time-consuming task of securing permissions for the use of protected materials.

Finally, the U.S. Supreme Court has never ruled that copyright violates the First Amendment; rather, the Court has upheld the constitutionality of the federal copyright law over the years. Recently, however, a number of questions concerning possible conflicts between copyright and free speech have been raised by legal scholars and by the parties to copyright infringement suits. In one instance a U.S. district court in Florida accepted a First Amendment defense in the 1978 infringement suit brought by *TV Guide* against the *Miami Herald*. Upon appeal, the circuit court upheld the decision of the court below in favor of the *Miami Herald,* but on fair-use rather than First Amendment grounds. Although the circuit court did not reach the First Amendment issue in its ruling, it did leave open the question of how to deal with a communication in which the *idea* must employ copyrighted *expression* (such as with a news photograph) in order to be effective. Five years later, in the case of *Harper & Row* v. *Nation Enterprises* (1983), the U.S. Court of Appeals for the Second Circuit interpreted the fair-use provisions of the Copyright Act within a framework of First Amendment principles to hold that *The Nation's* unauthorized publication of copyrighted material was permissible, in part because of the "great public import" (i.e., newsworthiness) of the information published. Here the Court made it clear that its decision was influenced by the weight of the journalist's freedom to communicate in the balance between the First Amendment and the Copyright Act. This case is on appeal to the U.S. Supreme Court, which has granted certiorari. Readers should be alert to the Court's decision in the matter.

EXERCISES

A. Classroom projects and activities.

1. Here are two questions phrased for classroom debate:

a. Resolved, that the First Amendment should protect the unauthorized use of copyrighted expression when the copyrighted expression is essential to the effective communication of an idea.

b. Resolved, that a national clearinghouse for the collection of royalties on all copyrighted materials should be established and its use mandated for all holders of copyright in the United States.

2. Here are the same two questions phrased for discussion:

a. Should the First Amendment protect the unauthorized use of copyrighted expression when the copyrighted material in question is essential to the effective communication of an idea? If so, what specific guidelines should be drawn up for determining whether or not the use of such materials is "essential"?

b. Should a national copyright clearinghouse be established and its use mandated for all copyright holders in the collection of royalties? What about the establishment of uniform royalty fees for specified categories of material (e.g., a standard fee for a line of poetry, for a page of fiction, etc.)?

3. Write to the Copyright Office, Library of Congress, Washington, D.C. 20559 for (a) a copy of Circular R-1, *The Nuts and Bolts of Copyright,* and (b) a list of current publications. Add the material to your notes for the course.

4. Invite representatives of a local newspaper and a local television station to visit the class to discuss the kinds of copyright problems they encounter and the policies they follow to deal with those problems.

5. Invite a local attorney whose practice includes a specialty in copyright law to speak to the class on "What Every Citizen Should Know About the Law of Copyright." Be prepared to ask the speaker some hard questions concerning the effect of copyright law upon free speech.

6. Is copyright really a necessity to motivate creativity? Discuss the following quotation from page 806 of attorney Harry N. Rosenfield's essay published in the *Notre Dame Lawyer* (see reading list): "The copyright law has become—or is fast becoming—irrelevant to the preponderance of creativity in nonprofit education, research, and scholarship. One of the most persistent characteristics of creativity in noncommercial education, research, and scholarship is the creator's desire for wide and untrammeled dissemination and circulation of his writings, regardless of financial royalties. . . . More bluntly, a substantial part of the copyright system's difficulties, in connection with nonprofit and noncommercial uses, is *its erroneous assumption of its own necessity as an incentive to creativity*." (Emphasis supplied.)

B. Topics for research papers or oral reports.

1. Using Copyright Law to Censor Content: A Historical Survey.

2. The Two Faces of Copyright: An Analysis of How the Law Both Promotes and Hinders Freedom of Communication.

3. A Short History of the Evolution of Copyright Law in the United States.

4. A Defense of *The Nation*'s "Hot News" Argument in the Case of *Harper & Row* v. *Nation.* (Discussed in the chapter above.)

5. A Defense of the Position of the Copyright Holders in the Case of *Harper & Row* v. *Nation.*

6. A History and Analysis of the Evolution of Content-Free Administration of the Copyright Laws of the United States.

7. A Comparison and Contrast Between the Copyright Laws of the United States and the Copyright Laws of Other Nations. (Select one or more foreign countries for your comparisons.)

8. A Study of Proposals for Facilitating the Securing of Permissions and the Paying of Royalties for Copyrighted Materials.

9. Judge King Was Right! A Defense of the First Amendment Position of the U.S. District Court in the Case of *Triangle Publications* v. *Knight-Ridder Newspapers* (1978).

10. Judge King Was Wrong! Arguments Against the First Amendment Position of the U.S. District Court in the Case of *Triangle Publications* v. *Knight-Ridder Newspapers* (1978).

SELECTED READINGS

Auer, J. Jeffery. "The Rules of Copyright for Students, Writers, and Teachers." *Communication Education* 30 (July 1981): 245–255.

Chickering, Robert B. *How to Register a Copyright and Protect Your Creative Work.* New York: Scribner's, 1980.

Comment. "The First Amendment Exception to Copyright: A Proposed Test." *Wisconsin Law Review* (1977): 1158–1192.

Comment. "The Obscenity Defense Denied: The Rise of a Rational View of Copyright." *Western State University Law Review* 9 (Fall 1981): 83 ff.

Comment. "Parody, Copyrights and the First Amendment." *University of San Francisco Law Review* 10 (Winter 1976): 564–585.

Denicola, Robert C. "Copyright and Free Speech: Constitutional Limitations on the Protection of Expression." *California Law Review* 67 (March 1979): 283–316.

Goetsch, C. C. "Parody as Free Speech—The Replacement of the Fair Use Doctrine by First Amendment Protection." *West New England Law Review* 3 (Summer 1980): 39–66.

Goldstein, Paul. "Copyright and the First Amendment." *Columbia Law Review* 70 (1970): 983–1057.

Howell, Herbert A. *The Copyright Law: Howell's Copyright Law Revised and the 1976 Act.* Washington, D.C.: Bureau of National Affairs, 1979.

Jacobson, Jeffrey E. "Fair Use: Considerations in Written Works." *Communications and the Law* 2 (Fall 1980): 17–38.

Johnson, Donald F. *Copyright Handbook.* 2nd ed. New York: Bowker, 1982. (A standard reference; recommended.)

Lawrence, John S., and Timberg, Bernard, eds. *Fair Use and Free Inquiry: Copyright Law and the New Media.* Norwood, N.J.: Ablex, 1980.

Leavens, Thomas R. "In Defense of the Unauthorized Use: Recent Developments in Defending Copyright Infringement." *Law and Contemporary Problems* 44 (Autumn 1981): 3–26.

Nimmer, Melville B. "Does Copyright Abridge the First Amendment Guarantees of Free Speech and Press?" *UCLA Law Review* 17 (1970): 1180 ff.

Note. "Constitutional Law—Commercial Speech—Copyright and the First Amendment." *Wisconsin Law Review* (1979): 242–266.

Note. "Copyright Infringement and the First Amendment." *Columbia Law Review* 79 (1979): 320–340.

Note. "Toward a Constitutional Theory of Expression: The Copyright Clause, the First Amendment, and Protection of Individual Creativity." *University of Miami Law Review* 34 (July 1980): 1043–1075.

Note. "Toward a Unified Theory of Copyright Infringement for an Advanced Technological Era." *Harvard Law Review* 96 (December 1982): 450–469.

Palumbo, Norman A., Jr. "Obscenity and Copyright: An Illustrious Past and Future?" *South Texas Law Journal* 22 (1982): 87–101.

Patterson, Lyman R. *Copyright in Historical Perspective.* Nashville: Vanderbilt University Press, 1968.

Phillips, Jeremy. "Copyright in Obscene Works: Some British and American Problems." *Anglo-American Law Review* 6 (July 1977): 138–171.

Preston, Elizabeth, comp. *A Writer's Guide to Copyright.* Boston: The Writer, Inc., 1982.

Rosenfield, Harry N. "The Constitutional Dimension of 'Fair Use' in Copyright Law." *Notre Dame Lawyer* 50 (June 1975): 790–807.

CHAPTER 11

Technology and Free Speech— Part II: From Loudspeakers to Broadcasting and Access Theory

"Just as the Government may limit the use of sound-amplifying equipment potentially so noisy that it drowns out civilized private speech, so may the Government limit the use of broadcast equipment. The right of free speech of a broadcaster, the user of a sound truck, or any other individual does not embrace a right to snuff out the free speech of others."

—Justice Byron R. White *in* Red Lion Broadcasting Co. *v.* FCC *(1969)*

At the outset of their unique publication, *The Medium Is the Massage,* Marshall McLuhan and Quentin Fiore announce that electric technology, the medium "of our time . . . is reshaping and restructuring patterns of social interdependence and every aspect of our personal life. It is forcing us to reconsider and reevaluate practically every thought, every action, and every institution formerly taken for granted. Everything is changing— you, your family, your neighborhood, your education, your job, your government. . . . And they're changing dramatically."[1] McLuhan and Fiore might have added that the principles and practice of freedom of speech have also been changed by technology, starting with the invention of the printing press in the middle of the fifteenth century, as noted in the preceding chapter, and accelerating rapidly in the twentieth century with the development of radio and television broadcasting, various disc and tape recording techniques, motion pictures, loudspeakers, photography, photocopy machines, and the transmission of messages by cable, microwave, and satellite.

[1]Marshall McLuhan and Quentin Fiore, *The Medium Is the Massage* (New York: Random House, 1967), p. 8.

Just as print technology created a need for copyright, so do a number of modern developments in electronic communication and private ownership of the mass media create special problems of freedom and control. For example, the invention of the motion picture and its commercial development so disturbed many of those who would supervise the morality of their fellow citizens that a policy of prior restraint upon this medium of communication was accepted by the U.S. Supreme Court early in this century. The licensing of films is such a significant chapter in the history of censorship in the United States that motion pictures are discussed in Chapter 9 under the heading "Prior Restraint." The remaining main topics of modern technology and freedom of expression are discussed below according to three areas: (1) loudspeakers, (2) broadcasting, and (3) problems of access to the mass media.

I. LOUDSPEAKERS

Loudspeakers have not stirred as much passionate free speech debate in American society as have some other technologies, such as film, radio, and television. No doubt the nuisance factor in sound amplification devices helps explain the lack of passion on the part of those who would defend the widespread use of loudspeakers in the public forum. Yet the devices continue to be used from time to time, and students of the First Amendment should be familiar with legal precedent on the subject. The U.S. Supreme Court has ruled on loudspeakers and the First Amendment in only two instances: *Saia* v. *New York* (1948) and *Kovacs* v. *Cooper* (1949). Both cases are summarized below.

In *Saia* the Court by a vote of 5 to 4 struck down as unconstitutional a Lockport, New York, ordinance that gave the chief of police *discretion* over who could use sound amplifying devices on the streets and in public places. When a city permits an official to ban loudspeakers "in his uncontrolled discretion," wrote Justice Douglas in an opinion announced by Justice Black, "it sanctions a device for suppression of free communication of ideas." The dissenters, led by Justice Frankfurter, would have upheld the ordinance, largely because of the nuisance factor. As Justice Frankfurter argued, "Modern devices for amplifying the range and volume of the voice . . . afford easy . . . opportunities for aural aggression. If uncontrolled, the result is intrusion into cherished privacy."[2]

The following year in *Kovacs,* and by another vote of 5 to 4 (but with a shift in the viewpoint of the majority), the Supreme Court upheld a Trenton, New Jersey, ordinance that banned from the public thoroughfares "any device known as a sound truck, loud speaker or sound amplifier, or radio or phonograph with a loudspeaker . . . or any other instrument known as a calliope or any instrument of any kind . . . which emits therefrom *loud and raucous noises* . . . ." (Emphasis supplied.) The Court found that since there was no discretion permitted under the Trenton ordinance (the ban applied equally to all), the language "loud and raucous noises" was adequately precise. Furthermore, noted Justice Reed writing for the plurality, the reasonable control of loudspeakers does not violate the First Amendment, for the opportunity "to gain the public's ears by objectionably amplified sound on the streets is no more assured by the right of free speech than is the unlimited opportunity to address gatherings on the streets."[3]

Since 1949 the Supreme Court has been satisfied to let state and local authorities deal with loudspeaker issues, presumably within the framework of principles set forth in *Saia* and *Kovacs.* Municipalities and state courts have decided the matter in a variety of ways, ranging from a flat ban upon all loudspeakers, upheld by the courts of Florida, to a qualified ban in California, which limits control to nuisance factors such as the loudness of the device.[4] What can one conclude from the cases to date? Evidently, "reasonable" state and local laws which are administered *without discretion* in order to control sound amplification devices creating "loud and raucous noises" are constitutional. These laws may, and do, vary from total prohibitions upon loudspeakers in public places to regulations focused upon specific matters of time, place, and loudness of the amplifier in question.

II. BROADCASTING

When the Italian scientist Guglielmo Marconi began his experiments with "wireless telegraphy" in 1894, he little realized that his discoveries during the next forty years would revolutionize communication. Following the success of his attempt to send telegraph signals over the airwaves (initially for the remarkable distance of 1½ miles), Marconi offered his invention to the Italian government, which showed no interest. Upon the advice of relatives, he journeyed to London, where he filed for a patent in June of 1896. Soon, and with the support and encouragement of a number of British scientists, Marconi improved his radio device so that he was able to send signals to ships at sea—first up to 9

---

[2]*Saia* v. *New York,* 334 U.S. 558 (1948).
[3]*Kovacs* v. *Cooper,* 336 U.S. 77 (1949).

[4]*State ex rel. Nicholas* v. *Headley,* 48 So. 2d 80 (Fla. 1950); and *Wollam* v. *City of Palm Springs,* 379 P.2d 481 (Cal. 1963).

FIGURE 11.1. GUGLIELMO MARCONI, INVENTOR OF "WIRELESS TELEGRAPHY."
The invention and development of radio by the Italian electrical engineer Marconi at the turn of the century marked the beginning of a revolution in human communication technology that continues to the present day. Among other things, this technological revolution has created a variety of media-centered issues of freedom of expression unforeseen by those who wrote the First Amendment to the U.S. Constitution.
Harper's Weekly, October 7, 1899.

miles, then 12 miles, and before long hundreds of miles away. On December 12, 1901, he stunned the scientific community by spanning the Atlantic with radio transmission. For the first time, the Gutenberg technology had serious competition.

Government Supervision of Broadcasting: Rationale and a Brief History

All technology has limits, of course, and communication by radio waves is no exception to this rule. Central to an understanding of free-speech issues in broadcasting is the physical fact that *radio waves are a scarce resource.* There are only so many "slots" (frequencies) available for use in the broadcast spectrum; when those "slots" have been allocated, there are no more. For this reason, and because radio waves do not recognize national boundaries, worldwide regulations have been developed by treaty through the International Telecommunications Union (ITU) located in Geneva, Switzerland. Within the framework of rules established by the 150 nations which are members of the ITU, each nation develops its own procedures for allocating the frequencies of the broadcast spectrum.

In the United States, federal regulation of broadcasting began with the Wireless Ship Act of 1910, which required most American passenger vessels to be equipped with transmitters. Following the ratification of the first international radio treaty by Congress in 1912, the Radio Act of August 13, 1912, was enacted in order to meet the terms of the treaty.[5] This statute required a license from the secretary of commerce for the operation of a radio apparatus—the first such require-

[5]The 1910 law is found at 36 *Statutes at Large* 629; the 1912 law is found at 37 *Statutes at Large* 302.

ment in the development of broadcast regulation. Unfortunately, the new statute did not address the matter of frequencies for use by private broadcast stations, an oversight temporarily remedied by the secretary of commerce, who unilaterally assigned the inadequate number of two frequencies for such use. Before long the demand for those two "slots" was so great and the resulting arrangements to meet the demand so unsatisfactory that court actions were initiated. In 1926 a federal district court in Illinois ruled that the secretary of commerce had no authority to impose restrictions as to frequency, power, or hours of operation upon the operators of private radio stations.[6] In reference to the mess created by the district court's ruling, U.S. Supreme Court Justice Felix Frankfurter later wrote that within months "almost 200 new stations went on the air." He continued:

> These new stations used any frequencies they desired, regardless of the interference thereby caused to others. Existing stations changed to other frequencies and increased their power and hours of operation at will. The result was confusion and chaos. With everybody on the air, nobody could be heard. The situation became so intolerable that . . . [President Coolidge] in his message of December 7, 1926, appealed to Congress to enact a comprehensive radio law . . . .[7]

In response, Congress approved the Federal Radio Act of 1927, which brought order to the chaotic situation by establishing a system of licensing to be administered by a five-member Federal Radio Commission (FRC), located in the U.S. Department of Commerce, with each member appointed by the president. Furthermore, the Radio Act set forth two key principles that were retained in the Communications Act of 1934 and which continue as foundations of public law and policy governing broadcasting in the United States, namely, (1) that the airwaves belong to the people of the United States—not to the stations using them, and (2) that broadcasting is to serve the "public convenience, interest, or necessity."[8]

Moving quickly to exercise its statutory authority to assign specific frequencies to would-be broadcasters and to deny applications for licenses when there was no room for additional stations, the FRC soon had commercial broadcasting on the AM radio band functioning smoothly. In 1934 the FRC was replaced by the Federal Communications Commission (FCC) as a part of the reorganization of government under the "New Deal" administration of President Franklin D. Roosevelt. This was accomplished by congressional approval of the Federal Communications Act of 1934, which remains the basic legislation under which broadcasting operates in the United States. Section 301 of the 1934 statute reaffirms the doctrine of public ownership of the airways in the following language:

> It is the purpose of this Act, among other things, to maintain the control of the United States over all the channels of interstate and foreign radio transmission; and to provide for the use of such channels, but not the ownership thereof, by persons for limited periods of time, under licenses granted by Federal authority, and no such license shall be construed to create any right, beyond the terms, conditions, and periods of the license. No person shall use or operate any apparatus for the transmission of energy or communications or signals by radio . . . ex-

[6]*United States* v. *Zenith Radio Corp.,* 12 F.2d 614 (N.D. Ill., 1926).

[7]*National Broadcasting Company* v. *United States,* 319 U.S. 190 (1943).

[8]The Radio Act of 1927 can be found at 44 *Statutes at Large* 1162.

cept under and in accordance with this Act and with a license in that behalf granted under the provisions of this Act.

In addition, Section 303 of the 1934 law charges the newly established FCC with sustaining the policy decreed by Congress in 1927 that broadcasting serve the "public convenience, interest, or necessity."[9]

The Federal Communications Commission

The Federal Communications Act of 1934 established the FCC as an *independent* federal regulatory agency (unlike the Radio Commission, which was located in the U.S. Department of Commerce) with its own staff, and under the direction of seven commissioners who are appointed by the president and confirmed by the Senate. Commissioners serve for a period of seven years, with the terms of office staggered so that only one office is open each year. The law mandates that no more than four of the commissioners may come from any one political party and that no person may serve who has a financial interest in any of the industries regulated by the agency.

The Communications Act codifies the *general* framework of responsibility for the FCC, leaving it up to the commission to develop and approve *specific* rules and regulations for

the administration of the act. The resulting decisions of the commission carry the force of law. Those who wish to challenge an FCC decision must begin by following a three-step internal process, as follows: (1) first, the complaint is heard by an administrative law judge; (2) second, the decision of the judge may be appealed to the FCC Review Board; and (3) finally, the commissioners (who exercise discretion over which cases they accept for review) may hear the grievance. If this procedure fails to resolve the problem, the complainant may then take the case to a federal circuit court of appeals and then, if necessary, ask the U.S. Supreme Court to review the case.

The Five Bureaus of the FCC

The staff of the FCC accomplishes most of its work through five departments or bureaus, each of which is assigned specific duties. The bureaus carry out policies established either by statute or by action of the commission.

1. *The Broadcast Bureau* is of primary concern to students of the First Amendment, for it is responsible for licensing and supervising the approximately 10,000 radio and television stations currently operating in the United States.

2. *The Field Operations Bureau* maintains offices in various parts of the country and is responsible for helping to enforce numerous FCC regulations by monitoring broadcasts, making visits to radio and television stations, checking on CB (citizens' band) violations, and the like. For example, if a radio station broadcasts at a power greater than that which is assigned, the Field Operations Bureau is responsible for having the situation corrected. The office is sometimes called the policing arm of the FCC.

3. *The Cable Television Bureau* is charged

[9]The 1934 law appears in 47 *U.S. Code* Secs. 151–606. The Federal Communications Act has been amended a number of times, of course. Furthermore, federal statutes proscribing the broadcasting of lottery information, fraud, obscenity, or profanity are located in 18 *U.S. Code* Secs. 1304, 1343, and 1464. Helpful to the student who is trying to follow the twistings and turnings of legislation governing broadcasting are histories and anthologies such as Sydney W. Head and Christopher H. Sterling, *Broadcasting in America,* 4th ed. (Boston: Houghton Mifflin, 1982); and Frank J. Kahn, ed., *Documents of American Broadcasting,* 4th ed. (Englewood Cliffs, N.J.: Prentice-Hall, 1983).

with oversight of the cable television industry. The FCC entered this area directly in 1966, promulgating complex regulations the effect of which was to constrain the development of cable in deference to established television stations. Under pressures of deregulation, FCC restrictions over cable transmission have been relaxed in recent years, thus permitting a more rapid growth in cable services in the United States.

4. *The Common Carrier Bureau* regulates interstate services and rates of utilitylike operations such as the American Telephone and Telegraph Company.

5. *The Private Radio Bureau* (formerly called the Safety and Special Radio Services Bureau) supervises amateur and CB service as well as marine, aeronautical, police, and a number of other two-way public and private radio communication systems.

The Licensing of Broadcasting Stations

Stations are licensed by the FCC for a maximum period of five years for television and seven years for radio (prior to 1981, both radio and television broadcasters were required to renew their licenses every three years). Whereas any person in the United States may start a newsletter, magazine, or newspaper without securing government approval, broadcasters—who are looked upon as temporary trustees of the public airways, licensed for a few years to serve the public convenience, interest, or necessity—have a complex series of hurdles to overcome before they are allowed to go on the air. The process can be outlined in five steps.

1. First, the applicant must determine that an unused frequency (i.e., a slot on the broadcast spectrum) is available.

2. Second, most television applicants (but not those applying for television "ministations") must conduct an ascertainment study in the community where the station is to be located. This study, which is no longer required of applicants for radio broadcasting, must be done by those who plan to manage the station and must include extensive information based upon interviews and other sources as to the needs of the community to be served.

3. Third, the would-be broadcaster applies for a construction permit and license. The application should include information to convince the FCC that the applicant meets the following seven standards: (a) is a citizen of the United States, as required by federal law; (b) is of good character; (c) is adequately financed with resources to build, equip, and run the station for at least one year; (d) does not own a daily newspaper in the same market area and is in compliance with other monopoly-prevention standards of the FCC; (e) has adequate plans for programming; (f) has plans to install equipment that meets technical requirements and to employ qualified engineers to install and maintain the equipment; and (g) has a program for meeting equal employment and affirmative action requirements in the hiring of women and racial minorities.

4. Fourth, challenges (if any) must be met. A challenge to the proposed license does not always occur, but when it does it usually originates from one of two sources: (a) an established licensee who attempts to prove that the proposed station will interfere with the reception of the signal from the established station or (b) a rival applicant. In the latter instance, the FCC policy is to grant the license to the superior candidate or, in cases of equally qualified applicants, either to make a judgment as to which will do the best job or to decide the matter by lottery—a procedure authorized by Congress in 1981.

5. Finally the application process is completed, the construction permit is granted,

and—after it has been determined that the completed project meets FCC standards—the license is awarded. At this point the station may commence broadcasting.

As the time of license expiration approaches, the station must apply to the FCC for a renewal of its permit to broadcast. Generally, the presumption favors the established licensee, and the burden of proof is upon any challenger to show why the license should not be renewed. This is not always so, however, especially if serious charges of biased programming or of unethical or illegal management practices are involved. For example, in 1969 the U.S. Circuit Court of Appeals for the District of Columbia required a commercial television station in Mississippi, which was charged with blatant racism in its programming, to assume the burden of proof to show otherwise; when the station was unable to meet the court-assigned burden of proof, the court set aside the station's license. Eventually, the station lost its license to broadcast.[10] An instance of nonrenewal for a different reason occurred several years earlier, when the FCC refused to renew the license of radio station WOKO of Albany, New York, because the management had made false statements under oath in its applications for a license and for renewals over a period of years. Although the station's programming was found to be satisfactory, the license renewal was denied, and the U.S. Supreme Court sustained the FCC when that denial was challenged.[11]

Enforcement Powers of the FCC

The FCC has a number of means of enforcement at its disposal, four of which are used most often.[12] From least severe to most severe, these are as follows:

1. *A letter to the station.* Letters may range in seriousness from an inquiry about an alleged problem to a warning or a reprimand.

2. *A fine (forfeiture).* Fines are often employed by the FCC and range from small amounts of $250 to $500 to large amounts of up to $10,000. For example, failure to keep a proper log might result in a fine of $500, whereas broadcasting information concerning a lottery—a violation of federal law—might result in a fine between $5,000 and $10,000.

3. *Short-term license renewal.* The FCC is not required to renew a license for the maximum period of five years for television stations and seven years for radio stations. In those instances where deficiencies in policy and operation merit review within a year or so after license renewal, the commission may simply grant a short-term permit of from six months to two years or so.

4. *Revocation or nonrenewal of a license.* The most severe sanction exercised by the FCC is to put a station off the air by revoking or refusing to renew that station's license. In 1975, for example, the commission refused to renew the broadcast permits for all eight stations of the Alabama Educational Television Commission on the grounds of racism in the operation of the system. The FCC observed that the Alabama commission "followed a racially discriminatory policy in its overall programming practices and, by reason of its pervasive neglect of the black minority . . . did not adequately meet the needs of the public it was licensed to serve." The state system was permitted to reapply for li-

---

[10]*Office of Communications of the United Church of Christ v. FCC,* 425 F.2d 543 (D.C. Cir. 1969).
[11]*FCC v. WOKO, Inc.,* 329 U.S. 223 (1946).

[12]In addition to the four listed here, the FCC is authorized to employ cease-and-desist orders. These are rarely used, however, because the other forms of enforcement are so effective.

censes after it had corrected its policies so that it better met the needs of "significant minorities in its service areas."[13]

Broadcasting and the First Amendment

Perhaps no free-speech development of the current century better illustrates the remarkable capacity of the American Constitution to meet changing needs and circumstances than developments in the area of broadcasting and the First Amendment. The electronic marvel of Marconi's wireless, unimagined by the Founding Fathers, has presented over the years a variety of free-speech challenges to legislators, judges, legal scholars, and public communicators in general. By means of discussion and debate, the government and the broadcasting industry have forged compromises and developed policies that represent a synthesis between the old constitutional principles and the new technologies of communication. The free speech issues in this process tend to coalesce around four topics: (1) licensing (who is to own and operate a radio or television station), (2) balance in programming and access to station facilities, (3) constraints over program content (including specific issues of censorship), and (4) special problems of cable transmission.

Licensing, Ownership, and Operation of Broadcasting Facilities

Originally, licensing was established by Congress as a means of bringing order out of broadcasting chaos by mandating rules and regulations by which scarce radio frequencies were rationed to superior applicants for their temporary use. This system was based upon the dual premise that the airwaves belong to the public and that they were to be used by

licensees to serve the public interest. The licensing policy itself did not attract a First Amendment debate when Congress established it in the broadcasting legislation of 1927 and 1934; evidently few, if any, members of Congress considered how the granting of an exclusive license effectively excluded those who had no license from speaking over the airwaves with their *own voice* and in their own way. Furthermore, a second issue developed over the years concerning how much cross-ownership of radio and television stations was to be permitted. The cross-ownership issue included not only the free speech rights of would-be owners but also the general concern over how monopoly control might lead to the suppression of dissent by rich and powerful "media magnates."

The two problems concerning licensing, ownership, and operation can be stated in question form, as follows: (1) Does the granting of an exclusive broadcasting license violate the First Amendment rights of those who were denied a license? (2) Do FCC regulations limiting the concentration of ownership of stations violate the First Amendment rights of those prohibited from owning a station under those regulations? Fortunately for public communicators seeking answers, the U.S. Supreme Court has dealt with both issues.

THE CONSTITUTIONALITY OF LICENSING. The question of whether or not licensing violated the First Amendment was decided by the U.S. Supreme Court in 1943 in the case of *National Broadcasting Co.* v. *U.S.,* a case that originated in 1941, after the FCC moved to diminish the power of the networks over local stations by issuing a set of regulations governing chain broadcasting.[14]

---

[13]*Alabama Educational Television Commission,* 50 F.C.C.2d 461 (1975).

[14]*National Broadcasting Co.,* v. *U.S.,* 319 U.S. 190 (1943). Justice Frankfurter's comments on the First

The networks challenged the new regulations in court and lost, for the Supreme Court not only concluded that the FCC's rules concerning chain broadcasting were legal but also that the FCC's licensing policies were constitutional. Justice Felix Frankfurter, speaking for the Court, addressed the First Amendment question directly:

> We come, finally, to an appeal to the First Amendment. The Regulations, even if valid in all other respects, must fall because they abridge, say the appellants, their right of free speech. If that be so, it would follow that every person whose application is denied by the Commission is thereby denied his constitutional right of free speech. . . . Unlike other modes of expression, radio inherently is not available to all. That is its unique characteristic, and that is why, unlike other modes of expression, it is subject to governmental regulation. Because it cannot be used by all, some who wish to use it must be denied. But Congress did not authorize the Commission to choose among applicants upon the basis of their political, economic or social views, or upon any other capricious basis. If it did, or if the Commission by these Regulations proposed a choice among applicants upon some such basis, the issue before us would be wholly different. The question here is simply whether the Commission, by announcing that it will refuse licenses to persons who engage in specified network practices (a basis for choice which we hold is comprehended within the statutory criterion of "public interest"), is thereby denying such persons the constitutional right of free speech. **The right of free speech does not include, however, the right to use the facilities of radio without a license. The licensing system established by Congress in the Communications Act of 1934 was a proper exercise of its power over commerce. The standard it provided for the licensing of stations was the "public interest, convenience, or necessity." Denial of a station license on that ground, if valid under the Act, is not a denial of free speech.**

The Supreme Court not only affirmed the constitutionality of the FCC's broadcast licensing system in the case of *NBC* v. *U.S.* but also sustained the commission's rules of 1941 on diversification of ownership. These rules prohibited any organization from operating more than one broadcast station in the same community. By agreeing to these limitations, the Supreme Court gave its nod of approval to the FCC for the development of reasonable antimonopoly regulations for broadcast outlets, a process which reached a high point in a 1978 Supreme Court decision, as explained below.

THE CONSTITUTIONALITY OF THE FCC'S ANTIMONOPOLY RULES. Prior to 1975, when the FCC announced a new set of rules on divestiture, the antimonopoly policies of the commission that were initiated in 1941 had been revised and expanded a number of times—most notably in 1953, 1964, and 1971—and the Supreme Court had in general sided with the commission in challenges to the revisions. Furthermore, the FCC is currently reconsidering its position on a number of antimonopoly regulations (including the seven-station rule, discussed below); readers should be alert to the strong possibility of change in one or more of the six areas summarized in the following discussion.[15]

The central First Amendment issue at stake in the diversification debate is that of achieving a balance between the rights of persons or organizations to own and operate more

---

Amendment are found on pp. 226–227 of this lengthy opinion.

[15]See *Multiple Ownership of AM, FM and Television Broadcast Stations,* 18 F.C.C. 288 (1953); 45 F.C.C. 1476 (1964); and 28 F.C.C.2d 662 (1971). For Supreme Court opinion in addition to *NBC* v. *U.S.,* ibid., see *U.S.* v. *Storer Broadcasting Co.,* 351 U.S. 192 (1956).

than one major media outlet in a community (and, in some instances, in the nation at large) and the rights of the public to be protected from media monopoly and the threat of thought control inherent in such a monopoly. To this end the FCC had developed the following rules before 1975:

1. The "network rule" restricts organizations to operating no more than one broadcast network and forbids networks from owning more than one standard broadcast station in a given community.

2. The "duopoly rule" forbids the common ownership of two or more of the same type of station ("type" meaning AM, FM, or TV) in a given community. Certain combinations of types are permitted, however, such as owning both an AM and an FM radio station.

3. The "seven-station rule" limits an owner to a total of seven AM radio stations, seven FM radio stations, and up to seven TV stations provided that only five of these are VHF stations. (In July 1984 the FCC announced that this rule would be phased out over the next few years so that by 1990 there would be no restrictions on the number of stations one person or one company could own. A few weeks after making this decision, in response to strong opposition in Congress and among media access advocates, the FCC voted to postpone putting the new rule into effect pending further study. Readers should stay alert to the commission's disposition of this issue.)

4. The "common-market rule" decreed that after 1970 no applicants would be licensed to own and operate both a VHF television station and any radio station serving the same market; those combinations already in place were permitted to continue.

5. The "regional-concentration rule" sets forth a formula by which the FCC limits

common ownership within a given region of the nation.

Following five years of study, the FCC announced the sixth rule in 1975, in which it addressed the issue of *newspaper* ownership of radio and television stations. In its opening statement the commission spoke in favor of "diversity of viewpoints from antagonistic sources" as essential to democratic society, noting that "it is unrealistic to expect true diversity from a commonly owned station-newspaper combination." Consequently, a new regulation was necessary, namely, the "colocation rule."

6. The colocation rule concerning newspaper–broadcast station joint ownership forbids, in the future, the awarding of a broadcast license to any applicant who owns, operates, or controls a daily newspaper in the same community in which the sought-after radio or television station would be located. In short, new "colocated" combinations were prohibited after 1975. Subordinate to this basic rule were three others: (a) divestiture within five years (by January 1, 1980) had to be undertaken in sixteen "egregious" cases where the only general-circulation newspaper in a community also owned the sole broadcast station; (b) other joint-ownership arrangements were "grandfathered" and allowed to continue; and (c) the "grandfathered" arrangements ended automatically if either the newspaper or the station was sold in the future, in which case the facilities were required to be sold to different owners.[16]

In 1978 the U.S. Supreme Court turned back a challenge to the FCC's colocation

---

[16]*Rules Relating to Multiple Ownership of Standard, FM, and Television Broadcast Stations, Second Report and Order,* 50 F.C.C.2d 1046 (1975), as amended upon reconsideration, 53 F.C.C.2d 589 (1975).

rule, holding unanimously that the regulation concerning the ownership of broadcast stations by newspapers was constitutional. Reminding the plaintiffs in the case that "the broadcast media pose unique and special problems not present in the traditional free speech case" and that the purpose of the FCC rule was "to promote free speech, not to restrict it," the Court concluded in an opinion authored by Justice Marshall:

. . . The regulations are a reasonable means of promoting the public interest in diversified mass communications; thus they do not violate the First Amendment rights of those who will be denied broadcast licenses pursuant to them. Being forced to "choose among applicants for the same facilities," the Commission has chosen on a "sensible basis," one designed to further, rather than contravene, "the system of freedom of expression."[17]

Balance in Programming and Access to Facilities

The potential for one-sided treatment of public issues, and for the showing of favoritism by broadcasters toward political candidates of whom they approved, did not escape the Congress when it passed the Communications Act of 1934. Furthermore, the problems of balance and access have certainly not been ignored by the FCC, which is charged with enforcing the 1934 legislation. These two sources—the FCC and Congress—are the originators of regulations governing broadcasting, with *administrative* regulation coming from the commission and *statutory* regulation coming from Congress. Although there is some overlapping of principles in the doctrines concerning balance and access formulated by the commission and by Congress, the result is adequately discrete for a two-part analysis, as follows:

1. *The Fairness Doctrine.* This administrative regulation, formulated by the FCC and announced in 1949, requires stations that editorialize and present opinions on controversial issues to do so in a balanced way so as to communicate "all responsible viewpoints" on that issue to the listening or viewing audience. Among the subordinate rules is the right to apply to personal attacks and to political editorials made over the airwaves. (Note that the scope of the Fairness Doctrine is much broader than that of the equal-time rule, which is limited to political campaigns.)

2. *The equal-time rule.* This statutory regulation, passed by Congress as Section 315 of the Communications Act of 1934, has been amended a number of times over the years to reflect the evolution of opinion in Congress about access to broadcast facilities by candidates for public office. Its basic purpose as stated in the 1934 law: "If any licensee shall permit any person who is a legally qualified candidate for any public office to use a broadcasting station, he shall afford equal opportunities to all other such candidates for that office in the use of such broadcasting station."

A more detailed analysis of these two areas of the regulation of public communication over radio and television is now in order.

THE FAIRNESS DOCTRINE. The contours of a doctrine of balance in the coverage of controversial public issues by broadcasters emerged from the labyrinth of FCC proceedings in 1941, when the Mayflower Broadcasting Corporation applied for the frequency assigned to WAAB, a Boston radio station. Mayflower presented a number of reasons to support its challenge, one of which was that WAAB was guilty of one-sided editorializing on matters of public concern. Although the FCC found Mayflower's arguments uncon-

---

[17]*FCC v. National Citizens Commission for Broadcasting,* 436 U.S. 775 (1978).

vincing, denied the challenge, and renewed the license of WAAB, it did use the hearing as a forum for considering whether or not a licensee should be permitted to editorialize. The commission concluded in what has become known as the "Mayflower Doctrine" that all broadcast editorials should be prohibited.[18]

"The broadcaster cannot be an advocate," said the FCC in *Mayflower,* and to justify this point of view the FCC argued that radio could not serve the interests of democracy if it were permitted to air one-sided opinions concerning causes and candidates. "Freedom of speech on the radio," the commission concluded, "must be broad enough to provide full and equal opportunity for the presentation to the public of all sides of public issues. Indeed, as one licensed to operate in a public domain the licensee has assumed the obligation of presenting all sides of important public questions, fairly, objectively, and without bias. The public interest—not the private—is paramount." As one can readily observe, the seeds for a full-blown doctrine of fairness were planted by this decision of 1941.

During the years of World War II (1941–1945), the dissatisfaction of the broadcast industry with the Mayflower Doctrine remained muted. However, the industry's concern came to the fore soon after the war ended, and in 1947 the FCC announced that it would take another look at its no-editorial rule and would at the same time examine the broader question of a station's affirmative obligation to present a balanced treatment of all sides of controversial public issues. Hearings were held beginning in 1948, and on June 1, 1949 the commission announced the results of those hearings by discarding the Mayflower Doctrine, substituting what has come to be known as the Fairness Doctrine.[19]

The new policy reversed the *Mayflower* position on editorials and announced that henceforth broadcast editorials would be permitted within the broad framework of a doctrine of fairness requiring that views other than those expressed by the licensee be aired. Furthermore, the FCC said, the principle of fairness included a "right to reply" for those who might be subjected to a personal attack over station facilities.[20] The commission summarized its revised position as follows:

> To recapitulate, the Commission believes that under the American system of broadcasting the individual licensees of radio stations have the responsibility for determining the specific program material to be broadcast over their stations. This choice, however, must be exercised in a manner consistent with the basic policy of the Congress that radio be maintained as a medium of free speech for the general public as a whole rather than as an outlet for the purely personal or private interests of the licensee. . . . Licensee editorialization is but one aspect of freedom of expression by means of radio. Only insofar as it is exercised in conformity **with the paramount right of the public to hear a reasonably balanced presentation of all responsible viewpoints on particular issues can such editorialization be considered to be consistent with the licensee's duty to operate in the public interest. For the licensee is a trustee impressed with the duty of preserving for the public generally radio as a**

---

[18]*In the Matter of The Mayflower Broadcasting Corporation and The Yankee Network, Inc. (WAAB),* 8 F.C.C. 333 (1941). For some reason the flat prohibition upon editorializing announced in this decision was never challenged in the courts.

[19]*In the Matter of Editorializing by Broadcast Licensees,* 13 F.C.C. 1246 (1949).

[20]The 1949 statement did not fully develop the personal-attack rule. The FCC clarified matters in an advisory statement issued in 1963, found at 63 F.C.C. 734 (1963); it then set out the governing principles more fully in a set of rules on personal attack announced in 1967. The 1967 rules as amended are given by Justice White in his opinion of the Court in *Red Lion Broadcasting Co.* v. *FCC,* 395 U.S. 367 (1969), at 373–375.

medium of free expression and fair presentation.

The legal test of the Fairness Doctrine began in November of 1964, when right-wing minister Billy James Hargis subjected Fred J. Cook, author of *Goldwater—Extremist on the Right,* to a personal attack over the facilities of WGCB, a Pennsylvania radio station owned and operated by the Red Lion Broadcasting Company. Cook, upon learning that Hargis had accused him of pro-Communist sympathies, claimed a right of reply under the Fairness Doctrine and demanded free time from WGCB for that reply. The station refused. After the FCC intervened on Cook's behalf to no avail, the case was reviewed by the U.S. Circuit Court of Appeals for the District of Columbia, which found that the FCC's position was both constitutional and correct under current regulations. The management of Red Lion appealed to the U.S. Supreme Court.

Soon after the *Red Lion* litigation began, the FCC announced a study of the personal-attack rule with the joint goals of clarifying the regulation and making it more enforceable. The results of this study were announced in 1967 and were promptly challenged on constitutional grounds by the Radio Television News Directors Association (RTNDA). In 1968 the U.S. Circuit Court of Appeals for the Seventh Circuit decided that the new rules violated the First Amendment, whereupon the government requested review by the U.S. Supreme Court. Upon the granting of certiorari, the Supreme Court combined this case with *Red Lion.* A few months later the Court, in a landmark opinion concerning broadcasting and the First Amendment, announced its conclusions concerning the issues raised in both appeals.

Justice Byron White began his opinion of the Court by reviewing the facts of the two cases at bar, after which he summarized the history of broadcast legislation in the United States, noting that over the years the federal courts had in general sustained the legality of the Communications Act of 1934 as administered by the FCC. Justice White stressed that Congress had decreed that broadcasting serve the public interest and had legislated a type of reply right when it approved Section 315 of the Communications Act (the equal-time rule, which applies to political campaigns). With the historical context established, he asserted that the FCC had acted properly when it ordered free time for Fred J. Cook over Station WGCB and when it issued detailed right-to-reply rules in 1967. Justice White then announced for the Court that because "the specific application of the fairness doctrine in *Red Lion,* and the promulgation of the regulations of *RTNDA,* are both authorized by Congress and enhance rather than abridge the freedoms of speech and press protected by the First Amendment, we hold them valid and constitutional. . . ."

Justice White then turned to the four arguments advanced by the Red Lion Broadcasting Company and by the RTNDA, namely, that the Fairness Doctrine and the right-to-reply regulations should be invalidated because they (1) violate the First Amendment, (2) compel self-censorship by stations seeking to avoid time-consuming and expensive controversies, (3) are excessively vague, and (4) have been made unnecessary by technological advances that have reduced frequency scarcity through a more efficient use of the broadcast spectrum. As one might expect, the First Amendment issue received more attention from the Court than did the other three; however, students of free speech should be aware of the Court's answers to all four objections.

Justice White addressed the *first* argument by summarizing the contention of the broad-

LANDMARK CASE
Red Lion Broadcasting Co. v. FCC, 395 U.S. 367 (1969)
Decided June 9, 1969

Vote: 8 to 0 upholding the constitutionality of the Fairness Doctrine and the personal-attack regulations as promulgated by the FCC.

Majority Opinion By: Justice White.

Concurring Justices: Chief Justice Earl Warren and Justices Black, Harlan, Brennan, Stewart, Fortas, and Marshall.

Dissenting Justices: (none)

Justices Not Participating: Douglas (because he missed oral arguments).

Summary: When author Fred J. Cook was refused reply time by radio station WGCB in Pennsylvania (owned by the Red Lion Broadcasting Company) to answer a personal attack against his patriotism by right-wing minister Billy James Hargis, the FCC sided with Cook and took the company to court to force compliance with the Fairness Doctrine. Soon thereafter, in a different case involving similar issues, the Radio Television News Directors Association (RTNDA) challenged the constitutionality of the FCC's personal-attack regulations. The Court of Appeals for the District of Columbia sustained the FCC and the Fairness Doctrine in Cook's complaint, but the Court of Appeals for the Seventh Circuit came to a contrary conclusion in the RTNDA case, deciding that the FCC's personal-attack regulations violated the Constitution. The U.S. Supreme Court moved to settle the matter by agreeing to hear both appeals, which it treated together in one opinion. In its landmark decision and by a unanimous vote, the Court ruled that the Fairness Doctrine and the personal-attack rules derived from it *are constitutional*.

Rule Established; Significance of Case: The Fairness Doctrine as applied to broadcast licensees by the FCC does not violate the First Amendment; rather, it promotes freedom of speech in that it helps to "preserve an uninhibited marketplace of ideas" by facilitating the communication of "social, political, esthetic, moral, and other ideas and experiences" to the public. Furthermore, the right-to-reply regulations based upon the Fairness Doctrine are also constitutional, as specifically set forth in the FCC's 1967 rules concerning personal attacks and political editorials. The rules: (1) when a *personal attack* is made upon an identifiable person or group, the station is required within one week to notify that person or group (including a transcript, tape, or accurate summary of the attack), and offer time for a reply over the station's facilities; also, (2) when in a *political editorial* a station endorses or opposes a candidate for public office the station is required within twenty-four hours after the editorial is broadcast to notify other qualified candidates for that office or the person opposed (including a script or tape of the editorial), and offer time for a reply over the station's facilities.

casters that "the First Amendment protects their desire to use their allotted frequencies continuously to broadcast whatever they choose, and to exclude whomever they choose from ever using that frequency." In short, WGCB and RTNDA claimed that the same principles of free speech that apply to speaking and publishing should apply to them. In rejecting the argument, Justice White stressed that the technological limitations of broadcasting justified the conclusion that broadcasting be governed by rules which differ from the traditional ones, especially since there existed a potential for censorship by licensees that was not present in the other media. To emphasize this point, he observed:

"Just as the Government may limit the use of sound-amplifying equipment potentially so noisy that it drowns out civilized private speech, so may the Government limit the use of broadcast equipment. The right of free speech of a broadcaster, the user of a sound truck, or any other individual does not embrace a right to snuff out the free speech of others." He then expanded his discussion of the constitutional question.

Justice White *delivered the opinion of the court:*

This is not to say that the First Amendment is irrelevant to public broadcasting. On the contrary, it has a major role to play as the Congress itself recognized in [Sec. 326 of the Communications Act] which forbids FCC interference with "the right of free speech by means of radio communication." Because of the scarcity of radio frequencies, the Government is permitted to put restraints on licensees in favor of others whose views should be expressed on this unique medium. But the people as a whole retain their interest in free speech by radio and their collective right to have the medium function consistently with the ends and purposes of the First Amendment. **It is the right of the viewers and listeners, not the right of the broadcasters, which is paramount. . . .**

Nor can we say that it is inconsistent with the First Amendment goal of producing an informed public capable of conducting its own affairs to require a broadcaster to permit answers to personal attacks occurring in the course of discussing controversial issues, or to require that the political opponents of those endorsed by the station be given a chance to communicate with the public. Otherwise, station owners and a few networks would have unfettered power to make time available only to the highest bidders, to communicate only their own views on public issues, people and candidates, and to permit on the air only those with whom they agreed. **There is no sanctuary in the First Amendment for unlimited private censorship operating in a medium not open to all. . . .**

Second, the broadcasters had argued that if the airing of controversial opinion, including personal attacks and political editorials, would trigger an obligation to grant free time for the use of a station's facilities to air views "unpalatable to the licensees, then broadcasters will be irresistibly forced to self-censorship and their coverage of controversial public issues will be eliminated or at least rendered wholly ineffective." In short, the Fairness Doctrine would have a "chilling effect" upon a station's coverage of certain subjects. In answer, Justice White pointed out that the argument "is at best speculative," for the doctrine had not worked in the past to reduce the broadcasting of controversial opinion; furthermore, the FCC had the authority if needed to insist that a station "give adequate and fair attention to public issues." He ended the Court's answer to this argument with a warning that broadcasters had a duty to present representative views on public issues, and that if they shirked this duty, then "Congress need not stand idly by and permit those with licenses to ignore the problems which beset the people or to exclude from the airways anything but [the station's] . . . views of fundamental questions."

Third, Justice White continued, the "litigants embellish their First Amendment arguments with the contention that the regulations are so vague that their duties are impossible to discern." Not so, he replied, for past rule-making by the FCC had made the regulations sufficiently precise. Certainly "there was nothing vague about the FCC's specific ruling in *Red Lion* that Fred Cook should be provided an opportunity to reply." Nor are the personal attack and political editorial regulations questioned by the RTNDA lacking in clarity. As for future applications of the Fairness Doctrine in "extreme" situations, the Court "will deal with those problems if and when they arise."

Finally, the broadcasters argued that technological development had made more frequencies available for licensing than were available in the past, thus making the fairness regulations unnecessary, since more voices could now be heard over the air. In answer, Justice White observed that hearings before the commission "between competing applicants for broadcast spectrum space are by no means a thing of the past. The radio spectrum has become so congested that at times it has been necessary to suspend new applications. . . . Nothing in this record, or in our own researches, convinces us that the resource is no longer one for which there are more immediate and potential uses than can be accommodated, and for which wise planning is essential."

In the years following the *Red Lion* landmark, two First Amendment issues concerning the Fairness Doctrine have been decided by the commission and the courts, namely, (1) the right of individuals and organizations to purchase broadcast time for the airing of opinion (i.e., editorial advertising) and (2) the right of individuals and organizations to be granted free time to answer commercial messages with which they disagree. Each of these questions was decided in the negative, as explained below.

1. *The right of access through paid editorial advertising.* Four years following the *Red Lion* landmark decision the question of a First Amendment right of access to the airwaves for paid editorial advertising reached the Supreme Court for review. (Editorial advertising is that which advocates an opinion on an issue such as foreign aid, the military, welfare programs, the environment, etc., as contrasted with commercial advertising, which

attempts to sell products or services.) The case of *CBS* v. *Democratic National Committee* concerned an FCC ruling that allowed the individual station to decide whether or not to accept editorial advertising.[21] Two groups, the Democratic National Committee (DNC) and the Business Executives' Move for Vietnam Peace, had been turned down when they tried to purchase time for their "paid editorials" from stations which did not accept such advertising. The policy was justified, the stations argued, because editorial advertising would trigger the Fairness Doctrine and require the granting of free time for those who wished to respond, and because it was preferable for the licensees to meet their public service obligations in other ways that did not threaten them with so much controversy and potential loss of revenue.

When the FCC sided with the stations, the DNC and the peace group entered the courts to argue a First Amendment right to air their views in paid editorials. Although the Court of Appeals for the District of Columbia ruled for the plaintiffs, the U.S. Supreme Court disagreed, reversed the decision of the court of appeals, and reinstated the ruling of the commission. Consequently, *the sale of editorial advertising by radio and television stations remains optional with each station.* Central to the reasoning of the Court, in an opinion authored by Chief Justice Burger, were the arguments that such advertising would be monopolized by the rich, thereby undermining the principle of balanced programming concerning public issues, and that the Fairness Doctrine itself (which places the responsibility for public accountability upon the station) would be jeopardized, since the affluent (who are not legally accountable for a station's public service policy) could by the purchase of time for

[21]*CBS* v. *Democratic National Committee,* 412 U.S. 94 (1973).

airing controversy in fact dictate a station's approach to fairness in the coverage of public issues.

2. *Commercial advertising and the Fairness Doctrine.* In 1967 the FCC decided that the national debate over cigarette advertising was an issue of such public interest as to initiate the Fairness Doctrine in response to cigarette commercials. When this ruling was challenged, the court of appeals sustained the FCC and the U.S. Supreme Court denied review of that decision.[22] Although the commission attempted to limit its ruling to cigarette advertising, opponents of other commercials—such as advertising for polluting automobiles and gasoline, and for military recruitment—insisted that they deserved reply time under the principle of fairness. In 1974 the FCC reversed its policy on the matter, announcing that the 1967 rule on cigarette advertising was a "serious departure from the . . . central purpose" of the Fairness Doctrine, and that hereafter "we will apply the doctrine only to those 'commercials' which are devoted in an obvious and meaningful way to the discussion of public issues."[23] The court of appeals upheld the right of the FCC to change the policy, and the U.S. Supreme Court denied review of the opinion of the court of appeals.[24] That is where the matter now stands, and students of public communication should be aware that whereas *editorial* advertising (on those stations that do accept it, for the choice is op-

tional with the licensee) does trigger the Fairness Doctrine, ordinary *commercial* advertising does not.

Despite the unanimous decision of the Supreme Court in *Red Lion* upholding the constitutionality of the Fairness Doctrine, criticism of the rule continued, primarily from broadcasters who felt burdened by it. In addition to the four arguments advanced by the plaintiffs in *Red Lion* (summarized earlier), others surfaced, including the view that a freer hand in broadcast journalism is needed in one-newspaper towns in order that a contrasting voice from the radio or television station or stations be present to counter the one-sided view of the newspaper—in a way, a kind of "fairness argument" from a perspective at variance with that of the FCC.[25]

In response to numerous requests for a review of the Fairness Doctrine following the *Red Lion* decision of 1969, the FCC began a study in 1971 that culminated in the publication of a comprehensive "Fairness Report" in 1974.[26] Here the commission stood firm in its belief that the doctrine was needed to guarantee that broadcasters serve "the legitimate First Amendment interests of the general public." The FCC added that this should be done with a minimum of government interference; nevertheless, licensees continue to have an affirmative obligation under the fairness regulations to cover important public issues (those identified by the broadcaster as important, controversial, and conducive to debate in the community at large) and to

---

[22]The commission ruling is *In re WCBS-TV,* 8 F.C.C.2d 381 (1967); the court decisions are *Banzhaf* v. *FCC,* 405 F.2d 1082 (D.C. Cir. 1968). *cert. denied,* 396 U.S. 842 (1969). Note: In 1969 Congress banned all cigarette commercials from the airwaves, and the statute was upheld by the Supreme Court in *Capitol Broadcasting* v. *Acting Attorney General,* 405 U.S. 1000 (1972).
[23]In the 1974 "Fairness Report," 48 F.C.C.2d 1 (1974).
[24]*Public Interest Research Group* v. *FCC,* 522 F.2d 1060 (1st Cir. 1975); *cert. denied,* 424 U.S. 965 (1976).

[25]For a further look at problems created by the Fairness Doctrine, see Henry Geller, *The Fairness Doctrine in Broadcasting: Problems and Suggested Courses of Action* (Santa Monica, Calif.: Rand, 1973); and S. J. Simmons, *The Fairness Doctrine and the Media* (Berkeley, Calif.: University of California Press, 1979).
[26]The official title of the "Fairness Report" is *In the Matter of the Handling of Public Issues Under the Fairness Doctrine and the Public Interest Standards of the Communications Act.* The report is found in 48 F.C.C.2d 1 (1974).

present a balance in programming concerning those issues.

A few weeks after announcing the "Fairness Report," the FCC published a revised edition of its *Broadcast Procedure Manual,* a guide for the general public concerning basic policies of the commission on a variety of matters together with instructions on how to go about registering a complaint if a person or group believes that a licensee is in violation of a regulation or a statute.[27] Section 12 of this manual summarizes well the Fairness Doctrine as developed over the years (and as it now stands).

Fairness doctrine. Under the fairness doctrine, if there is a presentation of a point of view on a controversial issue of public importance over a station (or network), it is the duty of the station (or network), in its overall programming, to afford a reasonable opportunity for the presentation of contrasting views as to that issue. This duty applies to all station programming and not merely to editorials stating the station's position. The station may make offers of time to spokesmen for contrasting views or may present its own programming on the issue. It must present suitable contrasting views without charge if it is unable to secure payment from, or a sponsor for, the spokesman for such views. The broadcaster has considerable discretion as to the format of programs, the different shades of opinion to be presented, the spokesman for each point of view, and the time allowed. He is not required to provide equal time or equal opportunities; this requirement applies only to broadcasts by candidates for public office. The doctrine is based on the right of the public to be informed and not on the proposition that any particular person or group is entitled to be heard.

To complete this concise statement concerning fairness, the public communicator should recall the following regulations and

interpretations, discussed previously: (1) persons have a right to reply under the Fairness Doctrine if they are personally attacked, and candidates have a right to reply to certain political editorials; (2) there is no First Amendment right of access to station facilities for the purchase of time to air one's "editorial opinions"; and (3) commercial advertising for products and services does not trigger the Fairness Doctrine.

THE EQUAL-TIME PROVISIONS OF THE LAW. As noted earlier, the equal-time rule and the Fairness Doctrine are not the same, for they have different histories and different (although overlapping) purposes as well. The Fairness Doctrine is a *regulation* developed by the FCC and officially announced in 1949; on the other hand, the equal-time rule is a *statute* enacted by Congress as Section 315 of the Communications Act of 1934. Whereas the purpose of the Fairness Doctrine is to guarantee a balance in the overall coverage of controversial public issues of all types, the equal-time rule is more narrowly drawn to focus upon political campaigns. The 1934 law reads: "If any licensee shall permit any person who is a legally qualified candidate for any public office to use a broadcasting station, he shall afford equal opportunities to all other such candidates for that office in the use of such broadcasting station."[28]

In 1959 Congress amended Section 315 of the Communications Act after the FCC ruled that even short radio and television news clips featuring a candidate required reply time from other candidates.[29] Soon after the commission's ruling, Congress held hearings on

---

[27]The Public and Broadcasting—A Procedure Manual (revised edition), 49 F.C.C.2d 1 (1974).

[28]See *Letter to Mr. Nicholas Zapple,* 23 F.C.C.2d 707 (1970).

[29]The ruling came about when Lar Daly, running for mayor of Chicago, claimed that he deserved equal time on newscasts which had earlier included some coverage of other candidates for mayor. The commission agreed with Daly's view in *Columbia Broadcasting System,* 26 F.C.C. 715 (1959).

the matter and then changed the law, saying that the following four types of media coverage do not constitute political campaigning and do not, therefore, trigger the equal-time rule: bona fide (1) newscasts, (2) news interviews, (3) news documentaries, and (4) on-the-spot coverage of news events. Also in this amendment Congress for the first time showed its approval of the Fairness Doctrine by stating: "Nothing in the foregoing . . . shall be construed as relieving broadcasters . . . from the obligation imposed upon them under this chapter to operate in the public interest and to afford reasonable opportunity for the discussion of conflicting views on issues of public importance."

One effect of the equal-time provisions of the Communications Act was to deter broadcasters from covering face-to-face debates between the two major candidates for the office of president of the United States because such coverage would require licensees to give equal time to the numerous splinter-party candidates for that office. Congress experimented with an exception in 1960, passing the "Great Debates Law" to permit a nationally televised confrontation between presidential candidates John F. Kennedy and Richard Nixon. This temporary suspension of Section 315(a) of the Communications Act applied *only* to the offices of president and vice-president of the United States, and *expired* automatically following the end of the campaign of 1960. It has never been renewed for subsequent campaigns.

Fifteen years later the FCC stepped in and changed its interpretation of the equal-time rule *as amended in 1959* (recall that in that year Congress made exceptions for bona fide news coverage) and by so doing made it possible for presidential debates to be broadcast as news events provided they were sponsored by a nonpartisan group. Under this interpretation of the law, debates were broadcast between presidential candidates Gerald Ford

and Jimmy Carter in 1976 and between presidental candidates Carter and Ronald Reagan in 1980. Both were sponsored by the League of Women Voters. In November of 1983—in time for the national political campaign of 1984—the FCC again liberalized its interpretation of Sec. 315(a)(4) of the Communications Act by agreeing to allow the *stations* to sponsor broadcasts of debates between legally qualified candidates provided the debates are presented as bona fide news events. Under this ruling, no nonpartisan sponsor, such as the League of Women Voters, is required. This was done, said the commission, in the hope that the new policy would result in an increase in the number of candidate debates, for such programs "ultimately benefit the public."[30]

The final development that must be explained to complete the picture concerning equal time and access for political campaigns began with the enactment by Congress of the Federal Election Campaign Act of 1971. Title I of this statute amended Section 312 (however, it did not change Section 315) of the Communications Act to grant the FCC the authority to revoke a station's construction permit or license "for willful or repeated failure to allow reasonable access to or to permit purchase of reasonable amounts of time for the use of a broadcasting station by a legally qualified candidate for Federal elective office on behalf of his candidacy." Note that this amendment, which is found in Section 312(a)(7) of the Communications Act, is limited to *federal* elections and that it does not grant free time—only the right of candidates

[30]The FCC change in policy which permitted the League of Women Voters and similar nonpartisan sponsors to organize debates for broadcast is found in *Petitions of Aspen Institute and CBS,* 55 F.C.C.2d 697 (1975); this 1975 ruling was sustained by the Court of Appeals in *Chisholm* v. *FCC* 538 F.2d 349 (D.C. Cir. 1976). The further liberalizing of the rule in late 1983 is found in *Re: Petitions of Henry Geller et al,* 48 Fed.Reg. 53166 (November 25, 1983).

to *purchase* reasonable amounts of time for campaign purposes.

In October of 1979 the access amendment got its legal test when the three national networks turned down a request from the Carter-Mondale Presidential Committee for the purchase of air time because, said the networks, it was too early to declare the 1980 campaign under way (ABC, for example, announced that it would begin selling time for federal campaigning in January of 1980). The Carter-Mondale Committee complained to the FCC, which agreed with the complaint; the networks then requested review by the federal courts. When the federal circuit court of appeals affirmed the FCC ruling, the networks appealed to the U.S. Supreme Court. On July 1, 1981, the High Court, by a vote of 6 to 3, sustained the FCC's position by upholding the decision of the court below. In an opinion by Chief Justice Burger, and for the *first time* in the history of broadcasting, the Court approved the constitutionality of a limited right of access to the broadcast media.[31]

In the words of the chief justice, it is true that the "Court has never approved a *general* right of access to the media. . . . Nor do we do so today. Section 312(a)(7) creates a *limited* right of 'reasonable' access that pertains only to legally qualified federal candidates and may be invoked by them only for the purpose of advancing their candidacies once a campaign has commenced." Chief Justice Burger concluded that the statute in question "represents an effort by Congress to assure that an important resource—the airwaves—will be used in the public interest. *We hold that the statutory right of access, as defined by the Commission and applied in these cases, properly balances the First Amendment rights of federal candidates, the public, and broadcasters.*"

[31]*CBS* v. *FCC,* 453 U.S. 367 (1981).

In summary, (1) Section 315 of the Communications Act of 1934, as amended by Congress in 1959, states that (a) licensees who grant time to one candidate are required to grant equal opportunities to all other legally qualified candidates for that office (or for his or her supporters) to broadcast their campaign message. The equal-time rule is not triggered, however, by a station's coverage of bona fide news events related to the campaign. (b) The broadcasting of debates between legally qualified candidates for public office no longer initiates the equal-time rule if those debates are sponsored by a nonpartisan group or by a radio or television station provided the broadcast meets the standard of a "bona fide news event." (2) Section 312(a)(7) of the Communications Act, passed by Congress in 1971, establishes a limited right of "reasonable" access to broadcast facilities by candidates for federal elective office for the purchase of time for campaigning. The Supreme Court has upheld the constitutionality of this limited access law.

Constraints over Program Content in Broadcasting

Recall from Chapter 1 that in 1769 the English jurist Sir William Blackstone proposed in his *Commentaries* that the "liberty of the press, properly understood" means "laying no *previous* restraints upon publications, and not in freedom from censure for criminal matter when published." According to this point of view, communicators, while free to speak or publish without first securing government permission, could still be punished if they communicated "what is improper, mischievous, or illegal."[32] Perhaps no body of American law better illustrates the Black-

[32]William Blackstone, *Commentaries on the Laws of England,* vol. 4 (Oxford: Clarendon Press, 1769), pp. 151–152.

stonian position for the post facto punishment of the content of expression than the law of broadcasting and the FCC regulations based upon it.

The Communications Act of 1934 states in Section 326 that "*Nothing in this Act shall be understood or construed to give the Commission the power of censorship over the radio communications or signals transmitted by any radio station, and no regulation or condition shall be promulgated or fixed by the Commission which shall interfere with the right of free speech by means of radio communication.*" Yet that same statute banned from the airwaves any language which was "obscene, indecent, or profane," and any information concerning lotteries. No doubt Blackstone would have approved of this arrangement which, while prohibiting the exercise by the government of prior restraint over broadcasting, authorized post facto sanctions for program content proscribed by law.

GENERAL CONSTRAINTS. Constraints over the content of broadcasting are both general and specific. Prior to a consideration of those specific statutes and FCC regulations that spell out what is forbidden on the airwaves, readers should take note of the plethora of general policy rules discussed earlier (including the Fairness Doctrine, personal-attack principles, etc.) as well as others ranging from commission-formulated requirements concerning programming to voluntary industry guidelines developed by the National Association of Broadcasters (NAB). For example, with its Prime Time Access Rule, the FCC has attempted to encourage creative programming by local television stations by restricting the number of hours for *network* programs during "prime time" (7 to 11 P.M.). One must then add to such government regulations the guidelines set forth by the NAB in its Radio Code and its Television Code. To illustrate, the Television Code, which is adhered to by the three major networks and by most television stations, includes among its many guidelines a section on program standards that recommends how broadcasters should handle content on a variety of subjects ranging from sex, drugs, and violence to religion and morbidity in reporting the news.[33]

One issue of general program content that reached the Supreme Court in the early 1980s concerned whether or not listeners and viewers had a First Amendment right to *receive* certain types of broadcast formats in their communities. The issue developed in the late 1970s when a number of stations, for one reason or another, changed from their traditional format to some other (e.g., from a classical music station to a hard rock station, or from a foreign-language station to an English-language station). The FCC, after considering the complexities of the issue at stake, ruled that "market forces" rather than the commission should determine a licensee's format. When several groups of listeners composed of persons who liked the original formats but disliked the new ones appealed the decision of the FCC, the U.S. Supreme Court sustained the commission's position in the matter. By a vote of 7 to 2, in an opinion by Justice White, the Court addressed the First Amendment "right to receive" argument. The Fairness Doctrine approved in the *Red Lion* decision of 1969, Justice White observed, "*did not imply that the First Amendment grants individual listeners the right to have the Commission review the abandonment of their favorite entertainment programs. The Commission seeks to further the interests of the listening public*

---

[33] *The NAB TV Code,* 21st ed. (1980). For a single free copy of either the radio or television code (specify which) or both, address: National Association of Broadcasters, 1771 N St., N.W., Washington, D.C. 20036.

as a whole by relying on market forces to promote diversity in radio entertainment formats and to satisfy the entertainment preferences of radio listeners. This policy does not conflict with the First Amendment."[34]

SPECIFIC CONSTRAINTS. In addition to state and federal legislation that prohibits the communication of fraud and false advertising in general (for more, see Chapter 7, "Commercial Speech"), radio and television stations are regulated under laws specifically directed toward the broadcasting of (1) lottery information and (2) language that is "obscene, indecent, or profane." A brief look at these two areas of censorship is appropriate at this point.

1. *Broadcasting lottery information.*[35] A prohibition upon the broadcasting of lottery information was included by Congress in the Communications Act of 1934. However, in 1948 Congress moved the antilottery statute from the Communications Act to the *U.S. Criminal Code,* where it now appears in Title 18, Section 1304. The law provides for a fine of up to $1,000 or imprisonment for up to one year or both for airing information "concerning any lottery." The statute has been amended by Congress in recent years to permit information about lotteries "conducted by a State acting under the authority of State law" to be broadcast by stations in the state, or in adjoining states.[36] Furthermore, the

FCC has its own rules based upon the antilottery law and enforces them by means of reprimands, fines, and threats of license revocation. A case in point occurred in 1975 when the commission refused to renew the license of radio station WOOK in Washington, D.C., because of convincing evidence that a concealed lottery, with its own special messages and code words not understood as such by the average listener, had been aired by the station over a period of time.[37]

2. *Broadcasting objectionable language.* The law against broadcasting objectionable language, like the antilottery statute, was moved from the Communications Act to the *U.S. Criminal Code* in 1948. It appears in Title 18, Section 1464 of the *Code,* and reads: "Whoever utters any obscene, indecent, or profane language by means of radio communication shall be fined not more than $10,000 or imprisoned not more than two years, or both." The statute generated little legal or regulatory activity until the 1960s, when listeners here and there began to complain about the growing candor in broadcast language. The issue was addressed several times by the FCC during the 1960s and early 1970s, only to reach a legal climax in the 1978 Supreme Court decision about George Carlin's comedy monologue "Filthy Words," which had been aired five years earlier by a radio station in New York City. Ironically, Carlin's routine concerned seven words "you couldn't say on the public airwaves."

An interesting example of FCC activity in this area occurred in 1961, when the commission refused to renew the license of radio station WDKD in Kingstree, South Carolina, in part because of the "indecent" language used by the station's disc jockey, Charlie Walker. According to the FCC report, Walker (who

---

[34]*FCC* v. *WNCN Listeners Guild,* 450 U.S. 582 (1981).

[35]In a variety of ways, state and federal laws control the communication of information about lotteries—and such controls are not limited to broadcasting. For example, federal law makes it illegal *to mail* a newspaper that includes lottery information, although the law has recently been amended to permit such mailings *within* states having legal state lotteries. See 39 *U.S. Code* Sec. 3005.

[36]18 *U.S. Code* Sec. 1307(a)(2)

[37]*In re United Broadcast Company* (WOOK), 75 F.C.C. 1018 (1975).

had earlier been convicted by a federal jury of violating the *U.S. Code*'s restrictions upon indecent language by broadcasters) had employed "coarse, vulgar, suggestive" language on a regular basis in his work as announcer and disc jockey. According to off-the-air tapes made by the FCC, Walker had invented "indecent" nicknames for several towns in the area, such as calling Greeleyville "Greasy Thrill" and referring to Bloomville as "Bloomersville." Also, he was constantly telling "raunchy" stories, of which these are typical:

> [A man says to me] "I believe that old dog of mine is a Baptist." I asked him why he thought his old dog was a Baptist and he says, "you know, Uncle Charlie, it is that he's done baptized every hub cap around. . . ."
>
> I don't wanta save everything I get my hands on. I had my hands on something last night and I guarantee you boy I didn't want to save it . . . you better believe that. . . .
>
> I can remember back when I was single boy. It is that my britches used to be wrinkled all the time too, but the reason my britches was wrinkled when I was single is because gals was always sittin' on my lap and that's why it is that my britches was always wrinkled. Man, times do change. Now what I got in 'em's wrinkled.[38]

In 1964, after receiving complaints about frank language in several programs aired by radio stations owned by the Pacifica Foundation (the complaints ranged from the playing of a recording of Edward Albee's *Zoo Story* to a talk show in which homosexuals discussed their problems), the FCC decided that the programs, while provocative, were not illegal and presented no barrier to license renewal.[39] However, in 1970 radio station

WUHY-FM was fined $100 for broadcasting a taped interview with musician Gerry Garcia in which Garcia answered some of the questions with "patently offensive words" and "expletives." In its report, the FCC gave no clue as to what the objectionable words were.[40] And in 1973, the same year that the Carlin case began, the commission effectively "chilled" a trend toward "adult" radio formats when it fined station WGLD-FM of Oak Park, Illinois, $2,000 for violating the obscenity and indecency clauses of the *U.S. Code*. The programs in question covered a variety of topics concerning sex, ranging from oral sex to female masturbation. One objection cited by the commission was that the discussions were broadcast during the day, when "significant numbers" of children were in the listening audience. The action of the FCC was sustained by the federal circuit court of appeals.[41]

The question of one's freedom to broadcast "indecent" language finally reached the U.S. Supreme Court for review in a case which began at 2 P.M. on Tuesday, October 30, 1973, when WBAI-FM, a New York City radio station owned by the Pacifica Foundation, aired a program about the attitudes of modern society toward language.[42] To illustrate the problem, the director of the program played George Carlin's satiric monologue "Filthy Words," which focuses on seven words that one may not say on the public airwaves—in Carlin's sequence, they are "shit, piss, fuck, cunt, cocksucker, moth-

[38]*In re Palmetto Broadcasting Co. (WDKD)*, 33 F.C.C. 265 (1961).

[39]*In re Pacifica Foundation*, 36 F.C.C. 147 (1964).

[40]*In re Eastern Educational Radio* (WUHY-FM), 24 F.C.C.2d 408 (1970).

[41]The FCC decision is found in 27 *Radio Regulations* 2d 283 (F.C.C. 1973); and the court decision is *Illinois Citizens' Committee for Broadcasting* v. *FCC*, 515 F.2d 397 (D.C. Cir. 1975). Note: The format involved is often called "topless radio."

[42]*FCC* v. *Pacifica Foundation*, 438 U.S. 726 (1978).

erfucker, and tits."[43] For the remainder of the recording Carlin pokes fun at the verbal taboos of contemporary society, employing the technique of constant repetition of the forbidden symbols, especially the word "shit." (As it turned out, the majority of the justices of the Supreme Court were not amused.)

A New York City member of the procensorship Morality in Media organization heard the broadcast while driving with his young son, and about a month later submitted a written complaint to the FCC about it (his was the only complaint received). After examining the facts, the commission granted the complaint by issuing a declaratory order that was placed in the permanent file of WBAI-FM to serve as a warning in the future. No criminal charges were filed, and no fine was imposed.[44]

The station appealed the charge as a matter of principle, even though the punishment was not severe—a move that pleased the FCC, which wanted a court determination one way or the other on the indecent-language provision of the law. The federal circuit court of appeals by a vote of 2 to 1 agreed with the position of the station.[45] The U.S. Supreme Court then granted review and, in an important decision handed down a year later, reversed the finding of the court of appeals and reinstated the FCC ruling in the case. By a vote of 5 to 4, and in an opinion by Justice John P. Stevens, the Court announced that Section 326, the anticensorship section, of the Communications Act did not deny the FCC the power to review the content of what is broadcast and to impose sanction if that content was found to be "obscene, indecent, or profane." Even though Carlin's language was not prurient, lustful, and erotic, and therefore not legally obscene, it was nevertheless *indecent,* said the Court—a problem magnified by the fact that the material was broadcast during the hours of the day when children might hear it.

In his opinion of the Court, Justice Stevens agreed that Carlin's monologue was "speech" within the meaning of the First Amendment. However, he cautioned, freedom of speech is not absolute and has been legally constrained in the United States for sedition, defamation, "fighting words," and obscenity. Here, he stated, "we must consider its context in order to determine whether the Commission's action was constitutionally permissible." Add the fact that the courts have "long recognized that each medium of expression presents special First Amendment problems" and that "of all forms of communication, it is broadcasting that has received the most limited First Amendment protection," and one can better grasp the two relevant distinctions between broadcasting and other media upon which the decision in this case rests.

Justice Stevens *delivered the opinion of the Court:*

. . . **First, the broadcast media have established a uniquely pervasive presence in the lives of all Americans.** Patently offensive, indecent material presented over the airwaves confronts the citizen, not only in public, but also in the privacy of the home, where the individual's right to be left alone plainly outweighs the First Amendment rights of an intruder. . . . Because the broadcast audience is constantly tuning in and out, prior warnings cannot completely protect the listener or viewer from unexpected program content. To say that one may avoid further offense by turning off

---

[43]From *Occupation Foole,* album #LD-1005, Little David Records. A similar recording entitled "Seven Words You Can Never Say on Television" is on *Class Clown,* album #LD-1004, Little David Records; the two monologues are not the same, however.

[44]*In re Pacifica Foundation,* 56 F.C.C.2d 94 (1975).

[45]*Pacifica Foundation* v. *FCC,* 556 F.2d 9 (D.C. Cir. 1977).

the radio when he hears indecent language is like saying that the remedy for an assault is to run away after the first blow. . . .

Second, broadcasting is uniquely accessible to children, even those too young to read. . . . Other forms of offensive expression may be withheld from the young without restricting the expression at its source. Bookstores and motion picture theaters, for example, may be prohibited from making indecent material available to children. . . . The ease with which children may obtain access to broadcast material . . . amply [justifies] special treatment of indecent broadcasting.

It is appropriate, in conclusion, to emphasize the narrowness of our holding. This case does not involve a two-way radio conversation between a cab driver and a dispatcher, or a telecast of an Elizabethan comedy. We have not decided that an occasional expletive in either setting would justify any sanction or, indeed, that this broadcast would justify a criminal prosecution. The Commission's decision rested entirely on a nuisance rationale under which context is all-important. The concept requires consideration of a host of variables. The time of day was emphasized by the Commission. The content of the program in which the language is used will also affect the composition of the audience, and differences between radio, television, and perhaps closed-circuit transmission, may also be relevant. As Mr. Justice Sutherland wrote, a "nuisance may be merely a right thing in the wrong place,—like a pig in the parlor instead of the barnyard." *Euclid* v. *Ambler Realty Co.,* 272 U.S. 365, 388. We simply hold that when the Commission finds that a pig has entered the parlor, the exercise of its regulatory power does not depend on proof that the pig is obscene.

If Justice Stevens's majority opinion settled the matter of communicating certain words over the airwaves—which, the Congress has determined, belong to the people and are therefore regulated by the government—it certainly did not prevent the sale of Carlin's records or the national discussion concerning whether the Supreme Court had acted wisely or foolishly over the "pig in the parlor." In fact, the publicity generated by the case boosted Carlin to such fame that in January of 1983 Home Box Office, a national pay television subscription service with about 8 million subscribers, presented via *cable* (but not via the airwaves, therefore avoiding FCC sanctions) a one-hour special entitled *George Carlin at Carnegie Hall*. In his monologue, the unrepentant Carlin not only discussed the controversy over the seven words one could not say over the air (pronouncing each of them without hesitation, to the obvious relish of the Carnegie Hall audience) but also announced that he had found at least two hundred more forbidden words, all of which he read from a scroll to enthusiastic laughter and applause from those in attendance. In this uncensored HBO program, the question of the regulation of content which is transmitted over the airwaves versus that which is transmitted directly by cable is highlighted. An examination of this issue completes the unit concerning broadcasting.

First Amendment Issues in Cable Transmission

The first commercial cable television systems began operating in the late 1940s and early 1950s as small companies providing an auxiliary retransmission service to isolated communities. The firms employed strategically located superantennas to pick up distant signals, which were then amplified and sent directly into the homes of subscribers by means of a wire called a coaxial cable. The service did not originate programs, but simply strengthened the over-the-air signals so that subscribers' homes would have a clear image on the screen.

The FCC left the new industry untouched for a dozen years, but in 1962 it entered the arena of cable regulation with rules governing microwave transmission to cable compa-

nies. The first comprehensive set of rules governing cable television were announced in 1966 in the commission's significant *Second Order and Report,* the rationale of which was not to censor programming but to restrict the industry in order to protect existing television stations. In short, the commission decided to prevent cable from growing much beyond an auxiliary service to isolated areas of the country. In 1968 the U.S. Supreme Court ruled that the *Second Order and Report* was constitutional, reasoning that since cable retransmitted television signals which were first sent out over the airwaves, the FCC was only exercising its duty to supervise broadcasting.[46]

During the 1970s the FCC began to accumulate evidence showing that cable's retransmission service was doing little, if any, damage to established broadcasters, thereby mitigating the initial rationale for tight controls over the new technology.[47] In addition, the courts on several occasions had found *for* the industry and against the FCC when certain regulatory constraints were submitted to judicial review. Consequently, the commission was stirred to consider and then initiate a process of deregulation—a move that gained momentum during the "deregulation fever" which struck Washington during the last half of the decade. By the beginning of the 1980s almost all of the FCC's restrictions upon cable had either been thrown out by the courts or abolished by vote of the commissioners. Within the short period of less than twenty years, cable had evolved from unreg-

[46]*Second Order and Report,* 2 F.C.C.2d 725 (1966); upheld by the Supreme Court in *U.S.* v. *Southwestern Cable,* 392 U.S. 157 (1968).

[47]Stanley M. Besen and Robert W. Crandall, "The Deregulation of Cable Television," *Law and Contemporary Problems* 44 (Winter 1981): 77–124; in particular, see pp. 104–106.

ulated to regulated and back again to generally unregulated—truly a unique development in the history of federal rule making.

The decision of the FCC to deregulate cable at the federal level has shifted the responsibility for industry regulation to state and local government. *Local government* has emerged as the major arena of cable administration, for it is here that the rules are devised for each franchisee. Consequently, even though uniform national standards remain in effect for radio and television broadcasters, there now exists little uniformity in the laws governing cable companies. Just as the law of defamation differs from state to state, so does the law of cable television—at least for the time being—differ from state to state and community to community. The individual who wishes to know the rules under which the local cable company operates will need to examine state law and local ordinances and contracts.

Before examining some of the First Amendment questions raised by cable technology, one should keep in mind the distinction between programs that are *first broadcast over the air and then retransmitted by cable* and *cable-only programs that are never sent over the airwaves* but are originated for, sent by, and received on the cable (e.g., Home Box Office). At least three First Amendment issues can be identified within the context of this over-the-air versus cable-only program dichotomy: (1) the extent to which the federal government should be allowed to regulate the interstate transmission of cable-only programs; (2) the extent to which state and local governmental bodies that grant franchises to cable operations should be permitted to set up and enforce standards for program content; and (3) the extent to which the rules of fairness and access that now apply to broadcasting should be applied to the rapidly growing cable industry.

FCC JURISDICTION OVER CABLE-ONLY PROGRAMMING. The 1968 Supreme Court decision in *U.S.* v. *Southwestern Cable,* which upheld the right of the FCC to regulate cable as a *retransmission* operation, did not address the question of the commission's authority over programs which were originated for cable only. However, in 1977 the U.S. Circuit Court of Appeals for the District of Columbia firmly rejected a set of FCC restrictions that were applied to *cable-only* programming, observing in *Home Box Office* v. *FCC* that the government was attempting to regulate the nonbroadcast activity of pay television in order to protect broadcasters. The court of appeals expressed doubts that such nonbroadcast programming was covered by the Communications Act, since no signal entered the airwaves; furthermore, observed the court, the alleged harm to existing broadcasters from cable-only programming was only speculative and for this reason was "simply impermissible." After the U.S. Supreme Court denied review, the FCC dropped the matter, and no further rules for cable-only services have been promulgated.[48] This regulation vacuum explains in part, at least, why George Carlin discussed "Filthy Words" with impunity (and added two hundred more to the original list of seven) over HBO in January 1983 and why no comparable program was aired by standard broadcasters. Future developments should be watched closely, for the question of federal regulation of cable-only is certainly not settled with any degree of finality. Perhaps the term "dormant" better fits the current status of this issue.

CONTENT CONSTRAINTS BY STATE AND LOCAL GOVERNMENT. In early 1983 the

[48]*Home Box Office* v. *FCC,* 567 F.2d 9 (D.C. Cir. 1977); *cert. denied,* 434 U.S. 829 (1977).

American Library Association in its *Newsletter on Intellectual Freedom* reported two developments that are, no doubt, harbingers of events to come as procensorship forces in local communities move to "clean up" cable entertainment. First, in Miami, Florida, following a call by the mayor for the formation of a cable censorship committee, the city attorney drafted an ordinance that would permit the revocation of the franchise of the city's cable service if "obscene" or "indecent" programs were allowed on the wire. And second, in Roy, Utah, despite strong protests by over six hundred local cable users who wanted no censorship, the city council adopted an ordinance that would permit the revocation of the cable franchise in that community if indecent programs (identified by ordinance supporters as certain adult entertainment originated by Home Box Office) continued to be allowed on cable.[49] When the Roy City ordinance was subjected to a legal challenge, the U.S. District Court for Utah declared the law unconstitutional on the grounds that a subscription service may not be censored by local ordinance unless and until it crosses the "pornographic line" established by the U.S. Supreme Court in the 1973 case of *Miller* v. *California.* Said U.S. District Judge Jenkins in the Roy City dispute, and concerning subscription television: "I need not hook up. I need not tune in. I may pick and choose among the programs and I may cancel. We need not approve, but we tolerate to the line of community standards drawn in *Miller* and applied in *HBO* v. *Wilkinson.*"[50]

A few months later, in another part of the country, the City of Cincinnati, Ohio, via the office of the county prosecutor, brought obscenity charges against its cable system, Warner Amex, concerning two films shown on the Playboy channel. The charges were dropped in June 1983, after Warner Amex signed an agreement not to permit X-rated films on its cable service to Cincinnati. Furthermore, the Cincinnati vice squad announced that it would monitor the Playboy channel for any future programs which might violate "community standards."[51] Clearly, the battle lines are being drawn over the standards of censorship for cable television programs; it would not be surprising to find Congress and the federal courts more deeply involved in the issue in the near future than was true in the years 1982 and 1983, when the above cases occurred. As students of free speech observe and participate in developments, a key fact should be kept in mind, namely, the programming in question is not sent over the airwaves and is voluntarily subscribed to and paid for by Americans who wish to receive it.

CABLE TECHNOLOGY AND THE ISSUES OF FAIRNESS AND ACCESS. The fact that cable-only signals make no use of the public airwaves appears to be highly significant to federal judges in determining the legality of various FCC cable regulations. For example, the Fairness Doctrine, the equal-time rule, and various other matters of balanced programming and access by which radio and television stations are regulated either do not apply or are of questionable application to the operation of a cable service. As a case in point, the FCC's 1972 access regulations, designed

---

[49]*Newsletter on Intellectual Freedom,* January 1983, p. 25.

[50]*Community Television of Utah* v. *Roy City,* 51 *Law Week* 2408 (1983). *HBO* v. *Wilkinson,* mentioned by Judge Jenkins, concerns an unsuccessful attempt by the state to censor HBO; this case is found at 531 F. Supp. 987 (1982). Also, in August 1983, the U.S. District Court for the Southern District of Florida declared the Miami, Florida, cable censorship ordinance unconstitutional. *Cruz* v. *Ferre,* 9 Med.L.Rptr. 2050 (1983).

[51]In "News Notes," Med.L.Rptr., July 12, 1983.

to prevent a company from exercising control over all cable channels in a given community, were rejected as without statutory foundation by the U.S. Supreme Court in 1979.[52] The way remains open, apparently, for Congress to pass legislation concerning fairness and access in cable operations, thereby plugging the statutory gap identified by the Supreme Court in *Midwest Video II*. Besen and Crandall observe in their study of the deregulation of cable that the access issue "is likely to become especially important" in the future "if large numbers of cable programmers are denied access to cable systems."[53] To this observation one might add that equal time and related access questions will almost certainly become a matter of congressional concern if and when cable operators permit much discrimination in political programming—especially if they allow only the cable company's point of view to be sent out over the franchised wire system. This question, like others similar to it, awaits resolution at some time in the future. Meanwhile, thoughtful students of the First Amendment should study the relevant issues and be prepared to participate in the inevitable public dialogue concerning not only cable television but also other channel-oriented technological developments such as the distribution of satellite signals directly to the home.

Broadcasting and the First Amendment in Brief

The Federal Radio Act of 1927 was the first comprehensive statute to be enacted by Congress for the purpose of governing broadcast-

ing in the United States. The 1927 law, which was made necessary by chaotic conditions in the fledgling radio industry (brought on by conflicts over use of the limited frequencies in the broadcast spectrum), was revised and expanded by the Communications Act of 1934, which, as amended from time to time, remains the basic "law of the land" for broadcasting. The Communications Act established the Federal Communications Commission (FCC) as an independent regulatory agency under the direction of seven commissioners appointed by the president and confirmed by the Senate. The FCC regulates radio and television in keeping with the Communications Act's standard that broadcasting serve the "public convenience, interest, or necessity." To this end, the commission licenses broadcasting stations for a limited period of time (seven years maximum for radio and five years maximum for television), after which the station must request a license renewal. Significant violations of a law by a licensee, or a failure to serve the public interest as determined by FCC policy, can result in the revocation or nonrenewal of a station's license.

In the years since the government began to regulate commercial broadcasting in the United States, four significant areas of First Amendment concern have emerged, namely: (1) licensing, (2) program balance and access to station facilities, (3) the censorship of content, and (4) special problems of cable television. *First,* the Supreme Court asserted in *NBC v. U.S.* (1943) that licensing did not violate the Constitution, for such a procedure was necessary because of the physical limitations of the broadcast spectrum. Also, the federal courts over the years have generally supported FCC rules designed to prevent monopoly ownership and control over stations, including regulations requiring diversity of ownership in local markets. *Second,* in

[52]*FCC v. Midwest Video Corp.,* 440 U.S. 689 (1979). This case is often called *Midwest Video II* to distinguish it from a 1972 case bearing a similar name.
[53]Besen and Crandall, p. 120.

BROADCASTING AND THE FIRST AMENDMENT: A CHRONOLOGY OF SIGNIFICANT DEVELOPMENTS

1. 1927 (by Congress), the Radio Act of 1927, 44 *Statutes at Large* 1162. Established the Federal Radio Commission (FRC) and a system of licensing; declared that the airwaves belong to the people, and that broadcasting was to serve the "public convenience, interest, or necessity."

2. 1934 (by Congress), the Communications Act of 1934, 47 *U.S. Code* Secs. 151–606. Reorganized the FRC into a seven-person Federal Communications Commission (FCC). This statute, as amended, remains in effect.

3. 1941 (by FCC), the Mayflower Doctrine announced, *In the Matter of The Mayflower Broadcasting Corp. and The Yankee Network, Inc. (WAAB),* 8 F.C.C. 333 (1941). Foundation laid for the Fairness Doctrine (which was officially announced in 1949) by ruling that stations could not editorialize, but should present "all sides of important public questions, fairly, objectively, and without bias."

4. 1943 (by U.S. Supreme Court), *National Broadcasting* Co. v. *U.S.,* 319 U.S. 190 (1943). Landmark decision, announcing that the licensing of broadcasting stations by the FCC was constitutional.

5. 1948 (by U.S. Supreme Court), *U.S.* v. *Paramount Pictures,* 334 U.S. 131 (1948). Although the case was concerned primarily with antitrust practices in the film industry, Justice Douglas in his opinion of the Court did affirm that broadcasting was "included in the press whose freedom is guaranteed by the First Amendment."

6. 1949 (by FCC), the Fairness Doctrine announced, *In the Matter of Editorializing by Broadcast Licensees,* 13 F.C.C. 1246 (1949). Here the FCC reversed its ban on station editorials (announced in 1941 in *Mayflower*) and in so doing ruled that advocacy by licensees should be a part of a "reasonably balanced presentation of all responsible viewpoints" on public issues and that a "right of reply" to personal attacks made over a station's facilities was now expected.

7. 1959 (by Congress), amended Sec. 315(a), the equal-time provision of the Communications Act of 1934, to establish four exceptions which did not trigger equal time: bona fide newscasts, news interviews, news documentaries, and on-the-spot coverage of news events. Also, Congress wrote the amendment in language which demonstrated its approval of the Fairness Doctrine.

8. 1960 (by Congress), passed the "Great Debates Law" which temporarily suspended Sec. 315(a) of the Communications Act of 1934 to permit a one-time exception allowing a television debate between presidental candidates John F. Kennedy and Richard M. Nixon without requiring equal time for splinter candidates.

9. 1966 (by FCC), first comprehensive rules for the regulation of *cable* television were announced, *Second Order and Report,* 2 F.C.C.2d 725 (1966).

10. 1969 (by U.S. Supreme Court), Fairness Doctrine declared constitutional, *Red Lion Broadcasting Co.* v. *FCC,* 395 U.S. 367 (1969). This landmark decision by a unanimous Court affirmed that both the Fairness Doctrine and the FCC's rule on the right to reply to a personal attack were constitutional.

the important *Red Lion* decision of 1969, the Supreme Court upheld the constitutionality of the FCC's Fairness Doctrine, requiring licensees to present a balance in their programming about public issues. Furthermore, the courts have sustained the statutory require-

11. 1973 (by U.S. Supreme Court), stations not required to sell air time for editorial advertising, *CBS* v. *Democratic National Committee,* 412 U.S. 94 (1973). The Court upheld the FCC's position that broadcasters were not required to sell time for editorial advertising.

12. 1974 (by FCC), "The Fairness Report" announced, 48 F.C.C. 2d 1 (1974). A comprehensive summary of the commission's support for the Fairness Doctrine; also, the FCC reversed its earlier position that commercial advertising triggered the Fairness Doctrine, hereafter excluding strictly commercial advertising from Fairness Doctrine claims.

13. 1975 (by FCC), announced new interpretation of political campaign news events, in *Petitions of Aspen Institute and CBS,* 55 F.C.C.2d 697 (1975). New rules permitted (a) full coverage of press conferences of incumbents or candidates if event is newsworthy and done without favoritism and (b) airing of candidate debates provided the debates are sponsored by someone (such as the League of Women Voters) other than the candidates or the broadcaster.

14. 1978 (by U.S. Supreme Court), divestiture regulations of the FCC upheld, *FCC* v. *National Citizens Committee for Broadcasting,* 436 U.S. 775 (1978). The Court ruled that the 1975 Multiple Ownership Rules were intended to promote diversification in the mass media, and were constitutional.

15. 1978 (by U.S. Supreme Court), FCC's reprimand of station for broadcasting George Carlin's satiric monologue "Filthy Words," upheld, *FCC* v. *Pacifica Foundation,* 438 U.S. 726 (1978). The Court held that the FCC could legally prohibit "indecent," "shocking," and "patently offensive" language from the nation's airwaves.

16. 1981 (by U.S. Supreme Court), stations may change overall formats without having an FCC review of the proposed change, *FCC* v. *WNCN Listeners Guild,* 450 U.S. 582 (1981). Also, the Court held that there is no First Amendment right to receive wanted programming.

17. 1981 (by U.S. Supreme Court), access to broadcast facilities guaranteed for federal candidates, *CBS* v. *FCC,* 453 U.S. 367 (1981). The Court upheld the FCC's efforts to enforce Section 312(a)(7) of the Communications Act (passed by Congress in 1971) assuring legally qualified candidates for federal office access to broadcast facilities to purchase "reasonable amounts of time" for campaign communication. This important decision for the first time grants candidates for federal office an *affirmative right of access* to the airwaves.

18. 1983 (by FCC), further liberalized the equal time rule by agreeing to permit stations (as well as nonpartisan groups—see item 13 above) to sponsor debates between legally qualified candidates for public office, and to broadcast those debates as bona fide news events; see *Re: Petitions of Henry Geller et al,* 48 Fed.Reg. 53166 (November 25, 1983). Sponsorship of such debates by licensees no longer automatically triggers the equal-time rule.

ment of the Communications Act of 1934 that stations grant equal time to candidates for public office; in the 1981 case of *CBS* v. *FCC,* the Supreme Court affirmed the constitutionality of the 1971 amendment to the Communications Act, which for the first time established a *limited right of access* to station facilities for candidates for federal elective office.

Third, the courts have upheld the specific content constraints placed upon broadcasting by the Communications Act and the *U.S. Code,* including those prohibitions upon the airing of lottery information and of using "obscene, indecent, or profane" language in broadcast programming. *Finally,* the rapidly growing cable industry, which for the time being has been generally deregulated by the FCC, presents three important questions for policy debate and future decision making: (1) To what extent should the federal government regulate the interstate transmission of cable programs, particularly that programming which is originated for cable only? (2) To what extent should state and local government, especially the franchising units, be permitted to set and enforce standards for program content? (3) To what extent should the established rules of fairness and access be applied to cable? These and similar questions concerning not only cable but also other channel technologies such as satellite transmission directly to the home remain to be settled in the years ahead. Meanwhile, persons who are curious about the regulations governing a local cable company should consult state and local laws on the subject as well as the terms of the specific contract under which the franchisee operates. (For a chronological summary of the material on broadcasting, see box.)

III. MODERN TECHNOLOGY AND THE "MARKETPLACE OF IDEAS"

In the year 1644 the English writer John Milton stated in his famous anticensorship tract *Areopagitica,* "And though all the winds of doctrine were let loose to play upon the earth, so Truth be in the field, we do injuriously by licensing and prohibiting to misdoubt her strength. Let her and Falsehood grapple; who ever knew Truth put to the worse in a free and open encounter?" In this way Milton demonstrated his belief in what some have called a "marketplace theory" of free speech—a viewpoint suggesting that ideas "grapple" in a field (or marketplace) open to merchants of all shades of opinion, and that after due consideration thoughtful consumers "buy" the product that to them represents truth. In more recent years this concept was articulated by Supreme Court Justice Oliver Wendell Holmes, Jr., in his dissent over the conviction of Jacob Abrams for passing out antiwar leaflets during World War I. In the conclusion of his argument against the conviction, Holmes wrote:

> . . . But when men have realized that time has upset many fighting faiths, they may come to believe even more than they believe the very foundations of their own conduct that the ultimate good desired is better reached by free trade in ideas—that **the best test of truth is the power of the thought to get itself accepted in the competition of the market;** and that truth is the only ground upon which their wishes safely can be carried out.[54]

Whether or not a truly open marketplace of ideas has ever existed in any society is a matter of dispute. Before the printing press there simply were no means of mass communication by which all in a society could participate in a clash of ideas (even if such a revolutionary thing had been permitted by the authorities, which, of course, it was not); after Gutenberg's invention made a national debate possible, restrictions such as licensing

[54]*Abrams* v. *U.S.,* 250 U.S. 616 (1919).

plus the chilling effect of the threat of severe post facto punishment served to restrict the marketplace to a small corner of the town square. Furthermore, after licensing was eliminated and post facto punishments reduced in severity, would-be professors of the truth confronted the fact that in many instances, as the adage so well puts it, "Freedom of the press is for those who *own* one!"

Post-Gutenberg technology has compounded the problem. Nowadays the individual who wishes to communicate to the general public must be concerned not only about who owns the printing press but also about who owns the radio and television stations, the networks, the cable systems, and the communication satellites. Although the U.S. Constitution constrains the hand of *government* from interfering with the efforts of public communicators to reach their intended audiences, the Constitution does considerably less to constrain the hand of *private* enterprise. And, as it turns out, most of the entrances into the marketplace of ideas—including the gates of press, radio, television, network, cable, and satellite—are privately owned and operated. Furthermore, the gates are operated for a profit, so that in many instances would-be communicators must pay extremely high prices to the gatekeeper if the message is to be permitted through. Finally, those who own the gates retain the authority to deny entrance to whomever they wish, and, for a variety of reasons, do exactly that. How can freedom of expression serve the public interest under such conditions? What, if anything, should be done to *require* the private gatekeepers to stop exercising discretion and start admitting all ideas into the marketplace? It is appropriate at this point (1) to examine some proposals for access to the media and then (2) to summarize the response of the federal courts to certain of those proposals.

Mandatory Access to Privately Owned Media

The idea that freedom of speech should be affirmatively promoted through law is not new—the nation's First Amendment is testimony to that, as is the copyright clause of the Constitution ("To promote the Progress of Science and useful Arts"), the Fourteenth Amendment, and numerous federal (e.g., the Communications Act of 1934) and state laws. Students of freedom of expression should observe that although many provisions of the Constitution and of federal and state statutes function in a negative way to constrain the authority of would-be censors by asserting "thou shalt not," these same documents serve positive functions as well, not the least of which is the educational one of reminding the citizens of the American democracy of their fundamental right to speak. In addition, the U.S. Supreme Court during the twentieth century has affirmatively supported freedom of speech in a number of decisions, as in opening up appropriate public places for parades, marches, and protests and in constraining the power of private enterprise in a variety of ways, ranging from *Marsh* v. *Alabama,* which said that company-owned towns must be open to the exercise of First Amendment rights, to the *Red Lion* decision affirming the constitutionality of the Fairness Doctrine as applied to radio and television.[55]

During the 1960s—appropriately called "the decade of dissent" because of the almost constant occurrence of protests and demonstrations from civil rights advocates and opponents of the Vietnam War—many speakers who attempted to reach the general public with their messages of "freedom now" or "withdraw from Vietnam" found that the

---

[55]*Marsh* v. *Alabama,* 326 U.S. 501 (1946); and *Red Lion Broadcasting Co.* v. *FCC,* 395 U.S. 367 (1969).

FIGURE 11.3. JEROME A. BARRON.
Jerome A. Barron, a leading advocate of the theory that access to the mass media should be considered a First Amendment right, is currently dean of the National Law Center of George Washington University, Washington, D.C. Despite a number of court decisions unfavorable to his theory of access, Dean Barron continues to believe that the privately owned mass media must be opened up if the system of freedom of expression is to serve its purpose of educating the public.
Courtesy of Jerome A. Barron.

privately owned media would not listen and would not permit the antiestablishment rhetoric to reach the marketplace of ideas. Much of the violence and civil disobedience of the period was later blamed on the frustration these would-be communicators felt when they were either ignored or denied access to the marketplace by the mass media. As one scholar concluded following a study entitled *Violence as Protest,* many rioters felt a sense of accomplishment because the destruction they had inflicted had attracted the attention of radio, television, and press and had therefore served as a "singularly successful attempt at communication."[56]

One of those who observed the efforts of antiestablishment communicators to reach the general public during the 1960s was professor of law Jerome A. Barron, who responded with a provocative proposal for a First Amendment right of access to the media. In his widely read essay published in the *Harvard Law Review* in 1967, Barron describes as an "anomaly" that feature of American constitutional law which extends protection to expression "once it has come to the fore" but is otherwise "indifferent to creating opportunities for expression."[57] The free-speech imperfection thus created was concisely stated a few years later in *Freedom of the Press for Whom?* In this work, Barron develops his theory of access more fully.

[56]Robert M. Fogelson, *Violence as Protest* (Garden City, N.Y.: Doubleday, 1971), pp. 85–86.

[57]Jerome A. Barron, "Access to the Press—A New First Amendment Right," *Harvard Law Review* 80 (1967): 1641–1678.

This book chronicles the struggle to open the media. It states the case for access. The basic premise is that our communications policy is presently in the grip of a romantic conception of free individual expression, an assumption that the marketplace of ideas is freely accessible. But "laissez faire" economic theory is inadequate and unsuitable to govern the interplay of ideas in American life. Private censorship characterizes both the print and the broadcast media. . . . Efforts of dissenting groups on both the left and the right to secure something as fundamental and simple as advertising space in their community newspapers are often futile. Similar problems exist in securing broadcast time. This book's basic argument is that the First Amendment should be restored to its true proprietors—the reader, the viewer, the listener. Freedom of the press must be something more than a guarantee of the property rights of media owners.[58]

Barron proposes that an interpretation of the First Amendment is needed which constrains the hand not only of government but also private groups. Neither should be permitted to censor ideas. What is unique about Barron's view is his recognition that modern communications technology in the hands of *private* owners threatens to undermine the goal of the Constitution to assure free and wide-open debate on public issues, and that something must be done about this if the system of freedom of expression is to remain viable. As he states in his *Harvard Law Review* essay, a way must be found to accommodate "the interests of those who control the means of communication" with the "interests of those who seek a forum in which to express their point of view."[59] The preferred route to

establishing a right of access is by legislation, he adds, although it can also be accomplished by judicial interpretation of the Constitution.

Proposals based upon Barron's thoughtful analysis of the marketplace of ideas in a day of high technology in the mass media were forthcoming from a variety of sources, ranging from professors of law to a special study group of the 1968 Biennial National Conference of the American Civil Liberties Union. Recommendations varied from those urging newspapers (and other channels of communication) voluntarily to provide space and time for the expression of minority views to those arguing that access be made mandatory under law. Thomas I. Emerson, in *The System of Freedom of Expression,* summarizes (but does not necessarily approve of) four things that might occur under a mandatory access rule: (1) a newspaper might be required to accept editorial advertising from those who wish to present controversial views to the public; (2) a personal-attack rule, similar to the one the FCC applies to broadcasters, could be applied to newspapers; (3) the letters-to-the-editor section of the paper could be expanded, with special attention to including expressions of opinion at variance with those of the newspaper; and (4) newspapers could be placed under a special type of Fairness Doctrine that would obligate them to provide in their overall coverage a balanced perspective on all newsworthy public issues.[60] Before long, cases began to reach the

---

[58]Jerome A. Barron, *Freedom of the Press for Whom?* (Bloomington, Ind.: Indiana University Press, 1973), p. xiv.

[59]Barron, "Access to the Press," p. 1656.

[60]Thomas I. Emerson, *The System of Freedom of Expression* (New York: Random House, 1970), p. 670; also, all of chapter 17, "Affirmative Promotion of Freedom of Expression," concerns the issue under discussion. For a brief survey of how the theory developed during the 1960s, see Thomas L. Tedford, "Freedom of Speech in the 1960s," chapter 22 in *America in Controversy: History of American Public Address,* ed. DeWitte Holland (Dubuque, Iowa: Wm. C. Brown, 1973), pp. 403–404.

federal courts which addressed the issue of mandatory access as a First Amendment right.

The Courts Respond to Access Theory

During the 1970s the federal courts were presented with a number of cases in which the issue of a constitutional right of access to the mass media was argued. The results were generally negative, as the rulings in five significant cases—two concerning newspapers and three concerning broadcasting—will show. First, the two newspaper cases will be discussed, after which a brief summary of three cases concerning broadcasting (as developed in the previous section of this chapter) will be added to complete the picture.

The first newspaper case began in the late 1960s, when the Amalgamated Clothing Workers of America (ACWA) attempted to purchase space for editorial advertising in the four daily newspapers then publishing in Chicago. ACWA wished to explain to the public the union's opposition to unrestricted importing of men's and boys' clothing. In support of its campaign, the union was picketing a major Chicago retailer, Marshall Field & Company, alleging that the store was contributing to the unemployment of Americans by selling so many imported goods. The proposed ACWA advertisement was rejected by all four Chicago dailies, whereupon the union entered federal court to insist upon the right to communicate to the public via paid editorial advertising. The federal district court rejected the argument that the First Amendment required such access to a newspaper; upon appeal, the federal circuit court upheld the newspapers' position that the press had absolute discretion over what it permitted in the way of advertising. The U.S. Supreme Court denied review.[61]

Second, a major test of access theory occurred in 1974 when the U.S. Supreme Court decided a case that had originated in Florida two years earlier in a controversy over that state's right-to-reply law. When a Florida newspaper refused to publish a candidate's response to that paper's editorial attack upon him, a legal challenge occurred, and because many of the elements of his "open-up-the-press" view were present in the case, Jerome A. Barron helped the candidate argue for a right of reply against the newspaper. The result was not a happy one for the advocates of access.

Chief Justice Burger writing for the Court first reviewed the circumstances of the case and the language of the statute in question, after which he summarized the basic views of access proponents as set forth in briefs and in oral arguments. He then concluded with the four reasons for rejecting access theory and for ruling in favor of the *Miami Herald*. (The selection below is organized around the four arguments as stated by the Chief Justice.)

Chief Justice Burger *delivered the opinion of the Court:*

However much validity may be found in the arguments favoring access . . . at each point the implementation of a remedy such as an enforceable right of access necessarily calls for some mechanism, either governmental or consensual. If it is governmental coercion, this at once brings about a confrontation with the express provisions of the First Amendment . . . .

[1.] The Florida Statute operates as a command in the same sense as a statute or regulation forbidding appellant to publish specified matter. Governmental restraint on publishing need not fall into familiar or traditional patterns to be subject to constitutional limitations on governmental powers. . . . [2.] The Florida

[61]*Chicago Joint Board, Amalgamated Clothing Workers* v. *Chicago Tribune Co.,* 307 F. Supp. 422 (N.D. Ill. 1969) sustained on appeal, 435 F.2d 470 (2d Cir. 1970); *cert. denied,* 402 U.S. 973 (1971).

Miami Herald Publishing Co. v. Tornillo, 418 U.S. 241 (1974)
Decided June 25, 1974

Vote: 9 to 0 delcaring the Florida right-of-reply law unconstitutional.

Majority Opinion By: Chief Justice Burger.

Concurring Justices: Douglas, Brennan, Stewart, White, Marshall, Blackmun, Powell, and Rehnquist.

Dissenting Justices: (none)

Justices Not Participating: (none)

Summary: In the fall of 1972 Pat Tornillo, candidate for election to the Florida House of Representatives, was severely criticized in an editorial published by the *Miami Herald*. Invoking the state's right-to-reply statute, a law passed in 1913 that required any newspaper attacking the character or official record of a candidate for public office to print free of charge the reply of that candidate, Tornillo insisted that the *Miami Herald* publish his response verbatim. When the newspaper refused, Tornillo entered the courts to compel compliance with the law. The circuit court in Dade County ruled the statute unconstitutional, but the Florida Supreme Court reversed the court below, ruling that the statute was constitutional. The U.S. Supreme Court granted review, and after hearing arguments (including those of Jerome Barron on behalf of Tornillo), unanimously reversed the Florida Supreme Court. Chief Justice Burger in his opinion of the Court gave four key reasons for ruling against access. Mandatory access to the press is prohibited by the Constitution, he asserted, because (1) just as restraint upon publication is a state action prohibited by the First Amendment, so is access *a command which is likewise prohibited;* (2) the *financial penalty* exacted from a newspaper (which must publish access materials free of charge) is not permissible; (3) the *chilling effect* upon the press is undesirable, for editors would become timid and avoid controversy rather than provoke demands for free access; and (4) the *editorial control* and judgment of the newspaper would be offended by such a requirement.

Rule Established; Significance of Case: The *Tornillo* decision is a major defeat for proponents of access to the press as a First Amendment right. Unless and until the ruling is tempered, there exists in the United States no constitutional right of access to the press—not even in "one-newspaper towns."

statute exacts a penalty . . . in terms of the cost in printing and composing time and materials and in taking up space that could be devoted to other material the newspaper may have preferred to print. It is correct, as appellee contends, that a newspaper is not subject to the finite technological limitations of time that confront a broadcaster but it is not correct to say that, as an economic reality, a newspaper can proceed to infinite expansion of its column space to accommodate the replies that a government agency determines or a statute commands the readers should have available.

[3.] Faced with the penalties that would accrue to any newspaper that published news or commentary arguably within the reach of the right-of-access statute, editors might well conclude that the safe course is to avoid controversy. Therefore, under the operation of the Florida statute, political and electoral coverage would be blunted or reduced. . . .

[4.] Even if a newspaper would face no additional costs to comply with a compulsory access law and would not be forced to forgo publication of news or opinion by the inclusion of a reply, the Florida statute fails to clear the barriers of the First Amendment because of its intrusion into the function of editors. A newspaper is more than a passive receptacle or conduit for news, comment, and advertising. The choice of material to go into a newspaper, and the decisions made as to limitations on the size and content of the paper, and treatment of public issues . . . constitute the exercise of editorial control and judgment. It has yet to be demonstrated how governmental regulation of this crucial process can be exercised consistent with First Amendment guarantees of a free press as they have evolved to this time. Accordingly, the judgment of the Supreme Court of Florida is reversed.

When the two access-to-newspaper decisions—*Amalgamated Clothing Workers* and *Tornillo*—are added to the three access-to-broadcasting cases, a picture emerges of almost total rejection of access theory by the Supreme Court. In the broadcasting area, the *first* case is *CBS* v. *Democratic National Committee,* in which the Court ruled that there is no constitutional right of access to station facilities for paid editorial advertising. *Second,* in *FCC* v. *Midwest Video Corp.,* the Court rejected regulations promulgated by the FCC that required a degree of access to a community's *cable* channels. *Finally,* in *CBS* v. *FCC* the Court did yield slightly to uphold the access provisions of the Federal Election Campaign Act of 1971, which requires broadcast licensees to sell reasonable amounts of time for campaign purposes to candidates for federal elective office. In holding that this *"limited* right of 'reasonable' access" does not offend the Constitution, the Court emphasized that it applied only to *federal* elections "once a campaign has commenced."[62]

Access to the Marketplace of Ideas in Brief

In the late 1960s and early 1970s, professor of law Jerome A. Barron and others argued that the belief that free speech functioned as part

[62]*CBS* v. *Democratic National Committee,* 412 U.S. 94 (1973); *FCC* v. *Midwest Video Corp.,* 440 U.S. 689

of an open marketplace of ideas was a romantic illusion which, if it ever existed in the past, certainly did not exist today. Rather than an open marketplace one found a closed system in which the channels of communication were owned and operated for a profit by *private* industry; unlike the government, private owners of the mass media were for the most part exempt from First Amendment constraints. What was needed, Barron asserted, was an interpretation of the Constitution that opened up the privately owned channels of communication so that all points of view might have access to the reading, listening, or viewing audience.

The federal courts—primarily the U.S. Supreme Court—rejected this argument as applied to newspapers and with one exception rejected it as applied to broadcasting and cable as well (although established rules of fairness and equal time under the Communications Act remained untouched). In the important case of *Miami Herald Publishing Co.* v. *Tornillo* (1974), the Court unanimously declared Florida's right-of-reply statute to be unconstitutional, and in so doing generally turned its back on the arguments of the advocates of access to the media. The specific principles that emerged from *Tornillo* and one other newspaper case, plus three access-to-broadcasting cases, are four in number: (1) there is no constitutional right to purchase editorial advertising either in newspapers or on radio or television; (2) there is no constitutional right of reply to an attack made against an individual by a newspaper (although the personal-attack rule remains intact for broadcasters); (3) the FCC's cable access regulations of 1972 were thrown out by the courts, and no substitute access require-

(1979); and *CBS* v. *FCC,* 453 U.S. 367 (1981). Note: For more details on these cases see the preceding section, which concerns broadcasting and the First Amendment.

ments have been proposed for the cable industry; however, (4) under federal statute there exists a limited right of "reasonable" access to broadcast facilities for candidates for *federal* elective office to *purchase* air time for the purpose of campaigning once a campaign has begun.

The overall picture for advocates of access as a First Amendment right remains gloomy, yet the issue continues to spark constructive debate with the reasoning of the Supreme Court in *Tornillo* being the focus of much of that debate. Whether students of free speech agree with either Benno C. Schmidt, Jr. (who finds the *Tornillo* decision to be unsatisfactory) or with defenders of the decision such as Floyd Abrams (who states that *Tornillo* is "an occasion for dancing in the streets"), all should continue to think about the best solution to Jerome Barron's core idea: that "the privately controlled media have a responsibility to provide opportunity for expression."[63]

CONCLUSION

Technological advances in the mass media during the twentieth century have greatly influenced—and continue to influence—the principles and practice of freedom of speech in the United States. *First,* loudspeakers, because of their high potential for creating a nuisance, have received less protection from the courts than have most other channels of communication. The U.S. Supreme Court has ruled on the subject in only two cases, asserting that local ordinances concerning permits for the use of a sound amplification device must be administered without discretion, and that narrowly drawn laws designed to control the "loud and raucous noises" emitted by loudspeakers are constitutional. The Court has been content in recent years to leave the matter up to state and local authorities; in some instances state courts have sustained ordinances forbidding *all* use of loudspeakers in public places.

Second, broadcasting presents unique challenges to the system of freedom of expression and to public communicators who function within that system. Because broadcast frequencies are limited in number, the federal government supervises the industry under the Communications Act of 1934. The Federal Communications Commission (FCC) established by that act is charged with regulating broadcasting in the United States for the "public convenience, interest, or necessity." Under the law, the airwaves belong to the people, and are only "loaned" to stations for a limited period of time under a license which is in effect for a maximum of five years for television and a maximum of seven years for radio stations, after which a renewal must be secured. Three significant issues concerning broadcasting and the First Amendment which have been decided by the U.S. Supreme Court are as follows: (1) the licensing of stations is constitutional, as are the rules of the FCC designed to prevent monopoly control over the industry; (2) the FCC's Fairness Doctrine, which requires licensees to present a balance in programming about important public issues, is constitutional (determined in the landmark *Red Lion* decision of 1969); and (3) constraints upon broadcast content that presents fraudulent information, lottery information, or language of an "obscene, indecent, or profane" nature are constitutional. Finally, cable transmission—particularly that which is for cable only, having never been broadcast over the airwaves—presents new

[63]Benno C. Schmidt, Jr., *Freedom of the Press vs. Public Access* (New York: Praeger, 1976), particularly pp. 217–254. Floyd Abrams, "In Defense of *Tornillo*," *Yale Law Journal* 86 (December 1976): 361–369, at p. 363. And Barron, *Freedom of the Press for Whom?*, p. xv.

problems of First Amendment law; for the time being cable is generally deregulated at the federal level; state and local laws and local franchise contracts determine what constraints apply to cable companies in a given community. Definitive legal principles concerning how the First Amendment applies to cable, satellite transmission, and similar new technologies await future decision making by the Congress and the federal courts.

Third, during the late 1960s and early 1970s a number of First Amendment scholars, led by professor of law Jerome A. Barron, proposed a theory of *access to the mass media* as a First Amendment right. In a day of concentrated private ownership of the mass media, these theorists argued, such a right was necessary to prevent the gatekeepers of press, broadcasting, and cable from keeping minority viewpoints from reaching the public. The response of the federal courts to this proposal for a right of access to the media was negative, as the following four results demonstrate: during the 1970s and early 1980s the courts ruled that (1) there is no constitutional right to purchase editorial advertising in newspapers or on radio or television; (2) the Florida law assuring certain persons a right of reply to a newspaper attack was declared unconstitutional (in a significant Supreme Court opinion that generally rejected access theory, *Miami Herald* v. *Tornillo,* 1974); (3) the FCC's cable access regulations of 1972 were rejected by the courts, and no new requirements for access to cable facilities have been announced by the commission; and finally, (4) the Supreme Court in *CBS* v. *FCC* (1981) did uphold a limited form of access when it declared constitutional a federal statute requiring broadcasters to sell "reasonable" amounts of time for campaign purposes to candidates for federal office during a campaign. Overall, access theory has won few adherents on the bench; however, it has

served—and continues to serve—the important purpose of stirring constructive debate about the influence of modern communication technology upon the system of freedom of expression.

EXERCISES

A. Classroom projects and activities.
  1. Here are three questions phrased for classroom debate:
    a. Resolved, that broadcasting should receive the same degree of First Amendment protection as do newspapers and public speakers.
    b. Resolved, that cable television, including that which is never sent over the airwaves, should be required to abide by the Fairness Doctrine, the personal-attack rule, and the equal-time rule, just as regular broadcasters do.
    c. Resolved, that this class supports the proposal of Jerome A. Barron for access to the press as a First Amendment right.
  2. Here are the same three questions phrased for discussion:
    a. Should broadcasting receive the same degree of First Amendment protection as do other means of communication, such as the print medium or public speaking?
    b. Should the Fairness Doctrine, the personal-attack rule, and the equal-time rule, which apply to broadcasters, be applied to cable-only transmission?
    c. Should access to the press (and to the mass media in general) be a First Amendment right?
  3. Invite a panel of managers of local or regional radio and television stations to the class for a discussion of First Amendment problems faced by broadcasters. Query panel members on how they meet the requirements of the Fairness Doctrine, the

personal-attack rule, and the equal-time rule.

4. Invite a panel of newspaper editors from your region, including the editor of your campus newspaper, to discuss Jerome Barron's theory of access to the press. Be sure to furnish each panel member in advance a summary of Barron's point of view.

5. In *Davey Johnson,* 54 F.C.C.2d 923 (1975), the FCC ruled that regular religious programming—such as church services, sermons, prayers, and religious music—does not trigger the Fairness Doctrine for atheists, agnostics, and others who might disagree with the content of such broadcasting. Is this fair? Is there a better solution? If so, what? Discuss.

6. Discuss why our society forbids the broadcasting of a routine such as Carlin's "Filthy Words" on the airwaves but permits news coverage of Nazi messages of racism and anti-Semitism, plus the use of the word "nigger" in political advertising on television by racist candidates for public office. Why is the word "shit" in a comedy routine considered unfit for the airwaves, whereas the word "nigger" in a political broadcast or commercial is not?

7. Discuss the following quotation from Barron's 1967 essay in the *Harvard Law Review:* "Our constitutional theory is in the grip of a romantic conception of free expression, a belief that the 'marketplace of ideas' is freely accessible. But if ever there were a self-operating marketplace of ideas, it has long ceased to exist."

8. Invite a professor of broadcasting, or a local radio or television administrator, to address the class on "Communications Technologies of the Future." Discuss what issues of freedom to communicate might emerge from the new technologies.

9. Secure a copy of your city's loud-speaker (and related noise-abatement) ordinance; duplicate and distribute to the class for discussion and evaluation. Does it apply equally to all, or are elements of discretion present? What improvements can the class recommend?

10. Secure a copy of state and local laws governing cable franchise agreements where you live. What content constraints, if any, are in effect in your community? Invite the manager of the local cable company to discuss First Amendment issues related to cable from the industry point of view.

11. Write for a list of publications from the FCC, and add the list to your notes for the course. Address the Federal Communications Commission, 1919 M Street, N.W., Washington, D.C. 20554.

B. Topics for research papers or oral reports.

1. Is the Grass Greener in the Mother Country? The Basics of British Broadcast Regulation (with Special Attention to the Freedom of Expression).

2. Is Deregulation the Answer? An Analysis of Proposals to Deregulate Broadcasting in the United States.

3. A Defense (or a Critique) of the Fairness Doctrine.

4. The Aftermath of "Pig in the Parlor": The Effect of *FCC* v. *Pacifica* (the 1978 Carlin case) on Broadcasting in the United States.

5. Cable Technology and the First Amendment: Problems and Proposed Solutions.

6. Monopoly Ownership and Control of Broadcasting: Problems and Proposed Solutions.

7. Communications Technology of the Future and Possible Effects on Freedom of Expression.

8. The Influence of Alexander Meiklejohn on the Law of Broadcasting.

9. Stopping the "Pollution" of the Airways: An Analysis of Federal Efforts to Keep "Obscene, Indecent, and Profane" Programming off the Air.

10. A Defense (or a Critique) of Barron's Theory of Access to the Mass Media.

11. An Analysis of Proposals for a Mandatory Right of Reply as a Substitute for Defamation Suits Against Newspapers.

12. The Citizens' Movement and Broadcasting.

13. Self-Regulation and Ethics in Broadcasting. (A study of the codes of the National Association of Broadcasters and other nongovernmental agencies concerned with radio and television.)

14. Sound-Amplification Devices and the First Amendment: Issues, Cases, and a Proposed "Ideal Ordinance."

15. Radio for "Mature Audiences Only": The Free-Speech Tribulations of the Pacifica Foundation.

SELECTED READINGS

Broadcasting, Cable, and Related Technologies

Barnouw, Erik. *A History of Broadcasting in the United States.* 3 vols. New York: Oxford University Press, 1966, 1968, and 1970.

Barnouw, Erik. *Tube of Plenty: The Evolution of American Television.* Rev. ed. New York: Oxford University Press, 1982.

Barrow, R. L. "Fairness Doctrine: A Double Standard for Electronic and Print Media." *Hastings Law Journal* 26 (1975): 659 ff.

Barton, Richard L. "The Lingering Legacy of Pacifica: Broadcasters' Freedom of Silence." *Journalism Quarterly* 53 (Autumn 1976): 429–433.

Besen, Stanley M., and Crandall, Robert W. "The Deregulation of Cable Television." *Law and Contemporary Problems* 44 (Winter 1981): 77–124.

Bittner, John R. *Broadcast Law and Regulation.* Englewood Cliffs, N.J.: Prentice-Hall, 1982.

Chamberlin, B. F. "The FCC and the First Principle of the Fairness Doctrine: A History of Neglect and Distortion." *Federal Communications Law Journal* 31 (1979): 361 ff.

Friendly, Fred W. *The Good Guys, the Bad Guys and the First Amendment: Free Speech vs. Fairness in Broadcasting.* New York: Random House, 1976.

Geller, Henry. *The Fairness Doctrine in Broadcasting: Problems and Suggested Courses of Action.* Santa Monica, Calif.: Rand, 1973.

Head, Sydney W., and Sterling, Christopher H. *Broadcasting in America: A Survey of Television, Radio, and New Technologies.* 4th ed. Boston: Houghton Mifflin, 1982.

Kahn, Frank J., ed. *Documents of American Broadcasting.* 4th ed. Englewood Cliffs, N.J.: Prentice-Hall, 1983.

Krattenmaker, Thomas, and Esterow, Marjorie. "Censoring Indecent Cable Programs: The New Morality Meets the New Media." *Fordham Law Review* 51 (March 1983): 606 ff.

Note. "Broadcast Deregulation and the First Amendment: Restraints on Private Control of the Publicly Owned Forum." *New York University Law Review* 55 (1980): 517 ff.

Note. "The Future of Content Regulation in Broadcasting." *California Law Review* 69 (1981): 555 ff.

Polsby, Daniel D. "Candidate Access to the Air: The Uncertain Future of Broadcaster Discretion." In *The Supreme Court Review: 1981,* pp. 223–262. Edited by Philip B. Kurland, Gerhard Casper, and Dennis J. Hutchinson. Chicago: University of Chicago Press, 1981.

Pool, Ithiel de Sola. *Technologies of Freedom.* Cambridge, Mass.: The Belknap Press of Harvard University Press, 1983.

Simmons, S. J. *The Fairness Doctrine and the Media.* Berkeley, Calif.: University of California Press, 1979.

Simmons, S. J. "FCC's Personal Attack and Political Editorial Rules Reconsidered." *University of Pennsylvania Law Review* 125 (1977): 990 ff.

Stebbins, Gene R. "Pacifica's Battle for Free Expression." *Educational Broadcasting Review* 4 (June 1970): 19–28.

Watts, Douglas R. "A Major Issue of the 1980's:

New Communication Tools." In *The First Amendment Reconsidered: New Perspectives on the Meaning of Freedom of Speech and Press,* pp. 181–193. Edited by Bill F. Chamberlin and Charlene J. Brown. New York: Longmans, 1982.

Woodby, Kathleen R., and Smith, F. Leslie. "The Cigarette Commercial Ban: A Pattern for Change." *Quarterly Journal of Speech* 60 (December 1974): 431–441.

Access to the Mass Media

Abrams, Floyd. "In Defense of *Tornillo*." *Yale Law Journal* 86 (December 1976): 361–369.

Bagdikian, Ben H. *The Media Monopoly*. Boston: Beacon Press, 1983.

Barron, Jerome A. "Access to the Press—A New First Amendment Right." *Harvard Law Review* 80 (1967): 1641–1678.

Barron, Jerome A. *Freedom of the Press for Whom? The Right of Access to Mass Media*. Bloomington, Ind.: Indiana University Press, 1973.

Carter, T. B. "Right of Reply Versus the *Sullivan* Rule: Time for a Second Look." *Loyola Law Review* 27 (Winter 1980): 41–68.

Cline, Timothy R., and Cline, Rebecca J. "Gaining Access to the Media: Some Issues and Cases." In *Free Speech Yearbook: 1975,* pp. 35–56. Edited by Alton Barbour. Falls Church, Va.: Speech Communication Association, 1976.

Compaine, Benjamin M., et al. *Who Owns the Media? Concentration of Ownership in the Mass Communications Industry*. New York: Harmony Books, 1979.

Emerson, Thomas I. *The System of Freedom of Expression*. New York: Random House, 1970.

(See chapter 17, "Affirmative Promotion of Freedom of Expression.")

Haiman, Franklyn S. *Speech and Law in a Free Society*. Chicago: University of Chicago Press, 1981. (See chapter 14, "Facilitation of Citizen Expression.")

Lee, William E. "The Problems of 'Reasonable Access' to Broadcasting for Noncommercial Expression." *University of Florida Law Review* 34 (Spring 1983): 348 ff.

Lively, Don. "Media Access and a Free Press: Pursuing First Amendment Values Without Imperiling First Amendment Rights." *Denver Law Journal* 58 (1980): 17–34.

Melnick, Alison. "Access to Cable Television: A Critique of the Affirmative Duty Theory of the First Amendment." *California Law Review* 70 (December 1982): 1393 ff.

Owen, Bruce M. *Economics and Freedom of Expression: Media Structure and the First Amendment*. Cambridge, Mass.: Ballinger, 1975.

Schmidt, Benno C., Jr. *Freedom of the Press vs. Public Access*. New York: Praeger, 1976.

Shapiro, Andrew O. *Media Access: Your Rights to Express Your Views on Radio and Television*. Boston: Little, Brown, 1976.

Silvers, Dean. "Access Right to the Mass Media: The Hidden Channels." In *Free Speech Yearbook: 1980,* pp. 40–50. Edited by Peter E. Kane. Annandale, Va.: Speech Communication Association, 1981.

Smith, Anthony. *Goodbye Gutenberg: The Newspaper Revolution of the 1980's*. New York: Oxford University Press, 1980.

Part IV

CONCLUSION

CHAPTER 12
Approaches to Free and Responsible
Communication

CHAPTER 12

Approaches to Free and
Responsible Communication

"If there be any among us who would wish to dissolve this Union or to change its republican form, let them stand undisturbed as monuments of the safety with which error of opinion may be tolerated where reason is left free to combat it."

—*Thomas Jefferson, "First Inaugural Address,"*
March 4, 1801

The eleven chapters preceding have provided the reader with a number of insights into how the nation got to where it is in its theory and practice of freedom of speech, including how the courts—the U.S. Supreme Court in particular—have applied the First Amendment to contemporary issues and cases. To conclude the text, this final chapter examines briefly the thinking of several First Amendment scholars concerning what each believes freedom of speech *ought* to mean; also, it urges the student to expand his or her study of communication freedoms to include the field of ethics in public discourse. The chapter, therefore, is organized around two main headings: (1) the views of four leading First Amendment scholars on freedom of speech and (2) some thoughts concerning the responsible use of that freedom.

I. FOUR PHILOSOPHIES OF FREEDOM OF SPEECH

Prior to the mid-twentieth century, those philosophers who argued for freedom of speech did so in general terms, attempting to justify the position that communication freedom is a social good and that more of it should be permitted. To this end John Milton, in his *Areopagitica,* published in 1644, urged that licensing of the press be eliminated; Thomas Jefferson, in numerous state-

ments of the late eighteenth and early nineteenth centuries, spoke on behalf of freedom to speak and to publish; and John Stuart Mill, in his essay *On Liberty,* first published in 1859, articulated with measured eloquence what many have called the finest defense of freedom of speech ever written. For example, Mill argued that freedom to express unorthodox ideas should be permitted for three reasons:

1. *The censored idea may be true and the accepted opinion may be in error.* "Those who desire to suppress [an opinion] . . . , of course deny its truth; but they are not infallible. They have no authority to decide the question for all mankind, and exclude every other person from the means of judging."[1]

2. *Even truth needs to be tested.* "However unwillingly a person who has a strong opinion may admit the possibility that his opinion may be false, he ought to be moved by the consideration that, however true it may be, if it is not fully, frequently, and fearlessly discussed, it will be held as a dead dogma, not a living truth."[2]

3. *There is likely some truth in all opinions.* "But there is a commoner case than [either of the two points above] . . . ; when the conflicting doctrines, instead of being one true and the other false, share the truth between them; and the nonconforming opinion is needed to supply the remainder of the truth, of which the received doctrine embodies only a part."[3]

As important as the views of Milton, Jefferson, Mill, and others were to the growing acceptance of the *idea* of freedom of expression in England and the United States, the specific questions about how a system of

[1]John Stuart Mill, *On Liberty,* ed. David Spitz (New York: Norton, 1975), p. 18.
[2]Ibid., pp. 34–35.
[3]Ibid., p. 44.

freedom of speech would work *in practice* were, generally speaking, left unanswered. By the middle of the current century, however, serious efforts were being made by legal scholars to formulate theories of freedom of speech and to apply those theories to the variety of specific cases that the courts were being asked to decide. Four of the most significant of these contemporary theories are summarized below, not only to inform the reader of the general position of the four theorists presented—Chafee, Meiklejohn, Emerson, and Haiman—but also to encourage the student of the First Amendment to read further in the literature of First Amendment theory (see the readings at the end of this chapter for some avenues of research).

Zechariah Chafee, Jr.: Protecting Speech That Serves the Social Interest

In 1941 Zechariah Chafee, Jr., Langdell Professor of Law at Harvard University, published his landmark study, *Free Speech in the United States*.[4] In this work Chafee pulled together his First Amendment thought, research, and writing of more than two decades to present both a history of free speech in America and a theory of what he believed the First Amendment should protect. Although Chafee discusses problems of preserving the peace, defamation, and "obscenity," his emphasis is upon political expression and the problem area of seditious libel. His theoretical position reflects this central concern for political speech.

Chafee's theory recognizes two general types of expression, namely, that which serves an *individual interest* (persons speaking on matters that are important to them "if life is to be worth living") and that which serves

a more general *social interest* (speech concerned with the "attainment of truth" so that citizens are well informed on public issues).[5] Then, without making an effort to develop fully and explain the area described as *individual interest* (Chafee believes that the individual type of expression is important, but that it does not weigh as heavily in the balance as does speech concerning the social interest), he states his answer to the question which concerns him most, namely: under what circumstances, if any, should speech of a *social interest* be constrained or punished?

> The true boundary line of the First Amendment can be fixed only when Congress and the courts realize that the principle on which speech is classified as lawful or unlawful involves the balancing against each other of two very important social interests, in *public safety* and in the *search for truth*. Every reasonable attempt should be made to maintain both interests unimpaired, and *the great interest in free speech should be sacrificed only when the interest in public safety is really imperiled,* and not, as most men believe, when it is barely conceivable that it may be slightly affected. In war time, therefore, speech should be unrestricted by the censorship or by punishment, unless it is clearly liable to cause direct and dangerous interference with the conduct of the war. [Emphasis supplied.][6]

As the above statement suggests, Chafee disapproves of the doctrine of remote bad tendency and approves of some form of the clear-and-present-danger test. As he says later in the book, "The . . . boundary-line of permissible speech is drawn back of the point where overt acts of injury to the state occur but not far from that point. The test laid down by the United States Supreme Court in the *Schenck* case still holds good,"

[4]Zechariah Chafee, Jr., *Free Speech in the United States* (Cambridge, Mass.: Harvard University Press, 1941).

[5]Ibid., pp. 31–34.
[6]Ibid., p. 35.

whereupon he quotes the words of Justice Holmes announcing the clear-and-present-danger test in the landmark case of *Schenck* v. *United States.*[7]

Although Chafee urges an expansion of the liberty of speech in the sociopolitical arena, he is not willing to extend the protection of the First Amendment to certain other types of speech, specifically that which he describes as profane, indecent, or defamatory. Such expression, he argues, is not essential to the analysis of ideas, is of "slight social value as a step toward truth," and must give way to the greater social interests of "order, morality, the training of the young, and the peace of mind of those who hear and see."[8] One year later the U.S. Supreme Court cited Chafee's point of view in the "fighting words" case of *Chaplinsky* v. *New Hampshire,* employing language similar to that used by Professor Chafee. In its unanimous decision upholding the conviction of Chaplinsky for cursing a police officer, the Court said that "the lewd and obscene, the profane, the libelous, and the insulting or 'fighting' words" are not protected by the Constitution. "It has been well observed," added the Court in a specific reference to Chafee, "that such utterances are no essential part of any exposition of ideas, and are of such slight social value as a step to truth that any benefit that may be derived from them is clearly outweighed by the social interest in order and morality."[9]

In short, Chafee proposes a maximum of protection for "worthwhile" speech that serves the social interest, while permitting constraints to be imposed when speech presents a clear and present danger to the community or to the nation. On the other hand, he allows the punishment of "worthless" speech—such as profanity or defamation—because he sees no constructive role for such expression in a free society's debate over ideas. In a sense, therefore, Chafee can be called one of the founding fathers (the other founders were on the Supreme Court in 1942) of the two-level system of free speech, namely, the "worthwhile" versus the "worthless" types of expression.[10]

Alexander Meiklejohn: A Theory of Absolute Protection for Political Speech

Alexander Meiklejohn, former president of Amherst College, professor at the University of Wisconsin, and director of the San Francisco School of Social Studies (which he helped to found), is a second First Amendment philosopher whose views have been highly influential in the legal community. Meiklejohn, at one time the teacher of Zechariah Chafee, Jr., developed a theory that provided for two types of freedom of expression, one absolute and the other subject to regulation by due process of law. Emphasizing that he saw freedom of speech as essential to self-government, Meiklejohn compared its function to that of a debate in a town meeting where community issues are decided and where the voters are made wise by means of free and robust discussion. What is needed in such a situation, he says, is not that each per-

[7]Ibid., p. 157. Also, Chafee specifically rejects the bad-tendency rule on pp. 23–24. The *Schenck* decision, discussed in detail in Chapter 3 of this text, is found at 249 U.S. 47 (1919). The rule announced by Justice Holmes is whether in every case "the words used are used in such circumstances and are of such a nature as to create a clear and present danger that they will bring about the substantive evils that Congress has a right to prevent."

[8]Ibid., p. 150.

[9]*Chaplinsky* v. *New Hampshire,* 315 U.S. 568 (1949), at 572, where Chafee is cited in footnotes 4 and 5.

[10]For more on the two-level approach to freedom of speech, see Chapter 6, which concerns provocation to anger. There the subject is discussed at the conclusion of the summary of the 1942 *Chaplinsky* case.

son be heard but that "everything worth saying shall be said."[11] Although the activities of
the meeting may be regulated by those procedures essential to orderly debate, the *ideas*
themselves must be expressed freely, without
fear of reprisal. Any effort to suppress ideas,
argues Meiklejohn, is absolutely condemned
by the First Amendment. As he so forcefully
puts it, "The freedom of ideas shall not be
abridged."[12]

Meiklejohn then develops his theory of absolute freedom for political discussion by
noting that Article I, Section 6 of the U.S.
Constitution grants to members of Congress
an absolute privilege of speaking and debat-
ing on the floor of both the House and the
Senate; for such speaking, the Constitution
states, members of Congress "shall not be
questioned in any other Place." Having identified this absolute privilege for congressional
debate, Meiklejohn argues for its extension to
political debate in general. Noting first that
under due process of law a person's "private
rights" to life and property may be regulated,
he states that under the Fifth Amendment the
"liberty of speech"—which he describes as a
private right—may be abridged by due process of law.[13]

Political expression, on the other hand, is
the "freedom of speech" of which the First
Amendment speaks, and for this reason it is
absolutely privileged and may not be
abridged—not even by the clear-and-present-
danger rule argued by Justice Holmes and accepted by Chafee. As Meiklejohn says:

. . . Individuals have, then, a private right of
speech which may on occasion be denied or
limited, though such limitations may not be
imposed unnecessarily or unequally. So says the
Fifth Amendment. But this limited guarantee of
the freedom of a man's wish to speak is radically different in intent from the unlimited
guarantee of the freedom of public discussion,
which is given by the First Amendment. The
latter, correlating the freedom of speech in
which it is interested with the freedom of religion, of press, of assembly, of petition for redress of grievances, places all these alike *beyond
the reach of legislation limitation, beyond even the
due process of law. With regard to them, Congress
has no negative powers whatever.* There are, then,
in the theory of the Constitution, two radically
different kinds of utterances. The constitutional
status of a merchant advertising his wares, of a
paid lobbyist fighting for the advantage of his
client, is utterly different from that of a citizen
who is planning for the general welfare. And
from this it follows that the Constitution provides differently for two different kinds of
"freedom of speech." [Emphasis supplied.][14]

In response to Meiklejohn's argument for
two kinds of speech, Chafee observes that
there is little, if any, specific historical evidence to demonstrate that the Founding Fathers had such a division in mind. Furthermore, asserts Chafee, Meiklejohn's argument
is seriously flawed because it "rests on his
supposed boundary between public speech
and private speech. That line is extremely
blurred." For example, continues Chafee, the
issue of the censorship of certain controversial novels, such as *Strange Fruit* (which deals
with a matter of race relations), is considered
by many to be a matter of private speech that
can be censored under due process of law; yet
Strange Fruit, as well as many other novels
that might be mentioned, also discusses im-

[11]Alexander Meiklejohn, *Free Speech and Its Relation to
Self-Government.* Collected with additional Meiklejohn
papers in *Political Freedom: The Constitutional Powers of the
People* (New York: Harper & Row, 1960). Citations here
and elsewhere are from the paperbound reissue by Oxford University Press, 1965. The quotation above appears on p. 26.
[12]Ibid., p. 28.
[13]Ibid., pp. 36–37.

[14]Ibid., p. 37.

FIGURE 12.1. *ALEXANDER MEIKLEJOHN.*
Alexander Meiklejohn, one of America's leading
First Amendment scholars, developed a theory of
absolute protection for political speech. Whereas a
person's private speech that was not a part of the
democratic dialogue could be abridged, argued
Meiklejohn, a person's public speech that
concerned the general welfare was absolutely
privileged. The photograph above was taken in
1953, eleven years before Meiklejohn's death in
1964 at age ninety-two.
From the Collection of Cynthia Stokes Brown.

portant social issues. Similarly, publications about birth control are concerned with both private and public matters. Where does one draw the line? "The truth is," concludes Chafee, "that there are public aspects to practically every subject."[15]

Despite the problem of drawing the line between public and private speech as proposed by Meiklejohn, the theory set out in 1948 when *Free Speech and Its Relation to Self-Government* was first published continues to exert an influence upon the thinking of many students of the First Amendment.[16] Both pi-

oneers discussed above—Zechariah Chafee, Jr., and Alexander Meiklejohn—deserve the careful consideration of all serious students of freedom of expression in contemporary society.

Thomas I. Emerson: The Expression–Action Theory

Thomas I. Emerson, Lines Professor of Law (emeritus) at Yale, is a third First Amendment theorist whose viewpoints on freedom of speech have exerted a considerable influence upon legal scholars. Proceeding from the position that neither Supreme Court decision making nor theoretical proposals from constitutional scholars (such as Chafee and

[15]From Chafee's review of Meiklejohn's *Free Speech and Its Relation to Self Government*, in the *Harvard Law Review* 62 (1949): 891 ff.

[16]For example, see Robert H. Bork, "Neutral Principles and Some First Amendment Problems," *Indiana*

Law Journal 47 (Fall 1971): 1–35. Bork argues that the First Amendment exists to protect *political* discourse; he calls upon Meiklejohn for support at pp. 26–27.

Meiklejohn) have managed to present a comprehensive, unified theory of freedom of expression, Emerson ambitiously attempts to remedy the situation with his expression–action theory. First appearing in book form in 1966, Emerson's theory was revised and published in 1970 with the title *The System of Freedom of Expression*.[17]

To begin with, Emerson argues that freedom of expression includes the right to form and hold beliefs on any subject and to communicate those beliefs to others by whatever medium one chooses—whether by traditional means, such as speech and the press, or by other means, including music or art. In addition, the principle of freedom of expression includes the right to hear the opinions of others, the right to inquire, reasonable access to information, and the rights of assembly and association.[18] Furthermore, the functions and values of a system of freedom of expression in a democratic society are fourfold, namely: as a means of (1) individual self-fulfillment, (2) discovering truth, (3) democratic decision making, and (4) "achieving a more adaptable and hence a more stable community, of maintaining the precarious balance between healthy cleavage and necessary consensus."[19]

Emerson then discusses what he characterizes as the "chaotic state of First Amendment theory" in the United States, a condition that he believes has resulted from the failure of the U.S. Supreme Court to formulate and apply any single theory to free-speech cases. The various tests used by the Court—such as bad tendency, clear and present danger, incitement, and balancing—are not only vague, Emerson says, but vary so much from case to case that they "can hardly be described as a rule of law at all."[20] The need is for a comprehensive First Amendment theory, he concludes, and in response to that need he proposes the expression–action position:

> The central idea of a system of freedom of expression is that a fundamental distinction must be drawn between conduct which consists of "expression" and conduct which consists of "action." "Expression" must be freely allowed and encouraged. "Action" can be controlled, subject to other constitutional requirements, but not by controlling expression. . . .
>
> The definition of "expression" involves formulating in detail the distinction between "expression" and "action." The line in many situations is clear. But at some points it becomes obscure. . . . In these [obscure] cases it is necessary to decide, however artificial the distinction may appear to be, whether the conduct is to be classified as one or the other. . . .[21]

Emerson devotes the remainder of the book to exploring various issues and cases, demonstrating the weaknesses and inconsistencies of the tests applied by the Supreme Court in the past and then explaining how the cases would be decided under his expression–action theory. The result is a generally libertarian approach to the First Amendment. Yet, even though Emerson is both thorough and thoughtful in his analysis, his conclusions are not always easy to agree on. In principle, the same question that Chafee asked of Meiklejohn ("Where do you draw the line?") can be asked of Emerson—only here the debate is over where one draws the line between expression that is fully protected and action

[17]Thomas I. Emerson, *Toward a General Theory of the First Amendment* (New York: Random House, 1966); and Thomas I. Emerson, *The System of Freedom of Expression* (New York: Random House, 1970).

[18]Emerson, *The System of Freedom of Expression*, p. 3.

[19]Ibid., pp. 6–7. Note: The first three of the four points were stated in similar language by Justice Brandeis in his concurring opinion in *Whitney* v. *California*, 274 U.S. 357 (1927); see Chapter 3 for more on this opinion.

[20]Emerson, *The System of Freedom of Expression*, p. 16.
[21]Ibid., pp. 17–18.

that can be controlled. Here are examples of Emerson's conclusions in four problem areas, namely, sedition, defamation, obscenity, and provocation to anger.

1. *Sedition.* "Seditious" opinion is classified as expression as long as it consists of advice and persuasion; antidemocratic views are protected, as are such symbolic means of communication as burning a draft card to protest a war or burning a flag to protest against the government. On the other hand, the following are classified as action: instructions and preparations that go beyond advice and persuasion; treasonous conduct; the physical obstruction of doorways, streets, etc.; and extreme forms of symbolic activity such as the pouring of blood on draft card files to protest against the draft.[22]

2. *Defamation.* In general, defamatory remarks are protected by the First Amendment under the expression–action theory, for such remarks are classified as expression as long as they concern public issues. In the area of *private* libel, the right of reply is preferable to a suit for damages. However, when libel is directed toward a private individual in a way that does harm to that person's feelings, it shifts from expression to action—comparable to an assault—and is no longer protected. A suit for damages would be permissible in such instances of "defamatory assault."[23]

3. *Obscenity.* Most of what society classifies as "obscenity" is a form of expression fully protected under the expression–action theory. This includes books, films, theatrical presentations, sculpture, paintings, etc.; the law of obscene libel as presently understood and enforced would be eliminated for the most part under Emerson's theory. How-

ever, action consisting of live conduct could still be punished. For example, sexual intercourse in public, even if done in the name of protesting repressive laws, would be punishable as conduct. Also, sexual materials thrust upon unwilling receivers so as to produce a "shock effect" would be a form of action which could be proscribed by law.[24]

4. *Provocation to anger.* Generally speaking, expression that is intentionally insulting or otherwise provocative is a form of speech protected by the Constitution—the audience, although angered, has a duty to restrain itself. On the other hand, when words are spoken face to face, in a *direct* encounter, so as to provoke a fight, the speech becomes conduct that is part of an act of violence and can be punished. Such "fighting words" are constrained, not for the reason of "worthlessness" stated by the Supreme Court in *Chaplinsky* but because they are "verbal acts" composing an assault upon the individual toward whom they are directed.[25]

In spite of the inherent difficulty of deciding where the line is to be drawn between expression and action in the many "gray area" cases between the two categories, Emerson's *System of Freedom of Expression,* as well as the expression–action theory which it advocates, is without question a landmark among efforts to develop a comprehensive theory of the First Amendment. This well-written and lucidly organized study should be on the "must read" list of all students of freedom of speech.

Franklyn S. Haiman: A Communication Context Theory of Freedom of Speech

In 1981 Franklyn S. Haiman, Professor of Communication Studies at Northwestern

---

[22]Ibid., chapters 4 and 5; in particular, pp. 70–90, 124–125, and 159–160.
[23]Ibid., chapter 14; in particular, pp. 537–543.

[24]Ibid., chapter 13; especially pp. 495–503.
[25]Ibid., chapter 9; pp. 328–345.

University, published his *Speech and Law in a Free Society*.[26] Although it is difficult to find a short label with which to characterize this thoughtful and significant study of freedom of speech, the term "communication context theory" comes close. Haiman avoids the pitfalls of the two-valued, either-or type of analysis attempted by Chafee (individual interest versus social interest), Meiklejohn (private versus public speech), and Emerson (expression versus action) by examining four context-centered problem areas and addressing the specific issues inherent in each of the four. The contexts identified by Haiman are (1) speech about other people (defamation, privacy, stirring to group hatred, prejudicing a fair trial); (2) speech directed to other people, including that which affects the social order (fighting words, objectionable messages, lies, intimidation, incitement to illegal action, conspiracies); (3) speech functioning within the general marketplace of ideas (problems of the affirmative promotion of freedom of expression); and (4) government participation in the communication marketplace (compelled speech such as loyalty oaths, secrecy, and communication by the various branches and agencies of the government).

Proceeding not only upon the communication scholar's insights into the processes of human communication—including the important area of symbolic or nonverbal communication—[27]but also upon several basic assumptions of democratic liberalism (e.g., the social order exists to maximize individual liberty, people are capable of free choice and are responsible for their own conduct, and the never-ending search for truth creates a need

for a free marketplace of ideas),[28] Haiman develops his four contexts, with interesting results, as summarized below.

1. *Communication about other people.* Concerning this general context, Haiman concludes: "Unless the harm done by an act of communication is direct, immediate, irreparable, and of a serious material nature, the remedy in a free society should be more speech. The law is an inappropriate tool for dealing with expression which produces mental distress or whose targets are the beliefs and values of an audience."[29] For example, Haiman would substitute a right of reply for defamation suits except in those cases where the alleged defamer refuses to provide for such a reply or when the time element does not permit it (such as the day prior to an important election).

2. *Communication to other people and that which affects the social order.* Concerning expression in these contexts, Haiman concludes: "Unless deprived of free choice by deception, physical coercion, or impairment of normal capacities, individuals in a free society are responsible for their own behavior. They are not objects which can be triggered into action by symbolic stimuli but human beings who *decide* how they will respond to the communication they see and hear."[30] The reader will readily observe that Haiman's solution departs sharply from the current assumptions of the law that hold the speaker—not the audience—responsible for what might occur in certain situations. For example, where questions of "obscenity" or "indecent language" arise, Haiman argues that it

[26]Franklyn S. Haiman, *Speech and Law in a Free Society* (Chicago: University of Chicago Press, 1981).
[27]Haiman's analysis of nonverbal communication and freedom of expression is a major contribution of the book; see especially ibid., pp. 25–38.

[28]Ibid., pp. 6–7.
[29]Ibid., pp. 425–427.
[30]Ibid., pp. 425–427. (Also, see the selections from William Bailey's essay, included in Chapter 6 of the present text, which address some of the same issues raised by Haiman.)

is better to depend upon the capacity of individuals to make wise decisions than to call for government censorship.[31] Likewise, those who allegedly incite to illegal conduct should not be held accountable for the actions of their listeners. Unless auditors are deceived, coerced, or mentally incapable of making a free choice, Haiman says, they should be held responsible for their own actions and not blame someone else "who may have planted an idea in their minds."[32]

3. *The general marketplace of ideas*. Concerning this topic, Haiman concludes: "So long as there is a free marketplace of ideas, where the widest possible range of information and alternatives is available, individuals will be the best judges of their own interests. The law is properly used to enrich and expand that communications marketplace and to insure that it remains an open system."[33] Specifically, government (and, by implication, society in general) should affirmatively promote diversity of communication, the views of nonconformists should be disseminated, constraints of time and place should be administered in a content-neutral way, and quasipublic private property (such as shopping centers) should make provision for nondisruptive communication with the public by community advocates.

4. *Government speech*. Haiman summarizes this area of concern as follows: "Government in a free society is the servant of the people and its powers should not be used to inhibit, distort, or dominate public discourse. There must be compelling justification whenever the government requires unwilling communication of its people or withholds information in its possession from them." Government communicators must not be al-

lowed to overwhelm other voices and points of view; thus, self-restraint and a respect for the general marketplace of ideas is required of those who exercise political power.[34]

Haiman ends his book with the philosophical observation that the principles of freedom of speech which he explicates and defends "require a strong and vigilant citizenry for their faithful implementation. The regime which they envision is not one for the squeamish or apathetic. It is not for those who lack the courage of their convictions."[35] Just as serious students of freedom of speech should be acquainted with the views of Milton, Mill, Chafee, Meiklejohn, and Thomas Emerson, so should they study carefully the analysis of Franklyn S. Haiman.

II. THE RESPONSIBLE EXERCISE OF FREEDOM OF SPEECH: A COORDINATE AREA OF STUDY

Since ancient times philosopher–critics as well as some leading practitioners of the art of persuasion have recognized that freedom to speak does not always result in thoughtful, "responsible" discourse—abuses of the liberty of speech inevitably occur. In the *Gorgias* (c. 387 B.C.) the Greek philosopher Plato denounces what he believes to be the teaching of gimmickry by the sophists of his day, whom he accuses of training others in the knack of achieving dishonest goals through trickery in public discourse. Aristotle, in the *Rhetoric* (c. 336 B.C.), recognizes that persuasion can be either a blessing or a harm, depending upon how it is employed. Although the *Rhetoric* itself is often described as a "morally neutral" textbook on persuasion,

---

[31]Ibid., chapter 9 generally, especially pp. 176–181.
[32]Ibid., pp. 277–278.
[33]Ibid., pp. 426–428.

[34]Ibid., pp. 428–429.
[35]Ibid., p. 429.

Aristotle clearly believed that the art of persuasion should be employed for honorable purposes; for example, he observes in Book I, Chapter 1 of the *Rhetoric* that although communicators should be able to understand the arguments of both sides of an issue "in order that no aspect of the case may escape us," this does not mean that persuaders should "advocate evil."[36]

Several centuries later, the Roman teacher Quintilian developed a philosophy of education intended to guide the training of a liberally educated orator whose public discourse would be for the good of society. In the *Institutes of Oratory* (c. 95 A.D.), Quintilian set forth his "good man" theory, which he discusses in considerable detail in Book XII, Chapter 1, as follows:

> The orator, then, whom I am concerned to form shall be the orator as defined by Marcus Cato, "a good man, skilled in speaking." But above all he must possess the quality which Cato places first and which is in the very nature of things the greatest and most important, that is, he must be a good man. This is essential on account of the fact that, if the powers of eloquence serve only to lend arms to crime, there can be nothing more pernicious than eloquence to public and private welfare alike . . . . Nature herself will have proved not a mother, but a stepmother with regard to what we deem her greatest gift to man, the gift that distinguishes us from other living things, if she devised the power of speech to be the accomplice of crime, the foe to innocency, and the enemy of truth. For it had been better for men to be born dumb and devoid of reason than to turn the gifts of providence to their mutual destruction. . . .[37]

Although the communication teachers of Greece and Rome remind us that contemporary concern over ethics in public discourse is nothing new, the questions remain concerning the specific standards for making an ethical judgment and the means by which the standards are enforced. Shall individuals decide these matters for themselves, or shall some powerful person or organization—such as the government, or some religious body— make the decisions for the society as a whole? One who prefers to let the individual make the choice is John Stuart Mill, who in 1859 concluded the chapter on "The Liberty of Thought and Discussion" in his famous work *On Liberty* by arguing that although abuses of freedom of speech are inevitable, governments should not intervene to enforce a standard of ethics in public discourse. Says Mill:

> . . . Undoubtedly the manner of asserting an opinion, even though it be a true one, may be very objectionable, and may justly incur severe censure. . . . The gravest of [offenses is] to argue sophistically, to suppress facts or arguments, to misstate the elements of the case, or misrepresent the opposite opinion. But all this, even to the most aggravated degree, is so continually done in perfect good faith, by persons who are not considered, and in many other respects may not deserve to be considered, ignorant or incompetent, that it is rarely possible, on adequate grounds, conscientiously to stamp the misrepresentation as morally culpable; and still less could law presume to interfere with this kind of controversial misconduct.[38]

One might ask, however, what about false advertising, or the dissemination of defamatory falsehoods? What should be the role of government in supervising such dishonest messages? Although one might be uncertain

---

[36]Aristotle, *The Rhetoric*, tr. Lane Cooper (New York: Appleton-Century, 1932), p. 6. For more on Aristotle's view of ethics in persuasion, see Richard L. Johannesen, *Ethics in Human Communications*, 2nd ed. (Prospect Heights, Ill.: Waveland Press, 1983), pp. 29–31.

[37]Quintilian, *The Institutio Oratoria*, ed. Charles Edgar Little, vol. 2 (Nashville, Tenn.: George Peabody College for Teachers, 1951), pp. 223–224.

[38]Mill, p. 51.

as to how Mill would respond to these specific questions, there should be little uncertainty about how modern society has responded, as specific legislation and various decisions of the courts will attest. For example, Justice Harry Blackmun addressed the matter of dishonest commercial messages in his opinion of the Court in the 1976 case of *Virginia State Board of Pharmacy* v. *Virginia Citizens Consumer Council,* making it clear that the Constitution does not protect false and misleading advertising.[39] And the Supreme Court's general condemnation of private libel is epitomized by Justice Potter Stewart's concurring opinion in the 1966 case of *Rosenblatt* v. *Baer,* where he asserts that the "right of a man to the protection of his own reputation from unjustified invasion and wrongful hurt reflects no more than our basic concept of the essential dignity and worth of every human being—a concept at the root of any decent system of ordered liberty."[40]

It would not be accurate, therefore, to say that government is denied authority in certain areas, such as false advertising and private libel, to enforce ethical standards in the marketplace of ideas. In religious, social, and political discourse in general, however, the First Amendment provides that individuals make decisions about ethics in public communication for themselves. It seems appropriate, therefore, to conclude this text about freedom of speech in the United States with the recommendation that students not only continue to broaden and deepen their knowledge of the theory and practice of communication *rights* but also that they expand their interests to include the theory and practice of communication *ethics.* Even though the study of speech ethics is beyond the scope of the present text, perhaps the brief discussion provided here will be a means of pointing the student to significant readings (see the list of sources at the end of the chapter), statements by professional organizations (see box giving the *Credo* of the Speech Communication Association), and courses in communication ethics offered by many institutions of higher learning.

CONCLUSION

In conclusion, four contemporary theories of freedom of speech are summarized: (1) Chafee's theory of individual interest versus social interest, which extends maximum protection to speech on social issues, permitting constraints only when the public safety is seriously threatened; (2) Meiklejohn's private speech versus public speech, which grants *absolute* protection to "public" speech but allows "private" expression to be regulated by the Fifth Amendment's "due process of law" provision; (3) Emerson's expression–action theory, which gives complete protection to "expression" but allows constraints over "action"; and (4) Haiman's communication context theory, which addresses problems of free speech in four kinds of contexts, namely: (a) speech about other people (the preferred solution: more speech), (b) speech directed to other people (trust the individual to respond in a responsible way), (c) maintaining the general marketplace of ideas (society should affirmatively promote diversity in communication), and (d) government participation in the public dialogue (those in government should show self-restraint, respect the marketplace of ideas, and not overwhelm other

---

[39]*Virginia State Board of Pharmacy* v. *Virginia Citizens Consumer Council,* 425 U.S. 748 (1976); also, see generally Chapter 7 of the present work for a survey of government efforts on behalf of truth in advertising.

[40]*Rosenblatt* v. *Baer,* 383 U.S. 75 (1966), at 92. This statement by Justice Stewart is quoted with approval by Justice Powell in his opinion of the Court in *Gertz* v. *Welch,* 418 U.S. 323 (1974).

CREDO FOR FREE AND RESPONSIBLE COMMUNICATION IN A DEMOCRATIC SOCIETY
Speech Communication Association

Recognizing the essential place of free and responsible communication in a democratic society, and recognizing the distinction between the freedoms our legal system should respect and the responsibilities our educational system should cultivate, we members of the Speech Communication Association endorse the following statement of principles:

WE BELIEVE that freedom of speech and assembly must hold a central position among American constitutional principles, and we express our determined support for the right of peaceful expression by any communicative means available.

WE SUPPORT the proposition that a free society can absorb with equanimity speech which exceeds the boundaries of generally accepted beliefs and mores; that much good and little harm can ensue if we err on the side of freedom, whereas much harm and little good may follow if we err on the side of suppression.

WE CRITICIZE as misguided those who believe that the justice of their cause confers license to interfere physically and coercively with the speech of the others, and we condemn intimidation, whether by powerful majorities or strident minorities, which attempts to restrict free expression.

WE ACCEPT the responsibility of cultivating by precept and example, in our classrooms and in our communities, enlightened uses of communication; of developing in our students a respect for precision and accuracy in communication, and for reasoning based upon evidence and a judicious discrimination among values.

WE ENCOURAGE our students to accept the role of well-informed and articulate citizens, to defend the communication rights of those with whom they may disagree, and to expose abuses of the communication process.

WE DEDICATE ourselves fully to these principles, confident in the belief that reason will ultimately prevail in a free marketplace of ideas.

(Endorsed by the Speech Communication Association, 1972, and reprinted here with the Association's permission.)

---

points of view). Also, the reader's attention is directed to the issue of "the responsible use of freedom of speech," with the suggestion that the study of communication *rights* ought to be expanded by each student to include a coordinate study of communication *ethics*.

Facing the threats to survival posed by a variety of modern weapons of mass destruction—and the pressures for censorship in the name of national security that grow out of those threats—plus the problems of sustaining a viable "marketplace of ideas" in an age of complex media technology (which is to a large degree in the hands of private "gatekeepers"), one cannot help but be concerned about the future of the system of freedom of expression. It seems appropriate, therefore, to conclude this book with a thought expressed forty years ago by the late Judge Learned Hand of the Second Circuit, U.S. Court of Appeals. On May 21, 1944, Judge Hand spoke to a large crowd, including a number of persons who had just been naturalized as American citizens, on "I Am an American Day" in New York City's Central Park. In a short address entitled "The Spirit of Liberty," Judge Hand in simple yet eloquent prose identified the source of human liberty, including our liberty of speech:

> I often wonder whether we do not rest our hopes too much upon constitutions, upon laws and upon courts. These are false hopes; believe me, these are false hopes. Liberty lies in the hearts of men and women; when it dies there, no constitution, no law, no court can save it; no constitution, no law, no court can even do much to help it. While it lies there it needs no constitution, no law, no court to save it.[41]

EXERCISES

A. Topics for classroom discussion.

1. John Stuart Mill's three reasons for permitting freedom of speech are explained briefly early in the chapter. They are (1) that the suppressed opinion may be true and the accepted view may be in error, (2) that even the truth needs to be tested from time to time, and (3) that there is likely some truth in all opinions (conflicting opinions often share the truth between them). Discuss each of these arguments in class. Is Mill convincing?

2. Which of the four major theories of freedom of speech summarized in this chapter do you prefer? Allow each student (or, if the class is large, selected students) to express a preference and to defend the choice. Discuss the results as time permits.

3. Alexander Meiklejohn urges that speech on public matters be given absolute protection, whereas Chafee responds that this is difficult to do because the line between "public" and "private" speech is "extremely blurred." Is it possible to classify speech as public or private, as urged by Meiklejohn, or is Chafee correct in his doubts? Discuss.

4. Franklyn S. Haiman suggests that a right of reply is a better solution to slander and libel than is court action for damages (in most cases). What do you think? Would you be willing to dispense with most defamation suits provided that a right of reply is assured? Discuss.

5. As this chapter mentions, the government does act to enforce standards of communication ethics in certain areas, such as advertising, and insofar as it permits suits for damages in cases of defamation. Can you identify other areas where the government works in similar ways to try to compel communicators to be responsible? Are there areas into which the government should move to try to assure the public a high degree of honesty in communications? Discuss.

B. Topics for research papers and oral reports.

1. Chafee's Theory of Freedom of Speech: An Analysis and Critique.

2. Meiklejohn's Theory of Freedom of Speech: An Analysis and Critique.

3. Alexander Meiklejohn: Advocate of Liberty. (A broad-based study of Meikle-

---

[41]Irving Dillard, comp., *The Spirit of Liberty: Papers and Addresses of Learned Hand,* 3rd ed. (New York: Knopf, 1960), pp. 189–190.

john's views on a variety of free-speech subjects, including academic freedom.)

4. Emerson's Theory of Freedom of Speech: An Analysis and Critique.

5. Haiman's Theory of Freedom of Speech: An Analysis and Critique.

6. Franklyn S. Haiman on the Responsible Use of Freedom of Speech. (A broadbased survey of Haiman's writings in the field of speech ethics.)

7. The Enforcement of Communication Ethics by the Government: A Study of Types and Methods.

8. A Study of Proposals for a Right of Reply as a Substitute for Court Action in Cases of Defamation.

9. A Personal Philosophy (or Theory) of Freedom of Speech.

10. A Personal Philosophy (or Theory) of Ethics in Public Communication.

SELECTED READINGS

First Amendment Theories

Baker, C. Edwin. "Scope of the First Amendment Freedom of Speech." *UCLA Law Review* 25 (June 1978): 964–1040.

BeVier, Lillian R. "The First Amendment and Political Speech: An Inquiry into the Substance and Limits of Principle." *Stanford Law Review* 30 (January 1978): 299–358.

Bork, Robert H. "Neutral Principles and Some First Amendment Problems." *Indiana Law Journal* 47 (Fall 1971): 1–35.

Brennan, William J. "The Supreme Court and the Meiklejohn Interpretation of the First Amendment." *Harvard Law Review* 79 (November 1965): 1–20.

Brown, Cynthia Stokes, ed. *Alexander Meiklejohn: Teacher of Freedom.* Berkeley, Calif.: Meiklejohn Institute, 1981.

Chafee, Zechariah, Jr. *Free Speech in the United States.* Cambridge, Mass.: Harvard University Press, 1941.

Chamberlin, Bill F., and Brown, Charlene J., eds. *The First Amendment Reconsidered: New Perspectives on the Meaning of Freedom of Speech and Press.* New York: Longmans, 1982.

Haiman, Franklyn S. *Speech and Law in a Free Society.* Chicago: University of Chicago Press, 1981.

Meiklejohn, Alexander. *Political Freedom: The Constitutional Powers of the People.* New York: Harper & Row, 1960. (Includes *Free Speech and Its Relation to Self-Government,* first published in 1948.)

Schauer, Frederick. *Free Speech: A Philosophical Enquiry.* Cambridge, Mass.: Cambridge University Press, 1982.

Siebert, Frederick S., Peterson, Theodore, and Schramm, Wilbur. *Four Theories of the Press.* Urbana, Ill.: University of Illinois Press, 1956.

Stevens, John D. *Shaping the First Amendment: The Development of Free Expression.* Beverly Hills, Calif.: Sage Publications, 1982.

Ethics in Public Communication

Andersen, Kenneth E. *Persuasion: Theory and Practice,* 2nd ed. Boston: Allyn and Bacon, 1978. (See chapter 15, "Ethics and Persuasion.")

Bok, Sissila. *Lying: Moral Choice in Public and Private Life.* New York: Pantheon Books, 1978.

Brembeck, Winston L., and Howell, William S. *Persuasion: A Means of Social Influence,* 2nd ed. Englewood Cliffs, N.J.: Prentice-Hall, 1976. (See chapter 10, "The Ethical Dimension of Persuasion.")

Christians, Clifford G. "Fifty Years of Scholarship in Media Ethics." *Journal of Communication* 27 (Autumn 1977): 19–29.

Christians, Clifford G., Rotzoll, Kim B., and Fackler, Mark. *Media Ethics: Cases and Moral Reasoning.* New York: Longmans, 1983.

Dieterich, Daniel, ed. *Teaching About Doublespeak.* Urbana, Ill.: National Council of Teachers of English, 1976.

Diggs, B. J. "Persuasion and Ethics." *Quarterly Journal of Speech* 50 (December 1964): 359–373.

"Ethics in Communication," entire issue featuring eleven essays on the subject. *Communication* 6 (1981): 145–322.

Eubanks, Ralph T. "Reflections on the Moral Dimension of Communication." *Southern Speech Communication Journal* 45 (Spring 1980): 297–312.

Ferre, John P. "Contemporary Approaches to Journalistic Ethics." *Communication Quarterly* 28 (Spring 1980): 44–48.

Flynn, Lawrence J. "The Aristotelian Basis for the Ethics of Speaking." *Speech Teacher* 6 (September 1957): 179–187.

Haiman, Franklyn S. "Democratic Ethics and the Hidden Persuaders." *Quarterly Journal of Speech* 44 (December 1958): 385–392.

Haiman, Franklyn S. "The Rhetoric of 1968: A Farewell to Rational Discourse." In Johannesen, *Ethics in Human Communication,* 2nd ed. Prospect Heights, Ill.: Waveland Press, 1983, pp. 177–190.

Haiman, Franklyn S. "The Rhetoric of the Streets: Some Legal and Ethical Considerations." *Quarterly Journal of Speech* 53 (April 1967): 99–114.

Hook, Sidney. "The Ethics of Controversy." *The New Leader,* February 1, 1954, pp. 12–14.

Hulteng, John L. *The Messenger's Motives: Ethical Problems of the News Media.* Englewood Cliffs, N.J.: Prentice-Hall, 1976.

Johannesen, Richard L. *Ethics in Human Communication,* 2nd ed. Prospect Heights, Ill.: Waveland Press, 1983. (Recommended as an introduction to the study of communication ethics.)

Johannesen, Richard L., ed. *Ethics and Persuasion: Selected Readings.* New York: Random House, 1967.

Johannesen, Richard L. "Perspectives on Ethics in Persuasion." Chapter 11 in Charles U. Larson, *Persuasion: Reception and Responsibility,* 3rd ed. Belmont, Calif.: Wadsworth, 1983.

Johannesen, Richard L. "Teaching Ethical Standards for Discourse." *Journal of Education* 162 (Spring 1980): 5–20.

Johnstone, Henry W., Jr. "Communication: Technology and Ethics." In *Communication Philosophy and the Technological Age,* pp. 38–53. Edited by Michael J. Hyde. University, Ala.: University of Alabama Press, 1982.

Marston, John. *Modern Public Relations.* New York: McGraw-Hill, 1979. (Includes a section on "Right and Wrong in Professional Public Relations.")

Merrill, John C., and Barney, Ralph D., eds. *Ethics and the Press: Readings in Mass Media Morality.* New York: Hastings House, 1975.

Minnick, Wayne C. "A New Look at the Ethics of Persuasion." *Southern Speech Communication Journal* 45 (Summer 1980): 352–362.

Minnick, Wayne C. *The Art of Persuasion,* 2nd ed. Boston: Houghton Mifflin, 1968. (See chapter 11, "The Ethics of Persuasion.")

Newsom, Doug, and Scott, Alan. *This Is PR: The Realities of Public Relations,* 2nd ed. Belmont, Calif.: Wadsworth, 1981. (Includes materials concerning ethics in public relations.)

Nilsen, Thomas R. *Ethics of Speech Communication,* 2nd ed. Indianapolis, Ind.: Bobbs-Merrill, 1974.

Nilsen, Thomas R. "Free Speech, Persuasion, and the Democratic Process." *Quarterly Journal of Speech* 44 (October 1958): 235–243.

Packard, Vance. *The Hidden Persuaders.* New York: McKay, 1957.

Phelan, John M. *Disenchantment: Meaning and Morality in the Media.* New York: Hastings House, 1980.

Rivers, William L., Schramm, Wilbur, and Christians, Clifford G. *Responsibility in Mass Communication,* 3rd ed. New York: Harper & Row, 1980.

Rogge, Edward. "Evaluating the Ethics of a Speaker in a Democracy." *Quarterly Journal of Speech* 45 (December 1959): 419–425.

Rubin, Bernard, ed. *Questioning Media Ethics.* New York: Praeger, 1978.

Sandage, C. H., and Fryburger, Vernon. *Advertising Theory and Practice,* 10th ed. Homewood, Ill.: Irwin, 1979. (Discusses ethics in advertising.)

Spero, Robert. *The Duping of the American Voter: Dishonesty and Deception in Presidential Television Advertising.* New York: Lippincott and Crowell, 1980.

Swain, Bruce M. *Reporters' Ethics.* Ames, Iowa: Iowa State University Press, 1978.

Thayer, Lee, ed. *Communication: Ethical and Moral Issues.* New York: Gordon and Breach, 1973.

Thayer, Lee, ed. *Ethics, Morality and the Media: Reflections on American Culture.* New York: Hastings House, 1980.

Wallace, Karl R. "An Ethical Basis of Communication." *Speech Teacher* 4 (January 1955): 1–9.

Weaver, Richard M. "Language Is Sermonic." In *Contemporary Theories of Rhetoric,* pp. 163–179. Edited by Richard L. Johannesen. New York: Harper & Row, 1971.

APPENDICES

APPENDIX I

The Federal Court System of the United States

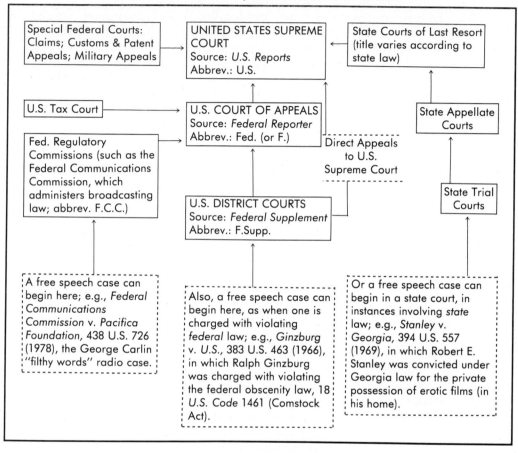

Special Federal Courts: Claims; Customs & Patent Appeals; Military Appeals

UNITED STATES SUPREME COURT
Source: *U.S. Reports*
Abbrev.: U.S.

State Courts of Last Resort (title varies according to state law)

U.S. Tax Court

U.S. COURT OF APPEALS
Source: *Federal Reporter*
Abbrev.: Fed. (or F.)

Direct Appeals to U.S. Supreme Court

State Appellate Courts

Fed. Regulatory Commissions (such as the Federal Communications Commission, which administers broadcasting law; abbrev. F.C.C.)

U.S. DISTRICT COURTS
Source: *Federal Supplement*
Abbrev.: F.Supp.

State Trial Courts

A free speech case can begin here; e.g., *Federal Communications Commission* v. *Pacifica Foundation*, 438 U.S. 726 (1978), the George Carlin "filthy words" radio case.

Also, a free speech case can begin here, as when one is charged with violating *federal* law; e.g., *Ginzburg* v. *U.S.*, 383 U.S. 463 (1966), in which Ralph Ginzburg was charged with violating the federal obscenity law, 18 *U.S. Code* 1461 (Comstock Act).

Or a free speech case can begin in a state court, in instances involving *state* law; e.g., *Stanley* v. *Georgia*, 394 U.S. 557 (1969), in which Robert E. Stanley was convicted under Georgia law for the private possession of erotic films (in his home).

A. Some Basic Facts About the Federal Courts

1. *U.S. District Courts*
    a. Number: there are 91 district courts, with at least one in each state.
    b. Jurisdiction: over cases that involve the U.S. Constitution, acts of Congress, and treaties (plus a number of other areas, such as when one state sues another). Free-speech issues involving federal laws, such as the Espionage Act of 1917, begin with a trial in the district courts.
    c. Number of judges sitting: one, as a rule (may be more for a major case).

2. *U.S. Courts of Appeal*
    a. Number: there are 12 federal judicial circuits, as follows:
        1st Circuit: Maine, Massachusetts, New Hampshire, Puerto Rico, Rhode Island.
        2nd Circuit: Connecticut, New York, Vermont.
        3rd Circuit: Delaware, New Jersey, Pennsylvania, Virgin Islands.
        4th Circuit: Maryland, North Carolina, South Carolina, Virginia, West Virginia.
        5th Circuit: Canal Zone, Louisiana, Mississippi, Texas.
        6th Circuit: Kentucky, Michigan, Ohio, Tennessee.
        7th Circuit: Illinois, Indiana, Wisconsin.
        8th Circuit: Arkansas, Iowa, Minnesota, Missouri, Nebraska, North Dakota, South Dakota.
        9th Circuit: Alaska, Arizona, California, Idaho, Montana, Nevada, Oregon, Washington, Guam, Hawaii.
        10th Circuit: Colorado, Kansas, New Mexico, Oklahoma, Utah, Wyoming.
        11th Circuit: Alabama, Florida, Georgia.
        12th Circuit: The District of Columbia.
    b. Jurisdiction: over cases tried in the district courts (i.e., the "courts below"), and those from federal regulatory commissions (such as the FCC or the Interstate Commerce Commission, etc.).
    c. Number of judges sitting: a minimum of three.

3. *U.S. Supreme Court*
    a. The U.S. Supreme Court is the nation's court of last resort.
    b. Jurisdiction: appellate jurisdiction over cases tried or reviewed in the courts below—the district courts, the courts of appeals, and the highest courts of the various states when federal questions are involved; in addition, the Supreme Court has original jurisdiction over certain matters, such as disputes involving ambassadors, ministers, and consuls.
    c. Number of judges sitting: nine.

B. Citation System for the Federal Courts

Most cases studied in a freedom-of-speech course will employ citations from the federal courts. The sequence of information is the same in each instance: (1) name of case, (2) volume number of reporting service in which case appears, (3) reporting service, (4) page where case begins in that reporting service, and (5) year of decision. Here is an example from the U.S. Supreme Court: *Miller* v. *California,* 413 U.S. 15 (1973). This citation should be interpreted as follows:

1. Name of case (from parties to the dispute): *Miller* v. *California.*
2. Volume number: 413.
3. Reporting Service: *U.S. Reports* (abbrev. U.S.), an official service of the U.S. Government Printing Office; only Supreme Court cases are reported in this publication.
4. Page where case begins: 15.
5. Year of decision: 1973.

In other words, the case of *Miller* v. *California* is found in *U.S. Reports,* vol. 413, page 15; you can tell at a glance that this is a Supreme Court citation by the abbreviation "U.S.," referring to *U.S. Reports,* for only Supreme Court decisions are published in this service; the Court announced its decision in 1973.

In addition to the Supreme Court citations, students should be familiar with how the decisions of the lower federal courts are reported:

1. U.S. district courts.
   a. Reporting service: since 1932 the decisions of district courts have been reported in the *Federal Supplement* (abbrev. F.Supp.); prior to 1932 they appeared along with decisions of the circuit courts in the *Federal Reporter.*
   b. Example: *Poxon* v. *Board of Education,* 341 F.Supp. 256 (E.D. Calif. 1971).
   c. Interpretation: Poxon sued the Board of Education; the decision of the district court is found in vol. 341 of the *Federal Supplement,* beginning on p. 256; the case was heard in Eastern District (E.D.) of the state of California, and the decision was announced in 1971.
2. U.S. courts of appeal (circuit courts).
   a. Reporting service: the *Federal Reporter* (abbrev. F., or Fed.); since 1925 the service has been renumbered in a *second* series (abbrev. F.2d).
   b. Example: *Torvik* v. *Decorah Community Schools,* 453 F.2d 779 (8th Cir. 1972).
   c. Interpretation: Torvik, who lost in the court below (winners do not appeal cases), is appealing the decision won by the Decorah Community Schools; the decision is found in vol. 453 of the *Federal Reporter,* second series, beginning on p. 779; it was announced by the Court of Appeals for the 8th Circuit in 1972.

Finally, students of the First Amendment should know about the following reporting services from the presses of private publishers:

1. Private reporters of decisions of the U.S. Supreme Court.
   a. The *Supreme Court Reporter* (abbrev. S.Ct.), issued by West Publishing Company.
   b. *U.S. Supreme Court Reports, Lawyers' Edition* (abbrev. L.Ed., L.Ed.2d—and occasionally simply L.2d—for the second series), issued by the Lawyers' Cooperative Publishing Company.
2. Weekly reporting service for recent decisions on all subjects (not limited to First Amendment cases).
   U.S. Law Week (abbrev. *Law Week*, U.S.L.W., or simply L.W.), issued by the Bureau of National Affairs in two sections, namely, a Supreme Court section and a section reporting decisions from other courts (both state courts and the lower federal courts).
3. Weekly reporting service for recent free-speech cases.
   Media Law Reporter (abbrev. Med.L.Rptr.), issued by the Bureau of National Affairs, is a valuable source of current decisions in both state and federal courts. Also includes news, bibliographies, and the texts of new government regulations affecting freedom of expression (such as policies of the FCC). The cases are reported under four headings: (1) Regulation of Media Content; (2) Regulation of Media Distribution; (3) Newsgathering; and (4) Media Ownership.

C. LEGAL RESEARCH AND THE COURT SYSTEM: SELECTED READINGS

Readings Concerning Legal Research

Cohen, M. L. *Legal Research in a Nutshell,* 3rd ed. St. Paul, Minn.: West Publishing Co., 1978.

Goehlert, R. *Congress and Law Making: Researching the Legislative Process.* Santa Barbara, Calif.: Clio Books, 1979.

Jacobstein, J. Myron, and Mersky, Roy M. *Fundamentals of Legal Research,* 2nd ed. Mineola, N.Y.: Foundation Press, 1981.

Jacobstein, J. Myron, and Mersky, Roy M. *Legal Research Illustrated.* Mineola, N.Y.: Foundation Press, 1977.

Lloyd, David. *Finding the Law: A Guide to Legal Research.* Dobbs Ferry, N.Y.: Oceana, 1974.

Price, Miles O., Bitner, Harry, and Bysiewicz, Shirley R. *Effective Legal Research,* 4th ed. Boston: Little, Brown, 1979.

Statsky, W. *Legislative Analysis: How to Use Statutes and Regulations.* St. Paul, Minn.: West Publishing Co., 1975.

A Uniform System of Citation: Forms of Citation and Abbreviations. Cambridge, Mass.: Harvard Law Review Association, 1967.

Readings Concerning the Legal System

Abraham, Henry. *The Judicial Process,* 4th ed. New York: Oxford University Press, 1980.

Baum, Lawrence. *The Supreme Court.* Washington, D.C.: Congressional Quarterly Press, 1981. (In particular, see chapter 4, "Decision-making.")

Berman, Harold J., and Greiner, William R. *The Nature and Functions of Law,* 2nd ed. Brooklyn: Foundation Press, 1966.

Congressional Quarterly's Guide to the U.S. Supreme Court. Washington, D.C.: Congressional Quarterly, 1979.

Farnsworth, Edward A. *An Introduction to the Legal System of the United States.* New York: Oceana, 1975. (Brief and well organized.)

Frank, John P. *Marble Palace*. New York: Knopf, 1961. (A standard study concerning the exercise of power by the U.S. Supreme Court.)

Kelly, Alfred, H., and Harbison, Winfred A. *The American Constitution: Its Origins and Development*. New York: Norton, 1955.

McCloskey, Robert G. *The American Supreme Court*. Chicago: University of Chicago Press, 1960. (Excellent short history.)

Mayers, Lewis. *The American Legal System*. New York: Harper & Row, 1964.

Post, C. Gordon. *An Introduction to the Law*. Englewood Cliffs, N.J.: Prentice-Hall, 1963.

Rembar, Charles. *The Law of the Land: The Evolution of Our Legal System*. New York: Simon and Schuster, 1981. (Recommended; written for the nonlawyer. Especially see chapter 3, "Taxonomy.")

Schmidhauser, John R. *The Supreme Court: Its Politics, Personalities, and Procedures*. New York: Holt, 1960. (Includes a useful discussion of how justices are chosen.)

Shapiro, Martin. *Freedom of Speech: The Supreme Court and Judicial Review*. Englewood Cliffs, N.J.: Prentice-Hall, 1966.

Sigler, Jay A. *An Introduction to the Legal System*. Homewood, Ill.: Dorsey, 1968.

Spaeth, Harold J. *An Introduction to Supreme Court Decision Making*, rev. ed. New York: Chandler, 1972. (Recommended brief explanation.)

APPENDIX II

Judicial Decision Making: The Two-Level Theory for Testing Freedom of Speech

Although not all decisions by state and federal judges concerning First Amendment questions fit neatly into a specific niche of the accompanying diagram (at the end of this discussion), most free-speech decisions can be analyzed and better understood if the principles of the two-level theory are applied to the case. The three steps in the application of the theory are as follows: (1) consideration of the due process standards of vagueness and overbreadth; (2) classifying expression as either "speech" as meant by the Constitution or as "nonspeech," which is described as "worthless" because it has little value to the democratic process; and (3) the application of the various tests to the expression considered worthwhile and deserving of the classification "speech." Each of these steps is discussed below, and each is illustrated on the diagram.

A. *Decision 1:* General tests of due process that are applied to *all* laws—vagueness and overbreadth.

1. *Vagueness.* In the case of *Connally* v. *General Construction Co.,* 269 U.S. 385 (1926) at 391, the Supreme Court said that a statute "which either forbids or requires the doing of an act in terms so vague that men of common intelligence must necessarily guess at its meaning and differ as to its application" violates the due process clause of the Fourteenth Amendment, and is, therefore, unconstitutional. An example comes from the "Speaker Ban Law" passed by the North Carolina General Assembly in 1963 and rewritten in 1965, which prohibited any person who "is a known member of the Communist Party" or who "is known to advocate the overthrow of the Constitution of the United States or the State of North Carolina" from speaking on a state college campus. A three-judge federal district court overturned the statute primarily on the grounds of vagueness, because the law's terms "known member" and "known to advocate the overthrow" were not clear. "Known to whom," asked the Court, and "to what degree of certainty . . . [and] according to what standard?" Also, does "known to advocate" include the advocacy of ideas, or does it mean "with force?" Finally, "Must the advocacy be public or private . . . [and is] the advocacy of peaceful change included?" The Court then announced that "it is sufficient to say that reasonable men might differ on the answers to these questions." *Dickinson* v. *Sitterson,* 280 F. Supp. 486 (M.D.N.C. 1968).

2. *Overbreadth.* A statute can be voided for overbreadth if it is worded so as to cover expression or conduct which is *protected* by the Constitution in order to "get at" expression or conduct which is not otherwise protected (figuratively speaking, it can be described as

"burning down the barn in order to get rid of the mice"). An example occurred in 1967 when the U.S. Supreme Court invalidated Section 5(a)(I)(D) of the Internal Security Act which employed language too broad in its attempt to exclude members of the Communist party from working in a defense facility. Chief Justice Earl Warren stressed in his opinion that the section of the law in question established "guilt by association alone" and could be interpreted so as to reach *protected* associations and memberships. Under the American system of law, he added, precision of regulation "must be the touchstone in an area so closely touching our most precious freedoms." *United States* v. *Robel,* 389 U.S. 258 (1967).

B.   *Decision 2:* Expression is classified as "speech" or "nonspeech." Expression that is lacking in ideas and in redeeming social value is placed in constitutional "outer darkness" at the level-two classification; such expression, which is called "nonspeech," may be constrained by due process of law without violating the Constitution. On the other hand, expression with potential social value is classified as "speech" and placed in level one, where it is permitted to continue unless brought into question, at which point it is tested (see *Decision 3* below). The position of the Supreme Court on "worthless nonspeech" is articulated in the case of *Chaplinsky* v. *New Hampshire,* 315 U.S. 568 (1942), in which Chaplinsky's conviction for cursing a police officer was upheld on the grounds that such "fighting words" were not essential to a democratic society. Said the Court:

> There are certain . . . narrowly limited classes of speech, the prevention and punishment of which have never been thought to raise any constitutional problem. These include the lewd and obscene, the profane, the libelous, and the insulting or "fighting" words . . . . It has been well observed that such utterances are no essential part of any exposition of ideas, and are of such slight social value as a step to truth that any benefit that may be derived from them is clearly outweighed by the social interest in order and morality. . . .

Among the types of "worthless" expression identified by the courts:

1.   As noted in *Chaplinsky,* lewd, obscene, profane, defamatory, insulting, or "fighting" words are not essential to the search for truth.
2.   *Commercial expression* which is false and misleading. In *Valentine* v. *Chrestensen,* 316 U.S. 52 (1942), the Supreme Court declared that commercial advertising (in this case, handbills being distributed on the streets of New York City) was not essential public information but rather expression for private profit. Such expression did not deserve the protection of the First Amendment, said the Court. However, during the 1970s the Supreme Court changed its mind and

moved *truthful* advertising of legal products and services to level one, where it was reclassified as "speech"; however, false and misleading advertising is still "nonspeech," and fits in level two. (For more, see the chapter on commercial speech.)

3. *Speech plus*—that expression which is accompanied by conduct such as picketing, marching, or sitting in a doorway so as to block the entrance to a building—receives less First Amendment protection than does "pure speech" (such as giving a talk to an audience in an auditorium). The principle is that the more "plus" (conduct) in the act of expression, the less that expression is protected by the Constitution. An example occurred in the civil rights case of *Cox* v. *Louisiana,* 379 U.S. 536 (1965), when the U.S. Supreme Court upheld a Louisiana statute prohibiting the obstruction of public passages, picketing near a courthouse, and breach of the peace. Expression mixed with certain forms of conduct is not free "speech" alone, said the Court, adding: "We emphatically reject the notion urged by appellant that the First and Fourteenth Amendments afford the same kind of freedom to those who would communicate ideas by conduct such as patrolling, marching, and picketing on streets and highways, as these amendments afford to those who communicate ideas by pure speech."

C. *Decision 3:* Expression that contains ideas and which has social value is classified as "speech" and is protected by the Constitution; it is permitted to continue until called into question by an apparent exception to the rule (such as inciting a riot), in which case the speech is tested—usually by one of the methods described below.

1. *Degree-of-Danger Tests.* A group of tests employed by the courts is based upon the degree of danger which the judges believe the speech in question created at the time of its utterance. The decision is usually stated in terms of one of the three types of danger tests listed below. (Since 1920 the courts have gradually become more liberal in this area, moving away from the restrictive "bad-tendency" test to the more liberal "incitement" standard. The variations should be thought of as representing positions on a continuum moving from tight restrictions to maximum freedom.)

a. *The bad-tendency test.* This can be called a "nip-it-in-the-bud" approach to judging expression, for it stops or punishes speech that the judges believe has a *tendency* to create a serious danger at some time in the future if it is allowed to continue. For this reason, it is also described as "killing the serpent in its egg" and "putting out the spark before the conflagration." A classic statement of this position appears in *Gitlow* v. *U.S.,* 268 U.S. 652 (1925), in which the Supreme Court upheld the sedition conviction of Benjamin Gitlow and in so doing stated: "A single revolutionary spark may kindle a fire that, smoldering for a time, may burst into a sweeping and destructive conflagration. It cannot be said that the state is acting arbitrarily or unreasonably when, in the exercise of its judgment as to the measures necessary to protect the public peace and safety, it seeks to extinguish the spark without waiting until it has enkindled the flame or blazed into the conflagration."

b. *The clear-and-present-danger test.* This test, more liberal than the bad-tendency doctrine, was advocated by Justices Holmes and Brandeis of the U.S. Supreme Court in the years following World War I. The test permits speech to continue until it creates a danger to society which is both *clear* (i.e., obvious) and *present* (i.e., immediate)—a position that differs markedly from the bad-tendency rule. Justice Holmes announced the test in *Schenck* v. *U.S.*, 249 U.S. 47 (1919), when he wrote that the "most stringent protection of free speech would not protect a man in falsely shouting fire in a theater, and causing a panic. . . . The question in every case is whether the words used are used in such circumstances and are of such a nature as to create a clear and present danger that they will bring about the substantive evils that Congress has a right to prevent." Eight years later, in *Whitney* v. *California*, 274 U.S. 357 (1927), Justice Brandeis explained the test in these words: "To justify suppression of free speech there must be reasonable ground to fear that serious evil will result if free speech is practiced. There must be reasonable ground to believe that the danger apprehended is imminent. There must be reasonable ground to believe that the evil to be prevented is a serious one. . . . There must be the probability of serious injury to the state." In general, this test and the incitement test have replaced the old bad-tendency doctrine in American courts.

c. *The incitement test.* Of the three tests described here, the incitement test is the most liberal, for it allows speech to continue past clear and present danger to a point just short of actual incitement to illegal conduct. The incitement position was announced by the U.S. Supreme Court in the case of *Brandenburg* v. *Ohio*, 395 U.S. 444 (1969), in which the Court overturned the sedition conviction of Ku Klux Klan officer Clarence Brandenburg for making a speech in which he threatened "revengeance" against those who opposed the Klan. Deciding that Brandenburg was "blowing off steam" rather than making genuine threats, the Supreme Court stated that "the constitutional guarantees of free speech and free press do not permit a State to forbid or proscribe advocacy of the use of force or of law violation except where such advocacy is directed to inciting or producing imminent lawless action and is likely to incite or produce such action."

2. *Balancing Test.* This is another commonly employed test; in "balancing" a judge weighs competing doctrines or issues against one another, then decides which prevails in the given case. Court decisions based upon the decision-making process of balancing can be classified according to two types: general balancing and specific or ad hoc balancing.

   a. *General balancing.* This form of balancing is employed when broad legal questions or constitutional issues are raised by the conflict being adjudicated, such as sometimes occurs over the Constitution's guarantees of *both* a fair trial and a free press, or over the government's need to maintain national security as contrasted with the right of the press to publish what it wishes in order to "inform the public." When a judge considers the competing claims of, for example, a fair trial versus a free press and then decides in favor of one over the other, the decision involves balancing. A case in point is *Nebraska Press Association* v. *Stuart,* 427 U.S. 539 (1976), in which a local judge issued a gag order against the press in a murder case as a way of preventing pretrial publicity that might prejudice the jury pool. In this instance, the rights of the media came into direct conflict with the rights of the defendant. After weighing the competing interests of these two rights, both guaranteed by the Constitution, the U.S. Supreme Court came down on the side of free press and overturned the gag order.

   b. *Specific or ad hoc balancing.* Specific balancing is similar to general balancing except that it involves the weighing of more narrow, localized issues than does the first category just discussed. For example, in *Kovacs* v. *Cooper,* 336 U.S. 77 (1949), the interests of a peaceful community as opposed to the free-speech right to use loudspeakers came into conflict via a local ordinance that prohibited the use of amplification systems producing a "loud and raucous" noise. The U.S. Supreme Court, without mentioning the term "balancing," considered the competing interests, noted that the ordinance was specific in that it forbade only those systems that emitted a "loud and raucous" noise, then weighed the scales in favor of the social interest of a quiet community.

   In truth, one cannot always classify a balancing decision as either general or specific with any degree of precision, for many occur somewhere between the two categories of issues concerning broad legal and constitutional doctrines and those concerning ad hoc clashes between limited individual or social interests. For more on the subject the student is referred to the case of *Barenblatt* v. *United States,* 360 U.S. 109 (1959), where the Supreme Court employed the balancing doctrine to sustain the conviction of Lloyd Barenblatt for refusing to answer certain questions before the House Committee on Un-American Activities. Not only is balancing specifically mentioned in the opinion of the Court but the doctrine itself is vigorously attacked by the dissenters to the Court's opinion. The criticism of Justice Black (see pp. 144–145 of the case report) is particularly instructive.

3. *Other Tests* (employed less often than those above).

    a. *Preferred freedom.* This test is based upon the conviction that freedom of speech is so important to American democracy that it has a "preferred position" in relation to other liberties; it follows that government must assume a heavy burden of proof when it attempts to curtail this highly valued liberty of expression. For example, in the case of *Thomas* v. *Collins,* 323 U.S. 516 (1945), in which the Supreme Court overturned the conviction of R. J. Thomas, president of the United Auto Workers, for speaking in Texas without first registering as a union organizer as was required by state law, the Court noted that because of the "preferred place given in our scheme to the great, the indispensable democratic freedoms secured by the First Amendment" that laws which attempt to "restrict those liberties must be justified by clear public interest, threatened not doubtfully or remotely, but by clear and present danger." (Careful readers will note that "preferred freedom" is a variation of the balancing doctrine.)

    b. *Less drastic means.* This test is similar to that of overbreadth, discussed earlier, for it emerges from a finding that a law or the government's interpretation and application of a law goes further than necessary to solve a problem. One might describe this test as an effort to discourage the employment of policies of "overkill" by the government. An example occurred in *Aptheker* v. *Secretary of State,* 378 U.S. 500 (1964), in which the Supreme Court invalidated Section 6 of the Internal Security Act, which prevented citizens from traveling abroad if they were members of groups classified as "subversive" by the government. The Court asserted that "Congress has within its power 'less drastic' means of achieving the congressional objective of safeguarding our national security," such as an improved security program; therefore, it is unnecessary to go so far as to deny a citizen's right to a passport.

4. *A Combination of Two or More of the Above Tests.* The various tests

THE SUPREME COURT'S TWO-LEVEL APPROACH TO TESTING FREEDOM OF SPEECH
1. The law is judged for *vagueness* and *overbreadth*.
2. What remains is classified as either *level-one* or *level-two* expression.
3. Level-one expression is worthy of testing; level-two is not.

LEVEL ONE: EXPRESSION THAT IS TESTED (HAS POTENTIAL SOCIAL VALUE)

Degree-of-Danger Tests

← Strict Control // Maximum Freedom →

Bad-tendency test	Clear-and-present-danger test	Incitement test

1.

2. Balancing (both *general* and *specific*)

Government/Social Interests → JUDGE DOES WEIGHING ← Freedom of Speech

(a) General government interests, e.g.,
(1) Fair trial
(2) National security
(b) Specific "ad hoc" interests, e.g.,
(1) A quiet community
(2) Litter-free streets

(a) General principles of freedom, e.g.,
(1) Free press
(2) Informing the public
(b) Specific "ad hoc" interests, e.g.,
(1) Use of loudspeakers
(2) Passing out leaflets

3. Other tests (used less often than the two above)
(a) Preferred freedom (in our system, freedom of speech holds a "preferred" position).
(b) Less drastic means (the goal sought should be achieved by other means).

4. A Combination of two or more of the above.

LEVEL TWO: EXPRESSION NOT DESERVING OF CONSTITUTIONAL PROTECTION

(The reason for this is that such expression is not important to the democratic process, is not essential for the exposition of ideas, and is of little value as a step to truth—as noted in the 1942 case of *Chaplinsky v. New Hampshire*. See the examples listed below.)

1. Includes the *lewd, obscene, profane, defamatory, insulting,* or *"fighting"* words.
2. False and misleading advertising (truthful commercial expression has been given a degree of First Amendment protection in recent years).
3. Includes "speech plus" (i.e., speech combined with action, such as blocking the entrance to a building while holding signs or shouting slogans). Such action is "nonspeech," or *conduct,* and is not essential as a step to truth. Therefore, "speechplus" is less deserving of First Amendment protection than is "pure speech."

FREE SPEECH CASE →

Decision 1
General tests of all laws:
1. Vagueness
2. Overbreadth

Decision 2
Expression is classified as:
1. Speech
2. Nonspeech

Decision 3
Level One
(Speech: Worthwhile expression is tested)

Level Two
(Nonspeech: Worthless expression is not even tested)

described thus far are often used in combination with one another; the balancing test in particular is regularly invoked along with one or more of the others. For example, in the case of *Schneider* v. *State,* 308 U.S. 147 (1939), the Supreme Court struck down the ordinances of three cities which had imposed an absolute ban upon the distribution of handbills on the public streets as a means of preventing litter. In deciding as it did, the Court used both an ad hoc balancing test and the doctrine of less drastic means. Justice Roberts delivered the opinion of the Court to say that (1) freedom of speech weighs heavier in the balance than do litter-free streets and (2) some other means of preventing litter should be employed. "There are obvious methods of preventing littering," observed Justice Roberts, such as "the punishment of those who actually throw papers on the streets."

JUDICIAL TESTS OF FREEDOM OF SPEECH: SELECTED READINGS

Barron, Jerome A., and Dienes, C. Thomas. *Handbook of Free Speech and Free Press.* Boston: Little, Brown, 1979. (See Chapter 1.)

Cahn, Edmond. "Justice Black and First Amendment 'Absolutes': A Public Interview." *New York University Law Review* 37 (1962): 549 ff.

Chafee, Zechariah, Jr. *Free Speech in the United States.* Cambridge, Mass.: Harvard University Press, 1941. (See Chapter 1, especially pp. 31–35.)

Emerson, Thomas I. *The System of Freedom of Expression.* New York: Random House, 1970. (See Chapter 1, especially pp. 14–20; Chapter 20; also use the index to locate Emerson's discussions of other tests.)

"The First Amendment Overbreadth Doctrine." *Harvard Law Review* 83 (1970): 844 ff.

Franklin, Marc A., and Trager, Robert. *The First Amendment and the Fourth Estate.* Mineola, N.Y.: Foundation Press, 1981. (Especially pp. 34–50 for a discussion of basic tests.)

Gillmor, Donald M., and Barron, Jerome A. *Mass Communication Law: Cases and Comment.* 3rd ed. St. Paul, Minn.: West, 1979. (See Chapter 1 for a discussion of the tests.)

Kalven, Harry, Jr. "Metaphysics of the Law of Obscenity." In *The Supreme Court Review: 1960,* pp. 1 ff. Edited by Philip B. Kurland. Chicago: University of Chicago Press, 1960. (This essay explains Kalven's concept of the two-level theory of worthwhile versus worthless expression.)

"Less Drastic Means and the First Amendment." *Yale Law Journal* 78 (1969): 464 ff.

Meiklejohn, Alexander. *Political Freedom: The Constitutional Powers of the People.* New York: Oxford University Press, 1965. (See especially lectures 2 and 3 of *Free Speech and Its Relation to Self-Government,* which are included in this collection of Meiklejohn's works.)

Strong, Frank R. "Fifty Years of 'Clear and Present Danger': From *Schenck* to *Brandenburg*—And Beyond." In *The Supreme Court Review: 1969,* pp. 48–80. Edited by Philip B. Kurland. Chicago: University of Chicago Press, 1969.

"The Void for Vagueness Doctrine in the Supreme Court." *University of Pennsylvania Law Review* 109 (1960): 67 ff.

APPENDIX III

Glossary of Terms

Absolutism.   The view that the First Amendment's words "no law" mean *no* law restricting freedom of speech—absolutely none. The First Amendment absolutist believes that all laws that constrain freedom of speech are unconstitutional.

Affirm.   A decision of an appellate court that agrees with the result in a case decided by the court below.

Amicus curiae.   Latin for "friend of the court." In practice, individuals, groups, or government agencies not party to a dispute before a court nevertheless participate in the case (such as by the submission of a brief arguing a view on the case) either by invitation of the court or on their own initiative. A brief submitted by a "friend of the court" is called an *amicus* brief.

Appeal.   When a case is brought to a higher court for review. Asking a superior court to review a decision of an inferior court.

Appellant.   The party who takes an appeal from one court or jurisdiction to another.

Appellee.   The party to an appeal who has an interest in upholding the decision of the lower court. Sometimes called the *respondent*. The party against whom an appeal is taken.

Bad-tendency test (also called "remote bad tendency"). See Appendix II.

Balancing test.   See Appendix II.

Brief.   A written document submitted by the attorney for a party in a case setting out the legal arguments in support of the position of that party.

Captive audience.   An involuntary audience, such as persons on a transit bus or on a plane; such persons cannot simply "walk away" from a message and are, therefore, described as a "captive audience."

Certiorari.   When a higher court agrees to hear an appeal from a lower court, as when the Supreme Court grants certiorari (at least four justices of the Supreme Court must vote to hear the appeal before certiorari is granted). Abbre-viated as "cert." Officially, certiorari is a command to the judges of a lower court to forward the records of a case to a higher court for review. In Latin, the term means "to be informed of."

Chilling effect.   A term used in First Amendment cases to describe the threat imposed upon communicators by some laws, regulations, or court actions that, because they are unclear, difficult to obey, or impose unusually severe punishments, have a "chilling" influence upon one's willingness to speak. To intimidate so as to silence.

Clear-and-present-danger test.   See Appendix II.

Commercial speech.   Commercial advertising for a product or a service.

Common law.   Refers generally to the legal system of England and of countries such as the United States which base their law upon that of England. More specifically, common law is based upon custom and upon court decisions, to be distinguished from statutes written into law by the legislatures. For example, self-defense is a common-law right with roots in antiquity. The term "common law" is often used to distinguish the legal basis for state action from *written* (i.e., statutory) law. The term "case law" is sometimes used as a synonym for "common law."

Complainant.   See "plaintiff."

Concurring opinion.   An opinion by a member of a court that agrees with the result reached by the majority but not with the reasoning of the majority. The concurring opinion is a means by which the reasoning of a concurring judge is stated for the record.

Court order.   See "injunction."

Defendant.   In criminal cases, the party accused of a crime by the state. In civil cases, the party against whom a suit is brought (the person who brings the suit is called the plaintiff).

Deposition.   See "discovery."

Discovery. Literally, uncovering that which was unknown (here, by the asking of questions). The taking of depositions (questions asked orally) and interrogatories (questions asked in writing), the answers to which are recorded in written form as a type of testimony under oath admissible later in open court as official testimony. Discovery occurs before the trial; its results are often used during a trial. For an example, see the defamation case of *Hebert* v. *Lando*.

Dissenting opinion. When a member of a court disagrees with the result reached by the majority of judges, he or she may announce a dissenting opinion stating the reasons for the disagreement.

Ex parte. Concerning one side of the case; acting on behalf or at the request of one party only. For example, an ex parte court order is one issued at the request of one party to a dispute without the presence or awareness of other parties involved.

Ex post facto. After the fact. In free speech cases, ex post facto (often shortened to simply post facto) punishment occurs *after* something has been said or published. To be contrasted with prior restraint, in which the expression is censored in advance.

Habeas corpus. Latin for "you have the body." A writ issued by a court to determine whether or not a person is legally detained or imprisoned. The prisoner named in the writ must be brought before a judge, who reviews the matter. Such immediate judicial review for detained persons is considered basic to civil liberties.

Heckler's veto. Loud, boisterous, and sometimes violent interference by members of an audience who oppose the views of the speaker, thereby preventing the effective communication of the message. By such disruption, the heckler is said to exercise a kind of "veto" over the speech.

Indictment. A written accusation of a crime, issued by a grand jury based on the presentation of enough evidence by the prosecuting attorney to convince the members of the grand jury of probable cause; when convinced, the grand jury issues an indictment, meaning that the case can proceed to trial. See "information."

Information. A written accusation brought to a magistrate (rather than to a grand jury) by the prosecutor. The magistrate, if convinced of probable cause, authorizes a trial of the accused. Not allowed in all states. Abused by the English in early sedition prosecutions (see Chapter 1), for it avoided the grand jury, whose members often refused to indict.

Injunction. An order from a court against a person or organization directing the party named to either do something, or to refrain from doing something, as specified in the order. Also called a court order. See "restraining order."

Judgment of the court. The decision of a court of law concerning the issues before it in a given case. To be distinguished from a verdict rendered by a jury; a judgment is rendered by a judge or group of judges.

Judicial review. The review of legislation or other action by the government by a court to determine whether or not the legislation or action is constitutional.

Litigants. The parties to a court case.

Majority opinion. See "opinion of the court."

Opinion of the court. The reasoning of a *majority* of judges in a case in which the law is expounded and the result (also called the judgment or the decision) is explained and justified. Not all decisions are supported by "an opinion of the court"—see "plurality opinion" below.

Overbreadth. See Appendix II.

Per curiam. Latin for "by the court." An unsigned opinion of the court in which no author is identified. Such opinions do not have to be unanimous; they simply express the collective view of at least a majority of judges.

Petitioner. Generally, any person who seeks judicial relief is called the "petitioner" by the courts. It applies, for example, to a person who files a petition with a court seeking review of a lower-court decision.

Plaintiff. The party who complains; the party who brings a lawsuit against another. Also called the complainant.

Plurality opinion. When an appellate court

consisting of more than three judges renders a majority decision announcing the *result* of an appeal but the judges composing the majority cannot agree upon a majority *opinion* in the case, the opinion agreed to by the largest number of judges voting with the majority is called the plurality opinion. For example, when the majority consists of 5 and the 5 divide 3 to 2 in their agreement upon opinions, the plurality vote is 3. Because plurality opinions do not represent the views of court majorities, such opinions do not carry the force of law, as do majority opinions. Cases that illustrate the subject: *Dennis* v. *United States* (Chapter 3) and *Hague* v. *CIO* (Chapter 8).

Post facto. See "ex post facto."

Preferred position. See "Preferred freedom," as discussed in Appendix II, p. 453.

Prior restraint. To stop a message before it is communicated, as when a war correspondent must submit his stories for "clearance" by military censors. Contrasted with "ex post facto," which is punishment of expression *after* it has been communicated.

Remand. To send back. When a higher court sends a case back to a lower court for reconsideration, usually in light of some mandate of the higher court.

Respondent. The party opposed to the granting of a petition.

Restraining order. Similar to an injunction but technically not the same. The restraining order, sometimes called a temporary restraining order (TRO), restrains the defendant for a time until the propriety of issuing an injunction can be determined.

Result. The decision in a case; not to be confused with the opinions of the judges who made the decision (the opinions give the reasoning for reaching the result). The result states *what* was decided; the opinion states *why*.

Reverse. When a higher court reaches a decision differing from that reached by the court below, the higher court reverses the result of the lower court. To overturn a judgment of a lower court.

Sedition. Expression—usually speech or writing—critical of the government and/or its officers, laws, or policies. Expression that allegedly promotes disaffection, hatred, or contempt toward the government, including that which urges public disorder or rebellion. Not to be confused with treason, consisting of overt *action* against the government.

Shield law. A law extending special protection to a reporter, thereby "shielding" that reporter from state actions which, in the opinion of some, interfere with the right to gather and report the news. For example, a law that permits a reporter to keep his or her sources of information confidential is one type of shield law.

Speech plus. A doctrine of the U.S. Supreme Court which describes speech conjoined with conduct or action, the *action* in the matter being the "plus." For example, burning a draft card to protest against a war may be a form of speech, but the *burning* is "plus"—action that goes beyond "pure speech." For more, see Chapter 8, where the doctrine is discussed in detail.

Stare decisis. Latin for "let the decision stand." The doctrine that a legal principle established in an early court decision should be allowed to stand. To determine the outcome of a current case by legal precedent. To hold to past decisions, thereby giving consistency and continuity to the law.

Statute. A written law, enacted by the legislature. To be contrasted with "common law," which is not written but based upon custom and court decisions.

Sub nom. Without an opinion, as in "affirmed *sub nom*," meaning that the court above affirmed without opinion the decision of the court below.

Temporary restraining order. See "restraining order."

Tort. A private or civil wrong which is not based upon a contract. Examples include defamation, invasion of privacy, trespass, and negligence. Usually relief is sought in civil court through a suit seeking monetary damages, as when newspapers are sued for libel.

Treason. Attempting to overthrow the government by overt acts or by betraying one's country to the enemy. The U.S. Constitution, Article III, Section 3, says: "Treason against the United States, shall consist only in levying War against them, or in adhering to their Enemies, giving them Aid and Comfort. No person shall be convicted of Treason unless on the Testimony of two Witnesses to the same overt Act, or on Confession in open Court." (See "Sedition," above.)

Vacate. To annul, set aside, or make void. For example, if the Supreme Court *vacates* a lower court decision, the lower court is required to reconsider the case.

Vagueness. See Appendix II.

Verdict. A decision rendered by a jury. Not to be confused with the decision rendered by a judge, which is called a judgment.

Writ. A written court order. The term has wide application in the law; in First Amendment cases it usually refers to a written order by a superior court to an inferior court to submit certain records in order that review might take place. Also an order to some designated recipient to do or not to do what is specified in the writ. Also, see habeas corpus.

Table of Cases

References to significant information are printed in *italicized* type.

461

Index

References to figures are printed in **boldface** type.

ABOUT THE AUTHOR

Thomas L. Tedford is professor of communication and theater at the University of North Carolina at Greensboro where, for the past fifteen years, he has taught a junior-senior-graduate course entitled "Freedom of Speech and Censorship." His Ph.D. in speech communication is from Louisiana State University. He has been active in the work of the Commission on Freedom of Speech of the Speech Communication Association since its inception in the early 1960s, having served as the commission's chairperson, editor of its newsletter, and editor of its annual *Free Speech Yearbook*. His publications concerning freedom of speech have appeared in the *Speech Teacher*, the *Free Speech Yearbook*, the *English Journal*, the *North Carolina Journal of Speech*, and the American Library Association's *Newsletter on Intellectual Freedom*.

In addition to his professional work in the free speech area, Tedford is active in the programs of the American Civil Liberties Union—particularly those concerning First Amendment questions. In 1965 he was named to the first board of directors of the newly chartered North Carolina Civil Liberties Union (NCCLU), serving three consecutive terms (nine years) during the formative period of the Tarheel Union. From 1975 to 1980 he edited *Liberty*, the quarterly newsletter of the NCCLU. He has worked on a number of NCCLU committees, including the Legal Committee, and is currently serving again on the NCCLU Board of Directors after being elected to a three-year term in the spring of 1984.